REFUGEES:
A PROBLEM OF OUR TIME

*The Work of The United Nations
High Commissioner for Refugees,
1951-1972*

by

LOUISE W. HOLBORN

with the assistance of
Philip and Rita Chartrand

Issued under the auspices of the Radcliffe Institute,
Cambridge, Massachusetts

VOLUME I

The Scarecrow Press, Inc.
Metuchen, N.J.   1975

HV
640
.H58
V.1

Library of Congress Cataloging in Publication Data

Holborn, Louise Wilhelmine, 1898-
    Refugees, a problem of our time.

    "Issued under auspices of the Radcliffe Institute,
Cambridge, Massachusetts."
    Bibliography: p.
    Includes index.
    1. United Nations. Office of the United Nations
High Commissioner for Refugees. 2. Refugees.
I. Chartrand, Philip, joint author. II. Chartrand,
Rita, joint author. III. Title.
HV640.H58   361.5'3   74-19471
ISBN 0-8108-0746-7

FOREWORD

Parallel to the stream of political and other, sometimes cruel, events which form the history of nations, there
is, as part of the emergence and the current of ideas and
philosophies that determine the development of civilizations,
the growth of man's concern for his fellow human beings.
In this century, which has been marked by so many profound and often violent changes, accompanied by suffering
on an unprecedented scale, there has been a remarkable
and increasing willingness on the part of citizens and governments to accept as an expression of their international solidarity an ever greater volume of responsibility to alleviate
human suffering.   This has been manifested in all fields of
activity--economic, social, humanitarian--through the creation of multilateral and bilateral systems of cooperation on
regional and world scales.   The United Nations and its
Specialized Agencies have within this framework a most
important role to play.

In the domain of humanitarian endeavors, the United
Nations, governments and voluntary bodies have built up
international systems which make it possible, even if at
present there is room for much improvement, to mobilize
impressive resources throughout the world and bring them to
the areas of distress where natural or man-made disasters
occur.   In the specific area of the protection of refugees
and the solution of refugee problems, the evolution in concept, approach and methods has led over the years to a
practice of international cooperation which in itself is truly
remarkable.   There is now an almost universal acceptance
of the humanitarian character of refugee work; granting
asylum, helping the displaced populations through migration
and local resettlement, agreeing to help the countries of
first asylum through financial contributions and the initiation
of permanent solutions projects--all of these have become
normal practices giving rise to little or no political controversies.   Modern methods have been introduced in the planning and in the implementation of refugee resettlement schemes
where assistance is designed as much to solve the individual

iii

problems as to promote the economic and social development of the host country.

Above all, a set of principles has been laid down in international instruments to define the legal status of the refugee and to ensure his basic rights as a human being. These principles have been formally accepted by many countries, and many others not yet parties to the international agreements apply them in practice. But there is, of course, still progress to be made before we can speak of their true universality. There are also certain domains where international thinking has not yet crystalized concepts, such as, for instance, the refugee's right to receive asylum.

What is perhaps most impressive when reviewing the history of this humanitarian work is, however, the trend towards universality and the ever-more flexible and understanding approach by governments and international bodies. One instance of this has been the introduction of the notion of "good offices" that allows the UNHCR to act in certain circumstances where otherwise difficult statutory problems might have slowed down its initial work and perhaps have created difficulties of a political nature. Another instance has been the decision to ask the High Commissioner to act as "focal point" for the United Nations system, taken by the Secretary-General, U Thant, in 1971 and unanimously supported by the General Assembly, when massive assistance had to be given to the East Bengali refugees in India, and by Dr. K. Waldheim in 1972 in response to a request from the Sudanese Government when seeking international assistance for the Southern region in the context of the rehabilitation of displaced persons and the repatriation of refugees who had left their homes during the years of internal unrest.

I am sure that to future historians it will be as important to study "how" and "why" this growth in humanitarian consciousness occurred and how the new practices developed, as it is to analyze the factors that have caused the changes in the political and social aspects of our world. For both fields offer the attentive student important lessons of success and failure, examples of errors to be avoided and of positive trends to be pursued in building the world of the coming generations.

In this respect the work of Professor Louise W. Holborn, tracing the history of the international concern for refugees since World War I, will be of great value. Not

iv

only does it bring together many of the elements that have created the international practice of protecting and assisting refugees as we now know it; it also draws a wide canvas of experiences that have been gained over the years. These will undoubtedly provide precious information to all those who are concerned with finding solutions to present and possible future refugee problems.

In preparing her book, Professor Holborn has, I hope, received encouragement from my Office, and she has been given access to thousands of UNHCR documents and files. She has also drawn on her own knowledge of and association with international refugee work and assembled and interpreted these from her own optic as an independent observer and historian. To her and to her assistants, I wish to express my admiration for the tenacity and skill with which they undertook and concluded their task.

Prince Sadruddin Aga Khan

Geneva, March 1973

ACKNOWLEDGMENTS

At the end of such a study one thinks with special appreciation of the wide range of persons and groups that have given so freely of their time and their expertise. It would be satisfying to name them all, but I trust they will recognize how much I appreciate the help and confidence they have contributed to my work.

My particular gratitude goes to Prince Sadruddin Aga Khan who provided the conception, the initiative, and invaluable encouragement and support throughout. My thanks go also to the UNHCR Headquarters Staff in Geneva, particularly to the officers of the UNHCR Public Information and to the UNHCR representatives in Europe and Africa who arranged my visits and contacts with government officials, with nongovernmental and voluntary agencies, and to the New York Office on which I had so constantly to call. Among the many who aided me greatly by providing information and perspective, my special thanks go to former High Commissioner Dr. Felix Schnyder, and the former Deputy High Commissioner James Read. Outside of the UNHCR, the staffs of the International Committee for European Migration, the International Council of Voluntary Agencies, the American Council of Voluntary Agencies for Foreign Services, the Lutheran World Federation, and the British Council for Aid for Refugees helped materially, as did many others.

I would like to acknowledge the assistance in particular through contributions by Philip and Rita Chartrand, Claire Fortier, Polly Barker and Ann Paden. Philip Chartrand, now Assistant Professor of Political Science at the Catholic University, in Washington, carried the major burden of preparing Part III and Chapter 18, and Rita Chartrand drafted much of the African sections. Both were associated with the work from the beginning. Mrs. Claire Fortier assiduously sifted documents and helped to prepare several chapters and the index. Mrs. Ann Paden has contributed unusually skillful editing and Mrs. Evelyn Katrak meticulous copy editing. Polly Barker provided secretarial and linguistic assistance during my 1969 visit to eight countries in West, East and Central Africa to study the operations of the UNHCR. Mrs. Marcella Martin has been a constant support in the latter stages of the manuscript through her cheerful typing and untiring work in turning messy manuscripts into beautiful typing and Mrs. Linda Murnik helped similarly at an earlier stage.

The generous support and hospitality of the Radcliffe Institute and its late director, Dr. Constance Smith, immeasurably aided the preparation of the book, and it is a source of particular satisfaction that it is published under the auspices of the Institute. The American Philosophical Society provided a grant-in-aid to attend the conference of the International Council of Voluntary Agencies in London in June 1968, and to spend six weeks at UNHCR headquarters. The constant interest and generous aid of Mrs. John Gordan helped materially in the preparation of the book. I would like to acknowledge also the financial contribution to expenses of the Bank of Equalization through the good offices of Dr. Eberhard Jahn. My colleague and friend, Professor Gwendolen M. Carter, Director of the Program of African Studies at Northwestern University, interviewed UNHCR officials for me in Hong Kong and Macao in 1969 and in Africa in 1972, and has been a constant source of help and encouragement.

Naturally I assume full responsibility for any factual inaccuracies or interpretive misjudgments that may mar this volume. None of the persons or groups mentioned above are committed by any opinion expressed herein.

Louise W. Holborn

Radcliffe Institute
Cambridge, Mass.
July 1973

TABLE OF CONTENTS

MAPS

Goennet einander den Platz auf fremden Boden und teilet,
Was Ihr habet, zusammen, damit Ihr Barmherzigkeit findet.

Aber ich taeusche mich nicht mit leichter Hoffnung in diesen
Taurigen Tagen, die uns noch traurige Tage versprechen:
Denn geloest sind die Bande der Welt. Wer knuepfet sie
      wieder
Als allein die Not, die hoechste, die uns bevorsteht.

         Wolfgang von Goethe, <u>Hermann und Dorothea</u>

Grant one another room on this strange ground and share
      freely
What you have, together, that you may meet with compassion.

I deceive not myself with light-hearted hopes in such days of
Sorrow, for they but promise sorrowful days for the future;
See, the bonds of the world are loosed; what shall bind them
      together,
Other than direst need, which on all sides clearly awaits us.

Translation by George F. Timson, London, The Mitre Press

PROLOGUE

This study describes in their vast dimensions the worldwide activities of the Office of the United Nations High Commissioner for Refugees (UNHCR) during its first twenty-two years, 1951-1972. Although the chief concern throughout the work is to describe the role of the UNHCR, its activities are placed in historical context and the environment within which the UNHCR has worked. This approach engenders a greater appreciation both of the complexity of its tasks and the extent of its achievements.

The UNHCR is widely acknowledged to be the indispensable agent of the international community in its efforts to handle and, where possible, solve one of the world's most anguishing and persistent issues, the problem of refugees. Throughout its existence the UNHCR has played a major role in extending international protection to refugees, and it has acted also as a catalyst to the efforts of many governmental and voluntary groups and international agencies. Whether it be the thousands of refugees who flee annually from Eastern Europe, the hundreds of thousands of African refugees scattered throughout that vast continent, or the millions of refugees who surged out of East Bengal (Bangladesh) into India, the response of the international community has been to turn to the UNHCR to provide legal protection, stimulate and coordinate material assistance, and seek long-range solutions.

In a world beset by a multitude of human problems, the plight of the refugee is among the most difficult. Isolated and deprived of the protection of a national government, the refugee carries handicaps that intensify the difficulties of meeting ordinary needs. His ability to move from one country to another--even to return to his country of birth--is restricted by his statelessness, de facto or de jure; moreover he is often discriminated against in educational opportunities, ability to secure a job, and right to social services. The primary function of the UNHCR is to alleviate those difficulties by providing the refugee with a legal status internationally accepted.

Only gradually has the world acknowledged the refugee problem to be a persistent and sustained phenomenon, not a transitory problem to be met and solved on an ad hoc basis as emergencies hit the headlines. It has come to recognize that a variety of approaches are needed to respond to refugee outflows. The initial reaction must be to provide relief to seek to alleviate destitution in an immediate and pressing situation. As long as refugee movements are looked on as temporary, relief will be the prime concern. As the problem endures, however, causing distress not only to the displaced themselves but also to the countries where they have found temporary abode, machinery must be organized to facilitate at least temporary absorption of the refugees. When it becomes evident that some, or most, of a refugee group are permanent exiles, wider schemes must be developed to attempt permanent settlement in the country of refuge or elsewhere.

Governments have begun to realize that traditional ways of extending international protection to individuals in such situations are inadequate in meeting the needs of substantial numbers of human beings in all parts of the world. Because refugee movements are caused by political changes and upheavals, it is inevitable that the nature of international action for refugees is affected by the political reaction of other states. As the product of political, religious, or racial discrimination by their governments, refugees can become a highly sensitive international political issue. Thus the question of what to do for refugees is affected by the political relations between the states of origin and of asylum, and between these and other states offering possible permanent settlement.

In this context the UNHCR has taken its place not as a temporary agency but as a well-established and, indeed, essential instrument of international action. Recognizing that the work of the UNHCR is non-political in nature, governments have contributed increasingly to its finances. Moreover, they have entrusted this international agency with many more and different kinds of situations than were originally envisaged. Thus, in the course of the years since its establishment in 1951 the UNHCR has become the focus for organizing major efforts on behalf of refugees undertaken by international, governmental and voluntary agencies on the international and national levels. This was never more apparent than in the decisive role in three major international crises over the establishment of Bangladesh, repatriation of the Sudanese refugees and expulsion of Asians from Uganda, all of which took place after the original termination date of this study and have been included because they confirm the indispensability of the Office. Through its humanitarian endeavors, as the following chapters make clear, the UNHCR has contributed effectively to the release of political tensions and thus to peace and security and, in addition, has made it possible for hundreds of thousands of former refugees to return to their native countries or to become contributing members of their adopted communities.

Almost all the material on the vital subject of the UNHCR lies buried in the voluminous and cumbersome records of the United Nations and the Office of the UNHCR itself and in the scattered and not easily accessible reports of international and national voluntary agencies. This study draws heavily on these records. In addition, it has made use of a wide range of published and unpublished contemporary material dealing with the broad political milieu within which refugee movements have occurred, and has drawn on substantial firsthand experiences with the operations of the UNHCR in Europe and in Africa.

The description in Part I of international efforts for refugees prior to the establishment of the UNHCR provides perspective on the ways in which the UNHCR was intended to differ from its predecessors, and on the extent to which, in time, it adopted certain devices and practices comparable to those of its predecessor agencies. At the same time, as will be seen in Part II, the UNHCR has operated in a setting different from that of the earlier international agencies concerned with refugees and has developed its own distinctive approaches and ways of action. A study of the UNHCR thus demonstrates both continuity and change in international action on behalf of refugees. The predominant continuity has been to meet the need of refugees for international protection. The response of League of Nations and UN High Commissioners for Refugees to this situation has, over time, alleviated to a great extent the problems arising from the refugees' lack of legal status and has in the process created a new body of international law by treaties and agreements. Part III deals entirely with the significant question of international protection.

Many studies have tended to treat refugee movements as isolated phenomena, without due reference to their political environment. Long experience with refugee problems, most of which involve both individual governments and the international community, leads to the conclusion that such problems can be understood and evaluated only within the general political, economic, and social framework in which they have taken place. It is for this reason that so much substantial background material is presented regarding the characteristics of the countries of origin and asylum and the general international setting at different periods of time. Although the activities of the UNHCR in Europe, North America, Latin America, Asia, the Middle East, and Africa overlap chronologically, they are described separately in Parts IV through VIII in the interest of clarity.

While the background to European refugee situations is comparatively well known, a more comprehensive approach was found necessary for dealing with refugee movements on other continents. In particular, greater detail on the setting and settling of the African refugees has been included. The High Commissioner's present role in African refugee situations is of very great importance and, indeed, since 1965 the Africa program has absorbed more than half his material assistance effort both in funding and in staff. Moreover, the general public has little background knowledge of the peoples and issues involved in African refugee problems, due in part to the fact that the news media ordinarily give them only scattered and superficial coverage.

This effort to spotlight specific African refugee situations has seemed warranted not only for its own sake but also for the numerous illustrations it gives of the size and complexity of the problems faced by African nations-in-the-making. It lends a certain specificity to what the "impact of modernization," "subsistence sector," "difficult communications," and the like mean in human terms. Indeed, a basic purpose of all the background sections is to modify the rather impersonal quality of the "refugee problem" by providing an account of the characteristics of some of the refugee groups, what their lives were like, why they left their homes, and what has happened to them thereafter.

PART I

INTERNATIONAL EFFORTS ON BEHALF OF
REFUGEES: 1921-52

What good is all the idle talk about corruption of our time
if our innermost self is not shaken by it?
What good does all the eternal light of truth
if we lack the inner light of human compassion?

--Johann Heinrich Pestalozzi,
translated from the German

Chapter 1

THE LEAGUE OF NATIONS AND INTERGOVERNMENTAL AGENCIES FOR REFUGEES, 1919-1946

In taking up its responsibilities in 1951 the Office of the United Nations High Commissioner for Refugees (UNHCR) was able to draw on the experience of a wide range of international efforts on behalf of refugees extending back to WWI. Both World Wars had produced large dislocations of population in Europe as well as great political changes. The political tensions and intolerance which resulted from these conflicts caused widespread persecution, or fear of persecution. Thus, many persons fled from their native states to seek asylum in adjacent countries. These persons were in great need of material assistance, but still more critical was the potential economic and social disruption in the receiving states caused by the sudden inflow of refugees. Moreover, in the international context the presence of the refugees often exacerbated ideological tensions between states. Thus the refugee problem caused by the World Wars was not only fraught with human need but also with dangerous national and international tensions that had not been present in previous migrations caused by political events. The resulting situations were clearly beyond the capacity of individual states to solve and gave rise to international efforts of ever-increasing scope.

Refugee Movements After World War I

A cursory view of the most extensive refugee movements that harassed Europe and Asia after World War I (WWI) provides some idea of the extent of the dislocations. In the years 1918-22 about 1.5 million Russian refugees were stranded, mainly in north, central, and southern Europe and in the Far East, as a result of the Bolshevik armies in European Russia in 1919-20, the Russian famine of 1921, and the breakdown of White Russian resistance in Siberian Russia in 1922. By 1923 there were also an estimated 320,000 Armenian refugees scattered throughout

3

the Near East, the Balkans, and other European countries
after their flight from persecution and massacres in Asia
Minor following the collapse of the Ottoman Empire and the
adoption by Turkey of a policy of nationalism. In addition,
the refugees included 30,000 Assyrian, Assyro-Chaldean,
Turkish and Assimilated Refugees--Christian minority groups
who before WWI lived in Kurdistan and Persian Azerbaijan.[1]
During the war they were driven from the Ottoman Empire
and they subsequently resettled, mainly in Greece, Iraq,
Lebanon, and Syria.

    The governments of the receiving countries, already
facing serious reconstruction problems--depreciating cur-
rencies, growing unemployment, and political unrest--were
ill-equipped for an influx of destitute people whose attitudes
and dubious legal status made them a political problem,
while their lack of money and goods and their poor or
weakened health involved serious economic and social difficulties. Thus, the countries of first asylum were not able
to absorb the refugees into their economic life. The "in-
truders," as they were regarded in many cases, became a
dangerous threat to political and economic stability in the
receiving countries.

The Need for Coordinated Effort

    Prior to 1921, efforts to cope with refugee needs
were undertaken mainly by private organizations, or voluntary agencies, and were predominantly in the form of relief.
No organized attempts were made at that time to integrate
refugees permanently into their countries of refuge, or to
move the Russian and other refugees to areas where they
might be settled under more favorable circumstances. Thus,
the large sums that were spent by governments and private
voluntary organizations on relief within the countries of
refuge provided only temporary alleviation of the situation.

    During 1920, various European countries undertook
bilateral negotiations aimed at transferring refugees from
their own territories to those of other states. These efforts
usually ended in failure because of the unsatisfactory legal
status of the refugees as prospective immigrants: some of
the Russian refugees, for example, held documents issued
by the Tsarist government, while most of the others possessed no identity papers of any kind and were in fact
stateless. Some of the host countries, such as Poland and

Czechoslovakia, issued papers of their own to refugees on
their soil.   These documents secured no international recognition however, and the refugees were confined to the issuing
countries in which they found themselves.

Refugees of the inter-war period also found closed
frontiers overseas: refugees are an anomaly in a nation-
state system.   The open migration policies of earlier times,
which were determined by the movement of capital and the
need for labor in the development of new territories, had
been replaced by restrictive legislation dictated not only by
local economic conditions but also by political and strategic
considerations.   Thus immigration had ceased to be purely
a national or even a bi-national problem to be solved between the giving and receiving countries.   Immigration policy
had become intimately linked with wider aspects of international relations.   In other words, it had become international in character.

It was increasingly recognized, therefore, that the
vast WWI refugee problem could be successfully tackled
only by internationally coordinated action.   The voluntary
organizations, whose resources were already overstrained by
their relief work in central and eastern Europe for these
starving and destitute persons involved in the exodus caused
by the movements of armies during the war and the redraw-
ing of frontiers after the armistice, found themselves overwhelmed by the task of meeting the needs of the disorgan-
ized masses of Russian and other refugees flooding into the
border countries.   Thus, they sought other ways of tackling
the problem. [2]

Appeal to the League of Nations

The first initiative to expand the base of refugee
operations came in February 1921, from a gathering in
Geneva of representatives of private relief organizations,
including some forerunners of agencies represented today
in the International Council of Voluntary Agencies (ICVA).
Following this meeting, an appeal was addressed through the
President of the International Committee of the Red Cross
(ICRC), Gustav Ador, to the League of Nations (LoN), suggesting the appointment of a League of Nations Commissioner
for Refugees and asking the League "to define the status of
Russian refugees, to secure their repatriation or their employment outside Russia, and to coordinate measures for

their assistance. " Mr. Ador underlined the fact that "the
800, 000 Russian refugees scattered throughout Europe are
without legal protection or representation. " He continued:

> It is not so much a humanitarian duty which calls
> for the generous activities of the League of Na-
> tions as an obligation of international justice. . . .
> All the organizations already at work would be
> glad to put forth fresh efforts under the general
> supervision of a commissioner appointed by the
> League of Nations, which is the only supra-na-
> tional political authority capable of solving a prob-
> lem which is beyond the power of exclusively hu-
> manitarian organizations. [3]

The appeal to the League was dictated by the wartime and post-war experience of the greater effectiveness of
coordinated efforts, and in particular, by the success of the
repatriation of German and Austrian prisoners of war from
Siberia which had been accomplished under the direction of
Dr. Fridtjof Nansen, acting as the League's High Commissioner for the Repatriation of Prisoners. In the course of
this transaction, 427, 886 prisoners of war were repatriated.
Moreover, Dr. Nansen gained the confidence of governments
and voluntary agencies and won the cooperation of the Soviet
Government and the executive assistance of the National Red
Cross Societies. In 1921 he also acted as Commissioner
for the organization of relief for famine-stricken populations
in Russia.

The ICRC proposed that the League should consider
three main aspects of the Russian refugee problem: first,
the definition of their legal status; second, their settlement
by repatriation to Russia, their immigration to other countries, or the organization of their employment in the countries where they were residing; and third, the coordination
of the various efforts already undertaken for the material
relief of the refugees.

The Covenant of the LoN did not include any specific
provision for international aid and protection for refugees;
however, reference to the general purpose of the LoN "to
promote international cooperation and to achieve international
peace and security, " and Arts. 23 and 25 were cited by
those in favor of the League's accepting responsibility for
refugees. [4]

On 27 June 1921, the League Council, after considering replies from member-states on the feasibility of international cooperation on behalf of refugees and the form it
should take, adopted the original ICRC proposal in principle
and instructed the Secretariat to make a preliminary investigation.

The First High Commissioner:
Dr. Fridtjof Nansen, 1921-29

On 20 August 1921 the Council of the League appointed
Dr. Fridtjof Nansen as "High Commissioner on behalf of the
League in connection with the problems of Russian refugees
in Europe. " He assumed the tasks of relief work for the
refugees: to determine the legal status of refugees, and to
seek a permanent solution through repatriation to Russia,
employment in the countries where they were residing, or
immigration to other countries. [5]

Dr. Nansen accepted the High Commission on 1 September 1921. He became the first international civil servant to deal with the refugee problem. The Council agreed
to pay the administrative expenses and to put its machinery
at the disposal of the governments involved, with the understanding that it would take no responsibility for the organization or financing of relief and that its work should be considered temporary. These two considerations always dominated the refugee work done under the LoN. [6]

The organization established for coping with the refugee problems was designed to provide the High Commissioner (HC) with channels: to the host countries, to private
voluntary agencies giving money and undertaking relief, and
to the refugees themselves. Governments were asked to ap-
point officials to communicate directly with the HC and to
receive specific proposals for action. Dr. Nansen also appointed his own representatives in those countries to keep in
touch with government officials and with the voluntary agencies. ICRC and the World Organization for Secours aux
Enfants (OSE) put their local representatives and their technical apparatus at Dr. Nansen's disposal. Through these
local officials and his own representatives, the HC maintained direct contact with the refugees. The work developed
to such an extent that in some places it was necessary to
set up a branch office.

In addition to conducting individual negotiations, the
HC consulted with representatives of interested governments
meeting together in inter-governmental conferences and with
an advisory committee of the voluntary agencies.   Though
the constituent societies maintained autonomy in their several
fields of activity and control over their own funds, coordination of their work was initiated to assure maximum efficiency.   The Office of the HC was able to serve as a clearinghouse for information and to fit individual efforts into an
overall plan and present them to the LoN.

LoN Participation in the Resettlement
of Greek and Bulgarian Refugees

Under an Agreement of 30 January 1923 Regarding
the Exchange of Greek and Turkish Population, 1,300,000
Greeks were transferred from Asia Minor, while 400,000
Turks were moved from the Balkans to Turkey.[7]   The LoN
availed itself of the relief services of the HC.   He organized the emergency relief action and also suggested the exchange of the people.   He also carried out some emergency
relief for Bulgarians who had been turned out of western
Thrace.   For the settlement of the Greeks, the LoN, under
the Protocol of 29 September 1923 signed by Greece and the
LoN, provided an international loan of £9,970,000.   The
Greek Government provided land, and under an autonomous
Office for Settlement, about 170,000 families (approximately
650,000 persons) were successfully settled by 1928.   This
settlement work in Greece was the first of its kind which
the LoN called into being.[8]

Along similar lines, a smaller project was carried
out in Bulgaria by which about 125,000 Bulgar refugees were
settled.[9]

In September 1923 Dr. Nansen was given responsibility for the Armenian refugees, including the right to issue
Nansen passports.   He devised schemes for transferring
many of these refugees to the Soviet Republic of Armenia,
and also drew up plans to settle some 40,000 in Syria.[10]

The Nansen Passport

During his period of office from 1921 to his death in
May 1930, Dr. Nansen was constantly concerned with the

question of the final disposition of refugees either by repatriation, employment in the countries of refuge, or resettlement overseas.   The dominant aim of the Office was
to turn as quickly as possible from relief and charity to
measures which would enable refugees to become self-supporting.   In order to do so, the HC needed information with
regard to the number, age, sex, and profession of the refugees.   With the cooperation of the International Labour
Office (ILO), Dr. Nansen carried through a census of refugees in the winter of 1921-22.   Subsequently, part of the
responsibilities of the HC were transferred to the ILO.
From 1 January 1925 to 1929, the ILO assumed the task of
finding suitable employment for refugees.   Handling technical aspects of the work for refugees--employment, emigration arrangements, and eventual settlement--ILO assisted
some 60,000 refugees to obtain work.   The task of the HC
in this period was restricted to legal and political matters.

For any long-range and permanent solution, the primary need of the refugees is a legal status that will give
them standing in the country of refuge and thus permit employment or enable them to travel from one country to
another in search of opportunities elsewhere.   The HC's
basic concern, therefore, was with legal problems and relevant political questions, and with securing a series of
agreements to provide refugees with identity and travel documents.   After careful preparation, Nansen called an inter-
governmental conference in Geneva (July 1922) to consider
a proposal for a legal status for registered refugees which
would be acceptable within and between countries.   The
Conference endorsed his proposal for a special certificate
of identity to be issued by individual governments to Russian
refugees in their territory.   Fifty-four governments ultimately agreed in principle to accept this certificate of identity for Russian refugees, a "Nansen Certificate, " known as
a "Nansen Passport"--although it was not identical with a
national passport. [11]

By an Arrangement of 31 May 1924, the same provisions were extended to Armenian refugees.   Thirty-eight
states agreed to recognize it.   In 1928 the provisions were
extended to Assyrian, Assyro-Chaldean, Turkish and Assimilated Refugees which thirteen governments accepted. [12]
In May 1935 provisions were extended to about 4,000 Saar
refugees--most of whom had entered France after the Refer-
endum held in the Saar. [13]

The Nansen Passport was an identity and travel document good for one year and renewable. Its crucial feature was that it gave the holder the right to return to the country issuing the document and thus permitted the refugee to travel elsewhere. While the certificates of 1922 and 1924 were not valid for return unless they contained a special statement to that effect, by the Arrangement of 12 May 1926, accepted by twenty-three states, the rule was reversed to make the certificate valid for return unless it contained a special statement to the contrary.[14] Nonetheless the certificate did not provide equal treatment for citizens regarding labor permits, social security, taxation, and other by-products of normal citizenship.

The importance of the Nansen Passport can hardly be overestimated. Through this first international identity paper, refugees of specified categories became the possessors of a legal and juridical status. Thus refugees, who were de facto or de jure stateless and without protection or representation from their native governments, were provided with both by the High Commissioner for Refugees, who acted for them in a quasi-consular capacity. This function is similarly of primary importance for the work of the UN High Commissioner for Refugees (HC).

Inter-governmental Arrangements of 1922-28: Extension of Consular Functions

On the basis of a League resolution the HC called a further international conference in Geneva, held in June 1928. A series of Arrangements were accepted:

First, as mentioned above, the Arrangements of 1922, 1924, and 1926 were extended to the Assyrian refugees.

Second, an Arrangement was concluded to define more clearly the legal status of Russian and Armenian refugees.[15] The activities of representatives of the HC up to this time had no basis other than the resolution of 27 June 1921. The Arrangement, adopted by eleven states, was only a recommendation, not legally binding, but it was an important precedent for the extended services of the present-day UNHCR. It recommended that the services, normally furnished to nationals abroad by consulates of their national country, should, in the case of the refugees, be carried out by the HC's representatives.   They could provide quasi-consular services in regard to

> certifying the identity of the position of the refu-
> gees; their family position and civil status, inso-
> far as these are based on documents issued or ac-
> tion taken in the refugees' country of origin; testi-
> fying to the regularity, validity, and conformity
> with the previous law of their country of origin,
> of documents issued in such country; certifying the
> signature of refugees and copies and translations
> of documents drawn up in their own language;
> testifying before the authorities of the country to
> the good character and conduct of the individual
> refugee, to his previous record, to his profession-
> al qualifications and to his university or academic
> standing; recommending the individual refugee to
> the competent authorities, particularly with a view
> to his obtaining visas, permits to reside in the
> country, admission to schools, libraries, etc.

Third, the non-obligatory nature of the latter Arrangement led the Belgian and French Governments to a
special Arrangement Concerning the Functions of the LoN
High Commissioner for Refugees, ratified by them on 2 and
21 May 1928 respectively. [16] It recognized the right of the
HC's representatives to exercise regular consular functions
regarding the provisions in Art. 1 of the above-mentioned
Agreement.

Officially, legal and political protection remained under the jurisdiction of the Secretary-General of the LoN,
but in fact it lay in the hands of the HC, who administered
his task by means of nineteen representatives established in
agreement with the respective governments of those countries in which they resided.   In the 1937-38 report of the
Nansen Office, 133,439 interventions were reported to have
been undertaken in the interest of individual refugees: to
obtain documents for them, to secure social security, to
liberalize employment restrictions, or to help them in other
legal matters.

By the middle of 1928 the number of unemployed refugees had been reduced from some 400,000 to approximately
200,000.   The majority of the remaining unemployed refugees were neither agricultural workers nor equipped for industrial work overseas.   Thus it appeared essential to

secure their absorption and assimilation in their countries
of refuge. Dr. Nansen believed that this task could be performed in ten years if adequate provision was made for
planning and carrying out a specific program to secure this
end. He proposed that the LoN's Secretariat should carry
these new responsibilities as well as continue to provide
legal and political protection for the refugees.

The International Nansen Office: 1931-38

Although the Assembly, by the Resolution of 23 September 1929, placed the HC under the Secretariat of the
LoN for one year, it contemplated a new comprehensive organization which led to the creation of the International Nansen Office for Refugees, with the stipulation that its work
be concluded at the latest by 31 December 1938.[17] It was
an independent body which, as designated by Art. 24 of the
Covenant, was to be "put under the direction of the LoN. "

The post of the HC was abolished, and supreme authority in the new International Nansen Office was exercised
by a Governing Body whose President was nominated by the
League Assembly. The President's coordinating role was
reinforced by his dual position as President of the Office itself. Professor Max Huber, then President of the ICRC,
was nominated. Georg Werner, Swiss, succeeded Max Huber on 1 January 1933, and in January 1936 a Norwegian,
Judge Michael Hanson, was appointed. Hanson served the
Office to the end of its existence in 1938. The Governing
Body consisted of three representatives of the Inter-Governmental Committee on Refugees (IGCR), three from the Advisory Committee of the private organizations (two of whom
were to be refugees), two representatives of the League's
Secretary-General, and the Director of the ILO.

The LoN's Secretariat was responsible for the legal
and political protection of the Russian and Assimilated Refugees, both in the interim period of 1929-30 and thereafter.
However, in practice, the Nansen Office undertook all phases
of the work for refugees in both periods.

While the League covered the annual administrative
expenditures of the Office, operational work was partly financed through the sale of Nansen stamps, a "fee for an
identity certificate in each country" similar to a national
passport fee.[18] In addition, a surcharge on French stamps

(totalling 326,000 f. francs) and Norwegian stamps (totalling 133,000 Norwegian crowns) was contributed to a revolving fund known as the Humanitarian Fund. The total income of this fund amounted to 1,300,000 Swiss francs. In addition, about twice this amount came from voluntary contributions by governments, and donations and legacies from private organizations and individuals.

Four unforeseen problems arose during the period of the Nansen Office which made it impossible to carry out the original plan of settling the remaining refugees in a ten-year period. The first was the worldwide economic depression which seriously affected the employment of refugees. It became increasingly difficult for refugees to secure labor permits, and even those employed were often forced to relinquish their jobs to nationals. Refugees without means of support were expelled from some countries and refused admission to others. A second major problem was the decline in the prestige and moral influence of the League due to the failure of the collective security in the Sino-Japanese and Italo-Ethiopian conflicts. In the third place, the entrance of the Soviet Union into the League strengthened the tendency to reduce League activities on behalf of refugees, since the Russian representatives bent their efforts to restricting endeavors on behalf of Russian refugees. The fourth factor was the new refugee problem that arose in Germany from 1933 on.

The High Commissioner for Refugees
Coming from Germany: 1933-39

The refugees coming from Germany after 1 January 1933 included both political refugees and persons who feared persecution on account of their Jewish extraction. Initially, their numbers were small. However, a quarter of a million were to seek refuge outside their homeland in the course of six years. By December 1937, the figures had already reached 158,000 (49,700 in Europe, 16,500 in North America and 43,000 in Palestine). The expansion of the "German Reich" led to new flights: 7,000 from the Saar territory in 1935; 60,000 from Austria after 1938; and a few thousand from Czechoslovakia after September 1938. By 1941 the number of Jewish refugees was estimated at 402,000 to 431,000; that of non-Jewish refugees at 32,000 to 36,000.

Compared with the former Greek, Russian, and Armenian movements, these were small totals, but the fact that these persons fled into other countries primarily to seek refuge and not settlement was a fundamental difficulty. The refugees were dispersed in an incidental fashion and without planned relationship to the economic, social, or political absorptive possibilities of their countries of refuge. While in the early years after WWI emigration to overseas countries had mitigated refugee pressures, the worldwide economic depression of 1931 had nearly stopped emigration.

In addition, political and military uncertainties were making all countries less willing to admit groups of aliens for permanent settlement. At the same time that the refugee problem became larger and more difficult, European countries had less capacity or will to solve it.[19]

In September 1933 the German refugee problem was brought before the Assembly of the LoN by the Netherlands representative. Because of the objections by the German delegation to direct action by the League, a compromise was formulated and the High Commission for Refugees (Jewish and other) Coming from Germany was set up on 16 October 1933, with its headquarters first in Lausanne, then London. It was an autonomous organization, responsible to its own governing body and not to the League Council, consisting of representatives of the countries of asylum and the private organizations. In contrast to the League's HC from 1921-29, the HC of the new office, Mr. J. G. McDonald, an American appointed by the LoN, had to secure from private sources not only funds for the settlement of refugees but also funds for their legal and political protection and for the administration of the Office itself. He resigned in 1935, pointing out that the work needed the authority of the League, and in fact, his resignation led to direct League involvement. On 14 February 1936, the Council appointed Sir Neill Malcolm, an Englishman, as High Commissioner for Refugees. He was a League official and obtained administrative expenses from the League, to which he was responsible. Thus his position corresponded somewhat to that of Dr. Nansen.

His mandate, confined to the improvement of the legal status of refugees and to finding refugee employment was extended to refugees coming from Austria following its annexation by Nazi Germany.[20] The humanitarian work was left to the voluntary agencies.

Convention Relating to the International
Status of Refugees: 1933

     The HC secured a travel-document arrangement for
the German refugees relatively easily, but the problem remained of securing legal and political protection similar to
the provisions for the Russian and Armenian refugees laid
down in the Arrangement of 1928.

     The world economic crisis at the turn of the thirties
continued to cause unemployment everywhere, and labor
regulations for foreigners had become very stringent in
many countries.   In addition, the rising costs for social
welfare led to less relief for destitute refugees.   Refoulement (expulsion) became more prevalent.   The urgent need
for a binding and comprehensive legal agreement which
would guarantee an international status to the refugees became more and more apparent.   In spite of the critical
time, a legal convention was achieved in 1933 under the
outstanding leadership of Max Huber. [21]   The drafting governments, referring to the Preamble of the Covenant of the
LoN ("in order to promote international cooperation by the
maintenance of justice") to Art. 23(a) of the Covenant and
to the Inter-Governmental Arrangements of 1922, 1924,
1926 and 1928, stated in the 1933 Convention:

> Refugees shall be insured the enjoyment of civil
> rights, free and ready access to the courts, se-
> curity and stability as regards establishment and
> work, facilities in the exercise of the professions
> of industry and commerce, and in regard to the
> movement of persons, admission to schools and
> universities.

It improved the Nansen Certificate system with regard to
the period of validity as well as the right to return to the
host country.   The Convention restricted the practice of expulsion, ensured the enjoyment of civil rights, and secured
most favorable treatment in respect to labor, welfare, relief, and taxation.   It was effective also for the so-called
Nansen refugees, under the Nansen Office. [22]

     A provisional arrangement for dealing with the Ger-
man refugees was finally signed at Geneva on 4 July 1936. [23]
It was replaced two years later by the more formal Convention Concerning the Status of Refugees from Germany,
signed at Geneva on 10 February 1938. [24]   In many respects

the latter was a repetition of the 1933 Convention.   It incorporated the following definition of refugee:

> Persons possessing or having possessed German
> nationality and not possessing any other nationality
> who are proved not to enjoy, in law or in fact,
> the protection of the German Government.
>
> Stateless persons not covered by previous Conven-
> tions or Agreements who have left German terri-
> tory after being established therein and who are
> proved not to enjoy, in law or in fact, the protec-
> tion of the German Government.

A further protocol to these above mentioned documents extended the provisions to refugees coming from
Austria. [25]

Effect of International Conventions
and Agreements: 1921-46

The major shortcomings of the legal arrangements
made on behalf of refugees during the period of the LoN
were the lack of universality in their acceptance and lack of
uniformity in application.   The more binding and comprehensive the nature of the agreements, the fewer tended to be
the states which ratified them.   Thus, while fifty-six states
eventually accepted the Arrangement with Regard to the Issue of Certificates of Identity to Russian Refugees of 5 July
1922, only eight states ratified the much more comprehensive Convention Relating to the International Status of Refugees of 28 October 1933, and only three states ratified the
Convention Concerning the Status of Refugees Coming from
Germany of 10 February 1938.   Many of the ratifications
were made subject to reservations.   In practice, the diversity of the administrative procedures of ratifying states
varied the application of the Arrangements, even when the
obligations accepted were identical. [26]   Moreover, at least
three of the Arrangements made during this period were
purely recommendations to governments and not of a binding
nature.   (Arrangement for the Issue of Certificates of Identity to Armenian Refugees of 31 May 1924; Arrangement Relating to the Legal Status of Russian and Armenian Refugees
of 30 June 1928; and Arrangement for the Issue of a Certificate of Identity to Refugees from the Saar of 23 May 1935.)

It must be emphasized, however, that, despite the difficulties encountered with the legal arrangements and agreements made concerning refugees in the period 1921-46, these instruments highlighted the specific problems facing the refugee, focused international attention upon finding solutions to the problems, and established important legal precedents for future international agreements regarding the status of refugees.   The precedents established during the period of the LoN were most important in that they developed and gained recognition for the concept of international protection for refugees exercised by an international agency on behalf of the community of nations.   In particular, the efforts of Dr. Nansen and his successors brought about a general acceptance of the need to provide refugees with a recognized travel document that would permit them to cross international borders in search of new and permanent homes. Moreover, the approach embodied in the Convention of 1933, of setting forth the specific economic and social rights which should be accorded by states to refugees, although not widely accepted at the time, served as the model for much of the substance contained in the more comprehensive and much more widely accepted Convention Relating to the Status of Refugees of 28 July 1951, the present "Magna Carta" for refugees.   And the forms and functions of the various High Commissioner's Offices created during the period of the League served as models for the shape and functions given to their eventual successor, the United Nations High Commissioner for Refugees, in 1951.

High Commissioner for Refugees Under the
Protection of the LoN: 1939-46

On 30 September 1938, the Assembly decided to amalgamate the two refugee offices, the International Nansen Office and the High Commissioner for Refugees Coming from Germany, under a single "High Commissioner for Refugees under the Protection of the League of Nations" for a period of five years.   Sir Herbert Emerson, a British civil servant, was appointed HC as of 1 January 1939 and became responsible for the legal protection of Russian, Armenian, Assyrian, Saar, German, Austrian, and Czechoslovakian refugees coming from the Sudetenland--totalling about 800,000 persons. [27]   The new HC was entrusted with the task of coordinating the humanitarian work, of promoting resettlement opportunities, and of supervising the application of the various arrangements and conventions in the field of international

protection. Following the precedent set in 1921, the LoN
supplied the yearly cost of the administrative expenditures
of the HC but did not provide assistance directly, as it had
done for Nansen's work. In brief, his role was essentially
that of an intermediary with a very limited staff. Funds
received from governments or private sources had to be allocated to those bodies which he considered best qualified
to administer the required assistance.

The Inter-Governmental Committee
on Refugees: 1938-47

The great difficulties caused by WWII crippled the
activities of the HC, as of course did the liquidation of the
LoN. On 31 December 1946 the mandate of the HC of the
LoN was terminated, and on 1 January 1947, the IGCR assumed responsibilities in London, outside the mantle of the
LoN. The first IGCR Director had been George Rublee, an
American; he was succeeded in February 1939 by Sir Herbert Emerson who served to the end of the Committee on
30 June 1947. This Committee had been created on the
initiative of President Roosevelt at an international conference held at Evian-les-Bains, France, July 1938 and it was
attended by representatives of thirty-two states including both
members and non-members of the LoN. The Committee's
original task had been to facilitate the exodus of refugees
from Germany and Austria and to seek resettlement for
them. As a result of the Bermuda Conference, held in April 1943, the mandate of the IGCR had been extended to the
Spanish refugees and to new refugee groups caused by WWII.
In 1946 its mandate was still further extended to all refugees
subsequently covered by the Draft Constitution of the IRO,
which took over all responsibility for refugees on 1 July
1947. The IGCR Conference held in London, approved on
15 October 1946 a travel document for those refugees who
came within the mandate of the IGCR and were not covered
by the previous agreements. 28   The Arrangement was signed
by sixteen states and entered into force on 13 January 1947.
The provisions were somewhat similar to those for the issue
of travel documents contained in the Arrangements for the
Nansen refugees and the Convention of 1938. The IGCR coordinated its activities with those of the HC of the LoN, the
newly created United Nations Relief and Rehabilitation Administration (UNRRA), the ILO and the War Refugee Board
of the US. Although no allied agency could halt the development of the Hitler policy toward the Jews, the IGCR by its

support of Jewish voluntary agencies operating in neutral
countries and by its assistance in the underground escape
routes, especially in France, Hungary, Italy, and Rumania,
brought several thousands to safety. (Others, fleeing over
the Pyrenees, were helped by allied agencies to reach North
Africa.)

The IGCR began its first resettlement operations in
1946, using financial contributions made to its operating budget, and thereby laid the foundation for the mammoth undertakings of the IRO. The IGCR also began negotiations with
countries in Europe and overseas that were interested in the
immigration of refugees. It concluded agreements with the
Belgians and with the Occupation authorities in the British
and US Zones of Germany for refugee miners; with the
French and Netherlands Governments, with Tunisia and with
Brazil, Venezuela and several other Latin American countries. Most of these agreements were later taken over by
the IRO.[29] The IGCR also acquired the first three ships of
what was to become the IRO fleet. In addition, it provided
legal and political protection and, through international conferences, developed agreements on identity and travel documents to supplement the "Nansen Passport."

Refugee work under the LoN from 1919 to 1946 and
under the IGCR responded to various needs and attempted
many approaches. Dr. Nansen's efforts, and later those of
J. G. McDonald, to strike at the roots of the problem by
negotiations with refugee-producing countries (in particular
with the Soviet Union and the German Government), were
unsuccessful. Thus the refugee agencies had to concentrate
on meeting the needs of refugees in such ways as to mitigate their plight, protect their dignity as human beings and
aid them in achieving a viable life.[30] In so doing, they
provided constructive precedents, techniques, and experience
on which subsequent refugee agencies, especially the IRO
and the UNHCR, have been able to build.

The outstanding figure during the early period of international refugee work was unquestionably Dr. Nansen. In
recalling Nansen's work on 24 October 1967, Prince Sadruddin Aga Khan pointed out that Nansen had

> concentrated his efforts on solving a problem which
> had accrued in Europe when Europe faced a tre-
> mendous accumulation of uprooted peoples and ref-
> ugees. Europe also had moral, social, and

philosophical precepts which allowed it to be the
first area of the world to establish certain concrete principles on refugee work--to define a refugee, to evolve the first legal instruments which
gave refugees a kind of entity, a kind of identification which they had never possessed until that
time. [31]

Dr. Nansen laid the foundations for the international
protection and assistance to refugees of the LoN and of its
successor, the UN. A man of great vision, humanity, and
warmth of heart, Nansen became, in the words of his successor Dr. van Heuven Goedhart, first UNHCR, the great
organizer of refugee work and the conscience of the LoN
and the international world. [32]

Notes

1. Otto Kimminich, Der Internationale Rechtsstatus des
     Flüchtlings, 1962: 206-26.

2. See UNHCR, The Red Cross and The Refugees: 7ff.

3. Ibid. : 8, and LoN, OJ, Mar. -Apr. 1921: 227.

4. Louise W. Holborn, "The League of Nations and the
     Refugee Problem, " The Annals, 1939: 124.

5. See Minutes of the Thirteenth Session of the Council,
     LoN, OJ, Annex 224, Sept. 1921, a summary state-
     ment in Annex C, Sec. II, to the record of the
     Sixth Meeting of the Second Assembly, 1921, LoN,
     Records: 105-6. See also the Nansen Report for
     1929, LoN A. 23, 1929, VII: 9.

6. The administrative expenses paid by the LoN were
     designated for staff salaries, the necessary branch
     offices, and the headquarters. Dr. Nansen's work
     was performed on an honorary basis. In the first
     phase, the expenditures amounted to an average of
     200,000 Swiss frs. yearly; in the second phase,
     during the work of the ILO, and then under the
     International Nansen Office, they averaged 300,000
     Swiss frs.

7. See Stephen P. Ladas, The Exchange of Minorities:

Bulgaria Greece and Turkey: 337, and Kimminich, op. cit. :   226-30.

8.   Werner von Schmieden, "Die Flüchtlingshilfe des Völkerbundes" in HIV Vol. 1:   235-37.

9.   See ibid. :   238.

10.   See ibid. :   233.

11.   This term was first officially included in the Saar Agreement of 1935, Arrangement of 5 July 1922, LoN, TS, Vol. 13, No. 355.

12.   LoN, TS, Vol. 89, No. 2006.

13.   Arrangement for the Issue of a Certificate of Identity to Refugees from the Saar, accepted by 17 states, LoN, OJ, June 1935:   633.

14.   LoN, TS, Vol. 89, No. 2004.

15.   Arrangement Relating to the Legal Status of Russian and Armenian Refugees, 30 June 1928, LoN, TS, Vol. 89, No. 2005.

16.   LoN, TS, Vol. 93, No. 2126.

17.   Res. of 30 Sept. 1930, LoN, OJ, Spec. Supp. No. 84: 157 ff.

18.   See Arrangement of 12 May 1926, par. 6.

19.   Walter Adams, "Extent and Nature of the World Refugee Problem" and "Refugees in Europe" in The Annals, May 1939:   26-44.

20.   LoN, OJ, 1938:   367.

21.   Convention Relating to the International Status of Refugees, signed 28 Oct. 1933.   LoN, TS, Vol. 159, No. 3363.

22.   For details of all these Arrangements and the 1933 Convention see Louise W. Holborn, "The Legal Status of Political Refugees, 1920-38. " AJIL, Vol. 32, No. 4, Oct. 1938:   680-703, and Kimminich, op. cit. :   231-40.

23. LoN, TS, Vol. 171, No. 3952.

24. LoN, TS, Vol. 192, No. 4461.

25. LoN, TS, Vol. 198, No. 4634, and by a Res. of the
     League Council to the Sudeten Germans on 19 Jan.
     1939, LoN, 1939, No. 72.

26. See Paul Weis, "The International Status of Refugees
     and Stateless Persons," JDI, No. 1, 1956: 4-69,
     esp. p. 22; and Holborn, "The Legal Status of Politi-
     cal Refugees," op. cit. : 680-702.

27. Additional Protocol of 14 Sept. 1939, LoN, Doc. C,
     258 M776, 1939, xii.

28. See IGCR, Preparatory Documents Concerning the Adop-
     tion of an Identity and Travel Document for Refugees
     Coming within the Mandate of the IGCR, London,
     1946. For text see UN, TS, Vol. 11, No. 73.

29. Agreement between the IGCR and the PCIRO, 27 June
     1947. For text see Louise W. Holborn, The Inter-
     national Refugee Organization, Its History and Work,
     1946-52, Oxford UP, 1956, pp. 591-92 (hereafter
     cited as IRO History).

30. See ibid. : 9.

31. Rep. to the Ex. Com. (XVIII), GA, (XXII) A/6711/
     Add. 1, 15 Nov. 1967, Annex 1: 12.

32. G. J. van Heuven Goedhart, "Refugee Problems and
     Their Solutions," Oslo, 12 Dec. 1955.

Chapter 2

AGENCIES OF THE UNITED NATIONS

During WWII and the immediate post-war period there took place the most formidable displacement of population the modern world had ever experienced. At the outbreak of the war there were more than one million refugees in various parts of Europe and Asia. This number was swelled almost beyond calculation by mass movements bringing vast human misery and suffering in their wake. Careful estimates by the Inter-Allied Committee on Post-War Requirements (Leith-Ross Committee) indicated that by 1942 there were more than twenty-one million homeless and displaced persons scattered throughout Europe, not including six million Germans who had been removed from West Germany under the Nazi regime into Nazi-occupied European countries. [1]

The Western Allies attempted to cope with this heavy burden, but they soon became aware that so complex and thorny a problem needed concerted international effort. The UK and the US first tackled the problem in the liberated areas and occupied countries. The British Middle East Relief and Refugee Administration (MERRA), which had been established with headquarters in Cairo on 1 June 1942, had by May 1944 cared for about 46,000 refugees from the Balkans (Greeks, Yugoslavs, and Albanians who had fled to North Africa). On 21 November 1942, President Roosevelt established the Office of Foreign Relief and Rehabilitation Operations (OFRRO) as a part of the Department of State under the direction of Herbert Lehman, later Director-General of UNRRA. Immediately after the landing of the Americans on 7 and 8 November 1942, a Joint Commission for Political Prisoners and Refugees in French North and West Africa began its activities. These agencies worked together with the Supreme Headquarters Allied Expeditionary Force (SHAEF), which had its own "DP Branch" for dealing with displaced persons, but the difficulty of maintaining separate spheres of responsibility of military and civilian authorities, particularly in the period of active warfare, soon became apparent.

In light of these inadequacies and the magnitude of the tasks, plans were developed to establish an international organization for relief and rehabilitation.

United Nations Relief and Rehabilitation Administration

Thus, the United Nations Relief and Rehabilitation Administration (UNRRA) was established by forty-four nations on 9 November 1943 as an operational and temporary UN Specialized Agency. [2] Its goal was "to plan and administer a relief program additional to the Allied armies" and "to prepare and undertake measures for the return of prisoners and exiles into their country of origin. "[3] UNRRA, which was set up before the establishment of the UN organization, became the first UN agency to deal in a comprehensive way with refugees and displaced persons. While it focused on the broad task of relief and rehabilitation in the more devastated areas, relief and repatriation of uprooted persons formed a significant part of its objectives. During the winter of 1944-45, local government agencies in cooperation with the civil affairs officers of the Allied Armies, operated assembly centers and camps for some 100,000 refugees; a very high percentage of these were Soviet-Russians, Poles, and displaced persons from other eastern European countries. By the end of the war, European war refugees were located mainly in the occupied countries of Germany, Austria and Italy, where they were partly under the control of the Western Allies and partly under the control of the Soviet Union. In Poland and other parts of Central and Eastern Europe they were under the control of the Soviet Union. In addition, there were displaced persons in the liberated countries--Norway, Denmark, the Netherlands, Belgium, Luxembourg, France, and Greece--and in several other countries in Europe and the Middle East. A complete statistical picture of these post-war multidirectional movements is not available. [4] From May to September 1945, SHAEF with the cooperation of UNRRA repatriated about seven million persons. In July 1945 SHAEF was liquidated, and its functions transferred to the Allied Control Council in Germany. The Soviet Union did not allow UNRRA to work in its zone; the three other Occupation powers concluded separate agreements with UNRRA.

UNRRA was the major civilian operating and coordinating agency in the liberated countries in Europe. Under its agreement it was to "plan, coordinate, administer or

arrange for the administration of measures for the relief of
victims of war in any area under the control of any of the
United Nations through the provision of food, fuel, clothing,
shelter and other basic necessities, medical and other services. " By the middle of 1945, more than 300 UNRRA
teams were in the field caring for displaced persons.   By
the end of 1945 UNRRA had supervision of 263 assembly
centers in Germany alone.

The UNRRA Council resolved that "it shall be the
policy of the administrator to enlist the cooperation and seek
the participation of appropriate foreign relief agencies to the
extent that they can be effectively utilized in relief activities
for which they have special competence and resources. "

Participation of the Voluntary Agencies
In UNRRA's Relief Program

During UNRRA's operations, more than sixty voluntary
agencies (ten operating internationally, and national societies
from twelve different countries) participated in UNRRA's program of relief.   They provided various services to displaced
persons and refugees, including distribution of basic relief
and supplementary feeding, health services, employment,
guidance, education, vocational training, spiritual and recreational programs, child-care programs, tracing services,
and resettlement.

The voluntary agencies did not operate independently.
Their activities had to be carried out under the UNRRA
"umbrella. "   As a result, long-established agencies with
diverse backgrounds and purposes were closely linked with
an official international agency.

After a long period of effort, to work out mutual assistance and to coordinate planning, a high degree of cooperation was achieved.   Cooperation fell roughly into four categories: (1) secondment or loan of agency personnel directly
to UNRRA; (2) development of supplementary projects by
agencies working in countries receiving UNRRA aid; (3) contributions of supplies by agencies directly to UNRRA or for
special groups or areas in countries where UNRRA operated;
(4) establishment of joint-planning committees or councils
with agencies, UNRRA, and governments in countries receiving UNRRA aid.   This kind of cooperation and complementary
effort between international organizations, governments, and

voluntary agencies became more formalized and more closely
knit during the IRO operations; such collective responsibility
has become even more significant in the UNHCR's work.

But coordinated relief was a temporary expedient.
Liberation and final repatriation were the main objectives of
the authorities sharing responsibility for displaced persons
in the early post-war period: the British, American, and
French armies, UNRRA and the IGCR. By 1945 it had become evident that a large number of displaced persons were
non-repatriable; they were reluctant or unwilling to return
to their homelands either because they had lost all ties with
their countries of origin or because of changed political conditions there. But at the same time many displaced persons
did not want to make their permanent homes in countries
where they had been brought against their will, in many
cases as slave laborers.

At the close of UNRRA, 30 July 1947, the great majority of displaced persons, about seven million, had been
returned home through organized repatriation by UNRRA.
However, the monthly number of those repatriated had rapidly declined after 1945. The issuance of special repatriation
food rations did not prevent a further decrease in the number repatriating. [5] These people, together with non-settled
pre-war and wartime refugee groups, represented the core of
the post-WWII refugee problem in Europe. In addition, in
the second half of 1945, a new influx of refugees had begun
into the overcrowded and war-devastated countries of Germany, Austria, and Italy. At the beginning of 1946, it was
estimated that there were close to two million persons who
had to be considered as refugees and for whom new homes
had to be found. They were a serious liability for the Allied powers. UNRRA was not in a position to deal with them
because its responsibility for refugees was only repatriation,
not settlement outside the countries of origin. The impending closure of existing refugee organizations (LoN High Commissioner, IGCR, and UNRRA) necessitated prompt action.

UN Deliberations

Emergence of General Principles. The solution of
the refugee problem and the creation of a comprehensive
refugee organization thus became the concern of the UN at
its very beginning. On the initiative of the Norwegian Government, the idea of creating a UN international refugee

organization had been discussed by the Preparatory Commission of the UN in May 1945 at San Francisco, but no action
was taken at that time.   In November 1945, the government
of the UK, one of the two main contributing members of the
IGCR, pointed out that after UNRRA's efforts for repatriating displaced persons were terminated, a refugee problem
would still exist.   It would be a matter which would concern
all members of the UN and could best be solved through the
UN.

On 13 December 1945, before Committee Three (Economic and Social) of the Preparatory Commission of the UN,
the UK delegate again stressed the urgency and importance
of bringing the refugee problem under the UN because of its
political and financial aspects and because of its concern to
all the member nations.   This, he said, would ensure the
free and open discussion of all questions relating to refugees, some of which involved difficult political problems. [6]

The question of refugees was put on the agenda for
the first part of the First Session of the General Assembly
(GA) under Item 17: "Matters of urgent importance, including the problem of refugees. "[7]   The matter was referred to
the Third Committee of the GA for consideration and report
to the Plenary Session.   More hours were devoted to the
refugee problem during the two parts of the First Session of
the GA than to any other single question except that of international security.   A vigorous debate ensued on the political
and technical implications of this humanitarian question as
well as upon the nature and scope of any new international
refugee organization.

The UK, the US, France, and other countries considered that the problem was "international in scope and character," and maintained that an effective solution could only
be achieved through an international organization.   International action was needed "in the interest of humanity and social stability" and to solve a problem which was "a source
of disturbance in the relationships of the nations. "[8]   The
Yugoslav delegate presented an alternative proposal, emphasizing that the problem of displaced persons had ceased to
be an important international question.   In his view no permanent international machinery was necessary to organize
assistance to such persons.   In the course of prolonged discussion in the Third Committee and in the following Plenary
Meetings of the GA, the Yugoslav view was upheld and elaborated by the Eastern European countries (Poland, USSR,

Ukranian SSR, and others). In their view, the solution of
the refugee problem was repatriation to be arranged as
quickly as possible, preferably through bilateral arrangements between the countries concerned, and denial of international aid to those who refused repatriation.

The different points of view on repatriation culminated
in an exchange between the US and the USSR delegates in the
Third Committee of the GA in 1946. [9] Mrs. Roosevelt, the
US delegate, supported the right of the individual to free
choice and Mr. Vishinsky, the USSR delegate, stressed the
paramount authority of the state over its nationals. The GA
rejected the Soviet point of view. While the West has considered repatriation to be the ideal solution for the refugee
problem, as did Dr. Nansen initially, the principle of "voluntary repatriation" in contrast to "forced repatriation" has
governed international practice to the present.

Following debate, the GA in a Resolution of 12 February 1946 (A/45) recognized that "the problem of refugees and
displaced persons of all categories" was "one of immediate
urgency, " and laid down three broad principles which should
govern future assistance to refugees: (1) the refugee problem should be viewed as "international in scope and nature;
(2) there should be no forced repatriation; (3) repatriation
for displaced persons should be pursued and assisted. [10] The
Resolution referred the matter to a special committee, to be
set up by the Economic and Social Council (ECOSOC) "for
thorough examination in all its aspects already considered in
the GA and to prepare a report for the Second Part of the
First Session of the GA. "

Character and Functions of a New Organization for
Refugees. Heated discussions among the representatives of
the twenty states on the Special Committee on Refugees and
Displaced Persons, spread over two months (8 April-1 June
1946), revealed not only the dimensions of the refugee problem but also discrepancies of opinion in regard to the need
for an international refugee organization and the form it
should take. The Special Committee examined more closely
the question of the term refugee in the light of the entirely
new situation created by WWII. It also studied how the general principles laid down in the Resolution of 12 February
1946 could be applied so as to give refugees and displaced
persons as well as interested governments the maximum
guarantee that their legitimate interests would be safeguarded.

The delegates discussed at some length the character
and functions of the agency which would best serve the purposes they had in view. A "truly representative and effective organization under the auspices of the United Nations"
was needed, which should "be given full authority to deal
with all classes of displaced and uprooted persons" and "be
assured of the necessary funds" to enable it "to cope adequately with this urgent complex, and inevitably long-term
problem. "11

Three possibilities were considered: (1) under Art.
22 of the Charter, the GA might establish machinery coming
directly under its own authority; (2) under Art. 68, a commission under ECOSOC might be set up; (3) under Arts. 57
and 63, a specialized agency could be created as an autonomous body linked with the UN by a negotiated agreement.
The British delegation was in favor of either of the first two
suggestions, mentioning the HC under the authority of the
League as a precedent. Members of the Commonwealth,
Belgium, France, and the Netherlands were also in favor of
the integration of the new organization with the UN and expressed doubts concerning the efficacy of any refugee agency
not under the authority of the UN. 12   However, the US favored a temporary specialized agency since "such a large
operational task, to be done well, must be able to function
quickly and with appropriate flexibility. " The US delegate
also pointed out that such a specialized agency would function
within the framework of the other agencies which were related to the UN, cooperating with it in accomplishing its purposes. In contrast, he felt that the UN itself was a deliberative body for discussing and deciding policy issues, in other
words a kind of parliamentary body.

The Draft Constitution which the Special Committee
prepared was discussed and amended in ECOSOC and the
Third Committee of the GA and finally adopted by the Plenary Session in a Resolution of 15 December 1946, by a vote
of 30 affirmative votes, five rejections, and 18 abstentions.
In spite of their basic differences, the final Constitution reflected an effort to meet the wishes and interests of all
members.

Creation of the International Refugee Organization

The IRO was created as a non-permanent Specialized
Agency of the UN (Art. 3) to deal with all categories of

refugees which had been the concern of other organizations
up to that time.   The beginning of its responsibility was set
at 1 July 1947, at which date UNRRA and the IGCR would
be liquidated.   Before the Constitution would come into
force, fifteen states had to ratify it, and a firm subscription
of 75 percent of the operational budget of the IRO had to be
secured.   By the Agreement of Interim Measures to be taken
in respect of Refugees and Displaced Persons, also concluded
on 12 December 1946, a Preparatory Commission of IRO
(PCIRO) assumed the responsibilities from 14 July until 20
August 1948, when this provision was fulfilled.   Only eighteen states out of fifty-four UN members became members
of the IRO: Australia, Belgium, Canada, China, Denmark,
Dominican Republic, France, Guatemala, Iceland, Italy,
Luxembourg, the Netherlands, New Zealand, Norway, Switzerland, UK, US, and Venezuela.

        The IRO, with headquarters in Geneva and about
ninety branch offices (BOs) throughout the world, was the
second operational or functional UN Specialized Agency.
The Director-General was nominated by an Executive Committee and elected by the General Council, the policy-making body.   He was entrusted with administrative and executive functions according to the decisions of the two governing bodies.   He was to be responsible to them and to report
on the work of the Organization twice a year.   The staff,
amounting to 2,877 persons at the peak of the IRO's operations, was appointed by the Director-General and worked as
international civil servants under the principles and conditions of Art. 101 of the UN Charter.[13]   The budget was
divided into administrative and operational expenses.   Over
a period of four-and-a-half years of operation--from 1 July
1947 to February 1952--the contribution paid by eighteen
governments amounted to the impressive total of $398,596,802,
with additional income of nearly $40 million from UNRRA and
IGCR, gifts, transportation, surplus selling, and Deutsch-
mark funds from the German economy.   Additional expenditures were made by individual national governments and
voluntary organizations.[14]

        The situation facing the IRO was considerably differ-
ent from that which had faced the Allied Armies and UNRRA
previously.   The figures available give only a partial view
of the general dimensions of the task.   When the PCIRO took
over operations on 1 July 1947, refugees and displaced persons under the IRO mandate were dispersed over a wide
geographical area and their total number was estimated as

being somewhere close to 1.5 million (not including those of
the Far East).[15] The difficulties facing the IRO in its performance of world-wide operations had a direct impact on
the minds of the refugees and demanded great flexibility and
adaptation in the Organization's attempts to stabilize the
position of refugees.

The wide range of IRO functions made it possible for
the first time to approach the refugee problem in all its
phases: identification, registration, and classification; care
and assistance; and repatriation or resettlement and reestablishment in countries able to receive those refugees who
were under the mandate of the IRO.[16] The majority lived
in the three Western Zones of Germany, in Austria, and in
Italy. Most of the remainder were in Belgium, France, the
Netherlands, Portugal, Spain, Greece, Sweden, Switzerland,
and Turkey. In addition, there were refugees in the Middle
East as well as in East Africa and India. In Shanghai,
Europeans of Jewish and White Russian origin were waiting
for an opportunity to leave China.

In terms of the kind of IRO assistance received, three
types of refugees were categorized: those refugees and displaced persons living in camps who were receiving care and
maintenance (that is, full livelihood); those living outside
camps who were receiving aid in resettlement and legal protection; and those who were de jure or de facto stateless
persons and receiving only legal protection.

These refugees were of some thirty different nationalities, the majority being Poles, Ukrainians, Latvians, Lithu-
anians, Yugoslavs, Estonians, Romanians and Hungarians.[17]
They were spread over twenty countries: in Africa, North
and South America, Asia, Europe, the Middle East and the
Far East.

The refugee population naturally fluctuated during the
period of IRO operations, and precise figures of the new
refugee flow which developed during IRO's activities are not
available. The information summary presented to the Second
Part of the First Session of the PCIRO (May 1947) by its
Executive-Secretary regarding the numbers of refugees and
displaced persons entitled to receive aid or protection from
IRO is shown in Annex 2.1.

This complex operation could be accomplished only
through joint effort by the member governments of the IRO,

the governments of asylum and of resettlement, the international and national voluntary agencies, and several UN organizations. They worked together in a three-phase effort
toward a final settlement of refugees: (1) temporary relief
activities of care and maintenance; (2) the movement of refugees out of the countries of temporary hospitality through
either repatriation or resettlement; (3) the establishment of
the refugee as a person possessing full citizenship and thus
adequate legal protection and the means of earning his livelihood.

During its four-and-a-half years of existence, the
IRO developed more formalized and closely intertwined cooperation among these partners, enhancing the concept of
collective responsibility. It "brought into effect a truly combined effort which enormously increased the organizational
resources which could be mobilized."[18]

For the purpose of carrying out these functions the
IRO was provided with wide powers in Art. 2.

Repatriation and Resettlement under the IRO

Organized repatriation, in contrast to spontaneous repatriation during the SHAEF and UNRRA operations, was accomplished for only 73,000 persons, including some 11,000
overseas Chinese who were moved back to China. In its
resettlement activities, on which IRO had predominantly to
concentrate, it built on the foundation of the IGCR, taking
over IGCR agreements with governments and private organizations, and concluding new agreements.[19] In contrast to
the overseas migrations of former centuries, post-war migrations were thus planned and coordinated to a large extent
by an international organization with enormous individual and
collective resources. The IRO's migration activities were
conducted under three approaches: (1) emigration under government selection schemes (mass settlement); (2) emigration
through personal nomination initiated by known sponsors in
the resettlement country (individual migration); (3) placement
of individuals with prospective employers or sponsors on the
basis of their qualifications or needs (Resettlement Placement
Service). The implementation of each of these three schemes
involved a wide variety of procedures. These procedures
and operational techniques, developed by the IRO in cooperation with its member governments, set new standards and
developed new methods for dealing with the problems involved
in twentieth century migration.[20]

In the immediate post-war years several factors had
been favorable for the resettlement of refugees. Above all,
governments were conscious of the precarious lot of the
refugees, the denial of human values and of the fundamental
human rights and worth of the human person--those principles which had been proclaimed in the UN Charter and had
been reaffirmed in the Universal Declaration on Human
Rights. Many also considered the solution of the refugee
problem of utmost importance in the maintenance of world
peace, because the inherent instability of the refugee situation as well as refugee discontent were factors likely to increase political tensions.

Governments also became aware of the fact that refugees could constitute an asset to their country. Among the
refugees were people with needed and valuable technical
skills as well as a large number of experienced farmers.
Western European countries needed additional manpower for
reconstruction and to fill the population gap caused by high
mortality and low birth rates during the war. Overseas
countries equally needed additional manpower for economic
development and to make up for the lack of immigrants
throughout the war years.

Furthermore, the member governments were anxious
that during the lifetime of the IRO--originally foreseen as
three years--the greatest possible use should be made of the
costly IRO fleet (at its peak of operation the IRO had forty
ships under its charge) by moving a large number of refugee
migrants. No less important was the impetus concurrently
to reduce cost for care and maintenance of the camp popula-
tion--80 to 95 percent of refugees in camps were massed in
the few countries bordering on their countries of origin
(Germany, Austria, and Italy) and were under the Occupation
Authorities, the main contributors to IRO funds.

Thus, the governments were as eager to relieve human misery and suffering as to lessen political tension.
They sought to counteract economic instability in the countries of refuge in such a manner that the refugees would not
become a political, economic, and social burden to either
the countries of refuge or the countries of final reception.
Accordingly, many governments progressively widened the
selection criteria by relaxing their immigration legislation,
culminating in the acceptance of "hard-core" cases, and by
preservation of the unity of families.

        In the earlier period of IRO, Belgium, France, and
the UK were the main receiving countries in Western Europe.
During subsequent years the movements to Western and
Northern European countries declined, partly because the
shortage of manpower could be met by admission of ordinary
migrants, and partly because the refugees availed themselves
of the overseas resettlement opportunities which became
more readily available through agreements concluded by the
IRO with some of the traditional overseas immigration countries: for example, the US, Canada, Australia, Argentina,
Brazil, and Venezuela.

        The US had admitted nearly 42,000 persons under a
directive issued by President Truman which transferred 90
percent of the regular immigration quotas for Central and
Eastern Europe to displaced persons in the US Occupation
Zone.   About 17,000 of those had been assisted under the
IRO.   As it became apparent that the available quotas would
be filled, several interested groups in the US, especially
voluntary societies, worked and lobbied for passage of a
special law which would make it possible for their country
to contribute more generously toward the solution of the
refugee problem.   The result was the passage of US Law
774, known as the "Displaced Persons Act of 1948," passed
by Congress on 24 June 1949 (amended by the Acts of 16
June and 29 June 1951), providing for the admission to the
US of about 400,000 persons between 1 July 1948 and 30
December 1951.[21]

The Legacy of the IRO

        The major difficulty which the IRO faced in the per-
formance of its functions was the constant change and development of international politics and economic conditions,
circumstances which had a direct impact on the case load
and on the minds of the refugees and of the governments
concerned.   The IRO administration was able to cope with
its task because of its continuous adaptation of procedures,
and through the combined efforts of eighteen governments and
of numerous international and national voluntary agencies.
The cooperation of international and national governmental
and non-governmental agencies, which had begun with the
efforts of Dr. Nansen in the LoN and became more extensive
and more formalized under UNRRA, was deepened and expanded under the efficient leadership of IRO Director-General
Dr. Kingsley and his staff.

Cooperation was the keynote of the entire effort of the IRO, on the part of not only member and non-member governments but also public and private agencies, religious organizations, and countless individuals. The success of the IRO was proof that such a machine could be built and made to work through international cooperation.

In all three phases of international activity for refugees, the IRO devised better methods for dealing with the problem. In addition to complete care and maintenance-- food, shelter, and medical care--the basic relief program of IRO comprised the wide range of social activities developed in any normal community. In this way, IRO sought to rehabilitate the uprooted people and make it possible for them to be useful citizens in whatever country they were destined to live.

Beyond this, IRO developed a new pattern of emigration. Never before had it been planned so carefully, so humanely, and on such a scale. The significant feature of IRO policy was that emigration was never compulsory. The task of the organization was to facilitate resettlement through liberalizing and humanizing opportunities for emigration.

For the residual category of those unable to emigrate, integration programs were developed with the countries of residence. In this field, new ways were found through the so-called "hard-core" program to help the aged and the chronically ill to secure institutional care. Thus, in accordance with the purposes and principles of the UN, the IRO fulfilled its mandate by bringing into effect "international cooperation of an economic, social and humanitarian character" and by "promoting and encouraging respect for human rights and for fundamental freedoms. " (See Annex 2. 2 for a statement of major items of expenditure under the IRO.)

But while IRO became a "landmark in international experience, " it was not able to liquidate the refugee problem. In setting up the IRO, the UN members had considered the refugee problem as an immediate post-war problem and assumed that it could be solved in a limited time by international cooperation and financing. Three critical problems were left unsolved: namely, material assistance for certain categories of refugees--for those for whom resettlement or repatriation was not in sight, for the continuing influx of new refugees, and for the "hard-core"; legal protection for those who had not the protection of their country of origin; and,

finally, plans and funds for permanent solutions. "The refugee problem, as envisaged in that resolution [12 February
1946], still exists and indeed other problems have been
added. Nevertheless, its size and urgency have been reduced. "22

From IRO to UNHCR, 1949-51

International assistance to refugees after 1921--as described in the preceding chapters--had been both humanitarian and legal in character, but the international agencies
dealing with refugees had been temporary organs, acting essentially pragmatically. The underlying assumption was that
the refugee problem was only a temporary phenomenon and
could be solved through national measures and international
cooperation. Furthermore, the international instruments
developed for providing legal status for refugees covered only
specific categories of refugees.

At no time during the IRO's operations did the General Council of the IRO or the UN lose sight of the organization's temporary character--its function being to solve an
emergency, and its aim "to bring about prompt liquidation of
one of the most tragic consequences of the Second World
War. "23 The expectation was that the IRO's three-year
program would be completed by 30 June 1950. As early as
May 1947, the Director-General presented to the PCIRO (at
the Second Part of its First Session) a document on the legal
and political protection of refugees in which he drew attention to the fact that, while the IRO would also look after the
legal and political protection of refugees in addition to its
main operational functions, this function would in time have
to be transferred to a successor organization. 24

The PCIRO also asked the Commission on Human
Rights at its Second Session in December 1947 to take action
to insure the legal protection of stateless persons by an international body, similar to that which governments grant
their own nations, and to establish the right of asylum on an
international basis. At the suggestion of the Commission on
Human Rights, the Sixth Session of ECOSOC in March 1948
took up the question of stateless persons and adopted Res.
116(VI) requesting the Secretary-General to undertake a study
on the position of stateless persons "in consultation with interested commissions and specialized agencies. "

By 1949, the question of the "rate of rundown" of
IRO operations was already being considered by the IRO itself and by its operational partners, the voluntary agencies
and member governments.   At its Second Session held from
29 March to 8 April 1949, the IRO General Council considered Preliminary Recommendations of the Director-General
with a view to the Termination of the IRO Program and his
proposals for Future International Action Concerning Refugees. [25]   The General Council requested the Director-General to present further recommendations for the "rate of run
down" of the present IRO program, "and for such subsequent
international action as may prove necessary" (Res. 36).

The General Council of the IRO continued to discuss
the completion of the IRO program and future international
action for refugees in lengthy discussions at its Third (Special) Session in June-July 1949. [26]   The member nations of
the General Council unanimously recognized that when their
mission came to an end, there would still be "a serious human problem" and they "wished to make it clear" that "they
will consider themselves as being relieved (by 30 June 1950)
of the responsibility which will rest upon them until then as
members of the Organization. "   They stressed that these
eighteen members had only "temporarily assumed" the responsibility "for the fulfillment of a particular task. "

The thirty signatories to the IRO Constitution had anticipated that the majority of the fifty-four UN member states
as well as other "peace-loving" nations would become members of the Organization and contribute to its expenditures.
(See Annex 2.3 for a statement of contributions made by
member governments.)   This hope had not materialized, and
the eighteen members of the IRO pointed out that they were
no longer willing to contribute to a costly and large-scale
operational agency which should be the responsibility of the
entire membership of the UN.   In short, they were not prepared to recommend a continuation of the IRO.

The General Council set 30 June 1950 as the completion date and instructed the Director-General "to discontinue
on 31 August 1949 all registration whereby refugees and displaced persons may be determined to fall within the mandate
of the Organization, " except unaccompanied children, refugees leaving their countries of origin after that date but
qualifying as under the IRO mandate, and those refugees who
were in need of legal and political protection.   Furthermore,
after 31 December 1949 the Director-General was to

discontinue admission of refugees to care and maintenance in
assembly centers and, after 31 March 1950, admission to
care and maintenance under cash-assistance programs.   By
30 June 1950 he was to discontinue care and maintenance for
all persons except those who were in process of repatriation
or resettlement and those persons (hard-core cases) for
whom permanent institutional or other satisfactory arrangements had not yet been completed (Res. 39).

In a memorandum the Director-General called the attention of ECOSOC to the fact that the IRO contemplated
termination of its operational activities on 30 June 1950 and
suggested that ECOSOC examine the problem of future international action on behalf of refugees, since "the situation
demanded a new organization corresponding to the facts. "[27]

The Director-General pointed out that there would be
large numbers of refugees, now still under the IRO's mandate in various parts of the world--mainly in Europe, and
more especially in Germany--who would not enjoy the protection of the government of their country of origin, and who
would not be rapidly absorbed into the national community of
the country of refuge.   In addition, there would be new refugees for whom the same problems would arise.

The General Council transmitted the memorandum for
consideration and action to ECOSOC with the following recommendations: that ECOSOC should determine that "international assistance in the protection of refugees should continue
unbroken"; that "an organ within the framework of the UN
should be entrusted with this responsibility" after the termination of the IRO; and that the question of the establishment
of an international fund to be administered by the organ for
such purposes as may appear necessary and desirable for
the material assistance of refugees should be dealt with by
ECOSOC.[28]

With Res. 39 the General Council had accepted as its
ultimate objective the termination of the IRO program and
had adopted "measures which should be taken to accomplish
this objective. "

Working Conference of IRO and
Associated Voluntary Agencies

In January of 1949, the Director-General of the IRO
held a combined conference at Geneva of representatives of

the IRO and associated voluntary organizations.   One hundred
and four IRO representatives from headquarters and from
fifteen field areas, and 100 representatives of forty-nine
voluntary organizations from thirteen countries or field areas participated.   This informal working conference for free
discussion of views on present and anticipated problems and
purposes in the operations of IRO and cooperating agencies,
discussed not only "operational requirements and objectives
for the remaining period of the IRO program" but, in great
detail, ways to facilitate future planning and cooperative effort once IRO operations came to an end.

Sir Arthur Rucker, Deputy Director-General of IRO,
pointed out that the prospective termination of the IRO was
only a year and a half away.   Governments could not be expected "to continue their very heavy contributions indefinitely, " and it was evident that "provisions had to be made for
certain parts of the work to continue--notably legal protection, tracing, and care of the residual group. " He continued
by saying that "possibly the UN might accept responsibility
for at least the first two functions.   The third is one we
hope the voluntary agencies will give considerable assistance.
While the solution of big social problems may require state
or official action, heart and soul are lacking if the work is
not supported by voluntary effort and the inspiration of the
charitable and religious impulse. " Mr. Myer-Cohen, Assistant Director-General, responsible for health, care, and
maintenance, stressed that the problem of refugees would
remain after the closure of IRO and the agencies should plan
their budgets and programs for the future accordingly.

Dr. Elfan Rees, Vice-Chairman of the Standing Conference of Voluntary Agencies (SCVA), noted that "there has
rarely, if ever, been achieved closer and more intimate
partnership between statutory and voluntary action than that
between IRO and its Associated Voluntary Agencies. " At the
same time he pointed out that there were fundamental differences between the voluntary agencies and the official organization not only in regard to basic and supplementary services but in the cooperative freedom the agencies had in contrast to the IRO which, by its constitution and official nature, was somewhat circumscribed in its role.   He also
stressed the continuing existence of the voluntary organizations; they had been there before the official organization and
would be there afterward as well.   Most important, voluntary
effort "does not stem from one parent or conform to one pattern" like the IRO.

Dr. Rees expressed serious concern that the remaining problems would be the "inevitable inheritance of the agencies." He emphasized that the voluntary agencies would, "as the agents of the private conscience," stick to their task, would continue their assistance in resettlement and their responsibilities for "reception and integration in new countries," and would assume new and long-term responsibilities for the "hard core," giving assistance through counselling and other services in the realm of social protection. However, the agencies' tasks were "the essential counterpart to official basic provision." In the interest of the refugees, and as long as their problem was unsolved, an official agency of the UN had to help them. He concluded by saying, "there will always be voluntary action, you can always rely on our help; but you would be unwise and unfair to cut [cast] us for the role of residuary legatee."

The Chairman sent a resolution, passed at the following meeting of the SCVA, to the Secretary-General of the UN which emphasized "the deepened concern of the plans for the premature closure of the IRO" (see Annex 2.4).

Termination Procedures

Although the IRO began the phasing-out of its operational programs as early as mid-1949, there was uncertainty for some time as to the date of termination. It was extremely difficult for the administration to develop liquidation plans, which entailed diverse and complicated problems, and for a variety of reasons it was necessary to extend the final date of the IRO operational program; the General Council at its Fourth Session extended the final date to 31 March 1951 (Res. GC/54 and 64 of 20 October 1949); at its Sixth Session the date was further extended to 30 September 1951 (Res. GC/78 of 13 October 1950). Liquidation finally occurred on 28 February 1952 (Res. GC/108). The period of operation after the initial 1950 deadline was known as the Supplementary and Closure Period.

Another complication in IRO termination plans was that, although the GA had decided on 3 December 1949 to establish as of 1 January 1951 a High Commissioner for Refugees, the final Statute of the Office was not adopted by the GA until 14 December 1950.[29] This Statute limited the competence of the HC to non-operational and predominantly promotional activities. Plans for a new migration agency were also under discussion; these led in late 1951 to the creation of the Inter-Governmental Committee for European Migration (ICEM) outside the UN, but its operation did not begin until February 1952.   Thus the transfer of resettlement equipment was to be in abeyance until then.

Procedural delays in refugee resettlement were a further complication in the termination of the IRO.   While the organization was striving to resettle as many refugees as possible overseas before termination, delays in processing and reception by governments--filling the numbers under the United States Displaced Persons (USDP) Act which expired on 31 December 1951, and changes in Canadian and Australian migration programs--made resettlement planning more complicated.   The transfer of residual groups, that is, those not yet resettled, to local authorities on 1 July 1950, required negotiations and arrangements which involved complex questions and interests for sovereign governments and voluntary agencies in Western European countries.   But on 1 July 1950, 111,000 IRO refugees became the responsibility of national governments in Western Europe, West Germany, and Austria.   Because of the difficult situation of the Italian Government, a very broad definition of the "resettlement pipeline" was applied in Italy, so that all eligible refugees in that country remained under the IRO's care, and transfer of responsibilities to the Italian Government was postponed until 1951.

After the transfer of responsibility for the residual group on 1 July 1950, the IRO still retained responsibility for care and maintenance of the so-called hard core cases. These were persons who had limited opportunities for resettlement because of problems of health, age, or family composition. [30]   From a functional point of view, these were people who either required institutional care or some special assistance without institutional care.   Those who were actually or potentially self-supporting fell into certain categories generally rejected by resettlement missions.

To speed up the process of finding solutions for the residual group as a whole, the Director-General, following the instructions of the General Council in the final period of the IRO program (Res. GC/39), brought to bear a variety of techniques and resources in order to deal with this complex problem: intensive counselling on a case-to-case basis; rehabilitation and vocational training programs; cooperative assistance of voluntary societies; and agreements in certain

areas for the establishment of institutions to be operated by
local welfare organizations.

In a survey presented to the GA on 27 October 1951
(Res. GC/97), the General Council provided a breakdown of
the residual group as follows:

Germany	80,000
Austria	24,000
Italy	24,000
Trieste	7,000
Greece	4,500
Turkey	300
Spain and Portugal	600
	140,400

In addition, 1,000 to 1,500 new refugees were entering Germany, Austria, Turkey, Greece, Trieste, and Italy monthly
from Eastern European countries. In all of the areas initial
reception resources for their care were inadequate and many
of these refugees had to move on westward to find opportunities for a livelihood. Their impact was thus felt in nearly
every country of Western Europe, where political asylum was
an established tradition. This continuous influx underlined
the long-term character of the refugee problem, particularly
in Europe, which had been a matter of concern to international bodies ever since the end of WWI. The survey also
mentioned three "outlying areas": the Middle East, with 90
European refugees; the Philippine Islands, with 150 on the
island of Samar; and China, where 5,000 refugees of European origin remained, of which 400 persons required institutional care because of age, illness, or other disability.

During its last year of operation, the IRO disbursed
$600,000 in direct care and financial assistance to provide
for the survival of approximately 3,000 refugees in the Far
East, the Philippines, Greece, Lebanon, Spain, Portugal,
and Turkey. In addition, the IRO gave an estimated
$800,000 a year to voluntary agencies to help them in their
work for these refugees, where national relief programs
were not of themselves sufficient to meet refugee needs.
During its final year an additional $3 million was given by
the IRO to aid voluntary agencies in Germany, Austria, and
Italy. [31]

ICEM was able to establish a revolving fund of $1
million to help individual migration--partly by a contribution

from the IRO which was administered by the voluntary agencies--and to provide a contribution to the administrative expenses of the voluntary agencies. In addition, the IRO transferred $500,000 for the establishment of a revolving fund for the resettlement of European refugees from Shanghai. A grant of DM 4,800,000 was transferred to the Special Department for non-German Refugees of the German Expellee Bank by the IRO. In the final disposal of its assets, the IRO, inter alia, transferred $236,698 to the UNHCR. (See Annex 2.5.)

In concluding its work, the General Council stressed that "although the problems inherent in the situation are clearly not of sufficient magnitude to justify the maintenance of the IRO, they are so grave in terms of human suffering that they call for urgent consideration by the UN. "32

Notes

1.   Foreigners who had been deported or recruited as workers in Germany or who took refuge there; see IRO, Constitution, in Holborn, IRO History: 584-85.

2.   For text of Agreement (Constitution) see Louise W. Holborn, ed. , War and Peace: Aims of the United Nations, Vol. 2: 159-61.

3.   George Woodbridge, The History of UNRRA, Vol. 3: 23 and 31.

4.   Figures available in connection with the bilateral arrangements made by France with the USSR and Poland indicate that from France, 2,000 Russian refugees and 3,500 Armenians returned to the Soviet Union; on the basis of a French-Polish arrangement 47,000 Polish refugees, slave-workers, and others returned from France to Poland; also, 400,000 to 450,000 Spanish nationals who had been refugees in 1939 had, by 1946, returned from France to Spain, reducing the estimated number of Spanish refugees to between 125,000 and 225,000.   For more complete figures see Jacques Vernant, The Refugee in the Post War World.

5.   Twelfth Report of UNRRA to US Congress.

6.   GA (I), Third Com., SR.

7.   GA (I), Off. Rec., Part I.

8.   GA (I), Third Com., 1947, SR, Annex 5A: 56.

9.   Quoted in IRO, GC/SR/94, p. 6, Ex. Com. (IX).

10. For text of this Res., see Holborn, IRO History: 589.

11. E/REF/52: 2 and E/REF/39: 1.

12. GA (I), Third Com., SR: 53.

13. Holborn, IRO History: 97ff.

14. The two largest operational supporters were the US
     with a contribution of 45.75 percent and the UK
     with 14.75 percent; 39.89 percent and 11.48 percent
     respectively for administrative expenses. Holborn,
     IRO History: 102ff.

15. Ibid.: 197-98.

16. Ibid.: 583.

17. IRO, The Refugee Problem, 1948: 4.

18. ECOSOC (XIV), E/211, July 1952.

19. See Holborn, IRO History, for respective Constitutional
     provisions: 693-94; for government agreements:
     594-680; for agreements with voluntary agencies:
     679-80.

20. For detail, see Ibid.: 365ff.

21. Ibid.: 411.

22. Rep. of IRO to ECOSOC (XIV), E/211, July 1952: 31.

23. GA (III), Third Com., Off. Rec., 12 May 1949: 435.

24. Doc. IRO/PREP/41, 29 Apr. 1947: 12.

25. IRO, Doc. GC/W/3 and Doc. GC/W/4.

26. IRO, Docs. GC/80 and GC/81; see Holborn, IRO History: 725-29.

27. IRO, GC/80, 11 July 1949.

28. ECOSOC (IX), E/1392, 11 July 1949.

29. GA Res. 319 (IV), 1949.

30. Unmarried mothers with children under 17; unmarried couples with or without children; those widowed, separated or divorced; those who had personal or occupational problems (criminal or security record; professional or specialist workers over 35 years of age; clerical, sales or other white-collar workers over 40 years of age); or uneconomic families (too large for self-support).

31. Res. 106 of IRO, GC (IV), Feb. 1952.

32. Ibid.

ANNEX 2.1

Refugees and Displaced Persons Entitled to Receive Aid
or Protection from International Refugee Organization, 1947

	Protection and help	Protection only
Germany, Fed. Rep. of	671,900	800,000
Austria	138,800	128,500
Belgium	5,000	-
China	13,500	12,000
Spain	482	482
France	431,200	150,000
Greece	2,000	-
Italy	146,500	146,000
Middle East	33,000	30,000
Netherlands	5,000	-
Portugal	230	230
UK	60,000	-
Sweden	40,800	-
Switzerland	13,200	12,000
Turkey	1,200	1,200
Total	1,562,812	1,280,912

Note: On 15 September 1948, the IRO published the following additional figures: As of July 1947. Protection and assistance: 704,000 refugees and displaced persons; protection only: 900,000 refugees (including 550,000 pre-war refugees); total for the two categories: 1,604,000.

SOURCE: UN, Dept. of Ec. and Soc. Aff. A Study of
             Statelessness, NY, Aug. 1949: 8.

ANNEX 2.2

International Refugee Organization--
Major Items of Expenditures (in US Dollars)

	1947-48	1948-49	1949-50	1950-52	Total
Administrative Expenses-- Total	3,475,306	4,299,985	4,489,730	5,437,803	17,702,824
Operational Expenses					
Personnel and establishment	11,370,714	13,482,953	15,468,431	12,877,268	53,199,366
Purchase and maintenance of vehicles	2,976,806	3,882,608	1,645,615	1,010,255	9,515,284
Health, care, and maintenance	42,476,834	43,227,193	28,146,399	33,575,709	147,426,135
Repatriation	1,483,057	668,332	233,666	82,945	2,468,000
Resettlement	13,844,765	65,012,461	67,742,120	48,283,652	194,882,998
Reestablishment loans	48,358	133,741	97,513		279,612
Losses on exchange		693,871	1,498,915	7,510	2,185,276
Program reserves		766,332	79,508		845,840
Operational Expenses--Total	72,200,534	127,867,491	114,912,167	95,822,319	410,802,511
Grand total	75,675,840	132,167,476	119,401,897	101,260,122	428,505,335

SOURCE: Holborn, IRO History: 125.

ANNEX 2.3

International Refugee Organization--
Contributions Made by Member Governments
1 February 1947-7 February 1952 (in US Dollars)

Member Governments	1947/48	1948/49	1949/50	Supplementary Period	Accumulated Totals 1 July 1947- 7 Feb. 1952
Australia	2,753,225	2,738,552	2,729,715	972,664	9,194,156
Belgium	1,575,405	1,567,062	1,561,355	558,433	5,262,255
Canada	5,440,717	5,411,553	5,396,117	1,916,287	18,164,674
China[4]	4,064,512	4,043,599	4,021,513	1,461,889	13,591,513
Denmark	1,059,462	1,059,961	1,055,961	376,525	2,491,948
Dominican Rep.	62,824	62,491	62,274	22,237	209,826
France	6,481,481	6,447,267	6,422,481	2,301,233	21,652,462
Guatemala	62,824	62,491	62,274	22,237	209,826
Iceland		31,965	31,812	11,495	75,272
Italy		3,525,351	3,514,373	1,250,985	8,290,709
Luxembourg		62,491	62,274	22,237	147,002
Netherlands	1,426,745	1,419,232	1,413,545	507,228	4,766,750
New Zealand	688,666	684,998	682,766	243,354	2,299,784
Norway	688,666	684,998	682,766	243,354	2,299,784
Switzerland		1,714,893	1,709,166	609,639	4,033,698

UK	22,832,464	22,709,603	22,650,524	8,025,495	76,218,086
US	71,024,899	70,643,727	70,447,729	25,000,000	237,116,355
Venezuela		358,481	357,289	127,425	843,195
Total Contributions Due	117,102,428	123,228,216	122,863,934	43,672,717	406,867,295
Less Total Contributions Unpaid		2,727,067[1]	4,081,537[2]	1,461,889[3]	8,270,493[1,2,3]
Total Contributions Received		120,501,149	118,782,397	42,210,828	398,596,802

1. China Contribution due $4,043,599, less amount paid $1,316,532   Amount unpaid $2,727,067

2. China Contribution due $4,021,513   Amount unpaid $4,021,513
   Guatemala " $ 62,274   " " $ 2,250 $ 60,024
   $4,081,537

3. China Contribution due $1,461,889   Amount unpaid $1,461,889

3. China Contribution due $1,461,889   Amount unpaid $1,461,889

4. The Chinese Gov. has made no contribution to IRO since 1948/49 when they were credited with $1,316,532 in cash and services, equivalent to approximately 32-1/2% of their contribution for that year. Although the contribution of China has been included in this statement, it has not been taken into the resources available to the Organization for expenditures subsequent to 1948/49.

SOURCE: UN, ECOSOC, E2211, Annex V, Apr. 1952: 37.

ANNEX 2.4

Communications From the Standing
Conference of Voluntary Agencies Co-Operating With
The International Refugee Organization (4 Oct., 1949)

17 Route de Malagnou,
Geneva

Mr. Donald Kingsley
Director-General
International Refugee Organization
Geneva

Dear Sir:

As you know, the Standing Conference of Voluntary Agencies
at its most recent meeting again gave serious consideration
to the problem presented by the decision that IRO should
terminate its activities as soon as possible after June 30,
1950.   Convinced that the cessation of international services
to refugees at that date would constitute a serious hardship
to hundreds of thousands of people, as well as a serious
breakdown in the scope of international effort, the Standing
Conference adopted the enclosed resolution and asked me as
its chairman to transmit it both to the Secretary General of
the United Nations and to IRO.   I therefore enclose in addition a copy of my letter of transmittal to the United Nations
and I hope that you will refer this matter to the appropriate
office within your own organization.

Sincerely yours,

(Sgd.) M. W. Beckelman
Chairman, Standing Conference
of Voluntary Agencies

The Conference has noted the proposals of the Economic and
Social Council of the United Nations for a successor agency
but points out that failing reconsideration of datelines now
established no new applications for assistance will be considered by the IRO and that there will be an inter-regnum

during which no international provision of even an emergency character will be available for new refugees.

If, in spite of these facts, member governments adhere to their present plan for the dissolution of IRO in June 1950, the Conference urges the continuation of at least those services which are a bounding international responsibility.

To avoid a breakdown in the complicated and smooth functioning emigration machine, there should be continuation of mass resettlement machinery and its ancillary services until such time as resettleable DPs have been moved to new homes; and continued provision and on a long term basis, of international machinery to facilitate individual migration.

Moreover, it is urged that renewed efforts be made to obtain whenever possible resettlement opportunities for hard core and to remove the remaining cases from countries of present residence, giving priority to those countries in which the long-term residence of DPs will be especially precarious. To the degree that the IRO fails to achieve this end the Standing Conference pleads for the immediate and permanent provision of Legal and Social protection and for the provision of financial assistance to those countries and agencies who undertake to assume responsibility for a share of this burden.

We wish to point out that the members of the Standing Conference will undertake to do all in their power to continue their services to refugees on a long-term basis, but our services are essentially ancillary to basic international provision and it will be quite impossible for organizations supported by private contributions alone to bear the whole future burden of refugee needs.   The resultant chaos and tragedy that will inevitably follow this untimely withdrawal of basic international provision will be catastrophic for refugees and DPs.

SOURCE: IRO, GC/115, 4 Oct. 1949.

ANNEX 2.5

International Refugee Organization,
GC Res. 106: Disposal of Assets

The General Council of the IRO

Having considered proposals for the disposal of any assets
of the Organization over and above those included in the
Final Plan of Expenditure

Resolves that such assets shall be disposed of in accordance
with the following schedule of priorities:

1.   the first charge shall be to meet unforeseen
     claims against the Organization and to defray any
     additional costs of liquidation which might be in-
     curred during the period of liquidation beyond
     those provided for in the Final Plan of Expendi-
     ture;

2.   the second charge shall be to reimburse the Pro-
     visional Intergovernmental Committee for the
     Movement of Migrants from Europe the costs of
     moving IRO eligible refugees who, by 1 February
     1952 had been visaed, but not moved;

3.   the third charge shall be to provide, after con-
     sultation with the United Nations High Commis-
     sioner for Refugees, to the extent of assets
     realized from a satisfactory settlement of the
     Food Replacement Account in Germany and from
     any assets which may be realized in Deutsche
     Marks, grants for assistance to residual refugees,
     such as grants for refugees in Trieste, to the
     Displaced Persons Department of the Expellee
     Bank, to Voluntary Societies and to Refugee Ser-
     vice Committees;

4.   the fourth charge shall be to establish a revolving
     fund in the form of a trust, to be managed by the
     Provisional Intergovernmental Committee for the
     Movement of Migrants from Europe, for the

movement of refugees who received visas after
1 February 1952.   Priority will be given to refugees now registered with the IRO

SOURCE: L. Holborn, IRO History: 748.

Part II

THE ESTABLISHMENT OF THE UNHCR: 1949-53

The UN is a peace-keeping and a peace-building organization. Its mandate is not only to maintain international peace, but also to create the conditions for stability and well being by employing international machinery for the promotion of the economic and social advancement of peoples.

Adapted from the Preamble of the UN Charter

INTRODUCTION

We have seen that the UN and its members were faced as early as 1948 with the realization that the organization which it had created two years earlier to take care of the problem of refugees, the IRO, was unable to fulfill its task in the allotted period. There was inevitably a residual group of refugees in countries of first asylum who had been neither repatriated nor resettled abroad or assimilated in their countries of asylum and, in addition, new refugees were arriving in the asylum countries every month. The issue was what, if anything, to do about the problem. The eighteen members of the IRO had agreed that they would no longer carry the burden of the refugee problem. But they were equally agreed that some further organized international effort would have to be made, and in this they were supported by the governments of the first asylum countries, by the concerned voluntary agencies, and to some extent by the countries of overseas resettlement as well. The international climate, however, in which the debates took place at the UN concerning the possibility of future action on behalf of refugees during the phase-out period of the IRO, was such that the issue was fraught with political as well as humanitarian considerations.

Two major kinds of political issues marked the process which produced the UNHCR from the debates of ECOSOC and the GA during 1949 and 1950. The first was a product of the growing tensions between the West and the East and was linked with the second, the very basic issue of what the international community should do with refugees. This discontent had been a major factor in the debates that had created the IRO and had also been a factor of great importance in shaping the way in which the IRO had operated, and in determining its successes and failures. These tensions had reached much more serious proportions by early 1948 with the Communist takeover of Czechoslovakia and the Berlin blockade and airlift. It reached its height in 1949-50 with the dispute between the USSR and Yugoslavia, the appearance of the People's Republic of China and the beginning of the

Korean conflict in 1950. In Europe, growing East-West tensions had brought about the declaration of the Truman Doctrine (12 March 1947), the initiation of the Marshall Plan economic aid program (June 1947), and the creation of the North Atlantic Treaty Organization (NATO) as the Western military shield against the threat of Soviet attack (April 1949). There was also the establishment of the Federal Republic of Germany out of Western-occupied Germany, and the setting up of the German Democratic Republic out of what had been Soviet-occupied Germany (May and October 1949). Moreover, the East in October 1947 had created the Cominform as the central organization for international communism. Thus Europe had become politically, economically, and socially divided, and the opposition of each side to the other had gravely hardened.

This basic ideological division between East and West was reflected in their division at every level and on every issue before the organs of the UN, and it affected the debates on future action for refugees as well. The basic Soviet and Eastern position was that all refugees should be repatriated forthwith to their homelands; any other action in some manner constituted exploitation of the refugees and violated international law by infringing on the sovereignty of the refugees' states of origin. The basic position of the West, as we have seen, was that repatriation could only be carried out with the voluntary agreement of the refugees themselves, and that all other refugees had a right to be granted a home elsewhere. While it had been possible to reconcile these two views somewhat in 1946 when the IRO was created, by defining that organization's functions as first repatriation and secondly resettlement, the split between East and West by 1949 made any common effort between them for future action on refugees impossible during the period of the establishment of the UNHCR. The East opposed further international action unless it was repatriation; the West continued to favor international action for refugees of some kind, but was divided over what the nature of that action should be.

During and after WWII the US had played the foremost role in designing and bringing into being the UN and its functional agencies, and it envisaged the UN as an instrument for "harmonizing the actions of nations in the attainment of ... common ends" (UN Charter, Preamble). The US Government had committed itself to an active international role and to collective responsibility. But the hardening of the Cold War had a deep impact on the foreign and domestic

policies of the US and brought about a fundamental reorienta-
tion of US foreign policy. Moving from a predominant reli-
ance on multilateral organizations, notably the UN, to a
strengthening of bilateral and regional ties with its allies,
the US less and less viewed the furtherance of the UN as a
significant cornerstone of its foreign policy. In a similar
development, many of the states of Western Europe were
moving towards closer regional cooperation as contrasted
with dependence on international organization.

     The profound change in US foreign policy resulting
from the changing international setting of 1949 and 1950 affected the government's policy in dealing with refugee problems. While the US Congress in 1946 had supported establishing a UN agency which included Soviet representation, by
1950 the East-West split had become so acute that Congress
vetoed the use of American funds for any international organization which would include Iron Curtain countries. The
US Government now preferred that its participation in UN
organs be held constant or be diminished and it proposed
that future action for refugees be handled through agencies
created outside the UN where only the US and its allies
would be directly involved. This was not an inflexible policy; it was recognized in the case of the Palestinian refugees
and the Korean refugees that aid programs must be set up
under UN auspices, and the US was a substantial instigator
and supporter of the United Nations Relief and Works Administration (UNRWA) in 1949, and of the United Nations
Korean Reconstruction Agency (UNKRA) after the Korean
War. The US was also not unconcerned with refugees in
Europe. Long after the issue of what the form of the
UNHCR should be was settled, American contributions to the
resettlement of refugees from Eastern European countries
who were fleeing Soviet domination continued through the
creation and support of ICEM and USEP (United States Escapee Program). But whenever possible, the US sought to
find forums outside the UN for such refugee activities and
to restrict the role of the UN in handling such problems.
In planning for European economic recovery, Will Clayton,
Assistant Secretary of State, in a State Department memorandum wrote that other nations might help with surplus food
and raw materials, "but we must avoid getting into another
UNRRA. The United States must run this show. "[1]

     There was another change in US policy in the period
between 1946 and 1949-50 that directly affected refugees; this
concerned the view of the need for continued large-scale
financial contributions.

A very large number of refugees had been resettled,
several years had passed since the end of the war, and
there was no longer the same willingness to accept refugee
immigrants, especially those who were more costly or less
useful to the host country. A great deal of money had been
donated by the US to the IRO, and there was strong feeling
that the time had come to terminate that support. Furthermore, the US had now turned decisively to the economic assistance of the European countries through the Marshall
Plan. Such aid, it was felt, would make it easier for these
countries to absorb the remaining refugees, who were after
all basically "their" problem. The US believed it had done
its share, and that in any case all that remained was to
"clean up" the remaining, comparatively small problem by
absorbing the refugees into the countries of asylum. In
short, there were both political and economic reasons for the
change in US refugee policy. Although the humanitarian aspect remained unchanged--concerned Americans did want to
see the problem of the refugees solved--the question was
how that was to be done in the light of the new US attitude
toward resettlement and toward making heavy contributions.

Meanwhile, the problem of refugees continued to
plague the countries of first asylum in Europe. They had,
of course, a great deal of assistance in diminishing the number of refugees who were on their soil, but the refugees remaining were in general those who seemed more a burden
upon their host countries than an asset. A truth about refugee resettlement is that countries are most willing to accept
refugees when they can see an economic benefit to themselves in so doing and least willing when only the humanitarian consideration is involved.

The Western European countries realized that, given
the new US policy, there was no realistic hope of the IRO
continuing to handle the problem of refugees by relieving the
countries of first asylum of their presence. Everyone, both
in Europe and overseas, realized that the major burden of
the remaining refugees would now have to be carried by the
countries of first asylum, and the issue to be decided was
what if any assistance the international community was going
to provide to those countries and the remaining refugees,
within that context. The governments which carried the brunt
of refugee influx as countries of first asylum wanted both
material assistance and assurance that the possibility of overseas resettlement remained open. The US and the other
countries of overseas resettlement sought to minimize

international action, because they wanted to reduce their financial contribution and because they felt the problem was essentially solved, the remnants being in fact someone else's responsibility. Within that context, they were more than willing to support the creation of a successor to the IRO--if the term "successor" is an appropriate one for such a different kind of organization.

In 1949 and 1950 then, two lines of international action for refugees were being simultaneously pursued. The IRO was working desperately to complete as much of its mission as possible before its time ran out. The member states, having established and contributed to the IRO, were anxious for the job to be completed. The deadline for its termination was extended and extended again, more funds were provided by its members, and other funds were sought in order to get the greatest possible number of refugees resettled. But at the same time, the existence of the so-called "residual problem" became clearer, along with the need for a long-term, albeit different, approach to that problem. Such was the setting in which debate was initiated on a future agency to handle the residual problem. The Director-General in his report on residual problems stressed that

> the whole nature of the refugee problem had undergone a radical change since IRO was established. Large numbers of displaced persons who were uprooted during the war and immediately afterwards, turned out in fact to be political refugees. This determines the essential nature of the IRO's plans and programs, dictating a shift in emphasis from repatriation to resettlement. As political tension increased, the displaced persons who became refugees because they refused to return home, were joined in the swelling numbers by those who fled from the same homelands and arrived as refugees in the areas of IRO operations. This exodus continues, and will continue as long as its causes persist. [2]

The East-West dispute, while the overriding issue of the period, did not affect appreciably the form of the action to be agreed upon within the UN. While the substance of the mandate was affected very considerably by the fact that the West was anxious to get along if it could with the East, by 1948 the Cold War was such that there was virtually no possibility for cooperation. The UN existed as a shell within which the two factions talked at rather than to each other. The East was full of recriminations for the way in which the IRO had, in its view, been used as a tool for the purposes of the West, in violation of the resolutions which had created it, and of its own Constitution. Charges were regularly hurled back and forth concerning the treatment of unspecified refugee groups and specific individual refugees during this period. The East objected at every step of the process that created the UNHCR; but its draft resolutions received little support, and when the time came for action, the West had more than enough votes to support its view. The question of what kind of action the Western states did desire was the more important issue in determining the form of the UNHCR and its powers.

In one major regard there was general agreement among the states of the West: the primary function of a new international refugee organization should be to provide international protection to refugees. This task, aimed at safeguarding the rights and legitimate interests of refugees and at overcoming any disabilities arising from their status as refugees, had been the major purpose of the refugee agencies set up under the auspices of the LoN and was one of the functions of the IRO as well. It was fully accepted by Western states that this protective function should continue to be exercised by some international body. There was such general agreement on this point that international protection was little discussed in the debates at the UN, although it was a most important factor in shaping the views of each delegation concerning the form and substance of the agency to be created. But while they agreed that international protection should be the agency's principal purpose, they did not agree on the implications that followed from that decision. Accordingly, the deliberations that went on within the organs of the UN for two years were centered around the two very different views held by the countries of overseas asylum on the one hand and the European states of first asylum on the other. The delegates debated the refugee problem itself; what international action beyond protection, if any, was needed; and what sort of international organization was therefore appropriate for the task.

The US, as the dominant spokesman for the states of overseas resettlement, sought a strictly defined agency with narrow authority and limited function which would be temporary (lasting three years), require a small staff and little

financing, and which would seek to achieve very limited objectives, notably the protection of the remaining IRO refugees until they were permanently settled and assimilated.
Specifically, the US favored the establishment of a refugee
service within the UN Secretariat rather than the appointment of a HC or the creation of a new specialized agency.
If there must be a HC, then he should be appointed by the
Secretary-General rather than elected by the GA (because,
it was felt, he should serve under the Secretary-General
and not exercise some independent authority where he might
exert influence on public opinion or on governments while in
office).   The US favored a very narrow definition of refugee
in order to limit the new agency to the protection of refugees, as set forth in the Constitution of the IRO.   It opposed
at first any broadening of the definition which might extend
the lifetime of the agency and perhaps, in time, again require the expenditure of sizable funds because of the appearance of new refugee groups.   The US also sought a very
narrow purpose for the new organization--merely the provision of international protection--and tried to rule out the
possibility of the new agency extending material assistance
to refugees.

As has been noted, elements within the country were
not without sympathy for refugees and their problems; many
Americans were deeply concerned and undertook very substantial efforts in the hope of alleviating refugee problems.
The US had been a substantial contributor to, and instigator
of, UNRWA and UNKRA and had not been unconcerned in regard to the European refugees.   But there was considerably
less public interest in the US in the problems of the residual
refugees than there had been in the heat of 1946-47, and
government desire to minimize involvement and cost was
correspondingly greater.

One can summarize the views of the Western European states toward the nature and purposes of the new refugee organization as being in most cases the opposite of the
US view.   There were, of course, differences of opinion
among them as there were among the countries of overseas
settlement.   France, for example, was a leader of the view
that the UNHCR should be a strong, permanent, multipurpose
organization with an independent HC, and most importantly,
with the power to raise funds and disburse them to refugees.
France also sought throughout 1949 to broaden as much as
possible the definition of the term refugee and therefore the
scope of the agency's authority.   There was a certain

realism in seeking a broader definition for a newly established organization, so that it could be influenced by the
Western European states to provide assistance when and if
the residual problem was swollen by new groups of refugees.
(Refugees from Eastern Europe were already appearing in
increasing numbers.) France's approach was also realistic
in that it sought to secure some action through the creation
of an agency and to assure that controversy did not result
in a stalemate.   In several crucial matters France gave way
(as did the US) in order to achieve a compromise position,
while other states, most notably Belgium and the UK, then
demanded broader and longer lasting powers than were urged
by either the US or France.

In short, the debates over wording as well as the
finally agreed provisions of the UNHCR Statute and of its
companion instrument, the Convention, reflect the process
of interaction and compromise between members of the
Western European and the overseas countries.   Without becoming excessively legalistic, Chapter 3 is aimed at focusing on specific issues which concerned UN members when
drafting the Convention and Statute, in order to discern the
broader views and concerns of member states regarding the
problems of refugees and the nature of appropriate international action.

Notes

1.   Quoted from Dean Acheson, Present at the Creation,
        My Years in the State Department, NY: 1969: 231.

2.   IRO, GC (VIII), 22-27 Oct. 1951.

Chapter 3

DELIBERATIONS IN THE UNITED NATIONS

From 1948 through 1950 lengthy deliberations concerning a new international refugee agency to succeed the IRO took place in three organs of the UN: ECOSOC, the Third Committee, and the Plenary Sessions of the GA. While debate during the process of negotiation ranged over every aspect of the pending Statute of the UNHCR, there was general agreement on the part of a large majority of states that the new agency should be established and that its basic function should be to provide international protection to refugees. Discussions centered about those provisions on which there was the most disagreement. These concerned the relationship between the new agency and the Secretary-General; the method of selecting the HC; the lifespan of the agency; questions of material assistance and funding; the extent of the activities to be pursued by the agency over and above international protection; and which refugee groups would come within the scope of its authority.

After debates had continued intermittently for over a year, the GA decided on 3 December 1949 to accept in principle the establishment of the Office of the UN High Commissioner for Refugees as of 1 January 1951, when it was expected that the IRO would terminate its activities. The Assembly adopted the Resolution on Refugees and Stateless Persons (GA [IV] 319) setting forth in a general way the form and functions of the new agency and requested ECOSOC to work out the details of the Statute which would serve as the agency's constitution. After debate the Assembly was ready to vote on the final text for the Statute of the UNHCR. This was based on the draft worked out by ECOSOC in response to the Assembly's earlier request and had been rewritten in the Assembly's Third Committee. Thus on 14 December 1950 the Assembly passed three companion resolutions: Res. 428(V) contained an Annex to the Statute of the UNHCR. Res. 429 (V) included in an annex the Draft Convention Relating to the Status of Refugees as prepared by

65

the Ad Hoc Committee on Refugees and Stateless Persons
and ECOSOC. The GA decided to convene a conference of
plenipotentiaries to complete the drafting and the signing of
the convention. By Res. 430 (V) the GA decided to address
to members and non-members of the UN an "urgent appeal"
to assist the IRO in its efforts and "in the absence of definite data" postponed until its Sixth Session the "examination
of the problem of assistance."[1]   On the same day the Assembly elected Dr. G. J. van Heuven Goedhart of the
Netherlands by secret ballot as the first HC for a period of
three years.[2]

Relation of the New Agency to the Secretariat

The earliest debate concerned the relationship between
the new agency and the existing organs of the UN and centered around two proposed alternatives: whether to place
the service of international protection within the existing
framework of the UN Secretariat, or to place it under an
independent HC who would be directly responsible to the
GA.[3]   At the plenary meeting of ECOSOC on 6 August 1949,
the French and Belgian delegates urged the immediate acceptance in principle of a HC to succeed the IRO. But the
US delegate urged that no decision be taken until further
study of the possible alternatives could be undertaken.[4]   The
US view prevailed, and in ECOSOC Res. 248(IX) A, the
Secretary-General was requested to prepare a more detailed
plan for the proposed new agency, bearing in mind the alternative forms which had been debated.

In response to the ECOSOC request, the Secretary-
General filed a plan for the new agency with the GA on 26
October 1949, indicating his preference for a HC "who would
enjoy a special status within the UN," and would "possess
the degree of independence and the prestige which would
seem to be required for the effective performance of his
functions."[5]   The Secretary-General's view appears to have
settled the issue, and in the Third Committee debates during
the Fourth Session of the GA in the fall of 1949, there was
already agreement that the use of a HC was the preferable
form for the new agency.

Selection of the High Commissioner

Debate in the Third Committee shifted to a closely
related point, the method for selecting the HC. Again

opposing positions were expressed by the delegates of France
and the US, with the former urging the election of the HC
by ECOSOC or the GA on the nomination of the Secretary-
General, while the latter urged his direct appointment by
the Secretary-General.

The debate on this issue was related to the earlier
one on whether the protective function should be placed within the Secretariat or under an independent HC.   The US argued that the HC would of necessity have to work very closely with and under the Secretary-General in order to achieve
his objectives, while France, joined by other members, emphasized that the HC would need the independent stature and
prestige which could only be provided by direct election.
The French delegate stated that in his view the appointment
of the HC by the Secretary-General would simply be another
way of reducing the new agency to the status of a section of
the Secretariat and was therefore as objectionable to him as
had been the earlier suggestion that protection should be provided by a service within the Secretariat. [6]   Voting in the
Third Committee on this point favored the French position,
especially after the French proposal had been amended to
make it clear that election would be by the GA.   Thereafter
this issue was no longer considered. [7]   The procedure of direct election on the nomination of the Secretary-General was
incorporated in the final Statute in par. 13.

The Life Span of the New Agency

During the meetings of the Third Committee at which
the method of selecting the HC was discussed, differences of
viewpoint also emerged concerning the life span of the new
agency.   The Committee had two detailed draft resolutions
before it concerning the new agency, the one submitted by
France and the other by the US.   The French draft made no
mention of a termination date, while the American draft
stated that the agency would function for three years unless
otherwise specified in the interim by the GA.   There was,
nevertheless, a consensus that even if the agency's only
function was to provide protection for those refugees who had
not yet received the effective protection of a government, its
work would need to be continued for considerably more than
three years.   Furthermore, its task would take even longer
if, as some states hoped, the agency was empowered also to
provide protection for refugee groups of the future.   The
point was underlined by the Director-General of the IRO when
he testified that the temporary nature of his organization had

made it impossible for it to complete the task of providing
protection. [8] But, consonant with the US position that the
new agency need only be concerned with the remaining IRO
refugees who were to be absorbed by the European states of
first asylum, the American delegate contended that the agency might need to operate for only a few years, and that its
utility certainly needed to be reconsidered by the GA after a
short time. When France and the US accepted the suggestions of several delegates and combined their draft proposals
into one draft resolution, both agreed to the inclusion of a
provision that the continuation of the new agency beyond a
period of three years would depend upon the decision of the
GA when it reviewed the work of the agency in 1953. Few
delegates at the Third Committee doubted, however, that the
agency would have to have its mandate renewed after three
years.

Material Assistance:
The High Commissioner's Authority

       During the UN deliberations on the UNHCR, two is-
sues involving material assistance were debated. The first
concerned the powers of the new agency directly: should
the HC have any authority to handle funds for material assistance to refugees? The second was whether to set up a
permanent international fund for material assistance in order
to institutionalize the raising and disbursing of some monies.
The two issues were debated separately at the UN during
1949 and 1950, although it was understood that if such a
fund was created it would be administered by the HC. In a
sense, the two issues concerned authorization and appropriation respectively: the first involved the legal power of the
UNHCR to handle funds, and the second the determination of
whether there would actually be any funds to disburse.

       The question of the establishment of an international
fund for material assistance to refugees was first discussed
at the Third (Special) Session of the General Council of the
IRO in July 1949, in connection with plans for future international action concerning refugees. The delegate from
France, M. Rochefort, argued that provision for financial
assistance should be considered to be as important as legal
protection, and his viewpoint was supported by the delegates
of Italy, Belgium, and most other Western European countries. Little enthusiasm for this point of view was shown
by the delegates of the US, Australia, and the UK. The

divergence of views was caused by the fact that the first
group of countries--those which bordered on the countries
of refugee origin--feared the great financial burden which
might result from the presence in and the influx to their
territories of large numbers of refugees after the IRO
ceased operations.   The resettlement countries, on the other
hand, were anxious that funds be devoted primarily to resettling the maximum number of refugees for as long as the
IRO fleet continued to operate.   The divergence was reflected
in the US desire simply to submit the question of material
assistance to the UN without recommendations, as opposed
to the French desire that the General Council of the IRO
specifically call on the UN to establish an international fund
for assistance.

     ECOSOC, meeting in August 1949, took account of the
European views on material assistance in Res. 248(IX) A
and requested that the Secretary-General's proposals on the
nature and extent of the powers of the projected refugee
agency include a proposal for "the administration of any assistance funds which the General Assembly might put at the
disposal of the United Nations for the benefit of certain
classes of refugees. "

     Pursuant to this request, the Secretary-General pointed
out to the Assembly that it was difficult to make specific
recommendations on the matter of assistance funds until the
Assembly had come to a decision regarding the amount and
types of assistance funds involved.   But he urged that as
a general principle the HC be allowed to accept both private
and public contributions, that he have the assistance of an
advisory committee in determining disbursement, and that he
not be responsible for disbursement of funds to individual
refugees but only to governments and voluntary organizations
for use in specific projects.

     The setting up of an Advisory Committee was dis-
cussed by the Secretary-General in his report on Refugees
and Stateless Persons.   He suggested that three functions
might be performed by such an Advisory Committee: (a)
the inclusion of non-members of the UN in the activities of
the UNHCR, especially since the ECOSOC Res. 248(IX) A
of August 1949 specifically asked the Secretary-General to
consider how non-members might be associated with the
work of the UNHCR; (b) "should assistance funds be contributed by Governments on a voluntary basis for use by the
HC, such a committee might appropriately exercise

supervision over the administration of such funds;" (c) "the question of the allocation of such funds [as the HC might receive] between areas, if the amounts are significant, may well require special consideration of the desirability of an inter-governmental committee or board combining the executive functions of allocation with the advisory functions noted in [point (a)] above." There was no detailed discussion of an Advisory Committee, however, until 1950, when the French draft for the Statute, discussed at the Social Committee of ECOSOC in August 1950, contained a provision for such an Advisory Committee. Discussion was inconclusive and the ECOSOC Resolution of that session (319[XI]A of 16 August 1950) simply said that the power to create such a committee should be given to ECOSOC in the Statute after the HC had expressed his views--the same wording that finally appeared in the Statute in par. 4.

The Secretary-General's recommendation found expression in the draft resolution for the Statute submitted by the delegate of France to the Third Committee in the fall of 1949. The French draft included permission for the HC to receive funds and disburse them to governments and private agencies as he saw fit. The draft proposal of the US for the Statute, on the other hand, made no mention of such a function for the HC, and in the debates that followed the US made clear its opposition to the inclusion of such a function in the Statute. Mrs. Roosevelt, for the US, argued that the UN was essentially a deliberative body which inappropriately was being pushed into becoming an international relief agency. The US Government, she said, favored responding to each situation on an ad hoc basis and objected to the general grant of authority to the HC to collect and disburse funds. Furthermore, involvement in material assistance would take up much time and require additional staff, both factors which were incompatible with the US view that the Office should be kept small and its operations very inexpensive.

The French rejoinder was that the US was somehow optimistically assuming that the HC would find no further relief work necessary, that he could raise few funds anyway, and that it would be better under the circumstances not to receive any funds for assistance at all. The French view, on the contrary, was that in many cases legal protection was useless without material assistance, and that even a little relief work undertaken by the HC was better than none at all. Mrs. Roosevelt replied that there might be times when material assistance would be of little value without legal

protection; and that legal protection had the additional advantage that it would require only a small staff and budget.
She went on to imply that the US would at least insist that,
if assistance funds turned out to be necessary, the HC would
have to seek the approval of the GA before requesting such
funds. "Even requests for material aid for the 'hard core'
should be presented to the General Assembly by the High
Commissioner only as the occasion arose," she said.

France and the US refused to compromise on the
question of material assistance; when their joint draft resolution was presented to the Third Committee on 14 November 1949, provisions reflecting both positions were included
and the Committee was invited to choose between them.   In
the final vote within the Third Committee the French provision on material assistance was favored, and the possibility
of the HC handling assistance funds was left open rather
than foreclosed.   The US then voted against the draft resolution as a whole.

At the GA's Fourth Plenary Session following the deliberations of the Third Committee on the general contents
of the Statute, the draft resolution adopted by the Committee
was debated again, and the US renewed its efforts to limit
the powers of the HC in the field of material assistance.
Having been defeated in the Third Committee on the issue of
the general authority to disburse funds, the US shifted its
position at the Plenary Session and sought instead to make
it difficult for the HC to receive funds for assistance.   The
US proposed that the Statute provision on assistance funds be
amended so as to require the HC to seek the prior approval
of the GA before making any general appeal for funds or any
appeal to governments.   Mrs. Roosevelt insisted that it was
preferable for the GA to retain control over such an important matter as assistance rather than to leave that issue to
the discretion of the HC.   The French delegate, M. Rochefort, expressed his willingness to accept the proposed US
restriction on the HC's fund-raising authority, and the GA
also accepted the restriction when it came to vote on the
general form for the Statute in December 1949.   The effect
of the Assembly's resolution was to make it difficult for the
HC to raise assistance funds, but possible for him to disburse whatever funds he might in the future receive.

The further question of establishing an international
fund for the assistance of refugees was not discussed as such
by either the Third Committee or the Plenary Session of the

GA in 1949, and the GA decided to defer consideration of
the fund question for a year, until its Fifth Plenary Session
in 1950.   At the Social Committee of the ECOSOC in the
middle of 1950, a proposal was submitted by the Belgian
delegate to the effect that the HC be allocated funds for the
purpose of granting material aid to hardship cases.   The
Belgian proposal was not adopted, and the ECOSOC resolution on the Statute only reiterated the substance of the limited provision on assistance funds adopted by the GA.   It
was this wording by the ECOSOC that was included verbatim
in the final form of the Statute as par. 10.

Other Activities: Repatriation and Resettlement

        An issue closely related to that of whether the HC
should be permitted to handle such assistance funds as he
might some day receive, was that of whether he should be
permitted to perform functions other than international protection.   Here again the US opposed broadening the authority
of the HC and objected to two amendments by Australia to
the joint US-French draft resolution before the Third Committee in 1949.   The first of these amendments would have
added a provision to the draft resolution noting simply that
in the future the GA could confer functions upon the HC other than protection; while the second would have added to the
list of functions appearing in the draft the words: "Engaging
in such additional activities, including repatriation and resettlement activities, as the General Assembly may determine."
There was little debate on these two amendments before the
Third Committee, and both were accepted by the Committee
in its final vote on the joint US-French draft resolution.   The
US, as noted above, voted against the amended draft.

        When the Third Committee's draft was submitted to
the Plenary Session of the GA, the US sought to have the
two Australian amendments deleted as part of its effort to
limit the HC's Office.   It was unwise, said Mrs. Roosevelt,
to mention such additional functions as repatriation and resettlement since no funds were to be provided for these services; this "raised hopes which might never be fulfilled."
And, speaking in regard to the US proposals for recasting
those parts of the Third Committee's draft resolution unacceptable to the US, Mrs. Roosevelt added, "Should the General Assembly find it possible to adopt the proposed US
amendments, the United States delegation would gladly support the draft resolution."

The French delegate, M. Rochefort, supported the various US amendments, including those seeking to eliminate references to "other activities," despite his earlier stance on some of the issues in the Third Committee.   This change in French policy may well have been made in the hope of ensuring US support for the new agency in the light of the US vote against the draft adopted by the Third Committee and the threat implicit in Mrs. Roosevelt's speech that the US might cast a similar vote in the GA. [9]   M. Rochefort maintained that the US amendments did not substantially affect the form that the French Government favored for the new agency.

With little further debate--the delegates of Australia and Mexico among others spoke in opposition to the US amendments--the GA voted on the Third Committee's draft resolution on the Statute.   The Assembly accepted some of the US amendments but rejected those seeking to eliminate all references to activities other than international protection.   In retaining a reference to such "other activities" the Assembly laid the groundwork for a most important addition to the authority of the HC.

When the Statute was drafted in detail in 1950 its first paragraph set forth two basic functions for the HC:

> the function of providing international protection
> ... and of seeking permanent solutions for the
> problems of refugees by assisting Governments ...
> to facilitate the repatriation of such refugees, or
> their assimilation within new national communities.

Scope of the High Commissioner's Competence: The Problem of Defining the Term Refugee

Of the issues that divided the drafters of the Statute, the one most difficult to resolve was that of determining to whom the benefits of the Statute would apply: that is, to what groups of persons was the HC to extend international protection? The issue centered around fixing a definition for the term refugee, for it was by this device, as the French delegate, M. Rochefort pointed out in 1950, that the scope of the HC's authority was to be established in the Statute.

What was the appropriate scope for the HC's

competence? While the issue of the nature of his authority
had tended to divide the drafters into two groups, the issue
of the extent of his authority produced many divisions. There
was the initial view of the US that the concern of the HC
should extend only to refugees covered by the definition in
the IRO Constitution. There was the view of the UK that he
should concern himself with all present and future refugees
as well as non-refugees who were lacking the protection of
a national government. And between these two views were
those of states which sought a number of different limitations on the HC's scope of authority, and those whose particular concern was the inclusion or the exclusion of some
specific groups of refugees.

        The first disagreement to arise during the process of
attempting to define the scope of the HC's concern was one
regarding statelessness. The IRO and its predecessors had
been concerned merely with the problems of refugees. The
Commission on Human Rights, the ECOSOC Resolution of
1948, and the Secretary-General's consequent recommendations that an international convention on the status of refugees be drafted and an international agency to meet the need
of refugees for international protection be established, on the
other hand, each included references to the problem of
stateless persons. At the time of the drafting of the Statute
and the Convention the distinction between refugee status and
statelessness was yet to be clarified. In the agreements
and arrangements concerning refugees drawn up during the
LoN, a refugee had been defined solely as a person of specified origin who no longer enjoyed the protection of his government. Nothing was said of the reason for his lack of
protection. 10

        While the needs of refugees, as opposed to stateless
non-refugees, have tended to be seen as more immediate and
more numerous--often including food, shelter, and medical
treatment as well as eventual settlement--both groups share
the need for some form of protection in order to ensure for
them at least certain minimal standards of treatment wherever they find themselves. It was the recognition of this
common need that led the Commission on Human Rights, the
ECOSOC Resolution of 1948, and the Secretary-General to
refer to stateless persons in general, meaning both refugees
and non-refugees, and to seek the provisions of international
protection for all those lacking the protection of a state, for
whatever reason.

During the debates within the UN leading up to the drafting of the Statute and the Convention, it became apparent that a majority of states preferred to deal separately with the category refugee, as opposed to stateless non-refugees, even when the issue was solely one of protection. Despite the efforts of a few states and the repeated recommendations of the Secretary-General, stateless non-refugees were eventually excluded from the competence of the HC by the adoption of a definition which included only those persons who both lacked protection and had a fear of being persecuted for reasons of race, nationality, religion, or political opinion. Stateless non-refugees were similarly excluded from benefiting under the terms of the Convention and were left to be the subject of a special international convention eventually drawn up in 1954.

Creation of the AD HOC Committee

Discussion of the Secretary-General's recommendation in the Ninth Session of ECOSOC was thus centered on distinguishing refugees from displaced persons, and both from stateless persons. The resultant ECOSOC Resolution, 248(IX)A of 6 August 1949, nonetheless failed to make clear a definition of the term refugee that would delimit the competence of the agency to be established.

The resolution's main thrust was to request the Secretary-General to prepare more detailed proposals for the structure and functions of the new agency in the light of the discussion which had taken place at the ECOSOC meetings, and to submit his further proposals to the Fourth Session of the GA in the fall. The Secretary-General thereafter reported that his interpretation of the ECOSOC resolution was that the Council was concerned only with the need for the protection of refugees as defined by the IRO; he was, he felt, not called upon to offer either new or modified definitions for the term.

In a companion resolution, 248(IX)B of 8 August 1949, ECOSOC took care of the matter of a possible further international convention on the status of refugees by passing that question on to a specially created Ad Hoc Committee consisting of representatives of thirteen governments. The Committee was empowered to consider the desirability of a further convention and, if they thought one desirable, to draft such a convention. No mention was made in this resolution

of the particular needs of the IRO refugees; the resolution
spoke instead of the broad needs of refugees and stateless
persons generally and seemed to be passing on with approval
the wide recommendations of the Secretary-General for a
new international agreement to improve the status of both
refugees and stateless persons.

The Secretary-General's conclusion that the members
of ECOSOC were interested only in the provision of protection for IRO refugees was refuted in the debate which took
place during the fall of 1949 at the Fourth Session of the
GA.   There was general agreement that the competence of
the HC should extend to groups of persons not included within the IRO's definition; this position was accepted even by
the US although it had proposed at first that the HC's competence be essentially identical to that of the IRO.   The
delegate from France was particularly outspoken in opposing
the transfer of the IRO definition to the HC's Statute and in
urging that the new problem of the day required a new and
broader definition.   Various special groups were mentioned
during the debates as being worthy of inclusion, including
refugees in Greece, India, Pakistan, and the Middle East;
while the UK delegation indicated a preference for the inclusion of all stateless persons, whether de facto or de jure.
No final determination was made during the Fourth Session
as to the scope of the HC's competence however; instead a
proposal submitted by the US was eventually accepted, which
left the question open pending a decision by the Ad Hoc
Committee on a definition of refugee for the draft Convention.   GA Res. 319(IV)A of 3 December 1949 indicated that
"for the time being" persons falling within the IRO's definition of refugee and displaced person would fall within the
competence of the HC, but the GA could add new categories
to that competence "from time to time" including such categories as might be covered by the terms of the Convention
yet to be drafted.

Definition by Categories

Delegates discussing the definition question at the
First Session of the Ad Hoc Committee in early 1950, as
well as at the subsequent Eleventh Session of ECOSOC and
the Fifth Session of the GA, tended to characterize the issue
as one of choosing between two contending solutions.   The
one solution, it was said, was to draft a "universal definition" that would specify the characteristics of refugees to be

included within the Statute or the Convention; the alternative was to draft a "definition by categories" that would enumerate the specific groups to be covered. Of the "definition by categories" it was said that this was the approach that had been used in all prior international instruments pertaining to refugees. [11]

Other delegates pointed out, however, that the experience of the IRO had shown that a "definition by categories" could be very cumbersome in practice. The IRO had required a trained body of eligibility experts and a semi-judicial tribunal of appeals in order to determine which refugees came within its mandate. Since the UNHCR was to be a much smaller organization it would be advisable to have a much simpler and more easily applied definition.

In support of the "universal definition" it was noted that it would provide the kind of simple definition that could be applied without elaborate legal machinery; that it was more in keeping with the broad humanitarian aims of the UN; and that it was more realistic in that it reflected the fact that future refugee groups were certain to emerge that would require the same assistance as groups already in existence. The objection to the "universal" approach was that it was difficult for states to commit themselves to a course of action the scope and duration of which were unknown. The traditional approach by categories was more likely to gain the approval of the large number of states needed to effectively implement the aims of the new agency and convention. If new refugee groups did appear in the future, it was said, then that was the appropriate time to determine what should be done for them.

The substantive views expressed by the delegates during the definitional debates, however, show that few of them saw the situation as essentially "either-or. "

There was a general agreement in delegates' speeches about several specific groups of refugees who should be included, and on several characteristics that refugees should have to be included, as well as considerable agreement on some groups to be excluded. The area of agreement was such as to discourage the adoption of a definition either exclusively "universal" or exclusively "categorical. " A "universal" definition sufficiently unrestrictive to include the refugees covered by the League arrangements (who had not had to "fear persecution") would have included as well many groups dislocated by WWII and its aftermath but not considered so much refugees as economic migrants. A definition composed solely of enumerated categories would have been much longer and even more complicated than that included in the Constitution of the IRO.

From the first major attempt to cast a complete definition of the term refugee at the first session of the Ad Hoc Committee in early 1950, to the final drafts--late 1950 for the Statute and mid-1951 for the Convention--elements of both the "universal" and "category" approaches were apparent. In all the drafts the definition was divided into three parts: the first two, referring to refugees of the inter-war period and to some or all of the groups that had been the concern of the IRO, were definitions by categories; the third, intended as a catch-all provision to cover all others considered in need of international protection as well, was a definition by characteristics. One part of the definition covered any person who in the period between 4 August 1914 and 3 September 1939 was considered to have been a refugee. A second part referred to two groups who had been among the major concerns of the IRO: those who were victims of the Nazi regime in Germany or of associated regimes, and those who were or had a well-founded fear of being victims of the Falangist regime in Spain. The more general third part referred to "any person who: (a) as a result of events in Europe after 3 September 1939 and before 1 January 1951 has well-founded fear of being the victim of persecution for reasons of race, religion, nationality or political opinion; (b) has left or, owing to such fear, is outside the country of his nationality, or if he has no nationality, the country of his former habitual residence; and (c) is unable or, owing to such fear, unwilling to avail himself of the protection of the country of his nationality. "

Debate went on among the delegates of many states concerning aspects of all three parts of the definition; but to the extent that their views can be said to have divided them into two camps, the issue that separated them was the phrasing of the third part. It was here primarily that those delegates who spoke of a "universal definition" were opposed by those who spoke of a "definition by categories. " The first group wanted an open-ended definition that would include refugee groups of the future, while the second preferred a definition limited to groups of the present.

Although the Ad Hoc Committee's report included the

comment that the cut-off date of 1 January 1951 did not "exclude persons who may become refugees at a later date as
a result of events before then, or as a result of after-ef-
fects which occurred at a later date," the inclusion of the
time limitation, and the geographic restriction contained in
the phrase "events in Europe," made this third part of the
definition unacceptable to the proponents of a "universal
definition."

At the meetings of the Social Committee of ECOSOC
in July and August 1950 both the Statute definition and the
Convention definition were under discussion, and the issue
raised at the Ad Hoc Committee meetings came up once
more.   Again the proponents of a "universal definition,"
namely the UK and Belgium, were defeated, and the ECOSOC
revision of the definition of the term refugee remained essentially that proposed by the Ad Hoc Committee for the
Convention, and that proposed by the US, now joined by
France, for the Statute.

Toward a Broader Definition: Separation of the Statute from the Convention

The definitional issue was debated in detail once again
by the Third Committee of the GA in November and December 1950, and once again the question of the coverage of future refugee groups divided the delegates.   But in this instance there were more states represented than at the Ad
Hoc Committee or ECOSOC and the proponents of a "universal definition" were more numerous.   The delegate of the
UK, now the spokesman for those states favoring a broader
definition for the Statute, made two proposals significantly
affecting the scope of application of the Statute.

First, it was proposed that the draft Convention,
which had been considered in detail by the Ad Hoc Committee at its First Session, reviewed in part by ECOSOC at its
Eleventh Session, reviewed again by the Ad Hoc Committee
at a Second Session, and was now under review by the Third
Committee, be drafted in final form by a specially convened
conference of plenipotentiaries from interested states rather
than completed by the GA.   The UK delegate argued that
there simply was not time for the Third Committee or the
GA to go over the Convention draft in detail, and therefore
such a special conference was required.   Furthermore, by
convening a special conference outside the structure of the

UN it would be possible to invite the participation of states who were not members of the Organization. This was especially desirable in that some of them were very concerned with the problems of refugees: Switzerland and the Vatican, because of their historic roles in working on behalf of refugees; the Federal Republic of Germany, Austria, and Italy because they were major countries of first asylum for refugees.

The definitional issue had been complicated by the fact that, at the time they were drafting the Statute, many of the same national delegates to the UN were also drafting the International Convention on the Status of Refugees. Both the Commission on Human Rights and the Secretary-General had supported the need for a convention and an international agency, and the Secretary-General's Study on Statelessness report had urged that the two should be linked in such a way that the agency would have recognized authority to supervise the carrying out of the terms of the Convention by those states which ratified it. For this linkage to be as clear as possible, it was assumed by the drafters who took up the Secretary-General's recommendation in 1949 that it would be necessary to have a common definition of the term refugee in order to determine the scope of application of each instrument.

Apart from the definition, however, the provisions of the two documents were to be quite separate and their legal implications quite different. The Convention would be directed toward national action, requiring government treatment of refugees to be at least identical with treatment of other aliens and, in some cases, with nationals. The Statute would be concerned with international action aimed at encouraging and supplementing the activities of states so as to safeguard the rights and legitimate interests of refugees and to overcome any disabilities arising from their status as refugees. The Statute would create an international agency which like many other agencies would have to seek to achieve its aim through whatever diplomatic pressures it could bring to bear on states. The Convention, on the other hand, would create binding new international legal obligations for those states ratifying its obligations which they would not otherwise have under customary international law. The implication of this difference in legal significance was that, regardless of how willing governments might be, as a humanitarian matter, to give the new agency a broad scope of concern, they were hesitant when it came to undertaking equally broad new

legal responsibilities themselves.   Thus, so long as the
scope of the Statute and of the Convention were to be the
same, as would be the case if both instruments had identical definitions of the term refugee, then the tendency, as
we have seen, was to restrict the definition to those categories of refugees regarding whom governments were in
practice willing to undertake obligations by a Convention.

However, the implication of the UK proposal for a
conference of plenipotentiaries was that it would no longer
make sense to define refugee in the Statute by a reference
to the definition in the Convention.   The proposed conference
could not possibly be convened before 1951, while the Statute
had to be completed before the end of 1950, as the HC was
due to commence operations on 1 January 1951.   Acceptance
of the UK proposal would thereby reopen the question of the
definition in the Statute.

On this second point the UK delegate had a further
proposal.   Stressing that it was not essential that the definition of refugee be the same in both documents, and that it
was desirable at least to have a "universal definition" in the
Statute even if the delegates were unwilling to commit their
states to undertake equally broad obligations under the Convention to both present and future refugees, the UK delegate
once again offered the open-ended definition of refugee his
country had advocated in the Ad Hoc Committee and in
ECOSOC.

Heated exchanges over the course of several meetings
of the Third Committee followed the introduction of the UK
proposals.   The US argued that the definition agreed upon
by ECOSOC included all refugee groups who were in need of
international protection and that it was inappropriate to make
decisions concerning future groups until they emerged.   If it
were solely a matter of protection, a very broad definition
of the term might be acceptable, added the US delegate, but
since the mandate of the HC had been broadened to include
the possibility of dispensing material assistance, and since
such funds were not available, the definition in the Statute
should be limited to those existing refugee groups who needed
protection and only protection.   The delegate of France also
opposed the UK position, not, he said, because his country
did not favor a broader definition, but because it favored a
broadly acceptable Statute and Convention even more.

But some Commonwealth and European states supported

the UK, and a compromise eventually had to be reached.
This compromise took the form of two draft definitions:
one for the Convention--which was essentially a restatement
of the definition accepted by the Ad Hoc Committee and
ECOSOC, although the geographic restriction "in Europe"
was omitted--and a second definition for the Statute which
repeated the definition now proposed for the Convention but
in effect omitted the time limitation of 1 January 1951.

The compromise Statute definition, accepted by the
GA on 14 December 1950, in Res. 428(V), marked a signal
victory for the proponents of the "universal definition" (although the UK abstained from the vote on the ground that
the definition was not yet broad enough) and meant that as
a new group of refugees appeared who exhibited the general
characteristics set forth in the Statute they would fall automatically within the competence of the HC.   But because the
Statute definition was different from that in the Convention,
its acceptance also meant that the competence of the HC was
broader than that stipulated by the Convention.   The result
was that in time two classes of refugees would emerge,
both of which would be entitled to the protection of the HC,
but only one of which would be legally entitled to the standards of national treatment laid down in the Convention.   This
disparity between the scope of the two documents was to
continue for sixteen years; it was largely eliminated through
the passage of the 1967 Protocol by the GA and its ratification by the signatories to the Convention.   The effect of the
1967 Protocol was to amend the Convention (as between
states acceded to the Protocol) by deleting its time limitation of 1 January 1951.

The Debate on Existing Groups of Refugees

In addition to the controversy concerning the coverage
of future refugee groups within the Statute and the Convention, there was another though less divisive debate as to how
many of the existing groups of refugees should be included
within the definition.   The delegate of Greece, for example,
urged consideration for the plight of some 700,000 Greeks
who had lost their homes during the course of the Greek
civil war.   The delegates of Pakistan and India each pointed
out that there were millions of refugees in need of assistance
within their borders due to their partition.   And the delegates
of the Arab states spoke of the needs of Palestinian refugees
in the Middle East.

The delegates of both France and the US expressed the general sentiment of delegates that it was inappropriate to include all existing refugees within the mandate of the HC. His function was to provide international protection for refugees who lacked the protection of any state. Those refugee groups who did not lack the protection of a government either because they were within the country of their nationality or because they were treated as nationals by the countries in which they had been granted asylum should be excluded from the Statute definition of refugee. While undoubtedly many of those excluded refugee groups were in need of material assistance the consensus was that this was not a criterion which justified their inclusion within the competence of the HC, insofar as protection was the main purpose of the establishment of the Office.

The culmination of the deliberations at the UN during 1949 and 1950 concerning a successor agency to the IRO was the passage of GA Res. 428(V) of 14 December 1950, with the governing Statute of the UNHCR set out in an annex. The effect of the Statute was to authorize the HC to carry out certain functions on behalf of the international community. Thereafter the HC had to look to the Statute as the source of his authority and to act within that authority, or seek new grants of authority from the GA as he found them necessary.

The Convention Relating to the Status of Refugees, which had been drafted and debated during the same period-- often by the same delegates who were drafting the Statute-- was referred by the GA for final drafting to a specially convened Conference of Plenipotentiaries representing the governments of interested states (Res. 428[V] of 14 December 1950). The Assembly did recommend to the Conference the text of a preamble for the proposed Convention and the text of a definition for the term refugee and recommended that the Conference members take into consideration as well the draft Convention worked out by the Ad Hoc Committee at the request of ECOSOC. In the same resolution, the GA also asked the HC to participate in the Conference of Plenipotentiaries.

The Conference met in July 1951, and some twenty-six governments, members and non-members of the UN, were represented. They redrafted the terms of the Convention and even the terms of the preamble and definition recommended for their consideration by the Assembly, although in most particulars they retained the text developed within the organs of the UN. [12]   The Final Act of the Conference was signed on 28 July 1951 and was thereafter open for signature and ratification by states.   The effect of the Convention was to establish a code of the basic rights of refugees, rights which signatories of the Convention pledged themselves to respect.

Notes

1.   For the text of these resolutions, see United Nations Resolutions Relating to the Office of the United Nations for Refugees, 2d ed. HCR/INF/48/Rev. 1 (hereafter UN Resolutions).   For the record of the deliberations which are the subject of this chapter see GA (III, IV & V), Third Com. and Plenary Sessions Off. Rec.; and ECOSOC (IX) and (XI).

2.   UN, GA (V), Off. Rec., Supp. No. 20 (A/1775): 48.

3.   Both of these alternatives and two others--the continuation of the IRO as a protective agency, and the establishment of a new specialized agency according to Arts. 57 and 63 of the Charter of the UN--were originally put forward as suggestions by the Sec. - Gen. in a very basic and significant report, A Study of Statelessness, NY: UN, Aug. 1949: 70-71; see also E/1112, Feb. 1949: 84-85.   But the GC of the IRO ruled out the continuation of the IRO as a possible approach to the problem, E/1392, 11 July 1949; 3, and the possibility of a new Specialized Agency was not raised again in the debates.

4.   ECOSOC (IX): 616ff.

5.   Refugees and Stateless Persons, Report of the Sec. - Gen., A/C.3/527--26 Oct. 1949.   The bulk of this report deals with the nature and extent of international protection as the basic function of the new agency and considers how the agency might be organized to perform this function.

6.   GA (IV), Third Com., Off. Rec.: 136.   The French delegate also noted that there were ample precedents for the direct election of the HC for Refugees.   Dr. Nansen, the first HC for Refugees, Sir Herbert

Emerson and the HCs for Refugees Coming from
Germany had been elected rather than appointed
(ibid. :   134).

7.   The suggestion that the GA elect the HC directly was
      made by the delegate of Lebanon (ibid. :   139); and
      the delegate of the UK expressed the approval of
      the majority of the Third Com. when she said that
      "the HC should be responsible directly to the high-
      est organ of the UN in order to maintain the high
      personal prestige and authority necessary for the
      exercise of his functions (ibid. :   1948).

8.   Ibid. :   127.

9.   M. Rochefort later implied that this was the reason
      for his position at the Plenary meeting.   See his
      comment on the need for compromise to win the
      widest possible number of signatures for the Con-
      vention and broadest possible support for the Statute
      (GA [V], Third Com. , Off. Rec. :   344).

10.   The requirement of persecution or fear of persecution
      was not an integral part of the IRO's definition of
      refugee.   While the organization's competence ex-
      tended to "victims" of various regimes, it also ex-
      tended to a general category who were defined in
      terms of their unwillingness or inability to avail
      themselves of the protection of the countries of their
      nationality or former nationality.   The term "per-
      secution" appears in the IRO definition as only one
      of the "valid objections" which a refugee can make
      to being repatriated to his homeland.

11.   The arrangements and agreements made under the
      auspices of the LoN had all followed the same for-
      mula of definition: persons to be covered had to
      be of some specified nationality (e. g. , "any person
      of Russian origin"), or from a specified country
      (e. g. , "refugees coming from Germany") who suf-
      fered the common disability that they no longer
      enjoyed the protection of the government of their
      nationality.   The IRO Constitution included within
      that organization's competence the same groups
      covered by the League arrangements, and added a
      further six categories: "victims of the Nazi or
      Fascist regime, " "Spanish Republicans and other

victims of the Falangist regime in Spain, " "Jews
from Germany and Austria not firmly re-established
in those countries, " "unaccompanied children, " "displaced persons, " and "persons who cannot or are
unwilling to avail themselves of the protection of
their country of nationality or former residence in
consequence of events subsequent to the outbreak
of the Second World War. "

12.   The most important of these changes in the definition
       was an amendment contained in Art. 1B of the
       Convention as an optional clause which permitted
       states to limit the words "events occurring before
       1 Jan. 1951" to "events occurring in Europe. "

Chapter 4

THE STATUTE OF THE UNHCR

The Statute of the UNHCR, contained in the Annex to GA Res. 428(V) of 14 December 1950, contains three chapters and thirty-three paragraphs detailing the general provisions for the Office, the functions of the HC, and the organization and financial arrangements of the Office.[1]

Functions of the High Commissioner

The first paragraph of Chapter 1 of the Statute sets forth two functions for the HC: that of "providing international protection to refugees who fall within the scope of the present Statute," and that of "seeking permanent solutions for the problems of the refugees."

Protection is not considered a permanent solution since it simply seeks to provide an international substitute for the diplomatic and consular protection of a state which refugees by definition lack. The purpose of international protection is to give refugees a recognized legal status analagous to that of other nationals living abroad. "Permanent solutions," on the other hand, refers to the economic and social integration of refugees in countries that have offered them asylum. It is through the implementation of both these functions that the HC can seek to minister to all the disabilities suffered by refugees owing to their position. But the HC's fundamental purpose is phrased in terms of international protection, which he may provide to refugees even after they have become integrated into the life of a national society. It is only when a refugee becomes a national of a state that he no longer needs international protection, and ceases to come within the mandate of the HC.

A major distinction is made in the Statute between the way in which each of the HC's functions is to be exercised. In acting to seek permanent solutions for refugee

problems, most notably through the extension of material assistance, the HC is directed to assist governments, whereas
no similar proviso precedes the grant to him of the authority
to provide international protection: the international protection function is exclusively the HC's to exercise as he sees
fit, independent of the approval or disapproval of individual
governments, or even of the Executive Committee.

The Statute paragraph specifies two ways in which the
HC may seek permanent solutions: he may "facilitate the
voluntary repatriation of such refugees or their assimilation
within new national communities." These are the two clas-
sic approaches that international agencies have undertaken
for the permanent settlement of refugees. Voluntary repatriation means facilitating the return of refugees who wish
to reacquire the nationality and protection they have lost or
have been denied. Assimilation means the legal and economic absorption of refugees by the country in which they
have sought asylum (integration), or by some other country
(resettlement), in the hope that eventually they will become
naturalized citizens of that country.

The first paragraph further specifies that in his function of seeking permanent solutions the HC is charged to act
"by assisting Governments and, subject to the approval of
the Governments concerned, private organizations." This
phraseology reflects the fact that the drafters of the Statute
agreed that the UNHCR should be, in contrast to the IRO, a
"non-operational" agency, by which they meant that it should
achieve its aims by enlisting others to carry out the actual
operations. The drafters assumed that the HC would have
neither the staff nor the funds to undertake such activities
himself, and that in many cases permanent solutions to refugee problems involved activities which could only be undertaken by governments. Even in regard to international protection, the predominant role of the HC was seen as being
to stimulate and encourage action by governments to achieve
more favorable treatment of refugees rather than to perform
direct services for individual refugees or groups of refugees
(see Statute, par. 8).

The role of the HC as delimited in the first paragraph of the Statute harks back to the role given to the HC
for Refugees under the LoN. There too the duty of the HC
had been to seek cooperation and to coordinate the efforts of
governments and voluntary organizations. Only during the
period of the IRO had the nature of international action for

refugees been fundamentally different, with the refugee agency itself undertaking direct and extensive action for the international protection, care and maintenance, repatriation, and resettlement of refugees.

In the second part of the first paragraph reference is made to the work of an Advisory Committee (Adv. Com.) to assist the HC in the exercise of his functions, especially in the determination of the eligibility of groups within his mandate. The fourth paragraph of the Statute elaborates the recommendation for an Adv. Com. Later resolutions of the GA and ECOSOC detail the powers of the various committees that have advised the HC, but it is sufficient to note here that on only one occasion, in 1952, has the Adv. Com. given advice as to eligibility, that being on the matter of certain Turkish refugees from Bulgaria. The question of the eligibility of Chinese refugees in Hong Kong was considered by the Adv. Com. and by the UN Refugee Emergency Fund Executive Committee (UNREF Ex. Com.) that succeeded it, but was eventually referred to the GA in 1957.

The Office as a Non-Political Agency

The second paragraph of the Statute contains the admonition that the work of the HC is to be "entirely non-political," despite, or perhaps because of, the charged political setting in which his work must take place. The refugees who have been the concern of international organizations since the time of Nansen have been in the main persons whose ties with their homelands have been broken for political reasons. The presence of refugees in countries other than their own has often generated further political problems, both in terms of the internal politics of the asylum country, and in terms of the relations between the asylum country and the country of their origin. The definition itself of the term refugee in the Statute contains as one of its essential elements a clause specifying that the refugee is a person who has a "well-founded fear of being persecuted for reasons of race, religion, nationality or political opinion." The inclusion of this clause within the Statute definition has had the effect of requiring the HC to take cognizance of the political situations which produce refugees, while at the same time his mandate requires that his actions must be non-political. In other words he must minister to the human needs of refugees without taking sides in the political controversies that made them refugees. While the effect of

these provisions in the Statute is to require the HC to tread
a very narrow path indeed, it is only to the extent that HCs
have been able to do so that they have been successful in
achieving their aims: the HC must have the cooperation of
governments to accomplish even minimal goals, and that cooperation can only be earned so long as the HC deals with
essentially political problems in an "entirely non-political"
or neutral way.

The Charge to Relate to Groups of Refugees

        The second provision of par. 2 of the Statute states
that the work of the HC shall "relate, as a rule, to groups
and categories of refugees. " This provision was aimed at
insuring that the UNHCR would not become another IRO
ministering directly to the individual needs of a multitude of
refugees but would instead remain a small office dealing
mainly with general refugee matters. It was also hoped that
this provision would make unnecessary the creation of an
elaborate procedure and sizable staff for the determination
of refugee eligibility, the assumption being that it would be
easier to determine the eligibility of an entire group than of
a large number of separate individuals, and that when an
individual determination had to be made it would be merely
a matter of determining whether or not the individual was a
member of an eligible group.

        The reference to groups was also included because at
least some of the drafters, especially M. Rochefort, the
delegate of France, conceived the function of international
protection not as acting on behalf of individual refugees (e. g. ,
by assisting individuals in their relations with national authorities) but rather as acting to promote better national
treatment for refugees as groups (e. g. , by encouraging new
international agreements or domestic legislation). The
UNHCR, it was stressed in the debates, would have neither
funds nor staff sufficient to take on the problem of a whole
host of individuals, but should oversee the national protection
provided to individual refugees by the country of their asylum.

        Practice turned out to be somewhat at variance with
these assumptions, however. The Office found that it was
required to consider the eligibility of refugees individually
by the very wording of the Statute. The definition of refugee
required that he be a person with a "well-founded fear of

persecution, " and it was difficult to see how this requirement could be met without an examination of the subjective
views of the refugee as well as his objective circumstances.
Furthermore, in carrying out the function of international
protection, the staff of the Office invariably became involved
in the provision of services to individuals.   The UNHCR has,
for example, dealt with individual cases when the problem
was one common to a group of refugees, for example, undertaking so-called legal test cases where the outcome might
create a precedent for other refugees or groups of refugees.
With the development of the "good offices" function of the
HC in the late 1950s a new basis for action emerged that
made it possible to deal with "groups and categories of refugees" without making an eligibility determination regarding
individuals.   As High Commissioner Felix Schnyder pointed
out in 1965, one advantage of the "good-offices" function was
that it reconciled the Statute reference in par. 2 to "groups"
with the Statute definition of refugee--two principles in the
Statute "which might originally have appeared to be in opposition or mutually contradictory. "2

Advisory Bodies

        The third paragraph of the Statute requires the HC to
"follow policy directives given him by the GA or ECOSOC. "
It is by making use of this provision that the Assembly has
from time to time given new authority to the HC to undertake specific tasks or to extend his regular activities to new
groups of refugees.   Subsequent resolutions of the GA pertaining to the HC must be read together with the Statute if
the full breadth of the HC's present authority and the full
scope of his responsibilities is to be understood.

        The fourth paragraph of the Statute concerns the cre-
ation and operation of an Advisory Committee to assist the
HC.   The Secretary-General had recommended the setting up
of such a committee of UN members for the HC, since this
is a standard procedure where UN agencies are empowered
to handle funds.   The French delegate had included a provision for such a committee in his 1950 draft for the Statute
as a way of involving those non-members of the UN who
were very concerned with refugee problems in particular,
Germany and Switzerland.   The French proposal was for a
committee composed of both member and non-member states.
But debate on the matter was inconclusive, with many delegates preferring to leave the question open until they could

hear the views of the HC.   Thus par. 4 was drafted simply
to permit ECOSOC to establish such a committee if it so
decided.   Following a favorable expression of opinion by the
first HC, ECOSOC implemented par. 4 and established the
Adv. Com. on Refugees on 10 September 1951. [3]   The Adv.
Com. was subsequently replaced by the UNREF Ex. Com.
in 1954 and that in turn by the Executive Committee of the
Program of the United Nations High Commissioner for Refugees (Ex. Com.) on 30 April 1958. [4]   The Adv. Com. was,
as its name implies, empowered only to give advice to the
HC on any aspect of his functions where he solicited its
views.   The UNREF Ex. Com. and the Ex. Com. on the
other hand, had the authority to issue directives to the HC
in the field of material assistance programs, but in matters
concerning international protection could only give advice.

Finally, Chapter 1 of the Statute contains a paragraph
which in effect limited the existence of the UNHCR to three
years, pending the decision of the Assembly to continue its
operations.   By subsequent resolutions the deadline set down
in this paragraph has been superseded as the Assembly extended the life of the Office for successive five-year periods:
1954-58, Res. 727(VIII) of 23 October 1953; 1959-63, Res.
1165(XII) of 26 November 1957; 1964-68, Res. 1783(XVII) of
7 December 1962; 1969-73, Res. 2294(XXII) of 11 December
1967; and 1974-78, Res. (XXVII) of 12 December 1972.

Interpretation of the Statute

It is in Chapter 2 of the Statute that the basic nature
of the HC's office is spelled out.   Here is found the lengthy
definition of the term refugee which specifies the scope of
the HC's competence as well as some specifications as to
what the HC can do to carry out the two functions, international protection and pursuit of permanent solutions, granted
him in the first paragraph of the Statute.   It has not always
been entirely clear what interpretation to place on certain of
the provisions.   HCs have themselves interpreted the wording, or if in doubt, have sought the advice of the Adv. Com.
or its successors, or, in the last analysis, the decision of
the GA.   From time to time, consideration has been given
to amending the Statute in order to clarify numerous provisions.   The project has never been carried through, however, because as long as the instrument is workable there
is reluctance to lay it open to redrafting by the organs of
the UN.   Legal niceties have taken second place to more

practical considerations. The problem of interpretation was eased at the start by the fact that the first HC, Dr. van Heuven Goedhart, was chairman of the Third Committee of the GA during the critical meetings of its Fifth Session in 1950 when the final details of the Statute were hammered out. He therefore knew the intentions of the drafters in each worked-over phrase of the Statute.

The Statute Definition of Refugee

Pars. 6 and 7 of the Statute define refugees within the "mandate" that is, those who come within the competence of the HC. While there are some differences between the definition in the Statute and that in the Convention, the only differences of substance--and they are crucial--are (1) that the scope of the Convention was limited to persons who became refugees as a result of events occurring before 1 January 1951, whereas the mandate of the UNHCR was to extend also to persons who became refugees as a result of later events; and (2) that states becoming parties to the Convention could further limit the scope of the Convention by declaring that the phrase "events occurring before 1 January 1951" meant for them "events in Europe occurring before 1 January 1951." With these two exceptions the discussion here of the Statute definition applies as well to the definition in the Convention.

The first category of persons within the competence of the HC (by par. 6A [i]) are those now known as "statutory" refugees--persons who have already been considered refugees under previous international agreements or under the Constitution of the IRO. The second category of persons included within the mandate (either by par. 6A [ii] or 6B) are persons generally accorded the status of refugee for the first time. It consists of two sub-groups, one of persons possessing a nationality (de jure), the other of persons not possessing a nationality (de facto). There are two conditions applicable to both groups: (1) they must be outside the country of their nationality or of their habitual residence, and (2) the reason for their alienation must be a well-founded fear of being persecuted for reasons of race, religion, nationality, or political opinion. For those persons having a nationality there is a third condition: they must be unable, unwilling owing to their fear of persecution, or unwilling for reasons other than personal convenience to avail themselves of the protection of the country of their nationality.

For those persons not possessing a nationality the third condition is somewhat different: they must be unable, unwilling
owing to their fear of persecution, or unwilling for reasons
other than personal convenience to return to the country of
their former habitual residence. If a person has more than
one nationality then he must satisfy the above conditions in
relation to each of the countries of which he is a national
(par. 7[a]). Furthermore, a person may be in this second
category even if he had been turned down by the IRO when
he applied to it for such a status (par. 6A [ii], the proviso).

"Fear of Being Persecuted" Clause

        The phrase "well-founded fear of being persecuted"
is the key to the definition in that it expresses what was
considered then to be the essential characteristic of a refugee. This phrase was not previously used in refugee definitions (although the terms "persecution" and "fear based on
reasonable grounds of persecution" were used in the IRO
Constitution, Annex 1, Section C), nor was any authoritative
interpretation of the phrase given in the Statute or the Convention. Its use primarily marked an attempt to move away
from previous definitions tending to categorize refugees by
nationalities, to an approach that would instead concentrate
on the essential personal characteristics of refugees. There
may be many reasons for a person being outside of his country and a variety of reasons for his unwillingness to return
to it, but only one motive has been singled out to characterize the refugee and to distinguish him from the victim of
natural disasters, the person who leaves his country for personal reasons, the fugitive from justice, and the ordinary
economic migrant: the refugee must fear "being persecuted
for reasons of race, religion, nationality, or political opinion. "

        The following general interpretations have developed
through the HC's application of this phrase from the Statute
and the practice of national authorities in applying the Convention.

1.   The term "fear" emphasizes that the major element to
      be considered is a subjective one: the psychological at-
      titude of the applicant must indicate that he has a genuine
      feeling of apprehension.

2. The term "well-founded" establishes an <u>objective</u> element: the applicant must be able to show <u>sufficient</u>, plausible grounds that in an evaluation of his case his apprehension is credible.

3. The refugee does not need to show actual persecution--he may have left his country before being persecuted or before the events occurred that now make him fear persecution; it is sufficient that he make it plausible that persecution exists and may be directed against him.

4. The fact that the refugee may have left his country for reasons other than well-founded fear of persecution is irrelevant if he can now show that he remains outside his country owing to such fear (persons who in effect became refugees after leaving their countries of origin are called <u>réfugiés sur place</u>).

5. The term "persecution" has been particularly difficult to define but would clearly include threats to life or freedom, and probably include any measure that made life seem intolerable to the refugee so long as his view of the measure was "well-founded."

6. The persecution must be attributable to the government either in that it initiated or encouraged the persecution, or that it could not or did not provide protection to its national from persecutory actions or threats by other elements within this society.

7. An economic migrant is not a refugee, but economic measures may often have racial, religious, or political aims behind them, especially if in intention or application they tend to discriminate against particular groups as sanctions, and in such cases may amount to persecution within the terms of the definition.

Despite the continued protestations of the UNHCR that determinations of eligibility do not imply political judgment of the policies of the countries of origin, the fact that a person or group is considered by the UNHCR as having a well-founded fear of persecution has sometimes been regarded as censure. In seeking to carry out its strictly "nonpolitical" role then, the Office has come to find that the "fear of persecution" element of the definition of the term refugee, which was meant to include all refugees in need of protection and had marked such an advance over the

narrowness of prior definitions based on categories, turned
out to have substantial disadvantages. It was as much to
overcome this disability as for any other reason that the Office moved in the late 1950s to create an alternative basis
for its authority and activities that did not require an eligibility determination based on the Statute definition. This
alternative basis was the "good-offices" function which is
discussed in detail in Chapter 18.

The Subjective Factor in the Protection Clause

In addition to requiring that the refugee be outside
his country owing to well-founded fear of persecution, the
Statute definition adds the requirement that he be unable or
unwilling for specified reasons to avail himself of the protection of his country of nationality or former residence.
While traditionally the element of lack of protection has been
a major part of definitions of the term refugee because those
definitions were based solely on objectively determinable
factors, it is of less importance in the Statute and Convention where the emphasis has been shifted to include subjective factors. It is essential to note that refugees within the
competence of the HC must be de facto stateless persons in
that they lack the protection of any state, since a basic
function of the HC is to provide international protection to
persons suffering such a disability. But by adding the word
"unwilling" as an alternative to "unable" the Statute in effect
establishes another subjective factor: a person seeking refugee status can either demonstrate that he is unable to obtain his country's protection or that he has good reasons for
not wanting to accept that protection even though it is available to him.

Cessation Clauses

Two sets of clauses in pars. 6 and 7 of the Statute
follow the basic provisions of the refugee definition: cessation clauses indicate the circumstances under which a person
shall cease to be a refugee within the HC's competence, and
exclusion clauses indicate types of persons who shall not be
within the HC's competence even though they might otherwise
meet the requirements of the definition.

The cessation clauses in the main simply repeat elements of the definition in order to make clear that if and

when a refugee no longer fulfills all of the requirements of
the definition then he no longer will be considered a refugee
within the mandate. If, for example, he reestablishes himself in his country of nationality or former residence, reac-
quires his former nationality if he had lost it, reavails himself of his country's protection, or acquires a new nationality and enjoys the protection of that nationality, then he
ceases to be a refugee within the mandate. Most of the
cessation clauses are phrased in terms of protection, underlying the fact that the major purpose of the definition has
been to determine those persons in need of international protection. But the HC also has the function of material assistance, and the criteria for determining whether a person
needs international protection are not necessarily the same
as for determining whether he requires material assistance.
This is a result of the narrow purpose intended for the HC
by some of the Statute's drafters and is an additional reason
why the UNHCR in time sought to escape complete dependence
upon the provisions of the Statute for its authority.

The two final cessation clauses in the Statute state
that if the circumstances in connection with which the person
was recognized as a refugee subsequently cease to exist, so that
he has no good reason for continuing to refuse to return
home or to refuse the protection of his country, then he
shall cease to be a refugee within the mandate. These
clauses are not worded the same way in the Statute as they
are in the Convention, where an exemption to each has been
included; but in practice they have been interpreted by the
UNHCR as if they did follow the wording in the Convention.
The debate at the Conference of Plenipotentiaries indicated
that there might be refugees, especially Jews from Germany,
who could not ever bring themselves to return because of
the "memory of past sufferings. " These exemptions were
included in the Convention's cessation clauses to permit them
to continue to be refugees.

Exclusion Clauses

There are three important exclusion clauses in the
Statute in par. 7, each of which was included in response to
particular objections raised during the drafting debates. The
first of these is known as the "ethnic exclusion clause" because it was intended particularly to exclude those persons
in Germany who had fled there after the Second World War
from countries of Eastern Europe and were considered to be

ethnic Germans (Volksdeutsche) regardless of their actual nationality. These Volksdeutsche had been specifically excluded
from the concern of the IRO by a special provision of its
Constitution, but the phrasing used in the Statute was somewhat broader, since the drafters intended to exclude other
similarly situated refugee groups from the mandate: those
refugees who are treated substantially like nationals by the
country of their asylum.

A second exclusion clause concerned the Arab refugees and others; so long as they were the responsibility of
UNRWA they were excluded from the HC's mandate.

The third exclusion clause covers three classes of
persons considered "unworthy" of international protection.
They are persons who may have committed war crimes,
serious nonpolitical common crimes, or "acts contrary to
the purposes and principles of the United Nations. " While
the wording of the exclusion was in large part so confusing
that even the drafters could not agree on a common definition of the terms, in general it can be said that its purpose
was to exclude fugitives from justice, broadly defined, from
the ranks of refugees fleeing unjust persecution. [5]

A fourth exclusion clause handles the problem of double nationality by ensuring that a national of more than one
country is not adjudged a refugee unless he satisfies all the
requirements already noted in relation to each of the countries of which he is a national.

International Protection

Par. 8 of the Statute is the only provision in which
the functions of the HC are spelled out in any detail, and
because of its specificity it has created as many problems
for the HC as have some other paragraphs of the Statute
owing to their vagueness. Par. 8 deals with the matter of
providing international protection for refugees within the competence of the Office and lists nine specific activities that the
HC may undertake in this regard. It has never been completely clear whether this list was meant to be exhaustive or
simply exemplary of what the HC might do in order to provide protection, but the consistent interpretation of the
UNHCR has been that par. 8 is not meant to be exhaustive.
This interpretation seems correct since some of the specific
international protection activities listed refer as much to the

function of seeking permanent solutions as to that of providing protection, and these two functions are clearly distinguished in par. 1 of the Statute; others refer to activities not of a legal character; and the rest hardly cover the breadth of activities undertaken by predecessor agencies of the UNHCR in providing the same kind of protection.

Until the Statute of the UNHCR was drafted, international protection was called "legal and political protection," a phrase that originated in a resolution adopted by the Assembly of the LoN on 30 September 1930.[6] Although, as has been pointed out by the foremost authority on international refugee law, "no precise definition of this term [legal and political protection] can be found in international instruments,"[7] the practices of refugee agencies under the LoN and of the IRO are best summed up in a definition of the phrase offered by the Executive Secretary of the PCIRO in 1948:

> It is one single form of protection, which is both legal and political in character. It is legal in so far as its object is to safeguard the rights and legitimate interests of refugees, and in particular to provide for, observe and regulate the application of existing agreements on the legal status of refugees; to provide, if necessary, for their revision; to supervise their day-to-day application in particular cases; to provide, if necessary, for the conclusion of new agreements; and to exercise quasi-consular functions ... this [legal] protection is at the same time of a political nature, in that it implies relations with the government.[8]

While the IRO decided to retain the phrase "legal and political protection" despite the initial objections to this implication of political activities, the phrase was almost casually replaced by the term "international protection" during the ECOSOC debates on the Statute in 1949.[9] As characterized by the list of activities appended to it in par. 8 of the Statute, the term "international protection" would seem to be quite different from "legal and political protection." The list includes no reference to quasi-consular activities or activities on behalf of individual refugees, leading one early commentator on the Statute to state that the authors of the Statute "seem to have been guided by a desire to restrict the scope of the HC's Office to functions of a higher order relating to the protection of the refugee at the international

level. "[10]   One of the major drafters of the Statute, M.
Rochefort of France, made the same point in stressing that
actual protection of refugees would be provided by governments, while the HC would have only functions "of a higher
direction, liaison and control service. "[11]   But from the beginning the practice of the UNHCR has been to ignore the
obscurities of par. 8 and to rely instead on the broad
phrasing of the paragraph and the general tenor of the Statute to support its contention that international protection
should be interpreted broadly.   High Commissioner van
Heuven Goedhart summed up this interpretation in 1953 as
follows: 'It is clear that the international protection for
which my Office is responsible is wider than the legal and
political protection with which previous international organizations concerned with refugees were charged. "[12]   The details of the activities of the UNHCR undertaken in the provision of international protection are given in Part III.

Material Assistance

Pars. 9 and 10 of the Statute reflect the compromise
achieved between those drafters who sought to limit the HC
to the function of providing protection and those who sought
to have him administer to all the needs of refugees.   The
paragraphs are worded in such a way that the HC is allowed
to engage "in such additional activities, including repatriation and resettlement, as the GA may determine"; however
he may have little money with which to do so and cannot
readily obtain funds without seeking the prior approval of the
GA.   But the restrictions included in par. 10 on the HC's
fund-raising activities were successfully eliminated by GA
Res. 538B(VI) of 2 February 1952 which permitted the HC
to raise funds for emergency aid to the most needy groups
of refugees, and by GA Res. 832(IX) of 21 October 1954,
authorizing him to make general appeals to UN members and
non-members for contributions to a permanent fund for the
solution of refugee problems.

Organization and Finances

The remainder of Chapter 2 and the whole of Chapter
3 of the Statute concern details of the organization of the
Office, its relationship to the other organs of the UN, its
staff, and its budget.   The only provision that has given rise
to differing interpretations is that contained in par. 20 which

insists that no expenditure of the Office other than administration expenditures shall be borne by the budget of the UN.
Administrative expenses are considered by the UNHCR to include salaries and expenses incurred by the Office staff, and
therefore include the cost of providing international protection insofar as that does not pertain to the provision of legal
assistance--as distinct from legal protection--for individual
refugees.   All other expenditures such as those arising in
the actual implementation of material assistance programs,
are to be financed by voluntary contributions.

As a result of the need indicated by the GC of the
IRO and of the recommendations made by the HC, the GA in
1952 agreed to give the HC in limited form the prior approval required by par. 10 of his Statute, authorizing him
to "issue an appeal for funds for the purpose of enabling
emergency aid to be given to the most needy groups among
refugees within his mandate."[13] This resolution was not a
full authorization to appeal for funds.   But subsequently, the
HC received funds for promoting permanent solutions from
the Ford Foundation, and on the basis of the activities thus
undertaken the GA fully authorized him to appeal for funds
for permanent solutions, namely the integration, repatriation
and resettlement of refugees.[14]

Notes

1.   For text of the Statute see UN Resolutions Relating to
        the UNHCR, 2nd ed., HCR/Inf/48.

2.   Felix Schnyder, The Good Offices and the Functions of
        the UNHCR in the Social Field, Doc. HCR/RS/32,
        p. 25.

3.   ECOSOC Res. 393 (XIII)B of 10 Sept. 1951.

4.   GA Res. 832 (XI) of 21 Oct. 1954; GA Res. 1166 (XII)
        of 26 Nov. 1957, and ECOSOC Res. 672 (XXV) of
        30 Apr. 1958.

5.   But see Ch. 11, below, on the question of the African
        "freedom fighters," which involves the interpretation
        of this clause.

6.   LoN, OJ, Spec. Supp. No. 84: 157-8; noted in UN,
        Study of Statelessness: 108.

7.   Weis, "International Status of Refugees": 211.

8.   IRO, PREP/266 of May 1948.

9.   See IRO, GC/SR/49 of 7 July 1949, reproduced in the
      Annexes to E/1392 of 11 July 1949; when George
      Warren of the US moved to drop the phrase "legal
      and political," the move was adopted almost without
      debate; see also the debates during ECOSOC, (IX)
      326th meeting: 626-32.

10.   Vernant, op. cit. : 42.

11.   GA (IV), Third Com. , Off. Rec. : 105.

12.   A/AC. 36/23 of 25 Mar. 1953: 5.

13.   GA Res. 538 (VI)B of 2 Feb. 1952.

14.   GA Res. 832 (IX) of 21 Oct. 1954.

Chapter 5

IMPLEMENTING THE STATUTE

The first step in implementing the Statute was the selection of a HC. Herein were evident the divisions which had permeated the deliberations on the functions and financing of the UNHCR. The Secretary-General, after unsuccessful efforts to get agreement on one candidate for the office, presented two candidates to the GA: Dr. J. Donald Kingsley, an American and the former Director-General of the IRO, and Dr. van Heuven Goedhart, a Dutchman. The GA by secret ballot elected the latter by a small majority (26 to 23), the voting split following the division between countries of overseas resettlement and those of first asylum, and between Western and Eastern countries.

The Office of the High Commissioner

Dr. van Heuven Goedhart was a distinguished lawyer and journalist. He was well known in the UN family. Active in the resistance movement in the Netherlands, he had been on a mission to London in 1944 and served there as Minister of Justice in the Netherlands Government-in-Exile. After the war he became a member of the Netherlands Senate. During the UN Conference on Freedom of Information in 1947-48 he had served as a member of the Netherlands delegation to this conference; in 1949 and 1950 he was chairman of the Third Committee of the GA. The fact that he was not the candidate of the US--and his passionate and vocal support of refugee interests--created tensions in the early years when it was expected that the HC's role would be that of a servant of governments. Dr. van Heuven Goedhart's example in the formative years of the UNHCR was to become decisive. He was supported by his Deputy HC, Mr. James Read, an American appointed by the HC, who served until the beginning of 1960.

In the first year of the Office, Dr. van Heuven

103

Goedhart relied greatly on the cooperation of the IRO, and throughout the final period of IRO's operations he maintained close liaison with that organization. Specific agreements were made between the IRO and the UNHCR on the timing and manner of the transfer of protection files, individual records, and so on. Not until 31 January 1952 did the UNHCR assume all protection functions previously performed by the IRO.[1] The IRO loaned to Dr. van Heuven Goedhart members of its own legal protection staff to make the necessary preparations for the transfer of protection functions, and at the time of liquidation transferred $236,698 to the UNHCR. But while the IRO had aimed at a smooth transition with no break in the continuity of the work for refugees, there were obstacles on every side. With the transfer of the IRO's operational activities to governments and voluntary agencies, the delay in the GA on a final decision on the creation of the UNHCR, and the limitation of the HC's functions, a serious break in the continuity of the work for refugees was unavoidable. It was known that the refugees themselves and the people who worked on their behalf were feeling doubtful and apprehensive about the transferral. The problems faced by the new HC were further complicated by the fact that the GA had made no allowance for a gradually decreasing budget in the transition period between the operations of the IRO and of the UNHCR. Despite the transfer of many of IRO's operational activities to governments and voluntary agencies in the countries of residence, the remaining burden was still very extensive, and the exceedingly modest UNHCR budget for 1951 ($300,000 intended for a nine-month period of preparation including the establishment of the Office--"a provisional estimate not based on fact or experience") could not cover even the most needed administrative expenses.

It will be remembered that UNHCR was non-operational and, in contrast to IRO, responsibility for care and maintenance of the refugees had been transferred to the countries of asylum. The majority of refugees, however, were residing in countries which were themselves having to contend with great domestic difficulties. The devastation of the war had been far-reaching in the countries of asylum, and their problems of physical reconstruction were more than matched by problems of economic, political, and social reconstruction. In view of this situation, Dr. van Heuven Goedhart was not yet able to count on the resources of the countries of asylum nor on their willingness to undertake new burdens. And from the countries of resettlement there

was a certain legacy of ill-feeling stemming from the controversy at the time of his nomination and election. Even
the physical setting for the HC's work had to be arranged
as well as the creation of an administrative structure and
the building up of staff.   The enormity of the tasks ahead
was evident.   "In January 1951 I found three empty rooms
in the Palais des Nations in Geneva," Dr. van Heuven Goedhart subsequently wrote, "and I had to start from scratch."

The HC's first priority was to insure that the structure and functioning of the Office were sufficiently flexible
to meet the continually changing conditions of the refugee
problem.   New situations were constantly developing, and
the Office had to be able to meet new needs immediately.
As the HC saw it, his headquarters staff did not need to be
large.   He looked instead to "a team at Geneva of highly
qualified collaborators devoted to the cause of refugees,
small but efficient," and he considered field missions to be
of overriding importance and essential to the proper discharge of his functions.[2]   "There is an absolute necessity
for permanent contact between my Office and the interested
governments," he pointed out.   Like his headquarters staff,
he envisioned the branch office staff as "small but efficient,"
comprised of no more than three professional officers.[3]
At the functional level, the branch officers were not to supervise the efforts of governments on behalf of the refugees,
as some governments were inclined to think but, he stressed,
to consult, advise, and stimulate.

Dr. van Heuven Goedhart saw himself, however, primarily as the representative of the refugees and, as such,
responsible for defending their interests.   As their custodian
and their representative at the UN, he felt strongly that they
should have the opportunity for direct contact with the Office.   Through his headquarters staff and the branch officers,
he wished personally to "maintain direct contact with the refugees themselves and also with the voluntary agencies working on their behalf."   But he assured fearful governments
that he had no wish to supersede their efforts.   "The interests of these governments and of my Office are parallel; we
both want to promote a solution to the refugee problem."[4]

The matter of branch offices was extensively discussed
in the Third Committee of the Sixth Session of the GA (January 1952).   The HC, referring to Dr. Nansen's experiences
in the early 1920s, noted that Dr. Nansen had emphasized
the need for delegations of the HC instead of national

commissions and had pointed out that, when the LoN had
withdrawn the delegations of the HC to save money, the refugees had encountered insurmountable difficulties, and en-
dured great suffering; some had even died. 5

Some governments feared that the proliferation of
branch offices would lead to an exercise in Parkinson's
Law: expansion for the sake of expansion within the UNHCR
and the creation of an unwieldy bureaucratic machine. They
wanted to stipulate the number of branch offices to be established and limit the number accordingly. Among some delegations there was also apprehension that the HC regarded
himself as a kind of government for refugees in contrast to
the GA's concept of the UNHCR as an instrument for collaboration with the national authorities. The majority of the
representatives, however, felt that the GA should not get
too deeply involved in specific operational decisions but
should rather lay down guidelines for the general policies to
be pursued by the HC with a view to increasing his effectiveness and lightening the burden of his responsibility.

In consultation with the governments concerned (see
Statute, par. 16), including agreement on a nominee for
each branch office representative, the HC established in the
first two years of his mandate eleven field missions in the
following countries, six of these in the latter half of 1951.

Austria (Vienna)

Germany (Bonn)

Greece, including the Near East (Athens)

Italy, including Trieste (Rome)

Belgium, for the Benelux countries (Brussels)

France (Paris)

UK and Commonwealth countries (London). This
    branch office was established mainly for liaison.

Thailand, for the Far East (Bangkok). The Bangkok
    office was closed after one year.

Colombia, for Latin America (Bogotá). The HC's
    representative in Latin America was accredited to

the governments of Bolivia, Colombia, the Dominican Republic, Ecuador, Guatemala, Honduras,
Panama, El Salvador, and Venezuela. His main
functions were to represent the interests of those
refugees who had been settled but had not yet acquired a new nationality, to inform all Latin
American governments of the plans and activities
of the Office and to promote the signing and ratification of the Convention of 1951.

USA (Washington, DC). This office was later moved
to NY, serving mainly as a liaison office with UN
headquarters New York, the bureaus of the US
State Department concerned with refugee problems,
and the headquarters of the US voluntary organizations.

Hong Kong. A representative was established by the
UNHCR jointly with the Provisional Inter-Governmental Committee for the Movements of Migrants
from Europe (PICMME) (later ICEM) to carry on
the operation begun by the IRO for the care,
maintenance, and resettlement of European refugees in China.

By the end of 1953, the HC reported that he had a
staff of ninety-nine persons, approximately half of these being professional officers and half secretarial personnel.
Some 40 percent of the staff was employed at headquarters
in Geneva, and 60 percent in branch offices.

Relationship of the UNHCR to the Governments

Although Dr. van Heuven Goedhart successfully established his own structure of administration in the first
three years of his office, it had to work, as he well understood, with and through national governments, inter-governmental and international agencies, and the voluntary societies. The latter had always carried and would continue to
carry the major operational responsibilities on behalf of refugees. Indeed, these relations were spelled out by the GA
and ECOSOC, the policy-making bodies for the UNHCR, in
policy directives in the Statute concerning the role of the
HC.

1. to keep in "close touch with the governments and

inter-governmental organizations concerned" (par. 8[g])

2. to establish "contact in such manner as he may think
    best with private organizations dealing with refugee
    questions" (par. 8[h])

3. to facilitate "the coordination of the efforts of private
    organizations concerned with the welfare of refugees"
    (par. 8[i])

These directives thus placed the work of the UNHCR
in a four-part framework, as had been the case with former
international bodies concerned with refugees. But since the
HC's mandate was different from that of earlier agencies,
his role with governments, international and inter-governmental organizations, and voluntary agencies has been a
different one as well. Basically, he has had to build up
new relationships, although to do this he has been able to
draw on the experience of earlier agencies.

As was apparent from the start, the various bodies
with which the UNHCR chiefly deals represent different interests and have varying ideas in regard to where the emphasis should be placed in refugee work. Even the Statute
definition of refugee was not interpreted by any in the same
way, and yet their several policies needed to fit into the
overall UNHCR planning. Not surprisingly, division of responsibility between government departments, inter-governmental organizations, Specialized Agencies, and voluntary
societies has confronted the HC with great problems of coordination. "The role of the Office of the UNHCR in binding
together within a larger framework the efforts of many dis-
parate organizations has been maintained" since the early
years of the HC's activity, wrote his Deputy, James Read,
in 1962, and "has assumed even greater importance as the
geographical scope of its operations has been extended and
its services multiplied."[6] During the course of its twenty-
one years of existence, UNHCR has become most effective
in building up a close network within the UN family as well
as with non-member states of the UN, and voluntary agencies.

It is appropriate at this point to indicate the character
of the relations between the UNHCR and the varied bodies
with which it is so essentially interrelated, since these relations form the framework within which its functions are
carried on. Although each relationship has been described

separately for purposes of clarity, UNHCR action should be viewed as a composite picture of complex interrelationships, and the overall picture of the activities of the UNHCR alters with the ever-changing needs of refugee groups.

The HC's most important relationships are with the governments of states, and constant interaction with participating governments on the international, national, and local levels characterizes the HC's activities. The governments of states are, as members of the UN, the HC's ultimate source of authority. His Office, as an international body, is created and maintained by the continued consent and co-operation of the states, who through their representatives at the GA and in ECOSOC make the final decision on all UNHCR policy. They are also a major source of funds--not just the administrative budget which is a part of the regular UN budget contributed by its members--but also of voluntary contributions by nations to UNHCR programs.

Individual state action is an essential ingredient in international protection with which the HC is charged. (It will be remembered that international protection is essentially a substitute for diplomatic and consular protection.) In fact, most of the legal and social disabilities suffered by refugees can only be overcome by state action--by changes in domestic law and in administrative practice--in order that refugees be accorded like treatment to that given other classes of persons within the state in question. Thus, the major elements in UNHCR's provision of international protection are: promoting the ratification of international conventions by states, thereby pledging them to accord these standards of treatment, and seeking to insure that contracting states fulfill the obligations they have undertaken. In this way the UNHCR acts much as a state would act in seeking through agreements to improve the standard of treatment given its nationals by another state, and, through its consular officers especially, seeking to ensure that the rights agreed to are in fact granted.

In getting states to ratify and to implement agreements on behalf of refugees, the UNHCR is dependent upon the cooperation of governments; but the governments are at the same time committed under the Statute to cooperate with the UNHCR. Specifically, the GA called upon governments--both members and non-members of the UN--to cooperate with the HC in his supervision of international conventions providing for the protection of refugees by granting asylum to

refugees, including the most destitute categories; by facilitating their naturalization; by providing refugees with travel
and other documents; and by informing the HC about the
number and condition of refugees received, and of existing
laws and regulations applicable to them (Res. 428[V], par.
1). The GA also urged governments to give the UNHCR
any support that would bring the refugee problem to a final
solution; that is, to assist his efforts to promote voluntary
repatriation, integration, or resettlement (Res. 428[V], par.
2).

It is noteworthy that the specific list of activities
given in par. 8 of the Statute as examples of the international protection function of the UNHCR, have as their corollary the list given in par. 1 (as summarized above), which
is directed toward states and what they are requested to do
in order to cooperate with the UNHCR.   (Not all of par. 8
is directed toward governments; a few activities listed there
refer to voluntary agencies.) In this way the drafters sought
to connect as closely as possible the obligations of states to
the rights and powers of the HC.

It should be noted that while power ultimately rests
with the states, the initiatory role in international protection
belongs to the HC. The HC's function has always been to
establish the goal and to indicate the steps necessary to
achieve it: to bring situations to the attention of governments, to urge them to alter conditions and to change laws
and administrative procedures, to call to their attention inequities in their legal systems, and so forth. He oversees
and seeks to gain their compliance with the standards that
they and he have agreed are appropriate for refugees.   The
HC's policy has had to be an elastic one taking into account
every facet of the problem.

Relationship to the Advisory Committee for Refugees

The HC has a particularly close relationship with
those governments that comprise his Adv. Com. or its successors, the Executive Committees.   These are generally a
cross-section of the states most concerned with refugee situations, either as countries of asylum or resettlement, and
in recent years, as countries of origin. From the beginning, the Committee was an important source of advice and
opinion for the UNHCR, and it has been essential that the

HC secure the support of its members for the implementation of his policies.

Pursuant to the ECOSOC Res. 393B(XIII) of 10 September 1951, the following fifteen countries (UN members and non-members) were selected by ECOSOC for membership on the Adv. Com. "on the basis of their demonstrated interest in and their devotion to the solution of the problems of refugees" (Statute, par. 4):

Overseas countries: Australia, Brazil, US, Israel, and Venezuela

European countries: Austria, Belgium, Denmark, Federal Republic of Germany, France, Italy, Switzerland, Turkey, UK, and the Holy See.

The Adv. Com. held its first session in Geneva in December 1951 and annually thereafter until it was reconstituted as the UNREF Ex. Com. in October 1954. According to its procedure "any State could attend the meetings without the right to vote, if matters particularly affecting its interests" were discussed by the Committee.[7] Specialized Agencies of the UN, and intergovernmental organizations, were entitled to be represented and to participate in the deliberations.[8] Nongovernmental organizations could submit oral or written statements in accordance with ECOSOC Res. 288B(X) of 27 February 1950, pars. 28-30, on arrangements for consultation with non-governmental organizations.[9]

Relationship to the Specialized Agencies of the United Nations

According to the Statute par. 8(g), the HC was advised to maintain close contact with international organizations and, on the urging of ECOSOC and the GA, the HC, following the practice of preceding international refugee organizations, established close contact with those UN bodies working in the wider field of migration, education, vocational training, and health. From the beginning UN members hoped that the Specialized Agencies could take care of refugee needs, in particular in the fields of migration, education, and health.

The HC was able to secure aid from the World

Health Organization (WHO), which at his request made a
valuable survey of tuberculosis cases in Trieste. From the
early beginning of his endeavors he also established a close
working relationship with the ILO. He was represented by
an observer at the ILO Migration Conference held at Naples
in 1951. In a statement made before the Third Session of
the Adv. Com. in 1953, the ILO representative affirmed
"the ILO's interest in the refugee problem and in particular
in questions concerning the integration of refugees and the
development of vocational training programs"; he also expressed the ILO's willingness, "within the limits of its possibilities, " to "collaborate to the greatest possible extent. "
The Director-General of the ILO acted as an advisor to the
HC in the Ford Foundation program, giving technical advice
on projects for vocational training. [10]

The United Nations Educational, Scientific and Cultural Organization (UNESCO) gave technical advice in the
cultural and educational fields. [11]   UNESCO also made sure
that refugees' interests were safeguarded in the International
Copyright Convention. [12]

Following the request of the Adv. Com. at its Second
Session, and in pursuance of a resolution adopted by the
Third Committee and subsequently by the GA itself (638[VII]),
a member of the HC's staff talked with the International
Bank for Reconstruction and Development (IBRD) in Washington about obtaining loans. But these negotiations produced
no concrete results, as the Bank under its constitution could
not make loans for the direct financing of programs for integrating refugees. It could only give loans for general development purposes and on the basis of national programs
which include measures from which refugees might benefit.

In the legal field the HC appointed Dr. Paul Weis,
formerly on the IRO's legal staff, as the UNHCR observer
on the UN Commission on Human Rights. In this area fruitful collaboration has developed which has aided not only the
refugees but also other UN endeavors in the field of human
rights.

While these contacts were of value to the HC, they
did not relieve the Office of its principal responsibilities.
The HC stressed that the handling of the refugee problem
could not be merged with such other related problems as
surplus population, manpower, employment, education, migration, or economic and social development. Although the

refugee problem was closely linked with all these issues, refugees had distinctive needs that could be met only by the UNHCR in its capacity as the "protector" of refugees. The GA expressed its agreement on this issue:

> The attempts to merge the refugee problem in any other problem has as a necessary consequence that the special conditions of the refugee are neglected, and that he is arbitrarily placed on an equal footing with any other candidates for the proposed solution of a larger problem, when, in fact the special circumstances of his misfortune require that he should be given special consideration. The refugee in all social and economic policies is the difficult case who does not fit into the generally accepted norm. [13]

Perhaps for this reason, it took a number of years in fact for interagency cooperation of refugee matters to become effective. Nonetheless, these early and pragmatic efforts toward cooperation between UNHCR and other members of the UN system led, in the course of the Office's first twenty-one years of existence, to closer and wider collaboration.

Relationship with the Inter-Governmental Agencies

In anticipation of the termination of IRO, various efforts were made to organize continuing services for the European refugees whose numbers were being constantly increased by the influx from Central and Eastern European countries. In the course of organizing collective efforts, there emerged two different organizations with which the UNHCR established close working relationship from the beginning:

1. The Council of Europe (CoE), created by international agreement under Art. 52 of the UN Charter by fifteen Western European countries on 5 May 1949, with headquarters at Strasbourg, France, effective 3 August 1949.

2. The Inter-Governmental Committee for European Migration (ICEM), with headquarters at Geneva.

The spur to the establishment of the latter organization was official recognition of the potentially explosive

problem of European overpopulation--a problem which had
become inseparable from that of the refugees--and the recognition of the overseas countries' need for additional manpower.   On 13 May 1950 the Foreign Ministers of the US,
UK and France meeting in London, issued the following joint
communiqué:

>The Foreign Ministers have recognized that the ex-
>cess of population for which several countries are
>suffering is one of the most important elements in
>the difficulties and disequilibrium of the world.
>They also believe that the systematic exploration
>of opportunities for greater population mobility can
>contribute significantly to the solution of this prob-
>lem.

The establishment of ICEM marked a decisive turning point
in the evolution of the intra-European and overseas European
migration, and thereby aided the settlement of large numbers
of European refugees.

The Council of Europe

The CoE, established "to achieve closer unity between
the European peoples and to develop their well-being with
due respect for human rights and fundamental freedoms,"
was concerned from the beginning with the acute problem of
refugees. [14]

At the first session of the Consultative Assembly in
August 1949 (the CoE operates through a Committee of Ministers whose members represent the eighteen participating
governments, a Consultative Assembly whose members are
drawn from all sections of opinion in the parliaments of
member countries, and a Secretariat), several parliamentarians drew attention to the refugee problem, in particular to
the problem of the "hard-core," that is, "sick and aged
people who cannot be absorbed into the economy of any country."[15]   On 8 September 1949 the Consultative Assembly
adopted an Order instructing the Secretariat of the Council
to collect data and to present to the Assembly full information on the European refugee problem and to make "contacts
with the UN and particularly with the IRO, with the governments of the various European states, competent administrative services and private institutions."   The Secretariat was
advised to investigate the legal status of various groups of

displaced persons, the possibility for these either to find
employment in Europe or to emigrate, and the material and
moral needs to be met (in particular for the hard-core),
and to study overlapping of already existing organizations in
order to determine those fields which were not yet covered
by any administrative organs.   The following year, in August 1950, the Consultative Assembly recommended that the
problem--the fate of all refugees, whatever their nationality,
race or creed--be considered in its entirety, and created a
Special Committee for Refugees.

The Committee made the distinction between "refugees
enjoying international protection" granted by the LoN,
UNRRA, IRO, and later by UNHCR, and "national refugees, "
those "persons who had been forced to leave their place of
origin and had settled in another part of their national territory, such as the refugees from the German territories
situated beyond the Oder-Neisse line and the Eastern Zone
of Germany, Greek victims of Communist aggression, and
Italian refugees from the former Italian colonies.   It also
included persons compelled to leave their homes and settle
in the country to which they ethnically belong, such as the
refugees of Italian ethnic origin from Istria or Dalmatia,
the Volksdeutsche, and the Turco-Bulgarians expelled from
Bulgaria and admitted to Turkey. "[16]

By 1950 the refugee problem had merged, as already
noted, into another still larger problem--that of overpopulation, or "surplus persons" ("surplus persons" being defined
as persons "unabsorbed in the economic life of the country
and so constituting a dead weight for that country"). [17]   Overpopulation in Europe was the result of the sudden increase
in population due to the continuing influx of refugees and of
a chronic disproportion between population growth and economic resources.   While, in former times, disproportion
between population and resources had been counteracted by
regular emigration, especially to the US, this migratory
flow had been curtailed since 1930, owing partly to restrictive immigration laws of the overseas countries but mainly
to the vast destruction and economic dislocation as a result
of WWII.   The effect of these developments was an accumulation of surplus population, mainly in Italy, Greece, the
Netherlands, and Western Germany, which could not be absorbed by progressive expansion within the domestic economies of these countries.   The CoE regarded the refugee and
overpopulation problem as a single issue.   While the presence of large numbers of refugees raised insoluble problems

of economic integration in any single country, the same factors also affected countries suffering from overpopulation
resulting from a lack of balance between the rise in population and domestic resources.

The Committee of Ministers convened a Committee
of Experts in the summer of 1951 to define the problem and
to propose effective solutions. Representatives of four international organizations took part--ILO, IRO, UNHCR, and
IBRD--and the US sent two observers. As a result, the
Consultative Assembly established a European Refugee Office
and a Committee on Population and Refugees, the latter being the first step toward linking these two issues and working toward a solution.

In an exchange of letters dating from 15 December
1951, the two Secretaries-General (CoE and UN) concluded
an agreement outlining cooperation based on principles common to both organizations.[18] Within the framework of this
agreement the UNHCR and the CoE instituted a certain collaboration which has become increasingly well defined. In
a three-sided exchange of letters (from May to August 1952),
the Secretary-General of the UN, the Secretary-General of
the CoE and the HC concluded that the agreement which had
been reached between the first two bodies should be extended
to the UNHCR.

Since that time the HC has maintained excellent relations with the Consultative Assembly and with the Committee
of Ministers. Specifically, since 29 August 1952 the HC has
presented the CoE with an annual report regarding the activities of his Office. This is studied by both the Consultative
Assembly and the Committee of Ministers, after which
recommendations and resolutions are made.

By Res. 53(35) of 12 December 1953, the Council of
Ministers appointed a Special Representative of the CoE for
national refugees and overpopulation, Dr. Pierre Schneiter,
former French Minister of Health and Population.[19]

In its activities the CoE put its main emphasis on the
"national refugees" according to a broader definition of refugees than that of the UNHCR.[20] In its efforts to improve
the status of "international refugees" the CoE concentrated
mainly on supplementing the activities of the UNHCR in the
field of international protection. Special refugee interests
were taken into consideration in the drafting of European
inter-governmental agreements and conventions.

The close cooperation between the CoE and the UNHCR has led to wider support of general UNHCR activities. At the request of the UNHCR, the Committee of Ministers resolved to invite member governments to "support action undertaken on behalf of the Berlin refugees by the UNHCR."21 The Committee on Population and Refugees provided for the building of several thousand temporary dwellings at a cost of DM 5,000 each. An appeal was made to member states to grant visas generously to the 1,500 "hard-core" refugees concentrated in Trieste.22 The Consultative Committee made two recommendations urging its member states to speed up the acceptance of Hungarian refugees in Austria (21 January 1959 and 21 January 1960). Two other recommendations furthered the World Refugee Year (WRY), 24 April 1959 and 21 January 1960. On the basis of the recommendation of 15 October 1958, member states of the Council, at the suggestion of the HC, provided planes for the evacuation of European refugees from Hong Kong in 1959.

The Inter-Governmental Committee
for European Migration

The creation of ICEM was more directly the result of concern about the growing problem of "over or surplus" population in Europe: Italy, where the problem of overpopulation was numerically greatest--due to the loss of the Italian colonies, the wartime halt in emigration, war devastation, and lack of capital--was strained by a surplus population of some three million persons. In Greece, where unemployment and lack of capital were chronic, recurrent strife and earthquakes had aggravated the problem. In the Netherlands, Europe's most densely populated country, limited land area and the return from Indonesia of thousands of Holland's former colonials, were responsible for the crisis. In Germany and Austria, the huge influx of refugees had been the chief contributing cause. Moreover, there was the rising influx of new refugees, called "escapees," from Eastern European countries and Eastern Germany. The remaining IRO refugees also needed resettlement.

The urgency of the overpopulation problem led to the establishment of an inter-governmental operational agency to provide migration assistance to refugees and European nationals. The Belgian Government in December 1951, on the initiative of the US Government, invited sixteen countries

concerned with migrants and refugees to an inter-governmental conference at Brussels to consider methods of alleviating overpopulation through overseas migration. As a
result, sixteen governments signed the Constitution of ICEM
and provided for PICMME to set up headquarters in Geneva
in February 1952 and carry on operations in the interim
period until the ICEM Constitution came into force on 30
November 1954. By 1971, the membership of ICEM had
increased to thirty-one Western European and overseas
countries. (See Annex 5.1.)

The mandates of ICEM and UNHCR are not identical.
ICEM was conceived as an instrument to restore an equili-
brium between the overcrowded and the undermanned nations,
through orderly migration of those Europeans who could not
move without international cooperative action. The experience of the immediate post-war years had proved that "normal" migration, taking place under bilateral agreements and
by private initiative, was not sufficient to meet the demands
of both the countries of emigration and the countries of reception. As an underlying principle, it was accepted that
planned and assisted migration on an international basis
should be linked with domestic governmental policy. Thus,
the objective of ICEM was to provide low-cost transport for
national migrants and "old" and "new" refugees who wanted
to emigrate from Western European countries to overseas
countries. For this program migration arrangements were
made between the Committee, the country affording asylum,
and the overseas country in need of manpower. The organization salvaged some of the valuable resettlement experience and machinery of the IRO; it absorbed 300 of the IRO
staff and took over twelve ships. When commercial shipping and air services returned to normal, ICEM arranged
special fares with the commercial agencies.[23] Over the
years it also developed pre-settlement and post-settlement
services as well as language and vocational training.

The cost of ICEM's operation and administration is
met by contributions from member governments, payments
from the migrants themselves or their sponsors, and revenue from voluntary organizations dealing with migrants and
refugee matters. In 1956 the Council, by a resolution, created a Special Refugee Trust Fund to be the repository of
monies from fund-raising campaigns for the transportation
of refugees. The organization itself is composed of a policy-making Council in which all member governments are
represented, a nine-nation Executive Committee, and an

Administration headed by a Director-General appointed by a
two-thirds majority of the Council.[24]   Currently, ICEM has
twenty-nine field missions overseas and in Europe.

Although ICEM was set up outside the framework of
the UN, it is international in scope and has maintained close
working relationships with the UNHCR, the UN Specialized
Agencies, and the voluntary agencies whose activities relate
to the movement of migrants and refugees.[25] ICEM's definition of refugees, like that of the CoE, is broader than
that of the UNHCR. This fact has led to "apparent statistical contradictions" in the course of their collaboration, but
a general understanding has been reached, leading to considerable cooperation.[26]   From its inception the UNHCR
has relied on ICEM's operational machinery to move European refugees within Europe and to overseas countries.
Following an expansion of its terms of reference, ICEM at
the request of the UNHCR has also been helpful in some
emergency situations beyond Europe, notably technical help
in repatriating Nigerian children in 1971 and transporting
Ugandan Asians in 1972.   The UNHCR maintains regular
contact with ICEM through a tripartite committee, composed
of representatives of UNHCR, ICEM, and USRP, which
meets in Geneva twice yearly.[27] It provides a useful forum
for the coordination of programs among the three organs
and helps to avoid overlap.

The Non-Governmental (Voluntary) Agencies

No element has been more vital to the successful
conduct of the programs of the UNHCR than the close partnership between UNHCR and the non-governmental organizations, commonly referred to as the voluntary agencies. For
while the UNHCR is the symbol and manifestation of the concern of the international community for the problem of refugees, the voluntary agencies have been the practitioners
who, through their dedication and long experience, permit
this concern to be translated into effective measures of aid.
They have been, and still are, agents of the private conscience.

The voluntary agencies have been a permanent factor
in refugee work since the early 1920s.   Not only have they
been a necessary adjunct to the work of public statutory organizations (international and national) but they have had a
great importance in their own right.   Under his Statute, the

HC is directed to seek permanent solutions to refugee problems by assisting governments and private organizations to
facilitate the voluntary repatriation of refugees or their assimilation within new national communities.   To implement
this directive the HC is to establish contacts with private
organizations in such manner as he may think best (Art.
8[h]) and facilitate the coordination of the efforts of private
organizations concerned with refugees (Art. 8[i]).   The Statute thus carries on the link forged in 1921 between official
international agencies dealing with refugee problems and the
voluntary agencies.   But while the HC could take advantage
of the experience of his immediate predecessors, UNRRA
and the IRO, in working with voluntary agencies the nature
of his relationship had to be different because his functions
and the political setting in which he had to work were different.   Whereas both UNRRA and the IRO were established as
operational bodies, acting directly on refugee problems and
with large budgets provided by governments, the UNHCR
was required to be non-operational, with a small budget only
for administrative expenses.   While international protection
was a function to be performed directly by the HC and his
staff, when it came to seeking permanent solutions his role
was to be that of stimulating, assisting, and coordinating
efforts of governments and voluntary agencies.   Thus it was
essential for the HC to find operational partners through
which he could work to achieve the goals set forth in the
Statute.   And it was equally essential that he find sources
of support that would make the fullest implementation of his
purposes possible.   It was to meet both these needs that the
HC turned to the voluntary agencies.

        Voluntary agencies come into being when private citi-
zens identify a human problem and out of compassion take
immediate steps toward remedying it.   For this purpose
they form an organization or a new division of an existing
one, and through the organization they rouse authorities to
find a solution for the problem.   When the end is achieved
the agency may either drop out of the picture or, as has
happened more frequently with agencies dealing with refugee
problems, so shape itself as to be able to serve as a partner of the official body which has assumed the responsibility.
Thus the voluntary agencies are the public expression of the
determination of many private citizens to assist their fellow
human beings.   Although more and more social needs are
being brought directly into the official sphere in every country, the assumption of these responsibilities by government
has not reduced the need for private action.   The needs of

post-industrial and post-war society have brought forth a variety of responses from the private sector, accounting for the staggering list of voluntary organizations in existence today.   To their role as organizations is now added their role as partners, in varying degrees of closeness, to official bodies both national and international.   The new partnerships and the increasing complexity of the problems with which the voluntary agencies deal have led to a growing need for professionalization in all spheres of philanthropy, from fund-raising to field-work techniques and program formation.   Trained, paid personnel are required for many voluntary agency activities, and efficient organizations have, in many cases, led to the formation of well-defined hierarchies.

Thus when the UNHCR came into being in 1951, there existed an array of voluntary organizations operating in virtually all fields of human need, many of them with great experience in the refugee field.   The assumption by official bodies of responsibility for the practical solution of refugee problems greatly increased the effectiveness of these voluntary efforts by providing official endorsement, and the network of experienced national and local committees which grouped voluntary agencies associated in the common cause, provided a readymade framework through which official refugee agencies could work to meet their own responsibilities. The pattern of "functional international cooperation" between official and private agencies which developed has, in view of the scope and complexity of present-day refugee problems, become an effective means toward long-range solutions.

Functions of Voluntary Agencies

Voluntary agency functions on behalf of refugees may be viewed from two aspects: their immediate practical services to the refugee, and their indirect service to him as intermediaries between him and official bodies dealing with refugee problems.

In terms of practical services, it is the voluntary agencies which are on the scene of disasters of both natural and political origin often long before official action can be taken.   Potentially they provide assistance to all refugees, including those who are not included in the mandate of the official international bodies, or for whom government bodies do not or cannot care.   This was very important in the past when the term refugee was narrowly defined and when refugees in desperate need could not be aided by official bodies. The presence of the voluntary agencies means that whenever there is a need, help is available on the basis of humanitarian rather than political considerations.

The voluntary agencies have operated at all stages of the work with refugees, from emergency-relief measures and assistance in and outside refugee camps to long-range projects for permanent solutions. Their personnel and financial resources are mobilized in emergency situations for stop-gap relief before official bodies can act. They bring food and clothing and medical assistance to refugees. They seek to provide shelter and the necessary physical comforts and to provide for the spiritual life of refugees wherever they are. Furthermore, the voluntary agencies provide counselling services on alternatives open for future settlement. They assist with child care and special care of the aged and handicapped. They operate tracing services so that refugee families may be reunited, and offer special counselling services for unaccompanied children.

In addition to emergency measures, voluntary agencies carry out practical services in relation to long-range solutions. They assist in the implementation of resettlement or camp clearance schemes. They may prepare emigrants for overseas resettlement by language training and orientation courses. In receiving countries they seek sponsorships for refugees, as well as employment opportunities. They meet ships transporting refugees to their new homes and often pay much of the cost of migration. In the new country, or in local integration schemes, they continue their assistance until each refugee is firmly settled. They seek housing, and grant loans to help establish refugees in their trades. They continue counselling so that refugees may take advantage of the public health, education, and other social services to which they are entitled under normal government programs, and supplement these services with loans or grants where they are insufficient to meet the refugees' special needs. To assist refugees to become economically self-sufficient they provide equipment--tools, sewing machines, and musical instruments, for example--as well as rehabilitation courses and programs for retraining professionals to meet requirements in the new country. By all these services and by encouraging local communities to accept refugees into their midst socially, the voluntary agencies attempt to minimize the inevitable disruption caused by the arrival in a community of sizable numbers of refugees.

In the provision of immediate practical services, agency personnel in the field, in direct contact with the refugees, are often able to create relationships which in themselves help fulfill refugee needs. Whether as compatriots, as members of the same religious group, or simply as fellow human beings, agency workers recognize the refugee's problems at the most basic level--illness, lack of food or clothing, separation from loved ones, and psychological conditions resulting from fear of authority or of persecution, from uprootedness, and from unemployment. They sympathize with his spiritual or educational needs and understand the kind of community he hopes to inhabit and the job he proposes to seek to become self-sufficient once again.

Voluntary agencies are also the agents of important indirect services, insofar as they function as intermediaries between the refugee and their own constituencies and between him and the official bodies seeking permanent solutions to refugee problems. A primary means of indirect assistance is that of lobbying before individuals, groups, private foundations, or official bodies concerned with refugees. Because of their firsthand knowledge of individual and overall needs they can stimulate individual generosity, act as pressure groups to encourage government or international action in behalf of refugees, and serve as reliable advisors to official bodies dealing with refugees. In their own constituencies the voluntary agencies mobilize the sympathy of compatriots or fellow members of a faith or the spontaneous generosity of individuals, and so obtain material assistance-- food, clothing, or money--as well as sponsorships and other support for special programs.

Because of their intimate knowledge and practical experience, coupled with their relative flexibility and freedom of action as compared with official bodies responsible to a multitude of divergent political interests, the voluntary agencies have been able to make bold experiments in the solution of refugee problems. If the experiments do not prove helpful, no official body is embarrassed or blamed. On the other hand, if they prove successful the voluntary agencies can work for their application by governments on a broad and official scale.

Functioning as a pressure group, voluntary agencies have combined to stimulate action at the international level as well. The voluntary agencies promoted the formation of official international bodies for dealing with the refugee and

pressed for the codification of his status and his rights.
The conference of 16 February 1921 which resulted in appointment by the LoN of the first HC was convened by the
ICRC. "The pattern established whereby voluntary agencies,
acutely sensitive to public opinion, clamored for organized
inter-governmental action to tackle the refugee situation"
was evident also in the formation of the IRO; the strongest
clamor came at the time of the premature closing of the
IRO. The SCVA, speaking for all member agencies, sent
a telegram to Mr. Trygve Lie, Secretary-General of the
UN, on 4 October 1949, calling for the UN to make provisions for continuing the work of IRO until some new mechanism was developed. It was largely through the lobbying
activities of the American voluntary agencies that the USDP
Act of 1948 was passed, without which IRO's program would
have failed.

Organizations for Voluntary Action

        The basis of all voluntary service to refugees is the
individual in his community working or contributing through
a local group which may or may not be part of a wider national or international voluntary agency. Of the voluntary
agencies concerned with assisting refugees, some are exclusively national organizations with overseas programs, for
example, the Oxford Committee for Famine Relief (OXFAM).
Others are massive international confederations basing themselves in fifty or more countries, such as the League of
Red Cross Societies (LRCS). Some undertake projects
amounting to thousands of dollars annually while others have
global programs running to twenty or thirty million dollars
per year. Some are formed specifically to meet new refugee problems, while others with long experience in counselling and welfare work have added refugee services to their
regular programs. Some have passed their fiftieth active
year--the World Alliance of Young Men's Christian Associations (YMCA), for example, has celebrated its one hundredth
anniversary.

        The largest of the voluntary agencies, those to whom
UNHCR first turned for assistance, are the denominational
agencies. These probably have the closest, most constant
relationship with their constituencies, while at the same
time they operate the broadest scope of programs for needy
persons. They have been entrusted by official bodies with
vast responsibilities for refugee welfare and have been

supported by sums amounting over the years to millions of
dollars.   Six of these--the World Council of Churches
(WCC), the Lutheran World Federation (LWF), the National
Catholic Welfare Council (NCWC), the American Friends
Service Committee (AFSC), the American Joint Distribution
Committee (AJDC), and the World Alliance of YMCA--are
internationally organized federations, the apex of a hierarchy
of individual denominational agencies which represent through
their membership hundreds of thousands of individuals.   They
have a long history of philanthropic work throughout the
Western World.   Other religious groups also work independently of these worldwide associations of denominational
groups.

In 1951, when the UNHCR first sought partners, many
non-denominational international voluntary organizations were
also operating humanitarian service programs from which
refugees benefited.   Some of these, such as the LRCS and
the ICRC, had long been known for their vast relief programs throughout the world.   In addition to these, however,
there were many smaller groups rendering services which
were to become important adjuncts to UNHCR programs,
some specializing in special services such as case work--
the International Social Service (ISS)--or serving particular
groups such as children and orphans, students, old or disabled persons, or intellectuals.   The agencies in this group
vary widely in scope, purpose, and organization.   For some
agencies, refugee work is their raison d'être--e. g. , the
Ockenden Venture, le Service social d'aide aux émigrants,
the International Rescue Committee (IRS) and the International Relief Committee for Intellectual Workers (IRCIW).
They operate independently, keeping their identity, but often
in close cooperation with other agencies.   In other organizations, such as the Red Cross, World University Service
(WUS), YMCA/YWCA, and OXFAM, refugee programs are
only one aspect of their work.

A third type of agency has been formed by ethnic
groups living overseas--for the most part in the US, Australia, and Canada--who wished to aid their refugee compatriots.   The American Fund for Czech Refugees, the
American Polish War Relief, and the Tolstoy Foundation are
examples in this category.   These and some other ethnic
agencies have performed useful services for refugees based
on specific knowledge not only of the language but of the
political, psychological, and historical background of those
they serve.   They have contributed relief supplies and

money and have been active in promoting resettlement for
refugees in overseas countries by finding sponsors and employment for them, by preparing them for emigration through
counselling, and by assisting their integration in the new
country.

UNHCR in Relation to the Voluntary Agencies

In order to receive recognition as co-workers with
international and national organizations, all types of voluntary agencies must meet certain basic requirements of stability and continuity. They must be properly registered in
their country of origin. Their programs must not be in
conflict with the purposes of the government of that country
or of the international governmental agency and must be in
keeping with their financial resources; and their staffs must
be qualified to execute them. In addition, they must be acceptable to the countries in which they are to operate, and
since they have no responsibility for matters involving national sovereignty they must avoid involvement in any political activity in those countries.

In addition to the above agencies, which are organized on an international basis and operate for mutual advantage with their national counterparts or branches, there are
many other agencies organized on a national level which
serve refugees.

As the mushrooming refugee problem placed ever
greater demands upon them and because of the part they
were now being called upon to take in support of official national government and international refugee programs, voluntary agencies of all types became increasingly aware of the
necessity for efficiency in their individual operations and for
interagency cooperation. Accordingly, in June 1948, thirty-
seven national and international agencies formed the SCVA
Working for Refugees "to provide for joint representation
in discussions with competent organizations or governments
on refugee problems," and to facilitate joint consultation
among the voluntary agencies concerning needs of refugees,
conditions of work of member agencies, and their status
with respect to one another. [28]   The SCVA has been given
official recognition and consultative status by ECOSOC,
UNHCR, ICEM, and USRP.

Many of the projects which the HC has promoted in

the course of his activities have been carried out by voluntary agencies.   They are the "operating arm," or executing
agent, of his program, and, in the words of Rev. Elfan
Rees, "the almoners of the High Commissioner." The field
workers of the voluntary agencies also often act as the link
between the refugee and the UNHCR, and the experience of
agency social workers and the information from them are of
primary importance to the UNHCR in planning programs.
At the program-planning stage, for example, the local HC
representative meets with the local Refugee Committee consisting of representatives from the HC, the government,
and voluntary agencies.   At these meetings the funds allocated to each type of aid are made known, and agencies are
invited to submit projects.   The HC initiates and coordinates
suggestions and calls for alterations when necessary.   The
voluntary agencies also have observer status in ECOSOC and
in the UNHCR Ex. Com.   In this way the experience of the
individual voluntary worker contributes to the development
of a program for the international community, to be coordinated by the HC.

Because there are vast differences in philosophy,
modes of operation, and constituencies among the voluntary
agencies and statutory bodies, coordination of programs by
the HC is an essential, though often remarkably complex
and difficult task.   Cooperation is not always easily achieved
in programs involving agencies--voluntary and other non-
governmental agencies, inter-governmental organizations,
and governments alike--with such diversity of views and efforts.   While over the long run, partnerships among these
bodies have been highly successful, there have been agencies
which have been more concerned about perpetuating their
own programs, more inclined to seek to aggrandize their
own empires, more likely to negate joint efforts, than to
recognize that aid is best provided in the most efficient and
rational way, and in cooperation with national governments
and inter-governmental organizations.

But although there have been differences among the
voluntary agencies, and between the agencies and the
UNHCR, over the long run, as Dr. van Heuven Goedhart
has stated, "the UNHCR has had the most excellent relations
with the voluntary agencies....   Their work is in a true
sense of the term indispensable and invaluable for the refugees to look for understanding and help.   Whenever the
story of the refugee problem is told or written, these agencies deserve that high tribute should be paid to what they
and their thousands of collaborators are doing."[29]

In the chapters to follow, the activities of governments, international and inter-governmental agencies, and voluntary agencies will be considered in the context of their combined work for refugees on the international, regional, and local level. Under the leadership of UNHCR in its role as "catalyst," there has evolved a loosely woven network for dealing with the plight of hundreds of thousands of uprooted people. The development of this international interdependence has become an increasingly important factor in the refugee's hope to lead a dignified and fruitful life.

Notes

1. IRO, GC/256, Semi-Annual Rep. of the Director-General of IRO.

2. A/AC. 36/24: 22.

3. Ibid.

4. Ibid.

5. LoN (IV), Eighteenth Plenary Meeting, 28 Sept. 1923.

6. James Read, "The United Nations and Refugees, Changing Concepts," IC No. 537, Mar. 1962: 14.

7. UN, GA, A/AC. 36/3/Rev. 2, 15 May 1964, Rule 6.

8. Ibid. , Rules 7 and 8.

9. Ibid. , Rule 9.

10. UN, GA, (VIII), A/AC. 36/SR 24, 9 June 1953: 11.

11. In a 1953 UNESCO Res. it was stated that "The Director-General is authorized to supply the HC, at the latter's request, with technical advice on the selection and preparation of such cultural and educational projects as the HC might wish to carry out on behalf of refugees under his protection." GA (VIII) A/AC. 36/SR 22, 9 June 1953: 6.

12. HC's Annual Rep. for 1953. GA (VIII), Off. Rec. Supp. No. 11, A/3294: 4.

13. GA (VIII), A/AC. 36/24, 1953: 20.

14. "No Room for Them?" Commentary presented by the
     Council of Europe on the problem of refugees and
     surplus elements of population in Europe, Stras-
     bourg, 1953.

15. Ibid. : 39.

16. Ibid.

17. Ibid.

18. In accordance with Art. 1, sub-par. c of its Statute,
     the CoE should act in order that "the participation
     of its members in work conducted through the Coun-
     cil will not in any way alter their contribution to
     the work of the United Nations or of other organi-
     zations to which these members belong. "

19. He took up his duties on 1 Feb. 1954.

20. "The term refugee shall be understood to mean any
     person who, as a result of political events of the
     two World Wars, is without established residence of
     his choice, having left his domicile under duress or
     under threat of violence owing to his political opin-
     ions, religion, nationality or racial origin. " CoE
     Rec. 2 of the Consultative Assembly.

21. CoE, Res. 53(21) of 7 May 1953.

22. CoE, Res. 53(10) of 5 May 1953.

23. See statement by Dr. Lindt at the ICEM Council (XII),
     6 May 1960, in UNHCR Ref. Serv., No. 18, July
     1960: 45.

24. The first Director-General was US Ambassador Hugh
     S. Gibson who served until his death in Dec. 1954.
     He was succeeded in May 1955 by US Ambassador
     Harold H. Tittman. The first Deputy Director-
     General, Pierre Jacobsen of France, served from
     1952 until his tragic death in 1957. Dr. Marcus
     Daly, an American businessman, was appointed in
     1958 and was succeeded in 1961 by Bastion W.
     Havemann, Dutch, who was in turn succeeded in

1969 by John F. Thomas, an American with over 25 years' experience in the refugee field.

25. For a detailed report, see US 90th Cong. , 1st Sess. , HR, No. 578 Washington, US GPO, 1967; see especially ICEM, Its Evolution During 15 Years, I. Refugee Programs: App. 6; 37-38. For a further discussion of its activities, see John F. Thomas, Planned International Migration and Multilateral Cooperation (ICEM at Work), Geneva, 1971.

26. See ICEM Constitution, Art. 1, sec. 3.

27. The US Escapee Program (USEP), later US Refugee Program (USRP), was created as a unilateral program by the US in early 1952.

28. For member agencies, see The Standing Conference of Voluntary Agencies Working for Refugees, Geneva 1955.

29. HCR/Inf. 18, 25 Apr. 1953.

ANNEX 5.1

INTER-GOVERNMENTAL COMMITTEE
FOR EUROPEAN MIGRATION

Member Governments

Argentina	Ecuador	Norway
Australia*	El Salvador	Panama
Austria*	Germany, Fed. Rep. of*	Paraguay
Belgium*	Greece*	Peru
Bolivia*	Honduras	S. Africa, Rep. of
Brazil*	Israel	Spain
Chile*	Italy*	Switzerland*
Colombia	Luxembourg*	US*
Costa Rica	Malta	Uruguay
Denmark	Netherlands*	
Dominican Rep.	Nicaragua	

*Governments represented at the Brussels conference

Observer Governments

Cyprus	Japan	Malta
Guatemala	Portugal	Turkey
Holy See	San Marino	Venezuela

Refugees

Main Asylum Countries

Italy
Austria
Germany, Fed. Rep. of
France
Greece
Spain
Belgium

Originating Areas	Main Immigration Countries	
Eastern Europe	US	276,965
	Israel	232,504
Middle East	Australia	193,474
	Canada	103,323
Cuba	Western Europe	63,540
	Latin America	29,992
Far East	S. Africa, Rep. of	10,063

NOTE: Countries are listed here in order of numbers of refugees (1952-71)

International Governmental Organizations Attending ICEM Council Meetings

UN, ILO, FAO, UNESCO, WHO, IBRD, CoE, OECD, CEC, OAS, TADB, UNHCR, and the Special Representative of CoE for National Refugees and Overpopulation.

International Non-Governmental Organizations Attending ICEM Council Meetings

ICFITU, ICVA, CCIA, CRS, ICMC, IRC, ISS, LRCS, LWF, United HIAS Service, WCC, ICRC, and a few others.

SOURCE: ICEM, Review of Achievements 1971: 42.

Chapter 6

THE SCOPE AND URGENCY OF THE TASK, 1951-53

High Commissioner van Heuven Goedhart's initial tasks were the organization of staff, the establishment of administrative procedures, and the building of relationships with governmental and non-governmental bodies. An urgent concern was to assess the needs of the refugees through statistical compilations and surveys, by extensive visits to refugee camps and areas of refugee concentration, and in consultation with governments. The results of these efforts upheld the HC's view, widely concurred in by Western European officials, that the need for international protection was only one aspect of refugee problems that would still exist after the liquidation of the IRO on 30 September 1951. The HC's investigations indicated that a primary need of thousands of European refugees was immediate material assistance, without which long-range planning to achieve permanent solutions for all mandate refugees would be fruitless.

The enormity of the task at hand was not immediately evident to the GA. The first three years of the Office's existence can be seen as a period during which the UNHCR struggled to identify the extent of the refugee problem, to bring to the attention of the international community its continuing nature, and to forge new approaches to effecting permanent solutions. In confronting this task, the HC was compelled to work within a framework of public opinion, reflected by the governments and in the UN, which perceived the urgent refugee problem of the post-war years as essentially solved and which sought to terminate its existing refugee programs as expeditiously and inexpensively as possible. The early years can therefore be considered a setting of the stage, an interim before the community of nations determined to pursue a permanent solution to the refugee problem.

It is important to establish the framework of events during this period--to indicate what the HC's early investigations disclosed, trace the development of an international

133

response to the situation, and show that ultimately Dr. van
Heuven Goedhart's vivid picture of the realities of human
suffering persuaded the GA in 1953 to expand the limited
range of the early activities of the Office.   The evolution
of long-range programs and the assumption of far wider responsibilities by the UNHCR than had even been contemplated during the original discussions on its mandate and
financing was thus made possible.   The programs which
were developed in response to refugee needs--despite the
limitations of the HC's terms of reference--and which so
greatly enlarged the scope of his activities will be considered in succeeding chapters (see Parts IV and V).

Statistics

It was essential that the HC determine the numbers
of refugees who fell under his mandate.   Data on numbers
of refugees under the IRO mandate were available as presented to the Executive Secretary of PICMME in May 1947,
but more information was needed.

The HC, feeling the need for an "independent and
scientific survey," was able to secure a grant of $100,000
from the Rockefeller Foundation.   This study was carried
out under M. Jacques Vernant, Professor at the French
Centre d'Etudes de Politique Etrangère.   It was begun in
June 1951 with visits by a team of assistants to most of the
countries of Western Europe and the Middle East.   The results of the preliminary survey were distributed in 1951.

The survey revealed that by the end of that year
some one million refugees would fall within the HC's mandate.   Of these, 410,000 refugees were in an IRO area and
not yet settled: 402,000 were in Europe, predominantly in
France, West Germany, Belgium, Italy, Austria, Sweden,
Greece and the Netherlands; 1,000 were in Middle East countries (Israel not included), and 1,700 were in miscellaneous
areas.   Of the total, 130,000 still lived in camps.   Since
several delegates objected to having this report distributed
by the UN, it was published as an independent and extended
study. [1]

At the request of its Adv. Com., the HC's branch
offices undertook a census of refugees in cooperation with
the governments concerned.   According to this census, it
appeared that close to 2,200,000 refugees would be eligible

under the mandate of UNHCR by 1 January 1953 (see Annex 6.1).[2] This figure, however, included persons who fell within the terms of the Statute, but who were unlikely ever to require the HC's material assistance or legal protection; it also included every refugee resettled overseas by the IRO, and in most cases these persons did not require the HC's protection.

Indices of reliability of the statistical data are only speculative, particularly since, unlike the IRO which kept an individual record of refugees applying for eligibility, the UNHCR of necessity based its figures on information provided by governments, by occupation authorities, and on evaluations by its staff and outside experts.   It must also be kept in mind that the problem of refugees is in a constant state of flux.   "The refugees are not a stagnant pool of statistics, but a slowly moving river of human beings, the overall composition of refugee groups is steadily changing in character."[3]   Statistics vary continuously in the light of developments in countries of origin and of asylum and in the light of fluctuating opportunities for resettlement in overseas countries.   Moreover, there are numerous persons who by definition are refugees but do not consider themselves such until, pressed by legal or other difficulties arising from their status, they become unhappily aware of their position and seek assistance.

The Need for Emergency Assistance

Regardless of whether the figures collected through governments or those identified by the Vernant study were accepted as the more authentic, the need for material assistance to refugees, particularly those in Shanghai, Samar, and in camps, was critical.   Thus, although legal protection was to be the primary function of the HC according to the Statute, material assistance was a practical concern of the UNHCR from the very beginning.   Indeed, the earliest report of the HC to the GA reflects a much greater concern with the securing of funds for carrying on some aspects of the assistance program of the IRO than with the provision of international protection.[4]

Dr. van Heuven Goedhart was convinced that the refugee problem could not be approached in the abstract.   Although figures were necessary for planning purposes, he was very much aware that, as Kathryn Hulme said, "statistics

tend to conceal the realities of human tragedy behind a curtain of useful administrative data. "[5]   Before presenting his
first report to the Sixth GA in January 1952 ("Observations
on Problems of Assistance"), Dr. van Heuven Goedhart
familiarized himself with the seriousness of the conditions
of refugees living in and outside camps by visiting countries
of asylum and contacting voluntary agencies. [6]   He was
alarmed by the grave circumstances of the people he met--
people adrift, many of whom had lost hope, initiative, and
integrity, and who had become increasingly unable to cope
with normal life.   Asserting that his Office would not merely "administer misery," he emphasized the increasing seriousness of the situation with which he was confronted, stressing the "constant influx of new refugees coupled with the
residual problems of refugees remaining in the countries
with their own national refugee difficulties."

        The continuing tide of refugees, mainly from Eastern
European countries, created enormous problems.   Most of
the refugees arrived destitute: their immediate needs were
clothing, food, shelter, as well as some sort of recognition
of status in the form of a document.

        Obviously their urgent need could not be met by legal
means alone.   The HC pointed out: "What does international
protection mean for a man who dies of hunger?   Passports
are necessary but hunger can't be stilled with them."

        But programs of material assistance required money.
Despite a grant of $236,698 from the remainder of the IRO
budget, the gap between emergency needs and available resources was large.   All possible ways of raising funds were
being used, the HC declared, even the sale for $14,000 of
an inherited bar of gold which the Nansen Office had purchased with part of the money accompanying its 1938 Nobel
Peace Prize.

Appeal for a UN Refugee Emergency Fund

        In earlier GA debates concerning the UNHCR, the
question of emergency assistance by the HC had been pushed
into the background.   In 1949 the Fourth GA had dealt only
with the creation of the Office, while the Fifth GA in December 1950 "in the absence of definite data," postponed consideration of problems relating to future international action
concerning the material needs of refugees until after the end

of the IRO's operation (that is, 30 September 1951), requesting the HC to present his observations and problems to the
Sixth Session of the GA.[7] Thus, Dr. van Heuven Goedhart
gave reports on the urgency of the situation to ECOSOC in
October 1951, and in January 1952 to the Third Committee
and the Sixth Plenary Session of the GA.[8]

He pointed out that although, as a whole, the refugee
problem throughout the world was not of sufficient magnitude
to justify the maintenance of IRO, it was nevertheless so
grave in terms of human suffering that it called for urgent
consideration by the UN. Dr. van Heuven Goedhart suggested three lines of action for coping with the problem he
described. He proposed first, the establishment of a limited
relief fund to provide for the basic needs of certain refugee
groups, particularly those in the Far East and Middle East,
which would be in desperate need after the ending of IRO
emergency relief. The fund would also be used for temporary emergencies arising from the influx of new refugees
into countries of first asylum. He requested the GA to authorize him to appeal for voluntary contributions and to administer this fund through his Office. The HC emphasized
that the governments of the asylum countries could not and
should not be expected to bear the entire burden. He
pointed out that "the HC was not entrusted solely with the
task of international protection but had also to seek lasting
solutions of the refugee problem by assisting governments
which were at the time confronted by very considerable difficulties. "[9]

Second, he recommended the adoption of long-term
plans "for financing and implementing economic reconstruction measures calculated to afford to residual groups in
some areas possibilities of a normal livelihood. " For this
purpose, governments and the appropriate Specialized Agencies "should be urged to work out in close collaboration with
his Office all suitable plans. "

Third, he suggested that those countries which were
making further internal efforts to promote migration take
measures to ensure the refugees "a fair share" in any available opportunities for migration.

Despite the urgency of the HC's appeal, the delegates
gave it a cool reception.[10] M. Rochefort, delegate of
France, said "that the lack of enthusiasm shown during the
discussion seemed to indicate that governments were no

longer interested in the refugee problem. In actual fact, the
problem still retained the same importance for those which
had set up IRO and those which were directly affected."
The delegates raised questions once more in regard to the
policy-making role of the GA and to the authority and functions of the HC. In an effort to neutralize objections, the
HC declared that the emergency fund of three million dollars
which he had requested would not affect the UN budget; the
GA was asked only to approve the launching of an appeal for
voluntary funds. Also, the collection of funds would not require additional staff since the contributions would be distributed by him to the various voluntary agencies concerned
with refugees, with the HC insuring coordination and efficiency of effort.

Nonetheless, debate continued on whether the situation justified an extension of the HC's mandate to include the
collection of funds. The majority believed that the GA
should allow the HC to appeal for voluntary contributions; it
was suggested that an amendment to the Statute was unnecessary, since par. 10(1) of the Statute authorized the HC to
administer funds from public or private sources for the assistance of refugees, although he had no right to solicit such
funds without the approval of the GA. Some members reiterated, however, the accepted principle that "the governments in whose territories [refugees] resided should care
for them as far as possible." The Canadian delegate asked
that exact information be presented to the GA on those refugees who would need assistance in addition to that already
supplied by ordinary governmental assistance services, the
intention being that international assistance should be authorized only as a supplement, and for a limited time. Mrs.
Eleanor Roosevelt, the US delegate, opposed authorization
of an appeal, reminding the delegates that contributions were
already required for the large relief programs in Palestine
(UNRWA) and Korea (UNKRA), as well as for UNICEF and
the UN Technical Assistance Program. She declared that
the UN was in danger of administering relief on a worldwide
basis and that her government opposed the precedent of authorizing a UN official to collect funds for a rather indefinite
program in competition with other and more definite UN
programs, and she announced that her government would not
contribute to such a fund and would abstain from voting for
the joint draft resolution introduced by Colombia, Denmark,
Lebanon, the Netherlands, New Zealand, the UK, and Uruguay, which embodied the HC's request for emergency assistance. [11] Mr. Beaufort, the Dutch delegate, stated:

"The High Commissioner should be authorized to make appeals for voluntary contributions--the mere fact of the GA's authorizing the High Commissioner to appeal for funds would not place governments under any kind of obligation to make contributions.   Furthermore, such authorization would not create a precedent, for there was the earlier example of the UN International Children's Emergency Fund. "

Eventually, the HC's poignant description of the refugees' plight convinced a sufficient number of the members of the GA to vote, somewhat reluctantly, for an emergency fund to which both member and non-member states and voluntary agencies would be asked to contribute regularly. [12]

The authorization proved to be only the first hurdle, however.   Response to the HC's initial appeal for the Emergency Fund was very poor: barely one-third of the target was reached by 31 March 1953 (see Annex 6.2).   The greater part of these funds had to be earmarked for refugees in China and the rest for relief programs to care for the most distressing cases during the winter.   At the Fourth Session of the Adv. Com., in March 1954, reporting on the response to his appeal for contributions, the HC stated that the results had been one of the "bitterest disappointments" he had ever experienced.   Authorizing him to seek funds for emergency relief "had made him what might be called an international beggar. "

While the Emergency Fund continued to be undersubscribed in the first years of the UNHCR's work (see Annex 6.3), the HC was to meet with a more sympathetic response in the Seventh and Eighth Plenary Sessions of the GA.   The Seventh recognized the need for a long-term program for assimilation and integration, and in the Eighth, resolutions were passed prolonging the mandate of the Office and affirming the governments' concern for refugees in need of emergency aid, those living in camps, and the hard-core.

The Need for Programs for Assimilation and Integration

At the Seventh GA, held in November-December 1952 the HC presented a comprehensive survey on The Refugee Situation in Different Countries. [13]   The survey focused on "the outstanding problems in the main areas where refugees" resided.   The HC requested the GA to assist him in solving three problems which he considered of such gravity as to

demand immediate action: (1) the distressing circumstances
of 8, 500 refugees of European origin in China; (2) the dis-
astrous fate of more than 130,000 persons under the HC's
mandate living in camps (in Austria, West Germany,
Greece, and Italy); and (3) the financing of integration, for
which he asked "without further delay the political and financial assistance required for an undertaking of such magnitude. "

In those refugee groups to be integrated were included: the hard-core (the old, the disabled, the invalid,
and the chronically ill); those in the Middle East; the children and the unemployed refugees in Europe; and the new
refugees constantly arriving at reception camps along the
borders separating Eastern Europe from the West. Dr. van
Heuven Goedhart again set a goal of three million dollars
for a twelve-month program of material assistance for the
most destitute groups in all parts of the world.

In this session the HC's report had considerable impact. The Dutch delegate, among others, was stirred by
the "alarming" and "moving picture of the desperate plight
of many refugees, in particular in Trieste and in the Far
East, " and like others, he was "deeply impressed by the
work that remained to be done. "14 He stated that in 1949,
the member states had perhaps not clearly understood the
facts of the case which the HC's report now disclosed.
However, world public opinion, he said, seemed to be turning to other matters, and "concern as to the fate of the refugees was giving way to the legitimate fears occasioned by
over-population. " He felt that "the inevitable conclusion
was that no permanent solution was possible without international action. "

The UNHCR, in view of the complexity of the problem
of integration and assimilation, had undertaken still more
comprehensive studies of the situation in the main countries
of asylum in order to enable the HC to recommend long-term
solutions to national authorities and to be able to ask for related assistance from the competent international bodies. 15
Dr. van Heuven Goedhart concluded on the basis of these
studies that as far as long-term assimilation was concerned,
a definite program would have to be initiated if the refugees
within his mandate were to be absorbed in the local areas.
He pointed out that the transfer of care and maintenance from
the IRO to the governments concerned, which had taken place
on 30 June 1950, had been in the nature of an administrative

transfer and did not provide a firm basis for the integration
of refugees into the economic life of the countries. He believed that his findings confirmed the fact that the implementation of a refugee policy called not merely for efforts
at legal protection, but for the adoption of special economic
measures or of measures related to a general economic development scheme.

Thus, on the basis of the HC's "further observations
and information," the Seventh Session of the GA, held in
December 1952, acknowledged that "voluntary repatriation or
resettlement in countries of immigration are not sufficient
in themselves under the present conditions to offer within a
reasonable time a permanent solution of that problem." The
GA invited the HC "in consultation with the IBRD, to examine
the situation with a view to exploring with the governments
directly concerned, what sources of funds might be available
and the most effective means by which such funds might be
utilized."16

Prolongation of the Office

In October 1953 the HC again reported on the complex-
ities of the refugee problem to the Third Committee of the
GA, drawing particular attention to the necessity for a certain amount of long-term planning. For "genuinely constructive work," he said, "a mandate of five years would seem
to be the minimum." Furthermore, "it had been proved that
a non-operational UN agency for refugees--chronologically
and geographically limited--was useful and worked efficiently
on condition that it was allowed, as was the UNHCR, to look
at all aspects of the problem, since all were inseparably related to one another. To have restricted the functions of
his Office to the legal protection of refugees would have
crippled it." However, in view of the non-operational character "its coordinating role became all the more important.
At that time the Office had an overall view of the various
projects that had been undertaken on behalf of refugees."
The HC urged that he be consulted before any further program of international action on their behalf was launched, in
order to attain better results. He stressed again the desperate living conditions of thousands of refugees, particularly
those living in camps, and stated that "the uncertainty as to
the availability of funds for financing emergency aid for the
most needy groups, made their situation continuously precarious. That situation was at variance with what the UN

owes to both the refugees and itself, and moreover threatened to frustrate part of the constructive work which the UN
had shown it was anxious to perform. "[17]

The Third Committee and the Eighth Plenary Session
of the GA in their considerations concentrated mainly on two
matters: the prolongation of the Office of the HC, and greater coordination of international action. In a memorandum to
the Third Committee, Secretary-General Dag Hammarskjöld
pointed out that the Report of the HC (A/2394 and Corr. 1)
showed that "there remains a need for a central international
organization concerned with the problem. It provides striking evidence of what can be accomplished by the UN in this
field through a small non-operational agency whose work is
supported by, and closely coordinated with that of other UN
branches and the specialized agencies. " But he went on to
stress that "despite the generosity of a number of governments, the total response to the Refugee Emergency Fund
has been inadequate. There will continue to be a compelling
need for emergency aid in several areas of the world in
1954, but the fund at present available to the High Commissioner for Refugees for this purpose will be exhausted by
the end of the present year. "[18]

The resulting discussion in the GA was marked by a
sharp difference of viewpoints. The majority of delegates
expressed their appreciation of the work of the Office, both
in providing international protection and in promoting permanent solutions for the different aspects of the refugee
problem, and emphasized the necessity for continued UN action through the Office, and the majority emphasized the
necessity of working for permanent solutions through integration in national communities or through resettlement by
migration. Some representatives, however--predominantly
those from the USSR, Byelorussian SSR, Ukrainian SSR,
Poland, and Czechoslovakia--were for disbanding the Office
and expressed strong criticism of the former IRO and of
UNHCR. They maintained that the Office perpetuated the
refugee problem, which should be solved through repatriation
as provided under GA Res. 8(1) of 12 February 1946.

In 1950, when the GA voted for the establishment of
the Office, the members of the UN had expected that the
refugee problem would gradually disappear with the progressive integration of refugees in the countries of residence.
But in the course of the three intervening years it had become clear that a continued UN role was needed. Thus, the

GA decided to continue the Office for five years beginning 1 January 1954, with a review to take place at the Twelfth Session of the GA in 1957. A vote was taken: 36 for, 5 against, 3 abstentions (Res. 727[VIII] of 23 October 1953), and Dr. van Heuven Goedhart was elected HC for the same period. The USSR, Byelorussian SSR, Ukrainian SSR, Czechoslovakia, and Poland opposed this nomination.

The general debate in the GA led to another resolution in which the GA noted "with concern the precarious situation of certain groups of refugees within the HC's mandate, in particular those in need of emergency aid, the considerable number still living in camps, and those requiring special care for whom no satisfactory arrangements have yet been made." It instructed "the HC to concern himself in particular with these groups of refugees" and called upon governments to intensify their efforts to promote permanent solutions. 19

These two resolutions are among the most significant events in the history of the UNHCR. The vote for the prolongation of the Office reaffirmed the international responsibility of the UN for the refugees, and the vote on the work of the UNHCR, while not changing its mandate, indicated a certain change of emphasis in the GA's conception of the Office. Convinced of the urgency of the need confronting European countries of asylum, the GA launched the UNHCR on the second stage of its activities, during which, while building on the foundations already established, it was to determine its indispensability not only in respect to the existing refugee problem but even more dramatically in relation to the new refugee pressures that were so unexpectedly to erupt in Europe and subsequently in Asia and Africa.

Notes

1. Jacques Vernant, Refugees in the Post-War World, London, Allen & Unwin, 1953.

2. As already suggested, the accuracy of this figure of 2,200,000 refugees was open to some question. See also Dr. van Heuven Goedhart, Refugee Problems and Their Solutions, Dec. 1955.

3. Rev. Elfan Rees, 28 Apr. 1953; for full text, see An. 1 to A/AC.36/28: 16.

4.   HC's Annual Rep. for 1952, GA (II), Off. Rec. Supp.
     No. 19, 19/2011, 1952.

5.   Kathryn Hulme, The Wild Place, Boston, Little, Brown,
     1954: 223.

6.   GA (VI), Off. Rec. Supp. No. 19 A/2011.

7.   GA (V), Res. 430, 14 Dec. 1950. 40 votes for, 5
     against, 7 abstained.

8.   GA (VI), Off. Rec. Supp. No. 19 A/2011.

9.   GA (VI), Third Com., Jan. 1952, Off. Rec.: 152.

10. GA (VI), Third Com., Off. Rec., 3 Jan. 1952: 163.

11. A/C. 3/L. 200.

12. GA (VI), Res. 538 (VI)B, par. 1, 2 Feb. 1952; 28 for,
     21 abstentions, 5 against.

13. GA (VII), Off. Rec., Supp. No. 16, A/2126 and Add.

14. GA (VII), Third Com., 9 Dec. 1952: 319.

15. See Docs. HCR/RS1: Summary of a report on the In-
     tegration of Non-German Refugees into the Economic
     Life of Germany, Rep. submitted to the HC by B.
     Lincke; and HCR/RS/3: The Financial Aspects of
     Integration of the Refugees in the Austrian Economy,
     Rep. submitted to HC by Gilbert Jaeger; HCR/W. 3:
     Refugees in Trieste, 19 Nov. 1953; HCR/RS/7:
     The Integration of the Refugees into the Greek
     Economy, 10 Feb. 1953.

16. GA Res. 638 (VII), of 20 Dec. 1952; 38 votes for, 5
     against, 12 abstentions.

17. GA (VIII), Third Com. Off. Rec., 13 Oct. 1953: 82.

18. Ibid.

19. GA Res, 728 (VIII), 48 for, 5 against, 4 abstentions.

ANNEX 6.1

PROVISIONAL STATISTICAL DATA ON REFUGEES PRESUMED TO COME WITHIN THE MANDATE OF UNHCR

All Countries (including Europe, the Middle East, Overseas Countries, and the Far East)	As on 1 Jan. 1952	As on 1 Jan. 1953
GRAND TOTAL	2,139,300	2,140,600
EUROPE		
Austria	274,200 (a)	229,300 (b)
Belgium	59,000	59,000
Denmark	1,150	1,150
France	400,000 (d)	400,000 (d)
Germany, Fed. Rep. of (c)	240,500	240,400
Greece	15,500 (d)	15,500 (d)
Italy	40,000 (d)	40,000 (d)
Luxembourg	800	800
Netherlands	14,100	14,100
Norway	2,000	2,000
Portugal	100	100
Saar	-	900
Spain	400	400
Sweden	44,000	44,000
Switzerland	10,000	10,000
Trieste	5,500 (d)	6,200 (d)
Turkey	2,250	2,250
UK	267,600	267,600
Yugoslavia	4,300	4,300
Total	1,381,400	1,338,000

(a) Includes 231,700 Volksdeutsche and 52,500 foreign refugees.
(b) As of 1 June 1953 - Includes 188,000 Volksdeutsche and 41,300 foreign refugees. The number of Volksdeutsche decreased during the period under review, mainly because many had been naturalized.
(c) Including Western Sectors of Berlin
(d) Provisional evaluation. Not including refugees within the mandate in Asia (except for China)

MIDDLE EAST AND FAR EAST

Egypt	2,300 (a)	2,300 (e)
Iran	2,000 (a)	2,000 (e)
Lebanon and Syria	400 (a)	400 (e)
China (mainly Shanghai)	8,000	15,000
Total	12,700	19,700

OVERSEAS COUNTRIES OF RESETTLEMENT (f)

Argentina	32,712	
Australia	182,159	
Bolivia	2,485	
Brazil	28,848	
Canada	123,479	
Chile	5,108	
Colombia	889	
French Morocco	1,446	
New Zealand	4,837	
Paraguay	5,887	
Peru	2,340	
US	328,851	
Uruguay	1,461	
Venezuela	17,277	
Other countries (500 or less), miscellaneous and not reported	7,433	
Total	745,212	782,855 (g)

(e) Not readable

(f) Figures based on the number of refugees resettled by IRO, not including 132,000 refugees resettled in Israel.

(g) The increase is due to the resettlement of 10,787 refugees by IRO in Jan. 1952 and of 26,856 refugees by ICEM during the period 1 Feb. 1952-31 Dec. 1952.

SOURCE: UNHCR, HCR/Stat/W.26, 17 Aug. 1953.

ANNEX 6.2

CONTRIBUTIONS TO THE UNITED NATIONS
REFUGEE EMERGENCY FUND, 31 MARCH 1953
(IN US DOLLARS)

Cash Contributions

Governmental

Germany, Fed. Rep. of	13,095	
Luxembourg	970	
Sweden	19,492	
Norway	14,104	
Switzerland	69,284	
UK	280,000	
Denmark	14,607	
Greece	1,000	
Australia	55,833	
Netherlands	10,000	
Austria	1,923	480,308

Other official contributions

IRO trust fund for Shanghai	236,698	
UK Control Commission for Germany	2,832	239,530
Private and individuals		19,874
Total		$739,712

Pledges of Cash

Governmental

Balance from Netherlands (guilders 95,000)		25,000
France (F. frs. 30,000,000)		85,714
Canada ($ Cdn. 100,000)		101,000
Belgium (B. frs. 200,000)		40,000
		$251,714

Refugees

Resulting from public appeals

Norway

70,000

Total

$321,714

SOURCE: HC's Annual Rep. for 1953 to GA, A/2394, 1953:33.

ANNEX 6.3

CONTRIBUTIONS TO THE UN REFUGEE EMERGENCY FUND
1 March 1952 to 31 December 1954

Government

Australia	$ 111,646.36
Austria	3,845.99
Belgium	40,000.00
Canada	152,097.40
Denmark	29,085.16
Germany, Fed. Rep. of	13,095.79
France	91,429.23
Greece	1,000.00
Holy See	3,000.00
Liechtenstein	467.29
Luxembourg	4,969.98
Netherlands	85,512.22
New Zealand	55,981.30
Norway	28,103.93
Sweden	38,814.34
Switzerland	127,695.28
Total:	$1,066,744.27

IRO

$ 246,698.49

Private

$ 159,227.50

Miscellaneous

$ 14,442.27

TOTAL INCOME

$1,487,112.53

SOURCE: UNHCR, Geneva.

PART III

INTERNATIONAL PROTECTION

The social, economic, educational and cultural conditions necessary for the fulfillment of personality and the maintenance of human dignity, as well as the political and civil rights of the individual are all implied in the dynamic concept of the Rule of Law ... Thus the concept of the Rule of Law stands for the value of a free society in which the fullest possible respect is accorded to the supreme value of human personality.

--International Delhi Congress, International Commission of Jurists, January 1959

INTRODUCTION

According to the traditional doctrine of international law, states are the subjects of international law, individuals are only its objects. In the leading textbooks on international al law, nationality is described as "the principal link between the individual and international law." In the case of the refugee this link is broken either because the refugee is stateless or because he does not have the protection of the state of his nationality; his nationality is "ineffective."[1]

It is a cardinal principle of customary international law derived from the long practice of states that a state has the right to protect its nationals even when they are abroad. It follows that a state also has the obligation to treat the nationals of other states in accordance with certain accepted principles that have been summarized as, at a minimum, respecting the person and property of the foreign national. If a state is derelict in this obligation then it may have to answer to the state of the foreigner's nationality since that state has the right to ask redress for wrongs done to its nationals.

Diplomatic protection then refers to the activities undertaken by states in seeking to insure that their nationals receive the standards of treatment to which they are entitled from other states. Such state activities generally include:

1. Espousing the legal claims of nationals against other states

2. Seeking to improve the standards of treatment to which nationals are entitled by the negotiation of bilateral consular treaties; trade agreements, immigration agreements, commercial agreements and other similar arrangements based on the concept of reciprocity

3. Seeking to assure that such agreements, once completed, are actually carried out and that nationals receive the rights to which they are entitled

4. Providing, often through consular officers, various documents that certify the identity of nationals and their personal or marital status or that certify the authenticity of documents and their conformity with the laws of the country of origin

5. Issuing passports to nationals to permit them to travel and to indicate to other states those to whom the agreed standards of treatment are owed

6. Repatriating those nationals who become distressed or indigent abroad. [2]

Under traditional international law the obligations owed by states to foreigners extended only to those possessing a nationality and enjoying the protection of a state. [3] The refugee, lacking the protection of any state, was an anomaly in customary international law: he had no legal standing or recognized status in any state and could be treated in any way any state pleased, while no state would espouse his cause. It is true that customary international law in regard to refugees has been changing through the acceptance of new doctrines and practices. Many states treat refugees much as they do alien nationals, in terms of domestic law, and a few states have equal treatment for all aliens enshrined as a principle in their constitutions. But in fact refugees continue to suffer to a greater or lesser extent from legal and social disabilities owing to their lack of status in most states. 'In the nation-state system of modern times, refugees, who by definition are either de facto or de jure stateless, and thus people of no-man's land, are an anomaly. Therefore, the general rules of international law had lacunae which have had to be filled with special provisions to secure a legal status for refugees. '[4]

International protection for refugees is a legal device developed over the course of the twentieth century as the means of remedying this gap in customary international law: first, through creating international conventions which set down standards of treatment to be accorded refugees--states that are parties to these conventions undertake contractual obligations in an area where customarily they had none; second, through establishing an international refugee agency which seeks, rather as a state does, to insure that those within its competence receive the treatment to which they are entitled.

International protection can only be a partial substitute for diplomatic protection, however, because international refugee agencies do not have the authority or standing of states.   They exist because they were created by states, and they operate only in those ways in which states have agreed to let them operate.   Thus some of those activities ordinarily carried on by states exercising diplomatic protection are carried on for refugees by international agencies, but others are carried on for refugees by the states themselves.   Perhaps the most important activity of international refugee agencies in this area has been promoting the conclusion and ratification of international conventions relating to the status of refugees and supervising their application by contracting states.   Such international agencies have also exercised what are called "quasi-consular" activities: the provision of documents and certificates for refugees which have almost the same legal significance as those provided a national by his consulate.   Refugee agencies have also interceded with national authorities on behalf of refugees, both individuals and groups, to seek settlement of specific disputes or the improvement of treatment generally.   But only in two countries, Belgium and France, have the representatives of an international refugee agency ever been accorded a status fully equivalent to that of foreign consuls. 5   The representatives have never issued passports or travel documents, even though at times the identity certificates they did issue have been accepted in lieu of travel documents or have been the only prerequisite for the issuance of such a document by a state.   International protection for refugees thus is complementary to the national protection of refugees provided by states on the basis of either their domestic laws or their international contractual obligations.

Legal protection is an essential factor in the integration of refugees into their new communities.   Without a satisfactory legal status, including the right to receive travel documents, to receive an education, to work, to own property, and to have access to courts, even the most generous material assistance cannot achieve a permanent solution.

This protective function is carried out at four levels. At the universal level it consists of "promoting the conclusion and ratification of international conventions for the protection of refugees, supervising their applications, and proposing amendments thereto" (Statute, par. 8[a]).   At the regional level it involves continuous contact with organizations such as the CoE and the EEC, the Asian-African Legal

Consultative Committee, the Organization of African Unity
(OAU), and the Organization of American States (OAS) in order to encourage member countries to become parties to the
international agreements concluded at the universal level; to
supplement the general agreements by regional instruments,
taking into account the special conditions and requirements
of the region; and to insure that refugees are included in the
benefits resulting from measures for regional integration.
At the national level the Office assists governments in the
preparation of legislation and administrative regulations by
which international instruments are implemented and seeks
to ensure that at every level of administration international
obligations pertaining to refugees are fully carried out.   At
the individual level the Office performs a variety of roles
by agreement with different governments, such as certifying
the eligibility of refugees or aspects of their personal status,
and it intervenes on behalf of individual cases where the
recognition of refugee status, the right of asylum, or the
principle of non-refoulement is at stake.   Activities in this
sphere on the part of the UNHCR's headquarters and field
staffs are, in the main, directed toward the adoption of
measures in the legal field which secure for refugees the
most satisfactory status possible, taking into account the
various interests of states called upon to deal with refugee
problems.

        The 1951 Refugee Convention, which is the basic and
comprehensive international instrument relating to refugees
and which underlies and supports so much of the HC's efforts to provide international protection for refugees and to
assist in achieving permanent solutions to refugee problems,
is the subject of Chapter 7.   The content and the significance of the 1951 Convention are there set forth in detail.
The activities of the UNHCR that have provided international
protection for refugees at the universal and regional levels
during the first twenty years of its operations, form the
subject matter of Chapters 8 and 9.   Activities of the Office
during the same period at the national and the individual
levels, pertaining to refugees in Europe, are described in
Chapter 10, as are details of refugee legislation in the major European countries of first and second asylum.   Chapter
11 sets forth activities of the Office at the national and individual levels as they pertain to refugees in Africa and
summarizes the refugee legislation which has been enacted
in that continent.   Legislation affecting refugees in the countries of overseas resettlement is described and discussed in
Part V.

Notes

1. Collection: 1.

2. An excellent discussion of the nature of diplomatic pro-
    tection can be found in the Sec. -General's Study of
    Statelessness, Doc. F/1112 of 1 Feb. 1949, esp. Ch.
    III; and see Paul Weis, "The International Protec-
    tion of Refugees," AJIL, Apr. 1954, 193-221, where
    diplomatic protection and international protection are
    contrasted.

3. There are two categories of stateless persons: de jure
    and de facto: "1. Stateless de jure are persons who
    are not nationals of any state, either because at
    birth or subsequently they were not given any nation-
    ality, or because during their lifetime they lost their
    own nationality and did not acquire a new one; 2.
    Stateless persons de facto, who having left their coun-
    try of which they were nationals, no longer enjoy the
    protection and assistance of their national authorities,
    either because these authorities refuse to grant them
    assistance and protection of their countries of which
    they are nationals. " See UN, Study of Statelessness,
    op. cit. Refugees de jure and de facto suffer from
    the same disability as stateless persons, but their
    situation is distinguishable in that they lack the pro-
    tection of the state of their nationality because of
    persecution or fear of persecution by reason of race,
    religion, nationality, or political opinion.

4. The laws and constitutional provisions of some states
    pertaining to refugees can be found in the Study of
    Statelessness: 18-19; while a complete record of
    such national legislation is contained in Vernant, The
    Refugee in the Post-War World; Quotation by Holborn,
    Bergen, Norway, Nansen Symposium, July 1951.

5. See Agreement of 30 June 1928, Concerning the Func-
    tions of Representatives of the High Commissioner for
    Refugees of the League of Nations, LoN TS, Vol.
    XCIII, No. 2126: 377-80; and see Weis, op. cit. :
    214.

Chapter 7

THE 1951 CONVENTION
RELATING TO THE STATUS OF REFUGEES

The drafting process described in Chapter 3 culminated in a specially convened UN Conference of Plenipotentiaries on the Status of Refugees and Stateless Persons, that
met in Geneva from 2 to 25 July 1951. There legal delegates from twenty-six governments, observers from two governments, representatives of twenty-nine non-governmental
organizations, two Specialized Agencies of the UN, and the
CoE, and the newly appointed first HC met to draft a Convention Relating to the Status of Refugees and a Protocol
Relating to the Status of Stateless Persons. The Final Act
of the Conference, adopted unanimously on 25 July 1951,
contained the text of the new Convention, the terms of five
recommendations which the Conference members felt to be
important but did not wish to include in the Convention, and
the agreement of the Conference members to make no decision concerning the status of stateless persons.[1] The Conference referred the matter of stateless persons back to the
appropriate organs of the UN for further study, and a special conference was convened in September 1954 to draft a
convention on this issue.[2] The Refugee Convention came
into force almost three years later on 22 April 1954, ninety
days after the sixth state, Australia, had become a party to
it by ratification. Australia's action fulfilled the ratification
requirement set out in Arts. 39 and 43 of the Convention.

The substance of the Convention is a specification of
the rights and duties of refugees vis-à-vis states, a specification that was most necessary in the light of the anomalous
situation of refugees in international law, and their resulting
lack of status in the domestic legal systems of many states.
In a large number of specific areas of domestic law, the
Convention sets down minimal standards of treatment that
must be accorded to refugees by states which accept the
Convention. Its aim is to insure that at the very least refugees will be accorded the same treatment as is generally

158

granted to other aliens in a state, and that in some matters refugees shall be accorded higher standards of treatment up to and including the treatment given to nationals of the country itself. The effect of the Convention is to place on a solid contractual basis the obligations of states, which were by no means clear under traditional international law, under which refugees tended to be ignored because the legal system was centered on the rights and duties of states as against other states and the nationals of other states.

The first Deputy High Commissioner, James Read, has pointed out that "the value of the rights set forth in this Convention may not be as important in some countries as in others. " Where refugees are admitted into countries on the same strict basis as immigrants and are subject to the same screening, they can be put on the same footing as other aliens because they have been admitted on the same basis. Special refugee legislation may not exist and may not be needed. But where countries, due to their traditional humanitarian attitude and their geographic location, have granted asylum to a large flood of refugees when admission may have been a matter of life or death, it has been more difficult--due to the economic, social, and political problems caused by the inflow--to grant refugees equality with other aliens, much less with nationals. "The fact that this Convention does equate refugees with nationals in so many respects, " noted Mr. Read, "is one of its most remarkable features. "[3]

Since 1921, when the international protection of refugees first became the direct concern of an international body, it has been accepted that the legal disabilities from which refugees suffer can be overcome only through two kinds of action: the creation and operation of international agencies charged with protecting and assisting refugees, and the establishment of multilateral instruments designed to define and improve the legal status of refugees. The two are connected in that it has always been of major importance to the concerned international agency to see that the existing multilateral instruments were fully implemented by their contracting parties and to initiate and promote the conclusion of further international instruments concerning the legal status of refugees. Since the most basic need of refugees is asylum, and since their lack of internationally recognized travel documents has been a major handicap in their movement, a number of international instruments have been entirely concerned with the establishment of a recognized travel document for refugees. [4]

But two treaties were drafted in the 1930s which went beyond travel documents to establish a broad set of regulations for the state treatment of refugees, the more important of these being the Convention Relating to the International Status of Refugees of 28 October 1933.[5] The second general treaty of the period was the Convention Concerning the Status of Refugees Coming from Germany but it largely repeated the provisions of the earlier convention, extending its terms to cover a new group of refugees.[6] While only eight states ratified the 1933 Convention, and some of them made substantial reservations, this instrument was the major model for the refugee Convention signed in 1951; other provisions of the 1951 Convention were based on articles of the earlier treaties concerned with travel documents for refugees.

The 1951 Refugee Convention served to consolidate and reinforce the series of multilateral instruments which had been drafted in the preceding decades. But its major significance lies not so much in its continuity with the past as in the changes which it has brought about in international law. For in addition to consolidating past treaty obligations the 1951 Convention broke new ground in five major regards:

1. It contained a far more general definition of the term refugee than had any of the earlier refugee treaties

2. It contained a much broader range of refugee rights

3. It specified in most cases higher standards of treatment for refugees

4. Many more states participated in its drafting and eventually ratified it than had done so with the previous treaties and

5. A direct and formal link was created, for the first time, between a refugee instrument and an international agency concerned with refugees, in that it was accepted by contracting states that an international agency would have the authority to supervise the application of the Convention's provisions.

Definition of the Term Refugee (Art. 1)

As with the Statute, the Convention begins by setting forth the definition of the term refugee in order to demarcate those persons eligible for the standards of treatment set down in the treaty.   The definition in the Convention is identical in practice with that contained in the Statute, except in two major respects which have the effect of narrowing the scope of the Convention.   Refugees as defined in the Statute are not eligible under the Convention unless they became refugees as a result of events occurring before 1 January 1951.   It does not matter when a person becomes a refugee; the operative concern is the date of the events of which his status is the result.   Thus, the Convention drafters noted that the instrument did not exclude "persons who may become refugees at a later date as a result of events before them or as a result of after-events which occur at a later date."[7]   On the basis of this interpretation the Hungarian refugees of 1956 were considered to be Convention refugees.   In addition, a further optional geographic restriction is available to contracting states in that they may declare, at the time of accession, that they choose to interpret the term "events" to mean "events occurring in Europe" rather than "events occurring in Europe or elsewhere."[8] This geographic limitation, first proposed by the Ad Hoc Committee on Refugees and Stateless Persons and confirmed by ECOSOC, was later dropped by the Third Committee of the GA only to be revived at the Conference of Plenipotentiaries and, largely at the insistence of France, accepted as an optional limitation available to signatories.[9]

The effect of these two limitations was that while the Convention's drafters hoped that states would accord Convention standards of treatment to all refugees (see Rec. E of the drafters in the Final Act of the Conference), contracting states are only legally obligated to accord such standards of treatment to refugee groups existing in 1951, or who appeared thereafter as a result of events prior to 1951.   For the some thirteen states which continue to invoke the optional geographic restriction, their obligation extends only to refugee groups resulting from events in Europe occurring before 1951.   With the eventual appearance of substantial refugee groups which did not relate to pre-1951 events there emerged a growing acceptance of the idea that something should be done to eliminate or minimize the effect of these two limitations.   The outcome of efforts made in that direction at the instigation of the HC was the passage of the 1967 Protocol to the Convention, described in Chapter 8.

While the definition of the term refugee is, with the exceptions noted above, the same in the Statute and the

Convention, the two documents charge different bodies with applying the definition. The decision as to who shall be accorded refugee status is, under the Convention, a matter for the authorities of the participating states. While in some states representatives of the HC participate in some way in the determination of refugee eligibility,[10] it is the decision of the state authorities which is binding. At the same time the HC has the final say as to who shall be considered a refugee under his mandate and therefore eligible for his international protection. But recognition as a refugee by the HC will not by itself either secure the refugee admission to a country or confer a legal status. And a determination of eligibility by one country does not, with the possible exception of the matter of travel documents, necessarily confer a refugee status upon the individual in other countries.

Admission and Expulsion (Arts. 31-33)

The first need of any refugee is for asylum; that is, to be admitted into the territory of a state other than the one from which he is fleeing. In most cases this means seeking asylum in a state which borders on the state where the refugee has a well-founded fear that his life or liberty is being threatened in the sense of Art. 1 of the Convention. States which have admitted large numbers of refugees coming directly from territories where they feared persecution are called states of first asylum, whereas states which accept refugees already granted asylum in other states are called states of second asylum or resettlement states.

International law does not recognize, however, nor did it at the time the Convention was drafted, an individual's right to be granted asylum by a state. While the growing practice of the great majority of states is to grant asylum to refugees, states have in the main steadfastly adhered to the traditional legal doctrine that the right of asylum is the right of states to grant asylum at their discretion. Attempts have been made on numerous occasions to gain recognition for an individual right of asylum or to create such a right by convention, but they have rarely succeeded. The 1933 Convention Relating to the International Status of Refugees provided that refugees had the right to be admitted to a country at least when they were at the frontiers of the country from which they were seeking to flee, but that treaty was accepted by only eight states, and the provision concerning admission was not included in subsequent conventions.

Proposals to add an individual right of asylum to the Universal Declaration of Human Rights in 1948 and to the Refugee Convention in 1950-51 were defeated. The final form of the Universal Declaration says only that everyone has the right to seek and to enjoy, not the right to be granted asylum. Nothing is said in the 1951 Convention about the right of individuals to be granted asylum, nor about the duty of states to admit refugees. The Convention's drafters did, however, include in their Final Act the recommendation that Governments "continue to receive refugees in their territories and that they act in concert in a true spirit of international cooperation in order that these refugees may find asylum and the possibility of resettlement" (Final Act, Rec. D).

In the period since the drafting of the 1951 Convention several significant steps have been taken toward general recognition of a refugee's right to be granted asylum, at least when he is coming directly from a country in which he fears persecution. These steps, and the part played by UNHCR officials in achieving them, are discussed in Chapter 9.

While nothing is said in the Convention as to the admission of refugees, a very important provision is included which embodies what has been called the principle of non-refoulement to the effect that once a refugee has managed to cross the frontier from the country where he fears persecution into the territory of a neighboring country, whether the crossing be achieved legally or illegally, the neighboring country (if a contracting party to the Convention) shall not "expel or return a refugee in any manner whatsoever to the frontiers of territories where his life or freedom would be threatened on account of his race, religion, nationality, membership of a particular social group or political opinion" (Art. 33).

The crucial importance of this principle of non-refoulement for refugees can be seen in the fact that the Convention's drafters required that no reservation could be made to this provision by states acceding to the Convention (Art. 42). Furthermore, even if the refugee illegally gains entry to the territory of a contracting state, the Convention requires that he not be punished for the illegal manner of his entry so long as he came directly from a territory where his life or freedom was threatened in the sense of Art. 1 of the Convention, and so long as he presents himself without delay to the authorities and shows good cause for his illegal

entry (Art. 31). A state is not required by the Convention
to grant such an illegal entrant more than provisional asylum, however, since expelling him to a third state is not
one of those penalties prohibited by Art. 31; nevertheless,
the expulsion cannot be carried out until the refugee has
been granted the necessary facilities and reasonable time to
seek lawful admission into another country (Art. 31, par.
2).

In addition to the provision on expulsion or return of
a refugee to a country of persecution, the Convention establishes safeguards concerning the reasons for which, and the
manner in which, refugees legally in a territory may be expelled to other countries. Under customary international
law any state is competent in principle to expel any alien
who has been admitted to its territory no matter how long
he has been there. The Convention permits such an expulsion only on grounds of national security or public order;
"only in pursuance of a decision reached in accordance with
due process of law"; and only, generally, after giving the
refugee the chance to defend himself before a duly constituted
judicial or administrative body (Art. 32). Even if the decision is validly taken to expel him, the refugee has the right
to "a reasonable period within which to seek legal admission
into another country" before the decision is carried out (Art.
32, par. 3).

Procedural Rights

Reciprocity (Art. 7). In seeking higher standards of
treatment for their own nationals abroad, many states--es-
pecially those whose civil law is based on the French Napo-
leonic Code--have made use of the device of reciprocity.
There are two kinds of reciprocity: legislative and diplomatic. The first is established by laws which grant certain
rights to foreigners in general provided that the home state
of the foreigner does the same for nationals of the state en-
acting the law. The second refers to rights especially accorded to the nationals of a second state by bilateral agreements.[11] Lacking a nationality, or at least an effective nationality, refugees find themselves unable to qualify for treatment accorded on the basis of reciprocity. States individually, and jointly through conventions, have moved to exempt
refugees from the requirement of reciprocity. The 1933 and
1938 Refugee Conventions provided for the complete exemption of refugees from reciprocity, but there, as in the

matter of the admission of refugees, are two of the very few instances where the 1951 Convention has not gone further in establishing refugee rights than prior international instruments.

The 1951 Convention stipulates that after three years' residence refugees will enjoy exemption from legislative reciprocity (Art. 7, par. 2). It does go on, however, to recommend that states grant refugees further exemptions from reciprocity (Art. 7, par. 4) and to require that exemptions from reciprocity previously granted to refugees be continued (Art. 7, par. 3). The significance of this requirement is that it preserves the more favorable position of those refugees who qualified for exemption under the more liberal provisions of the 1933 and 1938 Conventions in those states that are contracting parties to those two conventions.

Personal Status (Art. 12). Just as reciprocity is the prerequisite to the enjoyment of civil rights in some countries, so an alien's personal status is basic to his relations with other people under the law of a foreign country. Personal status refers to legal capacity (e. g., the age of majority); to marriage, divorce and adoption; to matrimonial rights (e. g., property rights of spouses); and to succession and inheritance. In most European countries and certain Latin American countries personal status is dependent upon nationality, so that an alien is considered to have the personal rights and be bound by the laws pertaining to personal status of the country of his nationality. In theory, stateless persons, such as refugees, do not possess any status whatsoever in such countries unless special provisions have been made for them under domestic law and, in practice, their position in regard to marital and family matters is very uncertain. This uncertainty makes it very difficult for persons seeking to establish or maintain legal relations with refugees (for instance, in making a contract with a married woman or a person under the age of majority). Even countries where personal status is determined on the basis of the domicile, as is the case with most common-law countries, the refugee may be in a difficult position if he has not yet established a domicile there and is held to be bound by the laws of the country where he was domiciled at birth.

The 1951 Convention follows the 1933 Convention in regard to the matter of personal status by establishing one rule for all refugees, whether de facto or de jure stateless, in all contracting states. Art. 12 states that the personal

status of a refugee "shall be governed by the law of the
country of his domicile or, if he has no domicile, by the
law of the country of his residence." This means that, in
the main, a refugee's personal status will be that accorded
by the country of asylum in which he has established his
residence. "The Convention embodied here, by this important provision, a principle which is increasingly gaining
ground in private international law."[12] It is a significant
advance in that it protects the refugee from "the operation
of a national law that has been amended according to the
social and political principles of a regime from which he
has escaped"; it assists the assimilation of the refugee into
the life of the asylum state by treating him in the same way
as nationals of the asylum state; and it frees him, to some
extent, from the need to somehow obtain documents relating
to his status from the country from which he has fled.[13]

Exemption from Exceptional Measures (Art. 8). While
refugees suffer some disabilities due to their loss of nationality, they have also at times experienced difficulty because
of their former nationality. In wartime refugees have sometimes found themselves, on the grounds of their former nationality, subjected to measures applied to enemy aliens,
even though they have fled in opposition to the regime of the
countries of their nationality. In Art. 8 the Convention requires contracting states not to apply such "exceptional
measures" against the person, property, or interests of the
refugee solely on account of his former nationality.

Documentation

Quasi-Consular Measures (Arts. 25 and 27). Nationals of a state can ordinarily obtain from their governments
at home or overseas such documents as birth, marriage,
divorce, or death certificates, as well as certificates of
identity, and certification that such documents as they have
are correct, properly translated, or in conformity with the
law of the country of their origin. Disabilities may arise
for refugees, however, particularly in those countries where
personal status is based on nationality, since they are unable
to have recourse to the national and consular authorities of
their countries of origin in order to obtain such documents
and certificates. This problem was recognized as early as
1928 when there was drafted at Geneva the Arrangement Relating to the Legal Status of Russian and Armenian Refugees,
which recommend that states entrust to the LoN HC the task

of providing to refugees these administrative services ordinarily performed for nationals by their own consular authorities. In so acting the HC, it was said, would be performing a quasi-consular function. (See Chapter 1 for details of the 1928 Arrangement.) The 1951 Convention requires that when the exercise of a right by a refugee would normally require the assistance of authorities of a foreign country to whom he cannot have recourse, the contracting state shall arrange for such assistance (generally in the form of the provision of documents) to be afforded to him (Art. 25, par. 1). The state is left free to decide whether to provide this quasi-consular function itself or to entrust the function to an international agency. In 1928 Belgium and France agreed to recognize the representatives of the then HC as having the status of consul for refugees in order to perform the functions set forth in the 1928 Arrangement. But today no state accords this status to the representative of the UNHCR, although in numerous states UNHCR officials play some part in the issuance of documents relating to the personal status of refugees.

Art. 27 of the Convention specifically requires that a contracting state issue identity papers to any refugee in its territory who does not possess a valid travel document, and here again the branch officials of the UNHCR in many states have come, on the basis of agreements worked out bilaterally with individual governments, to participate in the process of the issuance of such papers.

Travel Documents (Art. 28). It was the need to provide travel documents for refugees--a passport substitute that would make possible their legal movement to a state willing to grant them asylum--that first impelled the drafting of international instruments regarding refugees. The 1951 Convention requires that contracting states issue travel documents to refugees lawfully staying in their territories, "unless compelling reasons of national security or public order otherwise require" (Art. 28, par. 1). It also authorizes the contracting states to issue at their own discretion travel documents to other refugees in their territories, for example, those present illegally or temporarily (Art. 28, par. 1). Travel documents issued under the pre-existing international agreements and arrangements are to be recognized and accepted by contracting states of the 1951 Convention whether or not they were contracting states of the prior instruments (Art. 28, par. 2), and all contracting parties of the 1951 Convention are required to recognize the validity of travel documents issued in accordance with this Article and the detailed set of instructions appended to the Convention as a schedule (Schedule par. 7).[14]

Substantive Rights (Arts. 4, 7, 13-24, and 29)

The Convention does not set down the content of the social and economic rights which contracting states must accord to refugees, but rather requires, in regard to each of a large number of rights, that refugees must be treated in the same way as some other specified group within the population. For example, the Convention does not specify the amount of education to which refugee children are entitled, but says rather that the contracting states "shall accord to refugees the same treatment as is accorded to nationals with respect to elementary education" (Art. 22, par. 1). The Convention does stipulate, however, that its provisions shall be applied to refugees without discrimination by the contracting states as to race, religion, or country of origin (Art. 3) and that nothing in the Convention will impair any rights and benefits granted to refugees by contracting states apart from the Convention (Art. 5).

Four standards of treatment for refugees are established by the Convention, the first being the minimal one that contracting states at least accord to refugees the same treatment they accord to aliens generally (Art. 7, par. 1), while the other three specify treatment more favorable than for aliens generally in regard to a catalogue of especially important rights. The three higher standards are described in the Convention as (1) "the same treatment as is accorded to nationals" of the contracting state; (2) "the most favorable treatment accorded to nationals of a foreign country"; and (3) "treatment as favorable as possible and in any event not less favorable than that accorded to aliens generally in the same circumstances."

The same treatment as that accorded nationals is to be given to refugees in regard to the freedom to practice their religion and to conduct the religious education of their children (Art. 4). While refugees are to be granted free access to the courts of all contracting states, they are to be accorded the treatment granted to nationals in the states of their habitual residence as regards other matters pertaining to access to courts, such as legal assistance and exemption from cautio judicatum solvi (the requirement usually imposed on foreigners of a deposit to cover the court expenses of the other party in case the foreigner loses the case) (Art. 16); this same principle applies to the protection of their industrial property, such as inventions, designs or models, trademarks and names, and of rights in literary, artistic, and scientific works (Art. 14). Refugees shall be accorded the same treatment as nationals in any contracting state as regards rationing (Art. 20), elementary education (Art. 22, par. 1), the right to public relief and assistance (Art. 23), labor legislation and social security (with some qualifications) (Art. 24), fiscal charges (and in particular taxation) (Art. 29), and wage-earning employment--provided the refugee has completed three years of residence in the country, or has a spouse or one or more children, any of whom possess the nationality of the country of residence (Art. 17, par. 2).

In respect to wage-earning employment, where a refugee cannot fulfill one of the requirements that will entitle him to be accorded national treatment, he shall at least be granted the most favorable treatment accorded to nationals of a foreign country in the same circumstances (Art. 17, par. 1).[15] The most favored nation treatment is also to be given to refugees with regard to their right to form and to join "non-political and non-profit-making associations and trade unions" (Art. 15).

The standard of treatment "as favorable as possible and in any event not less favorable than that accorded to aliens generally in the same circumstances" is to be accorded to the refugee as regards "the acquisition of movable and immovable property and other rights pertaining thereto, and to leases and other contracts relating to movable and immovable property" (Art. 13); "the right to engage on his own account in agriculture, industry, handicrafts and commerce and to establish commercial and industrial companies" (Art. 18); the right to practice a liberal profession (if he holds a diploma recognized by the competent authorities of that state) (Art. 19); the right to obtain housing "in so far as the matter is regulated by laws or regulations" (Art. 21); and with respect to higher education--in particular, access to studies--the recognition of foreign diplomas, the remission of fees, and the award of scholarships (Art. 22, par. 2).

Role of the UNHCR (Art. 35)

        While the supervision of the application of internation-
al agreements relating to the status of refugees has been
considered an inherent part of the function of international
protection exercised since 1921 by various international
agencies, the 1951 Convention strengthened substantially the
role of such international agencies.   In a provision without
parallel in prior international instruments relating to refugees, contracting states undertake to cooperate with the
UNHCR or its successor agency in two ways: first, to
facilitate generally the exercise by the UNHCR of the functions entrusted to it by the GA and second, to facilitate in
particular the UNHCR's duty of supervising the application
of the provisions of this Convention (Art. 35).   Not only
then does the UNHCR have a supervisory duty over the implementation of the Convention, but the contracting states
have a legal obligation to recognize its authority.

Further Provisions (Arts. 11, 26, 30, 34, and 42)

        In addition to the provisions of the Convention dis-
cussed above, the following articles should also be noted.

        In Art. 11 of the Convention the first step is taken
toward stabilizing the positions of a comparatively small but
severely deprived group of refugees--those who serve as
seamen aboard ships carrying the flag of a contracting state.
At the time of the Convention there were refugee seamen
who could not leave their ships at all either in a port of
call or in the territory of the flag state.   The Convention
seeks to alleviate their hardship by requiring that contracting states consider sympathetically the requests of refugee
seamen for temporary admission to, or establishment in,
the territory of the flag state, and for travel documents.

        In Art. 26 a general right to freedom of movement
is accorded to refugees lawfully in the territory of a contracting state, including both the right to choose their place
of residence and the right to move freely within its territory, subject only to the regulations applicable to aliens
generally in the same circumstances.

        To promote and facilitate the resettlement of refugees
outside the countries of first asylum, the Convention stipulates in Art. 30 that a contracting state shall permit refugees

to transfer assets brought into its territory to a country of
resettlement and shall give sympathetic consideration to requests seeking the transfer of other funds, wherever they
may be, for the same purpose.

Since the only completely final solution for the problems of refugees lies in again acquiring a nationality and
the protection of a state, the Convention in Art. 34 requires
contracting states to facilitate as far as possible the assimilation and naturalization of refugees, especially by expediting naturalization procedures and reducing their costs.

The drafters of the Convention considered some of
its provisions more basic than others, so that while they
adopted a procedure, which until then had been a fairly unusual one in international conventions, of permitting signatories to unilaterally make whatever reservations they wished
to the text of the Convention at the same time they became
parties to it (in order to encourage as many states as possible to become parties), the drafters designated the articles
relating to the definition of refugees (Art. 1), non-discrimi-
nation (Art. 3), freedom of worship (Art. 4), access to
courts (Art. 16, par. 1), non-refoulement (Art. 33), and the
concluding procedural articles (Arts. 36-46) as ones to which
no reservations might be made.

In the years since the adoption of the 1951 Convention
in Geneva, the UNHCR has continually sought to increase the
number of states parties to the Convention so that it might
become a truly universal as well as a comprehensive international instrument with regard to the legal status of refugees.   The next chapter recounts the efforts of the Office
and its very considerable success in this endeavor.

Notes

1.   The text of the Final Act appears in UN Doc. A/
       CONF. 2/108 of 28 July 1951, and in 189 UN TS
       137; as well as in James M. Read, Magna Carta
       for Refugees, rev. ed., NY 1953 and Collection of
       International Conventions, Agreements and Other
       Texts Concerning Refugees, comp. Paul Weis, publ.
       in French and English by the UNHCR, 1971 (here-
       after referred to as Collection): 21-60.   Four com-
       mentators have described in detail the provisions of
       the Convention.   The most elaborate of these

discussions is Nehemiah Robinson, Convention Relating to the Status of Refugees: Its History, Contents and Interpretation, NY, 1953; see also Paul Weis, "Legal Aspects of the Convention of 28 July 1951 Relating to the Status of Refugees," BYIL, 1953, Vol. 30: 478-89; Weis, "The International Status of Refugees and Stateless Persons," JDI, 1956, No. 1: 4-69; C. A. Pompe, "The Convention of 28 July 1951 and the International Protection of Refugees," Doc. HCR/INF/42 of May 1958, first publ. in Dutch in Rechtsgeleerd Magazyn Themis, 1956: 425-91; and Eberhard Jahn, Der Völkerrechtliche Schutz für Flüchtlinge, Bonn, 1955.

2. The text of the Convention Relating to the Status of Stateless Persons appears in UN Doc. E/CONF. 17/5, 28 Sept. 1954, and in 360 UN TS 117.

3. Op. cit.: 4-5.

4. Weis, "The International Status of Refugees": 14 ff.

5. 159 LoN, TS No. 3663: 199-217.

6. 195 LoN, TS No. 4461: 59-81.

7. UN Doc. F/1618 of 17 Feb. 1950: 39.

8. See Art. 1B (1). Dr. Paul Weis said in a speech delivered in Washington, DC, Nov. 1969: "The question, whether the definition should be limited to events in Europe or not, led almost to a breakdown of the Conference [of Plenipotentiaries]. Only a proposal giving States parties to the Convention the option of declaring whether the word 'events' should be understood to mean 'events in Europe' or 'events in Europe or elsewhere' saved the Conference."

9. See Pompe, op. cit., esp.: 11-12.

10. Ibid.: 15.

11. While various commentators have differently defined the kinds of reciprocity, this was the interpretation of the Convention's drafters at the Conference of Plenipotentiaries; see ibid.: 23-7.

12.   Weis, op. cit. :   36.

13.   Pompe, op. cit. :   28, 29-30.

14.   Collection: 47-52.

15.   The phrase "in the same circumstances" wherever used
      in the Convention means that any requirements (such
      as length of stay, or concerning admission or the
      possession of certain documents) which the particu-
      lar individual would have to fulfill for the enjoyment
      of the right in question if he were not a refugee,
      must still be fulfilled by the refugee, unless by
      their nature they are requirements that a refugee
      is incapable of fulfilling; see Art. 6.

Chapter 8

EXTENDING INTERNATIONAL PROTECTION
TO NEW GROUPS OF REFUGEES

"The Law of Nations, or International Law," wrote
J. L. Brierly, "may be defined as the body of rules and
principles of action which are binding upon civilized states
in their relations with one another."[1] Until the nineteenth
century the major source of these rules and principles (in
the absence of any international legislature) was the customary practice of states. When a particular practice became
sufficiently widespread it came to be viewed as more than
mere habit or usage. It became a custom in the legal
sense: "a usage felt by those who follow it to be an obliga-
tory one."[2] As there is no text for determining precisely
when a practice has become a rule or principle of customary international law, particularly in the absence of a well-
developed court system capable of authoritatively propound-
ing the point, the growth of new customary international law
has usually been slow, and a precise formulation of the content of this body of law at any one time has been impossible.
In the last two hundred years states have turned more and
more to treaty-making so as to fill gaps in the body of customary international law and to make more certain their
rights and obligations toward one another. But while "conventional" international law, based on the written agreements
of states, is now more voluminous than customary international law, the latter continues to be of importance, and new
customs continue to become recognized, albeit slowly, from
the changing and developing practices of states.[3]

As has already been pointed out, the legal disabilities
of refugees are largely the result of their lack of standing
in customary international law. That body of law grew out
of a concern for the rights and obligations of states toward
other states and the nationals of other states. Refugees as
at least de facto stateless persons simply were not recognized as existing by traditional customary international law,
and therefore in theory had no rights whatsoever. Thus a

major purpose of the succession of international agencies
concerned with the protection of refugees has been to promote international law by binding states contractually to treat
refugees like their own nationals or the nationals of other
states.   The Statute of the UNHCR specifies first among the
list of activities that shall be undertaken by the HC for the
international protection of refugees: "Promoting the conclusion and ratification of international conventions for the protection of refugees, supervising their application and proposing amendments thereto" (Par. 8[a]).

In carrying out this provision of the Statute, the Office has sought: to increase the number of states who are
parties to international instruments that apply in whole or in
part to refugees, most notably the 1951 Convention; to promote the drafting of, and accession to, new instruments concerned with rectifying some particular disability of refugees;
to achieve the inclusion of provisions relating specifically to
refugees in conventions of more general applicability; and to
extend instruments concerned only with nationals of contracting states to include refugees.   In all these cases the Office
has been concerned with both international instruments of a
universal character and those open to accession of states
who are members of a particular regional organization.

But only states that agree to become contracting parties to an international convention are bound by the obligations it contains, and few if any conventions have been acceded to by all states.   On the other hand, all states are
bound to abide by the rules contained in the body of customary international law.   Thus in addition to promoting new
conventional international law, the UNHCR has also sought
to encourage more states to adopt liberal practices in their
treatment of refugees, and to encourage the recognition of
these more liberal practices as having the status of legal
obligations.   While this activity is not specifically mentioned
in the Statute, it is a natural part of the protective function
entrusted to the Office and has been a most important activity in areas such as the right of asylum where states have
resisted the inclusion of provisions in international instruments which would have recognized the right of refugees to
asylum.

Foremost among the conventions with which the
UNHCR has been concerned is the "Magna Carta for Refugees, " the 1951 Convention, as it is the most powerful instrument available to him in seeking to encourage the more

liberal treatment of refugees by states.   But the Convention
did not "legislate" for every refugee or every refugee disability, so that subsequent agreements have been sought to
supplement it.   Of primary importance among these, and
second only to the Convention in its impact upon refugee
situations, has been the 1967 Protocol to the Convention
which eliminated the time limit in the earlier instrument
that had confined its scope to refugees who were the result
of events occurring before 1 January 1951.   Going beyond
the two universal instruments relating to the status of refugees, it is appropriate to single out one regional convention
for inclusion in this chapter because of the potential impact
it may have upon the enormous number of refugees that are
in Africa and because the UNHCR was closely associated
with its drafting.   This is the 1969 OAU Convention Governing the Specific Aspects of Refugee Problems in Africa,
which has yet to enter into force.   While its aim is to complement the 1951 Convention by serving the special refugee
situations in Africa, in some regards its provisions are
more restrictive.   But the OAU Refugee Convention also
contains articles which break new ground in the recognition
of the rights of refugees.   The efforts of successive HCs
and their staffs in promoting the conclusion and ratification
of these three major instruments, as well as in promoting
all the further agreements and declarations detailed in Chapter 9 have brought about a profound change for the better in
the body of international law, both conventional and customary, affecting the status of refugees.

Promoting the 1951 Convention

        The first, and a most important continuing task for
the UNHCR in seeking to promote "the conclusion and ratification of international conventions," was to promote the
accession of states to the 1951 Convention.   While delegates
of twenty-four governments had adopted the draft of the Convention worked out in Geneva in July 1951, no state was
bound by its provisions until it formally adhered to the Convention and until at least a total of six states became parties to it.   As supervision of the implementation of this historic charter of the rights of refugees was to be a most vital
function of the Office, the ratification of the Convention was
an essential task of the newly created Office. [4]

        But the process of ratification of an international con-
vention can be a very slow one, especially when the

convention concerns a delicate domestic matter such as the treatment accorded to aliens. Despite the diplomatic efforts of High Commissioner van Heuven Goedhart and his staff, it took until January 1954 to get the accessions of six states in order to bring the Convention into force. These first six states were Denmark, Norway, Belgium, Luxembourg, the Federal Republic of Germany, and Australia, in that order. Australia's deposit of ratification on 22 January 1954 meant that the instrument would come into force ninety days later on 22 April 1954.

Since 1954 the Office has continued to promote accessions to the Convention, especially by states whose governments have appealed to the HC for assistance in meeting the problems of refugees within their borders. Of equal importance, the Office has worked through its branch representatives to see that at every level of government within contracting states the provisions of the Convention are fully carried out. In the case of those contracting states who made reservations to provisions of the Convention when they became parties, or who exercised the optional geographic limitation contained in the Convention (interpreting the phrase "events occurring before 1 January 1951" to mean only "events in Europe"), the Office has urged the withdrawal of the reservations and the dropping of the geographic limitation as soon as possible.

In some years only a few states were added to the list of parties, while in others when international interest in refugees has been high--such as WRY--there was a spate of ratifications. At the end of 1972 sixty-three states were parties to the Convention. (See Annex 8.1.) While only one of the Eastern European states, and not a single Asian state, had ratified the Convention by 1972, the contracting states who have acceded include almost every major state of first or second asylum in the world.

The 1967 Protocol Relating to the Status of Refugees

One of the major controversies which arose during the drafting of the Statute and Convention in 1949-51 concerned the extent to which the refugee groups of the future should be included within the coverage of either instrument. A compromise was eventually reached among the drafters[5] resulting in a definition of the term refugee in the Statute that was considered sufficiently broad to include many future refugee groups within the competence of the HC, while the Convention definition limited its benefits to refugee groups existing in 1950, or appearing subsequently as a result of events occurring before 1 January 1951. In addition, the Convention permitted contracting states to invoke an optional geographic limitation such that the phrase "events occurring before 1 January 1951" could be understood to mean only "events in Europe."

When the Convention and Statute were drafted it was recognized that their differing definitions of the term refugee meant that their scope of application would not be identical, but this did not generate a great deal of concern at the time because all known refugee groups generally considered in need of international protection were included within the scope of both the Convention and the Statute. The only situation where the Convention's definition might have caused a substantial problem, that raised by the flight of some 200,000 refugees from Hungary into neighboring countries in late 1956, was solved by the agreement of the Working Group of the UNREF Ex. Com. to treat the Hungarian refugees as ones who were a result of events occurring before 1 January 1951.

As new refugee groups emerged in the 1960s, however, particularly certain refugee groups in Africa, whose circumstances could not be related to pre-1951 events, the Convention's time limitation became a growing handicap for the HC as he sought to assist all the refugees within his mandate. While the Statute of his Office made many of these refugee groups the concern of the HC, his position in regard to them was weaker than it was in regard to those earlier refugee groups to whom the contracting states of the Conventions were bound as a matter of international law to accord certain standards of treatment. Thus by the 1960s the HC no longer had an international agreement to back up his efforts to gain Convention-type treatment on behalf of all the refugee groups within his mandate. As the numbers of such non-Convention refugees grew and their need for Convention standards of treatment became more pressing, the HC initiated action with a view to deleting the time limitation provision from the 1951 Convention. [7]

Following the GA's acceptance of Res. 1959 (XVIII) of 12 December 1963--a resolution that reflected the growing acceptance of the idea that post-Convention refugees should be entitled to the same treatment standards as Convention

refugees[8]--the deletion of the Convention's time limitation
was raised for the first time as an issue within the Ex.
Com.   At the Committee's Second Special Session in January 1964, and at its Twelfth Session the following October,
several delegates asked the HC what steps might be taken
to expand the personal scope of the Convention by removing
the time limitation. [9]

   High Commissioner Dr. Schnyder, who had been personally concerned about the matter for some time, readily
agreed to consider positive courses of action.   He was particularly ready to act at that time as the OAU had in the
same year decided to draft its own regional convention on
refugees, in part so as to overcome the time limitation in
the 1951 Convention.   The HC hoped--by making the 1951
Convention applicable to the new refugee groups--to maintain
its universality as a UN convention, so that a regional convention would only have to deal with specific African problems.   Therefore, he instigated, with the assistance of the
Carnegie Endowment for International Peace, a colloquium
of legal experts to consider what might be done to make the
Convention more relevant to the new refugee situations.
Some nineteen legal experts from Algeria, Colombia, France,
Ghana, Hungary, Italy, India, Norway, Switzerland, the UK,
the US, and Yugoslavia, as well as from international agencies, participated in a personal capacity in the Colloquium
held at Bellagio, Italy, during April 1965 and submitted their
recommendations directly to the HC. [10]

   The major issue for the consideration of the Colloquium was what legal proposals, acceptable to the states,
could be made for the coverage of refugee groups not covered by the Convention.   In his background paper submitted
to the Colloquium, the HC had proposed a variety of ways
in which the time limitation might be narrowed rather than
removed, but the Colloquium's recommendation was that the
time was ripe for the complete removal of the limitation. [11]
Furthermore, the Colloquium urged that the removal be accomplished by means of an entirely new international agreement which would contain directly or by reference all the
substantive provisions of the 1951 Convention with the exception of the time limitation.   While the new instrument was
to be called a "Protocol" to the Convention, it would be a
most unusual one in that far from simply amending the Convention it would restate it in broader terms such that a state
signing the proposed Protocol would in effect have signed the
Convention.   And the Colloquium urged that the Protocol be

capable of being adhered to by states who were not parties
to the original Convention. [12]

Having made its major recommendations without qualification, the Colloquium then suggested other ways in which
the suggested Protocol might be made more acceptable to
states hesitant to accept its broadened definition of refugee.
It voted to retain the optional geographic restriction in the
Convention which permitted contracting parties to limit their
obligations to those refugees who appeared as the result of
events in Europe occurring before 1 January 1951--though
only for those states which had invoked the restriction when
signing the 1951 Convention.   And a number of the Colloquium participants recommended that (a) contrary to the Convention, parties to the Protocol be allowed to reject the
compulsory jurisdiction of the International Court of Justice
over disputes arising out of the Protocol, and (b) contracting parties be allowed to suspend all their obligations under
the Protocol for successive periods of six months by the
simple declaration that "exceptional circumstances" made
them unable to meet their obligations. [13]

The UNHCR made use of the report of the Colloquium
in order to draft its own proposed Protocol in 1965, incorporating those recommendations of the Colloquium that it
deemed desirable--the elimination of the time limitation, the
incorporation of the substance of the Convention, the adherence by states not parties to the Convention, the optional
reservation on the compulsory jurisdiction provision, and the
retention of the geographic restriction--and rejecting the
other recommendations such as the provision for suspension
of obligations.   The UNHCR draft was sent to all states who
were members of the Ex. Com. or contracting parties of
the Convention, with the request that they respond with their
views on the draft. [14]   In addition, direct consultations were
undertaken with representatives from a variety of states in
order to further test the general acceptability of the draft
proposal.   In the course of the following eighteen months the
consultations and soundings as well as the debates at three
sessions of the Ex. Com. made clear that the groundwork
had been well laid for the acceptance of the new Protocol.

By the Sixteenth Session of the Ex. Com. the HC was
ready to urge that, on the basis of favorable replies from
twenty-nine governments and because of the urgent need for
the Convention to be widened, the Protocol be sent at once
for the approval of the GA and thence to states for signatures.

The Ex. Com. agreed to this course; with very little debate the Assembly "took note of the Protocol and requested the Secretary-General to transmit the text to States with a view of enabling them to accede"; and by September 1967 the necessary six states had accepted the Protocol bringing it into force as of 4 October 1967. [15]

The procedure used by the HC to move the 1967 Protocol so quickly and successfully from idea to reality was an innovation in international law. It combined the very closest search for the cooperation of all interested governments with a very high degree of personal control over the contents of the instrument the HC sought to have accepted. It avoided the traditional amendment process which would have required calling an international conference of representatives of every government that was a party to the Convention. Such a conference would have consumed a great deal of time, would have opened up the entire Convention to possible amendments, and would have meant that any amendment proposed had to be accepted by every contracting party before it took effect. The Protocol was short and direct, and as an independent international instrument went into effect after only a very small number of states had signed it. But perhaps the ultimate innovation was opening the Protocol for acceptance by states who had not ratified the Convention, and in so doing the HC was able to secure ratification by the US.

While the US had long supported the work of the UNHCR both financially and through its votes in the organs of the UN, and had participated in the work of the Ad Hoc Committee and in the Conference of Plenipotentiaries that drafted the Convention, it had in fact never ratified the Convention. There were a variety of reasons given for this lack of action, most notably the assertion that ratification was unnecessary in that the US already accorded treatment to refugees more favorable than that required by the Convention. [16] Probably more important in explaining the US refusal however, was (1) the fact that many of the matters regulated by the Convention were considered to fall within the jurisdiction of the respective states of the US, some of whose representatives zealously objected for years to any federal action which might tend to supersede state authority; (2) the fact that there has long been a general aversion evinced by the US to acceding to treaties regulating the relations between the individual and his government; and (3) the fact that until October 1965 there was a provision in US domestic immigration law that was considered to be

incompatible with the refugee definition in the Convention. [17]
With the removal of the domestic legal impediment, ratification of the Convention became a practicable possibility; and
when the whole spectrum of American voluntary organizations interested in refugees joined forces to urge US accession, the Government agreed. But rather than become a
party to the Convention, or to the Convention and the Protocol (as had been the case with all previous contracting parties), the US was the first and one of the few states to accede only to the Protocol. The unusual form given the Protocol paid a special dividend, for somehow it was more acceptable to the US Government than the Convention which it
incorporated.   The measure of its acceptability was that no
significant reservations were made by the US at the time of
accession. [18]

With the same speed with which it drafted the 1967
Protocol and had it accepted by sufficient states for it to
come into force, the UNHCR gained the signatures of additional states for it.   Unlike the slow pace at which states
had accepted the 1951 Convention--it had taken ten years to
have it ratified by twenty-seven states--it took less than
two years for twenty-seven states to sign the Protocol, and
by 1972 fifty-two states were parties to it.   (See Annex
8.1.)[19]

The steadily increasing acceptance of the 1967 Protocol has been of great importance to the work of the UNHCR
on behalf of new refugee groups.   While the Protocol does
not directly expand the scope of the HC's authority since it
applies to obligations undertaken by states, indirectly it has
strengthened his position substantially.   The definition of the
term refugee in the Convention as amended by the Protocol
is now identical in all significant regards with the definition
in the HC's Statute.   Thus in providing for the international
protection of refugees the authority of the HC is now broader
because the obligations of states are broader.   While previously he had the backing of the Convention only in regard to
refugee groups dating from before 1951, now he can require
states to carry out in regard to all refugees within his Statute mandate the legally binding obligations they have voluntarily accepted by ratifying the Protocol.   Through his successful efforts to amend the Convention and broaden its
scope, the HC has effectively broadened and strengthened
his possibilities for action in the field of protection.

The 1969 OAU Refugee Convention Governing the
Specific Aspects of Refugee Problems in Africa

        The African states have shown their deep concern for,
and interest in, improving the legal status of refugees
through the ratification of international agreements.   When
the UNHCR's direct involvement with refugees in Africa began in 1957, only one state in the continent, Morocco, was
a party to the 1951 Convention.   By the time the OAU decided to draw up its own regional instrument on refugees six
years later, fifteen states had ratified the 1951 Convention,
and the number in 1972 stood at twenty-four.   A large number of these states considered themselves to be bound to the
Convention by reason of declarations made before they attained their independence.   Exercising the territorial application clause (Art. 40) of the Convention, France and the
UK extended the application of the Convention, when they
signed it, to include not only their domestic territory but
also certain of "those territories for the international relations of which they were responsible."   On gaining independence most of the former dependencies in Africa have declared themselves willing to continue the obligation begun by
the earlier declarations, or have acceded to the 1951 Convention on their own.   And in the case of most of the ex-
French territories they have chosen to expand the original
narrow geographic limitation adopted by France limiting the
scope of the Convention to refugees resulting from "events
occurring in Europe before 1 January 1951," to include instead "events occurring in Europe or elsewhere."   Few of
the African states have made any reservations when becoming parties to the Convention.

        The interest of the OAU states in drafting and bring-
ing into force a regional convention that would govern the
status of refugees in Africa has grown primarily out of a
desire to remove refugees as a source of political tensions
among member states of the organization.   A deep-seated
fear of externally fomented subversion has sharply affected
government attitudes in Africa, toward the reception of refugees.   Since most refugee groups from independent African
states are the product of political instability and unrest,
there is a natural fear on the part of countries of origin
(shared by countries of refugee origin elsewhere in the
world) that at least the politically conscious among their
fleeing nationals may use asylum countries as a base from
which to seek the overthrow of the governments from which
they have fled.   The governments of countries of refugee

origin have often tended to view the action of neighboring governments in granting asylum to their fleeing nationals as an unfriendly act. Governments faced with an influx of refugees, therefore, have been torn between their humanitarian concern for the refugees and their desire to uphold the Pan-African ideal of eliminating all sources of tension between African states. Too often this has led them to regard refugees as a temporary phenomenon which will in time disappear, and to delay undertaking positive steps to promote the integration of refugees within their territories. If a special convention to which all OAU asylum states would become parties were to set down the standards of treatment and the rights to be accorded to African refugees, then the granting of asylum to persons fleeing from a neighboring state might no longer be considered an unfriendly act by the government of that neighbor. If, in addition, asylum states were obliged to prevent refugees from undertaking subversive acts against their home states, and to assist in the repatriation of those refugees who subsequently wished to go home, the effect of such a convention could be to depoliticize the refugee problem, transforming it into a more purely humanitarian issue more amenable to permanent solutions.

The fact that there was already a basic and comprehensive international instrument relating to the status of refugees in the form of the 1951 Convention did not deflect the OAU states, because the 1951 Convention did not legally encompass the refugees in Africa. In acceding to the 1951 Convention African states affirmed that it defined the minimum standard of treatment that should be accorded to refugees. But they, as contracting parties, were not legally obligated to accord any particular standard of treatment to refugees in Africa because few if any of these refugees come within a key provision of the 1951 Convention: that in order to be entitled to Convention coverage they must be refugees as a result of events occurring before 1 January 1951 (Art. 1). Thus, one of the first tasks the OAU set for itself after its formation in 1963 was the drafting of a regional convention which would govern the status of refugees in Africa and which would take account of the special concerns of African states.

The OAU's Council of Ministers at its Second Ordinary Session in Lagos, in February 1964, agreed to set up an Ad Hoc Commission on Refugee Problems in Africa consisting of representatives appointed from ten states. [20] The Commission was asked to examine the problems and to make

recommendations as to how they could be solved and as to
ways and means of maintaining refugees in their countries
of asylum. In its first report, drawn up at Addis Ababa in
June 1964, the Commission raised "most of the aspects of
refugee problems which have continued to occupy the attention of African States."[21] It urged that refugee problems be
solved in the spirit of the OAU Charter and in the African
context; that countries of asylum should prevent acts of subversion in their territory and should settle refugees away
from the border of their country of origin; that the states
concerned should enter into bilateral negotiations for the
solution of refugee problems; and that repatriation in particular should be assisted. Finally it proposed that the OAU
draft a special convention on the status of African refugees.
Accepting, inter alia, this final recommendation, the OAU
Council of Ministers at its Third Ordinary Session invited
the Refugee Commission to draft such a convention "covering all aspects of the problem of refugees in Africa."[22]

    The decision of the OAU to meet the drawbacks seen
in the 1951 Convention by drafting a separate instrument
posed a problem for the UNHCR. It had long been recognized that the 1951 Convention was not intended to benefit
refugee groups that emerged subsequent to its drafting--the
drafters had concluded that to leave the agreement's coverage open-ended would be like asking its signatories to sign
a blank check. Nevertheless the 1951 Convention set standards that, if accepted by a sufficiently large number of
states, would reflect a moral if not a legal undertaking by
states that would be of great value to all refugees. The
emergence of an instrument which in any sense superseded
or competed with the 1951 Convention would seriously impair
the universal character of the Convention which the UNHCR
had spent years fostering. Further, if the OAU Convention
did not contain the high standards of the earlier instrument,
refugees in Africa would be less well off than those elsewhere in the world; and if no provision were included giving
the HC supervisory authority over the implementation of the
agreement as was the case in the 1951 Convention, the
HC's role of providing international protection to refugees in
Africa might be affected.

    To make unnecessary just such an all-embracing re-
gional instrument the UNHCR moved to implement the plan
to remove the time limitation of 1 January 1951 from the
1951 Convention. During the same months of 1964 and 1965
when organs of the OAU were composing the first two drafts

of a regional instrument on refugees, the Bellagio Colloquium of legal experts was drawing up the recommendations which led to the acceptance of the Protocol in December 1966. But while African states were quick to welcome the Protocol as marking a great step forward in the quest for juridical solutions to the problems of refugees in Africa-- four of them were among the first six states whose ratifications brought the instrument into force--they continued to work on preparing their own regional convention as well.

The OAU Refugee Commission had composed its first draft of a regional instrument on refugees, known as the "Kampala Draft, " in December 1964. Covering the same ground as the 1951 Convention and following its form, the draft dropped the 1951 dateline but in other ways was much less liberal than its international predecessor. [23]

Following their consideration of this first draft, the Council of Ministers of the OAU, at their Nairobi meeting in March 1965, established a Committee of Legal Experts nominated by member states of the Refugee Commission to examine and redraft the OAU Convention in the light of comments to be submitted by African governments. [24] This legal committee met in Leopoldville (now Kinshasa) in July 1965, and prepared a revised form of the convention known as the "Leo Draft, " which "incorporated considerable improvements on the Kampala Draft, " as Prince Sadruddin noted subsequently; but which, he added, in the eyes of many OAU members, "on the one hand, overlapped with the 1951 Convention and, on the other, was still far less liberal than the 1951 Convention since it reduced its standards. "[25]

A substantial number of African governments shared the view of the UNHCR that these first two drafts were inappropriate both in scope and in content to meet the needs of African refugees and could raise conflicts between regional obligations and those owed to the world-wide refugee instrument. [26] The Administrative Secretary-General of the OAU accordingly presented to the OAU Conference in Accra a report on the Draft Convention which "brought these points into evidence. "[27] He urged that it would be most useful if the UNHCR were invited to send representatives to the Conference to present the HC's views on the Leo Draft. As a result, Prince Sadruddin, then Deputy HC, and two members of the Legal Division were invited to attend as observers the meeting of the Council of Ministers and the meeting of Heads of State and of Governments that took place in October 1965.

Following considerable discussion among national delegations, and between them and the UNHCR observers, the consensus of the meetings was that the Leo Draft was unacceptable. Most of the delegations agreed that instead of drafting a convention "covering all aspects of the problem of refugees in Africa, " the OAU should develop a convention which would "recognize the universal principles of the 1951 Convention and supplement the latter with a view to regulating certain aspects of refugee problems peculiar to the region in particular in so far as they concern relations between Member States. "[28] The African leaders stressed that they continued to regard the 1951 Convention as the basic instrument for the protection of refugees and encouraged the HC in his efforts to make the Convention include new refugee groups through the removal of the 1951 dateline. The member states of the OAU Refugee Commission were asked to provide "legal experts at the highest level possible" to reexamine the regional convention with a view to producing a draft in accord with the views expressed at the Accra meetings. [29] This decision was a most gratifying one for the UNHCR, especially when it was followed by an invitation from the Refugee Commission to participate in the preparation of the next draft.

Despite the views expressed at the Accra meetings, however, and although the regional representative for Africa of the UNHCR participated in the drafting sessions, the third draft of the OAU convention still tended to cover the same ground as the 1951 Convention, though its provisions were more liberal than those of the preceding drafts and it contained new articles felt to be essential for dealing with the refugee situations in Africa. [30] This draft failed as well to gain the approval of the OAU's Council of Ministers. At their 1966 meeting, in a unanimous resolution, the Council members turned the drafting job over to the OAU's Secretariat and this time embodied what had been the sense of the earlier Accra meeting as to the nature of the regional convention. They were, they said, "desirous that the African instrument should govern the specifically African aspects of the refugee problem and that it should come to be the regional complement of the 1951 UN Universal Convention on the Status of Refugees. "[31] This decision marks the turning point in the drafting of the OAU Convention; from then on drafts almost totally omitted any reference to matters already covered in the 1951 Convention and concentrated instead on matters particularly affecting refugees in Africa.

By the time the Secretariat's revised draft was presented to the Council of Ministers in September 1967, the
1967 Protocol had passed through the organs of the UN and
received three of the six accessions needed to enter into
force on 7 October 1967.   Nevertheless, it was agreed by
the OAU member states that in light of its complementary
character the regional convention was still necessary in order to fully meet refugee situations arising in Africa.   The
same conclusion was reached by the International Conference
on the Legal, Economic, and Social Aspects of African Refugee Problems held in Addis Ababa in October 1967, and the
recommendation of this Conference was endorsed by the
Tenth Ordinary Session of the Council of Ministers in February 1968.   But the revised draft of the OAU Secretariat required one further revision by the Refugee Commission's
Committee of Legal Experts before it was finally found acceptable by the Council of Ministers.   The fifth draft of the
OAU Refugee Convention, adopted by the OAU Refugee Commission in June 1968, received the unanimous endorsement
of the Council of Ministers in February 1969 with only minor
changes and was signed by the heads of states, or of governments, of forty-one independent African states on 10 September 1969.   By the end of 1972, eight states had ratified the
Convention; it will come into force when one-third of the
member states of the OAU, which in 1972 comprised 42 African governments, have ratified it. [32]

The final text of the 1969 OAU Refugee Convention
makes clear that it was drawn up to supplement and not to
supersede or conflict with the 1951 Convention and the 1967
Protocol. [33]   The latter instruments are explicitly recognized
in the Preamble of the text as constituting "the basic and
universal instrument relating to the status of refugees"; and
member states of the OAU who have not done so are called
upon by the Preamble to accede to both the earlier instruments "and meanwhile to apply their provisions to refugees
in Africa."   Art. 8 of the text, moreover, declares that the
OAU Convention "shall be the effective regional complement
in Africa of the 1951 UN Convention on the Status of Refugees."   The substantive articles of the OAU Convention create obligations to be assumed by contracting states in addition to those they have accepted by becoming parties to the
1951 Convention and 1967 Protocol--obligations deemed necessary by the drafters to cover the special problems that
have arisen in Africa relating to refugees. [34]

Art. 1 of the OAU Convention indicates its

complementary nature by first taking over the major definitional provision of the 1951 Convention:

> Every person who, owing to well-founded fear of
> being persecuted for reasons of race, religion,
> nationality, membership of a particular social
> group or political opinion, is outside the country
> of his nationality and is unable or, owing to such
> fear, is unwilling to avail himself of the protec-
> tion of that country....

It breaks new ground, however, by adding a further category
of persons to the definition:

> The term "refugee" shall also apply to every per-
> son who, owing to external aggression, occupation,
> foreign domination or events seriously disturbing
> public order in either part or the whole of his
> country of origin or nationality, is compelled to
> leave his place of habitual residence to seek refuge
> in another place outside his country of origin or
> nationality.

In other words, the 1951 definition was not intended
to cover individuals generally seeking refuge from the violence and devastation of war.   The essential requirement of
that definition was that the individual seeking refugee status
be able to show that he personally had a well-founded fear
of being individually persecuted.   "Persecution" as so used
implies an intentional injurious action or threat directed
against a particular person or group of persons.   Refugees
who flee from war or civil disturbance sometimes are not
fleeing from persecution or the fear thereof; they are simply
the unintended victims of an armed conflict.   Such persons
may intend to return to their homes when order has been
restored.   In the case of refugees from southern Africa and
from Portuguese-controlled territories, there is generally
little question that they fulfill the 1951 Convention definition
based on persecution.   But with regard to many of the Congolese refugees who fled from the breakdown of law and order, or at a later date even from rumors of a breakdown,
the matter is much more doubtful.   With the inclusion of the
additional refugee category in the OAU Convention all persons
compelled to flee across national borders to escape violence
of any kind or even foreign domination generally, and whether
or not in fear of persecution, will be equally entitled to the
status of refugees when granted asylum by a signatory state.

Thus, the OAU Convention offers for Africa a significantly broader interpretation of refugee than do the Convention and the Protocol.

However, in order to come within the competence of the HC so far as international protection is concerned, or to be eligible for the benefits contained in the 1951 Convention--even as modified by the 1967 Protocol--it continues to be necessary for the refugee to come within the scope of the definition based on persecution. If the OAU Convention with its different definition for a refugee comes into force, the result may well be the emergence in Africa of different classes of refugees--those who qualify for refugee status under all the international instruments, and those who only qualify under one--with a consequent confusion and disagreement among states and international agencies regarding to whom to accord which standard of treatment. For example, signatories of the 1951 Convention are required to respect the travel documents issued to refugees by other signatory states, that is, to accept the determination of refugee status made by the issuing state. But the OAU Convention makes all refugees, as it defines the term, equally eligible to receive travel documents. It remains to be seen what recognition will be given by states outside Africa to travel documents issued to OAU Convention refugees in cases where it appears the refugee does not fulfill the definition contained in the 1951 Convention.

In taking over, in the main, the definition of refugee used by the 1951 Convention and the UNHCR Statute, the OAU Convention also poses another problem of differential refugee treatment because its signatories are very likely to interpret one of the exclusion clauses of that definition differently from, for example, the UNHCR. The OAU Convention like its predecessors excludes from its coverage "any person with respect to whom the country of asylum has serious reasons for considering that ... he has been guilty of acts contrary to the purposes and principles of the United Nations" (Art. 1, par. 5[d]). Are the "freedom fighters" who are actively engaged in military operations or sabotage against colonial or white minority regimes barred from recognition as refugees by reason of this exclusion? The UNHCR, whose Statute contains a similar exclusion clause has, in spite of GA resolutions supporting the freedom struggle in Africa, ruled that because its role must be completely non-political and humanitarian such freedom fighters are excluded from the HC's mandate. But in view of the OAU's strong

commitment to the liberation struggle and its direct material assistance to recognized liberation movements, there is
little doubt that African governments will judge freedom
fighters to be OAU Convention refugees in those cases where
such a determination is relevant to the needs of the freedom
fighters.

In addition to the exclusion and cessation clauses
taken over from the 1951 Convention, the OAU Convention
has added one cessation clause which would permit contracting states to withdraw OAU Convention refugee status from
any refugee who "has seriously infringed the purposes and
objectives of this Convention"; and it has added an exclusion
clause exempting from the Convention's coverage any person
who "has been guilty of acts contrary to the purposes and
principles of the OAU" (Art. 1, pars. 4[g] and 5[c]).   One
authority has observed that since these purposes include a
commitment to the liberation of all of Africa, "dissidents
of the African liberation movement and those betraying the
specifically African cause could be excluded since their pro-
colonial attitude would be an obstacle to the emancipation of
African peoples. "35

The consequence of this exclusion clause, therefore,
may be to make even more prevalent the kind of problem
that arises on occasion today when African governments refuse to accord, or withdraw their conferral of refugee status
in cases where persons leave the ranks of the freedom fighters by choice or otherwise, or where dissident factions of
OAU-recognized liberation movements split off to form new
movements.   It is difficult now for the UNHCR to provide
international protection for persons who in the judgment of
the Office are refugees within the mandate, if they have
either been jailed or served with expulsion orders by African governments.   It may be even harder once the OAU
Convention comes into force if contracting states mistakenly
assume that their adherence to that agreement supersedes
their obligations under the 1951 Convention and the 1967
Protocol.

Going beyond problems of definition, the OAU Convention sets forth several provisions aimed at easing substan-
tively some of the major problems associated with African
refugees, and particularly to insure that in the words of the
Convention: "The grant of asylum to refugees is a peaceful
and humanitarian act and shall not be regarded as an unfriendly act by any Member State" (Art. 2, par. 2).   Thus

Art. 3 contains a pledge by "Signatory States ... to prohibit
refugees residing in their respective territories from attacking any Member State of the OAU." And in Art. 2 countries
of asylum are instructed, "for reasons of security ... [to]
settle refugees at a reasonable distance from the frontiers
of their country of origin"--an important step in maintaining
good relations between countries of origin and countries of
asylum. Art. 5 is a lengthy provision elaborating the process of voluntary repatriation, the most desirable solution
to refugee problems in Africa and in the view of some African governments the only satisfactory solution, but one about
which little was said in the 1951 Convention. Taken almost
wholly from a recommendation made by the 1967 African
Refugee Conference, Art. 5 sets forth the role that is to
be played by countries of asylum, by the OAU, and especially by countries of origin, in encouraging refugees to voluntarily repatriate: by easing their return to their homes,
assuring their safety, assisting their resettlement, and above
all granting them "the full rights and privileges of nationals"
and in no way penalizing them for having left.

The most important innovative feature in the new instrument is found in Art. 2. It deals with the refugee's
first and most fundamental need--asylum--and does so in
such a way as to put the African states ahead of any other
group of states in their willingness to give legal recognition
to an individual's right to asylum under certain circumstances. Previously no international convention has recognized that an individual could have a right to asylum, instead they affirmed that states had the right to grant asylum
at their discretion. The OAU Convention contains an absolute and unqualified requirement that no refugee shall be
subjected "to measures such as rejection at the frontier,
return or expulsion, which would compel him to return or
remain in a territory where his life, physical integrity or
liberty would be threatened" (Art. 2, par. 3). In this most
liberal recognition of the essential need of every refugee,
the OAU drafters have gone beyond the terms of the 1951
Convention and of the non-binding 1967 UN Declaration on
Territorial Asylum to insist that refugees have the right to
enter another country when coming directly from a country
where they fear for their own safety.

In addition, Art. 2 of the OAU Convention sets down
the requirement that as concerns all refugees within its definition, "Member States of the OAU shall use their best endeavors consistent with their respective legislation to receive

refugees and to secure the settlement of those refugees who, for well-founded reasons, are unable or unwilling to be repatriated" (Art. 2, par. 1). Finally, the Article urges contracting states to grant temporary asylum even in those cases when they feel they cannot grant permanent asylum; and it urges those African states which have not had to carry the brunt of the refugee burden "in the spirit of African unity and international cooperation [to] take appropriate measures to lighten the burden of the Member State granting asylum" when appealed to for help, by, for example, offering permanent asylum to refugees having only temporary asylum.

On the matter of travel documents for refugees in Africa the OAU Convention does not just repeat the provisions of the 1951 Convention but instead adds an exemption clause permitting a country of first asylum to dispense with giving travel documents with return clauses in cases where an African country of second asylum agrees to accept the particular refugees (Art. 6, par. 2). It is difficult to assess what effect, if any, this exemption will have on the matter of return clauses, since the mandatory duty to issue travel documents with return clauses under the 1951 Convention and the 1967 Protocol remains unaffected. African states of asylum have been hesitant to issue clause documents, because their view has been that the purpose of the travel document is to facilitate the dispersal of the refugees throughout Africa and thus to lighten the disproportionate burden of the refugee problem which they have shouldered. If African states not presently burdened by large numbers of refugees agree to accept refugees sight unseen from first-asylum states for permanent resettlement, then the absence of the return clause should pose no handicap to the movement of refugees. But if second-asylum states insist on a return clause and first asylum states continue to be hesitant to give it, then the refugee travel document may not serve to facilitate refugee movement and permanent settlement in Africa to the extent that it could and should do so.

The role of the UNHCR under the OAU Convention differs considerably from its role under the 1951 Convention in that, while the OAU Convention calls upon member states to "cooperate" with the UNHCR, no specific supervisory function over the implementation of the African Convention is entrusted to the HC (compare Art. 8 of the OAU Convention with Art. 35 of the 1951 Convention). Perhaps, however, by reason of the authority contained in the Statute of

his Office, the HC can encourage the ratification of the OAU
Convention, supervise its application, and propose amendments thereto, although his authority to do so is certainly
not binding upon states as it is in the case of the 1951 Convention.

The OAU Refugee Convention is potentially of signal
benefit to refugees in Africa because of its liberal and innovative provisions on the definition of a refugee and on asylum. Its incorporation of the central provision of the 1967
UN Declaration on Territorial Asylum, and its broadening
of the refugee definition to go beyond the concept of persecution, are developments of the greatest importance which
set an example for states throughout the world to follow.
Moreover, its inclusion of provisions aimed at eliminating
the political tensions occasioned by refugee flows through
prohibiting subversive activities and distinguishing the granting of asylum from the commission of "unfriendly acts"
should make it easier for African governments to undertake
permanent solutions, such as local integration or resettlement for refugee groups where repatriation is not yet possible. And by detailing the mechanism of voluntary repatriation, the OAU Convention may help to make this solution
more attractive to some refugee groups. Finally, the attention that has been focused on the legal needs of refugees
during the five-year process of drafting the OAU Convention
has led to wider recognition among African governments that
the permanent solution of refugee problems in the continent
requires that both material assistance and legal protection
be made available to refugees.

Notes

1.   J. L. Brierly, The Law of Nations, 6th ed., Oxford,
         1963: 1.

2.   Ibid.: 59.

3.   The Statute of the International Court of Justice lists a
         third source of international law in addition to the
         two mentioned here: the "general principles of law
         recognized by civilized nations" (Art. 38).

4.   In the first part of his report to the GA, June 1951,
         HC van Heuven Goedhart said, "I regard the early
         entry into force of this Convention as a matter of

the utmost importance. For my part, I shall do everything possible to carry out the responsibilities with which I am charged under the present draft of the Convention. In my opinion this Convention will provide an adequate status for very large numbers of refugees who do not as yet enjoy the benefits of any internationally recognized legal position, GA (VI) Off. Rec., Supp. No. 19, A/2011.

5.   See Ch. 3.

6.   Paul Weis, "The Concept of the Refugee in International Law," Doc. HCR/INF/49 of 2 Mar. 1960: 21; originally published in JDI, Vol. 87, Oct.-Dec. 1960: 928-1001; and see the Annex to UN Doc. A/AC.79/49, 17 Jan. 1957, where the decisions of states as to the eligibility of Hungarian refugees are noted.

7.   The process that led to the adoption of the 1967 Protocol, and its legal significance, are described by Paul Weis in the article, "The 1967 Protocol relating to the Status of Refugees and Some Questions of the Law of Treaties," BYBIL, Vol. 42, 1967: 39-70.

8.   The resolution contained a provision that urged governments to treat the new refugee groups "in accordance with the principles and the spirit of the convention."

9.   Rep. of the Ex. Com., Second Spec. Sess. App. 1 to GA (XIX) Off. Rec., Supp. No. 11, A/5811/Rev. 1, 1964, par. 14; and GA, Ex. Com. (XII) A/AC. 96/270 of 25 Nov. 1964, par. 33.

10.   Rep. of the Colloquium on the Legal Aspects of Refugee Problems, A/AC.96/INF.40 of 5 May 1965.

11.   Ibid.: 2. HC's Background Paper to the Colloquium is Doc. MHCR/23/65, Geneva, 1965.

12.   A/AC.96/INF.40: 3.

13.   Ibid.: 3-4.

14.   The HC's memorandum on the Rep. of the Colloquium,

including the HC's own proposed draft, is contained in Doc. HCR/RS/31 of 23 Sept. 1965, and was sent to governments under cover of a letter (Doc. MHCR/131/65) dated 13 Oct. 1965.

15.   The HC's recommendations and the replies from governments are set forth in A/AC. 96/346 of 12 Oct. 1966; the final draft form of the Protocol is contained in A/AC. 96/356 of 12 Oct. 1966; the action of the Ex. Com. on the draft may be found in Rep. of Ex. Com. (XVI), A/AC. 96/352 of 18 Nov. 1966, in par. 36-38; the GA action is in Res. 2198(XXI) of 16 Dec. 1966.

16.   Read, "The UN and Refugees": 52.

17.   "Until Oct. 1965, when the Immigration Act was revised, section 243(h) having to do with the authority of the Attorney General to deport aliens only gave him the power or the discretion to withhold deportation to a country where a refugee would suffer physical persecution.   That physical persecution (provision) was a very definite limiting factor (so far as US ratification was concerned)," said Laurence Dawson, then Acting Deputy Director of the Office of Refugee and Migration Affairs of the US Dept. of State, in testimony before Cong.; US Senate, Ex. Rep. No. 14, 90th Cong., 2d Sess., 20 Sept. 1968:   9.   It was a limiting factor because the definition of persecution in the Convention was clearly wider than the physical persecution provision of US law.

18.   See Message from the President of the US transmitting the Protocol Relating to the Status of Refugees, US Senate, Ex. Doc. K, 90th Cong., 2d Sess., 1 Aug. 1968:   vii.

19.   For text see Collection: 53-57.

20.   OAU, CM/Res. 19 (II).

21.   Eberhard Jahn, "Developments in Refugee Law in the Framework of Regional Organizations outside Europe," AWR Bulletin, Vol. 4, June 1966:   81.

22.   OAU, CM/Res. 36 (III) adopted in Cairo, July 1964.

23.   Dr. Eberhard Jahn, at that time Deputy Director of
      the UNHCR Legal Division, summed up in 1966 the
      drawbacks which the Office saw in the draft by say-
      ing: "there are omissions which, from the point
      of view of the international protection of refugees,
      are undesirable. The Draft does not contain any
      provision on such elementary rights as wage-earn-
      ing employment, elementary education, public re-
      lief, labour legislation and social security. It does
      not stipulate freedom of movement and it makes
      the issuance of travel documents merely optional
      and gives less protection against expulsion. " Jahn,
      "Development in Refugee Law": 82.   Furthermore,
      nothing was said in the Kampala Draft about con-
      tracting states' cooperating with the HC or as to the
      HC's supervising the application of the regional con-
      vention as had been provided for in Art. 35 of the
      1951 Convention.

24.   OAU, CM/Res. 52(IV) of 8 Mar. 1965.

25.   Statement by the HC to the Ex. Com. (XV), A/AC.96/
      310, 29 Oct. 1965: 1.

26.   A comparison between the provisions of the Leo Draft
      and those of the 1951 Convention which underlines
      the shortcomings of the Leo Draft is made by
      Kwasi Gyeke-Dako in an article reproduced by
      UNHCR.   "Some Legal and Social Aspects of Afri-
      can Refugee Problems, " MHCR/62/68, esp. pp.
      29-36.

27.   A/AC.96/310: 2.

28.   Ibid. :   3.

29.   OAU, AHG/Res. 26(II).

30.   The text is contained in Annex IV of the 'Report of the
      Third Meeting of the Legal Experts of the OAU Ad
      Hoc Committee on the Problem of Refugees, Held
      in Addis Ababa from 12 to 16 Sept. 1966, " OAU
      Doc. No. CM/134.

31.   OAU, CM/Res. 88(VII) of Oct. 1966.

32.   Because the OAU Convention uses the term "Member

States of the OAU" in many, though not all, of its
articles rather than the more usual treaty term
"Contracting Parties" it appears that the drafters
intended the Convention to be both a binding international agreement--among its contracting states;
and a hortatory declaration much like the 1967 UN
Declaration on Territorial Asylum regarding the
way in which all member states of the OAU should
act.   No African state is legally bound by the obligations on the Convention until it has formally ratified the instrument, but the fact that forty-one
heads of state and of governments in the continent
personally signed it gives the instrument very considerable authority even in the absence of ratification.

33.   See Collection: 255-62.

34.   The nature of these special obligations is the subject
of an article by the former Director of the UNHCR
Legal Division, Ousmane Goundiam, "African Refugee Convention, " MN, Mar. -Apr. 1970:   7-12.

35.   Ibid. :   9.

ANNEX 8. 1

RATIFICATIONS AND ACCESSIONS TO THE REFUGEE CONVENTION OF 1951 AND TO THE PROTOCOL OF 1967

Date for Convention Ratification, or Accession	Parties to the Convention	Date for Protocol Accession
4 Dec. 1952	Denmark	29 Jan. 1968
23 Mar. 1953	Norway	28 Nov. 1967
22 July 1953	Belgium	8 Apr. 1969
23 July 1953	Luxembourg	22 Apr. 1971
1 Dec. 1953	Germany, Fed. Rep. of	5 Nov. 1969
22 Jan. 1954	Australia	--
11 Mar. 1954	UK	4 Sept. 1968
18 May 1954	Monaco	--
23 June 1954	France	3 Feb. 1971
1 Oct. 1954	Israel	14 June 1968
26 Oct. 1954	Sweden	4 Oct. 1967
1 Nov. 1954	Austria	--
15 Nov. 1954	Italy	26 Jan. 1972
21 Jan. 1955	Switzerland	20 May 1968
17 Aug. 1955	Ecuador	6 Mar. 1969
30 Nov. 1955	Iceland	26 Apr. 1968
15 Mar. 1956	Holy See	8 June 1967
3 May 1956	Netherlands	29 Nov. 1968
7 Nov. 1956	Morocco	20 Apr. 1971
29 Nov. 1956	Ireland	6 Nov. 1968
8 Mar. 1957	Liechtenstein	20 May 1968
24 Oct. 1957	Tunisia	16 Oct. 1968
15 Dec. 1959	Yugoslavia	15 Jan. 1968
5 Apr. 1960	Greece	7 Aug. 1968
30 June 1960	New Zealand	--
16 Nov. 1960	Brazil	7 Apr. 1972
22 Dec. 1960	Portugal	--
25 Aug. 1961	Niger	2 Feb. 1970
10 Oct. 1961	Colombia	--
23 Oct. 1961	Cameroon	19 Sept. 1967
15 Nov. 1961	Argentina	6 Dec. 1967
8 Dec. 1961	Ivory Coast	16 Feb. 1970
27 Feb. 1962	Togo	1 Dec. 1969

30 Mar. 1962	Turkey	31 July 1968
4 Apr. 1962	Dahomey	6 July 1970
4 Sept. 1962	CAR	30 Aug. 1967
15 Oct. 1962	Congo, Peoples Rep. of the	10 July 1970
21 Feb. 1963	Algeria	8 Nov. 1967
18 Mar. 1963	Ghana	30 Oct. 1968
2 May 1963	Senegal	30 Oct. 1967
16 May 1963	Cyprus	9 July 1968
16 July 1963	Burundi	15 Mar. 1971
27 Apr. 1964	Gabon	--
12 Mar 1964	Tanzania, United Rep. of	4 Sept. 1968
30 July 1964	Jamaica	--
15 Oct. 1964	Liberia	--
21 Dec. 1964	Peru	--
19 July 1965	Zaire	--
28 Dec. 1965	Guinea	16 May 1968
16 May 1966	Kenya	--
7 Sept. 1966	Gambia	29 Sept. 1967
23 Oct. 1967	Nigeria	2 May 1968
8 Dec. 1967	Madagascar	--
10 Oct. 1968	Finland	10 Oct. 1968
6 Jan. 1969	Botswana	6 Jan. 1969
4 June 1969	Canada	4 June 1969
24 Sept. 1969	Zambia	24 Sept. 1969
10 Nov. 1969	Ethiopia	10 Nov. 1969
1 Apr. 1970	Paraguay	1 Apr. 1970
--	Swaziland	29 Jan. 1969
--	US	1 Nov. 1968
20 Sept. 1970	Uruguay	20 Sept. 1970
17 June 1971	Malta	15 Sept. 1971
10 Feb. 1972	Chile	27 Apr. 1972
12 June 1972	Fiji	12 June 1972

SOURCE: UNHCR, 1 June 1972.

ANNEX 8.2

MEMBERS OF THE ORGANIZATION FOR AFRICAN UNITY
(As of July 1973)

Algeria	Madagascar
Botswana	Malawi
Burundi	Mali
Cameroon	Mauritania
Central Afr. Rep.	Morocco
Chad	Niger
Congo, People's Rep.	Nigeria
Dahomey	Rwanda
Equatorial Guinea	Senegal
Ethiopia	Sierra Leone
Gabon	Somalia
Gambia	Sudan
Ghana	Swaziland
Guinea	Tanzania
Ivory Coast	Togo
Kenya	Tunisia
Mauritius	UAR
Lesotho	Uganda
Liberia	Upper Volta
Libya	Zaire
	Zambia

SOURCE: UNHCR, Geneva 1973.

Chapter 9

PROMOTION OF FURTHER INTERNATIONAL
INSTRUMENTS AND DECLARATIONS

In considering the substantial number of international instruments and declarations, other than the 1951 Convention, the 1967 Protocol, and the OAU Refugee Convention, which pertain to refugees and with which the UNHCR has been concerned, it is useful to classify them as follows:

1. Conventions relating to special refugee problems

2. Conventions relating to stateless persons and statelessness

3. Conventions containing special clauses relating to refugees

4. Conventions whose applicability is specifically extended to refugees

5. Conventions of general applicability that affect refugees

6. Conventions and declarations on asylum, and

7. Cooperative action on further declarations regarding refugees. [1]

Besides the UNHCR, many other international groups and agencies, governments, voluntary organizations, and individuals have played a role in initiating, drafting, and promoting accession to the variety of agreements and declarations affecting refugees. Due to the very nature of diplomatic negotiations it is not possible to document all the efforts of UNHCR in this area, nor is it possible to measure with complete accuracy its contribution. It is perhaps sufficient for an understanding of the overall achievement of the Office in this regard to point out that it is the only international agency concerned exclusively with refugees in general, and

international agreements and declarations affecting refugees
are not accepted by states unless very considerable efforts
are made by concerned persons to bring about this result.

In the seven sections of this chapter a variety of international instruments, both universal and regional, which
have a significant bearing on the content and the future development of international law relating to refugees are detailed, and the role of the UNHCR in regard to each instrument and each relevant drafting organization is set forth.

Conventions Relating to Special Refugee Problems

To this category of international instruments belong
those agreements that are concluded solely for the benefit of
refugees but which, unlike the 1951 Convention for example,
concern only one or a few of the legal disabilities suffered
by refugees.   Since the beginning of international efforts on
behalf of refugees these special conventions tend to have
been concerned with the fundamental need of refugees for
the facilitation of their travel.[2]

The Hague Agreement Relating to Refugee Seamen
(1957).   One of the first problems concerning protection
which was brought to the attention of the first High Commissioner, Dr. van Heuven Goedhart, on assuming his office, was that of refugee seamen.   While by international
law a ship is considered a piece of the territory of the
state whose flag it flies, many states do not equate time
spent by a seaman on board a ship flying their flag with
residence in that state.   Thus seamen who sought refuge by
serving on ships of states other than their own, or who
sought to exercise their calling as seafarers after gaining
refuge in a country of asylum, often found themselves in the
precarious position of having no country in which they could
legally stay, no valid identity or travel documents (or only
documents which had expired), and in an irregular status
everywhere.   Frequently such seamen were not permitted to
leave their ships in any port of call for lack of documents,
and thus were virtually condemned to sail the seas forever
or risk imprisonment when trying to land.

Discussions concerning the plight of these refugee
seamen were held between the IRO, the UNHCR, and the
ILO in early 1951, and led to passage of a resolution by the
concerned standing committee of the ILO, the Joint Maritime

Commission, on 24 May 1951.   The resolution urged governments to facilitate the acquisition of residence and travel
documents by refugee seamen especially by permitting them
to count time spent on board ship as residence in the territory of the state whose flag the ship flies.   On the initiative
of the ILO observer at the Conference of Plenipotentiaries
that drafted the 1951 Convention, an article (Art. 11) was
included in the Convention in regard to refugees serving as
regular crew members on board ship flying their flags.   The
article, with a view to facilitating the refugees' permanent
establishment, provides that a signatory state should give
"sympathetic consideration" to their establishment on its territory or permit their temporary admission and issue travel
documents to them.   No binding obligation was imposed on
signatory states.

The UNHCR and its branch offices continued to receive requests for assistance from refugee seamen.   Thanks
to the benevolent attitude of many governments, it was possible to solve some of the problems of these men, but others continued to pose intractable difficulties from a legal
point of view.   In October 1953, at the request of the HC
and in collaboration with his local branch office, the Netherlands authorities began an inquiry at ports in that country to
determine the extent of the problem.   Preliminary results
from that survey indicated that 25 percent of the refugee
seamen interviewed had no travel documents and that another
25 percent were in the precarious position of having expired
documents, or papers of doubtful validity.   The HC thus addressed a further memorandum to the ILO in November
1953.   Finally, responding to an ILO request for information as to compliance with the May 1951 resolution, the
Netherlands Government took the initiative and called a conference of eight Western European maritime nations to which
it submitted suggestions for a solution.   Three sessions
held at the Hague in 1955, 1956, and 1957 finally led to the
adoption of The Hague Agreement on Refugee Seamen on 23
November 1957. [3]   Both the UNHCR and the ILO were represented by observers who in fact participated in the negotiations.

The terms of the Hague Agreement provided that a
refugee seaman who has no country in which he may lawfully
stay be issued the travel document provided for by the 1951
Convention, and that he be accepted in its territory by the
contracting state under whose flag he has served for six
hundred days during the last three years or, if there is no

such state, by the contracting state where he had his last
lawful residence during the preceding three years.   For the
large number of seamen who would not be covered by these
conditions, more generous criteria were also included.
These provided that refugee seamen be issued a travel document and admitted to its territory by the contracting state
which last issued them travel documents valid for return
since 1945, even if the documents had expired; or, failing
this, the contracting state where they had last lawfully
stayed since 1945; or, failing this, the contracting state on
whose ships they had served for six hundred days during a
period of three years since 1945.

   A suggestion endorsed by the UNHCR and some of
the participating governments--that contracting states with
which the refugee seamen had a link as defined by the Agreement consider the men to be residents and grant them all
the rights accorded by the 1951 Convention--was the focus
of much debate. [4]   But as finally accepted, the Agreement
only required the contracting states to regard the seamen as
lawfully staying on their territory for the purpose of Art.
28 of the Convention, that is, for the purpose of being issued a travel document.   Nevertheless, these provisions
gave to a refugee seaman covered by the Agreement the
possibility of settling down in a state which accepted him.
(He would need to maintain a link with the accepting state
though, either by residing in it for some time or by serving
on its ships.)   Moreover, contracting states also undertook
to see that refugees serving on their ships were provided
with identity papers, and that refugee seamen were admitted
temporarily to their countries for shore leave, for taking
up engagements with other ships, or for health reasons.

   Following the signing of the Hague Agreement the
UNHCR at once sought to promote accessions to it, an activity in which it was again aided by the Netherlands Government.   That government submitted a resolution (after consultation with the UNHCR) to the Forty-First (Maritime)
Session of the ILO, urging member states of the ILO to accede to the Agreement and to inform refugee seamen of the
possibilities offered by the Agreement for regularizing their
position.   The resolution was adopted without a dissenting
vote in May 1958 by the General Conference of the ILO.
Moreover, the states that had participated in the Hague Conference tended to apply the principles of the Agreement even
before it was finally concluded in November 1957.   (The
UK, for instance, documented some 2,000 refugee seamen

in Britain during 1956-57.) Finally, by September 1961 all
eight of the original signatory states had ratified the Agreement, bringing it into force on 27 December 1961. As of
7 April 1970 a total of sixteen states had become parties to
the Agreement.

Following the coming into force of the 1967 Protocol,
the ILO Maritime Commission urged parties to the Hague
Agreement to extend, by declaration, the benefits of that
Agreement to post-dateline refugees as well as to refugees
covered by the 1951 Convention. Only Norway has informed
the ILO and the UNHCR that it will so apply the Hague
Agreement. In 1969 the Netherlands Government took the
initiative in drafting a protocol to the Hague Agreement
which would make the Agreement applicable to post-dateline
refugees, and the text has been circulated to the UNHCR
and to parties of the Hague Agreement for their comments.

In line with both the ILO resolution of May 1958 and
a reaffirming resolution of the Joint Maritime Commission
in September-October 1961, the HC won the agreement of
the Netherlands Government in March 1962 to the stationing
of a special counsellor at Rotterdam appointed by the UNHCR
branch office in The Hague. Previous measures taken by
the Office and by other interested bodies to inform refugee
seamen of the rights that were now available to them had
been only partially successful. The function of the special
counsellor, whose services were paid for jointly by the
UNHCR and the Netherlands, was to survey crew lists of
ships docking at Rotterdam in order to trace refugee seamen, and then to interview and advise the men how to claim
the benefits of the Agreement. In the first five years during which this guidance service was provided, over 2,000
refugee seamen were interviewed in the port of Rotterdam,
and the UNHCR was able to note that many of these men had
been helped to acquire adequate documents. However, there
remains the problem, as yet unsolved, of the refugee seamen serving on ships flying flags of convenience, notably
those of Liberia and Panama, which have no links with any
country party to the Hague Agreement.

The European Agreement on Abolition of Visas for
Refugees (1959). Concluded under the auspices of the CoE
and open to accession by member states of the Council, this
Agreement exempts refugees (the term refugee is defined in
the same way as in the 1951 Convention, Art. 1), lawfully
resident in the territory of a contracting party, who hold a

Convention travel document or a travel document issued under the London Agreement (signed 15 October 1946; 11 UN, TS 73), from the requirement of a visa for a visit of not more than three months' duration to the territory of another contracting party, provided that the refugee does not take up gainful employment.

The Agreement arose out of efforts made over several years by the UNHCR to facilitate the travel of refugees between states. The problem of refugee travel has long concerned the international community and was one of the principal reasons for the establishment of the first international agency for refugees in 1921. While the 1951 Convention included provisions requiring contracting states to issue travel documents to refugees and to recognize the Convention travel documents issued by other contracting parties, it took years for this part of the Convention to become fully implemented by the contracting states. There are still parties who do not issue travel documents or who issue ones that do not conform entirely with the requirements of the Convention.

Meanwhile, even with recognized travel documents, refugees found themselves up against additional formalities at national borders that complicated travel; they were required to have visas when nationals were not, or to fulfill additional conditions to receive a visa.

As part of the growing economic and social cooperation that occurred in Western Europe following WWII, the visa requirement for nationals was abolished between most European countries on a reciprocal basis; but refugees still needed visas. Frequently visa applications of refugees had to be referred by consuls to the central authorities, which caused delays, and the fees levied on the issuance of visas were sometimes considerable. The UNHCR sought to change this situation regarding refugee visas both through its branch offices at the national level, and through the personal efforts of the HC and his staff at headquarters at the regional level. The first break came in late 1954 when the three countries of the Benelux Union, Belgium, the Netherlands, and Luxembourg, decided through a series of bilateral agreements to waive the visa requirements for refugees holding Convention or London Agreement travel documents issued by any one of them, for the purpose of travel to any other of them for a temporary stay. With this precedent in mind, High Commissioner van Heuven Goedhart approached the CoE with a view to the adoption of measures for the facilitation of travel and the abolition of visas for refugees. [5]

In response to the HC, the Consultative Assembly of the CoE adopted a resolution on 25 October 1955 to the effect that all member states were recommended: to accede to the 1946 London Agreement or the 1951 Convention; to begin issuing travel documents as specified by the 1951 Convention if they were parties to it; to forthwith take steps to adopt the Benelux working arrangements for the exemption of visas for refugees; and, if not yet willing to waive the visa requirement, to give urgent consideration to the speeding up of procedures for issuing visas to refugees and to reducing the visa charge to a nominal sum, with the possible remission of fees in justified cases (Rec. 86[VII]).

A number of European states thereafter took unilateral or bilateral action to facilitate refugee travel. The Government of France, as from 1 January 1956, exempted refugees resident in France from the requirement of exit and return visas, an exemption hitherto applied only to "statutory refugees" (that is, those recognized under pre-WWII international conventions and arrangements). The Government of the Federal Republic of Germany decided as an interim measure to issue visas free of charge to refugees holding London Agreement or Convention travel documents; and on 12 May 1956 unilaterally waived the visa requirement for all refugees travelling to West Germany for temporary stays. Negotiations were begun between West Germany, France, Switzerland, and the Benelux nations as to the possibility of expanding the Benelux refugee visa arrangement of all those states.

In November 1957 the Special Committee of Senior Officials of Member States of the CoE for the Simplification of Border Formalities (set up some years previously to facilitate inter-European travel generally) considered the possibility of a multilateral agreement for the abolition of visas for refugees. The Netherlands delegation submitted a draft agreement patterned on the Benelux bilateral agreements already in force and was strongly supported by the UNHCR as represented by its Chief Legal Advisor, Dr. Paul Weis, who also urged passage by the CoE of a recommendation seeking the general relaxation of visa formalities and the reduction of visa fees for refugees pending the coming into force of the proposed multilateral agreement. The proposed UNHCR recommendations were taken over and issued by the

Committee of Ministers of the CoE as Res. 58(V) in March
1958, while the Netherlands draft agreement, after further
discussion and revisions, was also accepted by the Committee of Ministers and opened for the accession of states on
20 April 1959. [6]   Having received the necessary three ratifications, the Agreement entered into force on 4 September
1960.

Meanwhile, pursuant to the resolution of the Committee of Ministers and encouraged by the UNHCR, additional
unilateral and bilateral actions were taken by European governments to ease refugee travel.   On 15 May 1957 France
became a party to the Benelux agreements on the waiving of
visas for refugees, and on 1 May 1960 entered into a similar arrangement with Switzerland.   As from 1 July 1960,
refugees and stateless persons resident in Denmark, Finland,
Norway, or Sweden for at least one year were permitted to
travel to the other countries of this group without visa.   A
similar agreement was entered into by the Federal Republic
of Germany and Switzerland on 4 May 1962 for the benefit
of refugees seeking to travel from one state to the other for
visits of less than three months for purposes other than
gainful employment.   In addition, Norway and Luxembourg
stopped charging visa fees to all refugees, while the Governments of Austria, Greece, the Netherlands, Sweden, and
the UK agreed to waive visa fees under certain conditions
and in other ways to simplify and speed up the issuance of
visas to refugees.

At the renewed urging of the UNHCR, the Consultative Assembly of the CoE reiterated its recommendations:
that governments not yet parties to the European Agreement
on the Abolition of Visas for Refugees accede to that Agreement; that in the meantime they issue visas to refugees free
of charge and speed up the procedures for their issuance;
and that they not apply any measure of frontier control to
refugees not applicable to nationals of member states (Rec.
375[XV] of September 1963). [7]   The significance of the final
recommendation was that it would raise refugee standards
of treatment in the matter of travel to be identical with that
accorded nationals.   Following the passage of this resolution, additional states were successfully urged by the UNHCR
to join the Abolition of Visas Agreement; by March 1970
thirteen European states were parties to it.   The Benelux
Union expanded their visa exemption agreement concerning
refugees to Switzerland as of 15 June 1964 and signed an
agreement with Austria, which entered into force on 1 April

1965, with regard to the right of residence and the prolongation of refugee travel documents.

In a related development concerning the easing of
travel restrictions, the CoE in 1961 concluded an agreement
on travel by young persons on collective passports between
countries that were members of the CoE.   An article of this
agreement provided for an optional declaration extending its
provisions to young refugees and stateless persons.   By
April 1970 ten states had made such a declaration.

Other European Instruments Facilitating Refugee Travel.   During the same period that the UNHCR was working
through the CoE to facilitate inter-European refugee travel,
the Office also worked through the other major European
regional organizations, the EEC (or Common Market), the
OEEC (Organization for European Economic Cooperation) and
its successor the OECD (Organization for Economic Cooperation and Development), to further the same ends.   The issue in this case was the liberalization of the movement of
manpower for employment within Europe.   The HC's aim
was that refugees be treated as liberally in this regard as
nationals.   The Council of the OEEC adopted on 30 October
1953 a Decision on the Liberalization of Manpower Movements which required the authorities of member states to
grant, on application, employment permits to suitable workers who were nationals of other member states, if suitable
labor, forming part of the regular labor force, was not
available within the state for the employment in question.
As the result of consultations between the UNHCR and the
OEEC there was included in this 1953 Decision the provision
that refugees who at the time of the first application for
their employment were officially recognized as refugees in
another member state, were to be treated as nationals of that
state in implementing the provision of this Decision, provided that the refugees had the right to return to that member state.   The wording of the Decision made it doubly important to refugee workers that they be able to get travel
documents that would fully conform to the requirements of
the 1951 Convention including the right to return.

The UNHCR was represented at the Sessions of the
Manpower Committee of the OEEC held in 1957 and 1958 in
order to lend support to a French proposal that refugees
taking up employment in other member states under the
terms of the 1953 Decision should be issued a refugee travel
document valid for return for three years.   Certain countries

had difficulty in accepting this suggestion, but the Committee finally agreed on 17 July 1958 to urge the OEEC Council to adopt the French proposal with the right of return limited to two years.   The Council did so when it adopted Rec. C (58) 196 (Final) on 3 October 1958.   Thereafter the UNHCR worked to achieve national compliance with the Recommendation and to further the necessary bilateral agreements that would fully implement its provisions.

In a second move also directed at the OEEC, the UNHCR sought to extend another Council recommendation (C [55] 295) on the simplification of administrative practices governing the movement and employment of nationals of member countries to benefit refugees as well.   Acting with the backing of a recommendation of his own UNREF Ex. Com. (issued at its Fifth Session in June 1957), the HC had such a proposal laid before a working party of the Manpower Committee of the OEEC in April 1959, bolstered by evidence collected in the intervening months concerning the way in which refugees were actually treated under the Council's recommendation.   The proposal was accepted by the Manpower Committee, and on 9 May 1960 by the OEEC's Council which issued Rec. C (60) 65 (Final), that member states accord the same facilities as were granted to nationals to those refugees who wished to take up employment in another country and had the right to return to their country of residence.   The Recommendation provided for: the issue of entry visas free of charge, the granting of work permits and of residence permits valid for at least one year, and the exemption of refugees from the cost of health certificates and medical examinations.   In short it complemented the measure adopted by the Council in 1958 and thus further facilitated the movement of refugees from one member state to another to take up employment there.   When the OEEC was replaced by the OECD in 1961 the HC was gratified to have these measures regarding refugee travel for employment ratified by the new organization on 30 September 1961 (OECD/C[61] 41).

The Council of the EEC, whose decisions are considerably more authoritative for its six member states than are the recommendations of the OEEC or the CoE, carried the treatment of refugees one step closer to that of nationals in regard to travel for employment on 25 March 1964.   In the context of adopting a new regulation on the freedom of circulation of workers within member countries, the Council adopted a declaration of intention concerning the free circulation of refugee workers. According to the declaration, each member state of the Community was to give special consideration to the admission to its territory, for the purpose of taking up wage-earning employment, of refugees resident in another member state, with a view to granting such refugees as favorable treatment as possible. The UNHCR had hoped to achieve the complete inclusion of refugees and stateless persons within the new regulation on free circulation rather than their being the subject of a separate and less binding declaration. This was the course which, after UNHCR representations, the European Parliament, comprised of parliamentarians from the six member states of the Community, had adopted on 28 March 1963. But even the declaration finally accepted by the EEC Council was an advance; and it, in turn, led to a recommendation by the Consultative Assembly of the CoE to the Committee of Ministers that steps be taken to insure that refugees enjoy to the fullest extent possible in all member states of the Council the benefits of the six-nation EEC's new regulation on free circulation of manpower (Rec. 421 of 29 January 1965). Further action on this recommendation is still pending before the organs of the CoE, while the UNHCR continues to promote both additional action at the regional level on this matter and more complete implementation at the national level of decisions and recommendations already made by the EEC, the OECD, and the CoE.

Conventions Relating to Stateless Persons

It has already been pointed out that a stateless person is not necessarily a refugee; his reason for being outside his country of origin may not be due to a well-founded fear of persecution. But all refugees are by definition at least de facto stateless persons in that no state considers them to be among its nationals. De jure stateless persons, whether refugees or not, have been described as "rather an amorphous group" in that there are a variety of reasons for their lack of status. "There are those who are born stateless, i. e., persons born in jus sanguinis countries who do not derive a nationality from one of their parents (who are themselves stateless); persons who have lost their nationality without acquiring another in consequence of a change in their personal status, for instance by marriage; persons who have been deprived of their nationality by way of penalty or for political reasons; and lastly--and this is probably the largest group--persons who have become stateless in consequence of territorial changes. "8   In order to assist those refugees who are de jure stateless, the UNHCR has participated in those international activities that have sought to reduce present statelessness and eliminate future statelessness.   In addition, representatives of the UNHCR have been associated with international actions aimed at improving the status of existing stateless persons even though such persons, when not refugees, are outside the HC's mandate.   This association has taken place largely because of the expertise developed by the legal staff of the UNHCR in dealing with the problem of statelessness as it concerns refugees.

Despite the important progress brought about in this area by the drafting of the two multilateral instruments discussed here, there remains unsolved the plight of de facto stateless persons who are not refugees.   While both the Conference that adopted the Convention relating to the Status of Stateless Persons and the Conference that drafted the Convention on the Reduction of Statelessness also adopted recommendations urging contracting states to extend the provisions of these conventions to de facto stateless persons, the fact remains that this group has neither a recognized status in international law nor an international agency competent to provide it with international protection.

The Convention Relating to the Status of Stateless Persons (1954).   The 1951 Conference of Plenipotentiaries that produced the Convention Relating to the Status of Refugees was also charged with negotiating a Protocol concerned with the status of stateless persons.   However, the participants concluded that they lacked sufficient time to reach a conclusion on this matter and returned the question of stateless persons to the organs of the UN for further action. Thereafter, ECOSOC convened a special Conference of Plenipotentiaries to consider the draft Protocol relating to stateless persons, held in New York in September 1954.   The Conference discarded the proposed Protocol and instead adopted a Convention Relating to the Status of Stateless Persons which was opened for accessions on 28 September 1954, and entered into force almost six years later, on 6 June 1960, ninety days after it had been ratified by six states. 9 By 1972 twenty-six states had acceded to this Convention.

The Convention is modelled very closely on the 1951 Refugee Convention.   Most of its provisions parallel those of the earlier Convention, and it too sets forth in a number of areas the standards of treatment that are to be accorded to

de jure stateless persons by contracting parties.[10]   Such
persons are defined in the Convention as persons who are
not considered as nationals by any state under the operation
of its law (Art. 1).   In regard to a number of benefits and
rights, however, the Stateless Persons Convention is less
favorable than the 1951 Refugee Convention and certain provisions in the earlier Convention have no parallel in the
later one.   In particular there is nothing said about freedom
from penalties for unlawful entry (as in Art. 31 of the Refugee Convention), nor about prohibiting the expulsion or return of persons to countries of persecution (as in Art. 33
of the Refugee Convention).   Both of these points can probably be explained by the fact that, as Dr. Weis has pointed
out, "while fear of persecution is an essential element of
refugee status, this is not the case for stateless persons."[11]
Moreover, the Conference that drafted the Stateless Persons
Convention made the explicit declaration in its Final Act
that there was no need to include an equivalent to Art. 33
of the Refugee Convention, being of the opinion that that
article was an expression of a generally accepted principle.

The UN Convention on the Reduction of Statelessness
(1961).   The International Law Commission (ILC) of the UN,
as part of its examination of the question of "nationality,
including statelessness, " and in response to ECOSOC Res.
319 B III(XI) of 11 August 1950, between 1953 and 1955 prepared two draft conventions: one that would promote the
reduction of future statelessness; a second that would aim
at the elimination of all future statelessness.   Dr. Paul
Weis, Chief Legal Adviser to the HC, assisted the rappor-
teurs of the ILC in this task at their request.

The granting of nationality to individuals has always
been considered a matter within the exclusive jurisdiction of
each state regardless of the fact that the Universal Declaration of Human Rights contains the exhortation that "everyone
has the right to a nationality" (Art. 15[1]).   In order to
eliminate statelessness states will have to be brought to
recognize the Universal Declaration's exhortation as a binding principle of international law.   In so doing they will be
going substantially beyond what was asked of them in becoming parties to the Convention Relating to the Status of Stateless Persons; they will be committing themselves to accept
certain kinds of persons as full-fledged nationals entitled to
all the rights and benefits of that status.   In addition, they
will be giving up any rights they might have had to deprive
a person of his nationality if the effect of such action would

be to leave the person stateless. The members of the ILC and of the UNHCR's legal staff recognized that drafting a convention that would achieve these ends and yet be acceptable to a large number of states would be a most difficult endeavor. Both partial measures and all-embracing measures were included in the two ILC draft conventions.

At its Ninth Session in 1954, the GA considered the two draft conventions and decided that an Inter-Governmental Conference of Plenipotentiaries should be convened to conclude a Convention for the Reduction or the Elimination of Future Statelessness as soon as at least twenty states were prepared to participate in such a conference (Res. 896[IX] of 1954). It took almost four years to bring about notifications from twenty states to the Secretary-General that they were prepared to participate. The Conference on the Elimination or Reduction of Future Statelessness was convened on 24 March 1959 and a number of provisions for a convention were there agreed upon. But it required a second session, held in August 1961, to complete work on the Convention on the Reduction of Statelessness.[12] At both sessions of the Conference the UNHCR was represented by Dr. Weis.[13]

One of two basic legal principles serves as the basis for the nationality laws of most states: states tend to grant their nationality either to persons who are born on their territory, jus soli; or to persons, regardless of their place of birth, one or both of whose parents are nationals of that state, jus sanguinis. The approach adopted by the Convention in regard to eliminating future statelessness at birth has been summarized by Weis as striking a balance "between the obligations to be undertaken by jus soli and jus sanguinis countries: original statelessness is to be remedied by the subsidiary application of jus soli in jus sanguinis countries and, where this does not lead to acquisition of nationality, by the application of jus sanguinis by jus soli countries."[14] Additional articles clarify what have been at times controversial issues by specifying that foundlings shall acquire the nationality of the state where they are found, and that persons born on ships or in aircraft, wherever situated, shall be deemed to have been born in the territory of the state of the ship's flag or of the aircraft's registration.

Beyond the problem of original statelessness there is that of subsequent loss of nationality, whether as the result of individual action or inaction or as the result of state action. In Art. 5 the Convention covers all cases of change of personal status (e. g., marriage, divorce, adoption) so as to eliminate this as a cause of statelessness. Art. 7 contains provisions that seek to balance the desire to prevent statelessness and the aim of permitting the individual to sever his bond of nationality when he has recognized grounds for doing so, by enunciating a qualified principle that statelessness shall not result from a renunciation of nationality. The Convention contains an absolute prohibition against the deprivation of nationality on racial, ethnic, religious, or political grounds (Art. 9) which in the light of discriminatory individual and even mass denationalization in the past has been characterized as "a cornerstone of the Convention."[15] Deprivation of nationality on other grounds is permitted, however, so long as these occur by operation of law and on grounds existing in the national law of a contracting state and retained expressly by declaration. Furthermore, these grounds must be ones symptomatic of a breach of loyalty or the repudiation of allegiance to the contracting state (Arts. 7 and 8). Finally, concerning statelessness arising from territorial changes, whereby individuals have often lost their nationality in the past, the Convention requires contracting states to include provisions in treaties with other contracting states, and to endeavor to do the same when dealing with non-contracting states, ensuring that no person shall become stateless as the result of such a transfer of territory (Art. 10).

The Convention further contains provision (Art. 11) for the establishment of an international agency within the framework of the UN which will assist persons seeking to claim a nationality in relation to the authorities of the contracting parties. The body will have to be created, once the Convention has entered into force, by an action of the GA. The ILC drafts had made provision for the creation of an international tribunal as well, empowered to hear cases brought by the agency on behalf of claimants alleging a denial or deprivation of nationality in violation of the terms of the Convention. The Conference did not retain this proposal of the ILC however.

Despite the restrictions and conditions contained in the Convention that tend to limit the general application of its basic safeguards somewhat, the Convention on the Reduction of Statelessness can do much to remedy in time a distressing contemporary problem, that of the de jure stateless person. (Nothing is said in the body of the Convention concerning the de facto stateless.) But in order to come into force the Convention needs to be ratified by six states, followed by a delay of two years. As of 1972 only four states, the UK, Sweden, Norway and Austria, had acceded to it. But in that same year the HC stressed to his Ex. Com. the pressing need for further states to ratify this Convention, and, at his urging, the CoE's Committee of Ministers recommended to member states that they act on this matter without delay.[16]

Conventions with Special Clauses Concerning Refugees

In this category of international instruments there are two kinds of agreements within which some special provision affecting refugees have been included: treaties concerning extradition, and those concerning consular functions.

The European Convention on Extradition (1957). The jurisdiction of a state has always been considered to include all persons within its territory, but it may be defeated in exercising its consequential right to punish any of these persons for violations of its laws if they succeed in escaping to the territory of another state. However, the doctrine of state sovereignty is so important a part of international law that it contains an absolute prohibition against one state seeking to exercise its jurisdiction even over an escaped fugitive within the territory of another state. To further the ends of justice states have entered into bilateral extradition treaties which specify the circumstances and the procedures under which one state will surrender a fugitive from justice to the authorities of the other state. While these treaties originally were concerned with the return of political offenders, today the return of such offenders is generally exempted from extradition treaties. More specific generalizations as to the content of the doctrine of extradition are difficult to make as the mass of bilateral treaties on the subject vary considerably in content.

In order to bring about some degree of uniformity in this matter, the CoE promoted the drafting of a multilateral European Convention on Extradition which would supersede the bilateral agreements made between the member states of the Council.[17] The Convention contained in Art. 3 a provision that extradition shall not be granted if the party to whom the request is addressed considers the offence concerned to have been of a political nature; nor (at the request of UNHCR) where there are substantial grounds for believing that a request for extradition, made ostensibly for an ordinary criminal offense, is in fact for the purpose of prosecuting or punishing a person on account of his race, religion, nationality, or political opinion, or where the person's position might be prejudiced for any of these reasons. These provisions are important safeguards for refugees in upholding and strengthening the basic principle of non-refoulement being promoted by the UNHCR: that a refugee should not be returned to a territory where he has a well-founded fear of persecution on grounds of his race, religion, nationality, or political opinions. The provision exempting the extradition of a refugee in respect of an ordinary crime to a country where he may be subject to persecution has never previously been included in any international convention and is especially significant since there is often only a fine line between prosecution for "political crimes" and persecution for other reasons. This provision has been copied in several subsequent bilateral European agreements on extradition, and a very similar provision was adopted by the Commonwealth nations in 1966 as part of a scheme for extradition agreements within the Commonwealth.[18]

The HC was gratified when the Convention was adopted on 13 December 1957; with his encouragement there were sufficient ratifications to bring the treaty into force on 18 April 1960, and by January 1970 the number totalled ten.

The Office has taken a similar interest in the negotiation of extradition treaties elsewhere in the world, seeking to insure that the particular need of refugees to be safeguarded from political persecution is upheld.

The Vienna Convention on Consular Relations (1963). In accordance with GA Res. 1685 (XVI) an International Conference of Plenipotentiaries was convened in Vienna to draft a General Convention on Consular Relations; representatives of ninety-two states attended the conference, as did representatives of the UNHCR. Since most refugees are not de jure stateless but still possess a nationality, provisions relating to the protection of nations abroad by the consular officers of the state of their nationality would apparently apply also to them. At the request of the UNHCR a memorandum was circulated at the conference urging in effect that the consular function as it pertained to refugees be handled by the UNHCR.[19]

As a result of the HC's memorandum a proposal was made by the representatives of nine states that a Consular Convention include an article to the effect that a state was not obligated to recognize the consul of another state as entitled to act on behalf of a refugee from that state.   During the discussion that followed it was proposed that the article add that if a refugee wished to consult his consul he was entitled to do so; and the Greek representative suggested that reference could be made to the UNHCR's playing an intermediary role in such situations if necessary.   Little progress was achieved on these proposals as debate bogged down over whether or not a state had jurisdiction over all its nationals, refugees or not, abroad.   Deadlock resulted as the required two-thirds support could not be mustered for any proposal on this point, so the Conference members accepted a resolution not to take any decision on this question. 20

The outcome, marking one of the few failures of the UNHCR to get at least some action as the result of its efforts, left the state of international law regarding the relationship between a refugee and the consul of the state of his nationality unchanged, and also uncertain.   It is the hope of the UNHCR that further steps can be taken in the future to incorporate in bilateral and multilateral consular conventions provisions permitting refugees to take advantage of the international protection which is available to them, and insuring that national protection is not extended to them against their will.   Where it is up to the individual to choose which form of protection he wishes, states, it is hoped, will insure that the choice be made in complete freedom.

Conventions Extended to Apply to Refugees

There are a number of conventions that have been adopted since the advent of the UNHCR which would normally be applicable only to nationals of the contracting parties, but which have been specifically extended to cover refugees as well, by means of a special article or a protocol.   While such articles are an integral part of the conventions, the protocols are in the nature of optional amendments in that a state may ratify the convention with or without making the separate ratification of the protocol.   Where the effect of these conventions, if extended to refugees, would be to grant to refugees the same treatment as nationals of the signatory states in regard to some right or service such as social

security, then the UNHCR has assisted in their drafting and
has promoted their ratification by states.

Protocol No. 1 to the Universal Copyright Convention
(1952). At the Inter-Governmental Copyright Conference
which considered the Universal Copyright Convention in
Geneva during August and September 1952 under the auspices
of UNESCO, the UNHCR participated in order to urge that
in respect of the benefits of this Convention refugees should
be entitled to the same protection as the nationals of the country
of their habitual residence. The Conference decided not to include such a special provision relating to refugees in the body of
the Convention. Instead, it adopted on 6 September 1972 a Protocol concerning the application of that Convention to the Works
of Stateless Persons and Refugees. It provides that those persons
"who have their habitual residence in a state party to this Protocol shall ... be assimilated to the nationals of that state."[21] By
becoming parties to both the Convention and Protocol No. 1,
states would be granting rights to refugees in accord with the
principles enunciated in Art. 14 of the 1951 Convention relating
to the protection of the artistic rights and industrial property of
refugees.

The Protocol entered into force on 16 September
1955, and as of 1 April 1970 there were a total of fourteen
states parties to it.

The European Social Security Agreements. Art. 24
of the 1951 Refugee Convention includes among its provisions
the requirement that contracting states extend to refugees
the benefits of present or future agreements concluded between themselves concerning the maintenance of rights to
social security, subject only to the conditions which apply
to nationals of signatory states. It was in accordance with
this article that, on the initiative of the Belgian Government,
the CoE's Committee on Social Security adopted Protocols
in connection with the European Interim Agreements on Social Security by which the provisions of these agreements
would be extended to refugees as defined in the 1951 Refugee
Convention.[22] In the drafting and negotiating of these Protocols, the closest cooperation was maintained between the
UNHCR and the Secretariat of the Council, as has indeed been
the case in regard to all other questions relating to refugees.

The first of these Interim Agreements lays down the
principle that each contracting party will grant to nationals
of the other contracting parties the same social security

benefits relating to old age, invalidity, and survivors as it
grants to its own nationals.   This principle applies to both
contributory and non-contributory social security schemes;
however, invalidity benefits are payable only if the invalidity occurred in the country of residence.   The entitlement
to old age and survivor's benefits is made dependent on one
year's continued residence in the case of non-contributory
schemes.   Regarding social security agreements concluded
(or to be concluded) between individual contracting parties,
they are to apply also to nationals of other contracting parties to the Convention, in particular with respect to maintenance of rights acquired or in the course of acquisition,
and to the transfer of benefits (except for non-contributory
schemes).

The second Interim Agreement is very like the first
except that it covers a different area of social security--
namely sickness, maternity, death, employment injury, unemployment, and family allowances.   Benefits arising in
these areas of social security are to be granted to nationals
of any contracting party who are ordinarily resident in the
territory of another contracting party, except that in the
case of non-contributory schemes, there is a minimum residence requirement of six months.

The purpose of the Protocol to each of these two
Agreements is to extend their terms to refugees as defined
by the 1951 Refugee Convention.   Thus not only is equality
of treatment of refugees and nationals of their country of
residence concerning social security established, but refugees who have made social security contributions in more
than one country party to the Agreements will have these all
taken into account in calculating their benefits, and may--in
common with nationals--transfer acquired rights in regard
to pensions when moving from one contracting state to
another.

The basic principle of the European Convention on
Social and Medical Assistance is that each contracting party
will insure that nationals of the other contracting parties who
are lawfully present in its territory, and who are in need,
shall be entitled to social and medical assistance on a basis
of equality with its own nationals.   Social and medical assistance is defined as meaning all assistance which persons
without sufficient resources are granted as means of subsistence and care necessitated by their condition.   The Convention also provides that, subject to certain exceptions,

repatriation shall not be effected on the sole ground that the person concerned is in need of assistance. With the exception of the section designed to avoid repatriation of persons in need of assistance, this Convention is also applicable to refugees when contracting states become parties to the Protocol thereto. Thus the Protocol to this Convention is in conformity with the principle laid down in Art. 23 of the 1951 Convention.

The Convention and the two Interim Agreements as well as the respective Protocols were adopted by the members of the CoE on 11 December 1953 and opened for ratification. By January 1970 there were fourteen states parties to the Protocols on social security and thirteen to the Protocol on social and medical assistance benefiting refugees.

The ILO Convention Concerning Equality of Treatment of Nationals and Non-Nationals in Social Security (ILO Convention 118 of 28 June 1962). The UNHCR has been associated with the work carried out by the ILO in seeking to universalize the principle of equal treatment for nationals and non-nationals, including refugees, regarding social security rights and benefits by promoting the adoption of a general convention on this subject by all member states of the ILO. The first attempt to regulate this question in respect to all branches of social security goes back to the adoption of the Social Security (Minimum Standards) Convention by the ILO Conference in 1952. However, the part of that convention which concerned the equal treatment of nationals and non-nationals was recognized by the Conference to be only a partial solution to the problem, and the ILO Governing Board was invited to take further steps in dealing with the situation of the non-nationals. Following studies undertaken at the Governing Board's direction and the return of a questionnaire sent out to member states of the ILO, the Forty-Fifth Session of the ILO Conference discussed the terms of a proposed draft convention on social security rights for migrants in June 1961. At the following session, in June 1962, a Convention Concerning Equality of Treatment for Nationals and Non-Nationals was adopted, by a vote of 259 to one with 50 abstentions, and opened for ratification by member states.

The Convention covers the entire field of social security (except public assistance), but member countries may accept the obligations of the Convention in respect to one or more of the following branches of social security: medical care, sickness benefit, maternity benefit, invalidity benefit, old-age benefit, survivors' benefit, employment injury benefit, unemployment benefit, and family benefit. The Convention provides that a member country having ratified it shall grant within its territory to the nationals of any other member country which has also ratified it, equality of treatment with its own nationals under its social security legislation. Equality of treatment regarding the grant of benefits shall be accorded without any condition of residence as a rule, states the Convention, except that residence conditions of a specified time may be laid down in the case of benefits other than those the grant of which depends either on direct financial participation by the person protected or his employer, or on any qualifying period of occupational activity.

Art. 10 of the Convention specifically extends its provisions to apply to refugees and stateless persons without any condition of reciprocity.

The Convention entered into force on 25 April 1964 and there are presently twenty-two states parties to it.

With the adoption of the three European instruments on social security, and social and medical assistance, and the adoption of this ILO Convention, the UNHCR has turned its full attention to seeing that contracting parties implement to the full, both as a matter of domestic legislation and of administrative practice, the provisions of these instruments as they affect refugees. [23] There still remain two important problems to be dealt with in this field, however, which concern the UNHCR. While under a number of bilateral agreements as well as under the multilateral European Interim Agreements, refugees have been accorded equal treatment with nationals in regard to the accumulation of contribution periods earned in different countries and the transfer of pension benefits, no social security agreements have been concluded between European countries of first asylum and the main overseas emigration countries. And, of course, none of the existing agreements provide for refugees to benefit from periods spent and contributions made to social security schemes in their countries of origin.

Conventions of General Applicability

There is not space in this chapter to describe the great number of international agreements that have some impact on refugees because they affect all persons, both nationals and non-nationals, in some regard; nor even to describe the growing number of conventions and declarations in the area of human rights--an area of great interest to UNHCR. But it should be noted that staff members of the UNHCR have been associated with the efforts of regional organizations such as the CoE, and the OAS, as well as of the UN, to develop and codify man's basic human rights. For example, the Office cooperated fully in the planning and carrying through of Human Rights Year (1968) and welcomed the passage of the three Human Rights Conventions by the GA in 1965 and 1966.[24] The HC's interest in human rights, however, has always been grounded in the knowledge that refugees are, by definition, persons who have been deprived of basic human rights, and his consequent aim is that whenever possible the particular needs of refugees should be taken account of in the drafting of international declarations and conventions on human rights.[25]

Among the large number of conventions of general applicability there are two instruments with which the UNHCR has been particularly associated and which are of special relevance to refugees because they deal with problems to which refugees and their dependents are especially prone: that of certifying the death of missing persons, and that of collecting in one state maintenance obligations created by the courts of another state. Hence the inclusion here of the Convention on the Declaration of Death of Missing Persons, and the Convention on the Recovery Abroad of Maintenance Obligations.

The Convention on the Declaration of the Death of Missing Persons (1950). This Convention arose out of a memorandum submitted to the Secretary-General by the PCIRO on 3 June 1948, urging that action be taken to facilitate the provision of death certificates in the case of missing persons. The memorandum pointed out:

> In normal circumstances, it is easy to establish a person's death; hence a death certificate can be made out without difficulty. This is no longer true. Thousands of human beings have disappeared [in the course of WWII] without it being possible in the ordinary way to establish the fact of their death formally.... Failure to furnish such evidence of death gives rise to serious difficulties. Thus, for example, heirs cannot establish title and

so obtain possession of the property of missing
persons; a surviving husband or wife cannot re-
marry; and the guardianship of orphan children
cannot be definitely established.

Since in many cases these difficulties affected particularly
persons who came within the mandate of the IRO, and subsequently of the UNHCR, these two organizations were particularly concerned to see some international action to ease
the situation. The PCIRO memorandum led to a decision by
the GA (Res. 369[IV] of 3 December 1949) to convene a conference for the purpose of drafting and adopting a convention
that would regulate the issuance of death certificates for
missing persons. 26

The Convention, signed and opened for accession on
6 April 1950, established procedures whereby specified tri-
bunals could be asked to certify the death of missing persons; regulated the recognition of such certificates by other
contracting parties; and created an International Bureau for
the Declaration of Death (which was subsequently set up at
the European Office of the UN in Geneva) to act as a central
clearing house for persons seeking evidence to establish the
death of missing persons.

The Convention entered into force on 24 January 1952
on the ratification of two states, China and Guatemala. Because its subject matter was one of such special concern to
certain groups of refugees within the HC's mandate, Dr. van
Heuven Goedhart in 1952 addressed a joint letter with the
Director-General of the IRO, Mr. J. D. Kingsley, to governments expressing the hope that more of them would accede
to the Convention. 27 Thereafter additional states became
parties to it, although the number did not rise above eight
in all. Close liaison was maintained between the UNHCR
and the International Bureau established by the Convention,
and efforts were made to bring to the attention of concerned
refugees the provisions set down by the Convention.

Originally limited to a lifespan of five years, the
Convention was subsequently prolonged by means of a Protocol, so as to be valid until 23 January 1967, when it became
evident that it would not be possible to settle satisfactorily
all the cases to which the Convention might apply by its
original expiration date.

The Convention on the Recovery Abroad of Maintenance

Obligations (1956). The problem with which this Convention
is concerned arises when members of a family are separated
from the breadwinner due to his movement across a national
border either as a migrant or as a refugee, and the family
finds itself without his financial support. The breadwinner
may either have abandoned his family and be enjoying the
virtual immunity which exists by reason of legal obstacles
to effective prosecution in such cases, or he may find it
impossible to remit money to his family due to the restrictions imposed in a number of countries on the transfer of
funds because of a protracted shortage of foreign currency.
This kind of situation has become a social problem of international significance since WWII because of the mass movements of populations and the more frequent movements of
individuals. The UNHCR has been concerned with the situation because many of the families in need of maintenance
have been refugees. Thus from its beginning the UNHCR
participated in the discussions and the drafting of the texts
that led up to the adoption of this Convention, and since then
has promoted its ratification by states.[28]

The Maintenance Convention has its origins in an initiative taken by ECOSOC at its Fourteenth Session in August
1951 when it passed a resolution requesting the Secretary-
General to convene a Committee of Experts to formulate the
text of a model convention or model reciprocal law, or both,
concerning the recognition and enforcement abroad of maintenance obligations (ECOSOC Res. 390[XIV] of August 1951).
The UNHCR was represented at the meeting of the Committee of Experts in Geneva in August 1952, and urged that in
addition to making it easier for wives and children to collect support from husbands and fathers who have left them
to move to another country, the Convention should also provide for free legal aid to be made available in such cases.

The Committee could not agree to the inclusion of the
suggestions concerning legal aid, although in its report it did
appeal to the non-governmental humanitarian organizations to
continue their social services for indigent families and to
extend their arrangements for legal aid, and asked the Secretary-General to coordinate their activities in this field.
The Committee drafted both a convention on the recovery
from abroad of claims for maintenance and one on the enforcement abroad of maintenance obligations, the latter to
serve as a model for bilateral treaties or for uniform national legislation. At its Seventeenth Session ECOSOC resolved to transmit the findings of the Committee to member

states for their comments, and to ask the member states whether they considered it desirable to hold a conference to complete the drafting of a convention on the subject. Sufficient states responded affirmatively for the UN Conference on Maintenance Obligations to be held in New York in June 1956, and it was as a result of that Conference--in which again a UNHCR representative participated--that the Convention on the Recovery Abroad of Maintenance Obligations was opened for signatures on 20 June 1956. As of 1 April 1970 some thirty-two states were parties to the Convention and a lesser number had taken steps to facilitate the enforcement abroad of these same obligations.

Declarations and Conventions on Asylum

The fundamental importance of the principles of asylum and non-refoulement have been a concern of the GA since the inception of UN activities on behalf of refugees. Over the years High Commissioners have stressed how vital an element in the protection of refugees is international recognition of the right of an individual refugee to asylum and the corollary duty of states to grant asylum. To confirm this right and duty, they have sought again and again the acceptance of an international instrument legally binding on all states.

The UNHCR has played an important part in bringing about the adoption of several regional declarations and one crucial UN declaration, all of which recognize, in a limited form, the individual right to asylum. And it participated in the process that led to the adoption, in September 1969, of the OAU Refugee Convention which contains a similar provision concerning asylum that signatory states are required to recognize. Meanwhile, it continues to hope that "a legally binding international instrument will be drawn up" for all states to sign. [29]

While states in ever-increasing numbers have in fact accepted refugees seeking asylum from persecution, they have refused to admit that they have a duty to do so. And their refusal has taken the form of rejecting the inclusion of any provision that might establish such a duty in any international agreement that would be binding upon its signatories. [30] Attempts to include reference to an individual right to asylum in the Universal Declaration of Human Rights and in the 1951 Refugee Convention both failed, as described in Chapter 7.

The UN Commission on Human Rights had been charged, as early as 1947, with considering the inclusion of a right of asylum for individual refugees in an international instrument.   The Commission had sought, therefore, to do so in the Universal Declaration and considered the inclusion of the same right when it subsequently began drafting the Covenants on Human Rights.   However, some state representatives argued that there was no such right in international law; others argued that it was undesirable to try to impose on states in advance an obligation to accept whatever numbers and types of refugees might appear in the future. [31] It was moved and accepted during the Eighth Session of the Commission in 1952, therefore, that no reference to asylum would be included in the draft Covenant on Civil and Political Rights.   This outcome was reached despite a memorandum from the HC and the personal efforts made by the UNHCR's Chief Legal Adviser at the Commission's Eighth Session. The Office was disappointed at this setback and has sought reconsideration by the Commission on this point in subsequent years, but without success.   The Covenant on Civil and Political Rights which eventually passed from the Commission to ECOSOC and thence to adoption by the GA in 1966 did not contain a provision on asylum.

In 1957 a new and less ambitious tack was taken when at the instigation of France the Commission on Human Rights was asked to consider a draft Declaration on Asylum. [32] While legally speaking such a declaration cannot be more than hortatory as opposed to binding, experience with the Human Rights Declaration had shown that such declarations could in time come to approach the binding force of law. [33] While this lesser step was correctly calculated as being more acceptable to states than a convention on asylum, it still took ten years of continual effort, both within the organs of the UN and within influential regional and professional organizations, for the UNHCR in cooperation with sympathetic governments to move the draft declaration through the Human Rights Commission, ECOSOC, and the GA to adoption on 14 December 1967 as the Declaration on Territorial Asylum (GA Res. 2312[XXII]). [34]   The draft has taken three years to pass the Human Rights Commission, spent one year under consideration by ECOSOC, and then languished for almost seven more years in the GA.   It was debated by the Third Committee, then by the Sixth Committee, and by a special working party of the Sixth Committee, before finally being discussed for the last time by the GA at its Twenty-Second Plenary Session in 1967.   In the interim between each of

these discussions within organs of the UN, there were invariably requests made to governments for their comments
on pending drafts of the declaration, while resolutions were
adopted pledging final action on the instrument at the next
session of the GA.

Fully recognizing that even a truly significant declaration on asylum would require a virtually unanimous vote of
the members of the UN, the UNHCR early sought to stir interest and concern regarding this issue in as many ways as
possible.   In his annual reports to the GA and in his regular speeches to the Third Committee and ECOSOC, the HC
reiterated his hope for such a declaration and stressed the
need for it.   As High Commissioner, Dr. Schnyder noted to
the Ex. Com. (X) in 1963:

> I need hardly say how much we hope that a clear
> unambiguous text, constituting as it were the legal
> basis of a right which has not been embodied in
> an international instrument of this nature, will be
> adopted.   For, from the point of view of the ref-
> ugee, the right of asylum takes precedence over
> all others and should normally have its place
> among the many conventions or recommendations
> formulated under United Nations auspices. [35]

In addition, members of his Legal Division attended international meetings where asylum was a topic of discussion,
wrote articles on the subject, [36] and, most importantly,
sought to promote declarations on asylum by bodies other
than the UN.

In 1964, at the urging of the UNHCR as well as of
member states, the CoE resolved to charge its Committee
of Experts on Human Rights with considering the drafting of
a regional declaration on asylum.   The UNHCR was represented at the meetings of this Committee, and the HC himself emphasized the need for such an action in his speeches
to the Council's Consultative Assembly during this period.
The active concern of the UNHCR and others led the Committee of Experts to draw up a draft declaration on asylum
and submit it to the Council of Ministers in December 1966.
The adoption of that declaration by the Council on 29 June
1967 was a most important indicator of the liberal sentiments
of many European states experienced with the problems of
being countries of first asylum, and an important aid in mus-
tering support for the 1967 GA Declaration on Territorial
Asylum. [37]

In 1963, the United Arab Republic (UAR) had asked
the Asian-African Legal Comsultative Committee, an inter-
governmental advisory body of member governments in those
two continents, to include an item on the rights of refugees
in the agenda of its Sixth Session to be held in Cairo in 1964.
The Deputy Legal Adviser of UNHCR, Dr. Eberhard Jahn,
participated in the deliberations of the Committee, at its
Sixth, Seventh, Eighth, Tenth, and Eleventh Sessions, when
this agenda item was discussed.   Prince Sadruddin Aga
Khan, then Deputy HC, personally addressed the Committee
at its Sixth and Seventh Sessions, urging the adoption of
principles along the lines of the universally recognized UN
instruments relating to the status of refugees and to asylum.
The work of the Committee on this item led in 1966, at its
Eighth Session, to the adoption of a set of "Principles Concerning the Treatment of Refugees" which, to a large extent,
took into account the 1951 Refugee Convention and the Draft
United Nations Declaration of Asylum. [38]

In Africa, the UNHCR cooperated with the OAU from
1964 to 1969 on the drafting of a regional convention on refugees.   The central provision on asylum in that Convention
makes use of much of the phraseology that appears in the
UN's 1967 Declaration on Territorial Asylum.

In Latin America there is a long tradition favoring
the granting of asylum, and regional agreements exist which
spell out in considerable detail both the concept of diplomatic
asylum and that of territorial asylum.   The first of these
instruments was the treaty on penal law concluded in Montevideo in 1889 which contains a chapter on asylum; and since
then there have been concluded the 1928 Convention on Asylum in Havana, ratified by fifteen states; the 1933 Convention
on Political Asylum in Montevideo, ratified by fifteen states;
the 1954 Convention on Diplomatic Asylum in Caracas, ratified by eleven states; the Convention on Territorial Asylum
of the same year ratified by seven states; and the American
Convention on Human Rights, containing an article on asylum,
adopted in San José, Costa Rica in 1969.   In all of these
instruments, however, the right of asylum continues to be
described effectively as the right of states to grant asylum
at their discretion rather than the right of individuals to receive asylum.   For example, the 1969 American Convention
on Human Rights mentioning asylum says only: "Every person has the right to seek and be granted asylum in a foreign
territory, in accordance with the legislation of the state and
international conventions, in the event he is being pursued

for political offenses or related common crimes."39 The
one substantial development which has taken place within the
OAS with regard to the rights of refugees has been the inclusion in the 1969 Convention of a provision prohibiting the
deportation or return of an alien to a country where he fears
persecution--a provision which goes no further than did the
1951 Refugee Convention in recognition of the doctrine of
non-refoulement.

Even though the topic of asylum has been discussed
on more than one occasion by the Inter-American Human
Rights Commission, where the UNHCR has regularly been
represented by an observer, the long-standing division among
OAS members concerning the recognition of an individual's
right to asylum has continued to block the kind of legal development favored by the UNHCR.   Nevertheless, those
Latin American states that have long sought a regional convention on asylum as an individual right have had the opportunity through these discussions to reiterate their viewpoints,
and to express publicly their support for the kinds of innovative action being taken elsewhere.

Members of the UNHCR legal staff have also attended
a variety of meetings of non-governmental organizations
where asylum was a topic for discussion.   For example, the
matter was considered at the 1964 session of the International Law Association (ILA) at Tokyo, where Dr. Weis served
as a member of the Committee considering the legal aspects
of the problem of asylum.   The recommendations made in
the Committee's report led the Association to resolve unanimously that it was "Desirous of establishing the right of asylum of the individual in international law, in the light of the
current inadequate protection of human rights" and wished
the Committee to present draft rules on the subject at its
next international conference. 40   It required two further sessions of the Association, at Helsinki in 1966 and at Buenos
Aires in 1968, before the desire of the members was translated into agreed proposals concerning diplomatic and territorial asylum.   At both sessions the HC was represented.

The outcome of these efforts within the UN and elsewhere, as we have noted, was the unanimous adoption by the
GA in December 1967 of the Declaration on Territorial Asylum.   Three critical matters pertaining to asylum are dealt
with in the Declaration, and there are parallel provisions on
each of these matters in the OAU Refugee Convention, the
1966 Report of the Asian-African Legal Consultative

Committee, and the 1967 Refugee Resolution of the CoE (Res. 434). First, the act of granting asylum is a peaceful and humanitarian act and shall not be regarded as an unfriendly act by any other state. Secondly, the situation of persons seeking asylum is declared to be of concern to the international community both in the sense that international organizations can be involved in these situations, and in that states pledge to assist other states in lightening their burden when they find difficulty in continuing to grant asylum to refugees. Thirdly, the duty of states regarding the granting of asylum is spelled out in detail, including its limitations.

Much like the non-refoulement article of the 1951 Refugee Convention, the central provision of the Declaration on Territorial Asylum (and of the analagous regional instruments) prohibits the expulsion or return of refugees to states where they may be subject to persecution. The Declaration goes one very important step further, however: it also prohibits the rejection of a refugee at a frontier where the result would be to leave him in a country where he might be subjected to persecution. This "non-rejection" phrase, first used in the 1933 Refugee Convention, is a curious one, worded in the negative. It can be argued that the wording is such that none of these documents really recognizes an individual right to asylum at all but only expands the concept of temporary admission or provisional asylum which is a corollary of non-refoulement. A refugee may not be left in or returned to the country where he fears persecution, but he may find himself shunted to some third state or relegated to a legal limbo where he is physically present but has not been legally granted asylum and the rights that go with it. Even if this is as far as the Declaration goes its passage marks vital progress because it recognizes that right which is the most significant of all to a refugee--the right to get out of the country where he fears persecution into some other country. [41]   Admittedly, even that right is limited in these various instruments--with the important exception of the OAU Convention--by a provision that permits states to subject refugees to measures such as rejection at the border, return, or expulsion, for overriding reasons of national security or in order to safeguard the population, as in the case of a mass influx of persons. But in such cases states are asked at least to consider the possibility of granting to the persons concerned the opportunity, whether by way of provisional asylum or otherwise, of going to another state.

With the declaration by the GA of 1968 as the

International Year for Human Rights, the UNHCR made plans
to stress the special need of refugees for the recognition
and protection of their human rights--rights of which they
have by definition been deprived. The HC and members of
his staff continued to represent the Office at many international conferences and seminars held during that year in
order to encourage the greatest possible number of states
to accede to the various legal instruments directly affecting
refugees, and to promote consideration for the special legal
problems of refugees, most notably their need for asylum
and the fullest implementation of the principle of non-refoulement. Among those conferences in 1968 where support was
expressed for the adoption of an inter-governmental binding
legal instrument on the right of asylum was the Human
Rights Conference of Non-Governmental Organizations held
in Geneva in January, the Assembly for Human Rights held
at Montreal in March, and the Twenty-First Plenary Assembly of the World Federation of United Nations Associations
(WFUNA) held in April.

The HC was particularly gratified by the conference
action taken at the UN-sponsored Human Rights Conference
held in Teheran in May where, in response to the statement
and report submitted by the HC, a resolution was adopted
calling upon governments to accede to international agreements relating to refugees and affirming the importance of
the observance of the principle of non-refoulement and asylum. 42

In 1971 the Carnegie Endowment for International
Peace took the initiative to press for a broader and more
precise declaration on asylum. It organized in consultation
with the UNHCR a Colloquium on the Law of Territorial
Asylum. The Colloquium held in Bellagio, Italy, was attended by legal experts from fourteen countries and by the
HC and some staff members. They reviewed the question
of asylum in relation to international law and drew up a
number of articles for inclusion in an intergovernmental instrument on the subject. A further meeting of experts held
in Geneva at the beginning of 1972 elaborated the text of a
draft convention which puts the principle of non-refoulement
in the form of a broad and comprehensive legal obligation
(Annex 9.1). It also includes provisions concerning the
granting of asylum, non-extradition, the right of provisional
stay pending consideration of asylum requests and the right
of states to qualify the grounds for granting asylum. In
addition, it incorporates the principle of international

solidarity in alleviating the burden falling on countries which
grant asylum.   It further provides that the grant of asylum
constitutes a peaceful and humanitarian act and not an unfriendly action toward any other state. [43]

The HC forwarded the Draft Convention to the GA.
It was considered and discussed in the Third Committee of
the GA in 1972.   In the course of the debate, the Committee
felt that it was desirable that a Convention on territorial
asylum should be adopted under the aegis of the UN.   It
was, therefore, agreed that the HC would consult with governments on the matter and report to the next session of
the GA, with a view to paving the way for the convening by
the GA of a conference of plenipotentiaries.   In this way
the HC has sought to overcome the present anomalous situation whereby states "on the one hand continue daily to admit
new refugees in a true spirit of twentieth-century humanitarianism, while on the other hand, they stubbornly oppose efforts to put this situation on paper. "

Cooperative Action on Further Declarations Regarding Refugees

In order to better fulfill its Statute function of "promoting the conclusion and ratification of international conventions for the protection of refugees, " the UNHCR has always
worked closely with, and valued the cooperation of, certain
international and regional organizations which, inter alia,
share its concern for the legal status of refugees.   These
bodies include the two UN commissions particularly charged
with developing international law, the ILC and the Commission on Human Rights, and the ILO which shares a concern
for economic and social legislation affecting refugee labor
as well as, through its Joint Maritime Commission, a concern for refugee seamen.   The regional bodies with whom
the UNHCR has worked most often are the CoE, the OEEC
and OECD, the OAU, the OAS, the Asian Legal Consultative
Committee, and the International Committee on Civil Status.
While some aspects of this cooperation have already been
mentioned in setting forth the history of the major international conventions and declarations affecting refugees with
which the UNHCR has been involved, there are others that
also need to be detailed.

Personal contact has been maintained between the
UNHCR and these various groups: by the members of the
Office's Legal Division who have indefatigably attended the

sessions of any body when a matter relating to refugees was included in the agenda; by, on occasion, the HC or Deputy HC; and by the observers appointed by some of these organizations to attend meetings of the HC's Ex. Com. HCs have been pleased to accede to requests from the OAS, the OAU, the ILO, and the CoE that they be permitted to send observers on a regular basis to his Ex. Com. meetings. In the case of the CoE these ties are even closer, as it is customary for the HC to personally present an annual message and report to the Council's Consultative Assembly, for the Assembly to adopt a resolution in support of the HC's Program, and for observers of the Office to participate in the working sessions of the Council's various expert committees when refugees are the topic.

In addition to the recognition that has been given by the CoE to specific refugee problems in the formulation of regional conventions on social security, extradition, and the abolition of visas, its Consultative Assembly has twice reiterated its recommendation that the governments of member states incorporate clauses in agreements and conventions concluded or to be concluded in the context of European organizations to permit refugees within the mandate of the UNHCR and lawfully resident in the territory of contracting parties to these instruments to benefit from the facilities granted to nationals of other contracting parties under these instruments. (Res. 213[XIII] of September 1961 and Rec. 435[XVI] of October 1965.) Organs of the Council have also adopted recommendations and resolutions that

1.   Urged member states to become parties to the Hague Agreement on Refugee Seamen (Assembly Rec. 228[XI] of 1959)

2.   Recommended to member states that they relax statutory rules applicable to refugee doctors and dentists so as to enable them to exercise their professions in the countries in which they live (Assembly Rec. 253[XII] of 1960, and Res. [62]5 of the Council of Ministers)

3.   Recommended that action be taken to overcome the problems both of statelessness and multiple nationality (Assembly Rec. 87[VII] of 1955 and 194[XI] of 1959)

These recommendations led to the adoption by the Council of Ministers of the Reduction of Cases of Multiple Nationality on 6 May 1963 (43 ETS)

4. Recommended to member states that they facilitate the
    naturalization of refugees by removing certain legal ob-
    stacles, liberally interpreting other legal requirements,
    acceding to the 1961 Convention on the Reduction of
    Statelessness, and taking particular action for the bene-
    fit of refugee children. [44]

     As mentioned above, the Asian-African Legal Consult-
ative Committee played an important part in the development
of international refugee law in Africa and Asia. The Committee, established in 1956 by Asian states following the decisions of the Bandung conference, was subsequently expanded to African states. It has a permanent Secretariat in
New Delhi and gathers legal and judicial delegates of member countries for annual meetings where legal problems of
current interest are discussed with a view to forming a
common viewpoint of Asian and African states on these matters. The participation of the UNHCR at the sessions of the
Committee during which refugees have been discussed has
been valued all the more by the UNHCR since these sessions
have represented an occasion for discussing the status of
refugees among a great number of states which so far have
not acceded to any of the relevant international instruments.

     After preliminary deliberations in Cairo (1964) and in
Baghdad (1966) the Committee adopted at its Eighth Session
in Bangkok in 1966 a set of "Principles Concerning the
Treatment of Refugees," dealing with the definition of refugees, asylum, the right of return and the right to compensation, the minimum standard of treatment of refugees, expulsion, and deportation.

     These principles, besides creating a somewhat en-
larged refugee definition as compared with the 1951 Refugee
Convention, generally took into account the basic provisions
of the latter convention and of the then draft UN Declaration
on Territorial Asylum. In addition, the principles dealt
with the refugee's right of return to his country of nationality and the duty of that country to receive him, as well as
with the refugee's right to receive compensation from the
state which he has left or to which he is unable to return.
Still, at that Bangkok session the Committee did not see the
possibility of taking a position with regard to the question of
whether and to what extent the 1951 Refugee Convention
should be applied by member states. The Committee considered that "it would be up to the government of each participating state to decide as to how it would give effect to

the Committee's recommendations, whether by entering into
multilateral or bilateral arrangements or by recognizing the
principles formed by the Committee in their own municipal
laws. "

In 1967, the Government of Pakistan requested the
Committee to reconsider the "Bangkok Principles" in the
light of certain recent developments in international law, a
request which was supported by the Governments of Iraq,
Jordan and the UAR.   The UNHCR, which was also consulted, drew the attention of the Committee to the fact that,
since the adoption of the "Bangkok Principles, " a number of
new international instruments had entered into force which
called for review of these principles in the light of these
new developments.   At the Tenth Session in Karachi in 1969
it was not possible to give detailed consideration to the various suggestions made, but the Committee adopted a resolution on "Palestine-Arab refugees and other displaced Arabs"
and another resolution referring specifically to the 1967 Refugee Protocol, the UN Declaration on Territorial Asylum of
the same year, the recommendations made by the Addis
Ababa Refugee Conference in October 1967, and the then
draft OAU instrument concerning refugees.   The Committee
decided that the item should be taken up again at its next
session.

At the Eleventh Session in Accra in 1970, the Committee adopted a set of "Principles Relating to Displaced
Persons, " dealing mainly with the right of return and the
right to compensation.   The question of a review of the
"Bangkok Principles" was again discussed.   The Committee
was not able to come to final conclusions on this item, but
adopted a resolution expressing the view that "the above-
mentioned new instruments and recommendations made an
important contribution towards further development in international law relating to refugees" and requested the Secretariat to put the item on the agenda of its next session for
reconsideration of the "Bangkok Principles ... with a view
to bringing these Principles as far as appropriate in line
with the above-mentioned instruments and recommendations. "

It is not yet certain when exactly the refugee item
will be taken up again by the Asian-African Legal Consultative Committee, but the fact that the more recent international instruments and recommendations were generally viewed
positively by the Committee as important factors in the further development of international law relating to refugees is

certainly of importance for the HC's protection activities in the area concerned.

For a variety of reasons, neither the states of North America nor those of Latin America have ever been as interested in becoming parties to international conventions relating to refugees, as have for instance the European states. Both the US and Canada have tended to consider that their long-standing and liberal policies on the admission and integration of refugees made such ratifications superfluous--although both are now parties to the 1967 Protocol and Canada has also acceded to the 1951 Convention. As for Latin America, there has traditionally been a significant, though not large, number of Latin American nationals who have moved across national frontiers for political reasons. But they have not until very recently posed much of a problem either due to their numbers or to their needs. They have generally had sufficient means of support so as not to be a burden on asylum states; they have adjusted easily to life in countries where the culture, tradition, and language are much like their own; and they have tended not to sever all contacts with their countries of origin because they considered their exile to be temporary. Finally, because Latin American refugees have often maintained a strong, if not active interest, in the political affairs of their countries of origin, it would be very difficult for asylum governments to provide material assistance to them without running the risk of being accused of intervention in the affairs of a neighbor state. Thus until 1967 only Argentina, Brazil, Colombia, Ecuador, Jamaica, and Peru had adhered to the 1951 Convention and with the exception of Jamaica and Colombia, the other four contracting states had elected to interpret the Convention as covering only refugees resulting from events in Europe before 1 January 1951.

The problems of refugees come within the scope of two organs of the OAS: the Inter-American Human Rights Commission, and the Inter-American Juridical Committee, but in general both of these committees have been concerned with refugee problems only in as much as these pertain generally to human rights. Representatives of the UNHCR have attended as observers the meetings of the OAS Human Rights Commission held in April 1964, October 1965, November 1966, October 1967, and October 1969, where rights of refugees, in particular the matters of asylum and of travel documents, were discussed. In 1964 the Commission adopted a resolution demanding information concerning political refugees and inviting states to examine the possibility of issuing travel documents to refugees; a year later it recommended that travel documents like those provided for in the 1951 Convention be granted to refugees.   In November 1965 a special OAS conference requested the Inter-American Juridical Committee to plan a convention relating to refugees, but this work was never pursued.

It was only in 1967, with the passage of the 1967 Protocol and the appearance of very large numbers of refugees from Cuba, that the situation changed.   In that year the OAS Human Rights Commission finally recommended to member states that they ratify the 1951 Convention and 1967 Protocol, and since then Paraguay, Chile and Uruguay have acceded to both instruments and Argentina and Ecuador have ratified the 1967 Protocol.   The predominant refugee concern of the OAS continues to be in relation to the matter of asylum, however, and as indicated this concern has gone no further than to adopt a Convention on Human Rights which essentially restates the non-refoulement provision (Art. 33) of the 1951 Convention.

Dr. Eberhard Jahn has been the HC's representative at meetings of the International Commission on Civil Status (Commission Internationale de l'Etat Civil) which are attended by representatives of ten European countries.   At meetings held in Vienna in September 1965, at Strasbourg in April 1966, and at Athens in September 1966, discussions were held concerning the fuller implementation of Art. 25 of the 1951 Convention which requires signatories to arrange for the assistance of their authorities, generally through the provision of documents, to be afforded to refugees when the exercise of a right by a refugee would normally require the assistance of authorities of a foreign country to whom he cannot have recourse.   Dr. Jahn reviewed the special and often complex problems faced by refugees in matters such as marriage, adoption, registration of birth, and declaration of death, as a result of not having recourse any longer to the country of their nationality or prior residence.   The Commission, as a result of UNHCR suggestions, made three recommendations to member states at its 1967 session which would enhance the application of Art. 25.   The first asks governments to designate authorities in each country to issue the documents which would normally be delivered to a refugee by the authorities in his country of origin.   The second suggests that these designated authorities should have direct contact with one another, and the third provides for the international recognition of the documents so granted. These recommendations, if implemented, could assist in overcoming the continual difficulties experienced by refugees in proving aspects of their personal and civil status.

The especially close and fruitful interchanges that have taken place between the UNHCR and the OAU are the subject of a special section in Chapter 8.

Notes

1. These categories are adapted from those in Atle Grahl-Madsen, The Status of Refugees in International Law, Vol. I, Leyden, 1966: 32ff.

2. See Chs. 10 and 11 for developments in individual countries.

3. Text in ICLQ, 7(344), 1957; and Collection: 65.

4. Paul Weis, "The Hague Agreement Relating to Refugee Seamen of 23 Nov. 1957," Doc. MHCR/32/61: 7.

5. A/3123/Rev. 1: 20.

6. Text in 31 E TS and 376 UN TS 85; also Collection: 189.

7. For text, see Collection: 195.

8. Paul Weis, "The Convention Relating to the Status of Stateless Persons," ICLQ, 1961: 262; and see UN, The Study of Statelessness, Part II.

9. For text, see 360 UN, TS 117; also Collection: 87.

10. For a detailed discussion of its provisions and its drafting history, see Paul Weis, op. cit.: 255-64.

11. Ibid.: 260.

12. For text, see A/CONF. 9/15, 1961; also Collection: 109.

13. Dr. Weis has commented extensively on the problem of statelessness, the Conference, and the resulting

Convention in his article, "The UN Convention on the Reduction of Statelessness," ICLQ, II, 1962: 1073-96, on which the following discussion is based.

14. Ibid. : 1082.

15. Ibid. : 1084.

16. HC's Statement to Ex. Com. (XXI), 28 Sept. 1970.

17. For text, see 34 E TS; and 359 UN, TS 273.

18. See UK Doc. Cmnd No. 3008; and Weis, "The UN Declaration on Territorial Asylum," CYIL, 1969: 130-1.

19. See Annex 1 to A/AC.96/204 of 9 Aug. 1963 for the text of the memorandum.

20. For a longer account of the debate over this issue see Philippe Cahier and Luke T. Lee, "Vienna Convention on Diplomatic and Consular Relations," IC 571, Jan. 1969: 56-58; and A/AC.96/204 of 9 Aug 1963.

21. For text, see 216 UN TS 176; also Collection: 73.

22. European Interim Agreement on Social Security Schemes relating to Old Age, Invalidity and Survivors, and Protocol of 11 Dec. 1953 (12 E TS, 218 UN, TS 211); European Interim Agreement on Social Security Other Than Schemes for Old Age, Invalidity and Survivors, and Protocol (13 E TS, 218 UN TS 153) of 11 Dec. 1953; and European Convention on Social and Medical Assistance, and Protocol thereto (14 E TS, 218 UN TS 255) 11 Dec. 1953.

23. The UNHCR has also taken an interest in the drafting and adoption of a further instrument that, inter alia, concerns social security--the European Social Charter--which was drafted under the auspices of the CoE and opened for accessions on 18 Oct. 1961. But the Charter, which was drafted with a view to defining the goals of member states of the Council in the social field, does not directly benefit refugees; in its single reference to refugees it simply recommends that they be given treatment as favorable as possible with respect to the matters treated in the

Charter, over and above the rights provided in the 1951 Convention.

24. The International Convention on the Elimination of All Forms of Racial Discrimination of 21 Dec. 1965 and the International Covenant on Civil and Political Rights, and the International Covenant on Economic, Social and Cultural Rights, both of 21 Dec. 1966.

25. Such, for example, was the message of Prince Sadruddin Aga Khan to the International Conference on Human Rights held at Teheran, 25 Apr. 1968, Doc. MHCR/108/68.

26. For text of the Convention, see 119 UN TS 99; also Collection: 133.

27. A/AC.36/23 of 25 Mar. 1953: 24.

28. For text of the Convention, see 26 UN, TS 3; also Collection: 119.

29. A/7211, 1968: 11. For a comprehensive discussion of the right of asylum, see Otto Kimminich, Asylrecht, Luchterhand, Berlin, 1968.

30. The Conference which adopted the Convention on the Status of Stateless Persons of 28 September 1954 took the position on non-refoulement, which is the basic element of the right of asylum, that it was not necessary to include a provision on that matter in the Convention because it was a principle already generally accepted by states; UN Doc. E/CONF. 17/5.

31. UN Commission on Human Rights, Report of the Eighth Session, UN Doc. E/CN.4/699: 40. See also UN, The United Nations and the Human Rights, UN, 1968.

32. For an account of the "tortuous path" of the Declaration from initiation to final adoption, and an analysis of its contents, see Paul Weis, "The UN Declaration on Territorial Asylum," CYIL 1969: 92-149.

33. See E. Schwelb, "The Influence of the Universal Declaration of Human Rights on International and National Law," in Proceedings of the ASIL, 53rd

meeting, Washington, D.C., 1959: 217. Moreover, "A body of leading world authorities on human rights, meeting in Montreal, Canada, from 22 to 27 March 1968, declared that 'the Universal Declaration of Human Rights constitutes an authoritative interpretation of the Charter of the highest order, and has over the years become a part of international law';" quoted from William Korey, "The Key to Human Rights--Implementation," IC, 570, Nov. 1968: 8.

34.   For text, see Collection: 7.

35.   A/5511/Rev. 1/Add. 1: 13.

36.   See Paul Weis, "Territorial Asylum," IJIL, vol. 6, April 1966: 173-94; and Franz E. Krenz, "The Refugee as a Subject of International Law," ICLQ, vol. 15, Jan. 1966: 90-116.

37.   Res. (67) 14 of the Council of Ministers of the CoE. The text of Rec. 2 of the Res. is very much like that of the central provision, Art. 3, of the 1967 UN Declaration, although more clearly worded.

38.   See Eberhard Jahn, "The Work of the Asian-African Legal Consultative Committee on the Legal Status of Refugees," ZAORV, Vol. 27, Nos. 1-2, July 1967.

39.   Art. 22, par. 7.   For text see Collection: 263.

40.   The Res. is quoted in full in A/6011/Rev. 1: 5.

41.   Even before the Declaration on Asylum was adopted, Prince Sadruddin Aga Khan had stated in a speech in Oct. 1966: "Having regard to more recent developments [since 1951], the granting of asylum may to some extent already be said to be implied in the principle of non-refoulement, and it would seem now to be generally recognized that persons fleeing from persecution should be granted, at least, temporary asylum." Advance text of a lecture given by the HC at Copenhagen University, 20 Oct. 1966; UN Doc. No. 107/66: 6.

42.   Res. XIII of the Final Act of the International

Conference on Human Rights, UN Pub. Sales No.
E. 68. XIV. 2:   13.

43.   See Krenz, op. cit. :   109.

44.   CoE, Assembly (XXI) Rec. 564 of 1969 and Res. 70(2)
of Council of Ministers.

ANNEX 9.1

DRAFT CONVENTION ON TERRITORIAL ASYLUM
(15 January 1972)

PREAMBLE

The Contracting States,

Considering the obligation of States under the Charter
of the United Nations to promote universal respect for, and
observance of, human rights and freedom,

Recalling that the General Assembly of the United
Nations has solemnly declared that nations, irrespective of
their political, economic, and social systems or the levels
of their development should base their co-operation, inter
alia, on respect for fundamental human rights,

Mindful of Articles 13 and 14 of the Universal Declaration of Human Rights,

Recalling the Declaration on Territorial Asylum
adopted by the General Assembly of the United Nations on
14 December 1967, and recognizing the important advance
made by this Declaration in formulating principles upon which
States should base themselves in their practices relating to
territorial asylum,

Noting the present practice of States in granting asylum and the general acceptance of the principles of non-refoulement and the voluntary nature of repatriation, expressed
in various instruments adopted on the universal and regional
levels,

Believing that the conclusion of a convention based on
these principles will assist States to achieve those humanitarian objectives which are the common concern of the international community and will also thereby strengthen friendly
relations between States,

Have agreed upon the following articles:

I

GRANT OF ASYLUM, NON-REFOULEMENT AND NON-EXTRADITION

Article 1.   Grant of Asylum

1.   A Contracting State, acting in an international and humanitarian spirit, shall use its best endeavours to grant asylum in its territory, which for the purpose of the present article includes permission to remain in that territory, to any person who, owing to well-founded fear of:

(a)   Persecution for reasons of race, religion, nationality, membership in a particular social group, or political opinion, or for reasons of struggle against apartheid or colonialism; or

(b)   Prosecution or severe punishment for acts arising out of any of the circumstances listed under (a)

is unable or unwilling to return to the country of his nationality or, if he has no nationality, the country of his former habitual residence.

2.   The provision of paragraph 1 of this article shall not apply to:

(a)   Any person with respect to whom there are serious reasons for considering that he is still liable to punishment for

(i)   A crime against peace, a war crime, or a crime against humanity as defined in the international instruments drawn up to make provision in respect of such crimes;

(ii)   A serious common crime, or

(iii)   Acts contrary to the purposes and principles of the United Nations;

(b)   Any person who seeks asylum for reasons of a purely economic character.

3.   Asylum shall not be refused by a Contracting State solely on the ground that it could be sought from another State.

Article 2.   Non-refoulement

No person shall be subjected by a Contracting State to measures such as rejection at the frontier, return, or expulsion, which would compel him to return directly or indirectly to, or remain in a territory with respect to which he has well-founded fear of persecution, prosecution or punishment for any of the reasons stated in paragraph 1 of article 1.

Article 3.   Non-extradition

No person shall be extradited to a State to the territory of which he may not be returned by virtue of article 2.

Article 4.   Provisional stay pending consideration of request

A person requesting the benefits of this Convention at the frontier or in the territory of a Contracting State shall be admitted to or permitted to remain in the territory of that State pending a determination of his request, which shall be considered by a specially competent authority and shall, if necessary, be reviewed by higher authority.

II

INTERNATIONAL CO-OPERATION

Article 5.   International solidarity

Where, in the case of a sudden or mass influx, or for other compelling reasons, a State experiences difficulties in granting or continuing to grant the benefits of this Convention, other Contracting States, in a spirit of international solidarity, shall take appropriate measures individually, jointly, or through the United Nations or other international bodies, to share equitably the burden of that State.

Article 6.   Voluntary repatriation

If an asylee should voluntarily and in full freedom express his desire to return to the territory of the State of his nationality or former habitual residence, the State granting asylum and the State of the asylee's nationality or former habitual residence, as well as all other States concerned, shall facilitate his repatriation.

Article 7.   Co-operation with the United Nations

The Contracting States shall co-operate with the Office of the United Nations High Commissioner for Refugees, or any other agency of the United Nations which may be created for the purpose, as regards the application of the provisions of this Convention.   They shall in particular keep the Office, or agency, informed of all general implementing measures adopted by them and shall consult with the Office, or agency, regarding questions arising out of applications for asylum.

III

CHARACTERIZATION OF ASYLUM

Article 8.   Peaceful character of asylum

The grant of asylum in accordance with article 1, or the application of other articles of this Convention, is a peaceful and humanitarian act.   As such it does not constitute an act unfriendly to any other State and shall be respected by all States.

Article 9.   Right of qualification

Qualification of the grounds for granting asylum or applying the provisions of articles 2 or 3, appertains to the Contracting State whose territory the person concerned has entered or seeks to enter.

Article 10.   Régime of asylees

1.   States granting asylum shall not permit asylees to engage in activities contrary to the purposes and principles of the United Nations.

2.   Without prejudice to the provisions of regional conventions, a State incurs international responsibility for the actions of asylees to the same extent that it would be responsible for the actions of any other person living in its territory.

Article 11.   Good faith

All determinations and decisions called for in the

application of this Convention shall be made in good faith and with due regard to all ascertainable facts.

SOURCE: UNHCR, Geneva.

Chapter 10

REFUGEES IN EUROPE:
THEIR STATUS AND RIGHTS

While the legal staff at UNHCR headquarters is primarily concerned with the protection of refugees at the international level and with advising branch offices in the exercise of their legal functions, it is the branch officials who
bear the main burden of promoting the translation of international agreements into domestic legislation which is actually enforced, and of dealing with government officials on
behalf of individual refugees. Yet it is these activities which
form the core of the international protection function; without
them no international action taken for the benefit of refugees
can be truly effective. But the HC's representatives and
correspondents do not have the status of consuls in any
country. Their position and effectiveness depend very largely on their diplomatic skills and on the cooperation of the
relevant government authorities. Even though they are exercising the HC's authority under his Statute or under his
supervisory authority in accordance with the 1951 Convention, they can only succeed in assisting refugees by persuad-
ing governments to take the actions they recommend. Yet
the areas of their concern have political, economic, social,
and even religious implications at times, and involve a mat-
ter--the treatment of persons within the territory of a state--
which has long been regarded as exclusively within the domestic jurisdiction of states. It is in the light of these factors that activities of UNHCR personnel at the national and
individual levels affecting refugees in Europe must be viewed.

Activities undertaken by UNHCR officials at these two
levels can be divided into six categories depending on whether
they are for

1. Determining refugee status

2. Facilitating refugee movement

3.   Enhancing economic and social rights

4.   Promoting naturalization

5.   Securing legal assistance

6.   Administering the German Federal Indemnification Fund.

In the following sections the aims of UNHCR actions in five
of these six categories are shown in conjunction with the
legal position that exists, or the major legal developments
that have occurred, in European countries where refugees
have been granted asylum in substantial numbers.   The sixth
section concerns the origins and the administration of the
German Indemnification Fund, which has involved both the
headquarters and many BOs of the UNHCR around the world,
but grew out of negotiations conducted at the national level
with the Government of the Federal Republic of Germany.

          The legal position of refugees in European countries
is not yet everywhere identical with that of nationals.   It
differs from country to country but the years that have been
devoted by international and national agencies, public officials and private groups to improving the status of refugees,
and most especially the work of the UNHCR over the past
twenty years, has resulted in the agreement by most European countries to treat refugees in almost every way like
their own nationals insofar as economic and social rights are
concerned.   Further, the role of the UNHCR BOs in assisting in the determination of refugee status has helped to insure that the literally hundreds of thousands of persons in
need of asylum and of the benefits of refugee status have had
their needs recognized.

Determining Refugee Status

          The essential prerequisite for enjoying any of the
rights and benefits conferred by the 1951 Convention or any
other international agreement pertaining to refugees is that
the individual be determined to be a refugee as that term is
defined in the agreement.   In fact, in many countries the
1951 Convention definition is also the criterion used for determining to whom asylum will be granted.   The determination of refugee status or eligibility then is a decision of some
importance, yet there is no set procedure established in the
agreements for making this decision and it is the prerogative

of each state which is party to the agreements to conduct its own determination of eligibility. Recognition of refugee status by one contracting party, furthermore, does not bind other contracting parties although it will normally be accepted as a matter of international comity. The only exception concerns the issuance of travel documents where all contracting states agree to recognize such documents when issued in accordance with the Convention. As the document designates its holder to be a Convention refugee, persons travelling to other contracting states on such documents will be granted the status provided for by the Convention so long as they hold a valid Convention travel document.

The situation concerning eligibility or status is further complicated by the fact that the term refugee is defined differently in different international instruments. For example, while most of the regional instruments that relate to refugees adopted under the auspices of the CoE refer specifically to the definition contained in the 1951 Convention, there are other instruments such as the newly signed OAU Refugee Convention, which contain a considerably broader definition than does the 1951 Convention. With the adoption of the 1967 Protocol which changed the Convention's definition by eliminating its time limitation the question arose whether the variety of definitions should be allowed to multiply. (For one example of the effort made to amend an international agreement to bring it in line with the 1967 Protocol, see the case of the Hague Agreement Relating to Refugee Seamen.)

Because of the importance attached to the determination of refugee status, succeeding international agencies charged with the protection of refugees have paid particularly close attention to the determination procedures used by states, and in various ways and to a varying degree have been associated with these procedures. While eligibility determinations made by the UNHCR under its Statute are not as a consequence binding upon signatory states of the Convention, in a number of states representatives of the UNHCR play some role in the process that determines refugee status as the result of bilateral agreements entered into by either the UNHCR or pre-existing agencies such as the IRO and particular states. Elsewhere there may be no formal procedure, or the matter may be dealt with only when it becomes legally relevant as for example when travel documents are applied for or when deportation proceedings are being considered. [1]

An attempt will be made below to outline the main features of the procedures used for determining refugee status for the purposes of the 1951 Convention in a number of countries where the UNHCR is represented, paying particular attention to the role of the branch officers, and including legal arrangements relating to the admission, expulsion, and documentation of refugees. It is through its activities in this field that the UNHCR seeks to obtain for refugees that right which they need before they can enjoy any other--the right of asylum. To give some idea of the scope of such determination proceedings, the following figures indicate the number of persons who were recognized as refugees during selected years in those countries where the UNHCR takes part in the determination process. These numbers include those refugees who moved from one country of asylum to another, refugees who have lately arrived, and ones who, although residing for some time in the country, have only been formally recognized as refugees during the year. (The figures are taken from the annual reports of the HC to the GA in selected years.)

1958	29,900	1962	11,320
1959	24,000	1963	10,200
1960	16,232	1964	9,800
1961	16,000	1965	10,500

Austria. No special procedure for the determination of refugee status existed in Austria until 1956. Refugee status as such was not determined; instead different officials decided ad hoc on the refugee character of the person concerned for the purpose of the application of specific provisions of the Convention to him, without relation to the Convention as a whole and without there being the possibility of an appeal to a central authority. Negotiations were undertaken by the UNHCR with both the Allied control authorities and the Austrian Government to remedy this situation following Austrian ratification of the 1951 Convention in November 1954. (The Allied Commission was involved because by Four-Power Agreement it retained jurisdiction over prisoners of war and displaced persons for some years after WWII.) Following these negotiations an internal decree was issued by the Austrian Ministry of the Interior of 17 February 1956 (and amended on 29 March 1958) that established a comprehensive procedure for determining refugee status. Persons who crossed the border illegally and applied for asylum and persons who entered legally and subsequently applied for asylum were interviewed by security officials especially

appointed for this purpose. Originally this initial screening
took place in each province without the UNHCR's having the
right to interview the applicants, but the 1958 amending decree provided for eligibility advisers appointed by the
UNHCR to assist the security officials and to have the right
to be consulted when a negative decision was planned. In
November 1959, following the ebb of the tide of Hungarian
refugees, a federal eligibility center was established at
Camp Traiskirchen near Vienna and all persons seeking asylum were sent there for screening. UNHCR personnel were
permanently stationed at the new center thereafter, as well
as in the provinces with the greatest influx of asylum seekers. Under the 1956 decree illegal entrants determined to
be refugees were issued with certificates entitling them to
reside in Austria for six months subject to renewal, and upon
application would be issued a Convention travel document as
well. Administrative instructions which permitted the imposition of domiciliary bans on refugees whose presence constituted a danger to national security or public order, while
in accordance with Art. 32 of the Convention, caused difficulties for refugees and were as a consequence changed by a
decree of 1 October 1959.

The present Austrian eligibility procedure for refugees
is regulated by the Federal Law of 7 March 1968. The Law
has legalized the procedure, including the role of the
UNHCR, which hitherto had only been based on internal decrees. The UNHCR is to be informed of all cases where
the recognition procedure has been initiated, and is entitled
to express its views before a final decision is taken. Asylum seekers have the right to appeal against negative decisions, and the right to remain in the country until a final
decision on their status has been taken. And, as an additional advance, the Law expands the rights of refugees by
giving recognized refugees the right of residence within
Austria.

The established eligibility procedure could not be applied to the Hungarian refugees who poured across the Austrian border in 1956 and 1957 because of the numbers involved.
A special registration card was issued to these refugees by
the Austrian authorities, who agreed that in view of the circumstances under which this group had left its country of
origin, they would be considered as coming within the terms
of the 1951 Convention. This attitude, which was adopted as
well in most countries where Hungarian refugees coming
through Austria were given asylum, enabled the Austrian

authorities to carry out the registration of large numbers of the new refugees without delay. Those among the group who remained in Austria were subsequently registered and documented in the same way as other refugees in Austria.

An Advisory Council on Asylum (Asylbeirat), established by the Austrian Government to meet at monthly intervals or whenever necessary to advise the Minister of the Interior on questions concerning asylum policy and eligibility, began meeting in September 1965. The Council is composed of representatives of the Ministries of Foreign Affairs, Interior, and Justice, members of the Austrian Parliamentary Delegation to the Committee on Population and Refugees of the CoE, and the representative of the UNHCR in Austria, under the chairmanship of the Minister of the Interior. The Minister, before considering an appeal on a matter of eligibility or deportation of a refugee to his country of origin, may refer the case to the Advisory Council on Asylum and his negative eligibility decisions can be further appealed to the Austrian Supreme Administrative Court.

A special eligibility problem in Austria concerned the Volksdeutsche, refugees of German ethnic origin resident in Austria, who were excluded from the mandate of the IRO, although considered to be stateless refugees by both the Austrian and Allied authorities. The HC decided that they were within his mandate. [2] Volksdeutsche refugees in Germany, on the other hand, were specifically excluded from the HC's mandate and the Convention. When Austria enacted the Option Law of 2 June 1954, which permitted locally resident Volksdeutsche to acquire Austrian nationality, the question arose whether such refugees as did exercise the option should be disqualified from benefiting from the material assistance projects under the UNREF Program. The UNREF Ex. Com. agreed at its First Session that any refugee who was within the mandate on 21 October 1954 and subsequently opted for nationality under the Option Law could nevertheless be eligible for inclusion in the UNREF projects, but only during 1955. To act otherwise, decided the Committee, would discourage naturalization. [3] When the Austrian Government extended the deadline for exercising the option for nationality, the UNREF Ex. Com. decided that any person exercising the option should be included in the benefits of UNREF projects for one year from the date of his action, such eligibility not to extend beyond 30 June 1957. However, once accepted for inclusion in a project, such a refugee should be entitled to any benefits which it might provide, notwithstanding that the project might not be fully implemented within the one year period. [4] Volksdeutsche refugees in Austria opting for Austrian nationality would not be eligible for international protection however.

When by Art. 1 of the German Law for the Settlement of Questions of Nationality, enacted on 22 February 1955, German nationality was conferred on certain groups of Volksdeutsche refugees in Austria, the question arose again as to the effect of such legislation on the eligibility of such refugees under the Statute and the Convention. The Austrian Government ruled that all refugees coming within the scope of the German law who had not rejected the nationality conferred within the time period set by the law were no longer Convention refugees. The HC, acting on the advice of the UNREF Ex. Com., decided to exclude the same group from his mandate as concerned international protection, but to permit those within the group who would have rejected the nationality conferred had they been aware of the law before the 25 February 1956 deadline for rejection, to benefit from inclusion in material assistance projects under the UNREF program until 30 June 1957. [5]

Belgium. By a decree of 22 February 1954 the competence of the Belgian Ministry of Foreign Affairs to determine refugee status in accordance with the 1951 Convention has been delegated to the representative of the UNHCR in Brussels. While more than one European country turned over the function of determining refugee status to the IRO, Belgium is the only country where the UNHCR BO has continued to wholly exercise this function. On the basis of certificates issued after due examination by the BO, persons who are recognized as refugees under the Convention are accorded the rights and benefits attached to that status by the Belgian authorities. Before Belgium became a party to the 1967 Protocol, cases where the Minister of Justice--to whom all applications for asylum are first submitted--considered the applicant not to fall within the scope of the Convention due to its dateline of 1 January 1951, decisions on asylum were made by the Minister after consulting the Advisory Commission for Aliens. This Commission was composed of a judge, a lawyer of ten years standing, and a person experienced in the field of assistance to refugees. Since Belgian accession to the Protocol in 1969, arrangements have been made for the UNHCR to determine the eligiblity of all refugees in consultation, for certain special cases, with the Belgian authorities.

Executive ordinances issued for the implementation of the Law of 28 March 1952 concerning the Aliens Police, under which the Advisory Commission for Aliens was originally established, require that an expulsion order may only be issued against a recognized refugee after the advice of the Advisory Commission has been obtained. In addition, legal provisions ensure that the BO is informed of expulsion cases pending before the Commission and is thus able to make representations. Persons entering Belgium illegally and claiming refugee status are, according to these ordinances, to be granted a certificate that safeguards their position until their eligibility has been determined by the BO. These ordinances and the law to which they relate formed the subject of close consultation between the Belgian authorities and the UNHCR when they were drafted.

By a law of 14 March 1958 the Belgian Government further eased the burdens of being a refugee by ceasing to charge any fees for the issue and renewal of residence permits to refugees in the country.

France. The responsibility for the determination of refugee status which during its lifetime was carried out by the field missions of the IRO under agreement with the French Government, was taken over by the French authorities when the task of providing international protection was assumed by the UNHCR. The French Office for the Protection of Refugees and Stateless Persons (known by its French initials, OFPRA), created by the Law of 25 July 1952, is charged with the administrative and legal protection of refugees in France. The procedure for determining refugee status is laid down in Decree No. 53-377 of 2 May 1953, in accordance with which OFPRA issues two types of eligibility certificates, one to persons accorded refugee status but not entitled to the benefits of the Convention. Because France has declared that the words "events occurring before 1 January 1951" in the Convention's definition of refugee, were understood to mean "events occurring in Europe," refugees as a result of events occurring outside Europe and refugees as a result of events occurring after 1 January 1951 are given the latter certificate. OFPRA also provides recognized refugees with the documents needed to prove their personal status, which are recognized as official by the French authorities.

The representative of the UNHCR in France has a responsibility in connection with the supervision of the

implementation of all agreements concerning refugees in
France which is recognized by the law that established
OFPRA.   He is also a member of the governing body of the
French Office, as well as being one of the three members--
the other two being a member of the Conseil d'Etat and a
representative of OFPRA--of the Appeals Commission which
decides on cases where the French Office has refused recognition of refugee status.   The Appeals Commission is also
competent to examine the applications of refugees affected by
expulsion measures or measures restricting their freedom
of movement, and advises the Minister of the Interior on
their maintenance or cancellation.

       The Federal Republicy of Germany (West Germany).
The procedure for determining refugee status differs for
persons who entered West Germany prior to 30 June 1950
and for those who enter or have entered subsequently.   Refugees who were resident in West Germany before 30 June
1950 come under the provisions of the Homeless Foreigners
Act of 25 April 1951 and enjoy a more favorable status than
ordinary Convention refugees.   Homeless foreigners comprise in the main persons who could show proof that they
had been recognized as refugees by the IRO.   Their eligibility is determined by the local Aliens Police of their place
of residence.   The eligibility of newly arrived refugees not
eligible under the Homeless Foreigners Act was determined
in accordance with the Asylum Ordinance of 6 January 1953,
the Aliens' Law of 1955, and, after it came into force, by
the provisions of the Aliens' Law of 28 April 1965.   By
these three laws persons eligible for asylum are refugees
as defined by the 1951 Convention or as defined by Art. 16
of the German Basic Law (which includes persons not covered by the Convention due to the dateline of 1 January
1951).   Post-dateline refugees thus receive a status analagous to that of Convention refugees.   Persons recognized as
Convention refugees are issued with a travel document according to the provisions of the Convention as an identity
document, that of homeless foreigners being endorsed to that
effect.   Non-Convention refugees are issued with a German
travel document instead.

       Applicants seeking refugee status are directed to the
Federal Reception Center located until 1960 at Valka Camp
near Nuremberg, and since then at Zirndorf, where the
Federal Office for Recognition of Foreign Refugees is head-
quartered.   Until 1955 it was necessary for applicants to
appear in person, but in that year a procedure was adopted

whereby refugees who had entered West Germany since 1 July 1950 and whose residence had been authorized could apply for refugee status in writing. A similar procedure was adopted with regard to refugees who entered the Federal territory in Berlin and successfully passed a pre-screening process carried out in Berlin. Within the Federal Office there exist a pre-screening unit, several Recognition Boards, and a Recognition Appeal Board. In case of rejection by that Board, the case may be brought before the Administrative Court in Ansbach and thereafter before the higher Administrative Courts in Munich and Berlin. Applicants must be given the chance to contact the UNHCR for assistance, and a representative of the HC is entitled to be present at the sittings of both Recognition Boards and of the Appeal Board. The 1965 law provides for the participation in the recognition procedure of a Federal Commissioner as well, who is authorized to appeal against decisions taken by the Federal Office. The UNHCR was consulted by the German authorities during the preparation of both the 1953 and 1965 laws.

Over the years repeated efforts have been made by UNHCR BO's in the Federal Republic of Germany to have the eligibility procedures speeded up because in practice they had become very cumbersome. The legal assistance program financed by the UNHCR in the Federal Republic has always been larger than that in any other single country in part because of the need of refugees for legal counsel in submitting applications for eligibility and in dealing with the complicated procedure for appeals. In the case of Hungarian refugees seeking asylum in Germany during 1956 and 1957 the regular recognition procedures were suspended and these refugees were registered at transit camps where they were interviewed, provisionally recognized as Convention refugees, and issued with a certificate valid for four months. Once they had found a place of residence, however, the Hungarian refugees had to apply for recognition in the regular way, although they were not required to appear before the Federal Office in person.

In West Germany, the matter of expulsion orders is within the competence of the Länder without reference to the Federal Government. Noting the continuing practice of such authorities of issuing expulsion orders to refugees who entered the country illegally or have served prison sentences, officials of the UNHCR sought for several years either to have the practice discontinued altogether or at least to have the Office advised of such expulsion orders so that it might exercise its supervisory functions. While expulsion orders against refugees often cannot be executed, because such an action would violate the Convention's non-refoulement Art. 33, the fact that a person is under an expulsion order places him in a most irregular position. As a result of consultations between the competent authorities and BO personnel, instructions were issued in some Länder that such orders were not to be issued unless they could be carried out. Finally with the adoption of the 1965 Aliens Law some important safeguards were established with regard to both expulsion and deportation for all persons granted asylum. With respect to expulsion orders the Law goes beyond Art. 32 of the Convention, which permitted expulsion on the grounds of national security or public order, by limiting expulsion to cases where there are serious reasons for considering the individual a threat to public security or order. Currently a foreigner may not be deported to a country of origin where his life or liberty would be threatened on account of his race, religion, nationality, membership of a particular social group, or political opinion, unless there are serious reasons for considering him a danger to security, or if having been convicted in a final judgement of a particularly serious crime, he is considered to constitute a danger to the country.

Greece. Illegal border crossers requesting asylum in Greece are referred to one of the reception centers in the northern frontier region and are first examined by the competent police authorities. Thereafter, their status as Convention refugees is determined by the Minister of the Interior. In appropriate cases the UNHCR confirms whether or not the persons concerned are within the mandate of the Office.

Italy. An Agreement concluded between the Italian Government and the UNHCR on 18 February 1952, supplemented by an exchange of notes on 22 July 1952, established the procedures for cooperation between the two in determining the status of refugees in Italy. An Eligibility Commission consisting of two representatives of the Italian Government, one from the Ministry of Foreign Affairs and one from the Ministry of the Interior, and two UNHCR representatives, with rotating chairmanship, makes eligibility decisions based on the criteria of the 1951 Convention. All decisions must be unanimous. In April 1955 the Italian Government agreed to the establishment of an identical body to determine the eligibility of refugees arriving from Trieste, that commission to sit at Trieste where a transit camp for newly arriving refugees was established. There is no formal procedure for appeal, although the Eligibility Commission in Rome sometimes considers applications rejected by the Commission at Trieste, on appeal. Refugees recognized as eligible receive a residence permit, either permanent or renewable annually, and a travel document of the kind provided for in the Convention. From the establishment of the system, the Italian Government agreed that newly arrived genuine refugees who could give evidence of being self-supporting, would be left completely free to settle anywhere within Italy, while destitute refugees would be held in a reception center until arrangements could be made for their integration or resettlement.

Luxembourg. At the request of, and by arrangement with the Government, the UNHCR representative in Luxembourg determines the eligibility of refugees in that country in accordance with the 1951 Convention. The procedure differs from that in Belgium only in that documents of eligibility are issued by the Government, based on the findings of the UNHCR representative, rather than by the representative himself. Travel documents are only issued to refugees who are recommended by the UNHCR official. In expulsion cases, a decree was issued during 1955 according to which the UNHCR representative is entitled to be heard in expulsion proceedings against refugees, and the decision must be made in each case by the Government in Council after a formal hearing.

The Netherlands. Until 1955 the BO of the UNHCR in the Netherlands played no direct part in the determination of refugee status. However, in that year the Government requested the BO to establish certificates for refugees legally residing in the country, the possession of which would be necessary when applying for a Convention travel document or for any other facilities to which persons were entitled by virtue of their refugee status. The Office began issuing these "mandate certificates" during 1956, and the system was regularized by the issuance of a Royal Decree on 10 January 1957. Subject to that decree mandate certificates were required of all refugees whose residence in the country for three months or more had been authorized. Cases of refugees who arrived in the Netherlands illegally were examined by the Minister of Justice, in consultation with the Minister of Foreign Affairs and the UNHCR representative in the Netherlands. In cases where an application for status was rejected, or the withdrawal of refugee status or an expulsion order was being considered, the decision of the Minister of Justice--again in consultation with the UNHCR branch officer--could be appealed to the Standing Advisory Commission on Aliens, consisting partly of members of Parliament. The Commission also heard the views of the UNHCR representative, and the matter had to be reconsidered by the Government in the light of the advice given by the Commission. Since 1 January 1967, the procedures already described have been reaffirmed almost without change by the Aliens Law of 13 January 1965 and the Royal Decree of 19 September 1966, both of which entered into force in 1967. The new law makes it clear that all requests for admission as refugees, as well as the cases of all illegal entrants, are to be examined in the first instance by the Minister of Justice. The UNHCR was consulted in the preparation of this law.

Switzerland. Under Art. 69(b) of the Federal Constitution and Art. 21 of the Swiss Aliens Law of 1931, competence for the granting of asylum is entrusted to the Federal Council. In practice applications for asylum and recognition of refugee status are submitted to the Aliens Police of the canton in which the applicant is staying, from whence they are referred to the Federal Department of Justice and Police in Bern. In some cases applications are made directly to the Federal Department. Negative decisions may be appealed to higher bodies within the Department, and thereafter to the Federal Council. UNHCR headquarters maintains regular contact with the competent Swiss authorities in regard to general eligibility questions and individual cases. Beginning in 1961 Swiss authorities decided to make it possible for refugees to be released from control by the Aliens Police after five years residence instead of the statutory qualifying period of ten years applicable to aliens in general. On the basis of this release, favorable consideration can be given much sooner to applications for permanent residence permits by refugees, who will thus be exempt from the requirement of obtaining labor permits.

The United Kingdom of Great Britain and Northern Ireland. The procedure for determining refugee status in the UK has been worked out in practice rather than established by a specific law. The cases of persons seeking asylum are submitted to the Home Office where the determination is made by administrative officials, the final decision resting with the Home Secretary. It makes no difference if the person concerned is a Convention refugee or a refugee in a broader sense, as the definition of refugee applied by the Home Office can be very general. The Home Secretary also possesses the power to deport, and there was little in the way of an appeals procedure from negative decisions of the Home Secretary regarding either eligibility or deportation until 1969. Before that date an appeal against a deportation order was possible only where a person had resided more than two years in the country. Under provisions of the Immigration Appeals Act of 1969, an administrative appeals procedure was established to hear both claims to political asylum and claims against deportation orders, and the Act contains provisions for the participation of the UNHCR. The Committee on Immigration Appeals (the Wilson Committee) which recommended the new quasi-judicial procedure established by the 1969 Act received both written and oral testimony from the UNHCR representative in the UK and considered both the position of Commonwealth citizens and of aliens refused admission to or required to leave the country. More recently it has become the rule to ask the opinion of the UNHCR representative in the UK before a decision is made involving refugees or persons claiming to be refugees. [6]

Pursuant to a recommendation of the meeting of the Commonwealth Law Ministers held in London in 1966, several members of the Commonwealth have taken action to amend the Fugitive Offenders Act, 1881, which has remained part of the law of many Commonwealth countries. The Fugitive Offenders Act, 1967, in Britain, like similar Acts adopted in Australia, Swaziland, and Zambia, precludes extradition within the Commonwealth in cases where the person concerned may be prejudiced at his trial, or punished, detained, or restricted in his personal liberty by reason of his race, religion, nationality or political opinions.

Yugoslavia. A new Aliens Law was promulgated on 31 March 1965 which takes into account to a certain degree the special situation and needs of refugees. The law confers upon the Federal Secretariat for Internal Affairs the competence for deciding the refugee status of applicants, and specifies the grounds both for refusal and for withdrawal of that status. Provision is also made for the installation of and for assistance to persons recognized as refugees; for the establishment of reception centers for refugees pending their integration in Yugoslavia or resettlement elsewhere; and for the issuance of travel documents to refugees and stateless persons in accordance with the relevant international instruments, such as the 1951 Convention and the 1967 Protocol, to which Yugoslavia is a party.

Facilitating Refugee Movement

Refugees by definition lack an effective nationality and consequently do not have a valid passport. But in the modern world there are few national borders that can be legally crossed without a passport. Once granted provisional or permanent asylum the refugee is limited to the territory of the asylum state unless he can obtain some travel document which will be recognized by other states. Without such a document he cannot legally cross a national border whether for the purpose of resettlement, temporary employment, tourism, or for other personal reasons. The asylum state does not grant passports to refugees within its borders who are not its nationals: the passport has always been considered to certify only those to whom the issuing state extends its national protection. Since 1921 the solution to the need of refugees for travel documents has been seen as a special travel document, uniform in character and recognized by states generally, to be issued by states to persons within their borders whom they consider to be refugees. No state's protection accompanies these special travel documents; and the consular officials of the issuing state have no authority to intervene on behalf of refugees abroad holding such a special travel document. The "Nansen passport," the London travel document issued under the provisions of the 1946 London Agreement, and the Convention travel document (issued in accord with Art. 28 of the 1951 Convention), are all examples of such special refugee travel documents.

While contracting states of the 1951 Convention undertake to issue travel documents conforming to a certain style to refugees lawfully staying in their territory "unless compelling reasons of national security or public order otherwise require" (Art. 28), the UNHCR has found that in many cases there has been a considerable lapse in time between ratification of the Convention and actual issuance of Convention travel documents. For example, by 1962 only half of the signatories of the Convention actually issued the requisite travel document although all of them, and a number of non-signatories as well, were willing to recognize the travel documents issued by other signatory states to refugees. By 1970 about thirty-seven states parties to the 1951 Convention or the 1967 Protocol actually issued travel documents that conformed with the provisions of the Convention. In addition to urging Convention parties to draw up, print, and make available, travel documents for refugees, the UNHCR has encouraged the adoption of a format conforming to that of a specimen copy prepared by the Office in order to promote uniformity, and, as will be seen in the case of some African states, has actually printed quantities of the document booklet itself for distribution by the appropriate national authorities.

Over and above its continuing efforts to assure that all refugees in need of travel documents can obtain them, the UNHCR has sought the cooperation of governments in easing other travel restrictions and requirements that affect even refugees with valid and recognized travel documents. Governments have been urged: to waive visa requirements for refugees when they do so for foreign nationals, or in the alternative to eliminate or at least reduce visa charges; to enable refugees to obtain visas from consular authorities overseas without prior reference to central government authorities; not to apply any measure of frontier control to refugees which they do not also apply to foreign nationals. The signal success of its efforts in Europe along these lines is detailed in Chapter 9 as part of the consideration of UNHCR action on behalf of the European Agreement on the Abolition of Visas for Refugees of 1959.

Enhancing Economic and Social Rights

It has been generally accepted that while refugee status should be a temporary status, nevertheless it may be one that continues for many years. In order to make the lives of refugees as normal as possible until they receive some more regular status, more must be done than encouraging states to grant them asylum. For the benefit of both the refugees and of the countries which have received them, the refugees need to be integrated as fully as possible into the economic and social life of their new communities. In so far as this process is achieved by means of laws, it requires that states enact legislation assuring certain standards of treatment to refugees in regard to matters such as purchasing property, acquiring an education, practicing a religion, finding a job, opening a business, practicing a profession, gaining welfare assistance, security social security, and so on. The aim of the UNHCR has long been to see that in regard to these and all other economic and social rights refugees receive treatment as nearly as possible identical with that accorded to nationals by their own governments.

To the extent that the 1951 Convention is the source for the obligations undertaken by states to accord certain standards of treatment to refugees, the UNHCR has sought to make sure that the required standards are in fact applied to contracting states of the Convention and the 1967 Protocol. Further, where contracting states have made reservations to any articles of the Convention at the time of their signature or ratification--and the great bulk of these reservations have concerned the articles dealing with economic rights--the UNHCR has urged the rescinding of these reservations. And because in a number of regards the Convention does not require refugees to be treated equally with nationals, the UNHCR has encouraged the adoption of subsequent international agreements or measures at a national level that would confer a more favorable status on refugees.

Of the specific economic and social rights which have been of concern to the UNHCR, the three rights where it has been most difficult to achieve a liberalization of standards of treatment relate to social security, the right to work, and the practice of liberal professions. The steps undertaken by countries in Europe after consultation with the UNHCR to treat refugees more liberally in regard to these three particular rights form the subject of the following subsections.

Social Security. There have been fewer difficulties experienced by refugees in regard to social security than in regard to the right to work, as the latter is normally based on employment in the country rather than on nationality. The difficulties that exist in the field of social security relate to the transfer to one country of rights acquired or periods of time spent in another country. Art. 24 of the 1951 Convention requires contracting states to accord to refugees lawfully staying within their territory the same treatment as is accorded to nationals in respect of any social security scheme, and to include refugees among the beneficiaries of any bilateral or multilateral agreement concerned with "the maintenance of acquired rights and rights in the process of acquisition in regard to social security." It was in accordance with the latter requirement, which seeks to ensure that refugees can have the benefit of all the social security contributions they have made in whatever country when it comes time to receive the payments, that special steps were taken to include refugees with nationals as the beneficiaries of the multilateral agreements on the subject of social security entered into by members of the CoE in 1953, and by member states of the ILO in 1962. Art. 23 of the Convention also requires contracting parties to give the same treatment to refugees with regard to public relief and assistance as they give to their own nationals.

In Austria, as the result of two bilateral agreements entered into with the German Federal Republic in February and July 1953, Volksdeutsche refugees who were civil servants in their countries of origin and who on 8 May 1945 were entitled to pension payments from the German Reich or other German authorities, would receive pension payments in Austria in accordance with amounts received by Austrian civil servants; and social security rights acquired by Volksdeutsche refugees in private employment in specified countries of origin by the payment of contributions were recognized in Austria for the purposes of paying social security benefits under Austrian law. The German Government undertook to contribute to the expenditure resulting from the application of both these agreements by the Austrian Government. In 1956, the Austrian Ministry of Social Administration issued a decree making it possible for refugees who arrived during the winter when employment was difficult to find, to receive public welfare under a simplified procedure which obviated any delay. Thereafter, the Austrian authorities extended for successive periods, until 31 December 1962, the right of refugees in possession of an Austrian identity document to benefit from unemployment relief (as distinct from unemployment assistance, which is granted to refugees in the same way as to nationals).

In matters of public assistance and social security, refugees in Belgium enjoy the same benefits as citizens. Thus, for example, during 1956 Belgian authorities issued instructions that family allowances issued to nationals under the Belgian Social Security system were to be issued to refugees covered by the 1951 Convention as well. With the influx of Hungarian refugees, the Belgian Government decided to extend all social security benefits, including unemployment and sickness benefits, to all the new group of refugees irrespective of whether they had worked the 150 days required by law. Subsequently, the right to family allowances, normally reserved for those cases where children are brought up in Belgium, was extended first to Hungarian refugees and then to all refugees regardless of the location of their children. Mine workers, including refugee miners, suffering from silicosis have been permitted to benefit from a special retirement pension since 1960, provided that they have paid social security subscriptions for five years.

The special economic relationship which has been developing among the Nordic states of Denmark, Finland, Iceland, Norway, and Sweden impelled some of these states to make reservations to both Art. 24 and Art. 17 of the Convention, which would otherwise have obligated them to grant to all refugees the same benefits concerning social security and the same freedom to engage in wage-earning employment that were being accorded by each Nordic State to nationals of the other Nordic states. By a communication received on 25 March 1968 the Government of Denmark withdrew its reservations to Art. 24 entirely, thereby agreeing to be bound by all the requirements of that article on labor legislation and social security.

Refugees in France have continued to benefit from very favorable legislation in the field of public assistance and social security which practically assimilate them to nationals in these matters. As examples of how far this policy has been carried: the French Government has agreed, upon the suggestion of the UNHCR, that refugees be listed as candidates for low-rent public housing--a right previously reserved for French nationals; and during 1956 earlier decrees were extended to permit all refugee students to receive the social security benefits provided to French students under the law. Both of these actions go beyond the obligations assumed by France in becoming a party to the 1951 Convention.

In the Federal Republic of Germany, a new social security law promulgated on 16 April 1956 provided different treatment for German nationals and foreigners as regards unemployment benefits, but gave homeless foreigners (a class of refugees) the same rights as nationals. Other non-German refugees became entitled to these same benefits on 1 September 1956, after the European Social Security Agreements had come into force in the Federal Republic providing that they had resided there for at least six months. By an agreement drawn up with Austria during 1958, refugees who move from one of the two countries into the other may continue to draw disability or old age pensions in the country in which they settle. A new Aliens Pension Law passed in 1960 allows refugees to benefit in certain circumstances with regard to old-age, disability, and widows' and orphans' pensions in respect of periods of work completed in the refugee's home country.

The Government of Italy instructed the three Italian national insurance institutes in 1962 to extend to refugees in Italy the benefits of social security agreements concluded or to be concluded between Italy and other states having ratified the 1951 Convention. Moreover, the provisions of similar agreements concluded between Italy and states not bound by the 1951 Convention were also to be extended unilaterally to refugees, to the extent that such was possible. In a communication received on 20 October 1964 the Italian Government informed the Secretary-General that it had withdrawn the reservations it had made to Arts. 6, 7, 8, 19, 22, 23, 25, and 34 of the Convention, which list includes the article regarding public assistance.

Luxembourg undertook in 1955 to grant refugees the same unemployment benefits as nationals, which means, because these benefits are paid exclusively from public funds, that the country has exceeded in this matter the obligations contracted under the 1951 Convention. In 1959 invalidity pensions were granted to refugees after an identical work period with that required of nationals; while in 1960 family allowances (allotted beginning in 1958 to Hungarian refugees without regard to the required waiting period) were extended to all refugees, who now receive the same benefits as nationals of Luxembourg.

The Netherlands Government decided, in 1955, on initiating a new retirement pension plan for all nationals reaching the age of sixty-five, that refugees should benefit equally with nationals under the new law even though aliens normally would not be eligibile for the pension until they had resided for fifteen years in the country. An equally liberal position was taken by the Government in regard to the Act on the General Social Security of Widows and Orphans which came into effect on 1 October 1959.

Norway, which unlike Denmark, Finland and Sweden had reserved its position in regard to Art. 24 only insofar as certain laws relating to benefits for the disabled, and blind, and seamen were concerned, withdrew its reservations on 21 January 1954, within months of ratifying the Convention and as soon as the Government had amended the requisite laws so that thereafter refugees in Norway would receive equal treatment with nationals regarding social security. In

November 1966, the Government of Sweden notified the Secretary-General that it had withdrawn its reservation to Art. 24, par. 1(b), which had limited its obligation to accord to refugees the same treatment in regard to certain pension schemes as it accorded to nationals, and its reservation to Art. 24, par. 3, which had made that provision not binding upon Sweden. The latter reservation had originally been made in order to protect the special economic relationship developing between Sweden, Finland, and Norway. By rejecting its obligation under this provision, Sweden had made it possible to exempt refugees from the benefits which might be accorded to nationals of the other Nordic states in future agreements. To date there has been no withdrawal by Finland of its reservation to Art. 24, pars. 1(b) and 3.

On 4 October 1962, the Federal Parliament in Switzerland adopted a decree on the status of refugees with regard to old-age, survivors, and invalidity insurance. According to the decree, refugees are assimilated to Swiss nationals with regard to ordinary pensions in these fields. Provisions favorable to refugees with regard to extraordinary pensions and measures of rehabilitation as well as with regard to the payment of ordinary pensions to refugees who transfer their residence from Switzerland to another country, were included in the decree. Following the coming into force of the decree, the Swiss Government informed the Secretary-General that it had withdrawn the reservation to Art. 24 of the Convention made at the time Switzerland became a party to the Convention.

Right to work. There is no single right that is more important to the integration of refugees into their new communities than the right to work. And there is no better way of insuring that refugees do not simply remain indefinitely the objects of an international dole, but rather become participants in, and contributors to, the economic growth of the countries that have granted them asylum. The major effort of the UNHCR BOs in this field has been aimed at achieving the relaxation, in the case of refugees, of restrictions for the employment of aliens which exist in many European countries, as these have been a major device by which national labor markets have been protected from competition by aliens. In so acting the BOs are implementing Art. 17 of the 1951 Convention which provides that refugees shall be granted the most favorable treatment accorded to nationals of a foreign country as regards their right to engage in wage-earning employment, but that restrictive measures imposed on aliens or the employment of aliens for the protection of the national labor market shall not be applied to a refugee who was already exempt from them at the date of entry into force of the Convention, or who has been a resident for three years in the country, or who has a spouse or one or more children possessing the nationality of the country of residence. Some countries which have acceded to the Convention have made reservations concerning Art. 17, and these have been the subjects of consultations over the years with UNHCR officers.   Going beyond this, the BOs have sought to fully implement the recommendation also contained in Art. 17 that states assimilate the rights of all refugees with regard to wage-earning employment to those of nationals.   While some restrictions remain, progress has been achieved by the BOs in both of these endeavors.

The Government of Austria, when it ratified the 1951 Convention, made a reservation to the effect that portions of Art. 17 would be considered only as recommendations.   But with the encouragement of the BO in Vienna, administrative measures have been taken by the authorities which have exempted from the requirement of a work permit all Volksdeutsche refugees, all refugees entering Austria with the consent of the Austrian authorities for the purpose of family reunion, and all refugees who have been resident for three or more years in Austria.   (The final category was extended annually by decree to include subsequent refugees who had achieved three years residence until 1967 when a general decree was adopted granting access to employment to refugees automatically on completing three years of residence.)

In Belgium, the authorities agreed in 1960 to issue work permits for all professions, irrespective of the situation regarding employment, to refugees in Belgium within the mandate of the UNHCR who entered the country under group resettlement schemes.   The measure was estimated to affect some 10,000 refugees.   In 1963 the Government extended the liberalization and went beyond the requirements of Art. 17 of the Convention to grant work permits of unlimited duration to refugees who either fulfilled the Convention qualifications or had worked in Belgium for two years, and whose families reside with them in the country.   Beginning in 1966, refugees were permitted to apply for such permits themselves whereas in the past such applications had to be made by prospective employers.   And in 1969 Belgian authorities further decided to grant temporary work permits to persons for whom the process of refugee eligibility had been initiated.

At the same time that the Government of Denmark announced that it was withdrawing its reservations to Art. 24 of the Convention, on 25 March 1968, it also announced that it was partially withdrawing its reservation made to Art. 17, the effect of which had been to make that entire article not binding on Denmark. The Danish Government has now agreed to accord to refugees the most favorable treatment accorded to nationals of a foreign country as regards the right to engage in wage-earning employment, with the exception that they will not be entitled to privileges in this regard accorded to nationals of Finland, Iceland, Norway and Sweden. A similar reservation to Art. 17 by Norway has not yet been withdrawn; while Sweden has announced that it is ignoring the fairly minimal reservation made by its Government to Art. 17. Iceland and Finland have made no reservations to Art. 17.

In France, the Government declared at the time of ratification of the Convention that Art. 17 in no way prevented the application of the laws and regulations establishing the proportion of alien workers that employers were authorized to employ in France, or affected the obligations of such employers in connection with the employment of alien workers. In 1954 with the actual coming into force of the Convention, the French Government decreed that refugee workers fulfilling the conditions of Art. 17(2), particularly refugees resident for three years in France, would be automatically entitled to permanent work permits. Previously this permit had been available only to privileged residents who had spent at least ten uninterrupted years in France. Hungarian refugees received limited work permits soon after arrival and had the restrictions lifted in successive years until their permits were permanent and unlimited after three years residence. Beginning in 1969, French authorities decided to further relax employment restrictions by issuing temporary work permits to persons for whom the process of refugee eligibility had already been initiated.

Refugees who entered the Federal Republic of Germany before 1 July 1951 came under the provisions of the Homeless Foreigners Law and were treated exactly as nationals in regard to their right to work. A decree of 8 October 1954 applied to later arriving refugees and equally exempted them from the work permit requirement where they met the conditions laid down in Art. 17 of the Convention.

In Greece, non-ethnic Greek refugees continue to

require work permits as do all other aliens, and restrictive
laws on the hiring of aliens persist. But in 1961 the Greek
Government issued a circular to all Labor Offices in the
country instructing them to do everything possible to help
refugees find employment, and to issue them with work permits.

The Italian Government, upon ratification of the 1951
Convention, had made reservations to Art. 17 and Art. 18
of the Convention. But following negotiations with the
UNHCR BO in Rome, the Government agreed to provide work
permits to refugees included in UNREF programs for integration into the local economy in Italy; then to all refugees
who came within the scope of Art. 17(2) so long as they
were living outside camps on 27 March 1957; and finally to
all refugees who fulfilled the conditions of Art. 17(2). In
December 1963 the Italian Government further broadened the
categories of refugees who were to be granted the same
rights as Italian nationals with regard to employment.

While in Sweden a reservation has been made to Art.
17 of the Convention, the State Aliens Commission decided
in June 1953 that refugees would not be required to possess
work permits. In Switzerland, on the other hand, Art. 17
continues to be considered only as a recommendation by reason of the reservation made when ratifying the Convention.
But the Government there has stated that the competent authorities will make every effort to apply the provisions of
Art. 17 to refugees. The UK has maintained its reservation
to Art. 17 as well, one which exempts refugees from the
restrictions applicable to aliens as regards wage-earning
employment, but after four years of residence rather than
three.

Liberal Professions. Whereas most countries grant
labor permits to refugees, subject to certain limitations, for
wage-earning and salaried occupations and also for the independent exercise of crafts and trades, admission to the majority of the liberal professions has been virtually closed to
refugees in many countries because such admission is usually restricted to nationals and the 1951 Convention does not
prescribe a treatment more favorable than that accorded to
aliens generally. In a few countries, however, significant
measures have been taken towards liberalizing admission
criteria in this field, and a very important step has been
taken at the European regional level, particularly with regard to the medical profession.

The Austrian Government has long permitted the Volksdeutsche refugees who are lawyers, doctors, dentists, or
teachers, to practice their professions in Austria, provided
that they can meet certain conditions set up by professional
qualifying bodies and that they possess an Austrian diploma
or recognized foreign diploma. In March 1964, a law was
passed which permitted all refugee doctors who have obtained
their medical degrees abroad and who have been resident in
Austria for three years, to practice medicine even though
the conditions of reciprocity normally required may not be
fulfilled.

In Belgium, the law of 13 May 1955 provided that refugees studying medicine, pharmacy or dentistry at a Belgian
university, as well as refugees who had already obtained a
degree in one of these subjects from a Belgian university
would be permitted to practice their professions within Belgium even though they lacked Belgian nationality. In April
1967 further legislation exempted refugees from certain requirements in respect of the recognition of foreign academic
degrees and diplomas, particularly the requirement of reciprocity, while any refugee attaining a degree from a Belgian
university could by following a special procedure obtain recognition for that degree such that he could practice a liberal
profession within Belgium. A decree of the same time established that foreign diplomas of secondary education, including technical studies, would be considered equivalent to
Belgian diplomas, making it easier for refugees who had begun their education abroad to continue it in Belgium.

Refugees admitted to West Germany prior to 1 July
1950 have for many years been able to qualify for the practice of most liberal professions on the same conditions as
German nationals. By a Federal Ordinance of 5 June 1968,
this group was further benefited by receiving permission to
exercise the profession of pharmacist equally with nationals.
Refugee doctors having foreign degrees and medical students
upon graduation in the Federal Republic of Germany, regardless of when they entered the country, have since 1961 been
able to qualify through a special procedure for permission
to practice their profession as well.

On 26 May 1961, the Swiss Federal Council issued a
decree whereby all refugee doctors, dentists, pharmacists,
and veterinary surgeons (as well as refugee students in these
fields) who were admitted prior to 24 June 1960 with a view
to permanent residence would be allowed to take the Swiss

state examinations and subsequently to practice their profession in the country on an equal basis with Swiss nationals. This decree followed a similar one issued in June 1960 which applied only to Hungarian refugees.

Following consultations between the Secretariat of the CoE and the UNHCR, the Consultative Assembly of the Council adopted in September 1960 a recommendation concerning the position of refugee doctors and dentists in countries belonging to the Council (Rec. 253[XII]). The Assembly suggested the drafting of a European convention in which parties would undertake not to prevent refugee doctors and dentists from exercising their professions on grounds of nationality; grant them, as far as possible and without any condition of reciprocity, recognition of equivalence in respect of professional diplomas obtained in countries of origin; and facilitate by scholarships or otherwise such additional courses and examinations as might be necessary to fully qualify refugee doctors and dentists for local practice. At the same time, the Medical Women's International Association and the World Medical Association adopted resolutions along similar lines, urging their national member associations to promote measures designed to facilitate the admission of refugee doctors to medical practice. The Committee of Ministers of the CoE, to whom the Assembly's recommendation was addressed, did not take up the suggestion of a convention, but rather urged member states of the Council individually to undertake the steps proposed by the Assembly's recommendation. [7]

Promoting Naturalization

A basic assumption underlying all international action for refugees has been that it need only be temporary. It is assumed that each person who becomes a refugee will in time end that status either by voluntarily choosing to be repatriated to his country of origin or by being allowed to become fully integrated and eventually naturalized. The major purpose of international protection has been seen as providing refugees with a satisfactory interim legal status and paving the way for the termination of that status by voluntary repatriation or naturalization. For this purpose certain international instruments have been adopted, approximating the status of refugees in many respects, but not entirely, to that of nationals. In spite of this status, mainly regulated by the 1951 Convention, the refugee remains an alien who is subject to the relative political and economic instability which this inevitably entails.   He cannot expect to have full economic and social equality with citizens, nor to have their political rights, until he becomes a citizen as well.

It is generally recognized that the most satisfactory solution to a refugee problem is voluntary repatriation, and that is the possibility which is envisaged first.   There comes a time however when the hope of returning home is no longer realistic or when refugees are so firmly settled in a new community that they would no longer wish to return home even if they were able to do so.   Naturalization is then the only reasonable answer.   It is not possible to determine in advance how long it will take before this point is reached. Refugees must have a reasonable time to make up their minds, and countries of asylum need time to decide whether or not they will accept the refugees as citizens.   But refugees have much closer links with their countries of residence than do ordinary foreigners because they lack an effective nationality, and it has always seemed appropriate that their opportunities for gaining a new nationality should be made as easy as possible.   Art. 34 of the Convention makes this point by saying that "the Contracting States shall as far as possible facilitate the assimilation and naturalization of refugees."   The HC, both by reason of his statutory obligation to promote permanent solutions for refugee problems and as supervisor of the application of the Convention, has the duty to encourage governments to facilitate the naturalization of refugees.

In the new refugee situations in Africa and Asia, the question of the naturalization of refugees has not until fairly recently assumed any practical importance, though it will require full attention in the years ahead.   In the case of the traditional overseas countries of resettlement, mainly the Americas and Australia, refugees emigrate with the purpose of eventually becoming citizens of their new country-- as soon as this is permitted under its laws--and the country shares their desire.   No particular difficulty appears to exist in this respect since practically all these resettlement countries follow a very generous practice as regards naturalization.

The situation is different in Europe.   In certain countries refugees are accepted for temporary asylum only, pending their final resettlement elsewhere, so that the question of naturalization does not arise; but in other countries of first and second asylum there exists a tendency to consider naturalization not as an automatic right occurring after a certain period of residence, but as a favor to foreigners who have attained a certain degree of assimilation and who prove their attachment to the country concerned. Refugees who want to become naturalized in these countries are often faced not only with a very long residence period, ten to fifteen years is not uncommon, but also with restrictive administrative regulations imposing requirements which may be very difficult for a refugee to meet. In addition, there are still refugees in Europe who do not want to take the citizenship of the country of their asylum, giving rise to second and third generation refugee groups existing in some countries.

In order to promote naturalization the UNHCR has sought, through the cooperation of European states, to reduce the period of residence required for naturalization, expedite the administrative proceedings, reduce the costs, simplify the process, and free refugees from the requirement of a certificate of release from former nationality which exists under the laws of some states. Most often the efforts of the BOs have been directed towards assisting individual refugees to surmount the legal and administrative hurdles of the naturalization process. A substantial proportion of the legal assistance program financed by UNHCR and operated by a variety of voluntary agencies is aimed at facilitating this same process. But once in a while a major breakthrough occurs as new laws and administrative practices are instituted due in some part to the views put forward by the HC and his staff in the BOs.

In Austria, a law providing for the acquisition of Austrian nationality by refugees of German ethnic origin (the Volkdeutsche) by option, was enacted on 2 June 1954. It provided that refugees of German ethnic origin who established their residence in Austria between 1 January 1944 and 31 December 1949 and maintained their residence since 1 January 1950 could acquire Austrian nationality by declaration. The period for applying under the Option Law expired on 30 June 1956, and by the end of that year over 60,000 Volksdeutsche refugees in Austria had acquired that country's nationality under the terms of the law. Subsequently the Austrian Government requested its provincial authorities to ease naturalization by processing applications from foreign-speaking refugees without insisting on their producing expatriation permits from the authorities of their countries of origin.

The Austrian Nationality Act of 15 July 1965 has made it possible to reduce the period of residence from ten to four years if there are reasons particularly worthy of consideration, and the fact that an applicant for naturalization is a Convention refugee has been established as grounds for special consideration.

In Belgium, exemption from naturalization fees was extended to aliens including refugees engaged in the mining industry beginning in 1958.   In 1961 a law was adopted that greatly facilitated the acquisition of Belgian nationality by persons who were born or resident in the Congo (Leopoldville, now Kinshasa) or in the Belgian trust territories of Ruanda-Urundi.   According to this law, the stay of any persons including refugees in these African states for three years from the date of independence would be considered as a qualification for naturalization on the same basis as residence in Belgium.   The law of 28 February 1962 favored the naturalization of numerous refugee children resident in the country, whether born in Belgium or abroad, by permitting them to apply for nationality when they had completed five years of residence, so long as that residence began when they were less than fourteen years old.   Refugees generally are included in the category of privileged foreigners for the purpose of acquiring Belgian nationality by a law of 17 March 1964, which means that they may be naturalized after a residence period of three years, and that naturalization fees may be reduced under certain circumstances in the light of the financial situation of the applicant.

In France, an order was issued by the Ministry of Health and Population in October 1958 to the effect that refugee status should constitute a favorable element in the consideration of applications for French nationality through naturalization.

The Government of the Federal Republic of Germany enacted a Law for the Settlement of Questions of Nationality on 22 February 1955 which had the effect of conferring German nationality upon certain groups of Volksdeutsche refugees in Austria unless the grant was rejected by declaration made before 25 February 1956.   In the case of refugees within the Federal Republic, applications for naturalization are dealt with by the Länder authorities and are referred to the Federal Ministry of the Interior for final approval only.   However, the way was made easier for some refugees to acquire citizenship when, on 19 August 1957, a new federal law was enacted to promote the naturalization of foreign wives of German nationals and of former German nationals who had acquired another nationality after Nazi persecution. In addition, by an amendment to the Nationality Law of 1913 which came into effect on 19 December 1963, legitimate children of German mothers are now able to obtain German nationality at birth if they would otherwise be stateless--a provision which will benefit children of refugee fathers and German mothers born in Germany who would otherwise have been stateless.

In Greece, an amendment to the Nationality Act of 1955, Law No. 481 of 22 July 1968, waived the requirement of three years residence subsequent to the application for naturalization in the case of persons who have resided in Greece for at least eight years during the ten years preceding the application. These requirements do not apply to anyone born and residing in Greece, nor to the wife of a Greek who, having acquired Greek nationality by marriage, applies for official certification. This change in the law has made it possible for refugees, and especially those of Armenian origin, who fulfill the other conditions of the law to be naturalized at once.

During 1956 the Government of Italy instituted a special procedure which clarified the status of a number of refugees of Italian ethnic origin who had become Yugoslav citizens as a result of the Peace Treaty of 10 February 1947, by permitting them to reacquire Italian nationality. In 1968 the competent authorities in Italy decided no longer to require refugees to submit proof of release from their former nationality for the purpose of acquiring Italian nationality.

As a result of an amendment in 1959 to the Netherlands Nationality and Residence Act, widows and divorced spouses of refugees who possessed Netherlands nationality before their marriage can regain their nationality. A further amendment, which came into force on 1 October 1962, contains two articles benefiting certain refugees: one grants nationality to minors adopted by Netherlands nationals, and the second confers Netherlands nationality on any person who does not acquire the nationality of his alien father at birth but whose mother is a Netherlands national at the time of his birth. By 1964 a substantial number of the refugees acquiring citizenship each year were benefiting from provisions enabling refugees, in certain circumstances, to obtain naturalization free of charge or at a reduced fee in the

Netherlands, and from provisions permitting the reduction of the normal ten to fifteen year residence period to a minimum of five years where the applicant's assimilation within the country appears to be progressing satisfactorily.

The Federal Government of Switzerland has recently, with specific reference to Art. 34 of the 1951 Convention urging facilitation of naturalization, asked the Swiss cantons to give favorable consideration to applications for naturalization by Hungarian refugees whose status resulted from events in Hungary in 1956.

The CoE's Committee on Population and Refugees reported to the Consultative Assembly in September 1969 that there remained some 620,000 refugees in CoE member states, indicating that very substantial further steps needed to be taken by member states to facilitate the naturalization of refugees. [8] The report, drawn up with the cooperation of the UNHCR, concluded that the major impediments to naturalization continued to be the length of the residence period required, the condition of release from previous nationality, and the high naturalization fees. As a result of the report, the Consultative Assembly of the CoE and subsequently its Council of Ministers urged member governments to take a number of steps that would facilitate the naturalization of refugees, including acceding to the 1961 Convention on the Reduction of Statelessness, liberalizing their applicable domestic laws, and liberally interpreting those legal requirements they were unwilling to abolish. [9]

It was with the same aim of assisting refugees to acquire a nationality that the UNHCR became directly concerned with the drafting and adoption of the UN Convention on the Reduction of Statelessness of 30 August 1961. The object of that Convention is to reduce statelessness by requiring its signatories to grant nationality to certain groups of people, particularly children, who would otherwise be stateless. The Convention is of particular importance to the children of refugees who, due to the effective statelessness of their parents, would be de jure stateless at birth. Moreover, a resolution incorporated in the final act of the UN Conference that adopted the Convention on Statelessness contains a recommendation designed to facilitate the acquisition of an effective nationality by de facto stateless persons, many of whom are refugees, as well.

While the UNHCR has always sought to prevail upon

governments to facilitate naturalization, beginning in late 1968 particular attention has been paid to increasing the awareness of refugees of the advantages of acquiring the nationality of the country of their adoption. In Europe especially there exist within the refugee population certain attitudes which tend to resist the acceptance of a new nationality, even though most of them have fulfilled the period of residence required. Many of the refugees still hope that their exile may be temporary and that one day they may be able to return home. Furthermore, since they enjoy in general a rather liberal legal status they do not feel any obligation or any definite interest in acquiring a new nationality with all its obligations--such as military service. But as the UNHCR is now pointing out, naturalization is in the long run in the real interest of refugees. There is often a considerable difference between possessing a right and being able to exercise it. In the case of economic difficulties in a country it is a fact that priority of employment is likely to be given to nationals. Refugees who may do well in periods of economic growth find that their circumstances change when economic conditions become less favorable.

Adhering to the principle that refugee decisions must be arrived at voluntarily, the UNHCR does not under any circumstances try to force refugees who are unwilling to do so to apply for naturalization, even if there seem to be no valid reasons for their attitude. But the Office is seeking better ways to make clear to refugees that they have a moral obligation not to perpetuate a status for which there is no longer a need. The international community, which has assisted refugees when they have had difficulties and were in need, is considered entitled to expect that, when they have become established and qualify for naturalization, they take the opportunities offered and leave the limited international help available to the newcomers who do not yet qualify for naturalization. [10] For until they acquire a nationality or return to their countries of origin, refugees once within the mandate of the HC continue within that mandate by reason of the definition contained in pars. 6 and 7 of the Statute of his Office.

Securing Legal Assistance

While international protection is chiefly designed to promote measures to improve the legal position of refugees as a whole through international agreements, national legislation and administrative regulations, refugees also have individual and particular legal needs arising from their status as refugees which require individual legal assistance. This may be required in the form of legal advice, for refugees not fully acquainted with the laws and regulations of their countries of residence or with international rules governing their status; legal assistance per se, for securing their rights in administrative proceedings to work permits, social security pensions, recognition of foreign diplomas, naturalization, indemnification for Nazi persecution, and the like; or legal aid, for representation in court proceedings. In some countries special agencies have been created that assist refugees in their legal problems, or voluntary agencies seek to perform the same function. And in many countries refugees are eligible for free legal aid in some matters. Nevertheless, over the years an ever-growing number of refugees have also applied to the UNHCR and his BOs for assistance in personal legal matters.

The UNHCR has never been in a position to offer a full legal service to refugees. Its Statute discourages, though it does not necessarily bar, the provision of services to individual refugees by requiring that the activities of the Office "shall relate, as a rule, to groups and categories of refugees" (Statute, par. 2). Thus it has not been possible to win approval for the recruitment of legal staff in sufficient numbers with the necessary skills for this service as part of the administrative budget nor as part of the program financed through voluntary contributions. Furthermore, many of these legal services call primarily for the assistance of a lawyer practicing in the country where the refugee resides or where the legal proceedings take place.

Until 1957 the policy of the UNHCR was to give legal assistance to individual refugees only where their cases raised a general problem of legal protecting affecting a substantial number of refugees. "Nevertheless," as the HC's annual report in 1954 stated, "refugees who apply in person receive, whenever possible and within staff and budgetary limitations, advice on legal and other problems."[11] And the one legal adviser assigned to each of the BOs in Bonn and Vienna spent a substantial proportion of his time in providing help of this kind although he had other responsibilities as well. Other cases were referred by the branch officers, wherever possible, to voluntary agencies or other organizations under arrangements made with those agencies. Seeking to insure that every refugee did receive free legal advice

and assistance from specially qualified persons, branch offices regularly met with the existing voluntary agencies and
their legal advisers to coordinate their efforts, and sought
to assist in the setting up of appropriate bodies where they
did not exist.

In the Federal Republic of Germany and in Austria
legal counsellors were retained by a few voluntary agencies
for the purpose of assisting refugees, while the UNHCR BOs
in each country drew up a handbook for refugees in various
languages, and issued regular information bulletins explaining
the legal position of refugees and the authorities and organizations they might turn to for assistance. In Belgium, le
Centre d'initiation pour réfugiés et étrangers, an institution
created in 1953 by a group of Belgian organizations interested
in refugee problems, played a very valuable role in granting
legal assistance to refugees. In Greece two voluntary agencies, the Refugee Service Committee and the Greek Red
Cross, worked together to provide legal assistance to individual refugees; while in Italy legal aid was often granted by
the Assistenza Guindicale agli Stranieri. But by 1956, especially with the increased influx of refugees into Austria
(mostly from Hungary) and Germany, and with the reduction
of operations by some voluntary agencies in Austria, the HC
concluded that some new steps were necessary to provide
refugees with adequate legal assistance.

Considerable interest was shown in legal assistance
by the Conference of Non-Governmental Organizations Interested in Migration which set up working parties, where the
UNHCR was represented by an observer, that eventually
recommended the establishment of an International Center for
Coordination of Legal Assistance. The purpose of the Center, set up in 1958, was to encourage the establishment of
legal assistance services in countries where there was a
need, and to promote cooperation between such agencies because the nature of the legal problems of some refugees was
such that legal action was needed in more than one state.

On the basis of the generally recognized need, High
Commissioner Lindt won approval from the UNREF Ex. Com.
for a few small projects to be begun in 1957 for funding
legal assistance programs in Austria and Greece. Both of
these involved the UNHCR contributing to the salaries of a
handful of legal counsellors (often themselves refugees) who
would give day-to-day advice to refugees, and, in the case
of Greece, refer refugees in need of legal aid in court

actions to a panel of lawyers ready to give their services
free of charge.   Additional project funds were to be used to
defray stamp fees and court and other charges in civil cases.
A special contribution from the British United Nations Association to the UNHCR permitted the establishment of a fund
to pay lawyers' and court fees for refugees in Germany who
were in need of legal aid in court proceedings and could not
obtain it from other sources.

In 1958 and 1959 the UNREF Ex. Com. and its successor, the Executive Committee of the HC's Program,
agreed to the expansion of the legal assistance program and
its inclusion among the regular programs undertaken by the
UNHCR.   Contributions were thereafter made on a regular
basis for the provision of legal assistance to refugees through
counsellors employed by voluntary agencies in Austria,
Greece, Italy, and Germany (after the special fund was exhausted), and through funds intended to meet legal charges
of indigent refugees.   (Lawyer's services were generally
contributed without charge.)   A small contribution was also
made annually to the International Center for Coordination of
Legal Assistance in Geneva, which was run in close cooperation with the HC's own legal assistance efforts.   Attempts,
approved by the Ex. Com. to institute a similar program in
Latin America were less successful, and in the end the Office established a reserve fund at headquarters to be used
for the assistance of individual refugees with legal problems
elsewhere in the world.

At the suggestion of the Ex. Com. the HC in 1962 reviewed the need for continuing the legal assistance program. [12]
His conclusion, that the program should be continued, was
based on a finding that the need for such a service had not
ended and that the service was in fact complementary to his
material assistance programs and his international protection
function.   While some facilities for free legal assistance exist in nearly all countries, they do not in every case meet
the special needs of refugees for securing documentation,
overcoming language difficulties, and surmounting feelings of
fear and strangeness at being in a country other than their
own.   By solving legal problems the service of legal assistance also facilitates the permanent integration of refugees.
Legal assistance promotes the protection of individual refugees by securing them their rights within the country of asylum, and may obviate or lessen the need for material assistance where for example a right to a pension or to indemnification can be established.   The HC concluded:

> While the scope, extent and forms of legal assist-
> ance vary from country to country and require
> periodic adjustment to changing circumstances, in
> close consultation with the Governments concerned,
> the Programme as such must be regarded as con-
> stituting an integral part of the current tasks of
> the High Commissioner's Office. [13]

The HC's conclusion was accepted by the Ex. Com. and the
legal assistance program continues annually to take a relatively small but significant share of the Office's program
funds, the major cost continuing to be borne by voluntary
agencies and local associations. Some 5,000 to 7,000 refugees are now assisted by the program each year toward
achieving integration, resettlement, or repatriation. [14]

Despite the program of legal assistance and the guidelines established by the Office for the guidance of its BOs
in dealing with the legal problems of individual refugees, it
is very difficult to establish a clear line between assistance
and protection, and branch officers continue to find that the
provision of services to individual refugees is their single
most time-consuming task. When emergencies arise, when
local legal assistance is unavailable, when vital matters such
as travel documents, asylum, or non-refoulement are involved, or when the issue has diplomatic as well as legal
aspects, then branch officers of the UNHCR became involved,
whether the matter is one usually characterized as involving
international protection or legal assistance.

Administering the German
Federal Indemnification Fund

The immense human suffering inflicted upon millions
of innocent people by the National-Socialist regime of Germany gave rise, following WWII, to a number of legal measures aimed at affording at least some compensation for the
wrongs suffered. The most important of these measures
were the German Federal Indemnification Laws of 18 September 1953 and 29 June 1956. But these and other German indemnification laws treated some persecutees differently from
others: the extent of compensation varied under these laws
depending on the reasons underlying the persecution. Where
the reasons were the persecutee's race, religion or political
views, then indemnification was granted in respect of injury
to body and health and for deprivation of liberty.

Furthermore, dependents of the persecutee were entitled to
compensation for his death where such death was the result
of persecution.   But if the reason for the persecution was
the persecutee's nationality, then indemnification was granted
on a lesser scale and only in respect of a permanent injury
to body or health resulting in at least a 25 percent disability.   Surviving dependents of these persecutees had no claim
for indemnification.

The UNHCR regularly expressed its concern over this
discriminatory treatment of national refugees as opposed to
political refugees from National-Socialism and urged the
German Federal Government to amend the Federal Indemnification Laws.   The UNHCR was involved in the matter both
because its branch officers played an important role in certifying the refugee status of persons seeking to claim compensation under the indemnification laws, and because the welfare of such claimants was a matter that concerned the HC
under his mandate.   Although some changes were made in
the 1956 Indemnification Law as a result of UNHCR representations, the Office continued to urge the German Federal
authorities to eliminate the distinction between refugees persecuted on national grounds and other victims, in the matter
of compensation.   The breakthrough came following a UNHCR
proposal that a special fund be created, if the laws could
not be amended, from which payments could be made to
those refugee victims of persecution who did not receive
compensation under the law or who did not receive adequate
compensation.   The idea was supported by a number of governments, particularly the British Government, which also
expressed the desire that the fund be administered by the
UNHCR.   After numerous approaches by the HC to the German Federal Government, including direct discussions with
the German Federal Chancellor, Dr. Adenauer, the HC was
informed in October 1959 that the idea of such a fund was
accepted.   There followed a year of negotiation between
members of the German Federal Government and UNHCR
staff which concluded with the signing of an Agreement and
Protocol on 5 October 1960 establishing a UNHCR Indemnification Fund.

Under Art. 2 of the Agreement the German Federal
Government placed at the disposal of the UNHCR the sum of
DM 45 million ($11,250,000) to be distributed by the UNHCR
to certain persons who had been persecuted by reason of their
nationality in disregard of their human rights by the National-
Socialist regime.   In order to qualify for payments persons

had to have been refugees as defined by Art. 1 of the 1951
Convention on 1 October 1953, regardless of their subsequent
status or residence, and had to have obtained no indemnification payments under any other laws.   Surviving dependents
of persons who had died as the result of such persecution
were also eligible for indemnification under certain conditions.

Art. 1 of the Agreement provided that refugees who
had suffered permanent injury to body or health by reason
of their nationality would thereafter receive compensation on
the same scale as political and racial victims of persecution, instead of at a lesser rate.   This part of the Agreement was to be put into effect by the German Federal authorities who estimated that its implementation would result
in additional indemnification payments of about DM 50 million.   In the Protocol to the Agreement provision was made
for close consultation between the government authorities and
the UNHCR on both general questions and individual cases
arising under the Agreement, and for the Office to present
its views in cases where an application under Art. 1 was
rejected or where questions of fundamental importance arose.

A special Indemnification Section was established within the headquarters of the UNHCR to administer the Fund,
and a Consultative Committee was formed, composed of
representatives of voluntary agencies and of the refugees
themselves, to advise the HC, at his request, on matters
connected with the Fund.   In addition, an Appeals Board was
set up representing refugees, the voluntary agencies, and the
Office, to advise the HC on appeals against negative decisions taken by the Indemnification Section on applications received.   The GA at its Fifteenth Session authorized the regular budget of the UN to accept the costs of the legal and
administrative work involved in the implementation of the
1960 Agreement so that the whole amount of the Fund plus
interest could be devoted to the indemnification of the beneficiaries.

The procedure established for the administration of
the fund had two aims: to distribute the money on the basis
of the current need of the applicants as well as on the basis
of their past suffering, and to simplify the administrative
process so that payments could be begun as soon as possible.
But since it was not possible to know in advance how many
applications would be received and accepted, payments were
to be made in three installments: one when the application

was accepted, one when the total number of applicants accepted was known, and a final one when the residue of the Fund including the accrued interest would be distributed. With the very close cooperation of many voluntary agencies wide publicity was given to the Fund and its provisions, and refugees were encouraged to apply. The response was so large that the 31 December 1961 deadline was extended for three months, by which time almost 40,000 applications had been received. By far the largest group among the applicants were persons of Polish origin, followed by persons of Russian and Ukrainian origin; the most applications were received from people then living in the US followed by those in the Federal Republic of Germany, and in France.

The processing of applications, which in many cases required the Office to check with the files of the International Tracing Service in Arolsen and the Berlin Documentation Centre, and in other cases to examine voluminous documentation submitted by the applicants, took until 30 September 1964 when the HC declared the Fund closed so as to permit the final payments to be made in time for Christmas 1964. Of a total of 40,229 applications, 12,415 were decided positively; payments made as of 31 March 1965 amounted to $12,992,485, the amount available for payment having been increased beyond the original allocation as a result of interest accrued on investments and the revaluation of the Deutsche Mark in 1962. A small reserve was maintained in order to make payments where appropriate in cases still pending under the appeals procedure and the few cases in which screening was still in progress. The appeals against negative decisions totalled 3,652 by March 1966 and took until well into that year to settle finally.

Meanwhile further negotiations were undertaken by the UNHCR with the German Federal authorities, seeking compensation for persecutees who could not benefit from the earlier indemnification laws or from the UNHCR Indemnification Fund because they were not refugees on 1 October 1953. The Final Indemnification Law promulgated on 18 September 1965, which incorporated into law the 1960 Agreement with the UNHCR, also provided for compensation to be made to many of the persons previously not covered; by an exchange of letters with the HC in November 1966, the Federal Government agreed to provide the sum of DM 3.5 million ($875,000) for measures of assistance to those persons excluded from the 1960 Agreement between the Government and the UNHCR by reason of its 1953 deadline requirement for refugee status.   Implementation of the Supplementary Indemnification Fund began in December 1966; in August 1969 the fund was declared closed and all the monies distributed. Some 2,613 applications had been examined and favorable decisions made in 721 cases.   Payments to the beneficiaries totalled $867,620.

A third indemnification fund, the Residual Fund, has accrued from reimbursements made to the UNHCR by the German indemnification authorities in respect of applicants who succeeded with substantial claims in Germany after having received advances from the HC's Indemnification Funds. Under this Residual Fund applicants are considered who have not received indemnification from any other source.   An amount of $1,438,200 has been paid to 1,509 beneficiaries from this Fund as of 31 January 1971.

In addition to taking up the full time of a sizeable number of the HC's small headquarters staff for almost nine years, the handling of the two Indemnification Funds benefited heavily from the very considerable efforts made by a variety of voluntary agencies, "whose devoted participation was an essential element in the successful completion of this operation."15   During these same years since 1960 the HC has continued to be concerned with the carrying out of the obligations undertaken in the 1960 Agreement by the German Federal Government, especially to see that applications are settled as expeditiously as possible.   Questions have also been raised and settled concerning the exact scope of application of the Indemnification Agreement, and the action to be taken in regard to certain groups who had hitherto been unable to obtain indemnification.   By the end of March, 1971, a total amount of DM 214.5 million had been paid out under the terms of the above mentioned agreements to refugees who had suffered persecution by reason of their nationality.

A very large number of claims continue to await a decision, however, which has led the German Federal authorities, at the urging of the UNHCR, to approve an enlargement of the Federal Administration Office, the authority which adjudicates the claims.   There has also been in recent years a noticeable tendency towards a more liberal application of criteria by the Federal authorities.   While in 1968 the monthly average of positive decisions had been thirty-one, in 1969 it rose to fifty-three.   Cooperation on the completion of this program of indemnification is expected to take some additional years, during which time both voluntary agencies and the HC will continue to be involved in making representations on behalf of refugees before the appropriate German authorities.

Notes

1. For a consideration of both the legal nature of eligibility decisions and of the procedures used in European states for determining refugee status, see Paul Weis, "The Concept of the Refugee in International Law," JDI, Oct.-Dec. 1960: 928-1001.

2. A/AC.79/37 of 17 Apr. 1956: 1-2.

3. A/AC.79/22 of 17 Nov. 1955: 1.

4. A/AC.79/37: 9.

5. A/AC.79/41 of 12 June 1956: 28-30.

6. Grahl-Madsen, Status of Refugees in International Law, Vol. 1: 366.

7. Res. (62)5 of 1962.

8. The Committee's report is contained in CoE Doc. 2620, 16 Sept. 1969.

9. Rec. N. 564 of the Consultative Assembly, 30 Sept. 1969; and Res. (70)2 of the Council of Ministers of 26 Jan. 1970.

10. See UNHCR, note on the Naturalization of Refugees, Doc. MHCR 55/70, 21 May 1970.

11. GA (IX) Off. Rec., Supp. No. 11 (A/2648), 1954: 7.

12. His Report on Legal Assistance is contained in A/AC .96/157 of 28 Feb. 1962.

13. Ibid.: 11.

14. At times the assistance can achieve very substantial results indeed. For example, three of the legal counsellors in different regions of Germany succeeded during 1968 in obtaining retroactive indemnification

payments for refugees in an amount of $150,000.
One counsellor during the first half of 1969 obtained
$96,000 in retroactive indemnification payments and
$13,000 in retroactive pension payments for social
cases; A/AC.96/412 of 1969:   31-32.

15.   HC's Annual Rep. to GA(XX), Off. Rec., Supp. No.
      11, A/6011/Rev. 1, 1965:   7.

Chapter 11

REFUGEES IN AFRICA:
THEIR STATUS AND RIGHTS

While international protection has always been an important activity of the Office in Europe, only in recent years has it begun to attain a position of equal significance in Africa. The UNHCR has for some years encouraged the ratification by African states of international agreements relating to refugees, but its involvement with the provision of international protection at the national and individual levels has developed only in the recent past as the actual legal needs of refugee groups and individuals have developed in African asylum countries.

The most important need of refugees in Africa as elsewhere, asylum, has been granted freely by African states and has raised few important legal issues. Moreover, the overwhelming majority of refugees live in the subsistence sector of the economy where they seldom experience the kinds of legal problems that impede their economic integration into new communities. The two areas of the domestic law which principally affect them--the first relating to land use and ownership and the second to personal status (marriage, divorce, inheritance, etc.)--do not often differentiate between nationals and aliens so much as between members of one ethnic group and another. African rural refugees usually have had ethnic affinities with the people among whom they have sought asylum, with the result that their personal legal status is the same as that of the people around them. In other cases, legal status is ordinarily determined with reference to the traditional law of the refugee's tribe. Each man, as it were, carries his law on his back. The question of land use can be more of a problem when refugees are not settled among members of their own tribe, but even then the difficulties are comparatively minor since land for settlement is usually apportioned by the governments of asylum countries. Finally, there is an absence, at least in the

field of agricultural work, of legal obstacles arising from
regulations designed to protect national labor, as is the
case in Europe.   However, in several African countries
there are severe restrictions against the free movement
of rural refugees, and in a large number of African
countries it is difficult if not impossible for refugees to
become naturalized citizens.   With the exception of these
two matters, which are impediments to complete integration rather than to attaining economic self-sufficiency, refugees settled on the land in Africa have relatively little
need for international protection at present because they
have experienced few legal obstacles arising by reason
of their position as refugees.

However, within the period of UNHCR involvement in
Africa the legal situation of many refugees has changed.
The continent-wide drive to build unified nations and the effort to further economic development both require the creation of more complex legal systems.   One effect of this
process has been to differentiate increasingly between nationals and aliens to the detriment of aliens including refugees.   This is particularly the case in the monetary sector
of the economy where a growing number of skilled and unskilled refugees appear each year in search of employment
or education.   As the HC pointed out in 1967:

> The African state of today is developing into a
> modern state with an increasingly complex legisla-
> tion in respect to immigration, aliens control,
> social and economic rights, etc.   It is against this
> background that the legal problem of refugees in
> Africa must be seen and should be solved. [1]

For the skilled and educated refugees moving to the cities
the matter of an appropriate legal status is of the greatest
urgency.   Questions of residence permits, identity papers,
the right to work or to receive an education, social security, public assistance, and travel documents are of the same
importance to them as they have been to refugees in Europe
in like circumstances.

It is with the appearance of new laws and regulations
affecting rural refugees and, more especially, urban refugees, and with the appearance of new legal needs as refugees
seek greater integration into their new communities, that the
UNHCR has moved to emphasize that it has two functions to

perform in Africa as elsewhere: material assistance and international protection.   But in so doing the Office has been
affected by the legal basis which originally made possible
its assistance to refugees in the delicate political context of
contemporary Africa.   The basis for all UNHCR actions in
Europe, as concerns both material assistance and international protection, has been the Statute of the Office.   In acting under the Statute the UNHCR exercises an international
authority granted to it by the GA and recognized by states
generally.   In Africa, material assistance was what the governments originally needed and requested, and the UNHCR
has provided material assistance on the basis of the GA's
good offices resolutions.   Unlike the Statute, however, the
good offices authority can be exercised only when and for as
long as governments invite the HC to do so, and it applies
only to the provision of material assistance and other humanitarian initiatives.   At the same time, good offices does not
rule out the provision of international protection to those
refugees who come within the scope of the Statute.   But the
more recent and clearly valid assertion by the Office that it
had the obligation and the authority to extend its international
protection to mandate refugees in Africa went substantially
beyond the original good offices request of African governments and was a potential threat to the close relationship
that had developed between the governments and the Office. 2
Nevertheless the UNHCR has gradually expanded its international protection activities in Africa, and the steps taken by
the Office to promote such protection at the national and individual levels within the legal and political context of African refugee situations are the subject of this chapter.

While the legal needs of African refugees require
UNHCR action at the local level as well as at the international and regional levels, the division of activities at these
various levels between UNHCR headquarters and BOs has
not been as clearly demarcated in Africa as in Europe.
Members of the headquarters staff, particularly from the
Legal Division, have played and continue to play a prominent
role in protection activities at the national and individual
levels in Africa.

A major reason for headquarters involvement is that
on matters as politically sensitive as refugee affairs, most
African governments tend to make decisions only at the very
highest level.   On occasion it has taken meetings between the
HC or his immediate advisers and African governments or
heads of state before actions are actually taken for the legal

protection of refugee groups or even for some individual refugees.

An additional reason for headquarters involvement has been one of staffing. UN budgetary restrictions keep the number of UNHCR staff to an absolute minimum. In African countries the BOs are staffed by one or, at the most, two administrative officers with perhaps one or two secretaries. These small staffs have been kept very busy providing for the physical needs of refugees through programs of material assistance. As protection problems grew more numerous the Office found it difficult to substantially expand its legal staff in Africa without reducing staff elsewhere. Fortunately the changing character of international protection functions in Europe facilitated the reallocation of staff. By personnel transfer and subsequently by direct recruitment, the Office has been able to send legal officers to Africa for extensive surveys and consultations, to post officers with legal training as UNHCR representatives in Africa, and to establish two full-time legal positions: one for Eastern and Southern Africa at Dar-es-Salaam, Tanzania in October 1968 (the post was later transferred to Nairobi, Kenya); and a second at the BO in Kinshasa, Zaïre in 1969. As the need for international protection activities continues to increase, the Office plans to arrange for further legally qualified staff to be stationed in areas of the continent where the UNHCR is represented.

The periodic visits by senior officers of the UNHCR to a number of African states have served to supplement and reinforce the protection activities undertaken by branch officers by elevating the negotiations to a higher administrative level. The visits are also intended to extend the international protection function of the Office to a large number of African countries where there is no BO but where protection problems have arisen. In addition, these visits afford the Office an opportunity to inform governments in greater detail concerning their international obligations regarding refugees. Activities and legislation in other African states for the more liberal reception and treatment of refugees can be explained, and the point reiterated that states need no longer fear that the taking in and aiding of refugees will be interpreted as an unfriendly act against a neighboring state. Governments can be encouraged to identify the refugees within their borders and to take the actions necessary to permit their repatriation, their local integration, or their resettlement in other countries. Finally, in a continent where grave problems of communication still persist, these visits aid headquarters in pinpointing the nature and extent of protection problems so as to most usefully deploy its own limited staff.

While headquarters officials play an important part in the Office's total protection activities in Africa, a major role is played by the BO representatives themselves. Like branch officers elsewhere, they seek to promote accessions to international agreements relating to refugees, encourage the implementation of these agreements through the enactment of national legislation and administrative procedures, and find solutions for the legal problems of individual refugees. This last activity takes up a disproportionate amount of time in any country, but branch officials in Africa are finding their diplomatic skills being increasingly used in dealing with the comparatively small number of refugees with individual protection problems. The major reason why this particular activity is becoming such a time-consuming one in Africa, even though few refugees are involved, is that only about one-half of the major refugee-receiving states have yet taken steps to establish a legal infrastructure to deal specifically with the legal needs of refugees.

Even among those African governments that make any special recognition of refugee status, the majority tend to leave to the police, immigration officials, or local administrators such matters as the conferral of refugee status or its removal, the detention of refugees, or the restriction of their movements; and there is little direction or review by any specialized central government authority. When central governments do become involved in such matters the situation is often so highly charged politically that the decision is made outside the regular bureaucratic machinery. Too often the representative is left uninformed about decisions made regarding refugees by local governments, and is given no chance to make representations before those decisions are reached. Even when he finds out about a case, the representative may have great difficulty in discovering the appropriate officials or political leaders to whom to make his representations. The process has in many instances proved to be both time-consuming and frustrating, and yet it is an essential part of the role of the representative who is, as Dr. van Heuven Goedhart used to point out, a sort of consul for the refugee who has no consul. Efforts continue to be made by UNHCR personnel throughout Africa to gain greater recognition for the fact that the Office has both a material assistance function and an international protection authority, and to gain greater UNHCR participation in government decision-making affecting the status of refugee groups and individuals.

The general absence of governmental machinery especially charged with taking care of the legal aspects of refugee problems in Africa is one aspect of the widespread lack of refugee legislation. Only in Senegal has a law been enacted which deals comprehensively with the legal status of refugees. The Senegalese law includes a procedure for determining refugee status which is both centralized and semi-judicial; it provides liberal protection against expulsion or return and specifies a generous grant of social and economic rights to refugees accorded asylum in Senegal (see Chapter 42). Only four other refugee-receiving states have legislation specifically regarding refugees, but in each of these the law deals primarily with regulating the status of refugees and controlling their movements and activities, being concerned not with the rights to be accorded refugees so much as the obligations to be required of them. (See Tanzania, Chapter 41; Uganda, Chapter 43; Zambia, Chapter 45; and Botswana, Chapter 46.) In the great majority of African states, even those granting asylum to substantial numbers of refugees, the legal problems are handled as a matter of ministerial discretion, or under the provisions of broad immigration and aliens statutes intended to cover foreign nationals in general rather than the special situation of refugees.

This lack of administrative machinery and of refugee legislation stems quite naturally from the policy position of most African governments that refugees are a transitory phenomenon whose needs are material rather than legal, and which in that respect are met through the hospitality of the asylum state. In this period of strong nationalistic feeling there is a tendency for African populations to feel that such temporary residents can hardly expect to receive all the legal benefits of nationals. Then too, with the problems attendant upon economic development, particularly that of unemployment, there is opposition to sharing available resources equally with a foreigner who has his own country to which he will, in theory, eventually return. Finally, there is the matter of security. Constantly fearing, not without reason, that their borders are liable to penetration by trained foreign agents or armed groups seeking either their overthrow or the overthrow of neighboring governments, African governments are very wary of according generous rights to refugee

masses flowing into their territories. The preservation of
their newly-acquired independence, and the maintenance of
their internal and external security must, in their view, out-
weigh their desire to fully implement legal commitments.
Only with the gradual alteration of these policies and the attitudes which underlie them will the UNHCR be completely
successful in carrying out its role of promoting the international protection of refugees at the national and individual
levels.

The progress to date is not insignificant, however.
In the following sections, steps which have been taken by
African governments and the problems that remain to be
solved at these levels of international protection will be discussed in reference to:

1. Determining refugee status

2. Facilitating refugee movement

3. Enhancing the economic and social rights of refugees

4. Promoting naturalization.

Determining Refugee Status

Despite all the progress that has been achieved in
broadening the definition of the term refugee in international
agreements so as to better align the law with the actual
needs of displaced people, the crucial matter of interpreting
and applying the definition has always been left to the discretion of governments. No international agency can require
a government to recognize a particular person as a refugee;
and no international tribunal will reverse a government's
decision to refuse refugee status. Yet the UNHCR is also
authorized to decide who is and is not a refugee for the
purposes of administering its programs and of providing international protection, and is also empowered to supervise
the implementation by governments of the 1951 Convention
and the 1967 Protocol, which includes the way in which the
definition of refugee is applied. A UNHCR determination of
refugee status is not binding upon a government, which may
accord that status to anyone it chooses; but neither is a government's determination binding upon the UNHCR, which may
extend its international protection to persons refused refugee
status by a government, such as former freedom fighters.

In order to encourage the best application of the definition
and to avoid an unhappy situation in which the UNHCR and a
government disagree, the Office urges governments to establish a procedure for the determination of refugee status
which is as unbiased and divorced from political considerations as is the Office's own determination, and which permits the Office to make representation on behalf of the applicant seeking refugee status before the government body
empowered to decide the matter.

In European countries, where individual eligibility determination has always been the rule, various procedures
have been adopted which in the main conform to the semi-
judicial process preferred by the UNHCR. The HC's BOs
usually participate in these procedures, although the degree
of their participation varies from country to country. In the
new refugee situations which have arisen outside Europe and
more especially in Africa, it has not been necessary or even
feasible until recently for governments to resort to individual
eligibility determinations to any appreciable extent. Because
rural refugees tended to arrive in large numbers and were
often scattered over vast and remote areas, the administrative infrastructure could not carry out such a determination.
In these circumstances, when the flow became sufficiently
large so that some official determination was needed regarding the newcomers' status, it was decided to deal with the
problem en masse on the basis of the refugees' country of
origin or nationality. Because the groups in question dis-
played general features indicating refugee character, it was
possible for both the governments involved and the UNHCR
to consider members of these generally defined groups as
prima facie eligible, without raising considerations such as
fear of persecution, loss or refusal of national protection,
and so on in the case of each individual. This was particularly the case so long as the reason for making the determination was simply to specify who would benefit from certain material assistance programs authorized under good-
offices resolutions.

With the settlement of the refugees or shortly thereafter, some governments undertook the task of determining
specifically who was a refugee through the issuance of identity cards or permits to remain in the country.[3] In a growing number of African asylum countries including Uganda,
Zaïre, Tanzania, and the CAR, the UNHCR provides the
photographic equipment used as part of the process in making identity cards for refugees.

Whether or not a particular refugee-receiving state has specific refugee legislation, the process of determining individual refugee eligibility has been roughly the same. Through administrative decrees, classes of persons generally of determinable national origin or ethnic identity who have entered the country after a certain date are declared to be refugees. This means that they will not be imprisoned or returned to the country whence they fled simply because they entered the asylum country without proper papers or permission. They are, in short, exempted from the operation of part of the country's general immigration and aliens ordinances. It is then left to officials on the spot, either police, military, district officers, or even the staffs of voluntary agencies to decide which individuals come within the category of persons specified as refugees.

In African states which have refugee legislation the process of eligibility determination is more regularized and the discretion of determining officers more circumscribed, but most often it operates in the same way. In Tanzania, for example, following the procedure set forth in the relevant statute, the term refugee has been decreed to include persons ordinarily resident in Congo (Brazzaville), Zaïre, Malawi, Mozambique, Rwanda, or the Republic of South Africa, who have entered Tanzania after various established dates by methods other than in accordance with the provisions of the Immigration Act of 1963. [4] The same result has been achieved in Burundi through the issuance of a decree which defines as "Congolese refugees" simply "those persons of Congolese nationality who enter Burundi whether or not in conformity with the Immigration Law of 1 Sept. 1962, and who voluntarily claim the status of refugee."[5] A somewhat more rigorously worded decree two years earlier had defined Rwandese refugees as "persons leaving Rwanda who, after 1 Jan. 1959, have obtained asylum in Burundi, and who cannot or do not wish to claim the protection of the Rwandese authorities, or who cannot or do not wish to return to Rwanda."[6] There are two important exceptions in the matter of eligibility determination. In Senegal and in Botswana the applicable refugee statutes do not make use of a determination process based on national origin, but rather incorporate into their domestic legislation the definition of the term refugee which is found in the 1967 Protocol. [7]

While definitions based on nationality or country of origin hark back to those used in international arrangements and agreements concluded between the world wars for the

establishment of refugee status, and reflect an "open door"
asylum policy, there is another side to the coin. With the
exception of the law in Senegal, the purpose of African refugee legislation is--as the statutory titles indicate--the regulation and control of refugees to whom asylum has been
granted. The more general the definition used, the more
easily the governments concerned can insure that they have
the authority to control the presence and activities of aliens
within their territory in defense of their national security.
Thus in Uganda, Tanzania, and Zambia the onus is upon the
individual to prove that he is not a refugee--and therefore
immune from the application of the refugee control law--
rather than that he is a refugee as might be the case where
the purpose of the law was to accord rights or benefits to
refugees. Persons recognized as refugees under these control acts may be required to live in certain settlements, and
their movements and activities inside and outside these settlements may be regulated by the government. [8]

Going beyond the matter of definition, the refugee control acts of Zambia, Uganda, and Tanzania establish an almost identical procedure for the issuance to refugees of
"permits to remain" that can be used in derogation of their
liberal "open door" asylum policy. In Zambia every refugee
entering the country must obtain a permit to remain within
seven days of his arrival or face deportation or imprisonment for being unlawfully in the country. [9] In Tanzania any
class of refugee may be required by the minister to obtain
such a permit or risk being considered an unlawful entrant;
while in Uganda only refugees not living in settlements are
required by law to have a permit to remain. These permits
are issued by "authorized officers" who are variously defined
as including certain categories of police officers, administrative officers, military or prison officials, and designated
refugee officers. An essential part of the permit-issuing
procedure requires that such a permit shall not be refused
to a refugee if, in the opinion of the issuing officer, the result of the refusal would be the return of the refugee to the
territory whence he came, "and that the refugee will
[may] be tried [or detained or restricted] or punished [with-
out trial] for an offence of a political character after arrival
in that territory or is likely to be the subject of physical attack in that territory. "[10] The issuing officer need not give
any reason for refusing a permit, however, and an appeal
from his refusal is permitted only in Tanzania, and then only
if the refugee has been in the country at least three months.

While by use of the term "persecution" these statutes may seem only to be narrowing their generous refugee definitions to conform with the definition found in the 1951 Convention and 1967 Protocol, the concept of persecution embodied in these control statutes is much narrower than that found in the two international agreements. The Convention's use of the term "persecution" covers much more than physical persecution or political persecution; it refers to the entire breadth of discriminatory acts or threats which governments may apply to persons "for reasons of race, religion, nationality, membership of a particular social group or political opinion."[11] By leaving such broad discretion to issuing officers as to whether to issue or refuse permits to remain, limited only by a very narrow requirement as to circumstances under which a permit cannot be refused, these control acts make possible a much narrower "open door" asylum policy.

It is individual refugee determination procedures such as these which raise problems of international protection for the UNHCR because they do not fully conform to the internationally recognized standards for such procedures: definitions of "persecution" are too narrow, no reasons need be given for refusing a permit, and the right of appeal is not granted to all persons refused a permit. These shortcomings exist in other asylum countries as well. And in the large number of refugee-receiving countries which have no legislation defining refugee status or establishing a procedure for eligibility determination there is the additional problem that it is difficult if not impossible to determine on what basis refugees are being refused the right to lawfully remain in the country of asylum.

Unless there is a regularized, semi-judicial eligibility procedure established, subject to central review and control, the UNHCR cannot adequately carry out its international mission of representing the legal interests of refugees; nor can it ascertain, as its supervisory authority entitles it to do, whether states signatories of the 1951 Convention or the 1967 Protocol are fully implementing the international obligations they have undertaken. It is for these reasons that the HC has so welcomed the legislation passed by Botswana in 1967 and by Senegal in 1968, in which eligibility procedures were established which come much closer to the form considered essential by the Office for the full protection of refugees. The Senegalese procedure authorizing the direct participation of the UNHCR in the eligibility determination process is especially gratifying for the Office because it means that while the final power to decide who is a refugee rests with the government, the UNHCR is informed of every determination that is taking place and has the right to make its views known directly to the deciding authority.   In pursuance of its function of extending international protection to refugees at the national and individual levels, this is the kind of procedure the Office would prefer to see established in every asylum country for the determination of refugee status.

Beyond the problems associated with establishing appropriate procedures for determining individual refugee eligibility, there are other eligibility problems in Africa as well. The first of these concerns persons who are actively engaged in military operations or sabotage aimed at the overthrow of the government of the country from which they have fled. These rebels may be divided into two groups: those seeking the overthrow of an independent African government, and those seeking the overthrow of a white-dominated or colonial regime.   The latter category are called freedom fighters. In the case of rebels against independent African governments, regardless of how much they may embody the attributes of refugees, they are excluded from the coverage of the 1951 Convention, the 1967 Protocol, and from the competence of the HC because they are engaged in "acts contrary to the principles and purposes of the UN. "[12]

But the status of freedom fighters is less clear; their struggles have received the approbation of the UN on numerous occasions, for example in the Declaration on the Granting of Independence to Colonial Countries and Peoples.   Succeeding resolutions have reaffirmed the principles enunciated in that Declaration and have supported the struggle of peoples under colonial rule. [13]   Because OAU member states are committed to the support of this freedom struggle, the OAU Refugee Commission resolved in 1966 that freedom fighters should be considered refugees.   For its part, the UNHCR has tried to avoid all political involvement by adopting the position that it will not consider active freedom fighters eligible as refugees under its various material assistance programs, but leaves open the extent to which it might in extreme cases accord such persons its international protection. [14]

When freedom fighters seek to leave the armed struggle and become ex-freedom fighters even more difficulties are posed for African governments and the UNHCR.   While

freedom fighters may have left their countries of origin for
much the same reasons as refugees, they are sharply differ-
entiated by their intentions and their needs once they have
been granted asylum.   They intend to return to the country
they have left (not to re-avail themselves of its protection
but to bring down its government).   Their stay in the asylum country therefore is a temporary one, regardless of its
duration; their need is for a safe base for operations, not
for rights comparable to those of nationals.   They do not
need or seek the international protection of the UNHCR.   But
persons who try to withdraw from the armed struggle or who
are expelled from one of the liberation movements are in a
different situation.   Depending upon their intentions they may
then be eligible for refugee status.   But their withdrawal,
particularly if it was the result of a dispute within the liberation movement over tactics or ideology, may be considered
by both the movement and the governments which support
that movement to endanger the liberation struggle.   As a
consequence, a certain number of these dissidents have been
detained or imprisoned by African governments, or deported
to their country of origin or to some third state.   When and
if their cases come to the attention of UNHCR officials the
question arises whether such treatment was in accord with
the status of these persons.[15]   If the judgement of UNHCR
officers is that these persons have laid down their arms and
intend to lead a peaceful life and in all other ways fulfill the
criteria for recognition as refugees, action is taken to urge
the authorities concerned not to violate their country's international obligations by returning the refugee to "the frontiers
of territories where his life or freedom would be threatened,"[16] or by otherwise depriving him of his rights as a
refugee; and efforts are made to seek the release of the refugee and his resettlement in another country.

      At times dissidents from the freedom struggle and
other refugees have been declared "prohibited immigrants"
by some African governments.   This phrase, taken over by
independent governments from British colonial laws, has been
applied to persons in Kenya, Uganda, Tanzania, and Zambia,
held to have endangered national security or public order.
Moreover, these four states have agreed mutually that a prohibited immigrant in one of them shall be considered a prohibited immigrant by all of them.   When refugees are declared prohibited immigrants, it is considered by the four
governments to be a termination of their refugee status.
They are then either expelled from the country or, if that is
difficult, they may be indefinitely detained in prison under

the provisions of local security legislation.   The HC has
pointed out in reference to cases such as these that

> While governments have the sovereign right to ap-
> ply legislation in force, I feel that the special
> situation of refugees should be fully taken into ac-
> count.   Detention or extradition do not solve the
> problem but only postpone it.   The answer lies in
> speedier and more effective action on the part of
> UNHCR and the international community, and, at
> the same time, in a more cooperative attitude on
> the part of the country of asylum.[17]

The BOs' role in this is to point out to the governments concerned that it is inappropriate to withdraw the
status of refugee from a person otherwise eligible, on
grounds which are not mentioned in either the 1951 Convention or the 1967 Protocol.[18]   While all refugees are under
an obligation to obey the laws of the country of their asylum, they also retain the right to continue to be treated as
refugees even if they violate those laws.   The 1951 Convention does not provide states with the right to punish a refugee by withdrawing his refugee status once granted.   "It is
hoped, " noted the HC's 1970 Report to the GA, "that every
effort will be made by the Governments concerned in order
that the present practice of declaring refugees prohibited immigrants should be modified, bearing in mind the provisions
of the 1951 Convention."[19]

A final eligibility problem concerns the status of persons from Southern Rhodesia who have sought asylum outside
their country since November 1965 when the white minority
regime in that British Crown Colony unilaterally declared
its independence from UK control.   No country has yet accorded diplomatic recognition to the rebel regime in Rhodesia, and it is accepted that the UK continues to be internationally responsible for this territorial possession.   Thus,
since UK authorities are in law and in practice prepared to
provide that country's diplomatic protection to persons from
Southern Rhodesia seeking asylum, such persons do not
qualify as refugees either under the 1951 Convention, the
1967 Protocol, or the Statute of the HC's Office.   They are
not entitled to the usual international protection afforded by
the UNHCR to refugees.   Nevertheless, because of the nature of a certain number of cases involving Southern Rhodesia nationals, agreement was reached between the UK Government and the UNHCR in 1970 on the provision of UNHCR

assistance to Southern Rhodesians who, except for nationality reasons, could be recognized as refugees under the Statute. It is now possible for the UNHCR, after consultation with UK authorities, to use its good offices to provide such services as getting work permits, making arrangements for scholarships or travel to other countries, or providing limited material assistance to Southern Rhodesian refugees.

Facilitating Refugee Movement

There are two aspects to refugee movement both of which are the concern of the UNHCR. The Office seeks to promote the free movement of refugees within the territory of asylum states in accordance with Art. 26 of the 1951 Convention, and their free movement between states in accordance with Art. 28 and the Schedule to the Convention.

Except where a reservation has been made to Art. 26 by a contracting party to the Convention or to the 1967 Protocol, each party to these agreements is obligated to regulate the movement of refugees lawfully within its territory only to the same extent that it does "aliens generally in the same circumstances. " The point of this provision is that it recognizes the right of refugees to choose their place of residence and to move freely within the territory in search of the kind of employment and life style which they desire. In so providing, Art. 2b reflects both the drafters' concern for the complete integration of refugees and their desire to emphasize that refugees as human beings are entitled to enjoy those rights generally considered fundamental for all human beings.

In a large number of the refugee receiving countries in Africa, legislative or administrative controls have been drafted for the purpose of curtailing the free movement of any refugees to whom asylum has been granted. In some countries, such as Uganda, the law is lenient both as written and as enforced, with the result that two-thirds of the refugees do not live within the refugee settlements established by the Uganda Government; in others, such as Zambia and Tanzania, strict provisions and enforcement keep all but a very small number concentrated in rural settlements. Whether imposed for reasons of security, politics, or economics, these regulations afford governments the means of controlling the extent and manner in which refugees mix with the rest of the population. In fact, one of the reasons why rural settlement programs have appealed to some asylum governments is that they keep refugees together in remote areas of the country, separated from other elements of the population. At this stage it is an open question to what extent these restrictions on refugee movement, not imposed on aliens generally, are permanent restrictions which may impede the full absorption of the refugees in their new communities contrary to the spirit of Art. 26 of the Convention. Certainly encouraging the elimination of special restrictions on refugee movement is, in the long run, as important a task for the UNHCR as is the promotion of such substantive rights for refugees as the right to work and the right to receive an education.

In the HC's 1970 Report to the GA the point is made that some refugee control acts also permit the prolonged detention of refugees without trial or review although the Constitution and public security laws guarantee to all detained persons, including aliens, the right to a periodic review of their detention. "It is hoped that these laws," says the Report, "will be amended so as to bring them into line with the spirit of principles of the 1951 Convention, Art. 26 of which makes provision for the freedom of movement of refugees, subject to any regulations applicable to aliens generally in the same circumstances."[20]

In countries which have not yet ratified either the 1951 Convention or the 1967 Protocol, such as Uganda, or the Sudan, or which have become parties only to the Convention, such as Zaïre, there is no contractual obligation to permit refugees any degree of free movement within their territory. In such countries the efforts of the UNHCR to facilitate refugee movement are simply a small part of the principal effort which is to encourage these governments to become parties to the basic international conventions relating to refugees. In the absence of ratification, efforts to promote particular standards of treatment for refugees must rely on the argument that conformity with internationally recognized standards in this matter is a general duty of states. In the few asylum countries such as Botswana and Zambia where reservations were made to Art. 26 of the Convention, there is likewise no obligation to conform to the standard established in that article; and the UNHCR seeks here to encourage the removal of the reservations or the liberalization of regulations despite the existence of the reservations. Finally, in host countries which are contracting parties to the Convention and Protocol and which have agreed to be bound

by the provision of Art. 26, it has been the aim of the
UNHCR to see that domestic legislation and administrative
action fully accord with that provision.

With regard to external movement by refugees across
national frontiers, the UNHCR seeks to convince more and
more contracting parties of the Convention and Protocol to
agree to issue the Convention travel document referred to in
Art. 28 and the Schedule to the Convention, and then to issue the document liberally and expeditiously. The reasons
why refugees need an internationally recognized travel document have already been set out in Chapters 6 and 10; and
the particular issue of a return clause and the hesitancy of
African states to include such a clause in the travel documents they issue is included in Chapter 8. It is sufficient
to note here that the UNHCR has won a growing number of
asylum states to the recognition that the issuance of travel
documents with return clauses may well lighten, and cannot
increase, the refugee burden which they have shouldered.
At present the following African states have made public
their agreement to issue Convention travel documents and in
fact do so: Algeria, Burundi, Botswana, the CAR, Zaïre,
Ethiopia, Lesotho, Morocco, Senegal, Tanzania, and Zambia; however, Botswana, the CAR, and Ethiopia have not
fully clarified their position on the inclusion of return
clauses. The Zambian Government, which reserved its position on the inclusion of return clauses when ratifying the
Convention, has recently agreed, as one of a number of important concessions to refugees, to issue both the travel
document and a return clause. In the case of persons from
Southern Rhodesia who have been granted asylum in other
countries, those who are not supporters of the present illegal
regime and are not active freedom fighters may be issued
special British passports by the UK Government through its
diplomatic offices abroad when required. The document has
no return clause, however, so these persons can enter the
UK only in accordance with the general statutes regarding
the admission of aliens. [21]

It has sometimes been suggested that in the light of
the hesitancy of states to issue travel documents to refugees,
such documents might be issued by some international agency
instead. For example, one of the working papers for the
1967 International Conference on Refugee Problems held in
Addis Ababa suggested, inter alia, that this function be taken
over by the OAU. [22] But the possession of a travel document
is evidence of two facts: that the refugee resides in a

particular country and that he has the right to return to that
country after travel abroad. Both these matters require decisions that are within the exclusive competence of national
authorities to make. Since an internationally issued travel
document could not contain the same assurances, it would
not be of the same benefit to refugees. Nevertheless, by
reason of its assertion of governmental authority over Namibia, (former South West Africa), the UN Governing Council
for Namibia began in 1970 to issue travel documents (without
return clause) and identity documents to refugees from Namibia, and urged states generally to recognize these documents
in the same way as they do Convention travel documents.
The first group of these travel documents to be issued contained return clauses issued by the Zambian Government,
which permitted the holders to return to Zambia where the
documents were issued.

Where states have agreed in principle to issue Convention travel documents, the UNHCR has encouraged the
establishment of a routine, centralized procedure for their
issuance for much the same reasons that it has urged the
setting up of similar procedures for the determination of individual refugee eligibility. To make the issuance of these
documents easier and to assure that they conform as to text
and format with the model travel document drawn up by the
UNHCR, the Office has printed and distributed free of charge
small numbers of travel documents to some states which only
require the issuing government to insert the name of the
country concerned in order to be complete. Ideally, one result of the creation of a regular procedure for determining
individual refugee eligibility would be that registered refugees who could show a valid reason for travelling abroad
would find it much easier to obtain a Convention travel document. Until such procedures are generally established,
however, branch officers will probably continue to find that
the securing of travel documents for refugees is one of those
matters of individual protection which is very difficult to carry out with dispatch.

In countries which do not yet issue Convention travel
documents, branch officers trying to arrange for the travel
abroad of individual refugees, either for study, resettlement,
or other reasons, have sought to bring about ad hoc arrangements between the governments involved with the help of the
BO in the country to which the refugee wishes to travel.
Sometimes in return for the receiving country agreeing to
waive the need for a return clause, the sending country has

agreed to issue a Convention travel document or some other form of laissez-passer to the refugee which is sufficient for him to be permitted to travel to the country of his destination and to move in transit through the territory of intermediate states. When for some reason the refugee concerned is being held in restriction or detention by the country of his asylum, it is particularly difficult to arrange for the issuance to him of a travel document with a return clause, and in such cases all manner of documentary devices have been used to permit the refugee to travel to another country willing to accept him.

The facilitation of travel by refugees in Africa does not involve BOs only on that continent. Problems have also arisen due to the policies adopted by countries which are to some extent willing to receive individual refugees from African countries of first asylum. For several years, for example, the US was willing to accept refugees from Africa who wished to pursue educational studies, but was willing to grant some of them only a so-called "J-visa." The drawback of this visa was that it required the refugee student to return to his country of origin or go elsewhere upon completion of his studies. A certain time of residence outside the US was required for such students before they could return on a permanent basis if they desired to do so. By reason of the nature of the travel documents to which in many instances these visas had been affixed, a number of refugee students who had either completed their course of studies or ceased to be students, found themselves without any clear status at all--they could neither return to the country of original asylum nor be admitted to other countries, yet they could hardly remain in the US on a visa which accorded them few rights and specifically denied them the right to work. One of the immediate concrete benefits of US accession to the 1967 Protocol was that refugee students holding a "J-visa" were permitted to apply for an adjustment in their legal status so as to be accorded full rights of asylum without first leaving the country.

Enhancing Economic and Social Rights

Much has already been said in Chapter 10 about the need for insuring that refugees be accorded economic and social rights as much like those of nationals as possible. Experience has shown that refugees, if socially and economically integrated into the life of the host country, need not be a

burden for the country of asylum. Indeed, skilled refugees
can contribute to the host country's economic strength while
rural refugees can become a focal point for rural development. The integration of refugees into the social environment of the country of asylum can also eliminate the causes
of tension between states to which the presence of refugees
sometimes gives rise.

Moreover, the purpose of any material and legal assistance must be to enable a refugee, once he has been
granted asylum, to stand on his own feet at the earliest possible moment without further international assistance. For
well established psychological reasons and because assistance
funds are so scarce, relief and charity should not and cannot
be accorded to any refugee on a permanent basis. While
granting such legal rights to refugees as the right to work
does not make them full participants in the life of the society
they seek to join, it is the sine qua non for their assimilation. The right to work is no substitute for a job, but too
often refugees in today's world find that there are no jobs
for them until they have been specifically granted the right
to work and to enjoy the fruits of their labor. [23]

In order to facilitate the process of refugee integration, and also for humanitarian reasons, the international
community has attempted to define certain rights in the economic and social fields for refugees which, by reason of the
special dependency of refugees upon the countries of their
asylum, must often be more extensive than those rights enjoyed by ordinary aliens. The granting of these social and
economic rights to refugees is in line with the concept that
has now come to be generally accepted: that social rights
are a part of basic human rights. As early as 1948 the
Universal Declaration of Human Rights adopted by the GA included a number of individual social rights including the
right to work, and the right to an education, to social security, and to security in the event of a lack of livelihood in
circumstances beyond his control. [24] In each case the Declaration stated that the right was one belonging to "everyone,
as a member of society, " and not simply to every national.

The Universal Declaration was not proposed as an en-
forceable treaty obligation, but as a "common standard of
achievement for all peoples and all nations. " The importance
of its contents has been recognized in many ways by many
states, however, and it has been particularly accorded respect by African states. The constitutions of all

French-speaking African states express their adherence in one form or another to the Universal Declaration, as do the constitutions of Tanzania, Libya, and Ethiopia. The constitutions of English-speaking African states contain a bill of rights based on the European Convention on Human Rights, which is itself derived from the Universal Declaration. Furthermore, the Preamble to the Charter of the OAU, expressly reaffirms adherence to the principles of the Universal Declaration. [25] The 1951 Convention and the 1967 Protocol in effect translate into specific standards of treatment for refugees many of the social and economic rights enshrined in the Universal Declaration. With a few important exceptions every major African refugee receiving state has become a party to the 1951 Convention and the 1967 Protocol.

It can be argued that it is premature for the UNHCR to expand effort in Africa on the promotion of domestic legislation which would implement the economic and social rights of refugees set forth in the 1951 Convention and other international agreements. Few African governments presently have the financial resources to do more than establish a rudimentary structure of social legislation for their nationals. Elaborate social security or public relief and assistance schemes are rare, and primary education as a right rather than a privilege is a goal rather than a reality throughout most of the continent. Furthermore, until recent years there have been few signs that refugees or other foreigners would be excluded from the coverage of existing social schemes. Medical care, for example, has generally been given to refugees on the same basis as to nationals. In Europe, the UNHCR could work for the removal of specific provisions in domestic legislation which discriminated against refugees and could seek to insure that refugees were specifically included within the coverage of new and existing social legislation. In Africa the most that can generally be done today is to work for the passage of general legislation which would pledge governments to implement the social and economic rights of refugees as part of future legislation.

There are two reasons, however, which impel the UNHCR to act now for the establishment of an adequate legal status for refugees in domestic social legislation. First, it is clear that there is a growing trend among African governments to legislate against foreigners, including refugees, for the protection of nationals in employment. Burundi, for example, until 1967 did not legislatively impede refugees from competing freely and equally with nationals for the available

jobs. In that year, however, employers were required to
begin seeking permission annually before they could hire and
continue to employ a foreigner in Burundi instead of a national. The Uganda Government announced measures in 1970
that would require all employers in that country to replace
all foreign unskilled or semi-skilled labor (including refugees) with Ugandan nationals. Following consultations with
the UNHCR branch officer the government announced that
these measures would not require the dismissal of refugees
from employment.

The second reason for urging the establishment of an
adequate legal status for refugees is that the UNHCR has
more bargaining power now than it will have when its material assistance programs are completed. By emphasizing
that there can be an inter-relationship between its two functions of international protection and material assistance, the
Office can occasionally offer an exchange to the governments
of asylum countries. The success of this approach was
demonstrated by an agreement reached with the Uganda Government in 1969: following UNHCR assistance in the major
expansion of four Ugandan schools, the government gave refugees an equal opportunity with nationals to compete for the
available places in all Ugandan schools. The agreement thus
accorded to refugees in Uganda a standard of treatment even
more liberal than that set down by the 1951 Convention.

For these two reasons a much greater emphasis is
being placed on the provision of international protection at
the national level through the promotion of legislation for
refugees in Africa today than was the case even five years
ago. The HC said in May 1968 that it was particularly important that a legal basis should be established for the refugees in Africa, because, otherwise, when the cut-off date
for material assistance was reached, a new emergency might
be created. This legislation, which the Office is helping
these governments to draft, will still be used as the basic
instrument for the protection of refugees in the future when
African governments will have achieved a more developed
infrastructure. If it is not drafted before the African countries have become economically developed, it may become
more difficult to do so because new political problems may
appear which are even more difficult to solve than those
facing these countries today.

Senegal, which has been referred to as the pilot country in Africa insofar as refugee legislation is concerned, has

promulgated a statute which incorporates into its domestic
law the entire substantive content of the 1951 Convention
with regard to the rights of refugees; in five matters relating to the social and economic rights of refugees the statute
establishes more favorable standards than those contained in
the Convention.   These five matters are the right to work,
the right to receive an education, the right to practice a
liberal profession, the right to benefit generally from social
legislation, and the right to treatment without regard to legislative reciprocity.   No other African government has yet
been willing to go as far as the Government of Senegal in
according rights to refugees so nearly equal to those of nationals.   The action of that government serves as an impressive example of what can be done.[26]   The passage of
laws, no matter how generous, does not of itself achieve
permanent solutions to the problems of refugees: refugee
unemployment as well as national unemployment is a pressing problem in Senegal's urban areas.   The significance of
social legislation favoring refugees lies in the fact that it as-
sures them that as the country's economy and infrastructure
develop they will not be legally impeded from playing their
full part in the process.

Elsewhere in Africa the governments of asylum countries have been most ready to accord to refugees the right
to work when rural land settlement was envisioned.   Here
they have recognized how important the right to work is in
facilitating the integration of the refugee into the country of
asylum, and the contribution refugees can make by their
labor and skill.   "Governments have contributed generously
not only through making available free land to refugees on
which to work and through agricultural projects, but also
through a variety of technical services and advice," notes
one of the Working Papers for the 1967 Addis Ababa Refugee
Conference.[27]   But, as the paper goes on to point out, the
situation is somewhat different when it concerns activities
for which professional training is required.   Refugee doctors
and nurses have had little difficulty in exercising their right
to work in asylum countries because their skills are in short
supply.   Refugee lawyers and schoolteachers, on the other
hand, have found it much more difficult, particularly when
they seek to practice their professions outside refugee settlements.   The paper could well have added that the situation
is equally difficult for refugees who are skilled or semi-
skilled workers or who seek to be self-employed in a business or trade.   The kind of commitment which the HC would
welcome in the handling of refugee employment problems is

that originally made by the Government of Zaïre.   In December 1968 that government announced that, as of January 1969, all refugees granted asylum in Zaïre would be treated in the same way as nationals with regard to all labor legislation. However with the announcement of Presidential decrees in July and August 1970 barring the employment of foreigners in any field of public administration including teaching, and for the protection of national labor, there is some uncertainty as to the continued validity of the earlier policy announcement.

The commitments being made by African governments and the work being undertaken by the UNHCR in the furtherance of the refugees' right to an education have been detailed in Chapter 35.   As with other social and economic rights, consultations now occur on a regular basis in many asylum countries between UNHCR and government officials in an effort to insure that these rights are fully established through domestic legislation and that statutes and decrees to the contrary are modified to reflect the needs and rights of refugees in Africa.

Promoting Naturalization

In the past few years the UNHCR has placed increasing emphasis on the need for the naturalization of refugees. Refugee status should normally be a temporary status, pending permanent solutions through voluntary repatriation or complete assimilation in a new community.   Once repatriation is no longer a realistic solution, naturalization constitutes the final step in the refugee's integration in his new home country.   At both its Nineteenth and Twentieth Sessions, the Ex. Com. gave its firm support to the HC's efforts to encourage governments to facilitate the acquisition of new nationality by refugees and to encourage refugees who are eligible to apply on a purely voluntary basis for naturalization. [28]

Branch officers have sought to ensure that no artificial obstacles were placed in the way of the refugee's eventual naturalization.   In particular, they have urged that the interests of the refugee be kept in view by African governments when they are promulgating laws on citizenship and naturalization.   Because of the reluctance of certain African governments to acknowledge that some refugee groups are permanently within their borders and ought to be permitted

eventual naturalization, the HC has welcomed recent statements by the representatives of two African states.   At the
Nineteenth Session of the Ex. Com., the spokesman for
Tanzania announced that naturalization was possible for refugees granted asylum in Tanzania in those cases where they
intend to settle there permanently, show good character,
speak Swahili or English, give up their former nationality,
and reside in the country for at least seven years.[29]   At
the following session of the Ex. Com., the representative of
Zambia, in explaining his country's new Refugees (Control)
Act of 1970, announced that it did not prevent the naturalization of refugees after four years residence in the country.
It will be a continuing task of branch officers in Africa to
see that further initiatives like these are taken for the promotion of refugee naturalization in those cases where that is
a logical solution.

Conclusion

        The function of international protection, as exercised
at the national and individual levels in Africa has been an
important activity for the UNHCR for such a comparatively
short time that it is too early to make any far-reaching as-
sessments.   In some countries, Burundi, for example, well-
defined channels have not yet been established by governments through which problems of international protection can
be raised by UNHCR officials; in others, such as Zambia,
there is a well-developed system for consultation.   In countries such as Kenya, the UNHCR plays no formal role in
determining individual refugee eligibility and such determinations as do take place are based on ad hoc procedures.
Elsewhere eligibility machinery has been established and
branch officers regularly give advice and present their views,
as for example in Botswana.   In a few countries, notably
Senegal, these officials participate formally in the refugee
determination process.   The majority of asylum countries in
Africa have no specific refugee legislation, and there the effort of the Office has been to encourage the passage of legislation which would take full account of the needs and rights
of refugees.   Elsewhere the Office's concern has been more
with bringing existing laws into line with international standards for refugees set forth in the 1951 Convention and other
international agreements.   Similarly, on travel documents
there is a diversity of problems and no uniformity of achievement: government policies range from outright refusal in a
very few cases, through partial degrees of cooperation, to
full compliance.

In short, the major protection problems have been identified, and an increasing amount of time and effort are being spent on their solution. These efforts have led to some major breakthroughs and to the successful solution of the individual legal problems of a number of refugees. At other times the result has been frustration and failure. In the absence of full commitment to refugee integration it appears that the HC's international protection role in Africa is destined to continue for a very long time indeed.

Notes

1. Speech before the Conference on the Legal, Economic and Social Aspects of African Refugee Problems, Addis Ababa; 9 Oct. 1967; printed in App. 5(c) of the Conference's Final Report, May 1968.

2. The assertion is based on the authority granted to the HC by the Statute of his Office, pars. 1 and 8, an authority substantially strengthened in Africa by the fact that most of the major refugee-receiving countries there have become signatories of the 1951 Convention and 1967 Protocol, which authorize the HC to supervise the implementation of their provisions relating to the legal status of refugees by signatory states.

3. In some countries, for short periods of time, UNHCR officials have issued identity cards to refugees, e. g. in the Congo (Kinshasa) during 1963-64, but only for the purpose of facilitating the distribution of rations, clothing, blankets, tools, seeds, and so on.

4. See the Tanzania Refugee (Control) Act, No. 2 of 1966, sec. 3(1), and Government Notices Nos. 89 of 1966 and 433 of 1968.

5. Ministerial Order No. 020/782 of 5 Oct. 1965, Art. 2.

6. Ministerial Order No. 020. 692 of 30 Mar. 1963, Art. 1.

7. See Art. 1 of Senegal's Law No. 68-27 of 24 July 1968, set out in the Annex to Ch. 42; and the Schedule to Botswana's Refugees (Recognition and Control) (Amendment) Act, No. 37 of 1967.

8.   The refugee control acts of Zambia, Tanzania and
     Uganda contain identical provisions on this and many
     other matters because they have been modelled on
     each other. The Zambia Refugees (Control) Act,
     No. 40 of 1970, follows very closely the wording
     of the Tanzania Refugees (Control) Act, No. 2 of
     1966, which in turn was derived from the Uganda
     Control of Alien Refugees Act 1960 (Chapter 43).
     The Uganda Act itself is a revision of an earlier
     Uganda statute, the Control of Refugees from the
     Sudan Act, No. 35 of 1955, which expanded the
     Registration and Control Aliens Act, No. 23 of
     1949 (all three Uganda laws having been drawn up
     during the period of British colonial administration
     in Uganda).

9.   It is uncertain how this provision will be applied to
     refugees who have already entered Zambia since the
     Act was only passed in mid-1970.

10. Sec. 11(2) of the Tanzania Act. The same wording
     appears in the proviso to sec. 6(2) of the Uganda
     Act, while the bracketed words show changes and
     additions that have been made in sec. 11(2) of the
     Zambia Act.

11. Art. 1(a) of the Convention.

12. See exclusion clause in Art. 1F of the Convention, and
     par. 7(d) of the Statute. In practice, however,
     there can be a gray area between the refugee defi-
     nition and the exclusion clause when refugees are
     subject to pressures by forces seeking the overthrow
     of the government of the country of their origin;
     e. g. the Rwandese in the Congo.

13. GA Res. 1514 (XV) of 14 Dec. 1960.

14. Goundiam, "African Refugee Convention, " MN, Mar. -
     Apr. 1970: 9; and "Development and Scope of the
     Definition of the Term 'Refugee', " AFR/REF/
     CONF. 1967/No. 2: 10.

15. The political sensitivity of governments on this subject
     is such however that it is difficult to know what
     percentage of these cases ever come to the atten-
     tion of the UNHCR.

16.   Art. 33(1) of the 1951 Convention.

17.   HC's Opening Statement to Ex. Com. (XXI), A/AC. 96/447, 14 Oct. 1970, App. 1: 8.

18.   Art. 1 C of the Convention details the conditions under which a refugee will no longer be considered a refugee within the scope of that convention. In general, these are where the refugee has voluntarily returned home, renewed his legal ties with the country from which he fled, or acquired a new nationality.

19.   A/8012: 9.

20.   Ibid.

21.   For detail, see UK, HC Hansard, Vol. 766, 17 and 27, June and July 1968.

22.   AFR/REF/CONF. 1967/No. 17: 4.

23.   AFR/REF/CONF. 1967/No. 6: 1-2.

24.   See Arts. 22, 23, 24, 25, 26, and 28 of the Declaration, GA Res. 217A (111), of 10 Dec. 1948.

25.   AFR/REF/CONF. 1967/No. 6: 7.

26.   The CAR Government declared in 1967 that by becoming a party to the 1951 Convention and the 1967 Protocol it had incorporated their provisions into domestic law without the need of implementing legislation; and the Ghana Government announced in the same year that its refugee policy was based entirely on the provisions of the Convention and the Protocol, but it appears that no implementing legislation has yet been enacted.

27.   AFR/REF/CONF. 1967/No. 6: 10.

28.   A/AC. 96/403: 18; and A/AC/96/422: 18.

29.   A/AC. 96/SR. 194 of 11 Dec. 1969: 50.

Part IV

THE SEARCH FOR PERMANENT SOLUTIONS IN EUROPE

Statistics are only reference points for reality. We can summarize a million lives in a short paper, but eventually we must deal with human problems.

--Yul Brynner, Bring Forth The Children, New York, 1960.

INTRODUCTION

Although the primary function of the UNHCR as defined in the Statute was the provision of international protection for refugees, in reality the HC was confronted from the outset by the urgent need of refugees for material assistance, often at the level of mere survival. In the following chapters the story will unfold of the HC's struggle to secure material aid not only for the most desperately needy but on a far larger scale in support of material assistance programs aimed at the reestablishment of homes and livelihoods.

The expectation that the UNHCR would be able to effect a final settlement of European refugees within a few years had proven false. The task, which was to be an ongoing one, had been rendered even more difficult in the early years of UNHCR operations by the continuous influx of new refugee groups, which made additional demands on resources still burdened by the needs of residual groups of refugees.

This was a period when the HC would make strenuous efforts to persuade the governments of the extent and nature of the refugee problem and of the responsibility of the international community to assist in resettlement and local integration programs. "The decision which the United Nations must now take on the refugee problem," Dr. van Heuven Goedhart urged in the GA in 1954, "cannot be avoided, because it is inherent in the principles which have been accepted in the Charter. The continued presence of thousands of uprooted and unsettled refugees is a challenge to the sincerity of those who have subscribed to the basic principles of freedom which inspire the United Nations. "

While a critical need for funds plagued the HC throughout this period, the UNHCR developed an increasingly effective partnership with the voluntary agencies and out of their growing experience were forged new and workable solutions to refugee problems. Handicapped by a lack of money, these new approaches were characteristically expedient and pragmatic.

In response to the most urgent and immediate needs, the HC initiated local integration projects with the help of a Ford Foundation pilot project grant. In part, as a result of this successful program, the need for material assistance ultimately was recognized by the governments, and UNREF was established on 1 January 1955. UNREF was superseded on 1 January 1959 by a more comprehensive program, the High Commissioner's Program, which by 1963 came to be called the Major Aid Programs.

The scope of the HC's mandate was expanded to cover groups of refugees unforeseen by the 1951 Statute, and through the good offices concept the HC was enabled to offer emergency assistance to new groups of refugees.

There emerged in the collective response to the problems of refugees in Europe--both the residual problems and those created by new crises of the 1950s, notably the massive exodus from Hungary--a recognition that refugee movements are a phenomenon of the twentieth century, one requiring an adaptable worldwide machinery to stimulate and coordinate efforts to provide not only for refugee status in international law but also the material assistance necessary for final settlement.

Chapter 12

DIMENSIONS OF THE REFUGEE PROBLEM IN EUROPE

The classical methods for achieving a solution to the refugee problem have been repatriation, resettlement, and local integration; all three have been pursued as means toward a solution since the programs under the LoN.

Repatriation

Repatriation was and still is considered the ideal solution. But, as has been described above, it was the least possible solution. Dr. Nansen was the first HC to negotiate a repatriation agreement, that with the USSR. However, he experienced great difficulties and had to concentrate instead on assimilation within new national communities. After WWII UNRRA was able to repatriate many displaced persons (DPs). But, as we have seen in the deliberations on the creation of the IRO, East and West held opposing views of what was meant by repatriation, the East interpreting it in terms which the majority of the UN members considered to be equivalent to forcible repatriation. In practice, both the IRO and the UNHCR have considered it axiomatic that repatriation must be voluntary and that no person should be sent back to his country of origin against his will. The Soviet Union and the Eastern European states have repeatedly criticized the IRO and the UNHCR because of this policy and have maintained that IRO and UNHCR activities perpetuated the refugee problem. The refugee problem could have been solved long before by repatriation, the East maintained, had the HC adopted their interpretation of the terms of GA Res. 8(I) of 12 February 1946.

In response to a renewed accusation that he had not carried out the instructions of GA Res. 8(I) of 12 February 1946, the HC explained to the Third Committee of the GA on 16 October 1953, that under his mandate his task was not to insure repatriation or resettlement of refugees. His responsibility was to facilitate solutions of that kind, but he was not empowered to carry them out. [1] He elaborated on his position in a later statement:

> In accordance with the mandate of my Office any requests for repatriation which are received from individual refugees are referred to the appropriate authorities of the countries of origin. However, my Office is rarely able to obtain information on the action subsequently taken.

During 1955 various governments of the countries of origin renewed their efforts to encourage repatriation by sending repatriation missions to the countries where refugees were residing and through interviews conducted by members of diplomatic or consular missions. Publicity favoring repatriation, which called attention to recent decrees of amnesty and promised free transportation and loans to refugees wishing to return to their countries of origin, was also greatly increased. This resulted in a temporary increase in applications for repatriation. In the Federal Republic of Germany, fifty-six such applications were received during the summer and autumn of 1955. The return of 31 refugees of Soviet nationality before the expiration of their prison sentences for crimes committed in Germany was also reported. The Austrian Ministry of Interior notified the UNHCR BO that 263 persons had been repatriated from Austria between 1 April and 31 October 1955. But the HC stated, "my Office has no means of checking these figures nor of finding out how many of the persons concerned come within the mandate of my Office. "

In the Third Committee of the Tenth General Assembly, 1955, Poland, Czechoslovakia, the Ukraine, and Byelorussia introduced a draft resolution incorporating "voluntary" repatriation with reference to the Res. of 18 February 1946. Their countries, they maintained in the discussion of the Third Committee, had taken a number of administrative and legislative measures to provide for amnesty, protection, and employment. In the debate, however, other delegates pointed out that there were "displaced persons (who had wished to return to their home countries) who had been by UNRRA, and to a lesser degree by IRO, repatriated according to their wish, but that those who had not availed themselves of this opportunity had become refugees. " Since the Soviet draft resolution specified repatriation as the only permanent solution and did not include either resettlement or local integration, it was rejected.

The HC pointed out that in pursuance of efforts to solve the problems of refugees by repatriation while insuring due safeguards for their protection, he had requested the governments of the countries in which they were residing to insure that BOs were informed of any impending visit to refugees of a repatriation mission and that a representative of the UNHCR BO be invited "to accompany the mission in the capacity of an impartial observer to insure that no undue influence is exercised." He felt that this procedure was working satisfactorily since the BOs had been notified a number of times of such visits and their representatives had accompanied the missions. [2]

Only a small minority of the refugees were repatriated, although the UNHCR spared no efforts to promote and aid repatriation, as in Hungary, for example. With the exception of the repatriation of 180,000 Algerians from Morocco and Tunisia to Algeria, and of sizable refugee groups in certain other African countries, the numbers of repatriated refugees have been small in comparison to those who preferred resettlement or local integration.

Resettlement

Although the IRO had been able to achieve mass resettlement in overseas countries, the possibility of resettling refugees in immigration countries has been decreasing since 1950-51. Australia, Canada, and Israel, and to a lesser degree, the US, felt they had reached their absorptive capacity and could not, or would not, for the time being, admit many more refugees. Since economic development required considerable investment (in Australia in particular), the number of immigrants that could be admitted depended primarily on the capacity for capital expansion (e.g., in regard to family housing and creation of employment). Under the existing selection criteria for immigrants, fewer and fewer refugees in relation to the total case load were eligible. Also, the immigration countries were gradually reestablishing their traditional pre-war patterns of inter-continental migration (e.g., British migrants to Commonwealth countries; and Italian, Spanish, and Portuguese migrants to Latin American countries) and selection criteria thus favored national migrants over refugees. In 1952 there occurred a further decrease in migration opportunities as a whole, as a result of the increasing economic difficulties facing immigration countries.

Looking back over the years since the end of WWII, Dr. van Heuven Goedhart reminded UN members that in the UNRRA era repatriation had been the main point of the program; in the IRO period the main emphasis had shifted to the resettlement of refugees in other, mainly overseas, countries; but by the 1950s resettlement of refugees overseas was not, and could not be, the main approach to a permanent solution.

The "inevitable antagonism between the policies of the countries of emigration and of the countries of immigration due to their different self-interests," he pointed out, had worked to the disadvantage of the emigration countries. The immigration countries were now accepting only those persons capable of filling needs, often in clearly defined economic fields. Such restrictions on the selection of refugees for immigration operated adversely on the countries of asylum. The proportion of unskilled and aged refugees, and those in poor physical condition, increased considerably in Europe. Thus, while the selection of migrants in good health contributed to the general productive effort in the resettlement countries, it increased the proportion of refugees who could only be a burden on the social services of their countries of residence.

Furthermore, the urgency of the surplus population problem reduced the refugees' chances for migration, since the preference of the immigration countries went to nationals, who had passports and a protecting government, and were therefore in a more favorable position than the refugees who lacked both. Although ICEM had a small revolving fund of $500,000 with which to move those refugees already processed and visaed before the IRO was liquidated, it lacked funds for financing any large-scale movements of refugees. Under these circumstances a refugee could migrate only if he earned his own fare or if some voluntary agency would advance him the fare against eventual repayment.

Local Integration

The international community tended to regard overseas resettlement as the most apparent solution to the refugee problem, but as opportunities for migration lessened, the HC urged consideration of local resettlement as an equal alternative. In developing this new approach, economic considerations were brought forward in support of the soundness of proposed programs.   The cost of migration and the capital needed for the reestablishment of immigrants was proportionately high in comparison to the cost of local integration. The latter benefited by the difference in price levels, by the lower amount of investment required for substructure, and by the absence of inter-continental transport costs.   For these reasons, the HC felt it wise to concentrate on plans for "local integration," that is to say, economic integration--a process by which the refugee becomes incorporated into the economic activity of the country of residence, in accordance with his capabilities and with the standards applying to the population generally.

The mass departure of predominantly male, young, and qualified labor had left the emigration countries with what were called "residual" groups of refugees.   Dr. van Heuven Goedhart opposed the use of this term as well as the term "hard-core" and preferred to use the words "difficult cases" for those who had limited opportunities or no opportunities for resettlement.   The group obviously needed more individual counselling, retraining, and rehabilitation in order to prepare them for economic integration in their country of first refuge. [3]   With such counselling and training, however, Dr. van Heuven Goedhart believed that not only would the cost of maintenance borne by the country of refuge be reduced, but at the same time the national product would be increased.   This would compensate for the additional social welfare expenditure incurred in respect to the difficult cases. Moreover, he thought that economic integration would pave the way for the social assimilation of refugee groups as a whole.

Since the expansion of credit for such programs was beyond the economic capacity of the countries involved, the HC recommended that the UN should either through those of its members who were most concerned with the problems of reconstruction, or through the UN Specialized Agencies, provide the necessary economic support within the framework of existing arrangements or through special loans similar to those provided by the LoN for the reconstruction of Austria and Hungary and for the settlement of Greek refugees in 1923.   He suggested that it would be to the advantage of the overseas countries to contribute to the cost of local integration for some groups of refugees as well as to promote resettlement for others.

Thus the HC urged the Sixth GA, in 1952, that in

addition to promoting migration, long-term plans should be made and methods evolved for financing and implementing economic measures calculated to afford some local integration to residual groups of refugees. The GA responded to this request in Res. 538B(VI) of 2 February 1952 by asking the UNHCR to contribute to the promotion of activities designed to effect local integration; the HC thus was authorized to investigate and make plans to aid this process.

The UNHCR undertook area studies of the residual refugees concentrated in particular countries. Their situation is described in detail in the following sections. These data provided the basis for proposals for the economic integration and social assimilation of refugees which were contained in a Memorandum on the Economic and Social Integration of Refugees. [4] The HC pointed out that there were about 300,000 refugees under his mandate who were not yet permanently settled, adding that this number was constantly being increased by the arrival of new refugees. He spelled out some basic requirements that applied generally, although the measures required to cope with the problem of integrating specific refugees groups were bound to differ from country to country.

Refugees must be provided with decent living quarters, preferably in locations where the possibilities of employment were greatest; the employment of refugees must be fostered within the framework of general economic development, especially by means of occupational training or re-training; and refugees should have an opportunity to engage in independent occupations such as agriculture, trade, handicrafts, and the professions.

> Quite apart from the legal and other measures needed for the fulfillment of those general requirements, considerable capital will usually be called for. The governments of countries where the refugees are living should try to solve these problems satisfactorily and to provide the refugees, directly or indirectly, with the administrative, technical and financial means they require, as far as their resources permit.

While the legal protection of refugees might mitigate or even, in certain cases, remove the difficulties facing refugees, it was not sufficient for a permanent solution to the refugee problem. Moreover, the possibility of implementing

integration schemes was often beyond the capacity of countries weakened economically by the war.   Thus to achieve
the ultimate aim of the Statute, the HC felt it was essential
that the governments concerned "examine the possibility of
taking part in a scheme to provide from international
sources financial aid in securing the integration of refugees. "[5]

Refugees in the European Countries

The magnitude of the task of securing local settlement in the countries of refuge can best be gauged through
a detailed account of the post-war conditions in those countries and of the size and situation of their refugee groups.

The main group of residual refugees were located in
Germany, Austria, Italy and Trieste, and Greece, all concentrated on the borders of the countries of their origin.
These countries had experienced the destruction and damage
caused by the war, and serious dislocations had undermined
the fabric of their societies.   In addition, they were caught
between two opposed and ideologically irreconcilable power
centers.   In the other Western European countries (France,
Belgium, the Netherlands, Luxembourg, Denmark, Norway,
Sweden, Switzerland, and the UK) the numbers were less and
the refugees were predominantly residing outside camps.
However, with the exception of Sweden and Switzerland, all
these countries were preoccupied with the reconstruction and
rehabilitation of their war-torn territories and some had in
addition to cope with an influx of non-mandated refugees, for
example, the UK-Polish refugees (ex-soldiers); the Nether-
lands-Dutch Indonesians; and France-Spanish refugees and
returnees from Algeria.

The conditions of these refugees varied from country
to country, and the degree of assimilation possible differed.
Germany and Austria were occupied and ruled by the four
Allied powers.   Their territories were severely reduced and
they had to cope with a large group of "ethnic" or "national"
refugees in addition to aliens.   Greece and Italy also had to
cope with large influxes of ethnic refugees, and both countries suffered from unemployment and a severe housing
shortage.   All four of these principal countries of asylum
were in great need of international capital.

After the transfer of responsibilities for refugees

from the IRO to the countries of residence, the HC, exercising his basic function, concentrated first on arrangements
for their legal status, negotiating with the responsible governments in each country.

The work of the BOs developed progressively as the
IRO ended its operations in the field of international protection.   Officials of the BOs urged government officials in
each country to insure that the standards set by the 1951
Convention were implemented pending the entry into force of
the Convention.   These representations covered such matters
as the determination of refugee status, the regularization of
residence, the exercise of the right to work, travel documents, authentication of documentation, personal status, public relief and assistance, and social security.

The different tasks undertaken by the BOs in the
countries of residence in regard to the determination and
certification of refugee status were set forth in agreements
concluded with individual governments, relating to the establishment of such offices in their territories. 6

The Federal Republic of Germany

After Germany's defeat in WWII the Allies divided
Germany's post-war territory into four Occupation Zones
and Berlin into four Sectors and assumed supreme authority
over all Germany.   The failure of inter-Allied cooperation
resulted in the establishment of two separate states, the
Federal Republic of Germany in the West and the German
Democratic Republic in the East.   In 1948 the three Western Allies authorized the Germans to draft their constitution, known as the Basic Law (Grundgesetz), which was
promulgated on 23 May 1949.   The Government of the Federal Republic of Germany began to function in September
1949.

Under Art. XIII of the Potsdam Agreement of 2 August 1946 about ten million German citizens were expelled
(becoming expellees--Heimatvertriebene) from the Soviet
Zone Germany (now German Democratic Republic) and Poland, and 380,000 from Danzig who had lived as citizens in
the Free City of Danzig.   The rest were Volksdeutsche (people of German stock who had lived for centuries in Central
and Eastern Europe) who lived in the Baltic States and the
Memel territory (249,500), in Poland (one million), in

Czechoslovakia (3, 477, 000), in Hungary (623, 000), in Yugoslavia (536, 800), and in Rumania (786, 000).[7] All were
granted German nationality upon arrival, except about half
a million Volksdeutsche who went to Austria.

This tremendous influx not only raised great problems
of integration but also resulted in overpopulation with far-
reaching effects on economic reconstruction.

The new Federal Government administered and, under
Section 120 of the Basic Law, assumed full responsibility
for these German refugees under a Federal Expellee Ministry. Aid was concentrated on the most urgent need, housing. The government launched a policy to increase the supply of housing in the industrial areas. Two building subsidy
plans were carried out under two laws (24 April 1950 and
25 August 1953) from which the national refugees benefited
directly or indirectly; they were also covered by the general
welfare and social security laws.

In order to integrate the national refugees as quickly
as possible into the working population, two methods were
pursued: refugees were redistributed throughout the country, and capital was invested in the overpopulated area to
raise the level of employment. Thus the Federal Government carried out a policy of population transfer (Umsiedlun-
gen) to industrial areas to relieve overpopulated Länder. Of
a total of 1, 050, 000 national refugees, 850, 000 were transferred in the course of a few years. In addition, the government made credit available in districts where unemployment was greatest. Loans were granted for the expansion
of existing firms, the establishment of new industries, and
the construction of housing, including homes for the difficult
cases.

In addition to laborers there were many craftsmen,
tradesmen, and professional workers. To prevent these
self-employed workers or employers from sinking into the
proletariat, public aid was provided for them in the form of
long-term loans granted by the Expellees' and War Victims'
Bank, a central credit institution founded in 1950 for the
economic integration of German refugees, expellees and war
victims. This public loan policy (Equalization of Burdens
Act--Lastenausgleichsgesetz--of August 1951) was coupled
with tax relief.

Some 300, 000 farmers constituted an even greater

problem.   Although the government through two successive
laws (August 1949 and May 1953) tried to open up land for
new farms, many persons had to settle overseas.

All these schemes necessitated a large expenditure
and much economic planning.   They also demanded a great
adjustment of the political, economic, and social fabric of
the country.   The situation of the refugees under the mandate of the UNHCR must be seen in this setting.

The Transfer of Non-German Refugees to UNHCR.
Since 1945, under both the military occupation and under the
Occupation Statute, responsibility for non-German refugees
had been a subject reserved to the occupying powers, and
the status of non-Germans was largely regulated by occupation legislation.   Then a gradual transfer of responsibility
for alien refugee matters to the Federal German Government
took place.   This transfer of responsibility coincided with
the transfer of responsibility for the international protection
of refugees from the IRO to the UNHCR.

On 30 June 1950, IRO transferred to local authorities
its responsibility for the physical maintenance of all refugees
except those in process of resettlement, those in the institutional hard-core groups and unaccompanied children.   IRO's
public health programs, hospitals, homes for the physically
handicapped and for children, programs of occupational therapy, vocational training and medical rehabilitation, were
transferred to the West German authorities, assisted by the
voluntary agencies.

On 30 June 1951, IRO in agreement with the Allied
High Commission handed over the responsibility for DPs to
the German authorities.   The inter-Allied powers retained
considerable authority in refugee matters.   In October 1951
a joint memorandum addressed to the Chairman of the Allied
High Commission in Germany by the UNHCR and the Director-General of the IRO announced the assumption by the
UNHCR of responsibility for all measures connected with the
resettlement of IRO refugees within West Germany, all
measures connected with the protection of unaccompanied
children who would remain in Germany, supervision of the
execution of the agreements under which hard-core cases
had been placed in institutions, and supervision of the conditions existing in those institutions.   The UNHCR, as the
successor of IRO, was designated in various management
agreements regarding the disposal of institutional hard-core
cases.   The transfer was completed by 31 January 1952.

The HC also assumed IRO's responsibility in the DP Branch of the Expellee Bank Agreement. This agreement, concluded on 2 April 1951 between the IRO and the Equalization of Burdens Bank, Bank for Expellees and Sufferers from Damage (Lastenausgleichsbank, Bank für Vertriebene und Geschädigte), provided credit opportunities for non-German refugees to practice a handicraft, a trade or a profession. This agreement was supplemented several times. An additional loan plan was initiated in 1953 to provide housing for these refugees.

The IRO made close to DM 4.9 million available as capital for the granting of loans. Following up this initiative, the German Federal Government contributed approximately DM 30 million by the end of 1965. In addition, the UNHCR made available more than DM 8 million for the procurement of housing to effect camp clearance. Additional funds were contributed by other sources. Up to 31 December 1965, 2,597 economic establishment loans and 1,404 housing loans were approved in the amount of DM 49,706,000.[8] Between 1965 and 1972 the Bank was able to make a further 891 establishment loans.

In September 1951, when the UNHCR opened a BO in Bonn, there were 245,000 refugees in Germany, of whom 56,000 were living in 143 camps administered by the West German authorities. Some 48,000 of the refugees fell into the category of the difficult cases. Only one-sixth of the adult camp population was gainfully employed; almost two-thirds of the children attended neither schools nor vocational training courses. By 1952 the camp population had risen to 265,000.

Homeless Foreigners Law in Germany. Initially there existed a difficult psychological problem. The Occupation authorities as well as UNRRA and the IRO had kept the foreign refugees separate from the German population and had favored them from the legal and economic point of view. They had been kept apart from the German population as a matter of policy, the idea always being that they were to leave Germany, at first through repatriation and later through resettlement. At the beginning of 1950 only two or three in a thousand wanted to stay in Germany, then regarded only as a transit country. Six years of this privileged treatment had tended to divide the Germans and the non-Germans into two distinct groups. Under these circumstances the Germans had not developed any feeling of responsibility for the non-German refugees, and German public opinion was still too unprepared for any attempt at assimilation to be successful. The consequences of this separation of the two groups had to be overcome.

The Law of 25 April 1951 on the Legal Status of Homeless Aliens put refugees on the same footing as nationals, but practically speaking this had no effect, at least on the local level.

The Contractual Agreement signed on 26 May 1952 between the three Western Powers and the Federal Government brought about the final steps in the transfer of responsibility for non-German refugees from the occupying powers to the Federal Government. It undertook to implement the Homeless Foreigners Law of 21 April 1951, and promulgated appropriate legislation concerning the admission and distribution of new refugees and legislation concerning compensation to victims of Nazi persecution.

At the request of the UNHCR a circular was issued by the Ministry of the Interior in June 1952, explaining that the Homeless Foreigners Law now applied to all refugees under the mandate of the UNHCR who satisfied the residence qualification. Most of the provisions of this law were more favorable to refugees than were those of the 1951 Convention. The London Travel Document (and after the entry into force of the 1951 Convention in 1954, the travel document provided for in that Convention) was issued to all refugees within the UNHCR mandate.

Administration of New Refugees in West Germany. The administration of new refugees was governed by the Ordinance on Asylum of 9 January 1953. According to its provisions foreigners who crossed the frontier without entry permits seeking asylum as non-German refugees had to report to a collecting center. Refugees were received at the Federal Reception Center at Zirndorf near Nuremburg, from where they were transferred to a transit center.

Refugees had to remain in the collecting center pending determination of their status. Persons recognized as refugees were distributed to the various Länder by a Federal Commissioner, in consultation with the Länder and in accordance with a distribution scheme determined by criteria laid down in Art. 1 of the 1951 Convention. Distribution was determined by a Commission consisting of three members after pre-examination by the Chairman of the Commission. A person whose claim for refugee status was rejected could apply to an Appeal Commission of three members. The members of both Commissions were appointed by the Minister of the Interior, and the UNHCR representative attended the meetings of both Commissions. The BO in West Germany also undertook considerable work in connection with the protection of unaccompanied children.

Efforts were made to acquaint refugees with their rights and duties in Germany. The UNHCR in conjunction with the Federal Ministry for Refugees composed and distributed widely a handbook for refugees containing information on relevant legislation and existing organizations working on their behalf. In addition, the UNHCR BO circulated a monthly bulletin of up-to-date information concerning new legislation and regulations affecting refugees.

The BO devoted considerable effort to the creation of joint Refugee Councils (Beiräte), consisting of representatives of the German authorities and of the refugees, and in some cases of the voluntary agencies. In most of the Länder these councils were attended by a representative of the UNHCR BO.

The Republic of Austria

The geographical situation of Austria makes it a natural corridor for population movements in Europe. It borders on Czechoslovakia, Hungary, and Yugoslavia in the east, Italy and Switzerland in the south, and West Germany in the north.

From 13 March 1938 until 1945, Austria was under the Nazi regime through the Anschluss. Following the war, it was under four-power occupation for ten years. The last occupation forces were withdrawn in October 1955. Austria became a neutral state under the parliamentary declaration of 5 June 1955 and by the State Treaty of 27 July 1955 it was accorded the frontiers of 1 January 1938 (area 32,375 sq. miles).

At the end of WWII there were over 1,650,000 aliens in Austria, about one million of whom were non-German speaking. The majority of these persons could be repatriated with the aid of the Allied occupation authorities and

UNRRA. By August 1946 there were an estimated 482,000 refugees--about 176,000 non-German speaking and 306,000 German speaking. The group of non-Germans included DPs who had refused repatriation and those who since May 1945 had continuously arrived from Eastern European countries. In spite of emigration and naturalization in the following year the numbers did not decrease because of the continued influx of new refugees. Thus the total number remained in the years from 1946 to 1948 fairly constant and decreased continuously only from 1949 until the end of 1955. During this period German speaking persons predominated; they were mainly Volksdeutsche from neighboring countries.

The Allied powers in the beginning redirected the Volksdeutsche arriving in Austria to Germany. However, in the fall of 1946, at the request of the High Commissioners of the American and British Zones of West Germany, this population movement was stopped because of overcrowded conditions. The number of Volksdeutsche in Austria reached its height at about 400,000 persons in 1948. Some 100,000 DPs did not repatriate, and since 1946 a continuous influx of new refugees had arrived from the Eastern European countries. These were under the protection of IRO from 1 July 1947 to 31 January 1952. During this period about 147,000 non-German speaking refugees emigrated, and about 4,000 were repatriated.

When the UNHCR began its activity in Austria in 1952 there were about 228,000 refugees under his mandate; 193,000 Volksdeutsche and 35,000 non-German. Of these, 46,835 persons lived in 83 camps administered by the federal government. An additional 10,000 persons, mainly Volksdeutsche lived in about 130 camps which were administered by the Länder authorities, and private industrial firms. [9] At the beginning of 1950 there were two-thirds more men than women. Occupationally, about a third of the total were skilled and highly skilled workers; about a third were office workers, government servants, or practiced other non-manual occupations, and about a third were laborers, including a large group in agriculture, forestry, and fishery. [10]

The BO in Austria took all steps within its competence in agreement with the Allied and the Austrian authorities to help the refugees overcome their legal disabilities, to regularize their personal status, and to facilitate their assimilation in the Austrian community. In both Germany and Austria the IRO had maintained staffs of DP lawyers who

provided legal assistance to refugees.   When the IRO was
liquidated, arrangements were made with the voluntary agencies to assume some of the responsibilities for legal assistance.   A few of the voluntary agencies had lawyers on their
staffs and others had recourse to indigenous lawyers.   No
overall law existed in Austria concerning the status of foreign refugees similar to the Law on the Status of Homeless
Foreigners enacted by the Federal Government of Germany.

The Federal Government of Austria signed the 1951
Convention Relating to the Status of Refugees on 28 July
1951, but with important reservations.   At the urging of the
HC the Austrian Government withdrew these reservations
when it ratified this Convention on 1 November 1954.

At the end of December 1951, the HC asked Dr. Gilbert Jaeger, a Belgian economist, to investigate the question of economic integration of the refugees in Austria.
Many refugees, especially Volksdeutsche, had to accept employment in jobs far below the level of their education and
training.   The HC was unwilling to accept this situation as
permanent.

A great number of non-German speaking refugees were
resettled overseas with the aid of ICEM, but it was evident
that the majority of refugees remaining in 1951 would have
to be integrated into Austria.   The UNHCR pointed out that
the refugees would make a great contribution to the Austrian
economy if their abilities were fully used.   However, the
problem of overpopulation was particularly serious since the
proportion of refugees was relatively high in relation to the
normal population.   There was an urgent need for foreign
capital to facilitate economic integration.

The Republic of Italy

Like West Germany and Austria, Italy was a country
of first asylum because of its geographic situation on the
edge of the Eastern European countries.   It borders in the
northeast on Yugoslavia and, in the north, on Austria and
Switzerland.   Its total area of 116, 303 square miles is comprised of the mainland peninsula, the large islands of Sicily
and Sardinia, and about seventy smaller islands.   The Italian
economy at the end of WWII was predominantly agricultural.
The level of economic development varied from one region to
another, and there were a number of depressed areas.

Italy has always had a problem of overpopulation because of a marked disequilibrium between population growth
and natural resources.   Before WWI it relied on emigration
to keep its population at a level compatible with its resources.   From 1921 until the economic crisis of 1929-33
this outlet was, to a great extent, closed by restrictions on
the part of the major immigrant countries; it was entirely
stopped by WWII.   Serious unemployment was further aggravated by the return of 500,000 Italians from the former
colonies in Africa, the Aegean Islands, Venezia Giulia, and
Dalmatia.

UNRRA and IRO, as in the other countries, repatriated and resettled a large number of refugees.   IRO transferred the cost of material assistance to both "old" and new
refugees (including camp maintenance, cash allowances,
medical assistance, and hospital treatment) to the Government of Italy later than in the other residence countries because of the critical socio-economic situation in Italy.   Not
until June 1952 did the Italian Government assume responsibility through the Administration of International Assistance
Activities (AAI).   Under a supplementary agreement with the
IRO at that time, the Italian Government assumed full responsibility for material assistance to a group of approximately 9,500 refugees which had not been resettled or repatriated. [11]

In 1951, about 18,000 registered refugees had lived
in camps and around 2,500 lived outside camps.   In addition, it was estimated that 15,000 unregistered refugees
were in the cities.   New refugee groups continually arriving
added to a large group of difficult cases.

The procedure for the determination and certification
of refugees in Italy was based on an agreement made between the Italian Government and the IRO in December 1948.
With the closure of the IRO office in Italy these arrangements ended and a serious problem arose in connection with
the regularization of the status of new refugees.   On 2 April
1952 an Agreement was negotiated between the Italian Government and UNHCR for the establishment of a BO in Rome.
Under this Agreement it was provided that the office would,
at the request of the Italian Government, cooperate in the
determination of eligibility and issuance of identification papers to refugees.   A subsequent arrangement to implement
this agreement was negotiated in July 1952, under which
procedures were established: "Refugees are examined, with

a view to determining their status, by a joint committee
consisting of two representatives of the Italian Government
and two representatives of UNHCR, with rotating chairmanship. " Refugees recognized as such were granted asylum
as a political refugees.   They received a travel document
and a residence permit bearing the endorsement "eligible
under UNHCR, " valid for four months, which was automatically renewed.   The Italian authorities extended the validity
of the IRO identity documents until 31 December 1952.   Effective 1 January 1953, refugees within the UNHCR mandate
received the travel document provided for by the 1951 Convention, which served as an identity and travel document
and as a residence permit.

Newly arrived persons who claimed to be refugees,
and who could at the same time establish their identity and
their ability to be self-supporting to the satisfaction of the
authorities, were admitted freely to Italy.   They received
temporary residence permits pending regularization of their
status according to the procedure mentioned above.   New
arrivals who claimed that they were destitute were sent to
a collecting center.   If they were able to establish their
identity and were found to be bona fide refugees after provisional screening they were, within a period of not more
than thirty days, transferred to an "open section" of the
camps where they were examined for the regularization of
their status. [12]

The Italian Government agreed to the Convention on
1 August 1951 and ratified it on 15 November 1954.   The
Convention was regarded as giving effect to the principle of
"political asylum" already contained in Art. 10 of the Italian
Constitution:

> Any alien debarred in his own country from the
> effective exercise of the democratic liberties
> guaranteed by the Italian Constitution shall have
> the right of asylum in the territory of the Repub-
> lic, according to the conditions laid down by law. [13]

The Italian Government had frequently emphasized that
the economic and social situation of Italy caused by overpopulation and unemployment constituted a serious problem.
It refused to consider the integration of refugees as a possible solution and therefore considered Art. 17 of the Convention relating to wage-earning employment only as a
recommendation.   It regarded emigration as the only possible

solution for the majority of refugees. The situation in Trieste was particularly urgent, involving two distinct categories of refugees, those from Venezia Giulia and those from Yugoslavia and other Eastern European countries.

Refugees in Trieste

On 15 September 1947 Italy had signed the Treaty of Paris. The Free Territory was established and divided into two zones. Zone "A" was to be administered by the US-UK Military Government and Zone "B," which included 40 kilometers of the Istrian coastline, was placed under Yugoslav authority. The town of Pola at the southern tip of Venezia Giulia was entirely evacuated, and 30,000 people left the city of Fiume; only Yugoslav citizens and persons holding foreign passports remained. The city of Gorizia, at the north of the Gulf of Trieste, was returned to Italy. Italian nationals still in the Yugoslav zone were permitted to choose whether to stay or leave. Those who chose Italian citizenship under Art. 19 of the Peace Treaty proceeded to Italy. But the majority remained in Trieste where most had relatives and friends. However, at the beginning of 1950 the flow of refugees into Trieste greatly increased; many of them had hoped to take advantage of the resettlement schemes of the IRO, and intended merely to pass through Trieste en route to the IRO camps in Italy. But when the IRO announced the termination of its resettlement activities, large numbers of refugees found themselves stranded in Trieste.

Refugees in Trieste from Yugoslavia and Other Eastern European Countries. In 1948 the Government of Yugoslavia broke away from the Cominform, and a new refugee wave began, that of Cominformist sympathizers. The Allied authorities had to open new camps for large numbers of these exiles. The first large group reaching Trieste, mainly in 1950, were Nansen refugees of Russian origin. They had been given refugee status in Yugoslavia between the two World Wars and had acquired Yugoslav nationality by naturalization. After WWII, they had been led to resume their original nationality and could therefore not remain in Yugoslavia after it had broken off diplomatic relations with Russia in 1948. A fairly large number of Yugoslav refugees followed them and a smaller number of Bulgarians, Hungarians, Rumanians, and Czechs were received during 1950 and 1951.

International Assistance to Refugees in Trieste.   International assistance programming for refugees in Trieste
had been implemented, particularly for material aid and
for assistance in emigration.   IRO extended its emigration
activities until the end of December 1951 and at its liquidation made a grant of $200,000 to the Allied Military Gov-
ernment for settling a number of difficult cases.   ICEM,
which resumed emigration work at the beginning of 1951,
opened an office in Trieste, as did USEP (the US Escapee
Program).   Between 1 February 1952 and 30 September
1953, ICEM with the participation of voluntary agencies resettled about 1,100 persons, most of them refugees, and
some emigration schemes were financed by USEP.   ICEM
had at its disposal one million dollars for use in the placement of difficult cases in appropriate institutions.   The Allied Military Government, with the cooperation of voluntary
agencies, concentrated its efforts mainly on individual cases
emigrating to other European countries.

The following voluntary agencies had representatives
in Trieste: AJDC, ICRC, CICC, WCC, LWF, Tolstoy
Foundation, WUS, ISS, and YMCA.   Other agencies contributed to material aid and emigration: Aide Suisse à l'Europe, SRC, and Entr'aide Protestante and others.

In spite of these efforts, the number of refugees on
1 November 1953 was 6,200 (4,500 living in camps, 1,700
outside camps) because of the continuous influx of new refugees.

In January 1952, of the 5,000 to 6,000 refugees in
Trieste, 4,200 were living in four camps administered by
the Allied Military Government, while the Italian Government assumed responsibility for their care and maintenance.
In these camps (Opicina, San Sabba, San Sabba Annex, and
Gesuiti, a former prison) the refugees lived in overcrowded
and unhygienic conditions with almost no recreation facilities.   Among these camp refugees, 600 persons were categorized as difficult cases.

The HC paid special attention to the refugees in Trieste.   In one camp almost three hundred refugees had tuberculosis; at the HC's request WHO carried out an investigation of 279 tuberculosis cases at the end of 1951; 189 were
cured by the end of 1952.   A grant of $20,000 from the
Emergency Fund was used to improve the diet of the sick
and convalescent and the living premises for tuberculosis

patients treated during 1952; a special subsidy was granted
by the Ford Foundation Program to enable a number of refugees to participate in vocational training programs in preparation for emigration.

A small number of refugees were repatriated at their
own request to the USSR and Yugoslavia. But most of the
refugees had to emigrate to Australia, Canada, and the US,
with a smaller number going to Venezuela and Brazil.[14]

Greece

Greece occupies the southern tip of the Balkan peninsula and is bounded on the North by Albania, Yugoslavia,
and Bulgaria; on the east by Turkey; and on the southeast,
south, and west by the Aegean, Mediterranean, and Ionian
Seas, respectively. Its area is 51,182 square miles, including the Island of Crete and the Dodecanese Islands. A
naturally poor country, its resources had been severely
strained by the destruction of WWII and the subsequent Civil
War (1945-49).

In 1950 the Greek Government was faced with serious economic and social problems. During the Civil War,
about 750,000 peasants sought refuge in the towns. There
was a great housing shortage. In spite of a Government
housing program, there was still a shortage of 364,500
dwellings by the end of 1950. The Government also created
a work relief plan (1945-49) for the reconstruction of village
communities which gave refugees a basic means for support
and assistance.

Refugees in Greece were a heterogeneous group.
Some had arrived in the inter-war period, and others had
arrived after WWII. Their numbers were affected, as in
Germany and Austria, by continual fluctuations due to births
and deaths, but even more by the continuous arrival of new
refugees. On 1 July 1952, Greece harbored an estimated
15,400 refugees. Of these, 6,800 were Nansen refugees
(6,000 Armenians, 500 Russians, 300 Assyrians); in addition, there were 8,600 post-WWII refugees, 7,500 of whom
were of Greek ethnic origin (5,000 from Rumania, 2,000
from Russia, and 500 from other countries) and 1,100 non-
Greek refugees (including 450 Albanians, 350 Bulgarians and
250 Yugoslavians).

There were striking differences in the demographic features of this refugee population. The family composition of the inter-war refugees, who had been in Greece for some thirty years, was for the most part normal, except that among the Russian refugees there were a number of aged people without families. However, about 80 percent of the non-Greek refugees of the post-war period were men of working age without families.

The economic circumstances of the inter-war Armenian and Russian refugees were, on the whole, adequate.[15] But the post-WWII refugees were in need of immediate relief. Most lived in camps or reception centers where the physical conditions were poor, in spite of the good work done by the Greek Government. Their integration was greatly hampered by unemployment and underemployment. Morale among the refugees was low. Exile, poverty, and prolonged illness had lowered their self-esteem, as had the attitude of the population toward refugees of non-Greek origin and the fact that alien refugees were subject to security measures.

On 10 April 1952 the Greek Government signed the 1951 Refugee Convention of 1951. Although it was hoped that Art. 3 would afford equality of treatment for the refugees, Greece did not ratify the Convention until 5 April 1960, forestalling enforcement of that provision. Most of the refugees who were workers and employees needed to be granted residence and labor permits. The latter had not yet been given in general to the professions.

Because of the unemployment problem, the Greek Government was anxious that the refugees emigrate. Although refugees had priority with ICEM, emigration prospects were limited, partly because few immigrant countries wanted them, partly because a large proportion of the refugees were over the age of fifty. Those refugees who were able to emigrate had already done so. Thus by 1952, the only permanent solution to the problem was seen to be the integration into Greek social and economic life of an estimated 2,500 family units (including single persons).

Notes

1.   HC's GA (VIII) Off. Rec., 16 Oct. 1953: 99.

2.   An. Rep. to GA (XI), 1956, Supp. 11, A/3123/Rev.
     1.

3.   G. J. van Heuven Goedhart, "The Problem of Refu-
     gees, " Recueil des Cours, 1953.

4.   HCR/RS/4, 9 July 1952.

5.   Ibid. : 7-8.

6.   A/AC 36/23; 25 Mar. 1953.

7.   For detail, see G. C. Paikert, The German Exodus,
     M. Nijhoff, The Heague, 1962 and ILO, International
     Migration, 1945-1957, Geneva, 1959: 7-11.

8.   The Economic Integration of Non-German Refugees in
     the Federal Republic of Germany through Loans of
     the Equalization of Burdens Bank, Figures as of
     31 Dec. 1965, Bad Godesberg, Jan. 1966.

9.   Eugen Antalovsky, "Die Flüchtlinge und Osterreich, "
     in Theodor Veiter, Vertreibung Zuflucht, Heimat,
     Vienna, 1962: 160; Yvonne Van Stedingk, Die Or-
     ganisation des Flüchtlingswesens in Osterreich seit
     dem Zweiten Weltkrieg, Wien and Stuttgart, Wilhelm
     Braumüller, 1970, p. 138; and UN GA (VIII), Off.
     Rec. Supp. No. 11/A/2394/1953: 12.

10. See ILO Migration Field Mission, Austria, Vienna,
     reprinted in HCR/RS3, Jaeger, op. cit. : 69.

11. A/AC. 96/INF. 27, 8 Oct. 1954.

12. A/AC. 36/23. 25 Mar. 1953.

13. A/AC. 96/Inf. 27, 8 Oct. 1964.

14. See UNHCR Memo. of 26 Jan. 1953.

15. See HCR/RS/7, The Integration of Refugees in the
     Economy, Geneva, 10 Feb. 1953 and A/AC. 36/13,
     28 July 1952.

Chapter 13

THE FORD FOUNDATION PROGRAM

While the GA had acknowledged that plans for local integration were essential for a permanent solution in a reasonable time, it had not yet provided any tangible capital resources for implementation of such plans. Thus, the HC had to seek alternative methods of financing permanent solutions.

The HC was aided in this search by four major voluntary agencies: the WCC, NCWC, AJDC, and the LWF. The agencies worked internationally and served all major ethnic and religious groups, including new refugees and those not under the HC's mandate. They had offices or counterpart organizations in the countries of first asylum and had cooperated with IRO. Thus they were experienced in current situations, needs, and procedures. They had the staff and skills to carry out effective programs which were the common interest of the UNHCR, PICMME, and the agencies.

Request to the Ford Foundation

The four voluntary agencies, acting jointly with UNHCR and PICMME, approached the Ford Foundation in March 1952. They presented a document, The Plight of the European Refugees, requesting $10.5 million to support a humanitarian program in Europe.[1] The request from the agencies was backed up by a memorandum from the HC on Urgent Assistance for Refugees, PICMME's Plan for Cooperation with Voluntary Agencies in resettlement programs, and the detailed illustrations of Voluntary Programs for Local Integration.[2] They were moved to this action by two factors.

First, it was evident that existing provisions for refugees were inadequate even for emergency needs, and that refugees in most countries could not become self-sufficient

without help from the international community.   Although the
voluntary agencies had expanded their fund-raising efforts
far beyond normal, their resources were strained to the
limit by the programs they were carrying on--both as a
legacy from IRO and on their own initiative--programs which
had originally been envisaged as short-term undertakings.

Second, the successful operation of IRO resettlement
programs had proved that both official and voluntary agencies had achieved more through mutual aid and interdependence than they could have done separately.   This experience had "brought to light, unexpectedly, great opportunities
for complementary, integrated and combined operations of
intergovernmental and voluntary agencies. . . .   [It] was truly
a voyage of discovery in mutual aid and interdependence. "3
Implicit in these programs had been the belief that voluntary
action in humanitarian work is inherent in a free society,
and "essential to the growth and expression of democratic
relations in the international community. "4   The advantages
of voluntary work were: greater flexibility in experimenting
with new solutions, and greater effectiveness as the personal emissaries from democratic societies to victims of
authoritarian governments.

Survey of the Needs of Refugees

Drawing upon their operational experience, the agencies surveyed the needs of the refugees and the cost of operating the most essential projects.   They presented an
analysis of total funds available for these programs from
governments, inter-governmental organizations, and voluntary
agencies.   They estimated that a grant of $10.5 million
from the Ford Foundation would make up the difference between need and resources.

The projects for which the agencies requested the
most substantial support were those which they were already
operating or which they felt they should operate in cooperation with UNHCR and PICMME.

They pointed out that the following funds, supplementary to those from governmental and inter-governmental
agencies and international voluntary agencies, were urgently
needed:

$3,250,000 for immediate material assistance to

refugees located in Germany, Austria, Italy, Trieste, Greece, and Turkey, including newly arriving refugees daily crossing the borders; residual IRO refugees needing supplementary feeding for children and the sick; medical supplies, clothing, and shoes; hardship cases; the remaining refugees in Spain and Portugal; refugees not under the mandate of the UNHCR; and refugees in Shanghai.

$3,250,000 for resettlement, for promotion of resettlement opportunities, visa production, and services connected with integration in the resettlement countries; for establishing an additional travel loan fund to enable destitute refugees to reach a new country and begin a new life.

$4,000,000 for local integration projects; pilot projects similar to the Siedlungswerk (Germany), the Baugemeinde (Austria), and the French Farm Scheme; to provide opportunities for handicapped refugees to become at least partially self-supporting; to settle refugee farmers in areas where they could produce food; and to assist skilled workers in areas where employment was available.

The agencies' presentation revealed the need for immediate material assistance to four categories of refugees.

First, some 20,000 to 60,000 destitute refugees continued to flow annually into Austria, Germany, Italy (including Trieste), Greece, and Turkey. Their needs exceeded the regular provision made for new refugees by governments of these countries.

Second, for the 200,000 residual IRO refugees, for whom the governments of asylum countries provided minimum basic needs, minimum standards varied from country to country so that while in some countries, such as Germany, the voluntary agencies needed additional funds mainly for care of refugees with special handicaps--illness or old age-- in others, especially Greece and Italy, government provisions were grossly inadequate in all cases.

Third, some 200,000 additional refugees were

scattered through Europe who had hitherto not been under international mandate and whose needs had therefore not been officially assessed.   The agencies envisaged the needs of this third category of refugees to be at least as great as those of the residual IRO refugees.

Fourth, of the European refugees in Shanghai, for whom IRO had provided some assistance in resettlement, some 4,500 were still not resettled and were in serious danger of starving before resettlement opportunities could be found for them.

The desire of those presenting the report was not to continue stop-gap relief measures but to achieve permanent solutions, either through resettlement of refugees, or through local integration.   It was stressed that when existing refugees could become self-sufficient they would become an asset to the European community rather than a burden and that it would be easier to deal with new refugees before they became a problem.

Because of IRO's successful experience, resettlement suggested itself as one approach to permanent solution of the refugee problem.   However, because travel funds were insufficient, only a fraction could take advantage of the resettlement opportunities that were being found for them annually.   The voluntary agencies were supplying the essential personnel and organization for individual resettlement (at an estimated cost to themselves of one million dollars annually) and PICMME proposed to contribute one million dollars to establish travel loan funds, provided the voluntary agencies could match this sum.   Even with these facilities and the funds available, only 12,500 refugees, with an average travel loan of $200 each, could be resettled annually, although opportunities could be found for four times that number.

Increased provision for resettlement notwithstanding, many refugees would still be left in Europe.   Permanent solution to their plight could best be achieved through hitherto little tried programs of local integration.   The handicapped would have to be helped to become at least partially self-supporting, farmers would have to be settled in areas where they might produce food instead of receiving relief, and skilled laborers would have to be settled near areas where employment opportunities were available.

Voluntary agencies had initiated in West Germany and

in Austria small pilot self-help projects in the hope of winning support from local government and other sources.
Building schemes in Austria and Germany eventually won 80 percent of their support from those governments. Governments were also assisting in long-term loans for construction, and financing such enterprises as the Expellee Bank to aid in the establishment of small businesses. Nevertheless, the need for undertaking many more such projects was infinite.

Within this total request for $10.5 million the agencies listed priorities amounting to $6.75 million. This smaller figure was considered essential for assisting new refugees, establishing revolving funds for transportation, supplementing government assistance to difficult cases in Europe, maintaining displaced persons in the Far East, initiating long-range settlement projects in Europe, and promoting resettlement abroad.

Ford Foundation Response: Support
for Local Integration Programs

The Ford Foundation recognized the urgent need for finding solutions to the refugee problem. After personal deliberation with the HC, and consideration of the recommendations of George M. Shuster, who had made a four-month study of the problem, the Foundation, in July 1952, announced its decision to grant the sum of $2.9 million to the UNHCR to be expended by the HC through PICMME and the four agencies mentioned, as well as through the YMCA, the American Friends Service Committee (AFSC), and "such other agencies as he may select." The money was allocated for specific purposes:

For resettlement	200,000
For demonstration projects in social assimilation	$1,000,000
For training of youth	1,500,000
For youth centers in refugee camps	100,000
For cultural activities among refugees	100,000
	$2,900,000

Furthermore, strict criteria were outlined by which the HC was to judge requests brought to him by the voluntary agencies:

1. The work must help the refugees to help themselves.

2. Programs should be carried out without discrimination among refugee groups (which meant refugees not under the mandate of the UNHCR were also to be included).

3. The grants must promote the integration of the refugees in the communities in which they live as well as provide new resettlement opportunities abroad.

4. The work must not relieve governments of their normal responsibilities.

5. Programs of direct material relief should be avoided.

6. So far as possible the emphasis should be on youth.

    The amount of funds made available as well as their allocation contrasted sharply with the original recommendations and request. The total grant was less than one-third of the sum requested. Where local integration had constituted only 40 percent of the original request, it was now the focal point of the program, while substantial sums were allocated specifically for youth. Less than 10 percent was to go for resettlement abroad, and no provision was made for direct emergency relief, "in which the Ford Foundation does not engage."5

    The redirection of efforts from resettlement abroad to local integration reflected the combination of several factors. Although opportunities for resettlement were still available, many countries which had welcomed mass immigration after the war, especially of able-bodied workers, had, by 1952, reached a saturation point. Furthermore, refugees themselves, having become accustomed to local conditions, were reluctant to emigrate. Third, and perhaps the most important, the success of integration programs being carried out in Austria and Germany by the AFSC with a grant of $100,000 from the Ford Foundation indicated the great potential advantage of this new approach. Not only was it apparently a more satisfactory solution for many refugees, but experience had shown that capital invested in programs of local integration tended to attract considerable local financial support, sometimes doubling or tripling the original investment.

UNHCR as Administrator and Coordinator

The Ford Foundation originally intended to make the funds available to the HC for distribution to operating agencies.   Under Art. 10 of the Statute he could administer the funds, receive plans drawn up by the agencies, make a selection from them, coordinate those chosen, promote execution of his own proposed plans, and facilitate the implementation of all.   But because no legal basis could be found to exempt the UNHCR from taxes, it was decided that the money would go directly to voluntary agencies, which were tax exempt, for specific projects approved by the HC.

Once a project had been approved by the Geneva Office and returned to them via the BO of UNHCR in the country concerned, the voluntary agencies were given considerable operational freedom.   In the interest of speed, and because these programs were in fact often experimental--only the agencies operating them having had experience with them--the agreements were drawn up with a minimum of detail as to what was to be done and how much of the money granted was to go to each program.   On the other hand, the agencies were required to give detailed accounts of expenditures every three months so that the HC could make certain the money was being spent in accordance with the terms of the grant and with the overall principles laid down by the Foundation.   No administrative expenses were to be charged to the grant except the salaries of persons specifically employed full-time on a given project.   In addition, the agencies were to provide facilities for personal inspection of projects at the request of the HC.   These requirements provided a tighter control over their expenditures than the agencies had experienced under IRO: coordination and administration of the funds and responsibility for insuring their orderly and effective use had been assigned to the HC by the Ford Foundation.

Although the Ford Foundation allocated 2 percent of the principal ($58,000) for administrative expenses incurred by the HC in pursuance of his coordinating tasks, the HC pared these expenses down to less than 1.6 percent.   He hired only two professional officers.   Frans Kooijman, of the Netherlands, who had previously headed an extensive YMCA program for refugees in Germany, was to administer the program with the assistance of a former UN finance officer.

The combined concern for speed and economy had
certain drawbacks. The Ford Foundation stated in retrospect: "More time and money invested in preliminary checking and a larger allocation for travel to permit the Office to
maintain a closer supervision as the projects developed would
almost certainly have given the program more stability and
made it less vulnerable to false starts. "[6] A more adequate
evaluation system might also have been developed since reports were not uniform in terms of reference and, in many
cases, concerned themselves with overall programs rather
than exclusively Ford-funded ones. A comprehensive view
of the implementation of projects was not available, and the
actual numbers of refugees helped by Ford money could only
be estimated. A further consequence of the concern for
speed and economy was that opportunities for securing supporting contributions from other sources could not be sys-
tematically explored. The $5,568,470 which was forthcom-
ing was a spontaneous response rather than the result of
negotiations by the HC.

Before drawing up specific plans for projects to be
presented to the HC, the six agencies, in consultation with
the HC, agreed on the following provisional allocation of the
funds among themselves:

AFSC	$ 300,000
AJDC	$ 320,000
LWF	$ 495,000
NCWC	$ 890,000
WCC	$ 495,000
YMCA	$ 150,000
	$2,650,000

This left $250,000 to cover administrative costs and
requests from other agencies. These figures served as
guidelines for each agency in drawing up its specific project
proposals for HC approval. By this means, they avoided
competition and the waste of time entailed in preparing de-
scriptions of projects beyond the funds each was to receive.

Programs for Local Integration

Housing and accommodation accounted for about half of
the money allocated to integration projects. It was considered so important that it attracted more than 85 percent of
the total supporting contributions for all integration projects.

In housing, the prime function of Ford Foundation money was to reduce the amount of funds which had to be borrowed on the commercial market, where the rates ranged from 8 to 10 percent, by supplying loans either at very low rates or, in most cases, without interest. The saving could thus be passed on to the refugees in the form of lower rents. Without this rent subsidy, refugees would not have been able to compete on the commercial market with nationals who, not having been uprooted, could more often afford the down payments on housing or apartments.

However, local contributions could be obtained only if the housing conformed to government building standards. Where speed and economy were sacrificed to achieve compliance with standards for permanent housing, as for example in Germany, supporting contributions far outweighed Ford money.

In many cases, the eagerness of refugees to participate in building their own houses helped to make the money go further. Often, as soon as the basement was finished entire refugee families would install themselves, willingly accepting even worse conditions than in the camps, in order to be able to hasten the day when they would have a real home.

Agricultural projects were also important. A large percentage of refugees were from agricultural backgrounds. Pilot projects were carried out in efforts to resettle these people on individual farms or even to set up complete farm villages. The results were especially important in France and Greece, not only for the refugees concerned but also for the local areas. In some cases land that had been abandoned was again brought under cultivation, in others new techniques were introduced.

Revolving loan funds were the main device for helping refugees to help themselves. A sewing machine or a set of tools would have been impossible for a refugee to acquire without such loans. The success of these projects encouraged others to fund similar projects under UNREF. Almost half of the loan allocation from the Ford grant was used in Austria. Some 700 refugees were firmly settled with loans averaging $113, and another 430 benefited from the repayments on these loans. In Germany 220 were firmly settled and 50 others benefited under the original disbursement of $31,537, and 200 had been assisted from repayments up to 31 December 1957.

For many refugees who had lived in camps for years, the psychological difficulties involved in the decision to move were great. They needed support and continued counselling during the adjustment period. One great fear was that the rent would prove too high for a family on welfare or with a breadwinner only marginally employed. Changes in habits and, often, separation from friends had to be faced. Most non-German refugees did not feel welcome in Germany, although the situation was different in Austria. The aged were particularly reluctant to move, especially if the move involved entering an institution for the aged. Refugees feared that their liberty would be circumscribed by regulations, that they would not be permitted to take any possessions with them, that there were too few years of life left to them. Those who still hoped for emigration faced the loss of this hope.

For these reasons counselling received greater emphasis in countries of first asylum, whereas in countries of second asylum community centers were considered more useful.

The provision of youth homes and of educational and vocational training was an urgent need if young men and women were to become self-supporting. Where refugees were accommodated in apprentice homes during training, the projects had a distinct social value. After a childhood in various camps, a normal household life in a settled, indigenous community contributed greatly to an individual's development. There were young people among the new refugees who had been encouraged to escape alone by families which could not escape as a group, in the deep faith that life in a free world must be better for a child. These youngsters especially needed help and guidance.

Not only those whose work was in the trades and in clerical professions, but also the more gifted and motivated were in need of the chance to develop their capabilities and contribute to their new countries. Only in Germany were refugees eligible for government-sponsored scholarships. In other countries the only sources were private and these were usually inadequate to the needs of qualified secondary school graduates.

Resettlement Projects

      Mass emigration had ended with the IRO; the empha-
sis now lay on individual placement.   This meant that governments would no longer send selection missions to countries of first asylum to seek out suitable emigrants in relatively large numbers.   Visa applicants would be processed
in the usual way by consulates; but the task of finding work
and housing in reception countries rested on the refugees and
the international voluntary agencies helping them to meet the
various immigration requirements of different countries or
negotiating for the acceptance of groups of refugees under
sponsorship schemes.   The number of visas was very limited, in part due to the fact that agencies lacked adequate
staff and offices in overseas countries for visa work.   ICEM
carried out the actual transportation of refugees.   The HC
sought to stimulate the granting of more visas in the major
overseas countries.   Ford money contributed to the increase
of immigration, supplementing a network of offices already
set up by ICEM and USEP.

      The WCC, which had launched its resettlement pro-
jects on 1 September 1952, was enabled by the Ford grant
to expand its programs considerably in three areas of immi-
gration--Australia, Canada, and Latin America.   In Canada
a second office was established in the western regions of the
country and the first refugee was processed there on 1 November 1952.   In Latin America, the offices in Brazil were
enlarged, and new ones were opened in Chile, Paraguay,
Uruguay, and Venezuela.   In Australia, a resettlement office
was set up; field workers were employed to encourage individuals to sponsor refugees for admission and to provide a
job-placement service.   Under this sponsorship scheme, 418
persons, in addition to those admitted on the governmental
immigrant scheme, were helped to emigrate.   A special officer was engaged in Geneva to oversee the expanded WCC
operation.

      A supplementary WCC project to the Latin American
immigration project covered $10,000 for small loans to refu-
gees in Brazil, Chile, Paraguay, and Venezuela for 55 fam-
ilies--155 persons in all.   Owing partly to inflation in most
Latin American countries, repayment was not made in full.
However, aside from being of considerable help to the refugees in resettlement, the availability of the funds influenced
governments to grant immigration visas.

Individual placement involved intensive counselling in countries of departure and reception and follow-up facilities for refugees in their new countries.

The Ford program included an intra-European project for the difficult cases, providing for the rehabilitation in Norway and Sweden of refugees suffering from tuberculosis and from physical handicaps. Some 87 tubercular and post-tubercular refugees and 32 family members were resettled from camps in Austria, Germany, and Italy to Scandinavian countries where, after receiving treatment, they were helped to find work and become integrated. The funds were used to pay the costs of selected missions, transportation charges, and sums required by receiving countries as a contribution toward the cost of treatment and settlement. By the end of 1956, 150 refugees had been resettled in Sweden and 112 in Norway.

The Berlin Crisis

Germany had at the outset been singled out as being in need of special programs. Recognizing the urgent need for assistance, the Ford Foundation supported a large-scale program in West Germany "without discrimination of refugee groups." The federal, state, and local governments of West Germany had made heavy expenditures to cope with the continuing influx from East Germany.[7] The YMCA operated youth centers in eighteen refugee camps and the AFSC had made a six-month study of refugees in Austria and Germany. Considering the size of the problem, these were hardly more than preliminary efforts. Despite these endeavors, rioting had broken out. The 50,000 participants were reported in the press to be "embittered and homeless after eight years of living in ramshackle camps." The Ford Foundation warned that "the situation of the refugees can lead to an explosion that will wreck efforts to stabilize central Europe."[8] The Foundation's decision to apply a substantial segment of its grant to Germany served, in turn, to draw further attention to the problem and to heighten appreciation of the fact that what was going on in Germany would have vital implications for the whole of Europe.

However, the most dramatic phase of the Foundation program came in early 1953 when political developments caused a sharp increase in the influx of refugees crossing from Eastern Germany into the Federal Republic, particularly

into West Berlin.   The number arriving in Berlin rose from
15,787 in December 1952 to 28,276 in January 1953, and attained a high point of 48,000 in March 1953.   Existing camps
were inundated with newcomers; bombed-out factories had to
be installed with straw mattresses and other emergency
equipment, to serve as reception centers.   Those who qualified under German law as refugees were eligible for airlift
to West Germany but only 400 to 500 could be flown out
daily.   Furthermore, about a quarter of the arrivals did not
qualify as refugees and were thus not entitled to work.
These 150,000 persons were superimposed on West Berlin's
existing unemployed, about 270,000 in a total population of
2.2 million.

Although these refugees were not within the mandate
of the HC, he intervened, since as administrator of the Ford
Foundation grant he was required to supervise the funds for
refugees without discrimination.   He stated that the influx of
these refugees had overwhelmed available accommodation in
Berlin as well as in West Germany and, without immediate
action, would have "far-reaching effects on the integration
of the existing refugee population," including the 45,000 non-
German refugees within his mandate. [9]

On 29 January 1953 the HC cabled the CoE asking support for his efforts to reestablish the new refugees.   On the
following day he sent a cable to sixty UN member states proposing, in agreement with the Government of the Federal Republic, to initiate immediately with the international voluntary
agencies, projects for prefabricated housing near employment
centers in West Germany.   Ford funds were initially used.
The majority of the adult refugees were workers and craftsmen between the ages of twenty-eight and thirty-eight, so
there was a good chance for them to be finally settled once
housing could be provided.   Switzerland immediately put a
substantial number of prefabricated housing units at the disposal of the HC; other governments also responded favorably.
Publicity concerning the HC's intervention helped to arouse
interest in the emergency.   The HC coordinated the variety
of efforts made by the international voluntary agencies and
intergovernmental agencies.

Mr. Kooijman flew to Berlin on 2 February and pre-
sided over a meeting attended by representatives of the voluntary agencies, German and international Red Cross Societies,   and the CoE, and consulted representatives of the
three Allied High Commissioners and governmental authorities

of the City of Berlin. By 10 February the HC was able to inform governments that the Federal Government had agreed that it would doubly match any outside contributions toward the permanent housing projects which were part of the special Berlin program. In addition, an amount equal to the German contribution would be raised by German authorities from German banks. Thus, German sources matched outside contributions for permanent housing four to one. At the suggestion of the Federal Government the contributions were to benefit not only the new refugees in Berlin but also other categories of refugees, including homeless foreigners under the HC's mandate who were still living in camps.

In addition, German authorities increased the airlift out of Berlin to 30,000 refugees per month, so that refugees could be flown out after an average wait of six days, instead of four to six weeks.

On 16 February Mr. Kooijman presented an overall plan of action on behalf of Berlin refugees, covering emigration, immediate relief in West Berlin, and integration of refugees in West Germany. Ford funds were to be used primarily for permanent housing projects in West Germany, which had been drawn up by AFSC, NCWC, and WCC. The funds were also to be used for vocational training, counselling, and the construction in Berlin itself of a hostel and two Häuser für Alle. German agencies pledged to supply blankets, towels, soap, and reading material. The Norwegian Aid to Europe and Swiss Aid to Europe had already made substantial sums available to finance youth projects.

ICEM, together with the voluntary agencies, appealed to its member governments for cooperation in relieving the pressure on Berlin. In all, a total of $406,943 from Ford funds was applied to the Special Berlin Program, through the goodwill and flexibility of the agencies who made drastic readjustments within their allocations on very short notice. Supporting contributions from German sources totaled $1,065,140.

Governments contributed $527,950 for prefabricated housing units and furniture for the refugees. The US Government allocated through the Mutual Security Administration a further $300,000 to assist in reception and to provide equipment for hostels for young refugees. A contribution of $23,810 from the International Rescue Committee (IRC) brought the total value of aid under the Berlin program to $2,323,843.

During the summer months of 1953 the influx of new refugees decreased; in August only 10,000 arrived. While during the first half of the year, twelve buses had run constantly between the largest of the transportation centers for refugees and Tempelhof airport, by the end of September, one was sufficient. Overcrowding in some of the West German Länder, particularly North Rhine-Westphalia and Baden-Wuerttemberg, hindered some of the refugees from going directly to the area where they were to be settled, yet the main impact of the emergency on Berlin itself had been absorbed. The HC's experience in coordinating this emergency program proved of great value during the Hungarian emergency in 1956.

Effects of the Program

With a terminal grant of $200,000 in March 1954, the Ford Foundation had contributed a total of $3,054,651, while the supporting contributions from other sources amounted to $5,568,470 (see Annex 13.1). This sum was increased by $790,936 through sperrmarks and sperrschillings. With this total amount of $9,414,057, fifteen voluntary agencies carried out ninety-one integration projects--local and overseas-- 116 youth projects, and twenty-one resettlement schemes in seven European countries and in Turkey, Canada, Australia, and Latin America (see Annex 13.2). A total of 37,160 refugees benefited from the Ford-stimulated projects, and by 31 December 1957 an additional 33,300 refugees had been assisted under continuation of these projects (see Annex 13.3).

In addition to the immediate benefits to refugees, the Ford program had far-reaching consequences for subsequent international refugee work. It demonstrated how the UNHCR, although non-operational, could stimulate a variety of pilot projects and effectively aid in constructive operation by enlisting and coordinating the support of experienced operational partners and private initiative, and significantly develop greater efforts and interest in refugee problems on the part of governments. This led directly to the next great step taken by the international community--the establishment of UNREF in 1954. Ford allocations helped to develop projects out of which emerged long-range policies for permanent solutions, as well as a variety of new techniques and procedures; the program also demonstrated how money and effort could most effectively be used to help refugees to help themselves.

It permitted the voluntary agencies to expand their operations and to develop skills and efficiency and demonstrated that the problems of mandate and non-mandate refugees were interrelated. Finally, the program effected solutions to a variety of refugee problems.

Prior to 1952, as we have seen, refugee work had been carried out mainly in the areas of emergency relief and overseas resettlement. But the Ford Foundation program's emphasis on self-help programs for local integration resulted in trail-blazing experiments with housing, agriculture, youth projects, loan funds, vocational training, and educational assistance and counselling, all of which had previously been undertaken only on a very small scale. Projects of this kind led to permanent solutions and--especially considering the emphasis on youth and the sense of urgency with which programs were carried out--to the prevention of potential problems. As a result of their proven success these new techniques became part of the regular UNHCR program.

Moreover, Ford Foundation funds "were a prime factor in enabling the voluntary agencies to expand their efforts."[10] By 1952, although they had continued to receive some support as the phasing out of the IRO proceeded, they could no longer count on sustained financial help within the framework of a truly international coordinated effort to solve the refugee problem. The infusion of Ford Foundation funds into the programs spurred the voluntary agencies to renewed efforts. The general goal--to facilitate permanent solutions --was set, but it was up to the voluntary agencies to develop concrete programs. Their experience in doing so, combined with the prevailing sense of urgency and the demand for strict accounting, produced highly skilled operational partners for the UNHCR, essential not only for his regular programs, but also for meeting the emergencies of the Berlin crisis and later the Hungarian crisis. A measure of their effectiveness is the fact that they continue to be the major operational arm of the UNHCR in Europe.

With regard to the UNHCR, the program demonstrated decisively "the usefulness of a non-operational agency whose primary role was to coordinate efforts on behalf of refugees, not only in facilitating permanent solutions, but also in dealing with emergencies."[11] The expenditure of $3 million of Ford Foundation funds, plus more than $6 million in supplementary contributions, through more than 200 separate projects carried out by fifteen voluntary agencies in eight countries (not including receiving countries in resettlement projects) would inevitably have led to waste of effort and funds, if not to chaos, without the careful and imaginative coordination which the HC provided. This coordinated international assistance and technical aid provided by the HC and his operational partners, the voluntary agencies, benefited communities as a whole in an ever-increasing and effective manner. The aid was accepted in the knowledge that any action undertaken was motivated solely by social and humanitarian considerations. Thus the Ford Foundation allocations provided new experience and enabled the HC to fulfill the functions for which his Office was created.

Above all, "at a time when governmental interest in the refugee problem was at a low point the grants encouraged governments, private sources, and the general public to take greater interest, moral and material, in furthering a solution of the refugee problem."[12] The infusion of capital brought about a "peaceful chain reaction" in terms of supporting contributions. Of the overall program, 69 percent was financed by supporting contributions.[13] This fact, combined with the evident effectiveness of the programs in accomplishing their purposes, "played a major psychological role in establishing a pattern of more or less regular contributions by governments in favor of refugees on a continuing basis completely divorced from emergency relief." By focusing a bright light on the refugee problem, the Foundation's action "made it virtually impossible for nations who had in practice adopted the concept of the unity of mankind and the ideal of the UN to belittle such a major humanitarian problem."[14]

Notes

1. A Statement Prepared for the Ford Foundation, Mar. 1952.

2. Ibid., Apps. I-III: 12-27.

3. Yul Brynner, Bring Forth the Children, New York, 1960: 16.

4. Statement: 2.

5. Final Report on the Ford Foundation Program for Refugees, Primarily in Europe, July 1958.

6.   Ibid. : 22.

7.   "From 1949 to 1951 the Government of Western Ger-
      many spent more than 10 billion DM for assistance
      to refugees, more than 74 percent of which was
      spent on relief, unemployment, and similar efforts
      to keep them alive.   The expenditure for 1949 repre-
      sented 45 percent of all welfare costs and 12 per-
      cent of all government expenditures--federal, state,
      and local. "   Statement: 40.

8.   Report on the Ford Foundation Program: 40-61.

9.   Statement, op cit. :   42.

10. Ibid. : 14.

11. Ibid. : 42.

12. Ibid. : 14.

13. Ibid. : 24.

14. Ibid. : 18.

ANNEX 13.1

FORD FOUNDATION GRANT:
Overall Analysis of Financial Allocations to Projects
by Program, Country, Type of Solution and Source of Contribution
as of March 1954 (in US Dollars)

Program, country, Type of solution	Ford Found. Contributions	Est. total of support. Contributions	Total Contributions
A. LOCAL SETTLEMENT			
Austria			
Integration	419,450	855,305	1,274,755
Youth projects	310,392	305,380	615,772
Total	729,842	1,160,685	1,890,527
Belgium			
Integration	64,901	90,100	155,001
Youth projects	1,600	---	1,600
Total	66,501	90,100	156,601
France			
Integration	233,484	318,714	552,198
Youth projects	32,223	25,429	57,652
Total	265,707	344,143	609,850
Germany, Fed. Rep. of			
Integration	472,975	2,085,002	2,557,977
Youth projects	700,083	1,754,620	2,454,703
Total	1,173,058	3,839,622	5,012,680
Greece			
Integration	57,771	41,206	98,977
Youth projects	16,109	---	16,109
Total	73,880	41,206	115,086
Italy			
Integration	25,054	35,200	60,254
Youth projects	39,888	23,800	63,688
Total	64,942	59,000	123,942
Trieste			
Integration	---	---	---
Youth projects	42,426	13,000	55,426
Total	42,426	13,000	55,426
Turkey			
Integration	---	---	---
Youth projects	59,580	20,714	80,294
Total	59,580	20,714	80,294

(cont. on next page)

Total integration	1,273,635	3,425,527	4,699,162
Total youth projects	1,202,301	2,142,943	3,345,244
Total local settlement	2,475,936	5,568,470	8,044,406
B. RESETTLEMENT OVERSEAS	578,715	---a	---a
C. ADMINISTRATIVE EXPENSES	49,292	---	49,292
GRAND TOTAL	3,103,943b	---a	---a

a Supporting contributions for Resettlement Overseas are impossible to evaluate.

b The amount of $3,943 over and above the Ford grant represents a gain attributable to fluctuations in official exchange rates.

SOURCE: Final Report on Ford Foundation Program, Geneva, July 1958: 126-27.

ANNEX 13.2

FORD FOUNDATION PROGRAM:
Analysis of Funds Spent on Integration,
Youth Projects, and Resettlement Overseas
as of March 1954 (in US Dollars)
(Supporting Contributions are Underlined)

Agency	Integration	Youth projects	Resettlement overseas	Total
AFSC	150,578 (13)	156,887 (17)	---	307,465 (30)
AJDC	130,190 (5)	---	190,000 (3)	320,190 (8)
LWF	302,553 (12)	173,129 (17)	102,517 (6)	578,199 (35)
NCWC	353,717 (27)	462,124 (42)	161,500 (3)	977,341 (72)
WCC	221,664 (19)	238,266 (28)	111,890 (7)	571,820 (54)
YMCA	36,965 (6)	133,560 (8)	5,000 (1)	175,525 (15)
APWR	10,000 (1)	---	---	10,000 (1)
IRC	20,000 (1)	10,221 (3)	---	30,221 (4)
ISS	23,848 (3)	---	7,808 (1)	31,656 (4)
IUCW	8,000 (1)	---	---	8,000 (1)
MCC	6,000 (1)	---	---	6,000 (1)
ORT	---	10,000 (1)	---	10,000 (1)
USC	---	8,114 (1)	---	8,114 (1)
UUARC	10,120 (4)	---	---	10,120 (4)
WUS	---	10,000 (1)	---	10,000 (1)
GRAND TOTAL	1,273,635 (91)*	1,202,301 (116)*	578,715 (21)	3,054,651 (228)*

Country	Integration	Youth projects	Resettlement overseas	Total
Austria	419,450	310,392	22,000	751,842
	855,305	305,380	---	1,160,685
	(33)	(24)	(1)	(58)
Belgium	64,901	1,600	---	66,507
	90,100	---		90,100
	(5)	(1)		(6)
France	233,484	32,223	---	265,707
	318,714	25,429		344,143
	(13)	(6)		(19)
Germany	472,975	700,083	130,000	1,303,058
Fed. Rep. of	2,085,002	1,754,620	---	3,839,622
	(29)	(68)	(1)	(98)
Greece	57,771	16,109	---	73,880
	41,206	---		41,206
	(8)	(4)		(12)
Italy	25,054	39,888	45,808	110,750
	35,200	23,800	---	59,000
	(3)	(6)	(2)	(11)
Trieste	---	42,426	---	42,426
		13,000		13,000
		(5)		(5)
Turkey	---	59,580	---	59,580
		20,714		20,714
		(2)		(2)
Australia	---	---	40,167	40,167
			---	
			(4)	
Canada	---	---	67,490	67,490
			---	---
			(4)	(4)
Latin America	---	---	268,250	268,250
			---	---
			(8)	(8)
Miscellaneous	---	---	5,000	5,000
			---	---
			(1)	(1)
GRAND TOTAL	1,273,635	1,202,301	578,715	3,054,651
	3,425,527	2,142,943	---	5,568,470
	(91)*	(116)*	(21)	(228)*

*Total corrected to avoid duplication, some projects being
implemented jointly.

SOURCE: Final Report on Ford Foundation Program: 48.

ANNEX 13.3

FORD FOUNDATION PROJECTS FOR LOCAL SETTLEMENT: OVERALL ANALYSIS OF NUMBER OF BENEFICIARIES

Program Type of solution and further assistance---→ Country, stage of settlement	Integration[a] Total	Youth projects[a] Total	Total of actual beneficiaries[a] as of March 1954	Total of refugees assisted under continuation of projects up to Dec. 31, 1957[b]
Austria				
Firmly settled	3,460	930	4,390	...
Others	5,580	1,100	6,680	...
Total	9,040	2,030	11,070	6,200
Belgium				
Firmly settled	140	--	140	...
Others	660	40	700	...
Total	800	40	840	2,000
France				
Firmly settled	670	50	720	...
Others	3,110	300	3,410	...
Total	3,780	350	4,130	6,700
Germany, Fed. Rep. of				
Firmly settled	4,390	1,850	6,240	...
Others	5,810	4,990	10,800	...
Total	10,200	6,840	17,040	15,100
Greece				
Firmly settled	210	60	270	...
Others	1,150	120	1,270	...
Total	1,360	180	1,540	300
Italy				
Firmly settled	40	--	40	...
Others	80	930	1,010	...
Total	120	930	1,050	1,000
Trieste				
Firmly settled	--	--	--	...
Others	--	1,290	1,290	...
Total	--	1,290	1,290	1,800
Turkey				
Firmly settled	--	20	20	...
Others	--	180	180	...
Total	--	200	200	200
Total firmly settled	8,910	2,910	11,820	...
Total others	16,390	8,950	25,340	...
Grand Total	25,300	11,860	37,160	33,300

a All figures rounded to nearest ten.
b All figures rounded to nearest hundred.

SOURCE: Final Report on Ford Foundation Program: 124-5.

Chapter 14

THE UNITED NATIONS REFUGEE FUND

The HC continued his persistent search for permanent solutions. The positive results of the Ford Foundation pilot schemes and the prolongation of his office for five years spurred Dr. van Heuven Goedhart to proceed with practical planning for long-term programs. The HC considered the promotion of permanent settlement a "most important aspect of the work of his office." Indeed, "from the point of view of the refugee," he pointed out, "a permanent solution was more important than legal protection or emergency aid (that is to say, simple relief or welfare). The refugee's ambition was not to receive assistance from others but to become self-supporting."[1] In his observations on Problems of Assistance the HC warned the GA that "the solution for the economic problems of the alien refugees in Central Europe and the Near East [was] not in supplementary relief ... the task of international protection, conferred on his Office under Art. 1 of the Statute, did not merely imply legal protection, which was a continuing process, but also the promotion of permanent solutions for which long-term planning was necessary."[2] In addition to these two functions, the Office was also charged under Res. 538(VI) with responsibility for bringing emergency aid to the most needy groups of refugees. For this purpose the Emergency Fund of $3 million had been established. Only if these tasks--legal protection, methods of permanent settlement, and emergency aid--were undertaken together could the end defined in Art. 8 be achieved: namely, to reduce the number of refugees requiring protection.

To secure this end the promotional nature of the HC's activities were vital. Apart from inviting governments to sign and ratify the Convention, three lines of action had to be pursued: provision of emergency funds for the neediest refugees to keep them alive; a fair share in immigration schemes for those who wanted to be resettled; and long-term

370

programs for permanent solutions through strengthening the
economies of the countries of first asylum.

Need for Further International Aid
in Local Integration Programs

Important as had been the achievements under the
Ford Foundation's stimulus, there remained much to be done
toward integration of refugees.   Following the request of the
GA in 1953 (Res. 728[VIII] of 23 October 1953), the HC presented a detailed survey of those refugees still living in
camps in Europe, of those in need of emergency aid, and of
the difficult cases.   As of 1 January 1954, 87,677 refugees
lived in camps administered or supervised by governments
(see Annex 14.1).   These were often overcrowded, unsanitary, ill-equipped with heat and water, and without opportunity for work.   Life in them was inevitably degrading.   Furthermore, there were several thousand refugees who were
living in unofficial camps for which the indigenous authorities
accepted no direct responsibility, as well as over 14,000
refugees of European origin in China.

While living conditions in the camps varied considerably from country to country and while some improvements
had been made under the UNHCR, these camps--initially conceived as transit centers--had become an almost permanent
feature of the countryside.   They inexorably pressed the
"waiting people" into the mold of despair.   By 1954 many
of these people had been in the camps for nearly ten years.
Old people had died in them and many children knew no other
home.   "The time spent in the clusters of huts and barracks
is more than a terrible waste of precious years of life,"
wrote the HC.   "The anxiety about the future and the feeling
of isolation as social and economic outcasts sap morale and
health; skills depreciate, and initiatives needed to build up a
new life sink into the stagnation of mere existence, however
uncomfortable, for which neither work nor initiative is required."[3]   Fit and willing workers and their families were
compelled to subsist in degenerating idleness in countries
which excluded them from seeking or accepting work or in
camps located in isolated areas far from employment.

The HC pointed out that the integration of refugees
could not be left to the process of spontaneous economic development.   Compared with a country's nationals, the refugees had basic disadvantages; they could not be treated as a

normal group within the population.   Their special position
was characterized by their lack of knowledge of the language
and local conditions, their prolonged life under most difficult
conditions, and their need for special readaptation through
vocational training.   Any large-scale integration program, he
stressed, would require substantial funds which were beyond
the resources of most countries of residence.   International
financial assistance would be necessary, as the Ford Foundation results had proved if similar programs for permanent
solutions were to be developed.

However, the financial situation was most precarious.
All hopes of receiving funds from IBRD had to be relin-
quished by 1953.   The countries of asylum were not including the refugee groups in their reconstruction and economic
development plans and the IBRD was not, therefore, in a
position under its statute to provide international loans for
refugee settlement.   By August 1954 the Emergency Fund target of $3 million had not been met and the Ford Foundation
grant was exhausted.

The HC warned that "the dangers of a false optimism
concerning solutions of the refugee problem cannot be over-
emphasized, nor can the dangers of relying for complete
solutions on programs which only touch the fringe of the refugee problem."[4]   He submitted a five-year program for the
promotion of permanent solutions to be funded at a level of
approximately $12,000,000.   It was designed primarily to
assist those refugees still in camps and the difficult cases.
He hoped that this program would greatly accelerate the capacities of countries of residence and of immigration to absorb a relatively large proportion of the approximately
350,000 refugees who did not wish to be repatriated or who
had not yet been assimilated.[5]

The Establishment of UNREF

At the suggestion of the Adv. Com. in December 1954
the HC submitted his program to ECOSOC which--on considering his report and his request for the re-examination by
the Ninth Session of the GA of the implications of the provision of permanent solutions--recommended that the GA approve the HC's proposals to "ask the Negotiating Committee
for Extra-budgetary Funds" to negotiate with members and
non-members of the UN concerning contributions for his program.[6]

The HC submitted to the Ninth Session of the GA "the outlines of sample projects for Permanent Solutions."[7] This was in essence the UNREF Program. These sample projects, based on the Ford Foundation pattern, envisaged integration of refugees into agriculture, and their establishment in trades, small businesses, and professions; construction of housing in employment areas; assistance to university students; vocational training and retraining for integration; and support in migration.

The UNREF program was meant not only to provide permanent solutions for a limited number of refugees but was also envisaged as a "prime mover" in the field of permanent solutions. The indirect effects of the program and its stimulus on other programs were regarded as of equal importance with its direct effects.

The basic principle of the program, like that of the Ford Foundation project, was that contributions from outside sources were of a supplementary character and should not relieve the countries of residence of their responsibility for finding a solution for the problems of refugees within their own territory. It was expected that voluntary agencies and the major countries of asylum would contribute to the UNREF Fund.

The GA authorized the HC "to undertake a program designed to achieve permanent solutions within the period of his current mandate."[8] It stipulated that the governments in the agreements negotiated with UNHCR should give assurance that they would "assume full financial responsibility" if any of the refugees within the scope of the program still required assistance at the end of the program on 31 December 1958. It decided that this UNREF Program should be merged with the program of emergency aid. The Emergency Fund had, by 31 December 1954, not reached its target of $3 million. Only $1,484,112 in cash contributions had been received, of which about 75 percent had been devoted to the relief of the European refugees in China and their maintenance in Hong Kong while in transit for settlement. The small surplus of $238,530.99 was transferred to the new fund.[9]

Acceptance by the Governments of Their Obligation to Aid Integration and Resettlement Programs

In taking this action, the international community

recognized that, although care of refugees must continue to be the responsibility of the countries of asylum, certain countries, due to their geographic situation, had had to receive a particularly large number of refugees. The countries of asylum could not face alone the expense and social problems resulting from the presence of refugees on their territory. In the absence of adequate outside aid, these countries would not be able to assimilate refugees into their strained economies, and might therefore be compelled to adopt a restrictive attitude toward the refugees they were sheltering. If the granting of asylum were accepted as at least a moral obligation for all states, such an obligation must be matched by appropriate aid from the international community.

While the GA did not modify the functions of the HC, the UNREF program changed the emphasis of his work. It was generally recognized that these estimated 350,000 non-settled refugees in Europe could have become self-supporting after the IRO ended its work in late 1951 if international assistance to them had been continued. In the intervening years, however, their situation had deteriorated in spite of the efforts made by the governments of the countries of residence to achieve their integration. Consequently, as the HC stated in his Annual Report of 1959, a fuller and more expensive program had to be put into effect in 1954 than would have been the case if such a program could have been started in 1952. The interruption in international assistance had led not only to an increase in the number of refugees to be assisted but had affected also the morale of those who had been living in camps for too many years. It had further led, indirectly, to an increase in the number of refugees requiring emergency aid in order simply to survive.

The Adv. Com., at its Fifth Session in December 1954, at the request of the GA, reframed the program for the period 1 January 1955 to 31 December 1958 and established the total target for government contributions to UNREF at $16,000,000 to be sought by the Negotiating Committee for Extra-Budgetary Funds.[10] The decision of the Adv. Com. was confirmed by the UNREF Ex. Com. at its First Session, May 1955[11] and approved by the GA at the Tenth Session in October 1955.[12]

The Administration of UNREF

ECOSOC, as requested by the GA, established the

UNREF Ex. Com. as successor to the Adv. Com. [13] It consisted of twenty members and non-members of the UN who
were selected by ECOSOC and met twice a year.   On 24 April 1957 Canada became an additional member (see Annex
14. 2).   While the Adv. Com. had had only an advisory capacity, the new committee also had executive functions during
the existence of the Fund.   It gave directives to the HC in
carrying out this program and had overall control over spend-
ing by setting the annual target, approving the annual operational planning, and insuring the close cooperation of the HC
with governments and intergovernmental and non-governmental
organizations.   The HC was requested to submit to the
UNREF Ex. Com. an annual report containing a country-by-
country project analysis.   The UNREF Ex. Com. not only
approved the annual target for the projects but also assumed
the responsibility of urging the governments to provide the
funds--a two-way affair.   Thus the establishment of the
UNREF Ex. Com. brought about a closer cooperation between governments and the Office in the policy and planning
of the program.

During the first months of 1955 the HC concentrated
on developing a closer administrative structure with his
partners.   Immediately after the First Session of the UNREF
Ex. Com. an Implementation Committee was set up in the
UNHCR at Geneva with the task of negotiating agreements
with governments and voluntary agencies that had submitted
projects.   With the assistance of the BOs, the Implementation Committee was responsible for supervising the execution
of the projects by the voluntary agencies.

The projects covered a wide range and involved several countries with widely different conditions.   Differences
in source and distribution of funds for the various projects,
in type and number of refugees to be helped, and in local
laws and practices resulted in considerable variations, not
only among the various types of projects, but among individual projects of the same type.

The policy laid down by the Office requested that
agreements involving funds from UNREF should be comprehensive.   The agreements contained detailed clauses about
financing of the projects from various sources; on the number and type of refugees; on inspection and auditing; and on
regular semi-annual reporting.   For these reasons, the establishment of the agreements required many preparatory
discussions and deliberations at Headquarters, much

correspondence and many negotiations with governments and agencies. The UNREF Progress Report of 30 September 1956 indicated that seventy-three agencies were participating in carrying out programs. [14]

UNHCR officials both at headquarters and in the field kept in close and constant touch with such specialized agencies of the UN as ILO, UNESCO, and WHO and with the CoE, the OEEC, and others. Particularly close ties were developed between the HC, ICEM, and USEP. Monthly meetings were held between these three bodies to insure the coordination of their work on the resettlement of UNHCR mandated refugees. An overall agreement was reached between UNHCR and USEP under which USEP paid two-thirds of the grants for institutionalized difficult cases within USEP's case load. In addition USEP contributed to the joint operation for European refugees in China. A close collaboration was maintained among these three agencies in regard to the contribution of funds to the voluntary agencies in order to avoid duplication in the support given to these agencies.

The HCR also established a closer relationship with the voluntary agencies which played such an important role in the operational part of the UNREF Program. They needed to be consulted in the planning phases, both at field and headquarters level. Advisory boards consisting of representatives of the voluntary agencies and of governments were set up by the BOs in countries where the program was to be carried out. These boards assisted the UNHCR in drawing up projects for submission to the UNREF Ex. Com. At headquarters close contact was maintained with the voluntary agencies through regular meetings between the SCVA and the Office.

The First Session of the UNREF Ex. Com., held in May 1955, established its rules of procedure, revised the financial rules for the voluntary agencies, and established a Standing Program Sub-Committee, composed of 12 members. [15] (See Annexes 14.2 and 14.3.) On the recommendation of the Sub-Committee it approved the plan of operations for 1955 in the amount of $4,200,000.

The Committee's principles to be followed:

1. For each project there should be a reasonable supporting contribution from sources within the country where the project was to be carried out

2. Every project should, as far as possible, be so con-
    ceived that it could be completed with funds allocated in
    the plan of operations for the current year, without in-
    volving commitments for the following year

3. Projects should be submitted, as far as possible, in
    their final form

4. Projects should not involve the establishment of admin-
    istrative machinery that might tend to perpetuate itself

5. Priorities for the implementation of projects should, as
    far as possible, be agreed upon with the governments of
    the countries of residence

6. The progress reports on projects, to be submitted to
    the Committee in accordance with its terms of refer-
    ence, should indicate the number of refugees who have
    benefited from the projects and the reduction of camp
    population brought about accordingly. [16]

Implementation of the UNREF Program

The UNREF Program as adopted by the GA fell into
four parts:

1. permanent solutions with the primary aim of
    assisting the refugee camp population in Aus-
    tria, Germany, Italy, and Greece

2. the settlement of difficult cases

3. the Far Eastern Operation for the evacuation
    of refugees of European origin via Hong Kong

4. emergency aid to the neediest refugees.

The main emphasis was on reduction of the number of refugees in camps. [17]

Permanent Solutions.   The UNREF Program consisted
of a body of projects relating to housing, credit facilities,
vocational training, rehabilitation and education.   These projects were coordinated with each other and with special
counselling and placement projects.

The emphasis of the program was originally placed on the granting of loans to assist refugees in establishing themselves in industry, trade, and agriculture, and on the provision of housing close to employment facilities. Housing, however, proved to be the primary requirement to help refugees to leave the camps. In 1957, it was found that 55 percent of the camp population could be settled if they obtained adequate housing. Other projects were vocational training, aid to high school pupils and students, and physical rehabilitation. After housing, counselling and placement services constituted the most important part of the program. Special counselling projects proved indispensable in determining the most appropriate solution for the problems of individual refugees. As the most qualified refugees left the camp for resettlement and integration, there remained an increasingly higher proportion of economically weaker refugees, handicapped families, and difficult cases. More intensive counselling was required and new types of projects specially adapted to individual cases had to be drawn up. Thus an efficient and well-endowed counselling and case-work service for the fulfillment of the camp closure program was developed.

According to the UNREF Progress Report of 30 September 1957, the Office had under its direction fifty-six counsellors and ten case-workers (Austria had thirty-three counsellors and eight case-workers; Germany, eighteen counsellors and two case-workers; and Belgium, five counsellors). In Greece a pre-selection service under the BO in Athens built up files on each individual case. Many voluntary agencies also provided counselling service in connection with emigration projects and various vocational training projects. The counsellors did not live permanently in a camp, as their activities spread over several camps. They looked for vacancies and available accommodations and tried to find qualified candidates among the refugees. The case-worker, however, lived in a camp and tried to find the best solution for each inmate.

To enhance the value of counsellors and case-workers the UNHCR organized seminars at which they could talk to experts in social work and exchange their own experiences. The first seminar was held in September 1957 at Feldafing, near Munich, with the assistance of USEP, UN Technical Assistance Administration, and various voluntary agencies; High Commissioner Dr. Lindt attended this seminar.

Difficult Cases.   The establishment of projects for handicapped refugees was an extremely delicate task for the counsellors and case workers.   It was necessary to launch a number of special resettlement projects for refugees in this category.   In 1957 there were twenty of these projects in operation--in Austria eight, Belgium one, France two, Germany seven, and Italy two.   This program laid the groundwork for the later expanded program for handicapped refugees.

The resettlement program for difficult cases which had begun under the former Emergency Fund, made steady progress due to the generous support of some countries, especially the Netherlands, Norway, Sweden, Denmark, Belgium and France, which accepted difficult cases against a modest grant, or free of charge, and undertook to look after them until the end of their lives.   In addition, several homes were fitted out or built with the help of UNREF (by 1957 there were four in Austria, one in Egypt, one in France and seven in Greece).   The inmates were grouped according to their religion and their nationality of origin.

For young persons, vocational training projects were arranged with the result that these young people went into trades and professions where they could find employment and thus earn their own living.   Aid for university students and high school pupils was provided.   Most of the students studied subjects which qualified them for professions where openings were available.

Other Programs.   The Far Eastern Operation continued throughout this period.   Between February 1952 and the end of 1959, 14,000 refugees of European origin emigrated from China via Hong Kong (see Ch. 27).   The Emergency Fund concentrated aid in the form of supplementary food, medical aid, and direct financial assistance to needy refugees in Egypt, Greece, Italy, Jordan, Lebanon, Syria, and Turkey.   By the end of 1958, 11,500 refugees had been supported at a level of $348,424.

Obstacles to Implementation
of the UNREF Program

The UNREF Program had a slow start.   Not until June 1955 did implementation begin, and even then progress was slow because governments responded slowly to the appeal for contributions. In fact, the total target for 1955 was not reached and since the US had made its contribution on a matching basis, some of it was forfeited.

The target for 1956 also fell short, which made it necessary to postpone some programs. Another cause for delay was the attitude of the refugees themselves: many of them still had hopes of emigrating; others who had been living in camps for a long time were simply apathetic. Both groups were unwilling to leave the camps. Problems also developed in regard to the building programs.

The UNREF Ex. Com. , as well as ECOSOC, at its Twenty-Second Session, 13 July 1956, discussed these problems and requested that the HC submit a report on the effects of the shortage of contributions on the reduction of the camp population. [18]

However, the ECOSOC meetings were overshadowed by the sudden death of Dr. van Heuven Goedhart on 6 July 1956. Deputy High Commissioner James Read assumed the responsibilities of the HC until a new HC could be elected to the Office. At the end of October he was confronted with the great task of the large, unexpected influx of Hungarian refugees into Austria and Yugoslavia; this emergency demanded immediate concentration and pushed the UNREF program somewhat into the background. Since the experiences gained in dealing with the Hungarian refugees had a decisive impact on the last two years of the UNREF program, we turn now first, to the change of HCs and then to the Hungarian crisis which began in October 1956.

Notes

1.   Adv. Com. (IV), 16 Mar. 1954, A/AC. 36/33.

2.   GA (VI), Off. Rec. , Supp. 19, A/2011, HC's First Report, Part III: 6.

3.   Rep. to GA (IX), Supp. No. 13, A/2648, 1954.

4.   GA, Adv. Com. (IV), 29 Jan. 1954, A/AC. 36/32: 20.

5.   Ibid. : 4.

6.   ECOSOC Res. 549 (XVIII), July 1954.

7. GA (IX), 1954, <u>Off. Rec.</u>, Supp. No. 13B, A/2648/Add. 2.

8. Res. 832 (IX) of 21 Oct. 1954, 44 votes to 5 and 5 abstentions.

9. GA (X), <u>Off. Rec.</u>, Supp. No. 11, A/2902.

10. A/AC. 36/37.

11. A/AC. 79/12.

12. GA, Res. 952 (X), 51 votes to none and 2 abstentions.

13. GA, Res, 565 (XIX) of 31 Mar. 1955.

14. A/AC. 79/48.

15. For text, see GA (X), <u>Off. Rec.</u>, Supp. 11 A/2902 and Add. 1: 37.

16. <u>Ibid.</u>: 32 ff.

17. GA, Res. 925 (X), par. 2.

18. A/3123/Rev. 1/Add. 1.

ANNEX 14.1

REFUGEES LIVING IN CAMPS

	1 July 1952	1 Jan. 1953	1 July 1953	1 Jan. 1954
Austria	50,317	47,727	45,945	42,411
West Germany	42,529	41,949	36,339	35,296
Greece	2,700*	2,700*	2,655	2,471
Italy	4,000*	3,900*	3,900	3,900
Trieste	3,444	4,259	4,391	3,599
Total	102,990	100,535	93,230	87,677

SOURCE: <u>HC's Annual Rep.</u> to GA (IX) Supp. No. 13, A/ 2648, 1954: 9.

*Approximate figures.

ANNEX 14.2

MEMBERS OF THE UNREF EXECUTIVE COMMITTEE

Australia*	Iran
Austria*	Israel
Belgium	Italy*
Brazil*	Netherlands*
Canada (since 1957)	Norway
Colombia	Switzerland*
Denmark*	Turkey
Germany, Fed. Rep. of*	UK*
France*	US*
Greece*	Venezuela
Holy See	

*Members of the Standing Program Sub-Committee

SOURCE: UNHCR, Geneva.

ANNEX 14. 3

RESOLUTION NO. 2. THE ESTABLISHMENT
OF A STANDING PROGRAM SUB-COMMITTEE

The UNREF Executive Committee

A.   Decides to establish a Standing Program Sub-Committee
composed of the following twelve members, Australia, Austria, Brazil, Denmark, Federal Republic of Germany,
France, Greece, Italy, Netherlands, Switzerland, United
Kingdom and United States of America, and with the following terms of reference:

(1)   To examine programs and projects before sessions of the Executive Committee in the light of general
policies determined by the Committee in order to expedite
the latter's proceedings through appropriate preparatory
work;

(2)   Taking into account the priorities as determined
by the Executive Committee, to authorize the implementation
of projects which have been approved, subject to funds becoming available, by the Committee;

(3)   To authorize variations in approved projects in
cases in which changes in circumstances make it impracticable for the projects to be carried out as originally approved;

(4)   To take such further action with respect to projects or priorities as the Executive Committee may authorize;

(5)   To submit a report to each session of the Executive Committee.

B.   Requests the Sub-Committee to meet immediately before
each session of the Executive Committee and at such other
times as it may be convened by the Chairman, after consultation with the Chairman of the Executive Committee and the
HC.

Note: Amendment to par. A, 4 gave the Committee the necessary authority for approval of implementation between the
Sessions of the Executive Committee.

SOURCE: A/3123/Rev. 1/Add. 1: 37, and A/AC. 79/28,
        UNREF Com. (II), Jan. 1956.

Chapter 15

UNHCR ON THE EVE OF THE HUNGARIAN REVOLT

The sudden death of Dr. van Heuven Goedhart was announced at the opening of the session of ECOSOC, 9 July 1956, by its President, Mr. Hans Engen (Norway). He noted that the HC "was well known to all members of the Council for his vigour, honesty and singleness of purpose with which he had served the cause of the refugees. His death was a great loss to the UN, of which he was one of the most able and devoted servants." The delegate of the Netherlands, Mr. Striker, described him as "a great Dutchman," whose death was a tragic loss to hundreds of thousands of refugees all over the world. [1]

Dr. van Heuven Goedhart: "The High Commissioner of the Refugees"

Dr. G. J. van Heuven Goedhart's death was, in the words of the US delegate, Mr. Baker, "a serious blow not only to the cause of refugees, but also to the forces of good that were striving for a better world. His life had been an inspiration to all who had come under the influence of his devotion, courage, warmth of heart and singleness of purpose." Mr. Baker continued: "His death imposed an obligation upon all to re-dedicate themselves to the work for which Dr. van Heuven Goedhart had given his life." Expressions of many other delegates reflected "an air of loneliness and unreality" due to his absence.

In retrospect, the delegates realized what a difficult and often disheartening time Dr. van Heuven Goedhart had had. In assessing five years of the UNHCR, he had told the delegates to the Third Committee of the Tenth Assembly-- the last time he spoke to the Third Committee--that the Office had developed considerably since its "modest beginning." The developments had, in fact, been substantial. At the international level, the isolated and incomplete legal provisions governing refugee status had been replaced by the 1951 Convention Relating to the Status of Refugees. In 1950, no material assistance had been provided. By 1955, the UNHCR had the UNREF at his disposal and had embarked upon a four-year program for permanent solutions. [2] While Dr. van Heuven Goedhart admitted that "many defects" and "numerous failures" could be pointed out, in general he noted progress. He stressed the shift in emphasis from the single approach of resettlement to the recourse to integration. With this chance had come the widening role of the Office.

Dr. van Heuven Goedhart, a "tireless worker for the refugees," had outlined to the Third Session of the UNREF Ex. Com. (28 May to 1 June 1956) his recent six-week visit to eight Latin American countries: Argentina, Brazil, Chile, Colombia, the Dominican Republic, Peru, Uruguay, and Venezuela. The main objective of his trip had been to secure further accessions to the 1951 Convention, to obtain further contributions to UNREF, and to investigate the further possibility of having limited numbers of refugee families who were still living in camps admitted to these countries as immigrants. [3]

Only a fortnight before his death Dr. van Heuven Goedhart had also spent a week in the UK making preparations for a forthcoming UN Association campaign on behalf of refugees. The HC's staff, limited in its size, was not able to organize or carry out such campaigns by itself. But he and his staff stimulated many national campaigns and always kept in touch with them.

Many commentators on Dr. van Heuven Goedhart's death stressed the distinctiveness of his contribution. The refugees had lost "a great protagonist of their cause," declared James Read, his Deputy HC. Through his deep conviction, great humanity and untiring activity he had reawakened "the conscience of the world." [4]

The Israeli delegate, Mr. Shoram-Sharon, stressed that Dr. van Heuven Goedhart had never lost sight of the human suffering of the refugees. "He had brought hope and new dignity where despair had prevailed and self-respect had been lost through hardship; and had approached his mission with the sole object of eliminating human misery and helping the refugees to lead a free and independent life." [5] The British delegate pointed out that he "had valiantly championed their cause without fear or favour," and overcome obstacles with "imagination, tenacity and industry." [6]

Dr. van Heuven Goedhart had, in effect, been "the HC of the refugees," pleading their cause with untiring energy and singleness of purpose. His honesty, compassion and warmth had made him an effective champion of the distressed. He considered his office the link between the refugee and the rest of the world.

He had greatly admired Dr. Nansen, and was inspired by his "hard hitting, direct and courageous works," based on self-sacrifice and devotion. In 1954 he established the Nansen Medal as an award and inscribed the medal with a quotation from Nansen: "Love of man is practical policy," words which befitted his own actions. [7] On one occasion he reminded his audience of Dr. Nansen's reply to objections to a plan which Dr. Nansen had presented. When it was said, "This is extremely difficult; it seems even quite impossible," Dr. Nansen had answered, "the difference between the difficult and the impossible things is, that on difficult things you must start right away, but that on impossible things [you] must wait a little longer." Dr. van Heuven Goedhart added, "I make this reply mine."

Dr. van Heuven Goedhart worked unremittingly against the difficulties he encountered. He had to struggle on two fronts: on the one hand to convince governments that there was still an unsolved refugee problem of considerable magnitude left after the IRO closed its doors; on the other, to persuade the governments to contribute funds for permanent solutions. [8]

The London Times editorialized: "He was resolute in his dealings with governments, and sometimes made himself unpopular by his insistence that the final solving of the problem was the responsibility of the international community and could not be left to the states" of asylum. [9] He was very outspoken, and often went ahead with his plans without consulting the governments. The US Government, disappointed that its candidate had not been elected, had expressed concern over Dr. van Heuven Goedhart's stress on local integration at a time when the US State Department was anxiously trying to prolong the DP Act and did not contribute to the Emergency Fund. His anti-Communist outlook made him unacceptable to the USSR and to the Eastern European countries which voted against his re-election in 1953.

Achievements of the First Five Years

In reflecting on the achievements of the five years of the UNHCR under Dr. van Heuven Goedhart, it is worthwhile to recall briefly the different stages of his work and that of his staff. The HC built up a network of BOs with a dedicated and loyal staff. He achieved a more efficient working relationship with the governments through the Adv. Com. (later the UNREF Ex. Com.) and evolved better cooperation with the various UN Specialized Agencies; he also developed a complementary relationship with the CoE and close collaboration with ICEM and USEP and, above all, with the voluntary agencies. The last-named had been the backbone of his planning and programs; in fact their agencies had helped him, through the Ford Foundation Program, not only to develop programs, but also to convince the governments that economic integration and social assimilation were essential in the case of many refugees and that they should be regarded as complementary to resettlement. Largely at his urging, the governments had agreed to the establishment of the Emergency Fund (GA Res. 5388[VI]) and finally to the beginning of UNREF (GA Res. 832[IX]). He had taken a keen interest in the problem of international protection, broadening the concept to include the promotion of permanent solutions, and encouraging governments not only to ratify the 1951 Convention, but also to widen their national legislation to provide for refugees.

He had been convinced that the refugee problem could be solved in a given time; only money was lacking. Many times he had expressed his disappointment that the member states of the UN "had failed to give him the modest means required to carry through his programs as he had planned."[10]

Dr. van Heuven Goedhart had been awarded the Wateler Peace Prize for 1955 by the Carnegie Foundation; in the same year his office received the Nobel Peace Prize for 1954.[11] The Nobel funds were used to terminate the refugee camp on the Island of Tinos in Greece; the Wateler prize was distributed in the form of anonymous gifts to various refugee causes.

In 1956 Dr. van Heuven Goedhart was posthumously awarded the Nansen Medal in "recognition of his exceptional and inspired work ... [and] of the outstanding devotion and singleness of purpose" in his work for the refugees. On 2 May 1958 a memorial plaque was unveiled in the Palais des

Nations in Geneva, bearing his name, the dates 1951-56,
and the inscription, "With love and the example of our personal sacrifice the refugee problem can be solved" (GA Res.
1039[XI], B). Dr. van Heuven Goedhart left a permanent
mark on the Office and laid the groundwork for its future development under his successors.

Election of Dr. Auguste R. Lindt

On 10 December 1956 the Eleventh General Assembly
elected Dr. Auguste R. Lindt as the successor to Dr. van
Heuven Goedhart. He was proposed by the Secretary-General and elected by acclamation. As a Swiss he represented a
neutral country. Having been the Swiss observer to the UN
since 1953, he was a familiar figure to the members of the
UN. They respected "his ability, his experience, his devoted labours, and his enthusiasm for the cause of the UN."

Dr. Lindt had also been Chairman of UNICEF and its
Program Committee and President of the 1953 UN Opium
Conference, and had headed the Swiss Delegation to the Con-
ference on the Statute of the International Atomic Energy
Agency, held in New York in 1956. He had studied law.
As special correspondent of several European newspapers
from 1927 to 1940, he had traveled in Manchuria, Liberia,
Palestine, Tunisia, Rumania and Poland. He had served in
the Swiss Army from 1940 to 1945.

Dr. Lindt assumed his office at the height of the
Hungarian Revolt. This crisis tested to the full the foundations laid by Dr. van Heuven Goedhart. Under Dr. Lindt's
leadership the Office of the HC was to prove itself flexible
and effective, and in the aftermath of the Hungarian refugee
problem, he was able to mold, out of the machinery created
under Dr. van Heuven Goedhart, an even more comprehensive and responsive definition of the Office.

Notes

1.   ECOSOC (XXII), Off. Rec., 9 July 1956.

2.   GA (X) Third Com., Off. Rec.: 5.

3.   For report on this trip, see GA (XI) Off. Rec. Supp.
     No. 11A, A/3123/Rev.1/Add. 1 and 2, 1957.

4.   GA (X) Third Com., <u>Off. Rec.</u>: 44.

5.   GA (XI), Third Com., <u>Off. Rec.</u>: 14.

6.   <u>Ibid.</u>: 49.

7.   See his Oslo speech, 12 Dec. 1955, and GA (IX),
      Third Com., <u>Off. Rec.</u>, 1955.

8.   UNHCR <u>Pr. Rel.</u> PM/3105, 9 Dec. 1955.

9.   <u>The Times</u>, London, 10 July 1956.

10.   Norwegian Delegate, GA (XI), Third Com., <u>Off. Rec.</u>:
      47.

11.   After receiving the Nobel Prize Dr. van Heuven Goed-
      hart gave a party for the staff. He told the ninety-
      nine members of the staff, "everybody could say
      that he was one percent of the Nobel Prize winner."

Chapter 16

THE HUNGARIAN REFUGEES: 1956-57

While the camp clearance program for the "old refugees" was in full swing, Austria was suddenly confronted with a new and almost overwhelming refugee problem. The Hungarian Revolt started on 23 October 1956, and in the course of nine months an estimated 180,000 Hungarian refugees took refuge in Austria, and another 20,000 in Yugoslavia. This exodus represented the largest spontaneous movement of a civilian population in Europe since the Spanish Civil War.

The Hungarian Influx into Austria

Austria, after the State Treaty of 18 May 1955 between Austria and the four occupying powers, had regained its independence on 27 July 1955. The last occupation troops had been withdrawn in October 1955, and by early 1956 the barbed wire barriers between Austria and Hungary had been removed and the 354-kilometer border was no longer heavily guarded. By a constitutional law the Federal Republic of Austria pledged itself to permanent neutrality. Its economy had recovered remarkably in response to Western aid, and it enjoyed a relatively normal life, politically and economically. Yet, it still had to care for some 30,000 refugees and 150,000 Volksdeutsche who had not yet been fully integrated and many of whom still lived in camps. For these substantial help was provided by ICEM, USEP, UNHCR, and the voluntary agencies.

The Hungarian refugees were mostly peasants and residents of Hungarian border villages who began to cross the border and move into the adjacent villages after 27 October, but from 4 November on, the size of the influx swelled. Between 28 October and 16 November, in severe winter weather, 35,000 persons crossed the border. Cities such as Vienna, Graz, Linz, Innsbruck, Klagenfurt, Salzburg and others quickly became overcrowded.   The Austrian citizens responded compassionately and spontaneously.   (See Annex 16.1.)

On 28 October the Council of Ministers of the Austrian Government--stressing its neutrality--granted the right of asylum to all refugees and informed the Security Council of the UN.   The government provided accommodation, care and maintenance, and transportation from the border, but it was not able to cope with this problem alone, and needed international help.   On 4 November, Minister of Interior, Oskar Helmer, appealed to the UNHCR and to ICEM.   He cabled:

> As a result of the latest political events approximately ten thousand men, women and children from Hungary have sought asylum in Austria so far during the last week.   The Austrian Federal Government is undertaking all possible efforts to accommodate these refugees as quickly as possible. This situation has given Austria a new very difficult problem not only as regards monetary assistance but also and above all for the coming months.   I ask you urgently to inform the member Governments of the UNREF Executive Committee and other Governments and authorities who may be concerned by this situation and to convey a request of the Federal Government for help.   Financial aid is very necessary in order to ensure humane care and maintenance for these refugees during the coming winter months.   Furthermore early temporary acceptance of as great a number as possible of these refugees by European States is urgently requested.   The Federal Government appeals to the feeling of solidarity in helping refugees which has so often been evidenced in the past. [1]

Action of the GA

Deputy High Commissioner James Read, then Acting HC, immediately made available to the Austrian Government $25,000 from UNREF and made an urgent appeal to member governments of the UNREF Ex. Com. and to other interested governments for two kinds of assistance: financial aid and "at least temporary asylum" for the Hungarian refugees by countries which were less prone than Austria, by virtue of their geographic position, to a heavy influx of refugees.   He

stressed that the services of the Office were available to assist in selection and that ICEM was preparing its services to
assist in movement of refugees to countries willing to give
asylum and was contacting its member governments. [2]   He
emphasized that early reply to this appeal would facilitate
reception arrangements for refugees in Austria. [3]   Returning
from a trip to Vienna, he also brought firsthand information
to the Emergency Conference held in New York on 16 November by the ICVA.

On 9 November 1956, during its Second Emergency
Special Session, the GA "requested the Secretary-General to
call upon the HC to consult with other appropriate international agencies and interested governments, with a view to
making speedy and effective arrangements for emergency assistance to refugees from Hungary. " On 29 November 1956
the Eleventh Session of the GA, "recognizing the urgent need
of these tens of thousands of refugees for care and resettlement" requested "the Secretary-General and the UNHCR to
continue their efforts"; urged governments and non-governmental organizations "to make contributions ... for the care
and resettlement of Hungarian refugees, and to coordinate
their aid programs in consultation with the Office of the HC";
requested that the Secretary-General and the UNHCR "make
an immediate appeal to both Governments and non-governmental organizations to meet the minimum present needs" of
the refugees; and authorized them "to make subsequent appeals on the basis of plans and estimates made by the HC. "[4]

Eligibility

The Third Committee of the Eleventh GA (24 and 30
November to December 1956), while considering the Annual
Report of the UNHCR, dealt extensively with the Hungarian
refugee question.   Some delegates expressed doubt as to
whether the question should be discussed in the Committee,
since the GA dealt with the matter in its plenary meeting.
Doubt was also expressed as to whether the Hungarian refugees fell within the mandate of the UNHCR.   However, at the
initiative of Mr. Baroody, delegate from Saudi Arabia, the
Committee discussed the matter thoroughly on the basis of a
statement made by Deputy High Commissioner James Read. [5]

The majority of the Committee members agreed that
the problem should be discussed, in view of the interconnection between the HC's mandate under the GA's Res.

1006(ES-II) and 1029(XI) of 9 and 21 November 1956, and the
regular mandate of the Office. However, it was the understanding that "the discussions should be conducted solely for
the purpose of finding constructive solutions and that it should
not duplicate the discussion in plenary on the political aspects of the problem. "[6]

The majority felt that the matter fell definitely within
the HC's mandate; that "because of its past experience" the
Office "was well-qualified" and that "concerted action and efforts for emergency measures should be channeled through
this Office"; and that in agreement with the Secretary-General, no new machinery was needed for implementation of the
adopted GA resolutions on this subject.

In a statement before the Ex. Com. (IV) on 17 January 1957, Dr. Lindt, who had been to Austria for an on-the-
spot investigation before taking up his appointment as HC,
elaborated on the question of the eligibility of the Hungarian
refugees. He pointed out that "refugees from Hungary who
meet the terms of Art. 6B of the Statute of the Office are
within my mandate. " He further referred to Art. 1A (2) of
the 1951 Convention, and the Report of 15 February 1950 of
the Ad Hoc Committee on Statelessness and Related Problems
(E/1618) in regard to the dateline of 1 January 1957.   On
the basis of these provisions he concluded that, "it is reasonable to relate the departure of the refugees from Hungary
not merely to the events which took place in Hungary in November 1956, but also to fundamental political changes which
took place as a result of the last war.   It would follow,
therefore, that the refugees from Hungary who meet the other requirements of the Convention should be considered to be
within its scope notwithstanding the fact that their flight took
place after 1 January 1951. " He went on to say that "this
interpretation has been adopted by the Austrian authorities
who are prepared to consider the Hungarian refugees in Austria to be within the scope of the Convention and to issue
them with a normal eligibility certificate to this effect as
soon as it is technically possible, unless eligibility examinations show that any individual applicant should not be entitled
to the benefits of the Convention.   The attitude which has
been taken by the Austrian authorities on this question has
been followed in most countries where refugees of Hungarian
origin coming through Austria have been given asylum. "[7]

Repatriation

    The Czechoslovakian delegate, introducing a draft
resolution (A/AC. 3/44508), stressed that repatriation was
the best way to solve the urgent problem, and that therefore
the UNHCR should inform the refugees of the existing laws
and measures.   Other Eastern European countries, including
the USSR, stressed that for that reason amnesty decrees had
been issued by the individual countries and repatriation missions were ready to visit the refugees.   This resolution, after a prolonged debate with some political undertones on both
sides (reception countries and countries of origin) was rejected 43 to 10, with 15 abstentions.   Instead, a twelve-pow-
er draft resolution (A/C. 3/4510) was finally adopted by a
roll-call vote of 57 to none with one abstention.   This draft,
which included the requests of the above-mentioned resolutions, was adopted without change by the GA, Res. 1039(XI)
of 23 January 1957.

    The question of repatriation as a permanent solution
was raised again by the Hungarian observer in the Fourth
and Fifth Sessions of the UNREF Ex. Com. in 1957.   He
accused the HC of failing to facilitate repatriation.   His government, he maintained, had declared an amnesty and was
willing to accept those refugees who were willing to return.
For that purpose his government had presented a memorandum (A/3504) to the Secretary-General with the proposal that
funds allocated for projects for refugee youths and for integration of refugees in Austria (Doc. A/AC. 79/49) should be
used instead for the repatriation of unaccompanied children
and of refugees of school age and that the HC should insure
the necessary funds from the UN or other sources for the
cost of repatriating the refugees to Hungary.

    The Austrian representative stressed that his country
favored repatriation, but that no one would be compelled to
leave Austria.   After consultation with the HC, the Austrian
Government accepted a Hungarian repatriation mission.

    High Commissioner Lindt expressed his Office's guid-
ing principles for repatriation further at the Fifth Session of
the UNREF Ex. Com. [8]   He pointed out that the functions of
his Office, as stated in Art. 2 of the Statute, were fundamental for his policy; they were "humanitarian and social and
of an entirely non-political character."   He stated that, in
his opinion, "the Hungarian refugees, the minors as well as
other refugees, are under the territorial jurisdiction of the

country which has given them asylum.   Any decisions concerning these persons have, therefore, to be taken by the
authorities of these countries by virtue of their sovereign
rights.   In this matter, the role of my Office in the exercise of its functions is to advise and assist Governments.
My Office cannot take any decisions concerning the movement
of these persons, be it for repatriation or for resettlement. "
And turning to repatriation, he stated that "the functions of
my Office are two-fold: international protection and search
for permanent solutions for the problem of refugees by assisting governments to facilitate the voluntary repatriation of
refugees or their assimilation within new national communities.   These two functions are closely inter-connected. "

        Under the Statute and Resolutions, GA 925(X) and
1039(XI), he was required to provide international protection
and to safeguard the free choice of the refugees.   However,

> the arrangements for repatriation and the visits of
> repatriation missions are a matter to be decided
> by the Governments of the countries in which the
> refugees find themselves and subject to the agree-
> ments which they may have concluded with the
> countries of origin of the refugees in the exercise
> of their sovereignty.   Whenever Hungarian repatri-
> ation missions have interviewed refugees in coun-
> tries of asylum they have been accompanied by an
> impartial observer from my Office, whose task it
> has been to ensure that no undue pressure from
> any side is exercised upon refugees, and that re-
> patriation is in fact voluntary.   While a certain
> number of refugees have declared their desire for
> repatriation as a result of visits of repatriation
> missions, another not inconsiderable number have
> already returned to Hungary independently and of
> their own free will.   Whenever a refugee wishing
> to be repatriated has applied to my Office, he has
> been referred to the competent authorities and
> given such assistance as may be necessary to bring
> him into contact with the authorities of his country
> of origin, and his repatriation has, in this way,
> been facilitated.

He explained that the movement of unattached youth was the
responsibility of the country of asylum.   He could only, in
the exercise of his function of international protection, advise
and assist the competent authorities.   His Office was guided

"by the principle of family reunion and the best interest of
the minor in all its work concerning these minors. "

However, Dr. Lindt took pains "to have the Office
play a positive role in the voluntary repatriation of refugees. "⁹   He set up careful procedures to insure the voluntary repatriation of Hungarian refugees in Yugoslavia.   The
refugees were accompanied by UNHCR staff members to the
Hungarian border, assuring their free decision.   In regard
to the large number of unaccompanied minors whose parents
asked for their return, the international humanitarian office
proved of great value.   The Office kept in close touch with
the Hungarian authorities on this group and tried to guarantee
that within the countries of asylum procedures were followed
that allowed each case to be solved in keeping with the wish
and the long-term interests of the child concerned.   The HC
also encouraged governments to provide lists of Hungarian
minors in their territories to the ICRC, which was present
in Budapest, so that parents could get in touch with their
children through the Red Cross.   Dr. Lindt, himself carried
on various negotiations with the Hungarian Government, in
particular with regard to the repatriation of unaccompanied
children.   At the same time the refugees had to sign a
statement that the decision was taken of their own will and,
as stated by the HC, a Hungarian-speaking staff member accompanied Hungarian repatriation missions on their visits to
refugees.   Some 18,200 Hungarians returned from Austria
and Yugoslavia to their country of origin.

Immediate Outside Response to the Crisis

Since no estimate was possible of the future increase
of the influx, the emphasis was on immediate resettlement.
In response to the Austrian appeal to the nations of the world
to move refugees out of Austria as soon as possible, some
Western European countries immediately sent airplanes,
trains, and buses to Austria.   On 7 November the French
Red Cross flew a plane to Vienna loaded with medical supplies and brought refugees back to France.   Some British
private groups, and later commercial aircraft companies, on
their own initiative and at their own expense, shuttled their
planes between Britain and Austria for the British Red Cross,
bringing 7,500 refugees to the UK by 14 December.   On 8
November the first special train, from Switzerland, moved
more than 400 refugees.   And in the following days, buses
from Sweden and trains from Belgium and the Netherlands

returned with refugees to those countries. Governments and
non-governmental organizations responded quickly and spontaneously with generous contributions for emergency relief
funds.

About $10 million in cash and in kind were pledged
by twenty-five nations.   This included $4.5 million from the
US; 100,000 yards of cloth from Pakistan; $50,000 worth of
medical supplies from Bolivia; 100 tons of rice, 50 tons of
sugar and five tons of black tea from the Republic of China;
and 30 tons of raisins from Greece.   In addition, a total of
about $500,000 was given directly to the Austrian govern-
ment by Australia, Colombia, France, the UK, and the CoE.
The voluntary agencies, which had begun to house refugees
in hotels, contributed additional thousands of dollars to the
relief effort.

Organization for Coordinated Action

In view of this enormous and instantaneous response,
coordination was essential to the relief action in order to
avoid chaos and duplication of effort.   The HC, entrusted
with the task of coordinating all emergency measures, engaged in diplomatic and planning activities.   He established
close contact with the Austrian Government, the inter-governmental agencies, and the voluntary agencies in bringing
quick and effective aid to the Hungarian refugees; coordinated
the emergency aid; made appeals, in consultation with the
Secretary-General, for assistance to these refugees; and prepared a comprehensive assessment of the needs of these
refugees at the request of the UNREF Ex. Com.[10]

The UNHCR, USEP, and ICEM had had functioning offices in Austria since the closure of IRO, as had the voluntary agencies, representing the religious denominations
(CRS, NCWC, CWS of WCC, LWF, and AJDC); non-sectarian
groups (AFSC and IRC); and smaller organizations with ethnic
interests (United Ukrainian American Relief Committee, Polish American Immigration and Relief Committee, Tolstoy
Foundation) and other organizations such as ISS.

In Vienna, a Committee for the Coordination of Help
to Hungarian Refugees was set up in the first week of November under the chairmanship of the UNHCR representative,
Victor Beerman.   The Committee was composed of representatives of Austria (Minister of the Interior, Mr. Helmer),

ICEM and USEP, the IRC, and the LRCS, the international
and national voluntary agencies, and the Austrian National
Committee for Help to Hungarian Refugees.   This Committee, meeting every few days to exchange information, coordinated the activities of the various authorities.   The LRCS
(League of Red Cross Societies) was responsible for coordinating voluntary efforts in connection with immediate emergency assistance and, with ICEM, for registration, documentation, and transportation from Austria.   Various international and national voluntary agencies undertook emergency
assistance from their own resources and with the help of
USEP.

On 13 November 1956, the Austrian Government called
upon the UNHCR to coordinate overall operations; an agreement was concluded by the UNHCR, the LRCS, and the Austrian Federal Government, under which the UNHCR organized
and coordinated the whole operation.

Close contact was maintained between the Viennese
Committee and the corresponding bodies in Geneva.   At the
invitation of the HC, ICEM, USEP, and a number of voluntary agencies held a meeting at Geneva on 13 November. [11]

On 24 November the Deputy HC could state before the
Third Committee of the GA that "the response by the Governments to the appeal to take refugees, and the response
by various other agencies to aid in the task of immediate
emergency assistance has been most heartening, " but he
warned that "the proportions of the problem have grown so
in the last few days, and continue without abatement, so that
we cannot feel anything but a sense of the greatest urgency
and hope that Governments and agencies will continue their
interest and help to the UN and Austria in facing up to this
emergency. "[12]

In the first days large numbers of women and children (many unaccompanied) crossed the borders, but as time
went on more and more men arrived, together with students
and entire families.   Most of the refugees arrived in Austria
with nothing more than the clothes they were wearing.   The
immediate emergency needs were food, toilet articles, clothing, blankets, and bedding.   Thus emergency relief on the
borders of Austria and in Austria was the priority.

In his report on "assessment of the needs and recommendations for future action" submitted to the UNREF Ex.

Com. (IV) in mid-January 1957, the HC presented an overall picture of the influx of refugees in the past two and one-half months and gave an account of the action taken by UNHCR to secure emergency assistance (accommodation, care, and maintenance) and to facilitate the movement of refugees from Austria to overseas and other European countries. [13] It was an impressive picture. But in face of the needs, more financial aid and more opportunities for resettlement were urgent.

The Fourth Session of the Ex. Com. approved $290,000 for the implementation by the UNHCR of long-term projects for counselling and case workers, youth projects, and planning of housing programs, and at the suggestion of the HC agreed that studies of the long-term needs of the Hungarian refugees should be continued in conjunction with the Austrian authorities which should be the basis of recommendations submitted to the Fifth Session of the UNREF Ex. Com. [14]

The main burden, as pointed out earlier, lay heavily on the Austrian Government and on the voluntary agencies. From 18 October 1956 to 31 March 1957 an estimated $9,967,775 had been expended by the Austrian Government and further financial assistance had been promised. [15] Two outside organizations, the ICRC and ICEM, took part in the major operations. The first, in cooperation with the LRCS and the Austrian Red Cross, undertook the care and maintenance of the refugees in camps, while the second assumed responsibility for the large-scale movement of refugees to other parts of Western Europe and to the overseas countries.

By the end of October 1956, the Hungarian Red Cross had appealed to the ICRC for the dispatch of relief supplies for the population in Hungary. Large supplies came from all parts of the world, and arrangements were made between ICRC, the LRCS and the Austrian Red Cross for storing the material in Vienna. However, the situation changed quickly. More and more Hungarians moved into Austria and later into Yugoslavia. Thus the League concentrated on the refugees, and supplies already in Vienna were used for them.

With financial support from the HC, the host government, and the international community, the League progressively assumed responsibility for care and maintenance of an ever-increasing case load in camps in Austria. Fifty-two national Red Cross, Red Crescent, and Red Lion and Sun

Societies made experienced staff available (650 workers from fourteen countries) and contributed substantially in cash and kind. By March 1957 the League operated forty-four camps in Austria. The operations, originally planned for thirty days, were extended four times; in all they continued for eleven months. By 30 September 1957, relief action for the Hungarian refugees in Austria and Yugoslavia came to an end. Fifty-two countries had contributed 22,500 tons of relief supplies, valued at $14,200,000. The total for the operation of the relief programs (including cash and kind and personal services) was estimated at $19,200,000. In addition, half as much was spent on reception and resettlement services. [16]

Resettlement Programs

Technically speaking, ICEM's constitutional functions did not apply to the situation. There were no agreements between Austria and countries of immigration under which ICEM could act, and Austria, although a member of ICEM, had not contracted to pay a share of migration costs. Yet, in reply to Austria's plea and after the visit to Vienna of the Deputy-Director, Pierre Jacobsen, on 7 November, the Director of ICEM, Harold H. Tittman, acting in advance of constitutional authorization, cabled the Austrian Government's request to the member governments, suggesting an advance of $30,000 of ICEM's budget. [17]

ICEM undertook a large-scale resettlement operation, at first simply moving refugees to second-asylum countries in Western Europe, and soon after, from countries of second asylum or directly from Austria to overseas countries of immigration. It reported that in the first month (until 28 November) 90,000 Hungarians had crossed the border, of whom 21,669 had been moved out to ten countries:

3,917 to Switzerland	1,976 to the Netherlands
3,369 to Germany	1,172 to Italy
3,345 to UK	1,122 to Sweden
3,002 to Belgium	630 to the US
2,976 to France	151 to Eire

However, many problems had to be overcome before a fairly smooth operation was achieved; staff for registration and documentation, and for medical services were urgently needed. In late October 1956, ICEM had only thirty-nine

persons working in Austria, most of them in Salzburg, handling the processing of "old refugees" and of Austrian nationals
for overseas migration. In the course of the following weeks
more than 250 experienced staff members were transferred
from ICEM missions in Germany, Greece, Italy, and the
Geneva office to form the nucleus of the ICEM teams processing the refugee in camps with the aid of members of the
voluntary agencies. Later three separate centers were established for controlled and accurate registration, documentation, processing, and actual transporting of the Hungarians.
First, the refugees came to temporary reception camps
opened by the government, where they received care and
maintenance; next, they were transferred to one of five main
centers in Vienna, Salzburg, Graz, Linz, and Villach for
registration and processing; finally, they moved to so-called
"holding camps" near airports or embarkation centers where
they waited to emigrate as soon as transportation was available.

         Under the direction of Dr. Cleve Schou, a medical
officer of ICEM, the medical program was set up. It included medical processing, vaccinations, pre-embarkation
medical check-ups, and the securing of medical escorts and
medical supplies. He was able to perform these tasks with
the greatest possible speed, with a small staff and the help
of Hungarian refugee doctors and the personnel of the permanent migration missions from Australia, Canada, and the
US. [18]

         The HC and ICEM had urged the resettlement coun-
tries to speed up selection procedures, to relax their immigration requirements, and also to contribute to the transportation costs. The response was positive, and help came--
although not without some delays in regard to funding and
quota commitments--from more than thirty countries. Some
of the overseas countries dispensed entirely with their medical immigration criteria during the emergency and speeded
up procedure. Among the overseas countries Australia,
Canada, and the US received the largest number of refugees
(together more than half the total number) and provided substantial transportation at their own expense. From 7 November 1956 through 1 March 1958, 154,073 persons departed
from Austria--77,529 for overseas and 76,544 to other European countries. The UK, Germany, France, and Switzerland
combined received more than two-thirds of these refugees
settled in Europe (see Annex 16.2).

The wide and flexible range of services provided by the voluntary agencies brought a major contribution to the operation. Their fund-raising, expert help, unbroken experience, and unceasing pressure on the authorities were a significant factor in making the program a success in such a short time. To mention only a few: the WCC contributed $856,000; the NCWC carried full responsibility for moving over 38,000 Hungarian refugees, of whom 18,000 went to the US; HIAS provided material, medical, and spiritual aid; forty-three YMCA and YWCA groups raised $138,000 in cash and $45,000 in supplies and equipment. [19]

Operations in Yugoslavia

In December 1956, when the difficulty of getting into Austria increased, the refugees took the road to Yugoslavia. The Yugoslav Government, although in a precarious balance between East and West, granted asylum to the refugees, and at first helped the newcomers without outside aid. However, on 21 December, 1956, as the influx increased, the Yugoslav Government appealed to the HC. A representative of UNHCR, who investigated the situation, reported on 14 January 1957 that already 4,800 refugees had arrived and were being accommodated in sixteen centers. By the end of that month six more centers were added to house the ever-increasing numbers of refugees.

The HC reported on the Hungarian refugee problem in Yugoslavia to the Fourth Session of the UNREF Ex. Com. on 30 January 1957, making recommendations for future action. [20] The UNREF Ex. Com. agreed that the HC should extend his services to Yugoslavia, and an agreement between the Yugoslav Government and the UNHCR was concluded on 15 February 1957. The HC set up a provisional BO in charge of Mr. P. Brémont in Belgrade to coordinate emergency aid, superintend voluntary repatriation, and oversee action taken for the resettlement of refugees.

Most of the refugees preferred resettlement to the alternatives of repatriation or local integration. Therefore, at the request of the Yugoslav Government ICEM in mid-May 1957 assigned an experienced staff member, Edward B. Marks, with a team of twenty-one staff members to carry out a large-scale resettlement program under the auspices of the UNHCR, and in cooperation with the international voluntary agencies (AFSC, IRC, LWF, CRS/NCWC, UNHIAS and WCC) and USEP.

By that time the refugees in Yugoslavia were living
in about thirty camps spread over a wide area and varying
greatly in size, condition and administration.   The camp
population included 22 percent single males and 5 percent
single females, in addition to families; among these there
were an undetermined number of persons with medical and
social problems.   The camps were gradually consolidated as
the resettlement movements went on, and by October 1957
the number was reduced to three established camps, three
processing centers, one camp for unaccompanied youths, one
for convalescents, and two small transit centers for the decreasing numbers of new refugees.   Speed was of the essence.   Medical processing and selection procedure were
curtailed.   A unique airlift was established to speed up
transportation.   ICEM-chartered airplanes made twenty-seven
direct flights from Belgrade to New York City, carrying more
than 2,000 refugees.   Australia and Canada together accepted
over 3,000 refugees.   The Scandinavian missions were admitting tubercular and other handicapped refugees, and Belgium too used broad criteria in its selection.   France, of
the Western European countries, accepted the largest number, regardless of their physical condition. [21]

The total number of Hungarian refugees who had entered Yugoslavia was 19,857.   By the end of January 1958,
16,409 of them had emigrated, 2,773 had been voluntarily
repatriated, and 675 were integrated in Yugoslavia.   This
operation had been accomplished in one year.   The provisional BO, established on 15 February 1957, was closed on
4 February 1958.   High Commissioner Lindt stated, "This
provides an object lesson in what can be achieved if Governments tackle a refugee problem of known size with vigour
and determination. "[22]

UNREF Executive Committee Resolution of June 1957

Despite the fact that the flights of the Hungarian people had deeply stirred the public conscience of the Western
world and brought about such spontaneous cooperation between
governments, inter-governmental agencies, and voluntary
agencies, the efforts to bring the problem to a full solution
as quickly as possible weakened in the first half of 1957.
The momentum slackened before the job was finished.   The
danger was that a residual problem would be added to that of
the "old refugees" waiting for a final solution.

The turning point came as a result of the plea of Mr. Oskar Helmer, Austrian Minister of Interior, at the Fourth Session of the UNREF Ex. Com. (29 January to 4 February 1957). He pointed out that the influx continued despite winter conditions and measures designed to prevent the refugees from leaving. He acknowledged the assistance already given by the HC, ICEM, and the voluntary agencies, and expressed gratitude to those countries which had accepted refugees from Austria; he stressed, however, that the burden imposed on his country by the reception and care of so many persons was becoming too heavy to be borne alone. Austria was still lodging by far the greatest number of refugees. The Republic could not alone--on the basis of its geographical situation --carry the main burden. He went on to say:

> The way in which the refugee problem is solved by the States represents a crucial test for all the nations which have come together on the basis of the refugee convention. It is incompatible with our dignity to ask for the fulfillment of a duty which is equally incumbent on all free peoples.

> If Austria had not resisted with courage and determination all attacks on its democratic existence, if this country had not been such a reliable bulwark of democracy, the world would have found itself faced years ago with an Austrian refugee problem. [23]

No one in Austria, he added, was thinking of threatening to close the Hungarian frontier. Austria considered the right of asylum not only a democratic and international duty founded on law, but also a deeply moral and human responsibility, eine Herzensangelegenheit ("a matter of the heart"); therefore it would not close its frontiers. But the Western world, too, must remain aware of its responsibility to the principles of freedom and of international solidarity, and should not lessen its efforts until a humanly dignified future was secured for the last refugees. Mr. Helmer suggested that countries should accept Hungarian refugees from Austria on a quota system, and should accept them not exclusively on the basis of political, professional, or health considerations, since such selection tended to leave old and sick persons in Austria. Furthermore, he suggested that funds be raised to reimburse Austria for care and maintenance costs on the same quota basis. He also pointed to the complication which had arisen due to the fact that some overseas

countries, in particular the US, were not granting immigration facilities to refugees who had been moved to countries
of second asylum, which resulted in refusal of refugees to
leave Austria until final emigration was secured for them,
and also in the return to Austria of many persons from their
country of second asylum. He emphasized again the urgent
need for action in order to forestall the psychological depression induced by camp life.

After a two-day discussion, the Committee summed
up the deliberations about these problems in a unanimously
accepted resolution (see Annex 16.3), agreeing that "the fate
of the Hungarian refugees constitutes a challenge to humanity" and that "the care of refugees is a burden to be shared
by the whole world." The response of the countries followed
promptly. Although it was not feasible for them to accept
the Austrian proposed quota basis for immigration and funds,
in general both increased significantly; selection missions returned to Austria and further contributions for transportation
were made available. Denmark, Luxembourg, Costa Rica,
Venezuela, and others gave special contributions, and the US
provided $5 million; Norway agreed to take tubercular per-
sons; South Africa, Colombia, and Canada were ready to accept persons from countries of second asylum.

The revival of interest in as yet unsettled Hungarian
refugees was promoted by UNHCR by inviting a group of
world-renowned journalists to visit Austria and Yugoslavia.
This effort resulted in a major reporting campaign in the
world's leading newspapers, appealing to governments to continue action on behalf of the Hungarian refugees.

By January 1957, of the 170,000 refugees who had en-
tered Austria, some 70,000 remained within its borders. By
January 1958 that number had been reduced to 19,000 (see
Annex 16.4).

Permanent Solutions

The UNHCR responded to the renewed determination
demonstrated at the UNREF Ex. Com.'s Fourth Session by
preparing a program for permanent solutions. At its Fifth
Session, June 1957, the UNREF Ex. Com. accepted the HC's
proposal for a permanent-solution program for Hungarian
refugees in Austria and Yugoslavia, costing $3.5 million.
In a major effort to assist economic integration in those

countries 70 percent of the total sum was used for credit
and housing facilities, for establishing refugees in agriculture, and for educational projects--elementary schools, youth
projects, and aid to university students. Governments, voluntary agencies, and foundations contributed large sums to
meet the needs of the younger refugees. Finally, special
projects for intellectuals and care for unmarried mothers
were provided. [24]   The Austrian Government was enabled on
1 July 1958 to take over the large education program, using
funds made available under the US Surplus Food Program.

By 31 December 1960, the Hungarian refugee problem
in Austria had reached its final stage. [25]   Fewer than 9,000
of the total number of 180,000 remained. Of these 1,183
were still in need of material assistance and 570 lived in
federal and non-federal camps. (See Annex 16.5 for final
settlement as of January 1960.) The Ex. Com. approved
the closure of the fund for new Hungarian refugees by 21
March 1961. The residual needs of the refugees concerned
were absorbed in the regular program of the HC.

International Protection

While in the beginning all efforts tended to be concentrated on immediate relief and resettlement, the HC had
increasingly to pay attention to his basic task, international
protection. After final settlement, refugees were in need of
international protection until they acquired a new nationality;
legal provisions had also to be made in countries of second
asylum. Governments had to establish proper legal procedures with regard to unaccompanied children, taking into
consideration the parents as well as the child. Repatriation
also required diplomatic negotiations, particularly when the
country of origin was unable to cover the cost of return. At
the Seventeenth Session of ECOSOC, July 1958, the HC dealt
with these questions.

Results of the Hungarian Experience

The Hungarian experience taught a number of basic
lessons. All concerned realized that the refugee problem
was not a matter of past events, but a phenomenon of the
twentieth century. Furthermore, it was clear that, as maintained in 1951-52, countries of first asylum, whose geographical situation faced them with the practical necessity of

granting the right of asylum, could not cope with the burden alone. Above all, the Hungarian situation proved that a given refugee problem can be solved by a prompt and expeditious resettlement program, financial assistance, and multinational concern and compassion, and that refugees can be an asset to the receiving countries.

In the case of the Hungarian refugees it was evident from their composition that, notwithstanding the emotional and political overtones of their situation, they could in most cases contribute to the economic and social life of the settlement countries. The composition of the refugees according to age ranged from infants to those sixty-one and older, although younger people up to thirty-six years of age predominated. Men were more numerous, there being about seven men to four women. Professionally, 66.9 percent of the able working men could be grouped within seven professions and 47.5 percent of the able working women within five.[26]

The receiving countries made special arrangements for language and vocational courses for the refugees. The economic conditions in those countries at the time of the exodus was favorable to the refugees' economic integration.

The program also proved the need for maintaining international machinery for dealing with such crises. The UNHCR was essential as a coordinating and guiding body. The vigorous cooperation and close relationship between governments, non-governmental (voluntary) and inter-governmental agencies (ICEM and CoE), and USEP had, within eight months, reduced the Hungarian problem to manageable proportions. The HC's negotiating and diplomatic role in dealing with this human emergency had forestalled chaos and relaxed tensions. The delegate of the UK gave credit to the HC and to his staff by acknowledging that the Hungarian refugee problem had had a "tremendous impact on day-to-day work of the High Commissioner's Office" and that "it was greatly to the credit of the Office as a whole that they had caused so little dislocation, and that the staff had managed to shoulder its new and pressing problems without neglecting its more routine duty. The crisis had coincided with the appointment of the new High Commissioner, who thus had to start work in particularly difficult circumstances."[27]

The program demonstrated the close interconnection between the two functions with which the HC was entrusted by the UN: international protection and the search for permanent solutions. It demonstrated too that material assistance was essential in achieving final solutions, whether through resettlement, local integration, or repatriation. The voluntary agencies, international and national, had become the main operational partners in the countries of asylum as well as in those of resettlement.

At the meeting of the Third Committee the Hungarian delegate stated that he

> was glad that the general atmosphere of the debate enabled him to speak impartially on the question of the Hungarian refugees, which was of direct interest to his country. That favorable atmosphere was due in particular to the success of the HC who had managed in spite of great difficulties to carry on his duties in a purely humanitarian and social spirit in accordance with his terms of reference. The Hungarian Government was most grateful to the Governments, organizations and individuals that had helped to alleviate the sufferings of the refugees. [28]

The Rev. Elfan Rees paid tribute to the UNHCR by writing:

> The Hungarian crisis has surely proven, beyond further controversy, the need for maintaining permanent international machinery for dealing with such crises. No one attempts to deny or to minimize the chaos that clouded and confused the early weeks of the Hungarian influx. A multitude of concerned governments and a plethora of voluntary agencies had their representatives on the scene, each besieging the overwhelmed Austrian authorities with plans, proposals, and requests. Had the Office of the United Nations High Commissioner for Refugees not been in existence and available to give a hand, the chaos would have been fantastic. The High Commissioner's Office saved the day but not at once.... Its own approach to the crisis called for improvisation and trial and error. That order did emerge, however, from this chaos; that each agency was set to the task it was best equipped for; that border reception, emergency feeding and clothing, temporary housing, and ultimate movement

were planned and coordinated is irrefutable testimony to the importance of an Office of a United Nations High Commissioner for Refugees. [29]

Notes

1. GA (XI), Third Com., Off. Rec. A/C. 3/L. 507, 24 Nov. 1956: 1.

2. For text of Deputy Director of ICEM, P. Jacobsen, see Kern, Österreich, Vienna, 1959: 86.

3. This cable was followed by a letter from Mr. Read on 6 Nov.; for text, see Kern, ibid.: 285.

4. 1006-ES II; and GA (XI) 1129 by 69 affirmative votes, two against and eight abstaining; for greater detail see the Interim Rep. of the Secretary-General, Doc. A/337 and Add. 1 in GA (XI), Off. Rec. Annexes: 8 ff.

5. GA (XI), A/C. 3 to 507, 24 Nov. 1956.

6. GA (XI), Doc. A/3436. Rep. of the Third Com., 8 Dec. 1956.

7. A/AC. 79/49, Annex IV: 1-2, UNREF Ex. Com. (IV), 17 Jan. 1957.

8. For full text, see GA (XII), Off. Rec. Supp. No. 11, A/3585 Rev. 1: 58-9.

9. James Read, op cit.: 22.

10. UNREF Ex. Com. (IV), A/AC. 7949, 17 Jan. 1957.

11. SCVA, AFSC, AJDC, Brethren Service Commission, Comité international d'Aide aux Intellectuals, Conference internationale des Charitiés Catholiques, IRC, ISS, LRCS, LWF, NCWC, Tolstoy Foundation, UN HIAS, World Alliance of WMCA, World's YMCA, WCC, World ORT Union, WUS, and World Veteran's Federation.

12. GA (XI), Third Com., 24 Nov. 1956, op. cit.: 13.

13. A/AC. 7949, 17 Jan. 1957.

14. For detailed description of these programs, see A/AC. 79/73: 9-11.

15. A/AC. 79/73, 8 May 1957: 6.

16. UNHCR, The Red Cross and the Refugees, Geneva, May 1963: 19-22, and UN, GA. A/AC 79/52, 25 Jan. 1957.

17. For text of letter see Kern, op. cit.: 86.

18. Medical Rep. on the Hungarian Emergency Operation in Austria, Vienna; Apr. 1962, mimeographed.

19. For details, see Constant Companions, Voluntary Agencies and Refugees, MCR/270/64GE. 64-15450, Geneva: 29-31, and UN, GA, A/AC. 79/49 Add. Jan. 1957 and A/AC. 79/49, Annexes Rev. 1, 29 Jan. 1957.

20. A/AC. 79/54.

21. Edward B. Marks, "How the Yugoslav Camps for Hungarian Refugees Were Closed, " UN, Geneva.

22. GA (XIII), Off. Rec. Supp. 11, A/3828/Rev. 1: 4.

23. Author's transl., see Kerr, op. cit.: 62.

24. For details, see UNHCR Ann. Rep. GA (XIII) 1958: 3, 48 & 50.

25. A/AC 96/112 GA, Ex. Com. (V), for the HC's Program, 19 Apr. 1962.

26. For detail, see Kern, op. cit., Tables: 76-79, and Elfan Rees, We Strangers and Afraid, The Refugee Story Today, WRY 1969, N.Y.: 51. Some 72 percent of those refugees who had arrived in the US by May 1957 were between 16 and 45 years of age; 40 percent were single, predominantly males, most of them with skills, and many of them university graduates.

27. ECOSOC (XXIV), July 1957.

28. GA (XII), 5 Nov. 1957.

29. Elfan Rees, op. cit. : 52.

ANNEX 16.1

THE HUNGARIAN REFUGEE INFLUX INTO AUSTRIA, OCT. 1957 TO JUNE 1957

October	780
November	113,810
December	49,685
January	12,862
February	1,140
March	289
April	174
May	76
June	50

SOURCE: Friedrich Kern, with support of the Federal Ministry of Interior, Österreich: Offene Grenze der Menschlichkeit, Die Bewältingung des Ungarischen Flüchtlingsproblems im Geiste Internationaler Solidarität, 1958: 30.

ANNEX 16.2

THE DEPARTURE OF HUNGARIAN REFUGEES
FROM AUSTRIA, 7 NOV. 1956 TO 1 MAR. 1958

Country of Resettlement or temporary asylum	Cumulative Total from 7 Nov. 1956-- 1 March 1958			
	Transported by ICEM	Processed for movement with ICEM assistance	Other arrangements	Total Departure
Final Departures from Austria	82,165	55,725	16,183	154,073
Overseas Destinations				
Argentina	907	---	---	907
Australia	9,458	---	---	9,458
Brazil	986	---	---	986
Canada	15,839	3,588	3,148	22,575
Canada (via Netherlands)	---	1,960	---	1,960
Chile	258	---	---	258
Colombia	215	---	---	215
Costa Rica	15	---	---	15
Cuba	5	---	---	5
Cyprus	2	---	---	2
Dominican Republic	---	---	581	581
Ecuador	1	---	---	1
Fed. of Rhodesia & Nyasaland	52	---	---	52
Israel	1,896	---	---	1,896
New Zealand	960	---	---	960
Nicaragua	4	---	---	4
Paraguay	7	---	---	7
Turkey	79	---	426	505
Union of South Africa	1,309	---	---	1,309
US	12,003	23,182	---	35,185
Uruguay	37	---	---	37
Venezuela	611	---	---	611
Total	44,644	28,730	4,155	77,529
Within Europe				
Belgium	3,318	14	87	3,419
Denmark	58	1,090	26	1,174
France	9,345	---	887	10,232
Germany	191	10,506	3,577	14,274

Iceland	---	52	---	52
Ireland	540	---	1	541
Italy	3,487	---	362	3,849
Luxembourg	37	167	23	227
Netherlands	997	2,034	501	3,532
Netherlands (for Processing				
Canada)	24	---	---	24
Norway	1,106	---	57	1,163
Portugal	1	---	3	4
Spain	19	---	---	19
Sweden	2,358	3,041	54	5,453
Switzerland	67	10,091	1,815	11,973
UK	15,973	---	4,635	20,608
Total	37,521	26,995	12,028	76,544

Departures from Yugoslavia
(Provisional figures)   10,711   2,439   3,446   16,596

SOURCE: Jules Witcover, "The Role of ICEM in the Resettlement of Hungarian Refugees," REMP, The Hague, Mar. 1958: 21.

ANNEX 16.3

UNRFF Executive Committee Resolution (V) Concerning the Problem of Hungarian Refugees (unanimously adopted June 1957).

The UNRFF Executive Committee.....
Recalling General Assembly resolutions A/RESOLUTION/398 and A/RESOLUTION/409,

Recognizing that the fate of the Hungarian refugees constitutes a challenge to the conscience of humanity,
Having taken note of the data relating to the problem of Hungarian refugees submitted by the High Commissioner,
Recognizing that this problem causes most serious difficulties to certain countries of first asylum, notably Austria and Yugoslavia, in spite of the substantial contributions being made by many other countries,
Taking into account the need to ensure family unity,
Taking note of the statements made on behalf of the Austrian Federal Government by Minister of the Interior Oskar Helmer and Secretary of State Franz Grubhofer,

1. Declares that the care of refugees is a burden to be shared by the whole world in accordance with the capacities of the respective countries;

2. Supports the appeals made by the High Commissioner for Refugees in order that the countries of first asylum be enabled to meet the costs of the Hungarian refugee problem, and that countries which are in a position to do so accept the settlement in their territories of an increased number of refugees.

SOURCE: HC's An. Rep. to GA (XII), Off. Rec. Supp. No. 11, A/3585/Rev. 1, 1957: 41.

ANNEX 16.4

MOVEMENT OF NEW HUNGARIAN REFUGEES IN AUSTRIA
FROM OCT. 1956 TO DEC. 1961

	1956	1957	1958	1959	1960	1961	1956 1961
Number at Beginning of Period	--	71,500	19,200	14,900	9,600	8,900	--
Arrivals from Hungary	164,300	14,600	100	100	100	200	179,600
Arrivals from other countries	--	1,000	100	..	..	..	1,100
Other movements[a]	--	200	100	100	100	..	500
Gross increase	164,300	15,800	300	300	400	200	181,200
Emigration[b]	91,300	62,500	3,600	5,500	900	1,100	164,700
Repatriation	1,500	5,700	900	200	100	100	8,600
Gross decrease	92,800	68,200	4,500	5,600	1,000	1,200	173,300
Net variation during period	+71,500	-52,400	-4,200	-5,300	-700	-1,000	+7,900
Number at End of Period	71,500	19,200	14,900	9,600	8,900	7,900	7,900

a Natural increase.
b Including 1,183 naturalized refugees.
.. Less than 50.

SOURCE: A/AC.96/53, Annex II, Analysis of Position and Results Achieved in the
Implementation of the Fund for New Hungarian Refugees in Austria as of
31 Dec. 1961: 1.

ANNEX 16.5

FINAL SETTLEMENT OF THE HUNGARIAN REFUGEES
AS OF 30 JUNE 1959 AND JAN. 1960

Resettlement in Europe

	As of 30 June 1959	As of Jan. 1960
Belgium	3,461	6,000 (of which 900 left for other countries by 30 June 1959)
Denmark	1,178	
France	10,240	13,000 (of whom 4,000 left for other countries)
Germany	14,317	15,000
Italy	3,849	
Netherlands	3,547	3,800
Norway	1,232	1,500
Sweden	6,002	7,500 (inc. 400 TB cases)
Switzerland	12,131	13,000 (of whom 2,700 left for other countries by 30 June 1959)
UK	20,690	
Other European Countries	878	

Resettlement Overseas

Argentina	914	
Australia	10,156	15,000
Brazil	1,009	
Canada	25,513	38,000
Israel	1,897	
New Zealand	1,012	1,150
Union of S. Africa	1,323	
US	38,058	
Venezuela	706	
Other Overseas Countries (Chile, Columbia)	1,742	

SOURCE: Kern, Österreich: 68; figures for 1960 provided by UNHCR.

Chapter 17

1957: A DECISIVE YEAR

When Dr. Auguste Lindt assumed his task on 1 January 1957, in the third year of UNREF and in the midst of the Hungarian crisis, he was very much aware of the continuity of the international procedure dealing with the refugee problem, but also recognized that changed conditions and attitudes demanded new approaches.

Dr. Lindt was not discouraged by the magnitude and seriousness of the problems before him. He undertook his responsibilities with vigor and optimism. Inspired by the experience gained during the Hungarian refugee crisis he was convinced that the refugee problem was not an insoluble one. However, he was a realist, able to clearly outline to the governments the steps which had to be taken and to convince them that success depended mainly on the money available.

In his initial speech before the Thirteenth Session of ECOSOC in April 1957 and again before the Third Committee of the GA on 4 November of that year, [1] Dr. Lindt elaborated his approach to his duties as HC. He stressed that he would try to follow the path set by Dr. van Heuven Goedhart who had "succeeded by his tenacity and by his untiring efforts first to resuscitate and, afterward, to maintain general interest in a problem which, at the beginning of his term of office, was almost a forgotten one"; he paid tribute to van Heuven Goedhart's "creative imagination to think out ways by which the refugee problem could be approached," and reasserted, referring to Art. 2 of the Statute, that the work of his Office was of a humanitarian and social character and in no way political. In the work of "helping refugees, regardless of how or where they became refugees," he stressed the fact that his mandate did not apply to any particular region, but was of a global nature.

He laid great importance on the provision of international protection which would help in facilitating permanent

419

solutions. He assumed the widest possible freedom of choice in regard to these solutions, by repatriation, emigration, or local integration. The determining factor would be the free will of the refugee.

In seeking permanent solutions he emphasized that old refugees should be moved out of camps as quickly as possible. He considered the camps to be a sore on the body of mankind. "Refugees deteriorate rapidly" in such camps, he declared; they are "no place for human beings to live in." Camps should be only reception centers. He had in mind as a precedent the approach to the Hungarian refugees. "Due to an outstanding international effort, within approximately eight months" the problem had been reduced "to manageable proportions." In considering the problem of the old refugees he gave first priority to the clearing of camps.

Dr. Lindt envisaged a two-pronged attack on the problem. The countries of immigration should take a new look at the camps and relax their regulations as they had done for the Hungarians, taking into account that even if there was one difficult case in a family, the family as a whole could still be an economic asset to a new country. For the others, who needed local integration, houses had to be built (many refugees who were earning their living were still in camps because of the lack of housing, and thus were only half integrated), and counselling and vocational training and rehabilitation had to be organized. He pointed to the even more serious problem of the difficult cases--the physically handicapped or those difficult to settle because of social or economic handicaps. Institutional placement, rehabilitation, or some other permanent solution had to be found to fit each case. He referred to additional problems: the out-of-camp refugees and the European refugees in China. He stressed particularly the fact that to implement these plans money would be needed. He pointed to the shortfall of governmental contributions to UNREF.

Prolongation of UNHCR

The question of the UNHCR mandate was to be considered at the 1957 GA; Dr. Lindt urged prolongation. His Office, he pointed out, was charged with the supervision of the execution of the 1951 Convention, with determining eligibility procedures, or with helping to determine eligibility itself in certain countries. His Office was concerned with legal matters affecting the status and situation of the refugees. Although in 1956 approximately 55,000 refugees in Europe became naturalized (a great many in Austria), there were still around one million refugees in need of protection. Dr. Lindt concluded that prolongation of his Office was necessary because of the long-range nature of the problem of international protection. Because large numbers of refugees were not settled and an influx of new refugees continued, it would be necessary to provide for a continuation of UNREF programs which would not be completed by the end of 1958. Material assistance, however, was needed only as long as the refugee failed to become reestablished. The purpose of material assistance should be to deal with a problem as soon as it arose, in such a way as to provide a permanent solution as early as possible. The UNHCR could then intervene with enough speed and flexibility through the voluntary organizations. Otherwise there would be a residual problem, prolonging the need for material assistance.

Acting on the recommendation of ECOSOC (Res. 650[XXIV] of July 1957) the GA on 26 November (Res. 1165[XII]) acknowledged that "the need for international action on behalf of refugees would still persist" after 31 December 1958, and the GA in "considering the valuable work which had been performed" by the UNHCR both in providing international protection to refugees and in promoting permanent solutions for their problems and appreciating the "effective manner" in which it had been dealing with special emergencies, extended the Office for a further five years. It was decided that the election of the HC for a five-year period would take place at the Thirteenth Session of the GA in 1958. [2]

Intensification and Termination of the UNREF Program

In late 1956 and early 1957 the UNREF Program had been overshadowed by the urgency of the Hungarian crisis. When the great need of the Hungarian refugees had been reduced to manageable proportions, the Ex. Com. and the HC were very much concerned that the UNREF Program should be brought to its fulfillment.

At the Fourth Session of the UNREF Ex. Com. (29 January and 4 February 1957) Dr. Lindt stated that Dr. van Heuven Goedhart's "devotion and foresight in planning the UNREF Program was ... bearing fruit," but he added that a

considerable reappraisal was necessary to achieve the objectives within the given time. [3]

He reported that the UNREF Program had had a slow
start owing to the procedures required for its establishment
and to the non-fulfillment of government contributions. Also,
the implementation of projects had been delayed by the unexpected influx of the Hungarian refugees into Austria and Yugoslavia. In light of the experience so far gained and of the
forecast of the probable situation of the non-settled refugee
population in various countries by the end of 1958, he reported that additional funding at the level of $7,500,000
would be needed to achieve permanent solutions. Of this
sum, $2,700,000 represented the anticipated shortfall, and
$4,800,000 the amount needed over and above the UNREF
target. The total could be effectively used within two years
of the 1958 expiration date of the UNREF Program.

On the basis of the considerations of the UNREF Ex.
Com. and of ECOSOC Res. 650 C[XXIV] of 24 July 1957,
GA Res. 1166[XII] of 26 November 1957 (63 for, none against,
10 abstentions) requested the HC to intensify the camp clearance project and to continue to seek solutions for the problem of refugees outside camps. It authorized him to appeal
to governments and Specialized Agencies for the funds needed
for this purpose. He was further requested to bring the
UNREF Program to a conclusion by 31 December 1958.
"Bearing in mind that new refugee situations requiring international assistance" had arisen and had augmented the problem since the establishment of the Fund, and that other such
situations "would arise" in the future wherein international
assistance would be appropriate, the GA made far-reaching
decisions for the HC's future programs. They envisaged a
program that "should provide assistance to all refugees under
his mandate, in whatever part of the world they might be.
This program would be sufficiently flexible to adapt itself to
changing conditions and would enable new situations to be
met as they arose."[4] The HC was also authorized to appeal
for funds and to establish an Emergency Fund in the amount
of $5 million as of 1 January 1958. The GA, furthermore,
requested ECOSOC to establish a new policy committee, the
Executive Committee for the HC's Program (Ex. Com.),
which would replace the UNREF Ex. Com.'s executive and
advisory authority.

In the words of the US delegate, Res. 1166(XII)
"marked a significant development in that it recognized the

continuing nature of the refugee problem and its constantly changing aspects."[5]

During the last two years of the operation of the UNREF Program, the HC set out to achieve more realistic planning and implementation of the programs.

In order to assess accurately plans for intensification of the program, a survey to provide more precise statistics on refugees living in and outside camps was carried out in 1957-58 in six European countries under the overall direction of Professor Dr. J. Idenburg, Director-General of Statistics in the Netherlands.[6] This survey revealed that, as of mid-summer 1957, there were 58,200 refugees in camps and 120,000 non-settled refugees living outside camps (see Annex 17.1).

Of those living in camps, 24,500 were eligible for assistance under the USEP program or the UNHCR program for Hungarian refugees. An additional 31,300 were in need of aid. Within the non-settled groups living outside camps there were some 97,000 not expected to emigrate under normal schemes and not eligible for assistance under international programs.

The four-year UNREF Program carried out projects in thirteen countries settling permanently 50,349 persons excluding 11,500 beneficiaries from UNREF emergency aid. (For details, see Annex 17.2.)

By 31 December 1958, thirty-one governments and the Holy See had contributed $14,496,585, and contributions from sources within countries of residence amounted to an estimated $24 million. Additional private contributions from individuals and various bodies were $2,120,989.[7] Other income totalled $725,608. The value of UNREF projects reached to over $40 million, not including the cost of permanent care of difficult cases assumed by receiving countries, nor the cost of ancillary services provided by local authorities and voluntary agencies (see Annex 17.3).

The UNREF Program had various effects on international assistance to refugees. It served, as we have seen, to reduce the problem of the old refugees to manageable proportions. It also highlighted the complementary nature of the two activities: international protection and material assistance for achieving a permanent solution. Further, it led to a closer coordination among the UNHCR, governments, the Specialized Agencies, and inter-governmental and voluntary agencies working for refugees.

The Good Offices Resolution

The Chinese refugees in Hong Kong had posed a seemingly insoluble problem for the UNHCR ever since the Chinese Government in Taipei had first urged international action on their behalf in the earliest days of the Office's existence.   These refugees had long been felt to be of concern to the international community because of their need for increased material assistance--the kind of assistance that might be more readily forthcoming if sought by an international agency such as the UNHCR.   But the fact of the existence of two competing Chinese governments made it politically unfeasible for the GA to declare that the Chinese refugees in Hong Kong were within UNHCR's mandate, and without such a declaration, the Office felt itself powerless to aid these refugees.

In 1957 the problem had reached a serious crisis. All funds had been exhausted.   In Res. 1167 the GA acknowledged that "the problem of Chinese refugees in Hong Kong ... is such as to be of concern to the international community." Without reference to their eligibility under the Statute, the HC was requested to "use his good offices to encourage arrangements for contributions" to the Chinese refugees in Hong Kong.   The UNHCR was to play a part in the search for funds and in their distribution to the governments and agencies which would care directly for Chinese refugees.

In time the new responsibility, to act in a truly humanitarian manner without recourse in every situation to the legal strictures of the Statute, was to have a profound effect in permitting the HC to aid refugee groups on a global scale.

The three significant Resolutions, 1165, 1166, and 1167, passed by the GA in 1957, gave the HC a wider and more flexible role in coping with the old refugees as well as with any emergency relating to new refugees, not only in Europe but elsewhere.   The Office of the HC had been prolonged; the governments had accepted the interaction of international protection and material assistance, the latter for care and maintenance in case of need and for long-term solutions; the HC was authorized not only to appeal for funds,

but also to arrange financing for permanent solutions when
needed; and the scope of the HC's authority was significantly
expanded. Thus the year 1957 was not only a year of reappraisal and planning for European refugees, but also a year
that saw an expressed recognition that, as Dr. Lindt had
stated, the refugee problem was worldwide and a concern of
the international community.

Response of Voluntary Organizations and of US Citizen Groups

The programs for the Hungarian refugees also gave
impetus to the voluntary agencies to reappraise and intensify
their work for the old refugees.

In addition to the UN activities, voluntary agencies
and citizen groups showed a new concern for permanent solutions. They also felt the need for reappraisal and intensification of the work for refugees. They, like Austria and the
UNHCR, were concerned that despite the fact that the plight
of the Hungarians had

> stirred the public conscience in the free world,
> there nevertheless appeared weakness in the con-
> tinued efforts to bring this problem to as complete
> a solution as quickly as possible. It seemed as if
> this time again the momentum would die out before
> the job was done. It seemed as if this time,
> again a residual refugee problem would be added
> to the lingering problems since WWII. [8]

An emergency working conference on "The Refugee
Problem, Today and Tomorrow" was called in Geneva 27-28
May 1957, by the Conference of Non-Governmental Organizations Interested in Migration and the SCVA in association
with the UNHCR and ICEM. Over 150 delegates from seven-
ty-five agencies were present, and Dr. Adrian Pelt, Director
of the European Office of the UN; Ambassador Harold H.
Tittmann, Director-General of ICEM; Dr. Oskar Helmer,
Minister of Interior of Austria; and Dr. Lindt participated.

On the basis of their deliberations they urged governments and peoples to provide the means for reestablishing
the uprooted, taking into account the lessons of the Hungarian
emergency, and they formulated plans which could be put into
immediate operation in the event of another crisis. They

considered the refugee problem in the Far East (in Hong
Kong and Korea), the Middle East (Palestine Arab refugees),
and the general refugee situation in Europe, in particular
the recent influx of Hungarian refugees into Austria and
Yugoslavia.

As the presidents of the two convening organizations,
Edgar H. S. Chandler and James J. Norris, stated, the aim
of the conference was to mobilize "a large body of informed
opinions" in support of bold and imaginative action which
would make citizens as well as private, governmental, and
inter-governmental agencies aware "that whatever had been
accomplished in the Hungarian refugee emergency was not the
end, but the beginning of a long and difficult task, in itself,
and in addition only a part of a worldwide problem to which
humanity demands a solution. "[9]

At the same time the conference dealt with technical
questions involved in the reception, integration, and migration of refugees and drew up recommendations, based on
past experience, focusing on greater coordination and improvement in all three fields of permanent solutions.

In the US, too, leading citizens became concerned
that the success of the resettlement of the Hungarian refugees had created the impression that the refugee problem in
Europe was "solved" and that their rapid and compassionate
resettlement had produced a feeling of embitterment and
frustration on the part of those refugees still confined to
camps in Europe--many since the late 1940's--who considered themselves as the "forgotten men. " It was felt that the
successful resettling of the Hungarian refugees in such a
short time had established a pattern of emergency action
which might provide, with some suitable adaption, a solution
for the residual problem of refugees in Europe. This group
was concerned about the "apparent public indifference to the
problem" in the US which was due to a simple lack of awareness. Therefore, they aimed at better understanding and
clarification on the matter, not only for themselves, but also
to provide much-needed information for the public.

This representative group of prominent American citi-
zens established the Zellerbach Commission on the European
Situation, which conducted an extensive survey of refugees in
Europe in the fall of 1957.

A competent staff undertook preliminary research for

several months, before the Commission itself travelled
through Europe in October 1956.   They visited camps and
installations and had discussions with representatives of governments, inter-governmental agencies, and private organizations concerned with refugees.   They confined themselves
basically to studying those European countries which had the
greatest refugee concentrations--Germany, Austria, Italy,
France, and Yugoslavia.   But in a special report they also
dealt with Greece, Turkey, and the Scandinavian countries.

Their final report, An Appraisal of Some Salient
Problems Confronting the Free Nations as They Prepare for
World Refugee Year, [10] was widely distributed and discussed.
The series of recommendations designed to liquidate the re-
sidual refugee problem in Europe not only informed the pub-
lic but also had an impact on governments, particularly the
US.   In subsequent years, many of the Commission's recom-
mendations were realized, and ultimately World Refugee
Year (WRY) brought additional public support.

Notes

1.   GA (XI) Third Com. , Off. Rec.:   193.

2.   The GA re-elected Dr. Lindt as HC on 14 Nov. 1958.
      Before the election the Sec.-Gen. informed the As-
      sembly that Dr. Lindt, for personal reasons, could
      accept only for two more years.

3.   UNREF Exec. Com. A/AC. 79/78, 17 June 1957 and
      Doc. A/AC. 79/72.

4.   US Delegate, GA (XII), Off. Rec. , Third Com. , 3 Nov.
      1957:   221.

5.   Rep. on UNREF Ex. Com. (XII), 13-17 Jan. 1958.

6.   GA, UNREF Ex. Com. (VIII), A/AC. 79/111 and Add.
      1, 28 Apr. 1958, and Statistical Annex A/AC. 79/
      111, 21 Apr. 1958.

7.   Outstanding among the non-governmental contributions
      were over $400,000 by the UN Association of the
      UK and $1 million from the Netherlands Council for
      Aid to Refugees.

8.   Conference on The Refugee Problem, Today and To-
         morrow, Conf. Rep. 1957: 580.

9.   Ibid.

10. Rep. of the Zellerbach Com. on the European Refugee
         Situation, pub. by IRC, NY, 1957, and European
         Refugee Problems, 1959, a Special Rep., NY, 1959.

ANNEX 17.1

SITUATION OF REFUGEES IN EUROPE 1957

	In Camps	Outside Camps	Total
Austria	30,500[a]	28,500	59,000
France	--	36,000	36,000
Germany, Fed. Rep. of	20,700	40,000	60,700
Greece	1,400[a]	8,900	10,300
Italy	5,250	5,500	10,750
Turkey	346	750	1,196
	58,200	120,000[b]	178,000[b]

a.   Including refugees in unofficial camps

b.   Rounded figures

SOURCE: UNREF Ex. Com., A/AC.79/111, 21 Apr., 1958.

ANNEX 17.2: OVERALL ANALYSIS OF UNREF PROGRAM AS AT 31 DEC. 1958

Consolidated number of actual beneficiaries[a]

Program--Country	Firmly settled			Beneficiaries not firmly settled			All beneficiaries		
	From camps	Outside camps	Total	From camps	Outside camps	Total	From camps	Outside camps	Total
I. Permanent Solutions									
Austria	4,491	6,910	11,401	5,258	2,969	8,227	9,749	9,879	19,628
Belgium	-	781	781	-	1,074	1,074	-	1,855	1,885
France	-	765	765	-	65	65	-	830	830
Germany, Fed. Rep. of	4,290	1,070	5,360	8,900	1,700	10,600	13,190	2,770	15,960
Greece	425	390	815	262	227	489	687	617	1,304
Italy	431	889	1,320	680	420	1,100	1,111	1,309	2,420
Lebanon	-	5	5	-	5	5	-	10	10
Turkey	-	114	114	-	49	49	-	163	163
UAR	-	57	57	-	74	74	-	131	131
Total	9,637	10,981	20,618	15,100	6,583	21,683	24,737	17,564	42,301
II. Settlement of Difficult Cases									
Austria	223	35	258	-	-	-	223	35	258
China	-	382	382	-	-	-	-	382	382
France	-	66	66	-	-	-	-	66	66

Germany, Fed. Rep. of	60	–	60	–	–	–	60	–	60
Greece	52	264	316	–	–	–	52	264	316
Italy	84	82	166	–	–	–	84	82	166
Jordan, Lebanon	–	11	11	–	–	–	–	11	11
Turkey	–	52	52	–	–	–	–	52	52
UAR	–	53	53	–	17	17	–	70	70
Other countries[b]	–	17	17	–	–	–	–	17	17
Total	419	962	1,381	–	17	17	419	979	1,398
III. Far Eastern Operations	–	6,650[c]	6,650[c]	–	–	–	–	6,650[c]	6,650[c]
Grand Total	10,056	18,593	28,649	15,100	6,600	31,700	25,156	25,193	50,349

a   The figures given here excluding beneficiaries of UNREF emergency aid, estimated at some 11,500 refugees.

b   Refugees from Ethiopia, Morocco, Spain, and Yugoslavia resettled in other countries and refugees from Iran settled in homes there.

c   Excluding 372 difficult cases already included in Part II of table, under China.

SOURCE: GA (XIV), 1959, Off. Rec., Supp. 11, A/4104/Rev. 1: 21.

ANNEX 17. 3

GOVERNMENTAL CONTRIBUTIONS TO THE PROGRAM OF THE UN REFUGEE FUND AS OF 31 DEC. 1958 (IN US DOLLARS)

1. Regular contributions

Australia	503, 839
Austria	17, 200
Belgium	560, 000
Brazil	15, 000
Canada	671, 282
China, Rep. of	5, 000
Colombia	10, 000
Denmark	289, 560
Dominican Rep.	15, 000
Fed. of Malaya	1, 000
France	931, 429
Germany, Fed. Rep. of	685, 715
Greece	14, 333[a]
Guatemala	b
Holy See	1, 000
Israel	10, 000
Italy	6, 073
Korea, Rep. of	2, 000
Liechtenstein	2, 501
Luxembourg	11, 000
Morocco	6, 817
Netherlands	384, 000
New Zealand	196, 000
Norway	349, 998
Philippines	1, 250
Sweden	463, 948
Switzerland	619, 158
Tunisia	2, 000
Turkey	12, 858
UK	1, 064, 027
US	5, 139, 000
Venezuela	20, 000
Total	12, 004, 988

2. Special contributions

France	100,000
Netherlands	700,894
New Zealand	126,000
Sweden	1,353,180
Switzerland	17,523
US	194,000
Total	2,491,597
Grand Total	14,496,585

a Including contribution in kind of $6,000 not otherwise included in totals.

b A contribution of 100 quintals of coffee was promised.

SOURCE: GA (XIV), 1959 Off. Rec., Supp. 11, A/4104/Rev. 1: 21.

Chapter 18

A NEW CONCEPT: GOOD OFFICES

The term "good offices" was used in relation to refugees at least as early as 1949 when the Secretary-General recommended that one of the functions that might be performed by the international agency which was to succeed the IRO was to use its good offices to assist in the repatriation, migration or resettlement of refugees. [1] As used there and in international relations traditionally, good offices refers to the role of an impartial intermediary assisting in the solution of a dispute between two states.

The HC may act only where and as he has been authorized by the GA either through the Statute of his Office or through subsequent resolutions. Until 1957 he was able to act only on behalf of refugee groups which came within the refugee definition of the Statute. In 1957, however, a significant Resolution was passed, one which was to greatly expand the role of the HC.

In response to the desperate need for material assistance of refugees in Hong Kong, the GA requested the HC, without reference to the Statute, to "use his good offices" in seeking contributions for the relief of these refugees who could not have been considered to fall within his mandate (Res. 1167[XII], of 26 November 1957; 59 votes for, 9 against, 2 abstentions).

Res. 1167 should not be viewed as a broad new grant of authority to the UNHCR, but rather, as High Commissioner Schnyder pointed out in 1965, as a way to provide "an essentially pragmatic solution" to what was considered "an extreme case. "[2] The application of the "good offices" concept was nonetheless to have far-reaching implications for the work of the HC. High Commissioner Prince Sadruddin remarked on the good offices role before the Ex. Com. in 1971:

434

While the basic structure of UNHCR has remained
the same, the problem of uprooted people throughout the world has greatly developed in dimensions
and variety. As a result of the ever-changing nature of the situation of displaced persons, my Office has been called upon increasingly to perform
functions not foreseen when its original mandate
was evolved. The use of UNHCR's 'good offices'
role is a natural by-product of this evolution. By
striving to promote rapid solutions to refugee problems, UNHCR surely contributes to the lessening
of tensions between States. The more a situation
is complex and loaded with political overtones, the
more we are required to be flexible in our work
and diplomatic in our approach. While determination of refugee status remains a matter for the
host country to decide upon, we must spare no effort to alleviate human suffering. [3]

The Chinese Refugees in Hong Kong

A special survey of the Chinese refugees in Hong
Kong authorized by the HC in 1952 summarized the political
problems involved. [4] For those states recognizing the Government of the Chinese People's Republic situated in Peking
it was possible to consider the refugees in Hong Kong as fulfilling the criteria for refugees set down in the Statute. They
were persons who, inter alia, were unwilling or unable to
avail themselves of the protection of that government due to
their well-founded fear of persecution. But for those states
recognizing the Government of the Republic of China in Taipei it was difficult to accept that the Hong Kong refugees
were in fear of persecution from the Taipei Government or
deprived of its protection, particularly since that government
had made clear its desire to aid them. The situation was
further complicated by the fact that the UK Government,
which controls the territory of Hong Kong had recognized the
Government of the People's Republic of China in Peking and
therefore could not accept the argument of the Chinese Government in Taipei that the refugees were entitled to its protection. Furthermore, the UK Government did not consider
any of the Chinese in Hong Kong to be refugees legally, but
treated them all as different categories of residents. The
UNHCR, on the other hand, was a part of the UN, and the
government in Taipei had a seat in the UN while the government in Peking did not. Under these circumstances it would

have been difficult for the HC to act other than in a way which accepted the government in Taipei as the official government of China.

If the aid of the UNHCR were to be enlisted in the cause of seeking increased material assistance for Chinese refugees in Hong Kong, a basis had to be found for the Office's action other than the Statute provisions previously relied on. It was with this realization that the UNREF Ex. Com. accepted the suggestion of the HC in 1956 that the question of the Chinese refugees be referred to the GA for consideration, and the good offices function was devised. [5]

Through the use of a phrase redolent of impartiality and to which there was no reference in the Statute, the GA achieved the end desired--more aid for the Chinese refugees --without making any declaration as to the legal status of the refugees and thereby becoming embroiled in the perennially troublesome issue of the two Chinas. However, three years after adopting Res. 1167 the GA made it clear that the Chinese refugees were not considered to come within the mandate of the UNHCR; in Res. 1499(XV) of 5 December 1960 (66 for, none against, 10 abstentions), the Assembly referred to the Chinese refugees mentioned in Res. 1167 as being among those "who do not come within the immediate competence of the United Nations." Thus, the Assembly's action in Res. 1167 did not alter the Statute, nor did it bring the Chinese refugees within the mandate of the HC as defined by the Statute. Rather its effect was to add a new authority to that already delegated to the HC by the Statute: to seek material assistance funds for a specified group of refugees regardless of their legal position as refugees in relation to the Statute of his Office.

GA Resolutions on the Algerian Case

The term good offices was not used by the GA when next it authorized exceptional action by the HC in another "extreme case," that of the refugees from Algeria in Tunisia and Morocco. Nevertheless, GA Res. 1286(XIII) reflected the good offices approach in "noting the action taken in 1958 by the High Commissioner on behalf of refugees from Algeria in Tunisia," and recommending that the UNHCR "continue his action on behalf of the refugees in Tunisia on a substantial scale and undertake similar action in Morocco." The effect of the resolution was retroactively to validate the HC's efforts

A Problem of Our Time

as well as to authorize their continuation. [6] Res. 1389(XIV)
and Res. 1500(XV) again recommended that the HC continue
his efforts on behalf of refugees from Algeria in Morocco
and Tunisia.   In fact, the political situation of the Algerian
refugees, like that of the Chinese refugees in Hong Kong,
made it diplomatically impossible for the HC to do anything
for them on the basis of a declaration that they were refugees within his mandate.   It was not that such a declaration
of eligibility would have embroiled him in a dispute over
state recognition, but that it would in some eyes have seemed
to be an assertion that a founding member of the UN and a
strong supporter of international action on behalf of refugees
was persecuting some groups among its nationals. [7]

    The Statute definition of refugee based on the concept
of "well-founded fear of being persecuted," that had seemed
such an advance over prior definitions of the term based on
categories, now had become an impediment to effective
UNHCR action in providing urgently needed material assistance to some new refugee groups.   If the Office was to respond meaningfully to these new situations of a diplomatically
delicate nature, than it would have to have a new type of authority which would permit it to adhere completely to the
Statute requirement that its every action be "entirely non-
political."

    In short, the Algerian situation required an authoriza-
tion for UNHCR action along the same lines as the good offices function given to it in the Chinese refugees' case. [8]
What was required was material assistance; there was no
need of international protection and no chance of achieving a
permanent solution except through repatriation of the refugees to their homeland. [9]

    Read together with the Chinese refugee resolution, the
Algerian refugee resolutions are a strong indication that by
1958 the Assembly was willing to turn to the UNHCR whenever its services could be usefully applied in meeting the
needs of new and different refugee groups.   If the prerequisite of effective action was a grant of new authority apart
from that contained in the Statute, the GA's good offices
resolutions reflected its willingness to grant such new authority.   The Assembly requested the HC in 1961 to assist both
in returning the Algerian refugees to their homes inside Algeria and in resettling them once returned, even though the
Statute specifies that refugees are no longer within the mandate of the HC once they have in effect returned home (Statute par. 6A[ii] proviso [d]).

Expansion of the Good Offices Function

Meanwhile, in a resolution unconnected with the Algerian situation, the GA again made use of the term good offices in reference to the UNHCR and did so in such a way as to widen further this new basis for the agency's material-assistance actions.   In Res. 1388(XIV) of 20 November 1959 (66 votes for, none against, 12 abstentions), the Assembly authorized High Commissioner Lindt "in respect of refugees who do not come within the competence of the United Nations, to use his good offices in the transmission of contributions designed to provide assistance to these refugees."

In this, its second specific reference to good offices in the refugee context, the Assembly broadened the area of application of the function without appreciably enlarging its content.   After the resolution on the Chinese refugees, good offices meant the collection and distribution of funds for the material assistance of a refugee group which did not qualify for assistance under the Statute.   But, unlike Res. 1167 pertaining to the Chinese refugees, Res. 1388 left to the determination of the HC and his Ex. Com. the groups which could now benefit from the exercise of his good offices.

Dr. Lindt's successor as HC, Dr. Felix Schnyder, suggested in 1965 that this provision of Res. 1388 "must not, however, be regarded as being more revolutionary in character or intention than was actually the case."   Stirred by the general revival of interest in all refugees whether within or outside the HC's mandate occasioned by WRY, he said, "the Assembly was actuated by a desire to support and encourage wide humanitarian action on behalf of all these deprived persons, and certainly not by any desire to extend the future competence of the HC to any group of individuals who might have some grounds for claiming the status of refugees."[10]

Nevertheless, among the achievements of the WRY was that it tended to break down the distinction between mandate and non-mandate refugees by emphasizing that the international community had an obligation "to help solve important refugee problems, irrespective of the refugees' legal status."[11] The force of Res. 1388 was to permit the UNHCR to provide material assistance funds to needy groups of refugees who previously would have been outside its scope of authority. In addition, the passage of this resolution in 1959 seems to have served as a useful precedent when the Assembly came to consider a much more far-reaching resolution in late 1961.

By December 1961 the good offices function had developed through three stages as its usefulness was increasingly recognized. From being a narrowly defined activity ("encouraging arrangements for contributions") exercised on behalf of a specific group of refugees (the Chinese refugees in Hong Kong), the function had been expanded to permit the same activity to be exercised for a much wider variety of persons ("refugees who do not come within the competence of the United Nations"), and thence to authorizing a very broad spectrum of activities for a specific group ("refugees from Algeria in Morocco and Tunisia"). Two final steps in the development of the good offices function occurred in December 1961 when the GA adopted two further resolutions on refugees.

In Res. 1671(XVI) (67 for, none against, 2 abstentions), the HC was authorized "to continue to lend his good offices in seeking appropriate solutions to the problems arising from the presence of Angolan refugees in the Republic of the Congo" (Kinshasa, formerly Belgian Congo). But in fact the HC had begun activities in the Congo before the resolution was adopted, so that its effect was to validate retroactively the exercise of his earlier good offices authority to permit the expansion and continuation of his activities for the Angolan refugees.

Adopted on the same day, 18 December 1961, but much more far-reaching in its implications, was Res. 1673 (69 for, none against, 14 abstentions), in which the Assembly noted with satisfaction "the efforts made by the HC in his various fields of activity for groups of refugees for whom he lends his good offices," and requested the HC "to pursue his activities on behalf of refugees within his mandate or those for whom he extends his good offices."

Emergency Fund Allocations

The HC's stated purpose in asking for the passage of Res. 1673 was that he felt he needed the approval of the GA in order to make allocations from his Emergency Fund to refugees for whom he extended his good offices. The Fund, set at $500,000 when it was created by the GA in 1958 as part of the establishment of the HC's Program, was intended to give the Office an ever-ready source of funds when the need to respond quickly to a problem of refugees within the HC's mandate arose. But by 1961 such emergencies turned

out to involve good offices refugees rather than mandate refugees; for example, refugees in Togo, in Cambodia, and in
Congo (Kinshasa). Prior resolutions had limited the HC's
function in regard to refugees not within his mandate to that
of transferring funds especially earmarked by their contributors. Foreseeing that such emergency needs were going
to increase in the months ahead, High Commissioner Schnyder sought and received the approval of members of his Ex.
Com. in May 1961 for the allocation of Emergency Fund
monies to good offices refugees.[12] But he went further and
asked for the approval of the GA as well; an approval that
would clearly regularize the Emergency Fund allocations he
had felt he must make during 1961 following the discussion
with his Ex. Com. In addition, a GA resolution of the kind
envisaged by the HC would permit him to respond fully and
in a completely humanitarian manner to new refugee situations, such as that in Togo, where the political and diplomatic factors were such that action based on his mandate or on
the kinds of GA resolutions previously passed would not have
been possible. (For an explanation of the difficulties faced
by the HC in seeking to assist refugees in Togo, see Chapter 38.)

By reason perhaps of its somewhat vague wording,
Res. 1673--thereafter called the "Good Offices Resolution"--
covers much more than Emergency Fund allocations. Its
effect has been in fact to permit the HC at his discretion to
carry out a broad range of activities for a very broadly defined category of persons. No longer an exceptional device
to be invoked in unusual cases, the good offices authority became, by the force of Res. 1673 (reaffirmed by two subsequent resolutions in 1962 and 1963), part of "the normal basis of the UNHCR's work."[13] Assistance for good offices
refugees could thereafter be handled as a part of the regular
projects of the HC's Program.

The Good Offices Function in Africa and Asia

The formal authorization to exercise his good offices
function as he saw fit in order to meet the various material
needs of refugee groups was granted to the HC just in time,
for in the months after December 1961 increasingly large
numbers of refugees appeared in a variety of African countries, and the need for UNHCR assistance was immediate and
grave. It has been on the basis of the Good Offices Resolution that the UNHCR moved in to grant assistance to new

refugees in Africa and later on the Asian subcontinent at the invitation of governments.[14]

At least three specific reasons have been given by the UNHCR for acting in refugee situations such as those in Africa on the basis of good offices rather than on the basis of the Statute's provisions. First, the major and immediate need of these groups was for material assistance rather than international protection. Second, refugees in Africa have been so numerous and spread out and communications so difficult that it would have been impossible to make an individual determination of Statute eligibility before undertaking the vitally needed emergency assistance to save their lives. Third, as noted in a UNHCR document, "it would have been difficult in the African context to establish for each individual case the existence of well-founded fear of persecution in the same manner as in Europe." Invoking the Statute would have meant making an eligibility determination based on a concept of persecution. As High Commissioner Schnyder has observed, the issue of persecution has been "at the root of many misunderstandings with countries of origin, whose susceptibilities are offended by eligibility decisions which they tend to regard as more or less open criticisms of themselves."[15] The good offices basis for action, on the other hand, contains no assumption of persecution even by implication. As High Commissioner Prince Sadruddin noted, it permits the HC "to apply himself to a refugee problem without having to take any formal decision with regard to its origins ... which has tended to emphasize and strengthen the purely non-political character of the work of the High Commissioner."[16]

Good Offices and the International Protection Function

The drawback of the good-offices function has been that it appears to be a separate basis for UNHCR action distinct from the Statute's authorization for the provision of international protection. The good offices development took place in order to permit the HC to aid refugee groups who did not clearly come within the Statute definition, or for whom the HC wished to avoid making a Statute eligibility determination. The general good-offices resolutions of 1961-63 mention two categories of refugees, those who come "within the mandate" of the HC and those for whom he "lends" or "extends" his good offices, as if they were quite separate

groups. [17]   And more than one HC has spoken of good offices
as distinct from protection.   Dr. Schnyder, for example, in
1962 said that good offices could be used as the basis for
action "when the object is merely to give urgent material
help, " and "unless actual problems of legal protection
arise. "[18]   High Commissioner Prince Sadruddin described
the Office's early view of good offices as being an activity
"somehow different" from providing protection. [19]   If there
are two separate bases for UNHCR action and two distinct
types of refugees for whom the Office can act, the question
arises: To what extent can international protection be provided for good offices refugees?   Are good offices refugees
completely outside the HC's mandate by definition and thereby deprived of enjoying his protection?

So long as the major need of the new refugee groups
was for material assistance, the question of their relationship to the Statute was relatively unimportant.   But stressing
good offices and material assistance to the exclusion of the
Statute and international protection created its own problems,
as Prince Sadruddin pointed out in 1969:

> The necessity of concentrating on the material as-
> sistance aspect and the comparative ease with
> which rural populations could be settled in Africa
> may to some extent have diverted attention from
> the legal protection side of our work and may also
> in some measure have created the impression
> among African States that our main function is to
> assist refugees materially. [20]

Once refugees began to appear in Africa, especially
in the cities, who needed more than material assistance--
jobs, education, travel documents--it became important for
the UNHCR to emphasize that although the basis for its major operations in Africa was good offices, it also had the authority under the Statute to provide international protection
to those refugees entitled to that protection.   Prince Sadruddin, then Deputy HC, made this point to the Ex. Com. in
1963 when he said: "Action taken under the good offices
procedure can, of course, in no way prejudice the possible
eligibility or ineligibility of the refugees benefitting from
such action for assistance under the mandate. "[21]

As early as July 1965 Dr. Schnyder began publicly to
redefine good offices in order to relate it more closely to
international protection.   In a speech before the Hague

Academy of International Law, he contrasted the Good Offices
Resolution (1673) with prior resolutions using the same
phrase.   Even though two categories of refugees were mentioned in Res. 1673, he pointed out, the resolution did not
exclusively relate those refugees "who do not come within
the competence of the United Nations" to the good-offices
function.   Instead Res. 1673 referred to the HC's "various
fields of activity for groups of refugees for whom he lends
his good offices. "   The implication of this wording, said Dr.
Schnyder, was that good-offices refugees and Statute refugees
were no longer mutually exclusive categories of refugees entitled to different kinds of services. [22]   While protection
could only be granted to refugees who came within the mandate of the HC as defined by his Statute, good-offices refugees might also be Statute refugees and entitled to protection
and Statute refugees might also receive good-offices material
assistance funds.

By asserting that it also had the Statute function of
international protection to perform in Africa, the UNHCR
was reintroducing the concept of persecution which it had
previously sought to avoid in its activities in Africa.   In order to mitigate the possibility that this assertion might upset
any African states of refugee origin, the office made use of
a practical procedure which had been very helpful at the time
of its involvement with the Hungarian refugees in 1956-57:
the prima facie group eligibility determination.   Despite the
wording of the Statute that the work of the HC should relate
as a rule "to groups and categories of refugees" (par. 2),
the definition of the term refugee itself seemed to require an
individual determination of eligibility; and indeed prior to
1956 the issue of who was eligible for the protection of the
HC was almost always decided on an individual basis.   But
to quote again from Dr. Schnyder's 1965 speech:

> following the exodus of some 200,000 Hungarian
> refugees from their country, the High Commission-
> er's Office resorted to the concept of prima facie
> eligibility in order to avert the paralysis which
> would have resulted from a strict interpretation of
> the mandate.   The concept of prima facie eligibility
> was applied collectively to this group of refugees
> as a whole and no longer, as is customary, to
> isolated individuals.

Dr. Schnyder went on to point out the value of the Hungarian
development in establishing a precedent: "[t]here was nothing

to prevent the High Commissioner's Office from following the
same course again, whenever the conditions of eligibility appeared to be a priori fulfilled, as was in fact the case."23

Prima Facie Eligibility

The prima facie eligibility determination became an
essential aspect of the UNHCR's operations in Africa when
the Office sought to reassert its role of international protection.   It made particular sense to use this group eligibility
determination in Africa where sudden large influxes of refugees in need of immediate aid tended to be the rule.   And
so long as the Office was dealing with groups, nothing more
than a prima facie eligibility could be established anyway.
Furthermore, the emphasis on groups and group eligibility
reflected the Statute requirement that the work of the Office
should relate "as a rule, to groups and categories of refugees" (par. 2) and was in conformity with all the subsequent
GA resolutions authorizing specific or general activities by
the UNHCR, which have also been phrased in terms of acting
for groups of refugees.   But more important, the prima facie
eligibility determination made it possible for the UNHCR to
assume that at least most of these large new groups of refugees came within the Statute definition and were therefore
entitled to the protection of the Office, that is, they were
mandate refugees as well as good-offices refugees.   Prima
facie eligibility meant that groups in Africa who looked "on
the face of it" much like the kinds of refugees meant to be
included within the competence of the HC by the Statute were
a priori and without further ado Statute refugees.   No formal
indication of the reasons for such a determination was needed,
nor did anything have to be said regarding the way in which
the Office reached its determination.   On the basis of this
phrase, the authority of the Statute could be asserted without
reference to the specific elements of the Statute's definition.

However, when cases have occurred in Africa that involved the protection of individual refugees, as for example
in obtaining travel documents, BO's of the UNHCR have made
individual determination of eligibility in accordance with the
Statute's requirements even where prima facie group eligibility determinations had already been made.

Widespread acceptance of the Office's application of
the prima facie eligibility procedures has led to a reduction
in Africa in the emphasis on good offices as a separate

function of the UNHCR.   Instead, emphasis has been placed
on the fact that most of the major refugee groups in Africa,
such as those from Portuguese territories and from Rwanda
and the Sudan (as well as refugee groups elsewhere in the
world such as the Tibetans) are now considered to be prima
facie within the mandate of the HC.   However, to quote High
Commissioner Schnyder:

> It is certainly no exaggeration to say that the good
> offices procedure has infused new life into the orig-
> inal mandate--which would probably not have sur-
> vived unimpaired [due to] its inherent inability to
> meet new situations and concrete needs engendered
> by events themselves.... Without affecting the ac-
> tual substance or the basic principles which con-
> tinue to govern the activities of the High Commis-
> sioner's Office, an empirical structure has been
> gradually built up, founded on and parallel to the
> Statute, which it supplements and reinforces. [24]

By accepting the concept of good offices as a way of authorizing actions by the HC apart from and in addition to the authority granted him in the Statute of his Office, a highly po-
liticized GA has found a way to express the humanitarian
aim of its members to aid the new refugee groups without
involving itself or the HC in the political situations which
produced these refugee groups--an involvement which certainly would have made meaningful and speedy international action
more difficult.   And by connecting its good-offices authority
and its Statute authority, the UNHCR has gone one step further in creating for itself a broad and very flexible basis for
action in response to a wide variety of situations where the
need may be for material assistance or international protection or both.

As far as good offices are concerned today, it is the
view of High Commissioner Prince Sadruddin that

> we must adhere to the idea that we must assist
> refugees who 'prima facie' can be considered as
> eligible under the Statute, and must use the sys-
> tem of good offices in a most pragmatic way in
> cases, particularly in Africa, where individual
> eligibility is impossible and where it is difficult to
> determine clearly whether the persons concerned
> fulfill, even 'prima facie,' the criteria of eligibility
> under the Statute. [25]

Such, for example, has been the case with the Congolese refugees in Burundi and in the CAR, with Nigerian children repatriated from Gabon and the Ivory Coast, and with refugees
in Cambodia and Vietnam. "The underlying philosophy,"
Prince Sadruddin has said,

> must be that we can lend our good offices to gov-
> ernments in cases where groups of people have
> left their countries of residence or origin, and are
> facing suffering, destitution, or even death, if not
> helped with great speed. This action might at the
> same time contribute to peace and stability in the
> area, and perhaps even limit the influx. In such
> circumstances the High Commissioner has to exer-
> cise his own discretion and judgment, and with the
> assistance of his representatives in the field, de-
> cide whether or not he can use his good offices,
> not necessarily to protect the individual, since this
> would have to be based much more on a clear-cut
> eligibility determination under the Statute, but at
> least to help them to receive material assistance,
> which in some instances may even be procured
> from "out-of-program" funds. It is this flexibility
> which is our strength and which we should pre-
> serve. [26]

The underlying concept of the good offices was, and
continues to be, that the HC, while adapting himself to rapidly changing situations, should act speedily and efficiently.
When the Secretary General called upon the UNHCR, first in
India and then in Sudan, to act as focal point or coordinator
of the whole UN system, the HC was able to respond on the
basis of the good offices. The world community supported
UNHCR activities on behalf of millions of West Bengali refugees in India in 1971-72 and those undertaken in the repatriation of hundreds of thousands of Sudanese to their homeland
in 1972, in the realization that is only through the practical
coordination of complex multilateral apparatus that the UN--
in these cases through the HC operating under the good offices concept--can respond adequately to the challenges of
our time. In October 1972, with reference to the Focal
Point operation, the Ex. Com. "reaffirmed its support of the
good offices concept, which enabled the HC to contribute
without delay to the solution of delicate and complex humanitarian problems concerning, in particular, persons whose
situation is analogous to that of refugees who are the habitual
concern of his office" (Ex. Com. XXIII).

The good offices concept thus has provided the necessary flexibility to deal with large-scale and complex problems whose emergence was not envisaged at the time the Statute was adopted. The good offices has likewise been invaluable in enabling the UNHCR to intervene in marginal cases, as in the Middle East and Southeast Asia, where a given group of limited numbers are in a situation analogous to that of refugees and where UNHCR action can ameliorate their distress. By virtue of the non-political character of good offices, the use of good offices in the broad sense of the term has also made it possible for the HC to act as an intermediary in order to assist in bringing about a solution to an existing refugee problem or to avoid the emergence of a new one.

Notes

1. The Rep. of the Sec.-Gen. on Refugees and Stateless Persons, A/C.3/527 of 26 Oct. 1949: 14 and 17-18.

2. Schnyder, "The Good Offices and the Functions of the UNHCR in the Social Field," Doc. HCR/RS/32:19.

3. HC's Opening Statement, Rep. of Ex. Com. (XXII), A/AC.96/463, 20 Oct. 1971.

4. Edvar Hambro, The Problem of the Chinese Refugees in Hong Kong, Leyden, 1955: esp. 29-40; and Elfan Rees, "Century of the Homeless Man," IC, No. 515, Nov. 1957: 245-52; for a summary of the discussions on this issue in the Ad. Com. and the UNREF Ex. Com.

5. Rep. of the UNREF Ex. Com. (IV), in Annex I to GA (XII), Off. Rec., Supp. No. 11, A/3585/Rev. 1, 1957.

6. Dr. Lindt had in fact begun his humanitarian task on behalf of the Algerian refugees some months before the resolution was adopted because the need was so great, and he had at least the tacit consent of the governments involved.

7. See speech of HC Prince Sadruddin Aga Khan, "Refugees and Human Rights," in WFUNA-FMANU Bulletin,

XII, 1967-68: 48.

8.   The HC and his Office have always considered the GA
      resolutions on Algerian refugees to have bolstered
      the Office's good-offices function; see ibid.: 48-49.

9.   Ibid.: 48.

10.   Dr. Schnyder, op. cit.: 15.

11.   Jacques Vernant, "The Refugee Problem Since 1955,"
      1965 ICVA Conf. Doc. Nr 20/E: 7.

12.   Rep. to Ex. Com. (V), A/AC.96/127, 7 June 1961:
      28-9, and App. II: 4ff.

13.   Statement by the HC at ECOSOC, (XXXIV) Doc. MHCR/
      204/62 of 27 July 1962: 5-6.

14.   UNHCR, "24 Oct. 1966, United Nations Day," a back-
      ground paper on the UNHCR, Doc. 66-45767, Gene-
      va, 1966: 7.

15.   Dr. Schnyder, op. cit.: 24.

16.   Prince Sadruddin, "Legal Aspects of Refugee Problems,"
      speech delivered at Copenhagen University, 20 Oct.
      1966, UNHCR Doc. 107/66: 11.

17.   GA Res. 1673(XVI), 1783(XVII) of 7 Dec. 1962 (99 votes
      for, none against, one abstention), and 1959(XVIII)
      of 12 Dec. 1963 (adopted unanimously).

18.   Statement by the HC at ECOSOC (XXXIV) Doc. MHCR/
      204/62 of 27 July 1962: 6.

19.   Prince Sadruddin, "Refugees and Human Rights": 48.

20.   Doc. 6/1/UGA.

21.   A/AC.96/200 of Apr. 1963, App. II: 4.

22.   Schnyder, op. cit.: 17-18.

23.   Ibid.: 19.

24.   Ibid.: 25.

25. Prince Sadruddin, "Legal Aspects of Refugee Prob-
     lems, " speech, op. cit.

26. Ibid.

Chapter 19

THE WORLD REFUGEE YEAR, 1959-60

In late 1956 and early 1957 a wave of sympathy swept the free world, enabling governments and voluntary agencies to settle the victims of the Hungarian uprising in a short period. This generous and immediate help, however, stood in marked contrast to the insufficient aid to an estimated 170,000 refugees in Europe still in need of resettlement, over one million Palestine-Arab refugees in the Middle East, one million Chinese refugees in Hong Kong, and about 10,000 White Russian refugees in China and Hong Kong, apart from the millions of refugees within their own countries: India, Pakistan, Korea, and Vietnam.

The Birth of an Idea

In the spring of 1958, four young Britons, Timothy Raison, Christopher Chataway, Colin Jones, and Trevor Philpott, members of the Conservative Party's Bow Group (founded in 1951) proposed a World Refugee Year.[1] They pointed out the success of the UN International Geophysical Year of 1957 and suggested that the UK should take the lead in proposing a WRY as a period for arousing public opinion all over the world. They stated that "an imaginative, altruistic campaign could do much to dispel a prevalent feeling of frustration." They outlined a plan to create

> an organizing body either governmental, inter-governmental or simply representing those who care. Its aim would be to set in motion a year's concentrated drive toward solving the major international [refugee] problems. Its function would be to focus world opinion upon the outstanding needs, to spur on the raising of money, to assist and coordinate the work of voluntary bodies and national and international organizations, such as ICEM, UNHCR, UNRWA, USEP and others.

450

The value of such a plan was immediately apparent to British leaders of voluntary organizations working in the refugee field, such as the British Council for Aid to Refugees (BCAR), Inter-Church Aid and Refugee Service, and the Catholic Women's League, as well as to the representative of the UNHCR in London and Sir Arthur Rucker, former Deputy Director-General of IRO, Chairman of the Trustees of the UN Association's Refugee Fund. A letter in support of the proposal was published in The Times (London) in May 1958. A meeting called by the UN Association prepared preliminary plans which were submitted to leading personalities in industry, commerce, trade unions, religious bodies, political parties, and voluntary organizations. Dame May Curwen, the indefatigable and compassionate Chairman of the BCAR, who was the British delegate to the UNHCR Ex. Com., urged the British Government to take the lead on behalf of the voluntary agencies. After some hesitation the British Government responded, and the House of Commons voted unanimous support. The Ninth Session of the UNREF Ex. Com. requested the HC to bring the proposal, as envisaged by the government and the voluntary agencies in the UK, to the attention of the Thirteenth Session of the GA "as a practical means of securing increased assistance for refugees throughout the world, in accordance with the wishes and needs of each country. "[2]

This idea of a WRY--eminently democratic in origin-- led, in record time, to the adoption of a World Refugee Year Resolution by a large majority of the GA on 5 December 1958. [3] It resolved "to focus interest on the refugee problem and to encourage additional financial contributions from governments, voluntary agencies and the general public for its solution, " and "to encourage additional opportunities for permanent refugee solutions, through voluntary repatriation, resettlement or integration, on a purely humanitarian basis and in accordance with the freely expressed wishes of the refugees themselves. "

Thus WRY--a "humanitarian year"--was designed to provide a unified effort to tackle a problem of worldwide significance which constituted both a wastage of valuable human resources and a source of international instability and tension. Although it was not a program of the UN, WRY was a landmark in large-scale operations for humane purposes. No legal or political considerations entered into it; "any group of refugees qualified for help under the WRY. " This concept was a departure from LoN and UN policies, both of which, as

we have seen, had established restrictive criteria to define
which refugees the international organizations should help.

UN Leadership

The GA and the Secretary-General gave their full
backing to this plan, and High Commissioner Lindt and his
staff helped in many ways to promote and coordinate the
manifold plans and efforts in the individual countries.   UN
Secretary-General Dag Hammarskjöld pinpointed the task at
hand by saying, "the problem of the refugees is a humanitarian problem.   The challenge of the WRY is a humanitarian
challenge.   It is up to each of us to meet that challenge. "

The GA called upon all UN members and members of
the Specialized Agencies "to make a further worldwide effort
to help resolve the world refugee problem" in the WRY beginning in June 1959.

In conformity with the Assembly's Resolution, the
Secretary-General designated a member of his Executive Office, Mr. Claude de Kemoularia, as his Special Representative for WRY. [4]   A small staff was chosen mainly from the
UNHCR, UNWRA, and the UN Office of Public Information.
Headquarters for the WRY unit was established at Geneva,
with a liaison office at UN Headquarters in New York.   This
WRY center served as a promotion and coordination unit until
the end of 1960.   It worked closely with other UN offices involved in the promotion of the WRY, in particular with
UNHCR, UNRWA, and the UN Office of Public Information;
with the Permanent Missions of the member governments;
with ICEM; and with the non-governmental sector through the
SCVA. [5]

This WRY unit was not a planning staff; it prepared
and distributed information and insured a "cross-fertilization
of ideas. "   It prepared and distributed material including
feature pamphlets, a continuing newsletter, photographs and
enlargements for exhibition purposes, films and radio and
television programs.   This material dealt with all kinds of
refugee groups, both within and outside the HC's mandate,
thus breaking down the distinctions between these two groups
and so furthering the basic idea that all refugees are entitled
to material assistance--an essential aspect of the good offices
operations of the HC. [6]

The Special Representative, the HC, and their staffs, as well as the Director General of UNRWA, made themselves available to governments and national committees to assist with the promotion of campaigns. In the words of Dr. Lindt, who gave dynamic leadership to WRY: "Our main task ... is to help in making the idea snowball; we must look for every permissible device to reach that man in the street who, up till now, has seemed so elusive. We know that once he hears what it is all about, he will help. "

National Committees

The very nature of WRY called for no complicated administrative machinery. To turn the Resolution into reality, nothing more was needed than the willingness on the part of each nation to participate in a manner and form most suited to its own traditions and methods. The appeal was universal, and assistance could take a variety of forms. Stress lay on the flexibility and simplicity of WRY. Any country taking part could itself select the classes of refugees and the organizations it considered best suited for its purpose. Some extended the Year beyond the 30 June 1960 deadline, others decided to make their committees permanent.

To reach the people, more than thirty-eight National Committees for WRY were set up. These committees, often under the patronage of the head of state, usually composed of representatives from all interested groups, and occasionally with the participation of the government, assumed the task of coordinating publicity, directing fund-raising activities, and allocating the monies made available for refugees. Their activities varied from country to country. As a whole, these committees were "the most important single factor making for the success of the campaigns. "[7]

International Committee for World Refugee Year

Under the sponsorship of the SCVA the International Committee for WRY (ICWRY) was created in March 1959 at Geneva to enlist the maximum support of "We the People" in making WRY a success for the sake of the many millions of refugees still homeless. ICWRY was a unique organization. Never before had so large a number of voluntary agencies with so many bases of existence banded together for one

common objective. Eighty voluntary agencies and other non-
governmental agencies participated, representing a multitude
of church, youth, trade union, and other organizations around
the world. [8] They helped the national organizations to coordinate their activities and informed them of what was being
attempted. Delegates from these agencies met at regular
intervals throughout WRY to discuss, plan, and implement
WRY's programs. Eight Plenary Sessions were held between
April 1959 and January 1961. ICWRY also organized in Geneva two Conferences for National Committees on WRY, (12-
14 January 1960 and 16-20 January 1961) before terminating
its activities in May 1961. [9]

A Crusade of Good Will

Close cooperation was developed among international
UN organizations, governments, ICEM, the CoE, as well as
among the international and national voluntary agencies, in
an effort to bring before the public the critical nature and
scope of the refugee problem. Everywhere the media were
exploited to the full: press, radio, television, movies, and
the theater played an important role in bringing home to
people all over the world the plight of the refugees. A
series of publications were aimed at various segments of the
public. Documentation was provided for conferences, lectures, and exhibitions. The periodicals of voluntary agencies
dedicated special issues to WRY. Posters of all kinds and
sizes papered public buildings everywhere. The UN designed
two symbols: a pair of hands within a laurel branch arched
to protect a human figure, and an uprooted tree--the latter
was used for the special issue of WRY postage stamps. The
UK adopted the symbol of "The Open Hand. "

Fund-raising methods varied from community to community, but generally were directed toward the general public rather than toward the canvassing of organizations or
foundations. Events such as fairs, dances, and concerts
were run by local people in small towns and in city neigh-
borhoods.

On 6 October 1959, at the conclusion of the general
debate of the GA (XIV), the president of the Assembly
warned that despite its good beginning the success of WRY
was by no means assured. He urged all members to give
careful consideration to the contributions they would make to
the two UN refugee organizations, the UNHCR and UNRWA.

"In launching the WRY," he added, "we, the General Assembly, gave a new hope to millions of refugees around the world. It is our task to fulfill this promise."

The matter was discussed in the Third Committee and in the Plenary Session of the GA (XIV), leading to two Resolutions (1388 and 1390) on 20 November 1959. In the first, on the report of the HC, the GA (in two operative paragraphs) invited the members of the UN and members of the Specialized Agencies "to devote on the occasion of the WRY, special attention to the problem of refugees coming under the competence of the UNHCR" and authorized the HC "in respect of refugees who do not come within the competence of the UN, to use his good offices in the transmission of contributions designed to provide assistance to these refugees."

In the second resolution the GA noted with appreciation the support already given to WRY by governments, nongovernmental organizations, and the public. It urged them, however, to continue to focus interest on the refugee problem and asked the Secretary-General to continue his efforts in the promotion of WRY.

At the end of WRY, the gifts, large and small, amounted to over $91 million, of which some $14 million was contributed directly to the programs of the UNHCR.[10] More than two-thirds was contributed by the public, one-third by government donations. (See Annex 19.2).

World Refugee Stamp Plan

The UNHCR and UNRWA called on all states participating in WRY to issue special commemorative stamps. After two years of preparation, on 7 April 1960, the governments of seventy-seven countries--eleven in Africa, twenty-one in the Americas, twenty in Asia, twenty-three in Europe, and two in Oceania--simultaneously issued postage stamps dedicated to refugees. To inaugurate the Stamp Plan, three WRY stamp exhibitions opened in Washington, New York, and Geneva on 7 April. The launching of the stamp issue was also marked by special messages from heads of state, from Pope John XXIII, and others. The sale of the stamps contributed considerably to the financing of the programs of both agencies; a total of nearly $1.6 million was raised, which was distributed by mutual agreement, 75 percent going to the UNHCR and 25 percent to UNRWA.

A stamp plan for refugees was not new. Since the
end of WWI a number of refugee stamps had been issued:
by Lebanon in 1926; by Norway in 1935, with a portrait of
Dr. Nansen; two stamps by France in 1936; six by China in
1944; and by the UN in 1953. The uniqueness of the WRY
stamp program, however, was its world-wide character,
marked not only by its financial impact on refugee problems,
but also by its effect on public opinion. [11]

Achievements

WRY was a significant achievement in the history of
the UN and of international cooperation in a human cause.
Some seventy-nine countries and territories took part in one
way or another (see Annex 19. 3). WRY rallied heads of
state, governments, international organizations, religious
leaders, voluntary agencies, famous men and women, and
millions of the unknown citizens of the world. The people
welcomed the lead of the UN in offering them an opportunity
for active participation in seeking to solve a world problem.
The broader sense of universal responsibility for refugees
which WRY had sought was awakened, and achieved very
tangible results. "The depth of public generosity and the
good will of governments, the dynamic energy of voluntary
agencies and of public spirited individuals, the possibilities
of action and the prestige of the UN" combined, proved Mr.
Hammerskjöld right when, speaking on 10 December 1959,
he declared that "we are dealing with a situation in which,
quite literally, money and the understanding and sympathy
which should accompany it can work miracles. "

Speaking before the final conference of ICWRY in
Geneva on 16 January 1961, Mr. Thomas Jamieson, Director
of Operations of the UNHCR, stressed that WRY had brought
with it greater recognition of the problems facing the Office.
"It has made known, " said Mr. Jamieson,

> the problems of refugees from China, both those
> of European origin and Chinese refugees now in
> Hong Kong, on whose behalf we are authorized by
> the General Assembly to use our good offices.
> Before WRY, little was known of our activities and
> our efforts in North Africa or of our good offices
> functions on behalf of refugees not under the United
> Nations' mandate.... Perhaps the aspect of WRY
> which made the greatest impact was its truly uni-
> versal character.

At the Fourth Session of the Ex. Com. in October 1960, delegates pointed out that "this action had made it possible as never before to view the refugee problem in worldwide terms and to include a broader understanding of the sufferings and needs of refugees in Asia and Africa as well as those on the continent of Europe. "[12]

Progress was made during WRY in finding permanent solutions, by camp clearance in Europe, by help to out-of-camp refugees and handicapped people; by providing immigration opportunities; and by widening international protection.

In the field of immigration recognition of the contribution a refugee can make to the country of resettlement became firmly implanted in the public opinion of the countries concerned. One of the most positive effects of WRY was the tendency to eliminate in government and community thinking the notion that many refugees (the handicapped and those difficult to resettle) were "unemigrable. " The reappraisal of basic immigration procedures and policies which took place in a number of countries resulted in placing less emphasis on the physical qualifications of each member of a family and more on the economic viability of the family as a whole. [13] Not only did such reappraisal remove the dilemma that had confronted many families desiring to emigrate in the past but it also made possible the reunion of families already separated for such reasons. In addition, some countries of first asylum which had already accepted many severely handicapped refugees made special efforts to share the problem through the establishment and extension of houses designed for this purpose. The UNHCR reported that, thanks to the liberalization of immigration criteria by various countries, some 4,000 physically or socially handicapped refugees, along with 3,000 dependents, were resettled outside their countries of first asylum (see Annex 19.4). By comparison, in the seven years 1952-58, some 4,665 handicapped refugees and their families had been resettled.

Dr. Lindt anticipated also that with the supplementary financial contributions resulting from WRY efforts the solution of the camp clearance program would be secured. Moreover, WRY helped many refugees living in very poor conditions outside camps in Europe to become self-supporting in their countries of first asylum.

A certain amount of progress was also made in the

field of legal protection on the basis of suggestions submitted
to governments by the HC and the Special Representative of
the Secretary-General, to the effect that appropriate action
in this sphere constituted one form of contribution to WRY.
Three new states ratified the 1951 Convention and others
started the procedure of ratification.

In the field of employment, progress was achieved; in
particular some countries relaxed their restrictions in regard
to refugee intellectuals (relatively few in numbers) which had
prevented the majority of them from practicing the professions for which they were qualified.   Social Security benefits
to refugees were widely expanded and travel facilities improved, thanks to the great efforts of the CoE.

The financial contributions and practical achievements
described above were only two results of the new interest
aroused in refugee problems.   No less important was the
realization, much more widespread as a result of WRY, that
the refugee problem was still with us and still called for the
active assistance of both governments and peoples.   Mr.
Hammerskjöld, when he summed up the significance of WRY,
warned the world in these words:

> WRY in every respect should be regarded as a be-
> ginning, not an end.   The refugee problem will be
> with us ... forever, unless the world turns more
> peaceful. ...   But we should not believe this is the
> end of the road.   We must anticipate continued
> needs, and for that reason we must also count on
> continued assistance. [14]

A statement by ICWRY, handed to the Special Representative of the Secretary-General on 7 July 1960, also drew
attention to the fact that while the hopes of many refugees
had been fulfilled thanks to WRY "it is abundantly clear that
the refugee question continues to pose enormous issues not
only to the refugees themselves and their country of asylum,
but to the whole society.   The conclusion of the WRY must
not result in a curtailment of efforts to help those who remain. "

Further, the Fifteenth Plenary Assembly of the World
Federation of UN Associations (WFUNA), meeting in Warsaw
in September 1960, adopted a resolution in which the Federation emphasized that "notwithstanding these achievements,
WRY should be considered only a significant impetus, since

it was not intended to solve, and has not fully solved, the problem of refugees"; WFUNA and its member associations, together with other voluntary organizations and governments, were urged "to continue their efforts and to seek to eliminate the conditions which cause people to seek refuge."

WRY provided a spotlight on this critical problem, spurring the world to give it necessary attention. But it could only lead to the essential next steps. As Dr. Lindt stressed: "WRY must not be a one-time effort; it has to be the beginning of a new, purely humanitarian and more intelligent approach to refugee problems."

The next ten years of the activities of the UNHCR brought to realization Dr. Lindt's final appraisal:

> Beyond these very tangible effects, the real merit of WRY may prove in the long run to be that in an entirely non-political, in a social and humanitarian spirit, it awakened the conscience of the world to this great problem of our time.

International solidarity was no empty phrase during WRY. While Europe and America strove to reduce the problems of refugees in Europe, they also reached out to those of the Middle East, North Africa, and Asia. But it was also significant that even the less economically privileged countries of Asia and Africa made their contributions.

Notes

1. Crossbow, A Quarterly Journal of Politics, 1(3), Spring 1958: 10-12.

2. A/3828/Rev. 1/Add. 1, Annex II; for detail see World Refugee Year, Rep. of the UK Com., 1 June 1959 to 31 May 1960.

3. GA Res. 1285(XIII) (59 votes for, 9 against, and 7 abstentions).

4. Mr. John Kelly was seconded by the HC to serve as Deputy Special Representative.

5. For detail, see GA (XV), A/4546, 22 Oct. 1960: Assistance to Refugees, Report of the Secretary-General

by His Special Representative for WRY, 30 Sept.
1960-28 Feb. 1961.

6.   See Vernant, speech at ICVA Conference 1965, Conf.
      Doc. No. 20/E: 7.

7.   GA (XV), A/4546, 22 Oct. 1960, op. cit. : 3.

8.   For listing of participating organizations see ibid., An-
      nex C: 1.

9.   The ICWRY, 1959-61, Geneva, n. d.

10.   The major contributors were the UK with more than
      $21 million and the US with some $18 million by
      30 September 1960.

11.   UNHCR and UNWRA, Report on the Refugee Stamp Plan,
      UN, Geneva, 1962 and The World Refugee Year Pos-
      tage Stamps, publ. by UN Staff Fund for Refugees,
      Geneva, 1961.

12.   GA (XV), A/4546, 22 Oct. 1960: 29.

13.   A/AC.96/88, 21 Sept. 1960; and A/AC.96/SR36, 3
      Feb. 1967.

14.   Pr. Conf., 30 June 1960.

ANNEX 19.1

PROVISIONAL TABLE OF WORLD REFUGEE YEAR CONTRIBUTIONS
by participating countries and territories
as known on 30 September 1960 (in US$)

Countries or Territories	Government[a]		National Committee and others		T O T A L S		
	Cash	Kind	Cash	Kind	Cash	Kind	Total
Australia	336,021	15,125	1,568,100	–	1,904,121	15,125	1,919,246
Austria	7,846,153	–	211,538	–	8,057,691	–	8,057,691
Bahrein	28,366	–	420	–	28,786	–	28,786
Barbados	–	–	1,281	–	1,281	–	1,281
Belgium	–	–	655,018	–	655,018	–	655,018
Bermuda	2,800	–	27,510	–	30,310	–	30,310
Bolivia	–	–	980	–	980	–	980
Brazil	55,000	–	–	–	55,000	–	55,000
British Honduras	699	–	–	–	699	–	699
Brunei (Borneo)	10,000	–	–	–	10,000	–	10,000
Burma	2,092	–	262	–	2,354	–	2,354
Cambodia	572	–	–	–	572	–	572
Canada	600,000	1,020,000	1,834,931	–	2,434,931	1,020,000	3,454,931
Ceylon	1,000	–	–	–	1,000	–	1,000
Chile	8,520	–	–	–	8,520	–	8,520
China	12,500	–	218,600	–	231,100	–	231,100
Colombia	2,000	–	6,094	–	8,094	–	8,094
Costa Rica	–	–	–	120	–	120	120

Country							
Cuba	10,000	-	-	-	10,000	-	10,000
Denmark	376,429	-	796,293	-	1,172,722	-	1,172,722
Federation of Malaya	2,500	-	-	-	2,500	-	2,500
Finland	5,000	-	66,467	19,639	71,467	19,639	91,106
France	1,450,000	-	-	-	1,450,000	-	1,450,000
Gambia	30	-	-	-	30	-	30
Germany, Fed. Rep. of	1,767,857	-	2,779,761	-	4,547,618	-	4,547,618
Ghana	3,000	-	2,861	-	5,861	-	5,861
Greece	5,000	-	5,000	-	10,000	-	10,000
Holy See	4,000	-	-	-	4,000	-	4,000
Hong Kong	-	-	143,970	-	143,970	-	143,970
Iran	-	-	38,929	-	38,929	-	38,929
Ireland	16,800	-	178,684	-	195,484	-	195,484
Israel	5,000	-	2,222	-	7,222	-	7,222
Italy	805,152	-	65,818	-	870,970	-	870,970
Japan	5,000	-	-	-	5,000	-	5,000
Kuwait	112,013	-	-	-	112,013	-	112,013
Liberia	3,000	-	-	-	3,000	-	3,000
Luxembourg	3,000	-	50,000	-	53,000	-	53,000
Malta	-	-	7,156	-	7,156	-	7,156
Mexico	20,000	-	-	-	20,000	-	20,000
Monaco	2,000	-	-	-	2,000	-	2,000
Morocco	-	80,000	-	-	-	80,000	80,000
Netherlands	183,157	-	1,749,999	-	1,933,156	-	1,933,156
New Zealand	196,023	-	705,685	319,238	901,708	319,238	1,220,946
Norway	419,991	-	2,105,557	167,996	2,525,548	167,996	2,693,544
Pakistan	3,150	-	-	-	3,150	-	3,150
Panama	-	-	200	-	200	-	200
Philippines	-	-	28,221	137	28,221	137	28,358

Portugal	—	8,635	—	8,635	8,635
Qatar	84,010	—	—	84,010	84,010
Rhodesia and Nyasaland	—	30,308	—	30,308	30,308
Sierra Leone	700	—	—	700	700
Sweden	166,988	2,155,598	424,710	2,322,586	2,747,296
Switzerland	440,092	955,303	—	1,395,395	1,395,395
Thailand	—	—	—	—	6,250
Tunisia	6,250	—	6,250	—	6,250
Tunisia	700,000	—	700,000	—	700,000
Turkey	15,000	41,670	—	56,670	56,670
Uganda	7,280	235	369	7,515	7,884
Union of S. Africa	41,200	—	—	41,200	41,200
UAR	—	—	465,000	—	465,000
UK	1,120,134	15,493,713	5,046,303	16,613,847	21,660,150
US	5,049,375	13,076,621	—	18,125,996	18,125,996
Viet-Nam, Rep. of	5,000	60,000	—	65,000	65,000
Yugoslavia	—	—	18,900	183,900	183,900
Yugoslavia	165,000	—	183,900	—	183,900
Total cash	21,233,604	45,073,640	6,462,413	66,307,244	
Total kind	1,986,375				8,448,788
Grand total	23,219,979	51,536,053		74,756,032	74,756,032

a Paid, pledged, or promised subject to parliamentary approval.

SOURCE: A/4546, Annex E, Part 1: 1 and 2.

ANNEX 19.2

PARTICIPATION OF COUNTRIES IN
WORLD REFUGEE YEAR 1959-60

Europe	Western Hemisphere	Middle East
Austria *	Argentina *	Israel *
Belgium *	Bolivia ¨	Jordan
Denmark *	Brazil *	Lebanon
Finland *	British Honduras *	Saudi Arabia
France *	Canada *	Turkey *
German Fed. Rep. *	Chile *	UAR
Greece *	Colombia *	Yemen
Holy See	Costa Rica *	
Ireland *	Cuba	
Italy *	Dominican Rep.	
Liechtenstein	Ecuador *	
Luxembourg	El Salvador	
Monaco	Guatemala *	
Netherlands *	Haiti *	
Norway *	Honduras *	
Portugal *	Iceland *	
Sweden *	Mexico *	
Switzerland *	Nicaragua	
UK *	Panama *	
Yugoslavia	Paraguay	
	Peru *	
	St Lucia (West Indies)	

Pacific	Asia	Africa
Australia *	Afganistan	Cameroon
Indonesia	Burma	Ethiopia
New Zealand	Cambodia	Federation of
Philippines *	Ceylon	Mali
	China *	Gambia
	Federation of Malaya *	Ghana
	Hong Kong *	Guinea
	Iran *	Liberia
	Japan	Libya
	Laos	Morocco
	Pakistan *	Togo

Rep. of Korea *   Sierra Leone *
Thailand   Somalia
Vietnam *   Sudan
                       Tunisia
                       Uganda *
                       Union of S.
                         Africa

* Countries in which national committees were formed.

ANNEX 19.3

DISPOSITION OF HANDICAPPED REFUGEES
BY COUNTRIES OF RESETTLEMENT, 1959-61.

EUROPEAN COUNTRIES

Belgium: 50 handicapped refugee families from Europe and 250 non-rehabilitable refugees of European origin from the Far East.

Denmark: 50 handicapped refugees and their families.

France: 110 refugees from Greece, with no regard being paid to normal criteria, and 250 non-rehabilitable refugees from the Far East and elsewhere.

Norway: 100 handicapped refugees and their families.

Sweden: 900 refugees, the majority of whom were handicapped.

Switzerland: 100 handicapped refugees from Europe and the Far East, to be cared for by institutions in the country; in addition, a group totaling 200 persons including rehabilitable handicapped refugees.

OVERSEAS COUNTRIES

Argentina: 700 visas for refugees of European origin in the Far East.

Australia: 500 families, each with one physically handicapped member. (200 of these admitted under government sponsorship.)

Canada: 100 refugee families from Europe, each with one member suffering from active tuberculosis, and 200 families with no limitation on the number among them with active TB, all under government sponsorship.

Colombia: 150 refugee families.

Iceland: 20 refugee fishermen with dependents from Italy.

New Zealand: 240 families with handicapped members.

US: 500 refugees classified as difficult to resettle.

SOURCE: Meeting a Challenge, UNHCR, 1961: 10.

Chapter 20

THE HIGH COMMISSIONER'S PROGRAM
FOR REFUGEES AFTER 1958

Termination of the UNREF Program on 31 December
1958 marked the beginning of a new era in international assistance to refugees.   Res. 1166(XII), passed by the GA on
26 November 1957, explicitly recognized for the first time
that the refugee problem was worldwide and that new and
unforeseen refugee groups might continue to arise.   Within
the framework of this significant resolution the HC was directed to coordinate international assistance to all refugees
under his mandate, in whatever part of the world they may
be found, and was authorized to appeal for funds and to administer a newly established emergency fund.   A greatly expanded concept of the function of the UNHCR, to be known
generally as the High Commissioner's Program, was embodied in the directives of Res. 1166.   In large measure
this new period in assistance programs grew out of the experience of the Hungarian refugees, which had deeply involved the international community.   The beginning of the
HC's Program on 1 January 1959 coincided with the initiation
of WRY which, similarly, acted to arouse the public conscience in the world at large.

The HC's Program took a flexible approach and was
essentially dynamic and subject to rapid change in scope and
nature, in contrast to the four-year UNREF Program with its
specific financial target and defined programs.   The main
distinction between the two programs lay in the method of
planning.   Under the HC's Program separate programs of
international assistance were planned on a yearly basis, and
the entire work of the UNHCR was reviewed annually.   Programs were reduced or expanded as the need arose.   A
balanced approach to the total refugee problem was thereby
constantly maintained.   The separation of programs made it
possible for contributors to concentrate their funds on activities in which they were particularly interested.   Thus greater flexibility was given to planning and implementation of all

468

types of projects.

The guiding principle observed by the Office was that its activities in the area of material assistance should be, whenever possible, of an increasingly marginal and subsidiary character, whether they were to supplement international protection or were undertaken in support of good offices.

The aim of these programs was to assist the refugees to become self-supporting as rapidly and effectively as possible in accordance with their own free choice. Thus, the programs should help the refugee "to help himself." For this reason, assistance, as far as possible, took the form of loans to enable the refugee to acquire the necessary housing or to establish himself in a job, a trade or a profession. Most refugees assisted by loans respected their obligation to repay them. Assistance was given in the form of grants only in the case of weaker refugees, that is, the handicapped.

Administration of the High Commissioner's Program

In order to achieve "the widest possible geographical involvement and greater responsibility of those States with a demonstrated interest in, and devotion to the solution of the refugee problem," ECOSOC was requested by the GA to establish an Executive Committee for the High Commissioner's Program (Ex. Com.) to consist of representatives of twenty to twenty-five member states. The Fifteenth Session of ECOSOC (30 April 1958) elected to this new Ex. Com. the members of the former UNREF Ex. Com. and an additional four members: China, Sweden, Tunisia and Yugoslavia. The responsibilities of this Committee, laid down in Res. 166 were as follows:

par. 5 (a) To give directions to the HC for the liquidation of UNREF

(b) To advise the HC in the exercise of his functions under the Statute of his Office

(c) To advise the HC on international assistance to be provided through his office in order to help solve specific problems remaining unsolved after 31 Dec. 1958 or arising after that date

(d) To authorize the HC to appeal for

funds to enable him to solve the refugee problems referred to above

(e)   To approve projects for assistance to
refugees coming within the scope of
sub-par. (c)

(f)   To give directives to the HC for the
use of the Emergency Fund (not to
exceed $500,000, par. 7)

par. 6   To authorize the HC, under conditions
approved by the Ex. Com., to appeal
for funds to provide supplementary
temporary care and maintenance to,
and to participate in the financing of
permanent solutions for, refugees
coming within his mandate and otherwise not provided for. [1]

The principal function of the Office in implementing
assistance programs was coordination. To achieve this coordination, in addition to the headquarters staff, additional
branch offices were established by the HC in various countries.

With detailed information on the composition of the
case load and on the various solutions which were required,
the efforts of governments, voluntary agencies, and the
UNHCR could be fully synchronized. Also, systematic coordination could be maintained with other departments of the
UN, the Specialized Agencies, inter-governmental organizations and, to a very large extent, with non-governmental organizations. Representatives of many of these bodies have
taken part as observers on the Ex. Com., and the HC himself or a staff member has attended their meetings when
refugee matters were being dealt with.

The Ninth (Special) Session of the UNREF Ex. Com.
in September 1958 requested the HC to plan the 1959 Program for a level of expenditure of $4,700,000; it also au-
thorized him to appeal for an alternative figure of $6 mil-
lion. On this basis the HC presented two sets of figures to
the meeting of the Ex. Com. held in January 1959. (See
Annex 20.1.)

International Assistance Programs

While the HC's Program was designed to allow flexibility in implementation of measures on behalf of refugees,

certain programs were identified by the Ninth Session of the UNREF Ex. Com. for continuing operation on the basis of need and available funds. These were (1) camp clearance (a two-year program, 1959-60); (2) aid to out-of-camp refugees; (3) an emergency fund to meet the needs of individual refugees; (4) assistance to new refugees in Greece; (5) a Far Eastern Operation (to be of three years duration, 1959-61); and (6) legal protection. (The Far Eastern Program is discussed in Chapter 27, and the functions of the HC in providing legal protection are considered in Chapter 9.)

In the preceding years a wealth of experience had been gathered and a basic framework for material assistance had evolved, particularly in the last two years of UNREF. On this foundation the HC built structures involving greater participation and more funding of the projects by the public and the governments.

The methods and tools used by the UNHCR in its early activities, and to a large degree those used by the IRO, and even by the LoN, were basically the same. They had, however, to be constantly re-examined and further developed in response to the need for adaptation and improvement, as well as to continually changing conditions and new demands on the Office.

Camp Clearance. Programs for camp clearance had been a primary concern of the UNHCR from the very beginning, following in the footsteps of UNRRA and the IRO; but under the UNHCR, emphasis was predominantly on local integration to achieve permanent solutions.

Dr. van Heuven Goedhart, however, was able to use the meager contributions to UNREF for emergency aid to only the most needy. The expense of operations on behalf of refugees in China prevented the realization of many projects urgently needed to alleviate the most pressing needs of the camp population.

British voluntary agencies had started a Camp Adoption Scheme to raise the morale of refugees by individual contacts with the adopting community, with the latter taking a direct and personal interest in the welfare of the refugees by meeting some of their most urgent material needs. Dr. van Heuven Goedhart initiated this plan in 1954 in as many countries as possible as "a means of expanding and channelling the good will and generosity of private persons and

groups for the benefit of refugees. " To facilitate the working of the scheme, the Office, collaborating with the voluntary agencies, prepared summaries of information on some
forty camps in Austria, Germany, and Greece. The summaries were distributed to interested organizations in the
UK, the Netherlands, Switzerland, and others. In the UK,
the Standing Conference of BCAR promoted the scheme. In
Denmark, the suggestion was made that the Camp Adoption
Scheme might be linked with the UNESCO coupon plan. [2]
The HC reported in 1955 that a total of forty-two camps had
been adopted, forty of these by the UK, and that the scheme
had improved morale and living conditions in a number of
camps in Austria, Germany and Greece. [3]

In the fall of 1956 the British adopting groups ener-
getically collaborated in the UN Association fund campaign
for refugees. Money was allocated among the various countries in proportion to the total raised. Some $7,000 was
allotted for permanent solutions projects for individual refugees in adopted camps in Germany and Austria. Other funds
were allocated to the Adoption Committee for Aid to Displaced Persons, and the BCAR--the two British agencies coordinating camp adoptions in Germany and Austria--for purposes connected with the adoption. In 1957 the British
North-West Region of the Society for Mentally Handicapped
Children adopted the group of mentally-deficient refugee children at the Philipps Hospital at Goddelay (Hesse) in Germany
(one of the institutions transferred by IRO to the German
authorities). By 1958 there were seventy adopting groups
active mainly in Austria, Germany, and Greece (fifty-one in
the UK, eight in Sweden, six in Denmark, and five in Canada). [4]

The efforts to relocate refugees, begun by Dr. van
Heuven Goedhart and described earlier, were intensified
under Dr. Lindt. The Camp Clearance Program, which had
been an integral part of the UNREF Program, was carried
on as a separate operation within the 1959 Program in Austria, Germany, Greece, and Italy. Between 1 January 1955
and 31 December 1959, 16,712 refugees from camps were
firmly settled and most of the others were in the process of
settlement. At the end of that period, there remained
15,770 refugees in camps qualifying for camp clearance, the
majority in Austria and Germany. There were still 105 official camps to be cleared by UNHCR, of which forty-one
were in Austria (excluding two camps accommodating new
Hungarian refugees only), forty-nine in Germany, eight in

Greece, and seven in Italy. The Camp Clearance Program also concerned 141 small, unofficial camps in Austria. During 1959 the number of refugees had decreased by 5,500. Yet on 1 January 1960 there were still within the UNHCR's mandate 14,300 refugees living in camps, 1,820 new Hungarian refugees in Austria, and 200 in Greece; and some 3,800 refugees qualifying for programs carried out by other organizations. [5]

The Office implemented a series of new projects for 1959, for which the Ex. Com. had fixed a minimum target of $4.7 million. (As of 30 April 1959 governmental contributions totalled $2,870,482 [see Annex 20.2].) It also started the implementation for 1960 for which the Ex. Com. had approved up to $9.5 million out of an exceptionally high total target of $12 million, 1960 being the year of WRY. Within the 1959 and 1960 Current Programs priority was further given to the Far Eastern Program and to the Camp Clearance Program. [6]

Programs for Non-Settled Refugees Outside Camps. The priority given to the Camp Clearance Program had delayed the implementation of material assistance to non-settled refugees living outside camps. For the first time, the HC was enabled under the new program, to undertake larger projects on behalf of out-of-camp refugees, whose number as of January 1959 was estimated to be 97,000. While the Camp Clearance Program was concentrated mainly in Austria, Germany, Greece, and Italy, the HC extended assistance to non-settled refugees far beyond the borders of these countries, especially in North Africa, the Middle East, and Latin America.

The problem of the non-settled refugees differed markedly from those of the camp residents. They were spread over a large number of countries. Many lived in areas where living conditions differed from those to which they had been accustomed. Moreover these areas were often isolated and the refugees therefore less easily reached. In Western Europe the non-handicapped among them did benefit directly from the general economic expansion, particularly in West Germany and Austria, and shared the available opportunities with the nationals of their countries of residence; but the handicapped often suffered greater hardships than those living in camps. This was especially true in those countries where social welfare legislation was not fully developed or where no network of voluntary agencies existed.

The projects designed to assist these refugees had the same aim as those for camp refugees, namely, to enable them to become self-supporting. While the camp population was mainly in need of housing, refugees living outside camps required more assistance to become established: educational facilities, vocational training or re-training, rehabilitation, and counselling. Counselling was particularly difficult to provide in outlying areas where the refugees were difficult to reach and where few or no voluntary agencies existed. In many cases these refugees were resettled with the aid of small loans for establishment in crafts and trades. Handicapped refugees were given priority under the HC's program in accordance with the directives of the Ex. Com. Furthermore, priority was given to specific areas, such as Greece and Turkey.

The amount of the UNHCR's contribution was related to the supporting contributions of the countries of residence. A ratio was established by the Ex. Com. which took into account

1. the proportion of the handicapped population to the total population of the country
2. the total number of non-settled refugees, including those outside the mandate of UNHCR, living in the country and the total effort made on their behalf
3. the value of the project for the economy of the country in the sense that projects which increase the national capital (fixed assets) of a country should normally require higher supporting contributions than those projects which only provide services for refugees. [7]

Thus the degree of assistance by the UNHCR varied according to the economic and social conditions of the country of location.

By 31 December 1966 the final closure of the remaining camps in Europe was nearly achieved. Since that time, camps have been mainly used, as had been originally intended, for transit of newly arrived refugees. [8]

Special mention should be made of the early closure of the camp on the Greek Island of Tinos in the Aegean Sea, on 16 December 1957, under the devoted and able efforts of Helen Handropoulou, a UNHCR counsellor. The liquidation

of the camp was made possible by the use of $35,000 of the
Nobel Peace Prize money awarded to the UNHCR in 1955,
as well as by contributions of $10,000 each from the Nor-
wegian Refugee Council and Swiss Aid to Europe, with the
cooperation of the Greek Government and WCC. Of the 100
refugees living in this camp, many were able to emigrate,
the majority found work or were relocated on the land or in
small businesses, and the old and infirm were settled in an
old people's home opened on the island under an UNREF
project, or in another institution in Athens. [9]

Programs for Handicapped Refugees. Responsibility
for the hard core refugees had been transferred by IRO at
its liquidation to the countries of residence. They were
those who, mainly due to the restricted and selective immigration criteria of resettlement countries, had been rejected
as "unemigrable" cases. In the terminology of resettlement
countries, they were "difficult to resettle."They were people
with physical disabilities--amputees, epileptics, or persons
affected with tuberculosis, or heart or muscular diseases;
people with mental disabilities or personality disturbances,
such as alcoholics; or the socially handicapped--single
mothers with children, illiterates, and those with penal records.

From the moment Dr. van Heuven Goedhardt took office, one of his deepest concerns was for these difficult
cases. Of his first expenditures from the Emergency Fund
in early 1952, $20,000 was for clothing, supplementary food,
and medical supplies for the patients confined to crowded,
unhealthy barracks in Trieste. In the same year, the Ford
Foundation grant contributed to the upkeep of TB and post-
TB refugees in camps in Germany, Austria, and Italy.
Later the HC appealed to governments, particularly in Europe, to accept for treatment persons suffering from TB,
and to offer them the possibility of establishing themselves
permanently with their families.

The response to the problem of handicapped refugees
has been significant in Western European countries. Belgium, Denmark, France, Norway, Sweden, Switzerland, and
the UK have adopted special immigration schemes over the
years. Norway's programs for the handicapped began under
the IRO but, at the request of the UNHCR, admission criteria
were significantly broadened. Between 1954 and 1966, 441
refugees belonging to handicapped family units were admitted
and the handicapped placed either in rehabilitation programs

or under institutional care. Denmark, like Norway, has
pioneered the acceptance of handicapped refugees. Under
successive UNHCR sponsored schemes 265 handicapped cases,
with 163 family members, were admitted for settlement or
rehabilitation between 1954 and 1966. Before WRY, Sweden
had accepted roughly half the total number of handicapped
refugees resettled since 1953.

Sweden had long been a haven for refugees with tuberculosis. Since large numbers of Swedish TB institutions
were empty in 1950, Sweden arranged for the transfer of
refugees for medical care and a long-term stay in that country. In ten years 1,011 TB patients were transferred to
Sweden, accompanied by 935 relatives.[10]

Little was accomplished toward the liberalization of
immigration criteria by the overseas countries. The conditions of those refugees who were unable to emigrate or to
integrate in the asylum countries steadily deteriorated under
the stress of prolonged camp life, while their numbers increased. There were also many outside the camps whose
insecurity and economic need lessened their chances for a
permanent solution.

Arrangements were made to provide lifelong care in
appropriate institutions for the aged and permanently incapa-
citated refugees. A program of "housing with care" was
initiated for those who, although unable to earn their living,
were still anxious to lead an independent life. These projects varied according to local conditions and possibilities.
In countries with a developed social welfare system the refugees placed in such homes had access to welfare assistance. Those in countries where such assistance was not
available were given annuities.

Other refugees, whose condition and age did not require permanent care, received special rehabilitation or re-
training before they could resume a fully, or at least partially, independent life.

While the programs of camp closing and refugee relocation were being implemented, personality disturbances
among the residual refugees worsened. Reports of the
UNHCR and voluntary agencies revealed that years of camp
life had created personality disturbances that, in many
cases, made integration impossible without special rehabilitative treatment.

The HC took advantage of modern experiences in sociology and psychiatry to deal with and to rehabilitate refugees for constructive new lives. The HC appointed Dr. Strotzka as a mental health adviser for the purpose of determining the number and nature of those mental health cases which required treatment. At the time of the Hungarian revolt, Dr. Strotzka, in cooperation with UNHCR, dealt with approximately 18,000 difficult cases of Hungarians who were considered mentally or socially handicapped or both.

At the 1960 meeting of the World Federation for Mental Health he described the enormous variations in the social atmosphere of the camps, ranging from very abnormal to nearly normal living conditions. The differences seemed to be related to the number and composition of the population; to the economic, social, and cultural conditions inside and outside camps; and to the personalities of camp officials and counselling personnel. Only 10 to 15 percent of the camp residents appeared to have integration difficulties which met the criteria of social or mental handicaps. While the case load included psychotics, mostly schizophrenics, and all kinds of neurotics, the majority of patients were alcoholics or individuals who had lost, or believed they had lost, their ability to work. [11]

In response to Dr. Strozka's first report the Ex. Com., at its Third Session in April 1960, authorized pilot rehabilitation projects. [12] In addition to individual or group psychotherapeutic treatment in psychiatric clinics or in clinics for alcoholism, the rehabilitation of special cases involved the setting up of special types of sheltered workshops and the renovation or construction of special dwellings, providing, as previously mentioned, "housing with care."

In the effort to resettle handicapped refugees, appeals were made to countries of immigration to widen their immigration criteria. For many years there seemed to be little hope of finding resettlement for most types of difficult cases on a scale necessary to resolve the problem. With the exception of the plans of the Western European countries, already mentioned, there was no real change in the negative attitude of a number of governments, particularly the non-European governments, until WRY in 1959-60. A chain reaction during the period of WRY led to migration opportunities for some 4,000 handicapped refugees with 3,000 dependents. On the whole, the experience of these programs, undertaken with some hesitation, proved positive. One striking

example was Canada, which had formerly rejected immigrants with TB, but which now admitted 325 tubercular refugees in a period of fifteen months. By the end of 1965 only
three of these refugees were still in Canadian sanatoria, thus
providing that these apparently hopeless cases could be trans-
formed into healthy and useful members of society when
countries were willing to make the effort.

Despite the fact that WRY had demonstrated the possibilities of successfully relocating handicapped people,
there remained a residual group of people with handicaps
who were non-resettable even under the liberal criteria introduced. A "new look" in the presentation of such cases
had to be developed. Dr. F. A. S. Jensen, Chief Medical
Officer for the Australian Department of Immigration in
Rome, was seconded to the UNHCR by the Australian Government in 1961 to undertake a special survey of the residual handicapped case load. With the cooperation of ICEM,
and additional financing by USEP, he carried out a pilot survey in Italy.

Because of the highly individual nature of such handicaps, group planning was no longer practical. Each case
had to be considered separately. Dr. Jensen personally interviewed 317 handicapped refugees and their families who
wished to emigrate. Detailed dossiers were prepared for
each case, and this information was forwarded to governments and other interested agencies. The dossiers presented an adequate and honest picture of the handicapped
refugee--his character as well as his physical and mental
health. The more accurate the information on each individual refugee, the more helpful was this information for the
selection commissioners who knew the facilities for resettlement in their own countries. The reaction to the dossiers
was encouraging from the beginning. Governments, voluntary agencies, and private sponsoring bodies appreciated the
"in depth" data on each case so that they could judge the
special measures which were required for assuring successful settlement.

In February 1962 Sweden began the implementation of
the program by accepting 20 families. In March, Norway
and Belgium, followed by eight other countries, accepted
some of these difficult cases. Within nine months after the
dossiers had been made available to governments, the residual group in Italy was reduced by two-thirds.

The survey on Italy, titled Operation Fine Tooth Comb, presented by Dr. Jensen on 19 February 1962 to the Ex. Com., to ICEM, and to the voluntary agencies led to surveys in other countries: Austria, Germany, Greece, Hong Kong, Morocco, and Turkey. [13] These surveys were the result of the work of many hands and the cooperation of a variety of organizations and individuals. Dr. Jensen presented a general survey to the UNHCR and ICEM on 24 October 1962. [14] (Annex 20.3.) According to a final survey, completed at the end of 1963, 577 cases comprising 1,125 persons had been interviewed in the above-mentioned countries.

In addition, in October 1959, the HC appointed Dr. Peter Berner as Mental Health Adviser (under project RF/EUR/A.1/59), with the following terms of reference: to determine the volume and nature of the special cases and to make recommendations on the specific needs of the refugees, while maintaining close liaison with the UNHCR BOs and the competent authorities and institutions in the countries concerned.

Dr. Berner organized regional seminars attended by integration and follow-up counsellors, medical consultants, and expert advisers from the UNHCR branch officials. His main task was to seek solutions to the problems of special cases which were defined as: "Persons for whom special services are required to achieve the maximum degree of adjustment of which each person is capable." They included, "from a psychiatric standpoint, persons affected by psychosis, defects following on psychosis, or severe psychoneurosis, as well as psychopaths and persons suffering from varying degrees of mental deficiency. From a social point of view these disorders might reveal themselves through alcoholism, inability to work, social deterioration, isolation, or aggressive or promiscuous behaviour. "[15]

Dr. Berner presented his final report on the Mental Health of Refugees in the Special Cases Category in Austria, Germany, Greece, Italy and Turkey to the Tenth Session of the Ex. Com. [16] After preliminary investigations in 1960, the number of special cases was estimated at 1,530. A systematic registration and identification revealed that the case load amounted to 1,828 at the beginning of 1962, with an additional 891 cases still under treatment or observation. The UNHCR, at the request of the Mental Health Adviser, established a $6,000 psychiatric consultation and treatment

fund for refugees who could not obtain such assistance from
other sources, such as local health services, sickness insurance, or voluntary agencies. Dr. Berner later prepared
a similar survey for refugees in Latin America.

Despite the impressive efforts by the international
community, a group of handicapped refugees and their families had still not been finally settled as late as 1967. The
HC in that year presented a report which reappraised the
problem of severely handicapped refugees. [17] This report
resulted from conversations between Dr. Cleve Schou (Norway), Senior Medical Officer of ICEM and participant in the
Jensen survey, who had taken over Dr. Jensen's responsibilities at the end of 1965, and Mr. Thomas Jamieson, Director of Operations of UNHCR, with the permanent missions to the UN in Geneva (Australia, Canada, New Zealand,
the US, Belgium, Denmark, France, the Netherlands, Norway, and the UK). Information contained in the report came
from Dr. Schou's visits to the capitals of the Western European countries concerned and to the Field Migration Missions in Europe of the overseas countries.

As a result of these talks a clear-cut plan with well
defined stages evolved. The "Special Resettlement Dossier
Scheme," which had been carried on since the completion of
the Jensen Survey on 31 December 1963, continued over the
next two years. (Annex 20. 4.) The final effort on behalf
of the residual group was completed in August 1966. (See
Annex 20. 5.) Such cases were in the future handled under
the Current Program. [18]

In 1967, 531 persons were still left of the residual
group of handicapped in Europe. Dr. Schou could finally report to the Ex. Com. on 29 September 1970, that on 11
February 1970 he had personally escorted to London "the
last one of the so-called 'old' camp refugees" who had lived
for twenty years in a refugee camp in Italy. Dr. Schou
stated that while the problem of the old refugees had finally
been solved, it would not be completely solved until the
handicapped were brought back to a normal place in the community. This would only be possible, he noted, when all the
traditional receiving countries were prepared to accept on an
individual and continuous basis a certain number of handicapped refugees every year. Such a continuous program was
needed "to avoid accumulation in the countries of first asylum which have to accept every refugee whether he be blind,
lame, deaf-mute or otherwise handicapped. " To solve this

problem it had to be dealt with on an individual basis through
the established technique of the Special Resettlement Dossier
scheme.   He strongly appealed to the traditional receiving
countries among the Ex. Com. to help to achieve this.   He
mentioned, as examples, Switzerland which had accepted, on
an individual basis, fifty institutional cases every year, and
Canada which had agreed to accept fifty TB cases every
year. [19]

Assistance for Local Integration in Europe

        The general types of assistance for permanent solu-
tions undertaken by the UNHCR under the HC's Program is
described below.

        Statistics.   A new reporting system was devised which
not only improved the scope and accuracy of the implementation statistics but also created a basis for adequate control
of the program.   Instead of mere rolls of names, personal
history forms for each beneficiary were drawn up, avoiding
much duplication of names on the rolls and, at the same
time, providing a record of services rendered to a beneficiary until his final establishment.

        Case Work and Integration Counselling.   The mass
wartime and post-war movements of refugees had come to
an end (with the exception of Hungarian refugee settlement)
by the end of the IRO period.   It was imperative to approach
the remaining case load on an individual basis.   Many refugees living in camps were reluctant to leave their accustomed
abode, being afraid to live an independent life.   However,
with more intensive counselling, vocational training, aid to
high school and university students, and physical rehabilitation, a remarkable result has been achieved.   Pre-selection
counselling and follow-up services had to be further expanded
and refined.   Once the need of each case was determined,
the case-worker sought solutions through local means or by
drawing on the resources available from UNHCR, USEP,
ICEM, or voluntary agencies.

        Under Dr. Lindt the UNHCR improved and enlarged
the integration counselling system.   Each individual case required the closest planning and counselling.   This involved
more time for achieving a final settlement, since the remaining refugees were economically weak, many of them suffering from various physical and social handicaps that

impeded their integration or resettlement. Coordination of
the efforts of general and specialized social workers remained the main instrument in the implementation of the
program. A few social workers were employed on the staff
of the UNHCR BOs, but most such services were obtained
under contract with specialized voluntary agencies.

Housing and Employment. The two most crucial
problems to be overcome in developing integration opportunities were those of housing and employment.

The post-war shortage of housing throughout Europe
was a major problem facing every country, due to wartime
destruction and the movements of population. Nations
pooled their thinking and professional talents and dealt with
the question as an international problem. Since virtually
every country was without enough proper housing for its own
people, the need to shelter the refugees properly loomed as
one of the most serious obstacles.

Under the UNREF Program a promising beginning had
been made in providing housing; in fact, the largest amount
of funds spent under that program had been for UNREF
building projects in West Germany, Austria, and Greece.
(For a description of the Kåreas Refugee Housing Settlement
in Greece, see Annex 20.6.) But certain factors made this
an arduous and drawn-out process. The rising price of land,
increased building costs, and the lack of skilled labor delayed the completion of houses, particularly in Austria and
Germany. However, through difficult and time-consuming
negotiations, particularly where (as in West Germany) it was
necessary to deal with government authorities at the federal,
Länder, and local levels, the difficulties were surmounted.
Between 1955 and 1965, 10,164 housing units were completed
in Austria, West Germany, Greece, and France for the
benefit of 11,121 refugee households (comprising 35,790 persons). By 1970 the number of housing units completed was
12,500.

Since employment opportunities were available in some
countries and many refugees had the skills readily applicable
to fill those opportunities, a system of emergency or temporary housing was devised in some cities so that refugees
might be quickly accepted in cities of resettlement. A test
settlement, Wolfach, was developed in a cooperative undertaking between the Federal Government of Germany, UNHCR,
WCC, and LWF.

Establishment assistance was a useful complement to housing. It enabled refugees who had moved into their new accommodations to acquire the bare essentials of equipment and furniture which they were unable to purchase with their own low income.

The HC's Program was based on two principles. Rents had to be low and houses close to employment. Refugees belonged, in the main, to low income groups; many even depended on national assistance. Since most refugees could find work in industry, their houses had to be near industrial centers.

The UNHCR made strenuous efforts to reduce building costs and to find financing under favorable terms. In general the UNHCR followed the policy that economy and efficiency were most easily achieved by accommodating its plans to existing national or local building schemes. Cooperation with governmental authorities and building societies enabled the UNHCR to secure subsidies which reduced the cost of houses by as much as two-thirds. Such programs released the Office from the responsibilities of a landlord, while arrangements contained in the agreements with implementing agencies permitted the UNHCR to supervise the situation in those refugee settlements. These arrangements also stipulated that housing financed through UNHCR investment should be reserved for refugees for specified periods. Thus when the original refugee occupant left further refugees could be accommodated.

Old Age Institutions. Participation of the international community in the creation of old age institutions started under UNRRA and the IRO. With funds from the Ford Foundation the UNHCR financed a number of projects, the provisions of which differed from one country to another. In France, the UNHCR contribution was given toward the cost of construction, it being understood that the French Government would cover the cost of care and maintenance. French voluntary agencies assumed the obligation to accept refugees into these institutions as long as there were candidates. If the refugee population were to diminish to such an extent that there were no more candidates, then they would be authorized to take French citizens. In Belgium, and Italy, the UNHCR also contributed to the construction of old age homes, but the agencies had to cover the cost of care and maintenance which was not taken over by the government.

In Scandinavian countries, refugees have always been admitted into existing old age homes and no UNHCR contribution has been required. In the early days, the UNHCR made some contributions to Swiss voluntary agencies for additional beds in existing old age homes.

Contributions of the UNHCR were earmarked for settlement in institutions in the country of residence, or for settlement in institutions outside the country of residence. Over 3,200 places have been paid for in homes and institutions for the aged which, when vacated by the present refugee tenants, can be re-occupied by needy refugees for as long as the need exists. Similar facilities exist for the rehabilitation of handicapped refugees (homes for alcoholics, sheltered workshops). (Annex 20.7.)

Training and Education. Training projects were provided for young refugees, and after completion of their training they were helped to find employment in their trades. High school pupils and university students were enabled to complete their studies and became firmly settled.

A number of projects have been financed by the UNHCR to facilitate establishment in crafts, trades, and agriculture. The assistance was given either as loans or as grants. In Austria the UNHCR signed an agreement with the Ministry of Agriculture for the establishment of refugees in agriculture. Here again, the UNHCR contribution was given either as a loan or as a grant.

Supplementary Aid. Supplementary aid consisted mainly of medical assistance (particularly important in countries where public facilities were not available), supplementary food, clothing, heating and, in the neediest cases, small cash grants. Provisions were also made for credit facilities and small loans.

Notes

1. ECOSOC Res. 672(XXV), 30 Apr. 1958 and GA (XII), Res. 466.

2. HC's Ann. Rep., 1954: 11.

3. HC's Ann. Rep., 1955: 3.

4. Ibid. to GA for 1958: 20.

5. HC's Ann. Rep. , 1960: 15.

6. Ibid. : 3.

7. GA (XV), Ex. Com. (III), A/AC.96/78, 16 May 1960:
    10.

8. Ibid. , 1967: 16.

9. A vivid description of this task is given in UNHCR,
    Meeting a Challenge, Geneva, 1961: 36.

10. For a detailed report, see The European Seminar on
    the Social and Economic Aspects of Refugee Inte-
    gration, Sigtuna, Sweden, 27 Apr. -7 May 1960,
    UN/TAO/SFM/1960, Rep. 1: 48.

11. Henry P. Davis, "Involuntary International Migration;
    Adoption of Refugees," IM, Vol. VII (3/4) 1969:
    73. See also H. Strotzka, "Observations of the
    Mental Health of Refugees, " in WFMH, Uprooting
    and Resettlement, Geneva World Federation for
    Mental Health, 1960; ditto, "Action for Mental
    Health in Refugee Camps" in F. Thornton (ed.)
    Planning and Action for Mental Health, Geneva
    WMFH, 1961, and C. Schou, "To Cope with a Cri-
    sis; A Medical Report on the Hungarian Emergency, "
    IM, 1968, Vol. VI: 129.

12. HC's Ann. Rep. for 1960 to GA: 28 and 30.

13. Ex. Com. (VII), A/AC.96/Inf. 2, 21 Mar. 1962.

14. Dr. F. A. S. Jensen, UNHCR-ICEM-USEP Survey of
    Handicapped Persons, General Report, 24 Oct. 1962.
    Also "The Outcast from the Community: A Special
    Case, " in World Health, Geneva.

15. See Doc. A/AC.96/62, par. 9.

16. GA (XVII), A/AC.96/206, 24 July 1963.

17. A/AC.96/358, 23 Oct. 1967.

18. UNHCR Reports, "The Last of the Many, " Sept. -Oct.

1967, and A/AC.96/183, 23 Oct. 1967; and ICEM
MC/Inf. 121, 7 Oct. 1966, Special Report on Resettlement of Handicapped Refugees.

19.   Statement made by Dr. Shou at the Ex. Com. (XX)
       MHCR/99/70.

ANNEX 20.1 ANALYSIS OF REQUIREMENTS FOR THE HIGH COMMISSIONER'S PROGRAM, 1959 (in US $)

1.	Camp Clearance Program[a]		2,900,000[c]
2.	Far Eastern Program	3,300,000[b]	
	(a) UNHCR expenditure		
	Care and maintenance of refugees in Hong Kong	210,000	
	Administrative costs of Hong Kong Office..	25,000	
	Assistance for voluntary agencies......	108,000	
	Resettlement of difficult cases.............	337,000	550,000
	(b) ICEM expenditure		
	Transportation costs (not included in total)...............	(1,500,000)	
3.	Program for non-settled refugees living outside camps		
	(a) Permanent solutions for handicapped refugees............	1,000,000	
	(b) Registration and follow-up......	70,000	
	(c) Case-work and counselling......	120,000	
	(d) Promotion of education......	20,000	
	(e) Vocational training......	30,000	
	(f) Supplementary aid.............	80,000	1,320,000
4.	Emergency account for aid to individual cases		50,000
5.	Program for new refugees in Greece........		240,000
6.	Legal Assistance................		80,000
7.	Contribution to UNHCR administrative budget[a]		330,000
	Total		6,000,000

a An amount of $150,000 for administrative expenses is included in the figure for camp clearance.

b This figure is equal to half of the total allocation for the years 1959/1960 ($4.8 million) plus the value of the 1958 camp clearance projects likely to remain unimplemented for lack of funds (provisionally estimated at $900,000).

c This figure is equal to half of the total allocation for the years 1959/1960 ($4.8 million) plus approximately half the value of the 1958 camp clearance projects likely to remain unimplemented for lack of funds (provisionally estimated at $900,000).

SOURCE: GA (XIV), 1959, Off. Rec., Supp. 11, A/4104/Rev. 1: 29.

ANNEX 20. 2

GOVERNMENTAL CONTRIBUTIONS TO UNHCR PROGRAMS
FOR 1959 AS OF 30 APRIL 1959

	US$
Austria	12, 000
Belgium	50, 000
Cambodia	571
Canada	290, 000
China	5, 000
Denmark	72, 390
Dominican Rep.	5, 000
Federation of Malaya	1, 000
France	177, 143
Germany, Fed. Rep. of	209, 524
Ghana	3, 000
Greece	9, 000
Holy See	2, 000
Ireland	4, 667
Israel	5, 000
Italy	3, 000
Liechtenstein	1, 000
Luxembourg	3, 000
Monaco	2, 041
Morocco	2, 381
Netherlands	139, 211
Norway	98, 000
Rhodesia and Nyasaland, Fed. of	2, 823
Sweden	115, 987
Switzerland	156, 977
Tunisia	2, 000
Turkey	2, 667
UK	280, 000
US	1, 200, 000
Yugoslavia	15, 000
Total	2, 870, 482

SOURCE: GA (XIV), 1959, Off. Rec., Supp. 11, A/4104/
         Rev. 1: 22

ANNEX 20.3

JENSEN SURVEY OF CLASSIFIED HANDICAPPED
CASES FOR EMIGRATION (as reported 1962)*

	AUS.	GER.	GRE.	U.K.	ITA.	MOR.	TUR.	TOTAL
Physical Handicap								
Tuberculosis	5/10	6/11	-	-	16/39	6/11	2/4	35/75
Mental diseases	1/2	1/6	3/2	-	25/35	3/8	-	32/53
Paralysis and related diseases of the nervous system and sense organs	-	1/1	1/1	-	6/11	1/1	1/1	10/15
Diseases of respiratory (excl. TB) and cardiovascular system	-	2/10	-	-	16/40	5/24	-	23/74
Partial or total blindness	-	-	-	1/3	9/12	-	-	10/15
Deafness, mutism, deaf-mutism	-	2/2	-	-	-	-	-	2/2
Diseases of other systems	-	2/10	-	-	9/9	3/6	-	14/25
Amputation	1/1	-	-	-	1/4	-	-	2/5
Musculo-Skeletal deformity or impairment	2/4	-	1/1	-	12/31	-	-	15/36
Old age	-	5/6	-	2/3	11/16	2/7	1/1	21/33
Post-tubular	4/8	4/7	-	-	34/65	-	3/4	45/84
Other handicap (Alcoholism)	-	1/1	-	-	8/8	-	2/2	11/11
Social Handicap								
Single with child(ren)	2/8	1/5	-	-	10/30	-	1/2	14/45
Uneconomic families	-	-	-	-	1/8	-	-	1/8

	AUS.	GER.	GRE.	U.K.	ITA.	MOR.	TUR.	TOTAL
Employment difficulties	–	–	–	1/1	–	–	5/13	6/14
Family problems	–	2/2	–	–	2/2	–	–	4/4
Illiteracy	1/1	1/1	–	–	1/1	–	–	3/3
Penal record	–	3/11	3/7	–	28/44	1/4	–	35/66
Marital status	–	1/1	–	–	1/1	–	–	2/2
Others	–	–	–	3/11	8/11	–	–	11/22
Not handicapped but repeatedly rejected	–	2/2	–	1/2	23/40	–	1/4	27/48
Total	16/34	34/76	7/11	8/20	221/407	21/61	16/31	323/640

Composition of Residual Caseload

	AUS.	GER.	GRE.	U.K.	ITA.	MOR.	TUR.	TOTAL
Physical Handicap								
Tuberculosos	1/1	4/4	–	–	2/2	–	–	7/7
Mental diseases	3/12	2/5	–	–	11/4	3/7	1/1	10/29
Paralysis and related diseases of the nervous system and sense organs	2/2	–	–	–	–	–	–	2/2
Diseases of respiratory (excl. TB) and cardiovascular system	–	–	–	–	–	1/1	–	1/1
Partial or total blindness	–	–	–	–	–	–	–	–
Deafness, mutism, deaf-mutism	–	–	–	–	–	–	–	–
Diseases of other systems	–	–	–	–	–	–	–	–
Amputation	–	–	–	–	1/1	–	–	1/1

Musculo-Skeletal deformity or impairment	1/1	–	–	–	1/1	–	–	2/2
Old Age	–	–	–	1/4	–	–	–	1/4
Post-tubercular	–	3/14	–	–	3/3	–	–	6/17
Other handicap (Alcoholism)	–	–	–	–	–	1/1	–	1/1
Social Handicap								
Single with child(ren)	–	1/4	–	–	1/2	–	–	2/6
Uneconomic families	–	–	–	–	–	–	–	–
Employment difficulties	–	–	–	–	–	–	–	–
Family problems	–	–	–	–	–	–	–	–
Illiteracy	–	–	–	–	–	–	–	–
Penal record	1/1	3/4	–	1/1	3/6	1/1	–	9/13
Marital status	–	1/1	–	–	–	–	–	1/1
Others	2/2	1/1	–	1/4	1/1	–	–	5/8
Not handicapped but repeatedly rejected	–	–	–	–	–	–	–	–
Total	10/19	15/33	–	3/9	13/20	6/10	1/1	48/92

*The first figures refer to cases, the second to persons.

SOURCE: ICEM, <u>Spec. Rep.</u> on Resettlement of Handicapped Refugees, MC/Inf./121: 7 and 8.

ANNEX 20. 4

REFUGEES UNDER THE HIGH COMMISSIONER'S
MANDATE ACCEPTED UNDER THE JENSEN
SURVEY AND SUBSEQUENT SPECIAL RESETTLEMENT
DOSSIER SCHEMES (OCTOBER 1961 TO OCTOBER 1967)

| | Accepted for immigration and actually departed | |
	Cases	Persons
Australia	31	75
Belgium	101	193
Canada	42	80
Denmark	32	41
France	12	21
Germany	10	11
Netherlands	2	6
New Zeland	9	24
Norway	15	31
Spain	1	1
Sweden	67	122
Switzerland	29	44
UK	4	9
US	49	120
	404	778

SOURCE: UNHCR Reports, No. 48, Sept. /Oct. 1967.

ANNEX 20.5

STATUS OF THE JENSEN SURVEY
AS OF 31 AUGUST 1966

By Country of Departure

Country of Departure	Refugees examined		Accepted for emigration		Settled through local integr./ naturalization		Decreased Repatriated Withdrawn		Needing solution	
	Cases	Pers.	Cases	Pers.	Cases	Pers.	Cases	Pers.	Cases	Pers.
Austria	56	104	16	34	5	6	25	45	10	19
Germany	102	262	34	76	4	10	49	143	15	33
Greece	13	17	7	11	3	3	3	3	-	-
Hong Kong	14	36	8	20	-	-	3	7	3	9
Italy	335	561	221	407	16	28	85	106	13	20
Morocco	34	93	21	61	-	-	7	22	6	10
Turkey	23	52	16	31	-	-	6	20	1	1
Total	577	1,125	323	640	28	47	178	346	48	92

By Country of Admission

Country of admission	Accepted for emigration and actually departed		Of whom returned to country of origin or country of first asylum and resigned from emigration	
	Cases	Persons	Cases	Persons
Australia	26	64	1	1
Belgium	99	181	12	15
Canada	34	62	1	1
Denmark	11	18	1	1
France	12	21	-	-
Germany	6	6	-	-
New Zealand	7	20	-	-
Norway	14	28	2	3
Sweden	57	109	3	3
Switzerland	21	35	2	2
UK	3	6	1	1
US	33	90	1	1
Total	323	640	24	30

SOURCE: Ibid. : 6-8.

ANNEX 20. 6

KAREAS REFUGEE HOUSING SETTLEMENT
(GREECE), 1957-68

A project which played a prominent role in the camp clearance program in Greece was the Kareas refugee housing settlement. It is called Lindoupolis (after Dr. Lindt), and is located about four kilometers from the center of Athens on the slopes of Hymettus Mountain with a view of Athens, the Kiphissos and Illissos valleys, and the Saronic Gulf. At the time of the inception of the joint Greek Government-UNHCR program for permanent solutions for refugees in Greece, the site was virtually bare. The first road was opened in 1954. In 1968 25 apartment blocks and 61 flatlets housed 2,000 refugees.

Early in 1957 the land was bought by the government for the first 13 blocks of apartments to house approximately 360 families. The first 122 apartments were occupied in April 1958 by refugees from Rumania and Russia of Greek ethnic origin who were living in camps. Roads were opened, and provision made for rainwater and sewage disposal, electricity and water supply, and transportation, as well as for future extension.

The total cost has been approximately $2.5 million, with the UNHCR and the Greek Government each contributing $978,744. Construction was undertaken by the Greek Government, and facilities have developed which have attracted many local citizens to the area so that the danger of it becoming solely a refugee community has not arisen.

A refugee repays 55 percent of the actual cost of the apartments in semi-annual installments, with 2 percent interest. After a period of twenty years, when he has repaid the total amount due, he will receive a clear title to his apartment. The interest paid forms a fund to be used to consolidate the establishment of the refugee families. The average cost of a one-room apartment is 60,000 drs.; of a two-room apartment 100,000 drs.; of a three-room apartment 140,000 drs. Single people and childless couples are given the right to occupy the apartments for life, but do not become the owners; they pay a token rent of 40-60 drs. per month. Special provisions have been made for families who are genuinely unable to repay either wholly or in part.

For the accommodation of the aged, a special home was constructed where 96 refugees (25 couples and 46 singles) are accommodated in small one-room flats, each with a kitchenette. The project is under the care of the Ministry of Social Welfare. The refugees living in the flats have access to the Community Center and various cultural activities.

This kind of accommodation for aged people was entirely new for Greece, and the tenants of the small apartments encountered many difficulties of adjustment in the beginning. However, with the help of the counselling service of the UNHCR BO, the aged refugees are now well settled in their small flatlets. They have organized their own communities, the old men taking care of the administrative matters of the home and the women's committee taking care of recreational activities, cleanliness of the premises, decoration of the common rooms, and tending of the flower beds around the home. The government provides only for a caretaker and two charwomen. The Community Center provides overall supervision and help wherever necessary.

As the refugees in the settlement were of different nationalities, backgrounds and languages, the necessity for a Community Center soon became apparent which would serve to unite all the refugees into one community and also bring them into contact with the residents of neighboring community with a view to their more complete integration into Greek economic and social life.

Additional land (10,000-12,000 sq. meters) for a Community Center and school was requested in March 1959 by the Minister of Social Welfare from the Ministry of Agriculture. With the contributions of the Greek Government, Their Majesties Fund, Rädda Barnen of Sweden through the UNHCR, and the Caloust Gulbenkian Foundation, a Community Center was built in 1961. It is run by Their Majesties Fund.

The Center which was inaugurated in May 1962 provides recreation and education facilities for the refugees, and also offers courses in handicrafts. Through the specialized services of the trained staff of the Community Center the refugees are assisted to increase their self-reliance and to develop the necessary patterns of cooperation.

A 1969 report described the Center as employing four-teen staff members, six social workers, six teachers for various courses, one kindergarten teacher, and one teacher for sports and athletics. There was an excellent kindergarten attended by 94 children, half of them coming from the families in the neighboring communities. While of the 114 children in the study groups two-thirds were from families outside the Kareas settlement; 39 girls and young women were attending the housekeeping section.

For the aged, special programs such as films and slides, afternoon meetings, and excursions are organized. The members of this group also engage in various handicrafts as a form of occupational therapy, and through the sale of the articles thus produced a small income is earned which is divided among the members. In 1967, for instance, 307 pieces of embroidery were made by the old women's group, while the old men constructed 164 pieces of small furniture.

Meetings are regularly held by the refugees established in each housing block, with a view to achieving collaboration among the residents and electing committees responsible for upkeep of the buildings and grounds. In 1967, two thousand trees and one thousand bushes were planted. Furthermore, the Community Center organizes cultural and musical afternoons, concerts, and lectures which are attended by the majority of the population in Kareas. The regular members of the Community Center--those who participate in the training courses and the afternoon classes--number 500; but more than 1,000 people a month regularly attend the general activities of the Center.

Owing to the economic situation prevailing in Greece, plus a variety of factors which made it particularly difficult for the refugees to find employment--their lack of skills, the serious health problems of many of them, and the high percentage of handicapped--the need of a workshop became evident at the time that the first group of families moved into Kareas.

Through the efforts of the UNHCR and the contribution of the Caloust Gulbenkian Foundation, a separate building was constructed to provide the necessary space for a workshop.

Sewing, knitting, and embroidery machines, as well as looms were set up. With the supervision and help of the trained staff of the Community Center the refugees were able to produce articles in demand in the Greek market, in particular, articles appealing to tourists such as skirts, blouses, tablecloths, blankets, and handbags with Greek designs. The marketing of the refugees' products was entrusted in the beginning to Their Majesties Fund--this organization ran its own gift shops in the center of Athens--but as their handicrafts became known to a wider public the refugees were able to take direct orders from various organizations and individuals.

In 1967 the regular number of refugees working in the workshop reached 145, of whom 37 were occupied in the sewing and cutting section, 62 in the handicraft section, 14 in the carpentry section, 6 in the weaving section, 3 in the knitting section, and 23 in the ceramic section.

Almost one-half of the population established in Kareas (350 families) are refugees from Rumania of Greek ethnic origin. They are post-WWII refugees, the majority having arrived between the years 1948 to 1951, though a few families continue to arrive. Approximately 3,800 of this group lived in camps. The neediest families were included for housing in the first available apartments in Kareas.

The majority of these Greek ethnics from Rumania were well-established businessmen in the big urban centers in that country. They proved to be a most progressive group of refugees due to their good education and past high standard of living, hence they were able to use very constructively the assistance granted to them. The main handicap in this group is their advanced age, as the youngest and the more fit have migrated through the IRO and ICEM to the US, Canada, Australia, and the Latin American countries.

The second largest group housed in Kareas (278 families) are Armenians who arrived in Greece along with the 1,200,000 Greeks who had to leave Asia Minor after the Treaty of Lausanne in 1923. Their number was estimated at the time at 70,000. Many of them have emigrated overseas or "repatriated" to Soviet Armenia; however, approximately 10,000 are still living in Greece. The families who were moved into the Kareas settlement had been living for thirty-five years or more in primitive wooden shacks and mud huts which they had built on the outskirts of the big

cities when they arrived in Greece. One of the worst slum
areas from which Armenian refugees were moved to apartments in Kareas was the Dourgouti area, an area of 20,000
square miles where over 23,000 persons lived crammed into
a conglomeration of mud huts a short distance from the city
center.

This group, compared to the other two, has been
more difficult to integrate into Greek economic and social
life. Lack of knowledge of the language has been a problem
--the older generation speaks only Armenian and Turkish,
and the majority of the younger generation have been attending Armenian schools. Privation and hardship for so many
years, ill health and unemployment, and the fact that they
have kept very close together as a minority trying to keep
their national traditions and outdated mores and customs,
have kept the majority of them in the lower socio-economic
group.

The third group housed in Kareas (79 families) are
refugees from Russia of Greek ethnic origin. This group of
refugees first began arriving in Greece in 1921; up to 1939
they numbered about 50,000. During the Stalin regime they
were created as a hostile minority and were deported to
Kazakstan, and Siberia. They again started arriving in
Greece in small groups from 1957 onward. The majority of
this group are farmers, with a few skilled workers. The
seventy-nine families of Greek ethnics from Russia established in Kareas are on the whole a hardworking group, and
hence their integration has not caused much of a problem.
They are of good health and have the highest percentage of
young family members.

The last group, totalling just 12 families, are refugees from the neighboring countries; a few Albanian, one
Yugoslav, one Latvian, and a few White Russians.

The assimilation of these groups of different background presented a problem in the first years of their establishment in Kareas. However, through the efforts of the
staff which runs the Center many problems were overcome
and on the whole there is a good spirit of community life
prevailing in Kareas Settlement.

While it is difficult to speak with certainty about the
role of unemployment among the more employable refugees
settled in Kareas, it is a fact that the proportion of unskilled

handicapped, middle-aged and old refugees without any economic security is rather high.   Twenty-four percent of the
Kareas refugee population, it is estimated, have a monthly
income of less than 500 drs.   The UNHCR has assisted those
aged and handicapped refugees whose incomes were under
100 drs. by granting them life annuities of 500 drs. per
single person or 750 drs. per couple.

Of the remaining 76 percent of the population, 50 percent have a per capita monthly income not exceeding 1,000
drs.; 2 percent have reached a per capita income of 2,000
drs.; 6 percent have a per capita income of over 2,000 drs.
This last group consists of the small elite of professionals--
doctors, engineers, lawyers--and a few successful businessmen and shop owners.

The majority of the population in Kareas are unskilled
workers and small tradesmen.   Only 5 percent are university
graduates; at the other end of the scale, 5 percent are illiterate.   Some 30 percent have had only elementary schooling, while another 13 percent have not even completed elementary education.   High school graduates range between 16
and 18 percent and those who have graduated from a vocational training school are between 5 and 8 percent.   This
leaves a group of 13 to 15 percent, the majority women,
who have never attended school, although many of these have
had some kind of private education.

For refugees who had had past experience in a business, profession or trade, the UNHCR, through its joint
program with the Greek Government, allocated establishment
assistance up to 40,000 drs. per family.   Over 200 families
(600 persons) in Kareas Settlement have received some kind
of professional establishment assistance.   In addition, the
thirty-one shops of the Kareas Settlement market were allocated to refugees and, with a few exceptions, have become
flourishing businesses.

As 263 families of the 719 came from camps, and
the remainder from slum areas or sub-standard dwellings,
there is a high percentage of chronic illness, especially
arthritis, rheumatism, and heart disease.   However, serious mental illness accounts for only 2.5 percent of the
chronic disease; alcoholics and drug addicts number only a
very few cases.

In view of the health conditions of the population and

due to the fact that only a few have social security, the HC
has contributed toward their medical care by allocating a
yearly amount of $1,000 for medical care, drugs, etc. for
needy refugees.   No other kind of material assistance is
provided by the UNHCR for the refugees settled in Kareas.

Twenty-five blocks of family apartments and sixty-one
flatlets for old refugees now comprise the Kareas Housing
Settlement.   An asphalt road gives access to the community,
internal roads lead along the various blocks of apartments,
and a regular bus line has been established to serve the
2,000 refugees who have their homes there, as well as the
1,500 neighboring residents of the Kareas area.

SOURCE: UNHCR Branch Office in Greece, 27 Dec. 1969.

ANNEX 20. 7

INSTITUTIONAL RESETTLEMENT OF AGED AND SICK REFUGEES UNDER UNHCR PROGRAMS AND SPONSORED SCHEMES FROM 1952 TO JUNE 1963

Country	Number of places made available to refugees
Europe	
Belgium	709
Denmark	93
France	467
Germany, Fed. Rep. of	11
Ireland	44
Italy	40
Netherlands	100
Norway	119
Portugal	9
Sweden	344
Switzerland	442
UK	99
Overseas	
Australia	204
New Zealand	34
Total	2, 715

SOURCE: Ex. Com. (X), A/AC. 96/205, 6 Aug. 1963, Annex II: 10

Chapter 21

UNHCR IN EUROPE: THE SECOND DECADE

Dr. Auguste Lindt's Contribution

Dr. Lindt assumed his post as HC at the height of the
Hungarian crisis and at the moment when the Office was being approached for assistance to the Algerian refugees in
Tunisia. He found governments and the public eager to act.
During his service he governed his actions by his view of
"how best to help the refugees, regardless of how and why
they have become refugees. " By his initiative the GA expanded the activities of the UNHCR by a series of resolutions.
The most important of these recognized the continuing nature
of the refugee problem and authorized him to develop his
good-offices function and to establish an emergency fund to
enable him to deal with the new refugees in and outside of
Europe. [1]

Dr. Lindt combined humanitarianism with realism and
great drive, not sparing himself or those with whom he
worked. He contributed greatly to the concept and success
of WRY and gave a new and successful impetus to the immense work of camp clearance in Europe. He was skillful
in convincing governments and voluntary agencies in regard
to fund raising. He also started the indemnification program
in Germany. He travelled widely and tirelessly, especially
to the non-European countries of immigration to urge liberalization of their immigration criteria.

Dr. Lindt took pains to reconcile hostile points of
view. Under his leadership the Office played a positive role
in the voluntary repatriation of refugees; for example, the
HC himself visited Austria and Hungary, and through his efforts a large number of unaccompanied children were returned to their parents in Hungary. [2]

Dr. Lindt was convinced that the refugee problem was
soluble if the will to solve it and the money needed were

504

forthcoming. "Coordination is quite an easy task, " he maintained, "when it takes place in a concrete field, and when
all organizations have one common objective. " Thus he improved the performance of his Office by systematic planning,
by training his co-workers, and by drawing on specialized
knowledge in the economic and social fields. He was always
generous in his acknowledgment of individual service for the
common cause. Neither did he shy away from acting on his
own initiative, often with great courage, particularly in his
decision to participate in the delicate relief action for the
Algerian refugees in Morocco and Tunisia beginning in May
1959. The GA, by its Res. 1389(XIV) of 20 November 1959,
retrospectively noted this work "with appreciation" and recommended that he continue "his efforts ... pending their
return to their home. " During his period in office, the
machinery was established by which the UNREF Program
would be superseded by a more sophisticated and flexible approach to continuing needs for major assistance.

WRY ended in June 1960. In a speech to ECOSOC on
25 July 1960, Dr. Lindt noted the "stimulating effect" that
WRY had had in widening the role of the UNHCR. He
pointed out that the GA, in passing the WRY resolution, had
defined a refugee "purely from the social point of view without going into any legal definition, " and he went on to say
that "the GA first gave a demonstration of this tendency
when it passed" its good offices resolutions (1167 and 1388),
the latter of which authorized the HC "to lend his good offices for the transmission of contributions to benefit refugee
groups not within the competence of the UN. " "This tendency, " he said, "has strengthened the coordinating role of the
Office ... and the interest of the Office has been widened. "
Thus, he concluded, "in this development may be seen ... a
recognition of the refugee question as a whole as a social
and economic problem which is, on a purely non-political
basis, of international concern. "3

The GA itself reaffirmed the need to maintain the
impact of WRY in planning for further permanent solutions.
In its final Res. on WRY (1502[XV] of 5 December 1960) the
GA noted "with gratification the remarkable success of WRY
in many parts of the world, not only financially but also in
promoting solutions of problems to a large number, particularly those who are handicapped. " Stating that "WRY has
focused the attention of world opinion on the problems of
refugees, " it voiced the belief "that the enthusiasm and interest aroused by WRY, if maintained, [would] make a vital

contribution. " The GA also expressed "the hope that all
people everywhere will take into consideration the problems
of refugees and the need for sustained and increased efforts
for their ultimate solution" (71 votes for, none against, 10
abstentions).

In a press conference held at the Palais des Nations
at Geneva on 14 June 1960, the HC, however, cautioned
against "unfounded optimism. " While stressing the "very
important success" of WRY, he pointed out that "very large
amounts of money" were still needed "to meet the present
target, and to achieve ... the solving of the residual refugee problem in Europe. "[4] He reminded the public that the
Camp Clearance Program had solved only part of the refugee
problem in Europe. The Major Aid Programs were still
concerned with the old refugees who were within his mandate
before 31 December 1960. He emphasized that his current
program also included projects for out-of-camp refugees,
for new refugees in Greece, and for refugees in the Middle
and Far East, and that in addition to the normal program,
there was also the operation in North Africa on behalf of the
Algerian refugees in Tunisia and Morocco.

Introducing his last Annual Report to the GA, Dr.
Lindt declared "my Office must be flexible and elastic, " it
must be "ready to act where its intervention is needed, in
the consciousness of its global mandate which is unlimited
geographically and knows no preference for race or creed. "
It is essential, he emphasized, "to disentangle and isolate"
the refugee question "from the tensions and hazards of a
political nature. "[5]

Dr. Lindt had given dynamic and forceful leadership.
He had established a close relationship with and among all
his partners: the Ex. Com.; the governments of countries
of origin, asylum, and resettlement; the CoE, ICEM and
USRP; and above all, with the voluntary agencies. One of
his great strengths was his ability to inspire their confidence
and to kindle their full support. He spurred the social conscience of the world and moved his partners to act. International solidarity, during his term of office, achieved new
meaning.

The Swiss Federal Council announced on 13 July 1960
that Dr. Lindt had been nominated as Switzerland's Ambassador to the US. When the HC attended the Ex. Com. for
the last time on 11 October 1960, the chairman and all the

delegates in turn paid tribute to his work.   They spoke of
"his inspiration, patience, tact, perseverence, diplomatic
qualities, and wholehearted devotion to his task." Referring
to his "warm and human approach" they stressed that he had
earned the gratitude of "the rejects of the world who,
through his efforts, were now again respected members of
new communities."[6]

     Subsequently the President of the GA declared that
Dr. Lindt could take "proper pride" in two major achievements: his efforts "to gain acceptance by more governments
of the principles governing asylum and the protection of the
legal status of refugees," and his "efforts to secure a greater world consciousness of the tragic material plight still suffered by many refugees," efforts which have resulted in a
"remarkable increase in aid for these victims of oppression
and political strife, and in substantial progress toward permanent solutions which we have all witnessed." On 5 December 1960 the GA expressed "its thanks to Dr. Lindt and its
admiration for the brilliant and important work he has performed" (GA Res. 1501[XV], adopted by acclamation).

     When the GA approved Dr. Lindt's last annual report
in November 1960,[7] expressed in Res. 1499 (66 votes for,
none against, 10 abstentions) it referred once again to the
two resolutions of good offices (Res. 1167[XII] and Res.
1388[XIV]) and to its wish that the HC should, in case of
need, assist refugees other than those normally within his
mandate.   Thus, as his successor was able to point out,
without in any way abandoning what had been the essence of
the HC's mission, "the UN member states implicitly reaffirmed the universal and essentially dynamic as well as exclusively humanitarian and social nature of the mission of
the Office."[8]

The Office Under High Commissioner Dr. Felix Schnyder,
February 1961-December 1965

     By acclamation on 5 December 1960, the GA elected
Dr. Felix Schnyder, a Swiss citizen, as the new HC for the
period from 1 February 1961 to 31 December 1963.   He,
like his predecessor, was well known to the UN delegates
through his activity as Swiss observer to the UN and as
chairman of the UNICEF Executive Board.   His term was
subsequently extended by acclamation, to 31 December 1965.
At the same session the GA, considering its "valuable work,"

extended the mandate of the Office for another five years to
21 December 1968 by a vote of 99-0-1 (Res. 1783[XVII] of
7 Dec. 1962).

During Dr. Schnyder's period of service the UNHCR
passed through a most significant phase of its existence, one
in which the Office dramatically shifted its primary attention
away from Europe and Hong Kong, where it had focused its
concern and developed its expertise for the previous ten
years, to respond to the urgent and formidable needs of new
refugee groups elsewhere in the world, especially in Africa
south of the Sahara, where new policies and procedures had
to be developed. This expansion in the scope of the work of
the Office, as Dr. Schnyder pointed out in his first statement, was linked to the addition to the UN family of many
new states and "the ever-growing importance of the [ECOSOC]
Council's work on economic and social problems."[9] It was
Dr. Schnyder's major contribution to his Office that he carried through this drastic re-orientation and undertook the
search for permanent solutions to these new refugee problems without ever losing sight of the continuing needs of the
older refugee groups within his mandate.

As the number of still unsettled "old" European refugees declined, their problems had grown more intractable
and their needs greater. A major difficulty, as we have
seen, was to find settlement opportunities for the physically
and socially handicapped. If UNHCR programs for these
refugees were to be phased out it could only be done by
separately assessing and attending to the needs of each individual refugee. To achieve the speedy liquidation of residual problems--an aim of both Dr. Lindt and Dr. Schnyder--
much time and thought had to be given to even more imaginative and individually tailored programs, and additional efforts made to carry through the intricate negotiations with
governments and voluntary agencies for the transfer of the
remaining responsibilities to national bodies.

In the detailed report which Dr. Schnyder prepared
for 1962, he pointed out that the number of non-settled refugees had diminished from 270,000 on 1 January 1955 to
45,000 by 1 January 1963, despite the fact that there had
been an intervening influx of 310,000 refugees. Moreover,
as a result of a priority camp clearance scheme, there
were only 4,100 refugees still in camps.[10] This improvement in conditions was in part due to the favorable economic
conditions prevailing in the refugees' countries of residence

which had contributed, particularly in France and Germany, to the spontaneous integration of a considerable proportion of them. At the same time, the HC's Program had provided both the stimulant and a large cash contribution toward approximately one-quarter of the net decrease.

The residue of refugees would, however, be more difficult to settle, not only because of their own handicaps but also because there were unfavorable economic or demographic situations in some other states, their social legislation was still in a developing state, and the cost of living was steadily increasing. Moreover, there was a continuing stream of refugees from Eastern Europe of approximately 10,000 a year, and a new influx of refugees from Cuba into Spain.

Beyond Europe was the problem of European and Chinese refugees in the Far East, and the huge assistance program for Algerian refugees in Morocco and Tunisia which had begun by Dr. Lindt. The Office had also, since 1961, received a large number of requests for assistance from African governments, in particular, Togo, Congo-Kinshasa (Zaïre), and Tanzania in 1961, and Uganda and Burundi in 1962.

Confronted with this lengthening list of new situations in geographic areas where the Office had no previous experience, Dr. Schnyder responded by reordering his geographic priorities so as to make the best use of his very limited resources, and by making adjustments in his administration. Men who had spent years working with refugee problems in Europe found themselves opening up new BOs in tropical Africa and tackling very different situations on a trial and error basis. The Emergency Fund, authorized in 1958 by the GA as part of the HC's Program, came into its own that year as Dr. Schnyder drew upon it heavily for the first time to meet the most pressing needs of the new refugees. To achieve permanent solutions to these new problems the HC had stressed the development of new approaches, the establishment of new partnerships with non-governmental agencies experienced in these areas, and the strengthening of coordination with those new governments which found themselves directly faced with refugee problems in addition to all the other problems of independence.

In the ten years since the Statute and the Convention were drafted, the nature of refugee causes had changed, and

the need for the HC to act without reference to the political
situations which produced refugees was now far greater. International action on behalf of these new refugees was not
possible unless the HC could act so as not to offend the
countries of origin. In addition, the needs of the new refugees were such that material assistance had a higher priority than international protection. With these factors in mind
Dr. Schnyder built on the foundation which his predecessor
had laid for providing material assistance for refugees without reference to his mandate. The good offices function,
begun as a device for channelling aid to "extreme cases,"
was developed by Dr. Schnyder into a panoplied basis for
UNHCR action anywhere in the world through a series of
carefully prepared and executed diplomatic moves which won
the agreement of the GA membership to the general Good
Offices Res. 1673[XVI]. With the passage of this resolution
Dr. Schnyder had a basis for action uniquely adapted to the
new reality he faced: his humanitarian aims and responsibilities had been freed from any involvement with the political scene. The success of this approach was attested to by
the willingness of countries of origin as well as of asylum to
accept the HC's assistance.

What was now needed was a major effort both to
eliminate the inheritance of WWII, the old refugees, and to
launch a Current Program to meet current needs. Thus
1963 became a year of transition in which the GA approved
two significant programs for these purposes: the Major Aid
Program, and the Current Program for Complementary Assistance (subsequently the term "major aid programs" was
used with reference to international assistance programs in
Europe from 1955 onward).

Major Aid and Current Complementary Assistance Programs

The Major Aid Programs produced a wealth of lasting
accomplishments by 31 December 1965. Since 1955, 2,442
programs had been implemented at a cost of over $46,885,150
with additional supporting contributions of $59,300,000. The
cumulative figure of firmly settled cases totalled 96,522 refugees, and nearly 10,000 others were in the course of settlement, leaving a case-load of 14,700 identified refugees
not yet settled. By mid-1965 there were fewer than a
thousand still in camps. By 1966 camps had not only physically disappeared but, what was more important, the notion
of a camp as a dead end, a place of prolonged misery and

degradation, had been completely superseded by the concept of its use as a transit center where newly arrived refugees stayed while awaiting a solution, by either migration or local settlement.

Among lasting assets for the refugees which the Major Aid Programs produced were: over 3,200 prepaid places in homes and institutions for the aged which, when vacated, could be reoccupied by needy beneficiaries for as long as the need existed; nearly 10,000 housing units similarly available to new refugee tenants upon departure of previous beneficiaries; similar facilities for the rehabilitation of handicapped refugees (homes for alcoholics, sheltered workshops, a Protected Community in Capua, etc.); a loan fund of approximately $12,650,000 earning an average of some $320,000 a year. [11]

The Current Program for Complementary Assistance with a target of $1.4 million had a two-fold purpose. In the first place, it sought to insure that the Western European countries of first asylum would not be left, as they feared, without assistance in coping with the continuing stream of refugees coming from Eastern Europe. In the second place, it was directed to enabling the UNHCR to tackle new refugee problems wherever they arose, particularly in Africa. It was envisaged as "an essential means of action to insure the overall effectiveness of UNHCR's continuing role." In particular, the Ex. Com. directed the UNHCR to "make its services available so that new and current refugee problems would be met as they arose and that renewed, painful and resistant accumulation of refugee problems would be avoided."[12]

From that time on, the HC has each year presented a UNHCR Annual Assistance Program based on current refugee situations and needs. These annual programs now supplement, as necessary and warranted, the assistance rendered to refugees by host and other governments, local authorities, other members of the UN family, inter-governmental organizations (such as ICEM), and voluntary agencies. [13]

The 1967 Protocol to the 1951 Convention

Many of the new refugees did not come within the scope of benefits conferred by the 1951 Convention because they were not the result of events occurring before 1 January 1951.

The GA, on the HC's proposal and the recommendations of the conference of legal experts, accepted the Protocol Relating to the Status of Refugees eliminating the time provision of the Convention. The effect of the Protocol was to make the Convention a truly universal Magna Carta for refugees in all places and at all times.

The UNHCR as a Catalyst to International Action

Dr. Schnyder was well aware of the marginal character of his Office's actions, arising from the limitations of its mandate and from its limited resources. He viewed the role of his Office as being a critical one within the complex of national and international, public and private activities on behalf of refugees. "All action of the Office," he said, "is no more than the 'drop of oil' needed to start and maintain in operation machinery on a scale infinitely larger than that of our own action. In that whole operation the essential role of the High Commissioner ... is still primarily to provide a stimulus and to act as an intermediary of good will."14 On another occasion Dr. Schnyder used the chemical term "catalyst" in a way which perhaps best sums up how he personally viewed his job as HC:

> The function of the High Commissioner's Office ... is accordingly rather that of a catalyst capable, by reasons of its experience, of mobilizing or of making optimum use of the available resources by enlisting the cooperation of all the public or private organizations which can play a useful part in helping to solve the problems involved. There is evidence to show that joint and coordinated action by the High Commissioner's Office and the technical assistance services and other UN bodies or specialized agencies can, in many cases, be most useful and effective. By inviting this form of co-operation, by promoting or coordinating efforts, while not actually itself undertaking any operational scheme, the UNHCR will best be able ... to fulfill its obligations with respect to the new problems which arise almost daily. I think that the Office will also have to remind the governments concerned, at every opportunity, of their fundamental

responsibility as regards the welfare of the refugees on their territory and as regards the quest
for solutions adequate for the problems posed by
the conditions under which they live. [15]

In his last appearance before the GA, Dr. Schnyder
saw three resolutions favorable to the activities of the Office
approved unanimously. One resolution noted the difficulties
being encountered by the HC in obtaining funds to finance his
programs, and urged increased support from governments.
Another dealt with assistance to refugees in Africa and
stressed the need "to provide the means essential to uninterrupted continuation" of UNHCR's aid to refugees on that
continent. Finally the GA approved a resolution expressing
its sincere appreciation to Dr. Schnyder for his work as HC
(GA[XX], Res. 2039, 2040 and 2041 of 7 Dec. 1965). At
its Fifteenth Session the members of the Ex. Com. tele-
graphed Dr. Schnyder a tribute to his "distinguished leadership and outstanding competence" in the work of international
assistance for refugees, and expressed its "deep gratitude"
to him for his close cooperation. [16]

The Election of Prince Sadruddin Aga Khan

On 5 December 1965 the GA, on the recommendation
of the Secretary-General, elected by acclamation Prince Sadruddin Aga Khan (Iran) as HC for the period from 1 January
1966 to 31 December 1968. Prince Sadruddin, son of the
late Aga Khan, was well known to the UN family. In February 1962, Dr. Schnyder had appointed him Deputy HC, a
post vacant since the resignation of Mr. James Read in September 1960. He had previously served UNESCO in an
honorary capacity and had collaborated in a project relating
to Afro-Asian countries. Prince Sadruddin's cultural and
religious links with Islam had provided distinctive insight
and understanding for his visits to Iran, Burma, Thailand,
Malaya, Indonesia, the Philippines, Japan, Vietnam, Ceylon,
Kuwait, Bahrain, and Qatar as Chargé de Mission for the
UNHCR and during the WRY. As Special Advisor to the HC,
he had assisted at the Fifteenth and Sixteenth Sessions of the
GA (1960 and 1961) and at the HC's request had undertaken
a mission in order to discuss Angolan refugees with the Government of the Congo. He had taken a significant role regarding the repatriation of Algerian refugees in Morocco and
Tunisia and undertaken various missions to East, Central,
and West Africa and to Latin American and Western European

countries. He was well known to the members of the Ex. Com., to whom he had given a report on the development of refugee situations in a number of countries (Togo, Congo, Tanganyika, Uganda, and Burundi in Africa, and Macao in Asia), and a final report on assistance to Algerian refugees at the Eighth Session in October 1962.[17] He provided further insight into the refugee situation in Africa at the Tenth Session, October 1963, after his return from an intensive trip to nine African countries (Tanganyika, Uganda, Burundi, Ruanda, the Kivu Province of the Congo, Nigeria, Dahomey, Togo, and Ghana).[18] The purpose of this latter trip had been to assess progress and to promote understanding in Africa for the UNHCR's work. In October 1965 he attended the OAU Conference of Ministers in Accra as an observer.

The delegates of the Assembly greeted the new HC with great confidence and enthusiasm because, as the US delegate remarked, "of his valuable experience, his understanding of the problems involved and his compassionate concern for refugees throughout the world." The delegate from Tanzania noted that his work for refugees had "been eminently successful."[19]

On 11 December 1967 the GA voted to continue the Office for another five years from 1 January 1969 (Res. 2294[XXII], 96 votes for, 11 against, no abstentions) and by acclamation on 15 November 1968, reelected Prince Sadruddin Aga Khan to a five-year term of office from 1 January 1969.

As the GA had repeatedly stated, the settlement of refugees was the primary responsibility of the countries of asylum. The HC's function was to give supplementary assistance and to promote and coordinate the support of the international community. Prince Sadruddin continued negotiations with governments and voluntary agencies to phase out the HC's activities and assistance and to streamline his operations in Europe. The Office handed over many responsibilities to governments and private organizations in the countries concerned. While there were some delays in the completing of housing projects, particularly in Greece, by 1969 the task of material assistance to the old refugees in Europe had largely come to a successful conclusion.

At the same time, the flow of new refugees from Eastern Europe continued at the same rate as before, that is, approximately 10,000 a year. Moreover, the accumulation of Cuban refugees in Spain through the sixties, and

Czech refugees moving into adjacent countries following the
Soviet occupation in the late summer of 1968, continued to
make international action necessary. The continuing need
for such action was asserted again in 1970. The delegates
of the Ex. Com. agreed that, while the European refugee
problem had in general been solved, the UNHCR had ''to
maintain an effective presence in order to deal with the continuing flow of refugees, which might show a gradual or sudden increase, depending on political developments.''[20]

The Cuban Refugees in Spain

In October 1961 the Government of Spain asked the
HC for help in caring for the more than 5,000 refugees who
had arrived from Cuba. In cooperation with the Spanish authorities Dr. Schnyder had prepared a coordinated program
which enabled refugees either to settle in Spain or to emigrate as they wished and as opportunities were offered.
Two voluntary organizations working jointly with the government were providing temporary relief for these refugees but
lacked funds to meet the needs. The HC put $5,000, re-
ceived from OXFAM, at the disposal of one organization in
order to finance the most urgent needs for about two
months.[21]

The influx of Cuban refugees into Spain continued and
increased in the succeeding years. In 1964 there were an
estimated 10,000 to 15,000 Cubans in Spain of whom about
15 percent wanted to remain in Spain; most of the remainder
wished to go to the US. The UNHCR was called upon to
participate in the work of assistance. The Office provided
part of the help by allocating funds for counselling; for the
cost of amenities for the needy and aged; for assistance to
some to establish themselves in trades and professions; and
for temporary shelter for the refugees arriving in Spain.
Governmental and voluntary agencies, including the Anxilio
Social and Cantas Espanila, the Government Servicio Social
al Refugiado, and municipal welfare services took care of
the work for the refugees in Spain.[22]

The HC reported that in 1966 the flow of Cubans into
Spain still continued (averaging 300 to 450 monthly) and that
some 67,000 Cubans whose air travel from Cuba to Spain
had been financed by relatives, were waiting to emigrate to
the US eventually. Most succeeded in obtaining visas for the
US under the former non-quota immigration procedure.

However, with the enforcement, beginning on 1 July 1968, of a ceiling of 120,000 visas for all immigrants from the Western Hemisphere,[23] refugees from the Caribbean area had to compete with other applicants in the Western Hemisphere. These new provisions resulted in a sharp decrease in the issuance of US visas to the refugees in Spain, although certain ameliorative measures by the US Government resulted in a subsequent slight increase. However, not more than about 350 visas per month could be counted on.[24]

As a result of the disparity between the numbers of refugees arriving in Spain and the willingness of other countries to accept them, the backlog continued to increase and by the end of 1970 more than 12,000 persons were awaiting an opportunity to emigrate. The Spanish Government has had to increase assistance for food, medical care, inland transportation, etc. Local and international voluntary agencies have also intensified their activities and financial participation. The UNHCR has provided assistance toward local settlement, counselling and emergency assistance. With the help of the Cuban Welfare Society in Spain, the Spanish Migration Commission, and the IRC in cooperation with ICEM, efforts for resettlement have progressed.

In order to diversify the emigration pattern, ICEM set up an Information Service in Madrid in April 1968 to counsel and register refugees for other destinations, mainly Australia and Latin America. Of the some 2,300 refugees who received information on various resettlement possibilities on their arrival in Spain, 254 indicated an interest in other countries, 78 were registered for Australia and 176 for Latin American countries.[25]

Czech Refugees

The occupation of Czechoslovakia by the Soviet Union and four other Warsaw Pact countries in the late summer of 1968 created major new problems in that country.[26] Unlike the Hungarian crisis of 1956, however, the immediate result was not a movement of refugees seeking asylum in adjacent countries. At the time of the Czech occupation some 80,000 Czechoslovak nationals were abroad--most of them in Austria, Yugoslavia, Germany, Italy, France, the UK, and the US. These included tourists, students, and persons on official missions. Few of these chose at once to preclude their chances of returning to Czechoslovakia. The majority preferred to "wait and see" before deciding on a course of action. As time passed, thousands returned to their homes; but many within Czechoslovakia took advantage of still open borders to go abroad as ordinary travelers or as potential exiles. The majority of those who were in other countries, or who came out of Czechoslovakia after the beginning of the occupation, applied for prolongation of visas but not for refugee status.

In September 1968 the Czechoslovak Government urged its citizens abroad to return, promising that they were in no danger as a result of the recent political events. Despite this appeal, increasing numbers became refugees. In the spring of 1969 the number of registrations for emigration increased decisively. On 27 May 1969 the Czechoslovak Government announced an amnesty for all citizens who had left the country illegally after 9 May or whose permit to stay outside the country had expired, if they would return or regularize their status at Czechoslovak embassies before 15 September 1969. In October 1969 border exit points were controlled through new government regulations. By that time, according to official figures available to the US Department of State, there were some 42,000 Czechoslovak refugees: 12,500 in Austria, 1,500 in Italy, 12,000 in West Germany, 11,000 in Switzerland, and 5,000 in other Western European countries. [27]

Repercussions from the Czechoslovakian occupation in other Eastern European countries, resulted in an increasing number of persons seeking refugee status in the adjacent countries of asylum. The refugee flow brought serious problems to the host countries, principally Austria, Germany and Italy. All countries in Europe provided special emergency measures to facilitate housing, feeding, and regularization of visas. Special reception camps and centers were opened by governments and voluntary agencies. At the same time the UK and other Western European countries (in particular Sweden and Switzerland) and Canada, Australia, the Republic of South Africa and Iran offered resettlement opportunities. Financial support to refugees came through national and international organizations (AJDC, Tolstoy Foundation, ICMC, IRS, Polish-American Immigration and Relocation Committee, United HIAS, WCC and the American Fund for Czechoslovak Refugees, local Red Cross Societies, the asylum countries, ICEM, USRF (formerly USEP), and the UNHCR.

This group of refugees differed from the two previous groups who had left Czechoslovakia (those who fled from Hitler in 1939 and those who left after the Communist seizure in 1948). The new group was composed of much younger people--students, teachers, scientists, journalists, artists, and doctors. Many of them spoke English, French, and German. They were in possession of valid passports, and often had financial means.

Austria appealed for aid to the UNHCR. At the Nineteenth Session of the Ex. Com., October 1968, members of the Committee pointed out that the influx represented an additional burden, particularly in Austria. They stressed that this situation called for the increased attention of the HC. The HC had from the beginning offered assistance to those Czechoslovaks who sought refugee status, including assistance towards resettlement in countries other than that of first asylum, and emergency as well as integration assistance in host countries. Owing to the sympathetic and efficient handling by both the countries of first asylum and the resettlement countries and to concerted international assistance, this movement did not develop into a major refugee problem.

The UNHCR in Europe Today

The transfer of responsibility to governments of countries of residence and national private organizations had not eliminated all responsibilities of the UNHCR for international protection. [28] Most of the 650,000 refugees reported to be the HC's concern in Europe in September 1971 continued to require protection but were no longer in need of material assistance. On the whole, however, post-war refugees in Europe enjoy social and economic rights in their country of residence comparable to those of nationals.

UNHCR activities in Europe now are concerned primarily with assistance toward local settlement, the promotion of resettlement elsewhere, and legal assistance for individual refugees and with continuing appeals to governments and voluntary agencies for support for new UNHCR programs in Asia, Africa, and the Middle East. A new concern, which will be discussed in Part VIII, is the appearance in Europe of individual refugees from Africa.

Notes

1. GA Res. 1166 and 1167 (XII), 26 Nov. 1957; Res. 1388 (XIV), Nov. 1959; Res. 1499 (XV), 5 Dec. 1960.

2. James Read, op. cit.: 22.

3. Supp. to UNHCR Ref. Serv, No. 18, July 1960.

4. Ibid.; see also "HC Looks to Liquidation of Residual Refugee Problem in Europe," in UN Review, Sept. 1960.

5. HC's Statement to GA (XV), Third Com.

6. Ibid.

7. GA (XV), Off. Rec., Supp. 11, A/4378/Ref. 1, 1960.

8. Dr. Schnyder's statement to Ex. Com. (V) (his first contact with the Ex. Com.), May 1961, UN GA (XVI), Off. Rec., Supp. 11, A/4771/Rev. 1: 30.

9. Statement by the HC in presenting his Ann. Rep. to ECOSOC (XXXIII), 24 July 1961, E/3506/Add. 1: 1.

10. UNHCR Reports, No. 24, May-June 1963.

11. Ex. Com. (XV), A/AC.96/321, 31 Mar. 1966: 2.

12. UN, GA (XIX), A/AC.96/229, 15 Apr. 1964: 1.

13. GA (XIX), Off. Rec., Supp. No. 11A, A/5811/Rev. 1/ Add. 1: 5 and A/AC.96/Inf. and A/AC.96/226. Having considered the position of countries of asylum in Europe, the Ex. Com. "took note of the fact that the influx in Europe continues to constitute a burden for some of the countries of first asylum [and] recommends a continuous generous admission policy on the part of immigration countries in Europe and overseas, and to the extent possible, the integration of refugees wishing and able to build up a new life in their country of asylum."

14. Ex. Com. (XIII), A/AC.96/291, App. III, 25 May 1965: 6.

15.   Ex. Com. (VI) A/AC.96/146, Annex, Nov. 1961: 11.

16.   A/AC.96/334: 2.

17.   GA (XVII) Off. Rec., Supp. 11, A/5211/Rev. 1: 33;
      and a final report, A/AC.96/179: 33.

18.   GA (XVIII), Off. Rec., Supp. 11, A/5511/Rev. 1/Add.
      1: 15.

19.   For comments of other delegates, see UN, GA (XX),
      Plenary Meetings, 3 Dec. 1965.

20.   Mr. Sobotka, US Delegate, Ex. Com. (XXI), A/AC.96
      SR. 191, 1971.

21.   Ex. Com. (VI), A/AC.96/146, 14 Nov. 1961: 10.

22.   UNHCR, GA (XX), 1965, Off. Rec., Supp. 11, A/
      6011/Rev. 1: 13 and 12.

23.   US, PL 89-236, Immigration and Nationality Act.   Dec.
      1965.

24.   The Attorney General has exercised his parole author-
      ity under section 212(d)(5) of the US Immigration
      and Nationality Act to parole certain classes of
      Cuban refugees from third countries into the US.

25.   Ex. Com. (XX), 1969, A/AC.96/417: 11.

26.   UN, GA (XXIII), Off. Rec., Supp. No. 11 A A/7211/
      Add. 1.

27.   91st Cong., 1st Sess., Subcom. of the Senate Judiciary
      Com., US Assistance to Refugees throughout the
      World, 3 Nov. 1969: 76.

Chapter 22

THE VOLUNTARY (NON-GOVERNMENTAL)
AGENCIES IN EUROPE

The UNHCR, a humanitarian and non-operational
agency, acts principally in stimulating, planning, and coordinating programs and in administering funds solicited from
governments and other sources. The day-to-day implementation of projects is carried on mainly by a number of international and national voluntary and other non-governmental
agencies. These agencies maintain a direct and human link
with the refugee through a network of field missions operating both in countries of first asylum and in those of permanent settlement. In the words of Jacques Vernant: "Situated at the heart of the matter, because of their contact
with the bitter realities of a refugee's existence, the voluntary agencies know the needs of the refugees and how to
interpret these to governmental and international organizations."[1] Brian Neldner, Director of the LWF/TCRS defines
the unique function of the voluntary agencies in this way:

> The voluntary agencies have a specific and dis-
> tinctive contribution to make to refugee assistance,
> such as the humanising quality of their assistance;
> greater flexibility to deal with individuals, and
> with groups of refugees; speedy reaction to new
> situations, be they large or small; diversity of
> competence which can be found in the range of the
> family of voluntary agencies; and a more person-
> alised approach, especially in dealing with refu-
> gees as people and individuals.[2]

The voluntary agencies thus play an integral and essential
role in every stage of the work for refugees, from the moment of their arrival in a country of first asylum until they
are firmly established either within it or in a new country
(see Chapter 5).

The voluntary agencies played a very useful part in

521

the preparation and implementation of the UNREF program. Many of the projects in the program were initiated by them or established in consultation with them, and were implemented by their field staffs. The HC reported that in 1956, seventy-three agencies participated in carrying out projects of the UNREF Program. [3] By 1957 a realistic understanding of the social aspects of refugee problems had come about, and the greater emphasis on material aid which occurred at that time enhanced the role of the voluntary agencies and multiplied their already numerous tasks. Subsequent programs of the UNHCR have been formulated in such a way as to aid the voluntary agencies wherever possible in carrying out the resettlement of refugees.

WRY gave great impetus to the work of these agencies, as well as to the activities of the UNHCR itself, through the funds and publicity for their work which resulted from this worldwide effort. Since that time, the voluntary agencies have been able to intensify their already considerable efforts both in working jointly with the UNHCR in situations which fall within his mandate and in carrying on necessary tasks which do not fall within the competence of the UNHCR. [4]

The international and the national agencies which cooperate in the implementation of the programs of the UNHCR are autonomous bodies with specific aims and purposes. Most of them had been working on behalf of refugees long before the Office came into existence. To work out the most constructive means of cooperation between the UNHCR and the voluntary agencies has required a high degree of understanding and constant liaison. The administrative measures which have been evolved have, on the whole, been notably successful both in maintaining harmonious relations between the UNHCR and the voluntary agencies, and also in insuring that programs are carried out in accordance with the wishes of the countries of residence and of the donor countries that have contributed to the programs.

As we have seen, there were no accurate surveys of the refugee population in Europe when the UNHCR came into existence, either in regard to numbers or to the type of assistance which was required. This information was acquired under a Ford Foundation grant. It revealed the need for a great deal more assistance for large numbers of persons living both in and outside of the camps. With this information, and after consultation between the governments of the refugees

countries of residence, the voluntary agencies, and the
UNHCR, a series of measures were agreed upon to help the
refugees either to establish themselves in their country of
residence or to emigrate to other countries. These programs were approved by the UNREF Ex. Com. and later
came under the Ex. Com. of the HC's Program. While the
overall planning and coordination was done by the Office,
their implementation was largely the work of the voluntary
agencies.

At the inception of the UNREF Program the voluntary
agencies were concerned in the countries of first asylum
mainly with the provision of clothing, shelter, medical aid,
and cultural and spiritual assistance in rather broad and
general terms, and in the countries of resettlement with reception and placement services. Various international agencies had their own field offices throughout Europe and already had considerable staffs employed in these tasks. By
and large, these staff members were not trained social
workers but had acquired much experience and knowledge in
dealing with refugee problems. Various agencies employed
counsellors to work in specific refugee camps and areas,
particularly in Austria, West Germany, and Italy. These
counsellors compiled dossiers on individual refugees and
proposed the solution which would be most helpful to each
refugee family. The counsellors were under the direct
supervision of whichever voluntary agency employed them,
but the UNHCR made funds available for their salaries, per
diem, and travel in relation to the estimated size of the
case load of the particular agency as a means of strengthening these staffs. In general, also, assistance was given in
the fields of housing, education, supplementary medical aid,
and rehabilitation.

Each of these projects was outlined in a specific
agreement entered into jointly by the voluntary agency and
the HC which set forth the purpose of the project, its scope
in relation to the financial assistance to be provided, the
time period of the undertaking, and the agency's reporting
and accounting obligations. These agreements were reached
only after long and detailed negotiations, and constant liaison
was required thereafter to maintain satisfactory working relations. In some countries special committees were established composed of the representatives of the agencies working on the HC's Program and representatives of the UNHCR.
These committees met frequently to insure the smooth implementation of the programs being carried on and to plan

future programs.   Frequent meetings were also held by the
UNHCR with the ICVA, as well as with the headquarters offices of both international and national agencies.   A number
of voluntary agencies are represented as observers at the
meetings of the UNHCR Ex. Com.

The evolution of the concept of voluntary action, as
seen in the changing nature of the UNHCR's material assistance programs, is reflected in the voluntary agencies
themselves.   Voluntary action, while never free of the necessity for coping with emergency relief, has of necessity
broadened its scope.   The long partnership of UNHCR and
the voluntary agencies has hastened the evolution of organizational machinery and of operational patterns through which
the voluntary agencies have met the demands imposed by
this new concept of philanthropy.   In describing the period
dealing with residual problems in Europe with which the
UNHCR and the voluntary agencies were faced in 1951, Dr.
Schnyder said, "It was a question of everyone putting his
shoulder to the wheel and bringing whatever contribution he
could to the solution of this onerous problem."[5]

I: International Non-Governmental Agencies

In the following sections the major international organizations which have been partners of the UNHCR are described in some detail.   Other international organizations,
which have performed equally useful services, are not discussed here, as this account is intended to be representative
rather than exhaustive.   Similarly, the activities and programs conducted by many of these agencies in European
countries have been described in preceding chapters, and
those in the non-European areas are discussed elsewhere,
primarily in Parts VI-VIII.

Several of the international voluntary agencies that
have participated in the programs for refugees have been in
existence since WWI, although most were founded after
WWII.   A number of these international agencies have counterpart national organizations in several countries.   It was
logical and appropriate to combine the experience and material resources of these agencies with inter-governmental
programs on behalf of refugees, but the process of properly
coordinating these efforts was a complex one.   For example,
many international voluntary agencies had been established
through the concern of specific religious denominations in

countries outside of Europe, their main object being to bring
assistance to persons affiliated with their own religious de-
nomination.   As the pattern of organization and their approaches to the problem of bringing material assistance to
refugees differed among agencies, the guidance and coordination provided by the HC proved essential to the overall success of these efforts.

The International Council on Voluntary Agencies

A step of major importance taken by some seventy
voluntary agencies to gear themselves to the new tasks
brought to light by WRY was the creation, in March 1962,
of the ICVA.   In recognition of the fact that refugee problems were likely to be of a continuous, rather than an epi-
sodic nature, the ICVA was created out of a merging of
three existing bodies: the Committee of Non-Governmental
Organizations Interested in Migration, the SCVA and the
ICWRY.

ICVA is "the international confederation of citizens'
voluntary association--non-governmental, non-profit organi-
zations--engaged in worldwide developmental, social and humanitarian action. "   It works through a General Conference
and Governing Board, a series of program commissions and
working groups and a headquarters Secretariat, stationed in
Geneva.   It serves as an agent in the development, growth,
and improvement of member agencies, and promotes the establishment of groups or councils of voluntary agencies in
countries where such groups do not exist.   It thus encourages the spontaneous development of new agencies while at
the same time seeking a coordination of their efforts.   It
also encourages and stimulates studies designed to assist
refugees and other persons in need of international assistance.   It has no operations of its own, and is thus a neutral
platform on which agencies can meet to discuss specific
topics and occasionally to adopt common attitudes on programs (for example rehabilitation of Tibetan refugees; relief
of Bengalese refugees in India).

The ICVA Commission on Refugees and Migration
meets approximately every nine months in Geneva and its
members include the forty voluntary agencies which are most
frequently in contact on major or regular refugee programs
and which use ICVA as a forum for the exchange of information and the establishment of common services and policies
on specific or general situations or needs.

Official observers from non-member organizations
and from governments, the UNHCR, ICEM, FAO, ILO, and
other UN and public agencies interested in questions of refugees or migrants are entitled to participate in the discussions and in the formulation of recommendations, although
not to vote.   The General Conference reports are published
along with current reports on voluntary agency activities in
the Council's bi-monthly organ ICVA News.

Two other services of ICVA are those rendered by
its International Center for Coordination of Legal Assistance
(ICCLA) and the Kooijman Fund.   The ICCLA was established
in 1958 in Geneva under the auspices of the Committee of
Non-Governmental Organizations Interested in Migration as
a non-profit, humanitarian organization operating under its
own statute.   The Statute of ICVA makes the ICCLA part of
the ICVA.   The ICVA Governing Board, to which ICCLA
makes an annual report, appoints its officers in consultation
with the ICLLA bureau.   Legal aid is thus given an important place in the field of international philanthropy.   The
Kooijman Fund is designed to assist de facto refugees in any
part of the world by awarding one-time grants to individuals
for specific needs which cannot be met from other sources.
Thus, for instance, a refugee, whether or not he is under
UNHCR mandate, who is in need of financial assistance to
reestablish himself in his profession, may be helped through
the Fund.

1963 ICVA General Conference.   The 1963 Conference
was devoted to the theme "Voluntary Agencies: New Approaches to Human Needs in New Circumstances. "   Voluntary agency actions in the traditional fields of migration and
aid to refugees were analyzed, and their role was discussed
in relation to the task of relief and aid in the developing
countries and to the Freedom from Hunger Campaign (1960-
65) sponsored by FAO.   The Commission on Relief and Development was established at this time to concern itself
specifically with these matters. [7]

There was some opposition from Conference participants to ICVA's entering upon such a broad new field of
activity, and the belief was reiterated that the voluntary
agencies should supplement and complement the work of
governments and official agencies.   It was recognized that
"relief operations should go hand-in-hand with constructive
rehabilitation projects in order to avoid refugees becoming
dependent on relief supplies, and the emergency operations

becoming static." The ICVA Conference also stressed that "any effort to assist refugees must be closely related to the agricultural, industrial and public health needs of the country as a whole."[8] Thus, the 1963 Conference found the voluntary agencies looking both backward to their traditional role of relieving human misery through individual solutions, and forward to their role in the field of economic development as the solution to human needs.

1965 ICVA General Conference. The theme of the General Conference in 1965, "Dynamic Development: A Field for International Cooperation," indicates the nature of the problems and the acceptance of the new concept of philanthropy. The Conference was in itself a contribution toward International Human Rights Year as resolved upon by the UN. Its two hundred and twenty participants were drawn from sixty-five ICVA member agencies, forty-four other NGO's, seven governments, and fifteen inter-governmental organizations.[9] The membership also represented some individual organizations working internationally--The Tolstoy Foundation, the Heifer Project, and Find Your Feet, Ltd., are examples. A large proportion of the members, however, were either national councils drawing together the work of individual national agencies such as CORSO, ACVA, BOAR, and the Norwegian Refugee Council, or were themselves federations with member agencies in many countries, including many newly formed groups in developing countries.

1968 ICVA General Conference. The 1968 ICVA General Conference, "International Voluntary Action for Human Needs," held in London, in many ways marked a new stage in voluntary agency thinking and action. The agencies' long-recognized competence in refugee matters, to which UN Secretary-General U Thant referred in his opening message, had now been extended to a clearly defined ability and determination to play an increasingly active role in the world development process. The Conference constituted both a call to action and a collective declaration of readiness on the part of the non-governmental world to enhance its contribution to the elimination of human need and the attainment of social justice.

The HC in his message of June 1968 to this Conference summed up the role of the voluntary agencies in refugee work as follows:

An extremely close partnership has developed

between UNHCR since its creation in 1951 and
most of the Voluntary Agencies represented at this
Conference. To start with, the Voluntary Agencies were operational partners with UNHCR in the
welfare, resettlement, and integration of the hundreds of thousands of refugees in Europe who lived
in miserable conditions in camps and sub-standard
housing until they have now nearly all been settled. Later on when refugee problems in Africa
and Asia became more and more acute, the Voluntary Agencies continued to collaborate and are
still collaborating in the implementation of the programmes for assistance and settlement in those
areas. The funds raised by the Voluntary Agencies from their supporters for the refugee programmes across the world have been greatly instrumental in reaching the results so far achieved.
Furthermore, by their close and daily contact with
the refugees, the Voluntary Agencies have played
an outstanding role in the legal protection of refugees. I am convinced that the cooperation between us will grow even closer and closer as we
continue our work together. [10]

The Red Cross

The two sister organizations of the Red Cross, the
International Committee of the Red Cross (ICRC) and the
League of Red Cross Societies (LRCS) stand somewhat apart
from other agencies. The ICRC is the oldest of the non-
governmental organizations, and together with the LRCS is
defined as an "auxiliary to the public authorities." By
tradition the Red Cross acts in emergency situations, bringing help to victims of natural and man-made disasters, including refugees. The Red Cross owes its effectiveness,
in a large measure, to the fact that it is not hampered by
political considerations or bureaucratic procedures, yet it
has the privileged position of having full official backing for
its actions. Its fundamental principles reflect the strictly
observed neutrality which is the code of the Red Cross:
impartiality; action independent of any racial, political, or
economic consideration; the universality of Red Cross; and
the equality of the National Red Cross Societies.

The ICRC, with its headquarters in Geneva, was
founded in 1863 in Geneva and is formally recognized in

international law by virtue of the Geneva Conventions. While composed exclusively of Swiss citizens (a maximum of twenty-five), its work is international. It is private, independent, and strictly neutral in all political, ideological, and religious matters.

The ICRC recognizes any newly established or reconstituted National Red Cross Society which fulfills its conditions for recognition. The ICRC, jointly with the LRCS, received the Nobel Peace Prize on 10 December 1963 in recognition of its humanitarian activities.

The LRCS was founded after WWI (May 1919), as a non-political, non-governmental, and non-sectarian organization to encourage and promote in every country the establishment and development of a national Red Cross (or Red Crescent or Red Lion and Sun) societies and to coordinate international relief actions. [11]

After their services during WWI, the national societies federated in the LRCS to coordinate their services in peacetime in disaster situations. When one of the national societies calls for aid because the magnitude of disaster is too great to meet alone, the League intervenes immediately and unconditionally supports the national society of the particular country.

The League performs only a transitional action--a "survival" operation. It provides elementary relief for survival (food, shelter, clothing, medical care, etc.) but does not engage in any permanent action. It fills a gap while government and other organizations mobilize assistance. The meaning of transitional action, however, has changed due to circumstances. A representative of the LRCS has pointed out that "the notion of transitory is entirely relative, in time of war as in peace, and if certain relief actions in Europe lasted three weeks, in Africa they may sometimes last one or two years."

International governmental bodies have had close contacts with all three types of Red Cross organizations. It was the ICRC that took the initiative in calling the attention of the LoN after WWI to the need for long-term inter-governmental action on behalf of the refugees. [12] As a result the LoN appointed the first High Commissioner for Refugees, Dr. Nansen, in 1921.

A close cooperation and partnership between the HC and the Red Cross dates from the foundation of UNHCR. In addition to the significant role of the Red Cross as the operational partner to UNHCR in some of its refugee assistance programs, the Red Cross has also been able to act on behalf of refugees as a precursor to the UNHCR when the status of victims of an event is not yet defined, or pending appeals from governments to the HC.

One of the major efforts involving a complex UNHCR-Red Cross cooperative program was action undertaken on behalf of refugees from Hungary in 1956. The ICRC and the LRCS became the HC's partners in Hungary, Austria, and Yugoslavia. The LCRC was able to establish the support of fifty-two national Red Cross, Red Cresent and Red Lion and Sun Societies which provided assistance and services valued at just under $20 million. LRCS work in this operation was recognized when, in 1957, the organization was awarded the Nansen Medal for outstanding services on behalf of refugees.

Another UNHCR-Red Cross joint effort was the relief operation for refugees from Algeria in Morocco and Tunisia. This effort, which extended over a five-year period, was brought to a conclusion by the repatriation of more than 180,000 Algerians.

Other cooperative programs have been undertaken by the UNHCR in partnership with national Red Cross societies. The joint effort of the Ethiopian Red Cross and the Swedish Red Cross in providing services to Sudanese refugees is an example. In Nepal, the national Red Cross has been the channel for UNHCR assistance to Tibetan refugees, and the Nansen Medal was awarded to Princess Princep Shah, President of the Nepal Red Cross, in recognition of this work. Other joint UNHCR-Red Cross operations which have been carried out in respect to crises in Asia and in Africa are discussed elsewhere. [13]

International Social Service

The main purpose of ISS is to provide case work assistance to families and individuals faced with social or socio-legal problems resulting from past or contemplated migration and requiring action in more than one country. The service is not confined to refugees but has been operating since the foundation of ISS in 1921, for all persons whose problems are in some way related to another country. Its headquarters are in Geneva, and other offices have been set up in Argentina, Australia, Austria, Belgium, Brazil, France, Germany, Greece, Italy, Japan, Korea, the Netherlands, Switzerland, the UK, the US, Uruguay and Venezuela. Its programs are supported by private contributions.

In the fifties, the ISS was particularly active in Austria. The first grant made to ISS in 1952 by the Ford Foundation was for the establishment of a record center in Salzburg, Austria. ISS took over the administration of the records of refugees who had hitherto been assisted by the IRO. The second project implemented by ISS in Austria concerned a socio-legal aid service for refugees in Klagenfurt, for which the office was opened in December 1953.

On 1 July 1955, the UNHCR concluded an agreement with ISS under which ISS assumed the integration counselling for foreign refugees who lived in camps in Carinthia scheduled for closure and later in other camps.[14] The aim of the project was to integrate refugees into the economic life of Austria, primarily by providing for them housing, employment, vocational training, credit facilities, etc. The agency engaged two qualified German-speaking social workers, one of whom was a legal adviser familiar with the Austrian economic, social and socio-legal situation.[15]

In December 1956 the UNHCR concluded an agreement with ISS for a project on behalf of unaccompanied Hungarian youth in Austria. This project which was in operation until 31 December 1958, provided for individual case work service for unaccompanied Hungarian youth under eighteen years of age who were living in Austria and within the mandate of the UNHCR. For this project ISS employed six permanent and three additional temporary workers all of whom had special qualifications for this work. Apart from Austria, ISS also assisted Hungarian children in France, Italy, and in the Netherlands.

In Greece, ISS established an assimilation and resettlement service for refugees. The service pre-selected candidates for integration and resettlement schemes, assisted refugees in their dealings with government authorities and acted as a placement bureau. In Italy, ISS established a resettlement counselling service in Rome which was in operation for two years for the compilation of case files for refugees in Italy.

During the period 1961-64, ISS implemented legal assistance programs in Latin America for refugees within the mandate of UNHCR who were resettled in Latin America but not yet naturalized and were encountering legal difficulties. ISS undertook the legal counselling over a very widespread geographical area where the cooperation of experienced and competent lawyers was enlisted. These lawyers acted as counsellors to refugees who had arrived some ten to twelve years previously but had never had the possibility of receiving legal advice free of charge, and helped them to resolve legal and administrative problems connected with their refugee status.

In Argentina, for example, the lack of personal documents was a great obstacle because documents are of primary importance in civic life in that country. When papers are in order, refugees have the same rights and obligation in Argentina as the native born and immigrants. They can start working the day after their arrival if they so wish, and they can ask for naturalization whenever they decide upon it, just as immigrants can. Naturalized or not, they are entitled to a pension on retirement provided they have worked for a certain number of years. Without papers, however, none of these opportunities exist. ISS therefore provided legal advisers who helped the refugees settle these problems. They undertook the necessary legal and administrative steps to obtain identity cards and to replace or authenticate birth certificates which were required for naturalization and for registration of children in schools, and resolved difficulties in connection with diplomas, contracts of work, marriage certificates, successions, leases, etc. The majority of lawyers, like the Association for the Protection of Immigrants, and the Association of Lawyers in Argentina, offered their services, in some instances without charge.

The ISS also cooperated actively with the UNHCR in finding permanent solutions for refugees in Argentina, Paraguay, and Venezuela, such as the placement of old and sick refugees in institutions, provision of annuities, accommodation, medical assistance, and establishment and educational assistance. This particular project, in which several other voluntary agencies participated, was conducted in 1962. ISS has continued its social counselling activities in more recent times in Venezuela and Argentina, where complete studies of cases in urgent need of assistance have been made. The services rendered concerned economic problems, requests for citizenship, reunion with family members, health questions, professional orientation, etc.

From 1963 up to the present time, UNHCR has also
concluded repatriation agreements with ISS for refugees in
Argentina, Brazil, Venezuela, Chile, Uruguay, and Peru,
whereby ISS makes appropriate arrangements for the repatriation from countries of asylum to home countries of refugees
who are within the mandate of UNHCR.   The agency has to
ascertain that the decision to repatriate is entirely voluntary.
ISS then makes the appropriate travel arrangements and assists the refugees in obtaining the necessary exit permits,
vaccinations, visas, embarking and landing permits, passports, medical examinations, and so on.   Many applicants
for repatriation experience anxiety due to the tension between
the ties to the host country and the country of origin.   With
much understanding and insight, the social workers of ISS try
to help the refugees concerned in making a decision after
careful consideration of all factors involved, such as changed
political, economic and social conditions in the countries of
origin.

International Catholic Migration Committee

The great number of Catholics involved in migration
movements, including refugee resettlement schemes under
the IRO, evoked an intense effort on the part of the Catholic
Church.   In 1951 Pope Pius XII appointed a committee to
prepare plans for coordinated actions.   This committee drew
up the Statute of the ICMC which stated its goals and tasks.
Emphasizing concern for the family rights of migrants, including refugees, the ICMC seeks to improve and coordinate
services to migrants in both emigration and receiving countries, and to have governments adopt policies which will insure these rights.   Second, it provides technical, financial,
and advisory assistance to Catholic groups concerned with
these migrants, and performs functions in the field of international migration which cannot be carried out by national
agencies.   Third, ICMC represents "Catholic activities and
organizations before international organizations and conferences concerned with migration, refugee and population movements. "

With its headquarters in Geneva, ICMC has affiliates
in fifteen European countries: Austria, Belgium, Denmark,
France, Germany, Ireland, Italy, Luxembourg, Malta, the
Netherlands, Portugal, Spain, Sweden, Switzerland, and the
UK.   It operates in the following countries overseas: Ar-
gentina, Australia, Bolivia, Brazil, Chile, Egypt, Colombia,

Japan, New Zealand, Paraguay, Peru, the Republic of South Africa, the US, and Venezuela. Through its affiliates in receiving countries ICMC assists with the reception, placement, and integration of Catholic refugees and migrants sponsored by ICMC, the National Catholic Welfare Conference (NCWC), and others. In principle it assumes ultimate responsibility for all Catholic refugees throughout the world. 16

United Hebrew Immigrant Aid Society

Like its counterpart for Catholics, ICMC, UNHIAS is the international Jewish Migration Agency. It was established in 1954 as a consolidation of the seventy-year-old HIAS, the twenty-year-old United Service for New Americans, and the migration services of the American Joint Distribution Committee (AJDC). Its headquarters in New York coordinate the global activity of close to one hundred offices and cooperating committees in North America, Latin America, Europe, North Africa, Israel, Australia, Hong Kong, and elsewhere. It renders financial and technical services for the processing, transportation and integration of refugees and migrants.

The European headquarters in Paris is responsible for supervision of the emigration program in Europe and North Africa; headquarters in North Africa promotes resettlement opportunities in Canada and the US, the Latin American Office is responsible for promoting resettlement opportunities for Jews from North Africa, and from Egypt and Hungary as well. In the Far East, the Hong Kong office assists the remaining Jews of European origin still in Communist China with emigration to Western countries whenever exit permits are granted by Chinese authorities.

The World Council of Churches

The World Council of Churches (WCC) has its headquarters in Geneva. It is an ecumenical organization on a world level, established in 1948, and groups members from 180 denominations, including the major churches of the Protestant, Anglican, and Orthodox confessions. The stated purpose of its Service to Refugees Department is "to work for the material and spiritual welfare of refugees, and to appeal to its member Churches in receiving countries both to influence public opinion toward a liberal immigration policy and to welcome and care for those who arrive in their countries. "

Before the end of the war the churches which were to become
members of WCC had committed themselves to caring for
victims of the Nazi regime and had worked closely with
UNRRA and later with the IRO.   After 1948 this work was
coordinated and furthered through WCC.   Operating first with
refugees and displaced persons in Germany, its work gradually spread throughout the world.   It is now represented in
fifty countries and has a staff of 500 full-time paid personnel
operating in field offices wherever there are large numbers
of refugees in need of resettlement or integration assistance.
The central administration in Geneva is responsible for coordinating and managing the WCC resettlement program and
for administering a Travel Loan Fund.   Since the WCC's
work depends to a large measure on the support of inter-
governmental bodies and the UN, it has made special provision for representing refugee interests before these bodies
through its Commission of the Church and International Affairs.

Member churches contribute financially and in kind to
the refugee work of the WCC and provide for the spiritual
needs of refugees both before and after migration.   WCC also receives and administers funds from UNHCR, USRP, and
ICEM.

The principal countries, apart from the US, to which
refugees receiving WCC aid go, are Australia, Canada, and
Brazil.   The WCC has always concerned itself with difficult
cases, a substantial number of whom have been placed in
Belgium, the Netherlands, Sweden, and France, in homes
opened there with WCC assistance.   While in camps, refugees also benefit from the WCC Contributed Goods Program,
under which food and clothing are given by member churches,
individuals, or other organizations.

The Lutheran World Federation

The LWF has its headquarters in Geneva.   Founded
in 1947, the LWF "is an international agency for seventy
member churches from forty countries, embracing fifty-two
million baptized Lutherans.[17]   LWF is an outgrowth of the
Lutheran World Convention, formed in 1923.   Its services
to refugees stem from the belief that "both inter-church aid
and material assistance are natural consequences of the
faith."[18]

Immediately after WWII, Lutherans from the churches which had not suffered much from the war, especially those in the US, set about the task of assisting Lutheran pastors in refugee and DPs camps in Germany to provide for the spiritual life of interned Lutherans, and of revitalizing the shattered Church in Europe. One of the main functions of the LWF World Service Department (LWS/WS) is to support local Lutheran churches throughout the world where local resources are insufficient and to create new ones where none exist. These churches in turn assist in administering resettlement and material-aid programs for refugees.

LWF/WS aid projects initiate or expand activities in every major field of socio-economic development. They are carried out in two main ways: by direct operations through its field offices and by receiving and processing applications for help in specific projects.

Material assistance to refugees, begun in refugee camps on a small scale, has since become a worldwide program which benefits not only Lutherans, but any needy people, whether Christian or non-Christian. The LWF program in the Near East is the largest single program in that area. It also operates a program in Hong Kong, as well as an intensive integration program there, including housing schemes, medical aid, counselling, and loan projects.

Resettlement schemes begun in 1948 also grew to worldwide scale. By 1957 the LWF had resettled 93,478 refugees overseas, mostly in the US and Canada and had provided assistance to 12,000 refugees.

World Alliance of YMCA/YWCA

The World Alliance of YMCA (established in 1855) and the World YWCA (established in 1894) are separate worldwide Christian youth movements, being federations of autonomous national associations. Both movements, with central offices in Geneva, have actively served refugees and uprooted peoples since the end of WWI.[19] The programs of both movements in their work for refugees are designed to maintain and improve all aspects of normal community life in refugee camps and communities. Their work is carried out on an inter-confessional, international, and inter-racial basis. The two movements operate closely with all organizations, both governmental and non-governmental, wherever their aims and

objectives coincide.   Their work is carried on in Europe:
in Austria, France, the German Federal Republic, Trieste,
and the UK; in the Middle East: in Egypt, Gaza Strip, Jordan, and Lebanon; in Asia: in Pakistan, Hong Kong, and
South Korea.   Refugee work is planned and coordinated in
each organization by a special Refugee Committee.

Within each movement, national member organizations
carry on their own refugee services, but in countries where
the work is too great for a national movement to carry alone
the World Alliance and the World YWCA carry out separate
services for refugees.   Both movements operate (sometimes
jointly as with the World's YMCA/YWCA Service to Refugees
in Austria) vocational, language and leadership training programs: resettlement orientation courses, summer camping
for children and counselling for unaccompanied youth working
in industry, commerce and agriculture.   In Trieste, World
YWCA, in cooperation with WCC, concentrates on refugees
who cannot qualify for emigration.   Occasionally, both provide relief supplies, but their main focus is on training for
self-sufficiency and community life.   Through its national associations in resettlement countries, World YWCA also receives refugees and offers services leading to the integration
of newcomers.

World Union Organisation de Secours aux Enfants

The World Union Organisation de Secours aux Enfants
(OSE) is the federation of 29 national OSE agencies in Europe, Africa, the Middle East, North America, South America, and the West Indies.   It was established in 1912, with
headquarters in Paris.   The aim of OSE organizations na-
tionally, and of their federation, is the protection of the
health of Jewish populations all over the world, with special
attention to child care.   World Union OSE gives medical and
medico-legal assistance to Jewish refugees and displaced
persons and makes studies of socio-medical problems among
these peoples.   Its work is closely coordinated with AJDC,
HIAS, and other agencies assisting Jewish populations.

International Union for Child Welfare (Union Internationale de Protection de l'Enfance)

The International Union for Child Welfare (IUCW) is a
federation of national and international child-welfare

organizations. It came into being in 1946 with the merger
of the Save the Children International Union (which had been
established in Geneva in 1920) and the International Association for the Promotion of Child Welfare (established in Brussels in 1921). Its double aim is direct assistance to children in distressed conditions, including refugees, and promotion throughout the world of the principles of the Declaration
of the Rights of the Child (its own Charter) which was
adopted in 1923 and endorsed by the LoN in 1924. The principles are to relieve children in distress, to raise the
standard of child welfare, and to contribute to the moral and
physical development of children.

The IUCW has, since 1945, organized several conferences to stimulate interest in refugee problems, and in 1952,
at the request of UNESCO, the Union prepared a report on
the psychological, educational, and social adjustment of refugee and displaced children in Europe. Its member agencies
have been active in providing assistance for young refugees.
The British Save the Children Fund, for example, sent relief teams to Austria and Germany immediately after the war
and was supported in this work by contributions from other
Commonwealth branches. The Swedish Save the Children
Fund operated an extensive program in Germany which culminated in the setting up of hostels for young workers and
apprentices in and around Munich. The Danish Save the
Children Fund set up kindergartens and community services
for refugees in German camps and provided assistance to
refugees. In Argentina, the IUCW assisted new immigrants
by running language courses and taking temporary care of
refugee children while their parents looked for work. Among
those helped, a large proportion since WWII have been refugees, and it was to the IUCW that Ford Foundation granted
funds administered through UNHCR specifically for a program for refugee children on the Island of Corfu.

World University Service

The statutes of World University Service (WUS) require the promotion of international university solidarity and
mutual services within and between universities through the
extension of material aid. On this basis, university students
and professors participate in specific projects to meet urgent
needs of other universities. Since the early 1930s one of
WUS's principal concerns has been the plight of refugee students. Through scholarships and other forms of aid WUS has

enabled many to obtain academic and professional training
which qualified them for employment. In addition WUS provides welfare services and urgent relief to students and special cases. It operates programs in seventeen countries and
in addition to its central office in Geneva, has corresponding
offices in thirty-nine countries in all continents of the world.

International Relief Committee for Intellectual Workers

The International Relief Committee for Intellectual
Workers (IRCIW) was formed in Geneva in 1933 to assist
refugees formerly engaged in the liberal professions with a
view to facilitating their resettlement or integration. The
first group of refugees assisted by the Committee were
chiefly persons distinguished in the academic world and of
Jewish origin. The Committee provided relief for intellectuals who had escaped to Switzerland, and later to those who
were liberated from concentration camps. It administers
certain funds, in agreement with the German Federal Government, whereby restitution is made to persons who, persecuted by the Nazi regime, were forced into exile. It
grants loans, arranges language courses, assists in finding
employment, and procures the material necessary for these
refugees to pursue their work.

Two other organizations serve in a sense as the counterpart of the agencies especially established for assistance
to intellectuals and professionals who found particular difficulty in reestablishing themselves in new countries. Assistance to workers in general, and to refugees when they are
in need, is rendered by the International Confederation of
Free Trade Unions (ICFTU) and the International Labor Assistance (Entr'Aide Ouvrière).

International Labor Assistance (Entr'Aide Ouvrière)

The purpose of International Labor Assistance (ILA),
organized in 1950, is to strengthen the feeling of international solidarity and to supplement public welfare services in
countries of its member organizations. The present world
situation has compelled the ILA to direct a great deal of its
effort toward assistance to refugees. It assists in child
care, youth welfare, professional training, homes for the
aged, maternity aid, and emigration.

The ILA has member organizations, some of whose activities date back to 1900, in eleven European countries and operates through trade unions in other countries, particularly overseas, where the organization has no representatives.

International Confederation of Free Trade Unions

The International Confederation of Free Trade Unions (ICFTU), representing over fifty-five million workers in ninety-two countries, is a worldwide organization grouping workers' associations "free from the influence or control of governments, employers, or political parties." Its headquarters are in Brussels, and it has regional offices in Mexico for the Western Hemisphere, in Brussels for Europe, and in New Delhi for Asia and the Far East. To insure liaison with the UN, the Specialized Agencies and international organizations, Branch Offices are operated also in Geneva, Paris, Luxembourg, and New York.

ICFTU gives material and moral assistance to workers who are forced to leave their countries. Funds for assistance in integration are also provided.

World Federation of United Nations Associations

The World Federation of United Nations Associations (WFUNA), devotes itself entirely to gaining support for the UN and to making known to the public the aims and activities of the UN and its Specialized Agencies. As such it attempts to give public expression to the views of the peoples of the world. It has pointed up the need for permanent solutions for refugees and has made concrete suggestions to this end to the UN itself.

Although the Federation, founded in Luxembourg in 1946 by men and women of twenty-two nations, does not itself engage in direct assistance to refugees, many of its fifty-two national members have, in addition to these general promotional activities, raised funds for refugees, run work camps, and contributed volunteers to projects organized for refugee welfare or relief.

II: National Voluntary Agencies

The nature of the activities of the national agencies
is molded by the traditions, resources, and political setting
of the nation in which each has its roots.   In the European
countries many aspects of social welfare have long been
handled by official statutes and official bodies, or, at the
request of these public bodies, specific tasks are handled
by private organizations with the assistance of public funds.
Private philanthropy thus has assumed a modest place.   After the war, with limited private resources often wiped out
in just those areas where the most serious refugee problems arose, the voluntary agencies in Europe existed in
many cases as a framework through which overseas agencies,
particularly US private philanthropy, could act to bring help
to war-devastated areas, and so to refugees.

There exists, however, a network of voluntary agencies in the Western European countries, notably the UK,
France, Belgium, Netherlands, Switzerland, West Germany,
Austria, Italy, Greece, and the Nordic Countries.   Their efforts on behalf of refugees have been continuous and invaluable for fund-raising as well as for the implementation of
UNHCR programs in their respective countries.

To coordinate their activities with those of other national and international agencies, many of these have joined
together in national councils recognized by the government
as spokesmen for the country's agencies.   In each nation a
distinctive pattern of interaction has evolved between voluntary agencies, and between the agencies and their government.   The Norwegian Council for Refugees, the Danish Refugee Council, the Netherlands Committee for Aid to Refugees, the French Social Service for Aid to Emigrants (SSAE)
and the Schweizerische Zentralstelle für Flüchtlingshilfe, a. o.
are exemplary of such national organizations.

Attention will be focused in the following sections on
British voluntary activities, not with the intention of drawing
attention to the work of any one national council, but rather
by way of providing an example of the work which, in varied
forms and degrees, is duplicated in other countries.

British Voluntary Activities

In the UK, the UNHCR's work is strongly supported by

a number of voluntary agencies joined under the British
Council for Aid to Refugees (BCAR).   The British voluntary
effort in behalf of refugees--an unusually strong one--began
even before the end of the war.   When many separate voluntary agencies--some long established and others newly
formed in response to the plight of Europe--approached the
government seeking a chance to serve war victims, it was
suggested that, rather than "descend upon the theatre of war
without any organization and answerable to no one,"[20] they
should pool their experiences and coordinate their activities
under some unifying body.   Accordingly, in the fall of 1942
the agencies formed the Council of British Societies for Relief Abroad (COBSRA).   Under COBSRA many individuals
from constituent groups trained themselves for work in war-
torn Europe, even hiring a derelict house in London in which
they set up simulated field situations and organized relief
operations for "victims."   The government, with initial mis-
givings, did in fact call upon BCAR societies before the end
of the war to assist in relief of DPs and war victims, first
in Italy and Greece, and then in Normandy, Belgium, and
Holland.   The Army, itself, called upon COBSRA for six
teams (120 persons) to help with the thousands of people
found in the Belsen Camp.   Eventually, in British-occupied
zones some 1,200 BCAR workers operated in the field under
military government, and later under UNRRA.   When the
IRO was set up, COBSRA was the official agency responsible
for assisting (in cooperation with the appropriate departments
of government--the Ministries of Labour, Health, and Education, and the Foreign and Home Offices) in the selection and
settlement of 120,000 refugees brought to Britain under various Government labor schemes, as well as in the movement
of refugees in transit to other resettlement countries.

Establishment of BCAR

        As the emergency work in Europe diminished, and es-
pecially with the proposed closing of the IRO, the need was
felt for an organization which would turn its attention to coordinating the voluntary effort at home for refugees who were
already domiciled in the UK, as well as for those who might
come in the future.   On 24 January 1950, the Foreign Office
approached a group of voluntary agencies, convened by the
National Council for Social Service in London, to consider
the formation of a coordinating body for service to refugees.
No one existing agency seemed adequate for such a broad
range of needs as would have to be met for assisting refugees

to become self-sufficient and truly integrated into the British
economy and society. Following the successful experience
of voluntary work under COBSRA, it was decided to set up
the BCAR:

1. To promote all or any purpose for the benefit
    of displaced persons and refugees who have
    become domiciled in the UK ... and in par-
    ticular the advancement of the education, the
    furtherance of health and the relief of poverty,
    distress and sickness of these ... persons

2. To collaborate with the appropriate authorities
    and voluntary organizations in bringing to the
    UK, as and when possible, displaced persons
    and refugees who, on the grounds of age, ill-
    ness or physical handicap, are in need of spe-
    cial care and protection, and also the depen-
    dents of such ... refugees

3. To promote and organize cooperation in the
    achievements of the above purposes and to that
    end to bring together in Council representatives
    of voluntary agencies and stationary authorities
    engaged in the furtherance of the above pur-
    poses.

As a co-operative body, composed of bodies much
larger and more powerful than itself, BCAR from the beginning had available to it a broad range of services and considerable financial and personnel resources. Its initial members were largely those agencies which had been working under COBSRA (which itself became a member of BCAR).
British ORT and OSF, for instance, and the British Red
Cross (an advisory member) had well-developed programs
and widespread resources of both personnel and money.
Furthermore, some members, such as the Mental Health
Association, operated services which, though only marginally
concerned with refugees, might nonetheless be crucial to
them. In addition, BCAR's close cooperation with appropriate departments of government in all phases of its work
facilitated both its own and the government's work and meant
that the government "encouraged us and allowed us to develop
our work. "[21]

The IRO turned over to BCAR both its remaining work
in the UK, and the funds which were designated for that work.

Furthermore, the UK Government gave to BCAR the money which was to have been its final contribution to IRO. Thus the new organization could immediately set about the task of organizing its services to refugees in the UK and its program for encouraging the intake of many more refugees, especially the handicapped, from Europe and other parts of the world.

In addition to members with long experience in the field of refugee work, BCAR also had as members many newly formed ethnic groups. One of its first tasks in assessing its potential services and preparing its program was to assist these ethnic groups financially so that they could develop their very important work with refugees of their own nationality in the UK. [22] These groups were themselves united under the Central Coordinating Committee for Refugee Welfare Organization (CCCRWO). A second vital need was for hostels for elderly persons already in Britain as well as others whom the BCAR was able to bring over from Europe. BCAR set up local committees throughout the UK wherever there was a concentration of refugees, not only to assist them in becoming truly integrated but also to raise money for the further needs of refugees, especially for hostels.

Camp Adoption Scheme. When UNHCR announced the Camp Adoption Scheme in 1954, BCAR was in touch with the individuals through BCAR committees and the local offices of member agencies throughout the UK and so could publicize the scheme and set in motion a considerable flow of goods and money to refugee camps, especially in Austria, so that housing could be provided. Out of this scheme grew a permanent program of assistance to refugees in both Austria and Germany whereby individuals or groups in the UK could contribute to a fund for extending grants and loans to individual refugee families in those countries who would thereby become financially independent once more. The scheme operated continuously until after 1968.

2000 Scheme. At the same time, BCAR was closely involved in the "2000 Scheme" whereby families of refugees already in the UK were brought to join them. Many persons brought in under this scheme were aged, or ill and needed special care. It was to meet the needs of these handicapped refugees that BCAR bought an old house in London which became Agnew House, the first of several old-age and nursing homes which BCAR organized. It has operated Agnew House since that time for these and subsequently arriving refugees.

BCAR was also responsible for recruiting a certain proportion of the refugees for the 2000 Scheme as well as for their
welfare once they arrived in the UK.

    BCAR Hungarian Operation. In the midst of these
operations the Hungarian crisis broke out in 1956. Before
it was over 17, 000 Hungarian refugees had arrived in the
UK. BCAR, as the established organization which "could
speak for the welfare of refugees" while at the same time
taking into account the individual contribution which each
separate agency was able to make, was entrusted by the
government with total responsibility for their reception and
care. [23] The remarkably comprehensive program of services
to refugees developed to meet this crisis made the UK a
leader in the field of local integration.

    The Hungarian Operation, as it was called, involved
BCAR in all aspects of reception and local integration problems from emergency feeding through low-cost housing, a
revolving loan scheme, care of juveniles, education, and,
of course, counselling on all phases of life in the UK and
on employment. To provide all these services to the sudden flood of refugees, BCAR set up a separate Hungarian
Department. With BCAR the overall coordinating body, each
member society assisted according to its ability. The British Red Cross and the St. John's Ambulance Brigade played
a major role in the emergency reception arrangements at
London Airport and at the reception centers (in Army barracks provided by the Government). Although refugees often
arrived in groups of five or six thousand at a time, it was
possible for Sir Arthur Rucker to state, "I think it is hon-
estly true to say that none of the refugees arriving in this
country actually slept out or went without reasonable food or
were left cold or derelict. "[24]

    Housing Society. But reception was only a fraction
of BCAR's work with the Hungarian refugees. From the beginning it was considered of paramount importance that refugees be placed as soon as possible in permanent housing
near places of employment. In May 1957, the BCAR Housing Society was formed to provide such housing. The Lord
Mayor of London was president of the society, whose plan
was to purchase suitable houses in good employment areas
which might be made over into apartments for refugee families and which BCAR would rent to them at rates only high
enough to cover BCAR expenses and utilities. By Christmas
of that year (1957) BCAR had purchased fifteen houses and

had housed 100 refugee families.   The Women's Royal Voluntary Service (WRVS) provided much of the furniture for these
apartments.

Like the Camp Adoption Scheme, this Housing Society
program grew, and became a permanent operation of BCAR
from which all refugees arriving in UK could profit.   By
1968 the Housing Society was still receiving some applications
for its housing, although the successful economic adjustment
of many refugees, enabling many to buy their own homes,
permitted BCAR to sell off some of the properties it had
bought for refugee housing.

Hostel Program.   In addition to the housing provided
by the BCAR Housing Society, BCAR continued to run several
hostels throughout the UK, one of which for several years
was devoted exclusively to Hungarian refugees.   Many older
people preferred the security of one another's companionship
to the task of making a new life for themselves among their
British hosts.   The program of hostels, begun under the
IRO, and expanded of necessity after the Hungarian Crisis,
is another permanent aspect of BCAR's program for refugees, and has served a vital function for handicapped refugees brought to Britain under WRY.   Apart from the accommodations provided by the Housing Society and the hostel
program, individual societies, notably the WRVS, also found
places in private homes throughout the UK for thousands of
individual refugees, especially for unaccompanied youths.

Counselling and Welfare Department.   An effective
program for assisting Hungarian refugees to become truly
independent financially and well integrated into the local way
of life has involved BCAR and its member agencies in a
very wide range of welfare work which may be broadly classified under the headings of counselling, financial assistance
and education.   Detailed attention to the needs of refugees
long after their initial settlement and close cooperation with
appropriate government departments in meeting these needs
have distinguished the UK refugee program from the beginning.   The programs developed during the Hungarian Operation are still operable when the need arises.

The BCAR Advice and Welfare Department began operations right in the reception centers, sifting inquiries and
referring refugees directly to the appropriate source of assistance.   BCAR had first of all to assemble a corps of
interpreters and to establish liaison with these sources of

assistance--the various government departments and the member agencies with special services.   Refugees in UK are
immediately entitled to health, welfare and education provisions on the same basis as UK citizens.   The task of BCAR
was to provide counselling so that refugees would know how
to take advantage of these benefits.   Counselling was organized into the Citizen's Advice Bureau, the General Casework
Office, and the Red Cross Office to provide special welfare
for physically and mentally handicapped refugees.   Employment counselling was carried out in close cooperation with
the Ministry of Labour.   A special program of counselling
for unaccompanied youths was established, in which the
YMCA played a major role.

Housing Grants and Loans Committee.   Since the object of BCAR was to have refugees become self-sufficient
as soon as possible, BCAR also established a Housing Grants
and Loans Committee to operate a revolving fund for loans
and grants to refugees for a variety of purposes which would
lead them to independence.   Loans were granted for household furnishings, for tools or other equipment which would
allow a refugee to reestablish himself in his trade, for the
down-payment on a house, or for training which would lead
to independence.   Member agencies--especially church
groups--individuals, and the government as well contributed
to this fund.   As refugees gained independence and were able
to repay the loans, the fund grew and helped other refugees.
The operation of this fund has remained one of BCAR's major contributions to refugee welfare.

Education Programs.   Education of both adults and
children among the refugees has also been a prime concern
of BCAR.   English-language lessons were arranged in local
communities throughout the UK, as well as citizenship training courses for newly arriving Hungarian refugees.   Many
individuals were placed in institutions of higher learning for
special professional training as well as in universities.   WUS
was among the leading sources of assistance in this education program.   But other societies also played their part in
raising money for scholarships and in providing housing for
students during vacation time.   In addition, the YMCA and
the denominational agencies established comprehensive programs of education, counselling, and job training, especially
for the large number of unaccompanied youths who came with
the refugees.   The problems of these youths were difficult,
as many had been socially handicapped by the conditions from
which they had come.   A considerable number found difficulty

in adjusting to the jobs which were obtained for them, and some found their way to prison for various offenses. Many of these youths eventually returned home, with passage assistance from BCAR. Those who remained received regular financial assistance from BCAR to supplement their wages where these were insufficient.

To keep the Hungarian refugees in touch with one another and with events in the host country, the BCAR published a newsletter, in Hungarian The Hungarian in England, which was widely distributed in local committees and to individuals. Peak circulation of this newsletter reached 9,600, but as more refugees became proficient in English, the circulation diminished. An English-language newsletter, which still serves refugees, replaced The Hungarian in England.

Transit Centers. For the many Hungarian refugees who arrived in the UK in transit to other receiving nations--mainly Canada, Australia, and the US--BCAR also provided assistance. It operated holding hostels for these refugees and assisted the recruiting officers from those countries in the processing of refugees. In this operation the WCC, acting as agent for BCAR, set up offices with the LWF, the NCWC and HIAS in the BCAR main office. With this program Operation Airlift alone assisted 5,000 persons in reaching Canada in a period of only two months. Those who expected to go to other countries but were disappointed in their hopes became the responsibility of BCAR in the UK.

Very few Hungarian refugees returned home from the UK. The gradual reduction in demands for assistance in all aspects of the BCAR program indicates successful local integration of a very large percentage. In 1968 most of the calls for assistance came from refugees with special problems usually arising from old age or illness, and an increasing number of such cases were referred to BCAR agencies by Government welfare workers since their special problems did not fall within the range of regular welfare services. The experience acquired by BCAR and its member agencies in handling the Hungarian crisis continues to serve as the basis of UK leadership in the field of successful integration of incoming refugees.

BCAR WRY Program

BCAR was eminently suited to handle UK's part in the

WRY program. Not only did it raise large sums of money
for the WRY committees, but it constantly pushed for the
intake of more handicapped refugees from all over the world.
Many elderly White Russians from China came to the UK,
and many hard core cases who had been in refugee camps
in Europe for over ten years were brought to the UK to the
secure atmosphere of BCAR hostels. In three separate missions, over 1,000 refugees were accepted from camps in
Europe and brought to the UK for treatment and settlement.
BCAR was officially chosen as the agency responsible for the
detailed administration of these schemes, and one of its
representatives served on the various selection missions. 25

The stated objective of these missions was "not to attract workers for particular jobs; not to select families for
chosen homes; not to select families who are already or are
about to be integrated; our object is solely to help those in
greatest need if they want to emigrate to Britain. " This
objective was both more complex and more valuable than
ordinary immigration. 26 Since the persons most in need of
help were often those most hesitant to make the move, BCAR
published a leaflet, which the UNHCR contributed, designed
to reassure refugees by describing the sponsorship and settlement arrangements which were planned for them in the
UK. Where there was a wage earner in the family, BCAR
guaranteed all expenses until the family or individual became
economically independent. BCAR promised that no expenses
for maintenance would fall on public funds for at least three
years. Where there was no wage earner, BCAR guaranteed
maintenance for a minimum of seven years. BCAR received
widespread support for this program.

Large sums of money were raised by the British
Council of Churches, the Catholic Women's League, OXFAM,
and local WRY committees. The Central WRY committee
contributed £200,000 especially for the seven-year guarantee.
The Cala Sona Committee cooperated in settling several TB
families in Scotland. The Ryder-Cheshire Foundation agreed
to take responsibility for 40 families with chronically sick
members. Ockenden Venture undertook education for children in large families. WRVS sponsored 15 families.
BCAR also received help in this program from UNHCR,
ICEM, voluntary agencies abroad and at home, the Home Office, the Ministries of Health and of Labour and the National
Assistance Board. On the occasion of the entrance of the
one thousandth refugee the HC sent a scroll to Dame May
Curwen congratulating the UK for its part in the WRY program.

BCAR Activities in the 1960s

In 1961 the Hungarian Department was reincorporated into BCAR regular work. For many years thereafter the problem of resettling refugees undertaken as part of WRY became the central focus of BCAR. It was not until April 1967 that the Home Office took over responsibility for the maintenance of these refugees. (BCAR still is responsible for special welfare services to them.) Before that time BCAR made a survey of all refugees in the UK to assess their remaining needs, and one of its present tasks is to maintain this as a running survey. BCAR also has a central file of all refugees handled by itself or any of its members. In 1966 it set up a network of local committees to give friendship and assistance to those whose needs are revealed by this running survey.

By the end of 1969 BCAR had helped nearly 700 Czechs. They had originally been granted temporary asylum, but most of them settled permanently in the UK. They required considerable assistance with housing, requalification in the case of physicians, and financing in the case of students at technical colleges and universities. [27]

It is for her part in stimulating this comprehensive program for the refugees in the UK, as well as for her contribution to refugees as the UK's official representative to the UNREF Ex. Com. that Dame May Curwen (probably the most influential leader of voluntary action in the UK, even before the formation of COBSRA) was awarded the Nansen Medal for 1964. Many of the individuals who have been active from the beginning of the UK's voluntary efforts for refugees have also served as UK representatives or officers of international bodies assisting refugees. Their experience, as well as their courage and perseverance have made them leaders in service for refugees.

A British fund-raising agency, known as OXFAM (Oxford Committee for Famine Relief), began in 1942 as a small organization collecting mainly clothes for the war-torn West European countries. It channelled its aid through established agencies in the field. Clothing and other donated goods were valued at £33,181 in the year ending September 1948. Four years later, the figure was £146,449, roughly six times the value of the grant in aid. From 1952 to 1972 OXFAM contributed to refugees in Europe £330,047.50 (Annex 22.1). During that period it began to extend its aid to the Near

East, Asia, and Africa. It cooperates with several hundred
organizations working in the field to whom grants are made.
It has become an important supporter of the UNHCR, particularly in Africa (see Chap. 33).

Notes

1.   Jacques Vernant, The Refugees Problem Since 1955,
        ICVA Conference 1965, Conf. Doc. No. 20/E, mi-
        meo.

2.   Brian W. Neldner, Director of the Tanganyika Christian
        Refugee Service, "The LWF's Refugee Work in Af-
        rica, " in Working Together in Helping Africa's Ref-
        ugees, All Africa Conference of Churches, Nairobi,
        1970.

3.   GA, UNREF Program Rep. , Sept. 1956, A/AC. 11
        Dec. 1956; for list of the agencies see p. 95--a
        vivid eyewitness account of the activities of the
        UNREF Program was published at its half-way:
        To Have A Key, A Storybook of Human Drama,
        UNHCR, Geneva, Mar. 1957.

4.   For lists of voluntary agencies, see HC's Annual Re-
        ports to GA, 1966, 1968, 1969, and 1970. See also
        OECD-ICVA Directory, Development Aid of Non-
        Governmental Non-Profit Organizations, OECD Publ. ,
        Sept. 1967.

5.   Dr. Felix Schnyder, addressing ICVA General Conf. ,
        23 Sept. 1963, Conf. Doc. No. 17: 5.

6.   Statutes of the ICVA, Part A, Art. III--Purposes of the
        ICVA.

7.   In discussing the evolution of voluntary agency tasks
        from relief to development, Bishop Swanstrom de-
        scribed a project undertaken by the local counterpart
        of Caritas in a fishing village on the Caribbean coast
        of Colombia, in which distribution of powdered milk
        (from the US Food for Peace Program) for children
        and pregnant mothers led to the agency's involve-
        ment in creating a supply of pure water, and to the
        opening of a medical dispensary, followed by the
        opening of child care and home hygiene courses, a

community center, and eventually to a credit union. "But the story does not end there, " he wrote. "The microcosms of the local nuclei join into the city, province and nation-wide movements of social and economic development. Those diversify into agricultural and technical training centers, credit unions and cooperative federations, radio and TV literacy and basic education systems, medical and community improvement programs. These are conceived and directed by private leaders of the respective countries, who draw increasingly upon their own local resources for funds and technicals. " ICSVA, Conf. Rep. : 4 & 5.

8.   Working Group on New and Long-Term Refugee Problems in Africa and South East Asia, in Conf. Doc. 23: 13.

9.   ICVA, Human Needs and Social Justice: 5.

10. Conf. Doc. 11/E.

11. LRCS, Important Dates in the History of the League of Red Cross Societies, 1919-69, Geneva, 1969. The League, with its member societies in 115 countries, musters a strength of 225 individual members.

12. See Art. 25 of the Covenant of the LoN.

13. UNHCR, The Red Cross and The Refugees, Geneva, May 1963.

14. Camps Spittal, Feffernit, Parsch, Salzburg, Kufstein in Tyrol and St. Martin.

15. The Dutch Women's Federation for Relief contributed a considerable amount of money to ISS to enable this organization to grant loans to refugees for the purchase of furniture.

16. "World-wide Migration Services for the ICMC, " MN, 5, 1971.

17. Bernard Confer and Donald Anderson, Statement to Senate Subcom. to Investigate Problems Connected With Refugees and Escapees, Comm. on the Judiciary, "US Apparatus of Assistance to Refugees Throughout

the World," 89th US Cong., 2nd Sess., July 1966.

18.   Rep. to the Fourth LWF Assembly, Aug. 1957, Doc.
       No. 13: 5.

19.   The War Prisoners' Aid of the YMCA made possible
       educational, recreational, cultural and religious ac-
       tivities in prisoner of war camps to persons of all
       nationalities. The World YMCA cooperated actively
       with this work, especially for civilian internees and
       women prisoners of war.

20.   Lady Falmouth, Meeting of BCAR Council, 17 Mar.
       1965, London: 3.

21.   Dame May Curwen, ibid. : 8.

22.   In its first year BCAR assisted: Anglo-Rumanian Ref-
       ugee Committee, Assistance Comm. for Hungarians
       in Great Britain, Catholic Comm. for Poland, Bul-
       garian Welfare Comm., Czech Welfare Comm.,
       Slovak Welfare Comm., Yugoslav Welfare Comm.,
       and Russian Refugees Relief Assoc.

23.   Dame May Curwen, ibid. : 9.

24.   Ibid.

25.   WRY, the Report of the UK Committee, 1 June, 1959-
       31 May 1960.

26.   BCAR, Annual Rep. for 1959-60.

27.   See Ex. Com. (XXI), 1 Oct. 1970: Madam May Cur-
       wen and BCAR, Annual Rep. for 1968-69: 1.

ANNEX 22.1

OXFAM GRANTS FOR REFUGEES IN EUROPE, 1951-72

	£
Austria	135, 129
Germany	56, 034
Belgium	40. 50
France	26, 027
Hungary	26, 130
Yugoslavia	4, 050
Europe General	7, 972
Poland & Eastern Europe	3, 000
Turkey	8, 223
Greece	32, 470
Italy	11, 860
UK	13, 040
Spain	6, 072
GRAND TOTAL	£ 330, 047. 50

SOURCE: OXFAM, 1973.

PART V

RESETTLEMENT OF REFUGEES
IN THE OVERSEAS COUNTRIES

We urge the people of the United States to beseech God to render this country more and more a safe and propitious asylum for the unfortunate of other countries.

--George Washington
Thanksgiving Day
Proclamation of 1795.

Shall we refuse ... hospitality ... to the unhappy fugitives from distress?... Shall oppressed humanity find no asylum on this globe?

--Thomas Jefferson, 1801

INTRODUCTION

Resettlement is the third major means whereby refugees can establish new and permanent roots. As we have seen, repatriation was a possibility for only a relatively small number of European refugees. Under the IRO the predominant task was the settlement of refugees overseas, while the UNHCR developed means of maximizing opportunities for local integration. To a large extent the emphasis in the 1950s on local integration was a response to the fact that residual groups of refugees, incapable of resettlement abroad, remained unsettled. The advanced industrial condition of Western Europe, even during the decade of recovery after WWII, enabled European states to contribute to the painstaking process of finding the means that many refugees might become independent and reestablished within their borders, and that others, the difficult cases, might be incorporated within the welfare system of the state. In this significant process, however, the HC did not lose sight of the necessity of promoting resettlement overseas, as was recognized in the Statute (Arts. 8[d] and 9).

The existence in the Americas and Australasia of a "Europe Overseas" was a very basic factor in the process of resettlement. Because the people of the new world and those of Australia and New Zealand trace their ancestry, for the most part, to Western Europe, they identified with European refugees in terms of race, religion, and culture, and regarded these refugees as being capable of assimilating with their own populations. For this reason, as well as for humanitarian reasons and strategic and developmental purposes, many overseas countries were willing to admit substantial numbers of European immigrants. Further, they were prosperous enough to provide the infrastructure necessary for resettlement--homes, jobs, and welfare services--and in some cases to underwrite the costs of passage.

The principal overseas countries for resettlement have been: Australia in particular; Canada quite substantially but on a highly selective basis, and also the United States; and

559

New Zealand and the South American and Caribbean countries, which have remained hospitable to a more limited degree. Planned migration has been seen as a constructive means of filling gaps in manpower resources and thereby aiding economic development. Pursuing the aim of further industrialization, states have welcomed able-bodied and skilled refugees who could aid their economic growth. Because humanitarian sentiments have also played their part in shaping policies, there has also been a gradual liberalization of restrictive immigration regulations in some of the receiving countries, notably the US and Canada, particularly with regard to criteria affecting handicapped refugees and the uniting of refugee families.

Resettlement overseas is a distinctively different process from settlement in countries of asylum. In the latter, the refugees flood in through force of circumstance, and unconditionally they must be accommodated as best possible. Only gradually can arrangements be made for the local integration of those who will be settled permanently. Overseas, the process of admission is a much more regulated and thus selective one. Refugees fall into the general category of immigrants except where special provisions are made, and even then these provisions are carefully designed. There is, therefore, a two-fold urgency to stimulating overseas resettlement for refugees. In the first place, European countries are already industrialized, their opportunities for employment tend to be of a rather specialized variety, and the establishment of new communities, such as became common in Africa at a later date, has been virtually impossible. Faced with their own problems of reconstruction and development, the presence of large groups of refugees often cause serious political and economic strains. But beyond the immediate stress is the longer range prospect that further refugee movements might well take place which could unbearably overtax the asylum countries if they were not freed beforehand of a major part of their refugee burden. Such planning proved to have been essential in 1969 when Czech refugees flooded into the countries that in 1956 had received Hungarian refugees, most of whom had since been resettled overseas.

The responsibilities of the UNHCR in regard to moving European refugees overseas have been in two directions: encouraging countries of asylum to keep their borders open to receive possible new inflows of refugees; and seeking to find permanent settlement opportunities overseas for as many

refugees as possible. In this process the role of the UNHCR
is to maintain a presence in the countries of first asylum
that provide shelter to refugees awaiting resettlement; to
negotiate with governments overseas in seeking suitable resettlement opportunities and, in some cases, liberalization
of restrictive immigration criteria;[1] to coordinate the efforts
of governments, the Specialized Agencies, and the HC's
working partners, ICEM, USRP, and the voluntary agencies,
in the complex task of selecting, securing admission for,
and establishing emigrating refugees in overseas countries;
and at all times to maintain an overview of the practical and
political aspects of the immigration process.

During the years from 1951 to 1971 the UNHCR in the
field of resettlement--as in its other responsibilities--has
had to adapt not only to changing economic and social conditions in countries of asylum and of resettlement, it has had
to adapt also to changes in the psychological and physical
condition of the refugees. The long stay of many "old refugees" in camps or outside of the camps created a large
number of handicapped and difficult cases which needed initial rehabilitative treatment and vocational training in the
countries of residence before emigration. Political, economic and psychological factors often interacted insofar as
once refugees were accepted by their countries of destination, any delay in moving them could result in serious financial and psychological hardships for the refugees as well as
in unnecessary expenses for the countries concerned. Efficient means to insure the speedy movement of refugees was,
therefore, essential.[2]

Such means depended, as did the fulfillment of other
resettlement responsibilities, upon a close partnership between the UNHCR as the intermediary of goodwill, with the
governments of the asylum and of the immigration countries
on the one hand, and the Specialized Agencies, ICEM, USRP
(formerly USEP) and the voluntary agencies on the other.
This working partnership achieved a high degree of success
over the years under the leadership and guidance of successive HCs.

Since the admission of refugees depends on the immigration policies and laws of the receiving countries, the HC
has kept close contact at all times with the governments of
immigration and has urged them through diplomatic channels
to make it possible for refugees to migrate to their countries either in the normal way or through modified or

adjusted procedures. The UNHCR seeks particularly to maintain the unity of families, to secure admission of handicapped and difficult cases and to arrange for modification of age limit restrictions on entry, to reduce to a minimum the time spent in transit, and to provide legal protection to stateless persons. In countries of asylum and in the countries of overseas resettlement, the UNHCR has his own BOs which channel information and maintain liaison with the relevant government departments and various agencies concerned with refugee resettlement and integration. This coordinating function of branch representatives is supported from time to time by missions undertaken by the HC, and by headquarters staff. Since there is great variety in the immigration legislation and policies of different overseas countries and in the ways in which refugee problems have been handled, these are dealt with individually in the following chapters.

The UNHCR has relied on ICEM to carry out the movement of refugees from countries of asylum to countries of permanent settlement. The cooperation of ICEM, the use of its transportation facilities and technical knowledge, and the availability of its efficient and highly developed resettlement machinery has been an essential complementary element in the overall program of the UNHCR for providing permanent solutions for able-bodied as well as for handicapped refugees.

ICEM has provided a wide range of services in the field of refugee migration in countries of departure and of reception. The nature and extent of these services varies from country to country. In some cases they are carried out almost exclusively by ICEM, in others jointly with voluntary agencies and local authorities. [3]

ICEM, as we have seen, played a particularly essential role in the Hungarian crisis of 1956-57 and in WRY, 1958-59. The smooth-working machinery which had been developed over the years by UNHCR and ICEM also made it possible to avoid serious congestion in the European countries of asylum into which Czech refugees fled in 1969. The close relations which ICEM has with the major receiving countries, through the operation of its normal migration programs, has also proved useful in securing resettlement opportunities for refugees. One million refugees have been resettled in immigration countries in Europe and overseas with ICEM's assistance between 1 February 1952 and 23 May 1973.

The voluntary agencies have also played an essential role in the resettlement of refugees. In the countries of first asylum the voluntary agencies are in direct contact with the refugees and are responsible not only for advising them on realistic emigration possibilities, but also for the considerable administrative work involved in preparing dossiers and in bringing the refugees forward for interviews by selection missions. Each refugee is regarded as being on the case load of one or another of the international voluntary agencies concerned with refugees, which work in close association with their national counterpart agencies. The role of the voluntary agencies is equally important in the countries to which the refugees are migrating. In most countries of resettlement it is the local counterpart agency which secures sponsorships and makes arrangements for the reception of the refugees on arrival, finds housing and work for them, and generally guides them until they are assimilated into the local community.

The UNHCR seeks to secure as many resettlement opportunities as possible without UNHCR grants, both within Europe and overseas. However, where admission and final settlement of refugees is dependent upon them, UNHCR has contributed limited grants. [4] (It does not provide grants for refugees who, while within the mandate of the Office, qualify for assistance under USRP.) The dynamic nature of the refugee problem has necessitated a continuing change of emphasis in the distribution of UNHCR's funds for the promotion of settlement. Increasing numbers of refugees are being accepted by countries of immigration without UNHCR contributions, while at the same time higher per capita grants are needed to insure the resettlement of severely handicapped refugees or of groups of refugees presenting special problems when the financial responsibility is assumed by private organizations.

Part of the financial burden of resettlement operations has been borne by USRP, ICEM, and the UNHCR in the form of special grants to the agencies covering a wide range of services such as documentation costs, vocational training, language courses, salaries of staff members engaged in counselling and preparation of refugee emigrants, and reception in countries of destination. [5] Under agreement with ICEM, the agencies administer revolving loan funds by means of which the costs of the resettlement of refugees may be defrayed. These costs may include documentation, movement by air or sea, and inland transportation. The ICEM

Revolving Fund is financed jointly by ICEM and the voluntary agencies concerned.

In the course of the years changes in the character of refugee problems on a worldwide scale have led some international agencies to transfer their direct operations on behalf of refugees in countries of first asylum to indigenous agencies. This changeover has caused some dislocation and in some cases the local agencies have not been able to meet the burden without external financial and administrative support. In any case, international agencies which have transferred their former functions to indigenous agencies are still active through their revolving fund agreements with ICEM.

All immigrants, and especially refugees because of the earlier dislocation they have experienced, face immediate problems of adjustment in a new country of settlement. They may need help in order to learn a new language, and frequently must acquire new and more desirable skills in terms of local employment possibilities. They often face status dilemmas. Moreover, most migrants experience problems of self-imposed or enforced isolation within a new society whose history, traditions, and mores are necessarily unfamiliar to them. Their children frequently have special educational difficulties and suffer cultural conflicts. Only gradually have host governments and their people become more sensitive to the need for mutual adjustment within their expanding societies. Awareness that the refugees are adaptable and hard workers has facilitated their acceptance in local communities, however, while governments have become increasingly aware of their contribution to the country's economic development as well as to its cultural diversity and enrichment. The various manifestations of this process of mutual interaction, have played an invaluable role as will be noted in some detail in the chapters that follow.

Notes

1. In adopting the 1951 Convention, the UN Conference of Plenipotentiaries made a special recommendation that the unity of the refugee's family should be maintained, particularly in cases where the head of the family has fulfilled the necessary conditions for admission to a country. Since early 1952 consecutive resolutions of the GA have urged member states, states interested

in immigration, and the Specialized Agencies to give mandated refugees "every possible opportunity to participate and benefit from projects to promote migration" (Res. 538 B3 [VII] of 2 September 1952), to liberalize their immigration laws and regulations, and to include refugees in resettlement schemes (Res. 1388 [XIV] of 20 November 1959).

2.   A/AC.96/275, 24 Feb. 1965.

3.   In general the main activities with which ICEM is associated can be summarized as follows: 1) the compilation and maintenance of centralized records permitting governments, consular authorities, and selection missions to determine the numbers and categories of refugees seeking resettlement; 2) overall supervision of the preparation of the necessary documentation for specific resettlement programmes; 3) administrative arrangements to facilitate the work of selection missions for the interview of refugees; 4) provision of language training, counselling, and general orientation courses for prospective refugee migrants; 5) preparation for movement of refugee migrants who have been accepted by securing, inter alia, travel documents, transit and destination visas, and vaccination certificates; 6) provision of transportation by air or by sea; 7) provision of medical or other escorts where necessary; 8) reception assistance in countries of destination where necessary; 9) provision of the financing of refugee transportation.   A/AC.96/205, 6 Aug. 1963: 10-11.

4.   "A scale of maximum grants for intra-European resettlement schemes has been agreed upon between USEP (USRP) and UNHCR.   In cases where special circumstances relating to a scheme necessitate the payment of higher grants, consultations between the two organizations take place.   Similar grants are paid by UNHCR for the resettlement of refugees in overseas countries, mainly from the Far East, although higher contributions are frequently needed in respect of the family members in the age groups 40-60 years.   The level of grants is also determined by the type and overall cost of the solution provided" (ibid. : 18).

5.   In 1963, it was reported that "the scale of grants ranged from a minimum of $110 per person paid in special

circumstances for the resettlement of employable refugees and their dependents, to a maximum of $1,500
per person for the resettlement of handicapped refugees requiring special care and for non-rehabilitable
refugees admitted to newly established institutions"
(ibid.).

Chapter 23

REFUGEES IN THE UNITED STATES

The US, which has absorbed more immigrants than any other country in the modern world, has a long tradition of offering refuge. Its people have a deeply rooted sense of freedom. "The reasons for immigrating to America were many. Some came because of political, social or religious persecutions; some because of drought or famine; others because of war and its aftermath; and still others to achieve greater economic security or a freer way of life."[1] During the one hundred fifty years since the beginning of mass immigration (1820), the US has admitted a total of 45 million immigrants, a force which has contributed enormously to the country's development. Between 1945 and 1971, the US admitted more than 1.5 million refugees and spent $2 billion 800 million on refugee assistance around the world.

US Policy and Legislation

In reviewing the history of immigration legislation, it is apparent that US ideals of an open society have not always been matched by US policies. While an enormous flood of migrants had been accepted by the US in the period before WWI, demands for restrictions on immigration after that led to the adoption of restrictive legislation between 1921 and 1929. First a quota system was imposed, limiting the annual inflow from any one country to the actual number that had entered the US from that country in 1920. Subsequently immigration was further limited by a "national origins" system which effectively excluded would-be immigrants from certain areas of the world. To the extent that immigration was permitted thereafter it favored persons coming from Northern and Western Europe, and in the years from 1921 to 1940 very few immigrants born in Eastern and Southern Europe were admitted. Germany had been allotted a large quota in the immigration law; in consequence, between 265,000 and 285,000 refugees entered during the period from 1 July 1933 to 30 June 1943.[2] But because, apart from

special and belated provisions, all refugees have had to enter
the US as immigrants (with the exception of those from Cuba,
for whom the US has been a country of first asylum), the effects of the restrictive and selective immigration Acts
passed in the 1920s long curtailed the admission of refugees
from Europe and elsewhere.

Nonetheless, concern about the European refugee program grew in the US following the arrival of those who were
fleeing from the Nazi regime, and the spread of the news
about the unprecedented persecution and the extermination of
untold numbers of civilians for reasons of race, religion, or
nationality during WWII.[3]   Interest and humanitarian concern
were given official recognition first in 1938 when President
Roosevelt took the initiative in convening the Evian Conference, attended by Latin American and Western European
countries, at which the IGCR was established, and subsequently in 1943 when the Bermuda Conference was called by
the UK and US.   Not only was the scope of the IGCR's activities extended to all refugees in Europe, but the member
governments agreed to contribute funds for operational activities.

War Refugee Board.   Parallel to stimulating international action for refugees, President Roosevelt felt that the
US should also act directly.   In 1944, therefore, he established within the Executive Office a special agency for assisting refugees, known as the War Refugee Board, composed
of the Secretaries of State, War, and the Treasury.   President Roosevelt directed the Board to "take all measures
within its power to rescue victims of enemy oppression who
are in imminent danger of death, " and to develop "plans and
programs and the inauguration of effective measures for the
rescue, transportation, maintenance, and the relief of the
victims of enemy oppression, and the establishment of havens
of temporary refuge. "[4]   This decision was followed by the
establishment of the Office of the Advisor on Refugees and
Displaced Persons within the Department of State.[5]   The
Board, functioning from January 1944 to September 1945,
worked closely with the voluntary agencies, and the funds
for its operations came mainly from them.

Displaced Persons Act.   Although the restrictive legislation of the 1920s was revived by the passage of the Immigration and Nationality Act of 27 June 1952 (the McCarran-
Walter Act), concrete steps were taken at the end of WWII
to handle the admission of refugees and DPs separately from

the admission of other immigrants.   Since 1945 Congress
has repeatedly approved special emergency laws at the urging of Presidents Truman, Eisenhower, Kennedy, and Johnson, in response to the vast dislocation of peoples in Europe,
the Middle East, the Far East, and Asia.   These laws, in
contrast to the regular immigration laws, were not so much
concerned with the origin, race, and place of birth of the
immigrants, as with facilitating the admissions of refugees
in critical need of resettlement in the US.

President Truman took the first of these concrete
steps for refugees by his Executive Order of 22 December
1945 which set into motion a corporate affidavit program
whereby voluntary agencies could surmount one of the restrictions in existing immigration laws by giving guarantees
that specified refugees would not become a public charge.
These affidavits facilitated the admission of refugees to the
US.   Thereafter, President Truman's State of the Union
Message of 6 January 1947 and the unstinting efforts of a
sizeable number of Congressmen and of powerful citizen
groups led the way to the enactment of the Displaced Persons
Act of 25 June 1948 (PL 80-774) and its amendment of 28
June 1951 (PL 81-60) which extended the law until the end
of 1952, eliminating some of its inequities and facilitating
its administration.   A total of 410,000 persons (including
54,744 German expellees) were admitted under this law (one-
third of the case load of the IRO).

The Displaced Persons Act marked a turning point in
American immigration policy and in American foreign policy.
It "developed a new pattern of immigration, focused a coordinated community approach to immigrants, and welded together religious, nationality, and welfare groups, and public
and private agencies."[6]   The DP program was not an immigration program in the normal sense of that term.   It was
rather "a resettlement program.   A comprehensive system
of public and private social service agencies was established
and coordinated to help the new American adjust to his new
homeland."[7]   The position of refugees admitted under the
DP Act was different since most of them were sponsored by
voluntary societies, acting on behalf of the American community as a whole, while ordinary immigrants were usually
sponsored by relatives or friends.

In general, three facts accounted for the success of
the Act.   In the first place, the composition of the group included a high proportion of persons who were prominent in

their own country, and of professional people, artists, skilled technicians, etc. Many were highly educated; many spoke more than one language and many realized the importance of knowing English and lost little time in acquiring such knowledge. In the second place, their entry into the US took place under favorable circumstances. The immigrant aid societies could command the latitude, the financial resources and the moral support which enabled them to perform a comprehensive, efficient job and to assist the newcomers generously. Third, their arrival largely coincided with the industrial expansion and need for manpower of the post-war period.

However, many voluntary agencies testified in 1952 before the President's Commission on Immigration and Naturalization as to the necessity of still more tolerant emergency legislation that would help ameliorate refugee problems throughout Europe, the Middle East and the Far East. [8]

On 22 April 1953, President Eisenhower urged Congress to enact emergency legislation. He wrote:

> It is imperative that we join with other nations in helping to find a solution to these grave questions. These refugees, escapees, and distressed peoples now constitute an economic and political threat of constantly growing magnitude. They look to traditional American humanitarian concern for the oppressed. International political considerations are also factors which are involved. We should take reasonable steps to help these people to the extent that we share the obligation of the free world. [9]

Refugee Relief Act (RRA). Following the enactment of the McCarran-Walter Act of 27 June 1952, which had been passed over the veto of President Truman, Congress passed the Refugee Relief Act (RRA) of 3 August 1953 (PL 83-203). For a second time immigration barriers maintained for decades were temporarily set aside. Passed at the height of the tension between the West and the East, it provided for the admission of 189,021 refugees to the US from Communist dominated countries in Europe. It also made visas available for 4,000 war orphans, 3,000 Chinese refugees, and 2,000 Arabs. This was a departure from US immigration policy which, to that time, had virtually excluded Asians. The law was extended by an Amendment of 6 March 1956 to 31 December 1956.

Execution of the RRA was put under the Administrator
of the Bureau of Security, Consular Affairs and Personnel in
the State Department. It is well known that bureaucratic
procedures hamstrung the use of this act in the beginning and
thus affected the relations of the US with European countries.

The unfinished work of the RRA and the unexpected
Hungarian uprising in October 1956 called for a further
emergency provision. PL 85-316, passed on 11 September
1957, liberalized the admission of refugees who were formerly excluded. In addition to the criteria of the RRA, it
was possible for families to be reunited who had been separated because members suffering from tuberculosis had previously been refused visas. This law provided for 18,656
non-quota visas for refugees: 2,500 for ethnic Germans,
1,600 for Dutch nationals who had fled from Indonesia, and
14,596 for refugee-escapees from communist and certain
Middle East countries. Eighteen percent of the 29,000 refugees who arrived under its provisions were Hungarians.
The Hungarian immigration quota quickly became oversubscribed. There was no time for new legislation, but by an
Executive Order of the President provision was made for the
admission as parolees of 32,000 Hungarian refugees. A
parolee is ineligible for permanent alien registration until
two years after entry (Section 212[d][5] of the Immigration
and Nationality Law of 1952). Legislation was later passed
permitting the Hungarian parolee to adjust his status after
two years' residence. [10]

Fair Share Refugee Act. President Kennedy also took
an active interest in immigration and refugee problems. As
Senator from Massachusetts he had introduced in the Senate
on 17 June 1959, just before the opening of WRY, a joint
resolution on refugees (introduced in the House by Congressman Frances E. Walter of Pennsylvania) to "vest in the Attorney-General permanent authority to cope with the continuing problem of admission of refugees into the United States. "
Mr. Kennedy had declared before the Senate that "WRY is
about to begin in the US by Presidential proclamation on 1
July. There could be no better occasion for the adoption of
a permanent law concerning the admission of refugees into
the US. "[11] However, the resolution was not passed by Congress, which passed instead the Fair Share Law of 14 July
1960 (PL 86-648).

The Fair Share Act provided the first permanent US
refugee legislation. Twenty-five percent of the number of

refugees who had been admitted to other countries during previous periods could be admitted to the US. In addition, it provided for the "difficult to resettle" cases, such as persons with tuberculosis or other physical disabilities, and large families, if appropriate resettlement arrangements were made. Some 19,700 persons entered the US under this Act.

At the height of the refugee emergency in Hong Kong, President Kennedy authorized, as a humanitarian move, the parole of specified groups of refugees on 4 June 1962. It was mainly a family reunion program (two-thirds of those admitted had close relatives in the US, whether citizens or resident aliens; almost one-quarter of them had professional or technical training). More than 15,000 persons have been admitted under this program.

Upon taking office in January 1961 President Kennedy pursued his personal concern for refugees and took the initiative to widen US direct assistance programs. Within a month he established the Cuban Refugee Assistance Program under the Department of Health, Education, and Welfare to provide the Cuban refugees with initial care and maintenance, language, professional and vocational training, medical care, and education as well as with resettlement and employment opportunities throughout the US. He approved the liberal exercise of the Attorney-General's parole power to admit Cubans under Section 212 (d)(5) of the Immigration and Nationality Act. Under this law over 400,000 Cubans had entered the US by 1971.

Migration and Refugee Assistance Act. Following the recommendation of President Kennedy in a message to Congress on 11 July 1961, Congress enacted, in June 1962, the Migration and Refugee Assistance Act (PL 87-510). [12] This law grants permanent authorization for annual funding to the multilateral organizations, UNHCR, UNWRA, and ICEM and the unilateral programs for refugees from Eastern Europe (operated by USRP), the Chinese in Hong Kong and Macao, the Tibetan refugees, and the Cuban Refugee Program. In addition, it makes available to the President from the foreign aid contingency fund, up to $10 million annually "in order to meet unexpected urgent refugee and migration needs." For the first time in the history of US immigration and refugee legislation, the President and the executive branch have, on a permanent basis, a broad and flexible mandate for dealing with refugee affairs. Finally, President Kennedy, in a special message to Congress on 23 July 1963, called for the elimination of the national origins quota system. [13] This formula had resulted in wide discrepancies since 82 percent of the total quota was assigned to North and West Europe, 16 percent to South and East Europe, and only 2 percent to the rest of the world.

Immigration and Nationality Act. President Kennedy's proposals were vigorously endorsed by his successor, President Lyndon Johnson, in his State of the Union message of 4 January 1964, and again in a January 1965 message to Congress, in which he stated: "A change is needed in our laws dealing with immigration. Four Presidents have called attention to serious defects in this legislation. Action is long overdue." He called for a basic and realistic immigration reform. This goal was reached when Congress enacted the Immigration and Nationality Act of 3 October 1965 (PL 89-236). Congressman Emmanuel Celler and Senator Philip A. Hart, persistent advocates of reform, exerted vigorous efforts in Congress on behalf of this legislation.

This Act was, in fact, the product of a 40-year-long educational effort by religious, ethnic and other citizens' organizations. The support of organized labor, which in earlier decades had been hostile to immigration, also contributed to the change. One of the main groups heading the drive for this reform was the American Immigration and Citizenship Conference (AICC).

In Washington, the National Committee for Immigration Reform, an ad hoc pro-immigration lobbying group formed early in 1965, made an important contribution in consolidating support for immigration reform. It was composed of individuals rather than organizations, and included among its members former presidents Harry S Truman and Dwight D. Eisenhower.

The law not only eliminated the quota system, but for the first time inserted a permanent refugee section into the immigration law. Under Section 203(a)(7) visas were reserved for refugees "who ... because of persecution or fear of persecution on account of race, religion, or political opinion ... have fled from any Communist or Communist-dominated country or area, or from any country within the general area of the Middle East, and are unable or unwilling to return to such country or area on account of race, religion, or political opinion" (this included refugees from Libya, Turkey, Pakistan, Saudi Arabia and Ethiopia). [14]

Many provisions of the Fair Share Refugee Act, which expired in 1965, were continued as an integral provision in the amended Immigration and Nationality Law of 1965. However, refugees and escapees were now named "conditional entrants" with a two-year parole period. Visas were reserved for 10,200 refugees from Communist and Communist-controlled countries, and easy admission granted to unite separated families.[15]

Partly due to the backlog, partly to a sudden increase in applicants from Czechoslovakia and other Eastern European countries, the quota for refugees was exhausted by the end of the fiscal year 1968-69. In view of the shortage of seventh preference numbers (which reserves an annual quota of 10,200 for refugees), the Immigration Service approved the referral of family members to unused non-preference numbers. When this quota was filled the Attorney-General, after several months, authorized the use of Section 212(d) (5) for parole of refugees into the US. The Visa Office allocated for refugees some 500 visas for December 1969 and 2,700 for January 1970.

The Policy of Asylum for Refugees

Since the early beginnings of the country, the US "has provided asylum for those fleeing from persecution or oppression and seeking freedom."[16] The US has supported the efforts of the UNHCR to extend the principle of asylum for refugees worldwide. The extent to which the American people recognize this principle as long established in the national tradition was evident in the public response to the attempted defection in November 1970 of a Lithuanian seaman, Simas Kudirka. When Kudirka, a crewman on a Soviet vessel moored to a Coast Guard cutter in US territorial waters, attempted to defect, his return was requested by the Soviet captain and through a series of inept decisions and bureaucratic bungling a Soviet party was allowed to board the US vessel and forcibly seize the sailor. The public and the press were outraged, and distraught citizens from all over the country poured letters into Congressional offices. Within days the President had ordered an immediate report, and a full Congressional Hearing was held in December.[17] During this period the US Government also received a reprimand from the HC for the apparent violation of the 1967 Protocol.

The ultimate result of this unfortunate incident was the issuance of new Guidelines by the Secretary of State, approved by the White House on 4 January 1972 to Reinforce US Policy on the Right of Asylum. In this statement the President "re-emphasized the United States commitment to the provision of asylum for refugees and directed appropriate Departments and Agencies of the United States Government ... to take steps to bring to every echelon of the United States Government which could possibly be involved with persons seeking asylum a sense of the depth and urgency of our commitment." The Guidelines insisted that "the request of a person for asylum or temporary refuge shall not be arbitrarily or summarily refused by US personnel," and stated that the basic objective of the policy on right of asylum was "to promote institutional and individual freedom and humanitarian concern for the treatment of the individual."[18]

US Assistance Programs

Overall US contributions for on-going refugee assistance are channelled through both multilateral and directly operated US programs. These provide interim emergency care and maintenance, and assistance in the rehabilitation and reestablishment of refugees within their countries of asylum or in other countries.

US assistance in most refugee situations has been given through programs administered by the Office of Refugee and Migration (ORM) Affairs of the Department of State, as well as through US support of international organizations, including ICEM, IRCS, and UNHCR, and American voluntary agencies. US funds for refugee assistance in 1972 totalled $263.5 million.[19] The greatest part of this expenditure was allocated for assistance to Cuban refugees in the US ($139 million), but large contributions were made unilaterally for assistance in special refugee emergencies. The US, in addition to its annual contribution of more than $1 million to UNHCR, responded to a 1972 appeal for UNHCR for aid in assisting Sudanese repatriation and resettlement with support totalling more than $10 million in food and cash (a situation which was reminiscent of earlier US contributions of $5.7 million to Hungarian refugees and of $2.5 million to Algerian refugees). Ugandan Asians, who entered the US under the parole authority of the Attorney-General, were supported at a level of $1.5 million, and a contribution of $270,000 was made to the Burundi refugees (administered by the

Catholic Relief Services in Rwanda, CAR, and Tanzania).
The US Government supported through USRP the movement
of Soviet Jews from the Soviet Union to Israel with a contribution of $2.9 million in 1972.[20]

     In addition to participation in inter-governmental and
international agencies with concern for refugees, the US has
provided direct assistance by two US programs (Europe and
the Far East) which are funded and administered by ORM.
The larger of the two is the European Program, the US Refugee Program (USRP), called until 1966 the US Escapee
Program (USEP). This program was established by President Truman acting under the authority of the Mutual Security
Act of 1952, Section 101 (a) (1) (the Kersten Amendment); it
was continued under the authority of the Mutual Assistance
Act of 1954, as amended and codified later in the Migration
and Refugee Assistance Act of 1962 (PL 87-510). The program was initiated on 22 March 1954 with a fund of $4 mil-
lion.[21]

     US Refugee Program (USRP). While conceived pri-
marily on the basis of humanitarian considerations, the Escapee Program was also shaped by political thinking, namely
to demonstrate to the refugees and to the world the contrast
between the free European nations and those under dictatorial
regimes. It was intended to serve the "new" refugees: those
who had escaped from Eastern European countries, including
East Germany since 1 January 1948 (except that ethnic East
Germans were ineligible) and those in the Middle East. The
new refugees were located mainly in West Germany, Austria,
Greece, Trieste and Turkey, and their numbers were estimated at that time as 30,000. War and common criminals
were debarred from the program.

     In the course of discussions on coordination in the
Adv. Com. the US representative pointed out that "the program has been established because it had become apparent
that additional services for refugees would be required even
after the establishment of UNHCR and ICEM."[22] In the
Seventh GA the Czech delegation introduced a resolution
charging the US with subversive activity under Section 101
(a) (1) of the Mutual Security Act, in contravention of the
principles of the UN Charter. This resolution was rejected
by a vote of 41 to 5, with 14 abstentions.

     The primary purpose of USRP has been to assist ref-
ugees from Communist countries in Eastern Europe to

become reestablished, supplementing the assistance given by the countries of asylum, UNHCR, ICEM, and the voluntary agencies, in material aid, counselling and processing for resettlement by emigration and local integration. This program is directly administered by the Department of State, and the operational responsibility rests with the Refugee Migration and Red Cross (RMRC) Section of the US Mission in Geneva. Actual field work is carried out by eight American and international voluntary agencies under contract with USRP. The US allocated $64,230,000 to the program in the period 1952-71.

As noted earlier USRP is in working partnership with the UNHCR and ICEM. From 1952-69 the case load under this program was 316,510 refugees (from Albania, Bulgaria, Czechoslovakia, Hungary, Poland, Rumania, USSR, Yugoslavia and others). Of these, 79,057 resettled in Australia, New Zealand, Canada, the US, South Africa, and Rhodesia; 11,980 in Western and Central European countries; 7,359 in Latin America and 12,390 in other countries.

The USRP caseload in the spring of 1970 was about 25,000 refugees. About half were Czechoslovaks. Other nationalities, in order of numbers, were Polish, Hungarian, Rumanian, Albanian, Bulgarian and Russian. These are registered by voluntary agencies working in Europe and the Middle East. On an annual basis USRP is assisting roughly 55,000 refugees at a per capita cost of about $100 from ORM appropriations for the program of about $5.5 million.

The Far Eastern Refugee Program (FERP), funded and administered by ORM, was initiated in 1954 to assist the British Government and the Hong Kong authorities in their efforts for local settlement of Chinese refugees in the Crown Colony and in Macao. FERP assistance is programmed in coordination with the Hong Kong and Macao Governments and is implemented primarily through projects carried out by voluntary agencies under contractual arrangements with FERP. Such projects have included emergency assistance to new arrivals, integration assistance, vocational training, housing, medical services, educational facilities, resettlement abroad and the distribution and conversion of Food for Peace foodstuffs under the Agency for International Development (AID) and the Department of Agriculture. Since 1954 the US has allocated a total of $16,370 million through FERP in support of such projects.

The Food for Peace Program (PL 480), directed by
AID and the Department of Agriculture, provides surplus US
foods to needy peoples throughout the world, including refugees (especially in the Far East and Africa). An estimated
500,000 refugees in Hong Kong and Macao have received direct or indirect assistance through Food for Peace and FERP
activities.

Cooperative Action by Government and Voluntary Agencies

In the field of refugee assistance aspects of the activities of the voluntary agencies in the US were an essential
counterpart of government immigration programs. The voluntary organizations played a very important part, as they
had in wartime relief, in making immigration possible for
thousands of individuals through sponsorships, and in assisting with their integration in US communities. Overseas, as
economic conditions improved, voluntary agencies were able
to devote more attention directly to the needs of refugees
rather than to general relief.

Private voluntary agencies have not only spent since
the end of WWII more than $1 billion from private sources
to assist refugees, but have also made the implementation
of government resettlement legislation a success by helping
in the countries of asylum through counselling, language and
vocational training, and rehabilitation courses, and in the
US by securing sponsorship and helping in the reception and
integration of refugees in their newly adopted homeland.

Philanthropy in the US, although originating from the
same traditions as its European and, in particular, its British counterparts, developed along somewhat different lines.
American frontier society cultivated certain patterns of individual initiative and independent efforts for selfsufficiency
which were less evident in other societies. In isolated
frontier communities, helping one's neighbor in time of ca-
tastrophe, and mutual aid for tasks which were beyond the
individual's capabilities, were an integral part of society.
The philanthropic associations which grew up influenced by
these conditions were solely dependent upon their own resources for providing aid. This tradition of self-sufficiency,
combined with their enormous material resources, has been
a major factor in the vitality and multiplicity of voluntary
agencies in the US, and also helps to explain the ideological
conflict when, after WWII, many of them faced the prospect

of requesting government subsidies for their work, and of accepting government regulation of their activities. [23]

In their concern for their "neighbors" abroad, Americans have followed the precepts of the Old World, which had repeatedly come to the aid of the new nation from colonial times onward, not only with material assistance after such disasters as the Chicago fire, but with support for its educational, cultural, and religious institutions. Americans in their turn evinced similar concern through such agencies as the Relief Association for Ireland, which responded with material assistance to the great 1847 famine, the Northern Ohio Relief Association (1871) for relief to the needy of France and Belgium, and many others. Relief work which was undertaken under the leadership of Herbert Hoover after the invasion of Belgium in 1918 was continued after the Armistice in other countries of Europe, and in 1923 was extended to the Soviet Union for famine relief. The Spanish Civil War again evoked private US overseas philanthropy, over which, for the first time the government exercised limited controls. After the outbreak of WWII the private agencies "again made ready to carry out as best they could the tasks which they had never doubted it was their duty to meet."[24]

Among the American voluntary agencies which exist today, some of the earliest to respond to the needs of peoples overseas were the YMCA, the YWCA, the AFSC, the AJDC, and the Near East Relief Committee (now the Near East Foundation). Following WWI many additional agencies were founded. The outbreak of WWII, however, gave an impetus for spontaneous and, in some sense, chaotic expansion of private philanthropy from which the present-day structure has emerged. Not only did the denominational philanthropic agencies consolidate their work through the formation of vast relief organizations--NCWC, CWC, LWF, and UNHIAS--but a proliferation of ethnic agencies stirred the compassion of Americans for the plight of their compatriots abroad. Other secular groups were formed for assisting those suffering from the war without regard to their religion or nationality, such as CARE and IRC. By the end of 1939, 545 agencies were registered with the State Department alone. [25]

Simultaneous with the development of these agencies has been the increasing participation, especially after 1938, of the US Government in overseas philanthropy, not only as

the public expression of a humanitarian concern but also as
an important aspect of its foreign policy.   The present organization of relief and rehabilitation activities through voluntary agencies, and the pattern of interaction between these
agencies and the government, and between them and other
public bodies took shape during and immediately after WWII.

To channel the spontaneous outpouring of generosity
evoked by the war, and to protect its policy of neutrality,
the government in November 1939, through the Neutrality
Act, imposed certain restrictions on economic assistance to
belligerents, and required registration of all agencies handling
relief in those nations.   When the US entered the war the
government set up under Executive Order of 25 July 1942,
the President's War Relief Control Board (WRCB), which
further regulated the agencies, controlling their methods of
soliciting funds, and consolidating those with similar purposes.   The Board reduced the number of agencies operating
in the US from 545 in 1939 to 223 in 1942, and by 1945, to
90.   The President took an active interest in the operation
of the voluntary appeals, which, at his suggestion, were consolidated into a few major annual campaigns--the National
War Fund, the United Jewish Appeal and the United National
Clothing Collection.   Through these appeals $251 million in
funds and goods to the value of $186 million were col-
lected. 26

At the suggestion of the President's WRCB, seventeen
agencies in 1943 formed the American Council of Voluntary
Agencies for Foreign Service (ACVA) as a clearinghouse for
information on their activities.   The ACVA, which later grew
to 55 members, also served as a link between the voluntary
agencies and various government bodies, including Congress,
where its representatives were frequently asked to testify at
hearings.   In addition, the Council established criteria for
membership, including proof of financial stability, of humanitarian rather than propagandistic motives, and of acceptance
of certain standards for solicitation, which served to assure
the government of the reliability of member agencies.   During the latter years of the war, ACVA set up parallel councils in overseas areas for coordinating the work of agencies
operating in those areas.   This agency is today still the major link between American public and private overseas philanthropy.

America's part in post-war relief and reconstruction,
as well as its post-war assistance to the uprooted people of

the world, has been carried out through a partnership of
public and private agencies.   Emergency relief needs were
too vast for private organizations to meet unassisted.   Yet
the government recognized the value not only of the private
contribution, but of the special person-to-person manner in
which relief was administered.   In order to "tie together
the governmental and private programs in the field of foreign relief" (President's Directive of 14 May 1946) the President, simultaneously with the dissolution of the President's
WRCB and the removal of most of the restrictions on voluntary agencies, set up the Advisory Committee on Voluntary
Foreign Aid in 1946.   This board established registration
procedures and became the channel through which government support and subsidies became available to registered
voluntary agencies. [27]   The partnership was made concrete
when Congress appropriated funds for reimbursing private
agencies for the transportation costs of their relief supplies,
and by negotiation of special agreements with the governments of countries receiving such supplies exempting them
from import duty or taxes.   Surplus agricultural products
were also made available by the Department of Agriculture
for distribution by private agencies in support of their own
overseas programs.   The value of the supplies and facilities
through which government subsidized the voluntary agencies
enabled them to operate their programs with maximum effectiveness.

Emergency relief, however, was recognized by both
voluntary agencies and government as being only part of the
overall need for social and economic development.   Thus
when President Truman established a massive program for
technical assistance for economic development to overseas
countries in 1949, his program contained provision for cooperative actions by government and voluntary agencies.
Not only did the agencies develop, alongside their relief
programs, their own schemes for technical assistance for
self-help in the fields of agriculture, health education, and
so on; at times they also carried out government-initiated
assistance programs financed in whole or in part by the government under specific contracts. [28]

As has been said of the "people-to-people" quality of
voluntary philanthropy, "This relationship, while no substitute for governmental grants, has an indispensable quality
that no government-to-government aid can duplicate.   It has
created sympathy and good will between our citizens and their
fellowmen in allied and former enemy countries, and has

fostered an understanding of common problems. This humanitarianism is a force of enduring strength that can bind together the peoples of the world. "29

The voluntary agencies met a new challenge in late
1959 when the US became a country of first asylum for the
first time, and the government and voluntary agencies expanded their efforts to encompass refugee problems not only
abroad, but also at home.

The Cuban Refugee Program

Following the Cuban revolution of 1959 large groups
of Cuban refugees sought refuge in the US, confronting the
US suddenly with a challenge and problems already familiar
to European countries. Although many of them went to
Spain or to Latin American countries, the largest number
flooded into the US, because of its geographical proximity
and because of the close connections many Cubans had with
it through business, educational institutions, relatives, and
friends. More than 650,000 Cubans have come to the US
since Castro came to power.

The principal port of entry was, and continues to be,
Miami. The people of Miami and of Dade County, Florida--
the first to experience the impact of the refugee influx--or-
ganized through civic and religious groups a remarkable
emergency program. But the ever increasing Cuban population in that city soon exceeded the capacity and resources of
the local community. Because of this and because the problem was seen as a national one, President Eisenhower in
December 1960 and President Kennedy, soon after taking office in January 1961, made federal funds available to help
cope with the problem. On 27 January 1961, the Department of Health, Education and Welfare was directed by the
President to develop and administer a program of assistance
designed to deal with the Cuban refugee problem.

The program sought to help the refugees to adapt to
their new life by enabling them to become self-supporting
and to retain their self-respect. The emphasis of the program was on resettlement in order to reduce the refugee
population in Miami and the economic and social impact on
the community.

The program had to be implemented in an atmosphere

of great political tension and uncertainty.   Until the ill-fated
Bay of Pigs invasion on 17 April 1961, refugees, as well as
the American authorities, considered the program to be a
brief stop-gap one.   However, until 23 October 1962, when
all commercial flights were stopped, the influx of exiles into
Miami rose to between 1,500 and 2,000 each week, raising
the total number of arrivals in the area from 37,000 in
February 1961 to 150,000 in October 1962.

The program, operating since 1962 under the Immigration and Refugee Act of 1962 (PL 87-510), is responsible
for the following services: reception and registration of refugees upon arrival in Miami; classification of job skills; re-
imbursement to the states for welfare assistance and services to needy refugees; educational and health services; and
resettlement from Miami to homes, job opportunities, and
reunion with relatives in other parts of the US.

The program has been administered by the federally
operated Cuban Refugee Center, which opened its door on 7
December 1960 in Miami.   It has served as a focal point
for refugee registration and resettlement activities, and has
coordinated local aspects of the federal government's program, with state and local agencies participating.   Four national voluntary agencies (NCWC, CWS, United HIAS and
IRC) are under contract with the Federal Government to resettle Cuban refugees.   They work with their affiliates in the
states and local communities.   From 1961 to 71 the US allocated $585,000,000 to the Cuban refugee program.

The movement of Cuban refugees to the US can be
divided into three stages.   The influx began when the Communism of the Castro regime became apparent.   It reached
its first peak in the late fall of 1960 and continued until the
missile crisis on 22 October 1962, when the flights from
Cuba stopped.   During this period 153,534 Cuban refugees
were registered, of whom less than one-third, 48,361, were
resettled.

From October 1962 until November 1965, with no direct transportation available, only 30,000 refugees were
registered.   They came on Red Cross ships and on planes
returning from Cuba where the RC had taken medical supplies
in exchange for prisoners of the Bay of Pigs invasion.   In
the decade since 1961 an additional 11,282 persons crossed
the Straits of Florida in small boats at the risk of their
lives, while others reached the US via Mexico and Spain.
(These countries have maintained flights to and from Cuba.)

The third stage, that of the US airlift, followed statements on 28 and 30 September 1965 by the Prime Minister
of Cuba, Fidel Castro, declaring that Cuban citizens who
desired to join their families in the US or others wishing to
live in the US would be permitted to leave Cuba. In answer,
President Johnson on 3 October at the Statute of Liberty in
New York, declared

> that those who seek refuge here will find it. The
> dedication of America to our traditions as an asy-
> lum for the oppressed will be upheld. I have di-
> rected the Departments of State; Justice; and
> Health, Education and Welfare to make all neces-
> sary arrangements to permit those in Cuba who
> seek freedom to make an orderly entry into the
> United States. Our first concern will be with those
> Cubans who have been separated from children,
> parents, and husbands and wives now in this coun-
> try. Our next concern is with those who are im-
> prisoned for political reasons.

A fleet of small boats hurried to the coast of Cuba
to pick up refugees. Following a Memorandum of Understanding between the Embassy of Switzerland in Havana,
representing the interests of the US, and the Foreign Ministry of Cuba, concerning the movement to the US of Cubans
wishing to live in the US, regular flights from Veradero
Beach to Miami International Airport began on 1 December
1965. The airlift of refugees from Cuba was administered by
the Department of State, with costs of the airlift being borne
by the federal government. The airlift has brought refugees
to Miami at the rate of 800 to 900 a week.

Between February 1961 and 30 June 1972 the Cuban
Refugee Center in Miami registered a total of 445,150 refugees, with an overall resettlement rate of 66.4 percent of
registrations. From 1 December 1965 through 30 June 1972
persons coming in by airlift numbered 256,351 in 2,998
flights. The rate of resettlement away from Miami runs at
72.1 percent of airlift arrivals. As of 30 June 1972 nearly
300,000 Cuban refugees had been resettled to self-support
opportunities in all fifty states and more than 3,000 communities (see Annex 23.1).

In sum, it has been recognized that the refugee problem is of direct concern to the foreign policy and security
interests of the US. Programs for refugees have helped

those interests and been in line also with the traditional humanitarian role of the US in helping the persecuted and distressed, many of whom have relatives and friends in the US. Moreover, the refugees whether from Europe, Asia, or Cuba have proved a real asset through their professional qualifications, needed skills, and dedication to those "values which led to US independence. "[30]

Notes

1. Arthur Greenleigh, "Aliens and Foreign Born," Social Work Year Book, 1957, American Book-Stratford Publ. , New York, 1957: 105.

2. "How Many Refugees Are There in the United States?" Monthly Review, Immigration and Naturalization Service, Feb. 1944, 1(8): 3.

3. L. W. Holborn, "Refugees," The Annals, May 1939 and "Deutsche Wissenschaftler in den Vereinigten Staaten, " Jahrbuch für Amerikastudien, 1956: 15-26.

4. Exec. Order No. 9417, 22 Jan. 1944; for a detailed story of rescue operations of refugees, see Abba P. Schwartz, Open Society, NY, 1968: 162-67.

5. George L. Warren, Sr. was appointed by the President as the Advisor on Refugees and served as such as US delegate to the IGCR, IRO and ICEM Councils and to the UNHCR's Ex. Com. In his devotion to the refugee problem and his tireless efforts within the administration, he was one of the prime motivators before Congress for more liberal immigration legislation.

6. The DP Story, The Final Report of the US DP Commission, Washington, 1952: 211.

7. Ibid.

8. Whom We Shall Welcome, Rep. of the President's Commission on Immigration and Naturalization, US Govt. PO. , Washington, DC, 1 Jan. 1953.

9. Senate Rep. 629, 83rd Cong. , 1st Sess. , First Semiannual Report of the Administrator of the Refugee

Relief Act of 1953, US GPO, Washington, 1954: 1.

10. US, 85th Cong., 1st Sess., Senate Com. Print, 15
     Nov. 1967: 67.

11. US, 86th Cong., 1st Sess., Cong. Rec., Part 8, 17
     June 1959: 1014.

12. For text, see Immigration and Nationality Act, 5th ed.,
     revised through 31 Dec. 1965, US GPO, Washing-
     ton, DC, 1966: 197.

13. This system distributed among all the countries of the
     Western Hemisphere (except Jamaica, Tobago, and
     Trinidad) an annual total of nearly 157,000 quota
     numbers. The number of openings assigned to a
     given country was determined by the proportion of
     the US white population which its nationals or their
     descendents composed in 1920.

14. Immigration and Nationality Act, op. cit., 1966: 28-
     29.

15. John F. Kennedy, A Nation of Immigrants, rev. & enl.
     ed., NY, Harper & Row, 1964; "The New Immigra-
     tion," The Annals, Sept. 1966; Sidney Liskofsky,
     "US Immigration Policy," Reprint of American Jew-
     ish Year Book, Vol. 67, 1966 and US 89th Cong.,
     HR No. 745 and SR No. 748.

16. Attempted Defection by Lithuanian Seaman Simas Kudir-
     ka, Hearings before the Subcom. on State Dept. Or-
     ganizations and Foreign Relations, HR, 91st Cong.,
     2nd Sess., Dec. 1970, Washington, D.C., 1971: 8.

17. Ibid.

18. US Foreign Policy 1972, A Report of the Secr. of State,
     Dept. of State Publ. 8699, Apr. 1973: 164 and 557.

19. In 1971 the US contribution to UNHCR was $1 million;
     to ICEM $3 million; and to USRP $2.1 million; $.5
     million was allocated to FERP; and $27.5 million
     was made available to the closely related Food and
     Peace Program. Additional funds were maintained
     for designated groups of Southeast Asian and African
     refugees. The largest single US assistance program

was that for Cuban refugees in the US, $112 million in 1971. US Foreign Policy 1971: a Report of the Secretary of State, Dept. of State Pub. 8650, May 1972: 311.

20. US Foreign Policy 1972, op. cit.

21. Dept. of State, Bulletin, 14 Apr. 1952: 602.

22. George L. Warren, "The Escapee Program," JIA, 7(1), 8 Jan. 1954. A/AC.36/20, Sept. 1952: 10-11.

23. "Development Aid of American Voluntary Agencies," working paper of ACVA Conference on Development Aid of Private Organizations, Nov. 20-25, 1963.

24. Merle Curti, American Philanthropy Abroad, Rutgers UP, 1963: 480.

25. Registration was at that time a requirement only for agencies with programs of relief in belligerent countries. Many others served the still neutral countries. Arthur C. Ringland, "The Organization of Voluntary Foreign Aid: 1939-53," Dept. of State, Bulletin, 15 Mar. 1954: 391.

26. Ibid.

27. See US 89th Cong., 2nd Sess., Hearings of Subcom. ... July-Aug. 1966: 285 ff.

28. "Development Aid of American Voluntary Agencies," op. cit.: 3.

29. Quoted in Ringland, op. cit.: 1.

30. See hearings before the Senate-Subcom. on Refugees and Escapees, Mar. 1966, and Senate Hearings before the Committee on Appropriations, Foreign Assistance and Related Programs Appropriations, 92nd Cong., 1st Sess., Fiscal Year 1972, Washington, D.C. 1966 and 1971.

ANNEX 23.1

CUBAN REFUGEE PROGRAM
REGISTRATIONS AND RESETTLEMENTS, FEB. 1961-JUNE 1972

TOTAL REGISTRATIONS   TOTAL RESETTLEMENTS
      445,150   295,816

RESETTLEMENT BY VOLUNTARY AGENCIES SINCE
FEBRUARY 1961

	Registered	Resettled
USCC (Catholic)	297,664	188,126
IRC (Non Sect.)	91,887	61,870
CWS (Protestant)	51,092	43,092
HIAS (Hebrew)	4,459	2,838

OCCUPATION AND OLD AGE CATEGORIES OF AIRLIFT ARRIVALS

		Ages	
Professional, semi-prof., managerial	6.0%	0 - 5	10.1%
Clerical & Sales	11.2%	6 - 18	24.2%
Skilled	9.0%	19 - 29	8.6%
Semi-skilled	4.2%	30 - 39	19.5%
Service occupations	3.2%	40 - 49	15.7%
Farm-fishing	2.1%	50 - 60	10.4%
Children, students, housewives	64.3%	61 - 65	4.1%
		Over 65	7.4%

STATES AND D.C., OUTSIDE FLORIDA WITH THE
GREATEST NUMBERS OF RESETTLED REFUGEES
AS OF 30 JUNE 1972

New York	80,314	Massachusetts	8,147	Georgia	2,358
New Jersey	58,562	Texas	5,322	Ohio	2,353
California	39,040	Pennsylvania	3,857	D.C.	2,315
Illinois	22,146	Connecticut	3,817	Virginia	2,097
Louisiana	8,259	Michigan	2,779	Maryland	1,803

SOURCE: US Dept. of HEW, Fact Sheet, 30 June 1972.

Chapter 24

REFUGEES IN CANADA

Canada, as a "nation of immigrants, " has been among the foremost countries for reception of refugees since WWII. From the point of view of the HC, ever seeking favorable resettlement conditions for refugees in his charge, Canada, by virtue of its almost unlimited absorptive potential, its traditional and evolving immigration policies and the advanced administrative machinery for implementing them, and the sympathetic and cooperative attitude of both public and private agencies in regard to refugee problems, continues to provide excellent opportunities for uprooted people throughout the world to start life anew.

Official statistics of refugees have not been kept separate from those of other immigrants except for certain indentifiable refugee movements.[1] Canada's total intake of immigrants from 1945 to July 1969 was 3,176,634, of which a very large number were refugees.[2] Most of these immigrants are from Britain and the Western European countries. In recent years, however, immigration from Europe has been declining while it has been increasing from the US, Asia and the Caribbean (see Annex 24.1).

Canada's Immigration and Refugee Policies

Canada's enormous size and great natural resources are the crucial factors in its developing need of people. There are vast timber and agricultural lands, extensive mineral deposits, almost untapped sources of rich oil supply, great hydro-electric power supplies and great fisheries in both salt and fresh water. Successive waves of immigrants have, over the years, provided Canada with a large proportion of the manpower with which to develop these resources, and immigration is still a primary source of population expansion.[3]

589

Canada's population of 1,681,000 (1971) is composed primarily of the two ethnic strains which were its original settlers: French, who were the first permanent settlers and who, with their descendants and new immigrants formed 28.09 percent of the population in 1961; and British who, though coming later than the French, surpassed them in numbers, and continue to increase in numbers through immigration more than any other group representing in 1961 almost 58.45 percent of the population. The remaining 13.5 percent represent other groups predominantly of European origin.

Principles of Selective Immigration. Up until the first decade of the twentieth century Canada had an open door for immigrants, although those who entered came mainly from the British Isles, and from British stock in the US. Restrictions were first placed on immigration in 1910 when the Canadian Immigration Act excluded certain categories of persons: physical or moral defectives, conspirators, etc. This Act came at a time of peak immigration which continued until the outbreak of WWI. After that time a series of Orders-in-Court restricting various aspects of immigration were eventually embodied in the Revised Immigration Act of 1927 whose effect was virtually to reverse the open door policy; thenceforth immigration was prohibited for all persons with the exception of immigrants from certain countries who met stipulated occupational or skill requirements, as well as health and character standards. British and US immigration was not affected and was, in the British case, encouraged by such measures as transportation loans and reduced fares. This restrictive policy was pursued inconsistently and was subject to political considerations and economic trends, as well as to humanitarian considerations, until 1929 when, with the onset of the Great Depression, highly restrictive measures were enforced. The outbreak of WWII further reduced immigration. By 1941 immigration and natural increase had brought Canada's population to just over 12 million.

Post-war economic expansion in Canada again called for greatly increased manpower resources. Canadian immigration policy, including the admission of refugees has been "to increase the population by bringing forward carefully selected immigrants in such numbers as can be absorbed into the Canadian economy."[4] The foundations for this policy were laid by Prime Minister Mackenzie King in a statement before the House of Commons on 1 May 1947:

1. ... to foster the growth of the population of
    Canada by the encouragement of immigration.
    The Government will seek by legislation, regu-
    lation and vigorous administration to ensure
    the careful selection and permanent settlement
    of such numbers of immigrants as can be ad-
    vantageously absorbed in our national economy.

2. The objective of the Government is to secure
    whatever population we can absorb, but not to
    exceed that number. The figure that repre-
    sents our absorptive capacity will clearly vary
    from year to year in response to economic
    conditions. [It may be added that it also varies
    seasonally.]

3. The people of Canada do not wish as a result
    of mass immigration to make fundamental al-
    teration in the character of our population.
    [This refers primarily to Asiatic immigration.]

4. ... Canada is perfectly within her rights in
    selecting the persons whom we regard as future
    desirable citizens.

5. British subjects from the UK, Ireland, [and
    other Commonwealth countries] and citizens of
    the US who desire to enter Canada will only be
    required to meet certain standards of health
    and character and to show that they are not
    likely to become public charges. [Citizens of
    France were given similar privileges in 1948.]

6. During the depression and the war immigration
    was inevitably restricted but now the categories
    of admissible persons have been considerably
    widened. Special steps will also be taken to
    provide for the admission of carefully selected
    immigrants from among the displaced persons
    in Europe. [5]

Administration and Procedures.   To carry out these
broad principles the Canadian Government, through its Department of Citizenship and Immigration, organized a well-
trained administration for recruiting, screening, receiving,
and settling immigrants selected according to Canada's
changing needs. Selection was made not on a numerical or

national-quota basis, but rather on the basis of need within
certain categories of "admissible immigrants. " Thus, within
admissible categories, if prevailing conditions in Canada call
for persons in certain occupations such as lumber men, carpenters, or farm workers, applicants who possess those
skills and meet other qualifications of health and character
have been accepted. If openings in these fields did not exist in Canada, even though such workers qualified on other
grounds, they were rejected until such time as openings
again existed for their skills. Thus, both immigrants and
Canadians have been protected from unemployment which
might be caused by oversupply, through immigration, of manpower in particular occupations.

"Admissible immigrants" fell into two categories:
those who applied directly to government recruiting agents
for admission--unsponsored immigrants--and those whose admission was sponsored by a relative or other person who
was a Canadian citizen. After 1947, citizens of the countries
in Western Europe, DPs and refugees, could apply for admission as unsponsored immigrants provided they met the
health and character requirements, and in addition that they
were called forth by the Department of Citizenship and Immigration, or by the Department of Labour for placement in
available employment for self-establishment in agriculture,
business or industry, or for domestic service. Most refugees who came to Canada under the IRO were in this category. Nationals of countries outside of Western Europe (including refugees, unless special provisions were made) were
barred from unsponsored immigration.

Canadian citizens could sponsor the immigration of
relatives, in broad categories, who were citizens of these
Western European countries (including in this case Israel,
Turkey, Egypt, Lebanon) or of the Americas. Sponsorship
of relatives from all other countries was limited to immediate family--husband, wife, children under 21, mother over
60 or father over 65. All other relatives in the nonpreferred
countries were barred. Sponsored immigrants were also
required to meet health and character requirements and usually, although not always, skill and employability requirements as well. Thousands of refugees have rejoined their
families in Canada through the sponsored immigrant plans.

Changes made in subsequent years had the effect of
liberalizing criteria for these admissible categories: in the
unsponsored category, by permitting citizens from additional

countries to apply or by relaxing economic assimilability criteria; in the sponsored category, by permitting Canadians to sponsor an increasingly wider range of relatives from additional countries, as well as persons who were not relatives.[6] Furthermore, Canadian immigration practices have always allowed exceptions to the rules to be made, on humanitarian or other grounds, by means of Orders-in-Council. It is through this means that thousands of handicapped refugees have been permitted to enter Canada who did not meet regular immigration requirements of health, or probable economic assimilability.

Group Movements and Sponsorship Plans.   Refugees have been admitted to Canada either in group movements or under close relative and individual sponsorship plans.   The group movement plan, including those recruited by government for farm, domestic, or other unskilled labor, and those recruited by private industry to work in the garment industry, lumbering and railroad development, etc., was adopted soon after WWII both for humanitarian reasons, and to fill Canada's need for particular types of labor in its post-war economic development.

Beginning in July 1946, several movements were initiated which, while not specifically for refugees, nevertheless included a large number.   In July 1946 the Canadian Government authorized the admission of 4,000 Polish veterans from England or Italy (4,527 eventually arrived) to work for a minimum of two years as farm laborers.   They were later permitted to have their families join them.   In 1949 when conditions in Shanghai were becoming desperate, Canada accepted several hundred European refugees from the Far East without examination.   During 1948-49 over 1,000 persons from Baltic countries arrived in small boats on the shores of Canada, and were admitted, eventually permanently.   To avoid the possibility of further dangerous voyages, Canada set up offices in Europe at which such refugees could apply for admission.   The government also authorized the movement of 10 blind refugees to be sponsored by the Canadian National Institute for the Blind, and of 2,000 orphans who were to be placed for adoption by regular Canadian adoption services.   In 1949, the government permitted the International Student Service to sponsor refugee university students.   One of the most interesting movements was that of 15,000 farm owners from the Netherlands, whose lands had been inundated by the German Armed Forces.   Through the combined efforts of the Dutch and Canadian Governments,

places were arranged in Canada, and agriculturists were
selected in the Netherlands who came to Canada first as
laborers, but with the understanding that they would eventually acquire farms of their own. They were dispersed to
all provinces for settlement.

          Resettlement of DPs. By far the largest movement
was that of DPs from camps in Europe. On 7 November
1946 the Prime Minister announced that the government had
approved emergency measures to bring certain DPs and refugees to Canada. Arrangements were completed with the
IRO to facilitate their movement. Canadian selection teams
from the Departments of Health, Immigration, and Labour
examined persons collected by the IRO in centers of occupied
territories. (Canadian selection teams were among the first
in Europe after the war.) Those selected by reason of
health, character, and occupational suitability were eventually settled in Canada where, once established, they could
submit application for first-degree relatives. There were
also some DPs in occupied territories who did not come
within the mandate of the IRO; an organization was formed
in June 1947, the Canadian Christian Council for the Resettlement of Refugees (CCCRR) to assist in the processing
overseas, and the movement to Canada of these immigrants.
Of the 165,697 persons settled in this movement between
1947 and 1952, the largest occupational categories were do-
mestics, farm workers, miners, wood workers, hydro-con-
struction workers, railway workers, and clothing industry
workers (in that order). This movement, although motivated
by humanitarian considerations, nevertheless recruited immigrants who met existing Canadian immigration requirements
and manpower needs.

          Immigrants recruited under this plan, usually single,
or unaccompanied male workers, in most cases had employment arranged for them by the Department of Labour before
their departure from Europe. Canadian employers seeking
laborers under this scheme were required to sign an agreement whereby they guaranteed to the immigrant at least one
year's employment at prevailing wage rates, and suitable
accommodation. By the end of 1951, 56,609 refugees--
53,028 workers accompanied by 3,581 dependents, some of
whom were themselves also placed in industries--had been
admitted. Later, workers admitted under these group movements were able to have their relatives admitted. To fill
labor requirements of private industries, representatives of
various industrial associations also went to West Germany to

assist in the trade-testing of refugees admissible under "un-sponsored immigrant" provisions. In many cases industries agreed to bear the cost of rail transport from immigration ports in Canada to the final destination--as did the Department of Labor for its recruits.

Social Services and Provision of Citizenship. Government concern for an immigrant's welfare does not cease with his arrival under these arrangements. Like other aliens, the refugee benefits from the assistance of many branches of federal, provincial and local government, and, except for certain privileges such as voting, has full civil rights under law, may join a labor union, and enjoys the benefits of unemployment insurance, labor legislation, and a wide range of social welfare benefits. Aliens must fulfill residence requirements in order to benefit from federal Social Security (20 years for old age benefits and ten for blind persons' benefits). However, provincial government benefits are usually available after a shorter period of residence. (The Province of Ontario in 1959 reduced the period of required residence for handicapped refugees to six months.) Both the Settlement Division of the Department of Citizenship and Immigration, and the National Employment Service assist when necessary in finding employment for immigrants after their guaranteed year's employment ends, or if it is unsatisfactory. Refugees, in particular, also benefit from the Order-in-Council providing that any refugee taken to Canada under the group movement plan who becomes ill during the first six months of residence will receive medical assistance at the expense of the Department of Labour. The cost of illness occurring during the second six months is shared by the Dominion Government and that of the province in which the refugee resides. In addition to his right to benefit from regular educational programs in each province (the provincial government is responsible, for example, for education) refugees may also participate in special two-year language and citizenship classes held wherever six or more immigrants are gathered.

Certain difficulties were experienced in spite of these arrangements. Many refugees, unaccustomed to the isolation of a Canadian farm and separation from their countrymen, eventually drifted to the more populated areas and already crowded cities, thus defeating the hope of their even distribution throughout the nation. Furthermore, many eventually settled in national enclaves, rather than becoming integrated with Canadian society. Language difficulties contributed to

this trend, and to the inability of certain immigrants to hold
dangerous jobs in the lumbering industry.   Some employers,
for their part, attempted to employ immigrants only season-
ally rather than steadily, and some failed to provide suitable
accommodation.   The difficulty of matching professionals'
training to Canadian requirements was also a problem.   But
on the whole, immigrants, including refugees, were successfully settled by these programs.

        Since 1950 one of the conditions of admission has been
the applicant's suitability for eventual citizenship.   Under the
1947 Canadian Citizenship Act (amended in 1950) a refugee
or DP, like any other alien or immigrant from continental
Europe, may become naturalized after declaring his intention, and after five years of continuous residence.   Naturalization of parents implies also naturalization of children,
for each of whom, however, separate application must be
made.   Many refugees, however, do not avail themselves of
the opportunity to become citizens, although the average
waiting period to do so has been reduced from twenty years
in 1947 to eleven in 1951. [7]

Voluntary Agencies

        Immigration before WWII had been largely of English-
speaking persons who did not require the detailed follow-up
help which it is the custom of voluntary agencies to give to
foreign immigrants.   Canada's post-war determination to
step up the rate of population increase by means of active
recruitment of immigrants in Europe, although backed by
public opinion, was not backed, except in the case of Jewish
voluntary agencies, by a well-organized network/of private
organizations such as had developed in the US.   The government itself was obliged to organize the services required by
immigrants both overseas and in Canada.   It fell to local
church and welfare groups, however, to assist immigrants
with the many individual problems they faced after arrival.
Both French- and English-Canadian agencies geared themselves immediately after the war to meet the many demands
of the fast-growing immigrant population, of whom a large
proportion (up to 60 percent in some years) were refugees
who spoke neither English nor French.   Between 1946 and
1952 more than 600,000 immigrants--almost 5 percent of
the total population--entered Canada. [8]

        <u>Coordination of Voluntary Efforts.</u>   Shortly before

WWII, attempts at coordination resulted in the formation of the Canadian National Committee on Refugees (CNCR) whose double purpose was to arouse Canadian public interest and make known the plight of the refugees, and to induce the government to modify its restrictive immigration policy so that refugees and victims of persecution might be admitted to Canada. Throughout the war and afterwards the Committee pursued its educational campaign; it established practical means of assistance to immigrants; it maintained liaison with key officials in the government, putting constant pressure on them for modification of policy; and it kept in close touch with the IGCR and, later, with the IRO. As a result of public pressure on government generated by the Committee's campaign, the first Order-in-Council was approved in 1947, authorizing the admission of 5,000 DPs. This marked the beginning of a government policy of liberalizing the immigration laws and regulations for which the CNCR had been striving for many years. Its principal objectives having been accomplished, the CNCR disbanded, just at a time when Canadian immigration was on the upswing.

Coordination of voluntary efforts, much needed after that time, was accomplished through provincial organizations, some of which were more successful than others. The Montreal Council for New Immigrants, for instance, formed in 1949, coordinated all major ethnic and religious welfare agencies. After establishing effective functional liaison with the Department of Citizenship and Immigration in 1951, it was instrumental in altering deportation practices formerly affecting immigrants who had gone into debt to pay their passage to Canada. After 1951 the French-Canadian agencies, which had deep-rooted differences in approach from their English counterparts, withdrew from the Council and established their own program under the Service to New Canadians of the Montreal Commission of Catholic Schools; the French concentrated on welfare services, education, and language and vocational training for the children of German, Hungarian, Slovak, Polish and Ukrainian immigrants. The French-Canadian attitude toward immigration before the war had been rather negative, in view of the fact that the predominance of immigrants of British or American origin tended further to increase the imbalance of the population, but in the post-war period their attitude was reversed, both in response to the Vatican's expressed sympathy for DPs and refugees, and because of the much higher proportion of non-English speaking immigrants in post-war movements.

The most advanced of the English-Canadian efforts was developed in Ontario, which received the bulk of the immigrants. Activities of a wide range of agencies were coordinated in the Canadian Welfare Council (CWC), but services to immigrants and refugees were not, in most cases, separated from ordinary welfare programs, except for special programs of child care, vocational training, and recreation and health schemes. Since education was one of the primary needs of new immigrants, the CWC cooperated with the Canadian Citizenship Council (CCC, an offspring of the Canadian Education Association). The CCC not only promoted immigrant education at home, but in 1951, at the request of the IRO and of the Canadian Department of Citizenship and Immigration, organized orientation and counselling services for prospective immigrants in refugee centers in Germany, Austria, and Trieste.

In order to assist Canadian voluntary agencies to develop their organizations for promotion of resettlement opportunities, the UNHCR, in 1952, allocated $12,890 to the WCC, and $22,600 to LWF from Ford Foundation Funds. In 1953 the WCC was able to sponsor the entrance into Canada of 2,588 refugees, and the LWF of 4,000. By the time of the Hungarian Crisis in 1956, voluntary agencies were able to assist in the placement and integration of many of the 282,164 persons who migrated to Canada in 1957, its peak year of immigration. Their efforts during WRY were at the core of the large-scale assistance given to refugees during the years of high immigration rates, and five of them were officially entrusted with the responsibility for sponsoring handicapped refugee families entering during and after those years.

Jewish Relief Agencies. The Jewish share of efforts in behalf of post-war immigrants (27,500 or about 5 percent of whom were Jewish) was undertaken by established organizations. Canada's oldest voluntary agency, the Jewish Immigrant Aid Society (JIAS), has been operating welfare services since 1922, and specialized in pre-emigration and reception activities. By 1939 the United Jewish War Relief Agencies (UJRA) of the Canadian Jewish Congress (CJC) were organized into committees each with its special role, or with responsibility for a particular group of immigrants before they entered Canada.

The CJC was authorized by the 1947 Order-in-Council to bring to Canada 1,000 Jewish war orphans, for whose

complete care (physical and educational) UJRA was to be responsible for a period of five years.   In addition, UJRA assumed responsibility for three trade schemes which they had
promoted, whereby a group of 2,500 DP tailors, 500 furri-
ers, and 300 milliners were admitted to Canada, even though
only about half of them were Jewish.   UJRA paid all travel
costs within Canada.   Jewish agencies also extended services
to European refugees from Shanghai to whom Canada had
granted temporary visas while they awaited resettlement opportunities in the US, and obtained government permission
for those refugees, for whom no opportunities in the US could
be found, to remain permanently in Canada.   When the great
post-war IRO movement of refugees brought many Jews to
Canada, Jewish voluntary agencies were well prepared to receive them.

Response to Refugee Needs Since 1951

        In the post-war years Canadian immigration policies
have been adjusted to a greater extent "to the requirements
of the world in which we live and less to the needs and pre-
ferences of our own Canadian society."9   The most important feature of the new Act passed in 1952 was its flexibility.
The Act, as in Australia, merely established "prohibited
classes" of immigrants.   The actual flow of immigrants was
regulated from year to year by Orders-in-Council.10   George
F. Davidson, Deputy Minister of Citizenship and Immigration,
elaborating on the Canadian policy, stated that "our refugee
program today divides itself into three main streams ...
economic, social and humanitarian."   The economic stream
is the unsponsored or "open-placement" scheme.   The social
stream is the family-reunion program in which persons with
relatives in Canada have preference over those who have
none, and in which refugees are permitted to enter Canada
in family units rather than as employable individuals.   The
humanitarian stream is represented specifically by the flow
of handicapped refugees to Canada, sponsored by private individuals or voluntary agencies, who are admitted without
regard to their potential economic or social contributions to
Canada, or even to their ability to become self-sustaining.11
Increasingly liberal attitudes have enabled growing numbers
of the world's refugees in each of these streams to find permanent homes in Canada.

        Liberalization of Immigration Policies.   Canada's
generous attitude toward refugees was manifest most strongly

in its response to UNHCR pleas for resettlement opportunities, first for Hungarian refugees in 1956, and later for refugees in Europe and those of European origin in the Far East at the time of WRY. Canada accepted some 38,000 Hungarian refugees with virtually no screening, at a cost to the Canadian Government of more than $15 million, with additional sums provided by provincial governments and private organizations. This was the largest group of persons yet accepted into Canada who were not specifically selected for their potential economic contribution to the nation.

During the winter of 1955-56 Canada also allowed "winter movement" of refugees from overseas. Such movement had previously been barred because of the difficulty of finding accommodation and placement, especially in agriculture, during the winter months. Although there are no refugee camps as such in Canada, the government set up hostels for the reception of immigrants awaiting placement by the Department of Labour. Conditions in these hostels were relatively austere, and it was preferred that they not be used in winter. Nevertheless, in view of transportation difficulties and because of the pressure of the Hungarian crisis, and later the closure of refugee camps in Europe, Canada has permitted, although not encouraged, arrival of immigrants during the winter months.

Although the problems resulting from these huge movements were amazingly few, medical and institutional care of some kind was required for approximately 1,500 of these refugees. The movement also included 1,000 university students who required assistance of a special nature.[12]

Canadian Contribution to World Refugee Year. Canada's response to WRY was outstanding. The government took a number of special measures to help achieve one of UNHCR's main objectives--the closing of refugee camps in Europe. The Canadian Government was one of the early supporters of the concept of WRY and led the Canadian fund raising campaign by strong, publicly announced support of its purposes, and by reiterating the necessity for both public and private effort to achieve them. Canada was surpassed only by the US in its contribution to UNHCR for the period, and was third, after the US and the UK, in the value of its contribution of food and money to UNWRA.[13]

Several schemes for the admission of handicapped refugees, which were announced by other governments as special projects for WRY, were almost identical with the normal sponsorship program which had been carried out by Canada for years. Under this sponsorship program, relatives or one of five recognized church agencies could sponsor specific refugee families even though they suffered handicaps of health or age, if they undertook certain responsibilities to prevent these families from becoming a public charge. During 1960 alone, in addition to refugees and families being sponsored by relatives in Canada, 100 cases, totalling 249 persons, were sponsored by community groups, or voluntary or religious organizations.

Canada's special contribution to WRY, and to the problem of refugees in subsequent years, was a novel program, later followed by other immigration countries, of admitting tubercular refugees and their families to Canada for treatment and rehabilitation. Taking into account the fact that large numbers of refugees who had been in European camps for a prolonged period had developed TB and that it was extremely difficult to persuade countries of immigration to accept these refugees, the government initiated conversations with the HC, and consulted the provincial governments in Canada to work out possible arrangements for alleviating the situation in Europe. The HC termed this program a "breakthrough." With modern methods of treatment available in Canada, patients responded quickly. In view of the success, the provinces agreed to an extension of the program in which they participated by accepting the cost of treatment in provincial sanatoria while the federal government paid all other expenses (transportation, and maintenance where necessary until the families were reasonably able to support themselves). Selection criteria were worked out with the UNHCR. Canada's only major restriction on eligibility was in regard to mental and criminal cases, and that those with contagious diseases other than TB would not be accepted.

During WRY, also, the traditional "Assisted Passage Scheme" (begun in 1951) whereby immigrants could receive interest free loans for travel, to be repaid after they had become settled in Canada, was broadened to include additional categories of immigrants, and refugees and their families.

Changes in Immigration Regulations After WRY

The enthusiastic and generous response of Canadians

to the emergency of 1956 and to WRY were largely maintained in Canada's attitude toward subsequent refugee immigrants; furthermore, changes in immigration regulations
themselves "were brought about as much because of world
opinion, influenced by the efforts of UNHCR and by WRY, as
by the drying up of Canada's traditional sources of immigrants, who were, by now, needed for the economic development of their own countries in Europe. "14

A "Global Policy." In 1947 The MacKenzie King
principle of maintaining the balanced composition of Canada's
population gave way officially to a "global policy, " in which
qualified persons from any nation are potentially admissible
as immigrants. Revised Immigration Regulations, effective 1
February 1962, eliminated most restrictions based on nationality, and placed primary stress on individual merit and
education. In addition, they permitted non-citizens to sponsor a broad category of relatives and friends after only six
months' residence, thus, greatly favoring family reunion
from countries which had previously been non-preferred and
from which many refugees came. 15 The Assisted Passage
Scheme was now extended to this category also. Furthermore, certain hardship cases were permitted to enter, provided the sponsor could indicate ability to provide for the
newcomers, even if they did not meet health or occupational
standards. The regulations provided for the reunion of families from Asia and the Middle East in particular on a
broader basis than had been possible before. 16

Among the special refugee movements carried out by
the Canadian Government under the new regulations was the
movement in 1963 of 100 Chinese refugee families from Hong
Kong. This brought to some 25,000 the number of Chinese
who had come to Canada from Hong Kong and China since
1950. 17 Authorization was given for 50 families of stateless
persons from the Middle East to be settled in Canada under
private auspices in 1962, and another 50 in 1963. A total
of 251 persons was involved in this movement. The movement to Canada on an experimental basis of an unspecified
number of handicapped refugees was also authorized in 1962.
Refugees in this movement were to be at least partially employable, or to have at least one employable person in the
family so that they would not need extensive public assistance.

1967 Immigration Regulations. Changes in Canadian
economic and social life, and in world economic conditions
have caused Canada to retreat to some extent from the

high-point of non-restrictive immigration policies of 1963. This retreat has not reversed the fundamental concepts of the "global policy," but has considerably stiffened criteria for admission. In 1966 a slackening of employment opportunities for unskilled workers, along with increased demand for skilled and "white collar" workers, suggested the need for immigrants whose education was sufficient to permit them to adapt to changing conditions in Canada. With other developing countries competing for skilled workers, Canada, in order to discourage the entry of unskilled labor, and thus to avoid an over-supply of unemployable labor, drew up new immigration regulations. Policies, announced in 1966 by The Hon. Jean Marchand,[18] were embodied in new Immigration Regulations which took effect on 1 October 1967 (PC 1967/1616).[19] Responsibility for immigration, formerly residing in the Department of Citizenship and Immigration, was placed in the newly created Ministry of Manpower and Immigration.

In the economic stream--unsponsored immigrants selected by government or industry--few changes were necessary, since the policy of selection according to need allowed for the redirection of recruitment efforts to the desired categories of immigrants. In the social stream, however, previous policies had allowed the potential mushrooming of the very category of immigrants for whom it was now most difficult to find employment. Refugees and other immigrants had been permitted to sponsor a broad range of relatives with little regard to their employability in Canada, and these in turn, after six months of residence could sponsor additional everwidening circles of relatives. It was precisely in this category of immigrants that educational standards tended to be lowest and skills the least adaptable to changing employment opportunities in Canada. "In Canada's advanced economy, if those entering the work force, whether native-born or immigrants, do not have the ability and training to do the kinds of jobs available they will be burdens rather than assets."[20] The new regulations, therefore, stated that all sponsored immigrants proposing to enter the labor force should be literate and have the equivalent of a Canadian primary education, or possess a skill which Canada needed. Sponsors of any but immediate dependants would, in the future, have to be Canadian citizens, as an indication of their own firm settlement in the country and their ability to assist the sponsored immigrant to become established. On the other hand, all remaining nationality restrictions were removed from all categories of immigrants. Regulations for sponsoring

immediate family members and true dependants were not
changed. Some potential immigrants from among refugee
groups have undoubtedly been prevented by these regulations
from entering Canada, but the growing number of immigrants
from countries with refugee problems indicate that many refugees are still able to resettle in Canada as members of the
labor force.

Humanitarian Concerns. Canada is perhaps most
noteworthy, insofar as refugees are concerned, for the "humanitarian stream" of immigration. This stream persists
regardless of fluctuations in the economic and social streams.
Humanitarian motives have underlain immigration policy in
both the economic and social streams. Yet it is important
to note that certain programs, such as those for TB and
handicapped refugees, have had humanitarian considerations
as their central purpose, and that admissions under the
sponsored programs have included many persons who could
never become independent of their sponsors or of the society. Canada has accepted, at considerable expense to itself,
responsibility for the care and welfare of these refugees who
can in no way contribute materially to the nation. The degree to which this responsibility commits the sponsor is indicated in that "the basic duty of the sponsor is to meet any
situation that might develop."[21] This implies limitless responsibility, regardless of the sacrifice involved. And this
responsibility has been shared, in Canada, by federal, provincial, and local governments, by voluntary agencies, and
by private individuals who have acted with true humanitarian
motives in behalf of many helpless persons.

Even in 1966 when announcing the restricted regulations, Mr. Marchand stated, "There will be a continuing obligation to accept individuals or families who have fled their
own country for one reason or another. However, neither
the extent of the obligation nor our capacity to fulfill it can
be predicted with any accuracy. The former depends essentially on conditions from time to time throughout the world
or in particular countries. The latter is contingent on the
Canadian economic, social, and political structure remaining
strong and healthy." This principle applied equally to in-
capacitated members of Canadian families, whose cases
should be determined individually. "The important thing is
to retain the capacity to make exceptions in deserving circumstances without having the exceptions become the rule."[22]

The Canadian Effort Abroad and at Home

Canada has from the earliest period supported international efforts on behalf of refugees. It became a member of the IRO in 1947 and contributed about $18.1 million to the organization. It has been a member of the UNHCR Ex. Com. since 1957. Its contribution from 1951 to 1969 reached $4.7 million, and it donated $650,000 in 1956-57 to the Canadian Red Cross for assistance to the Hungarian refugees. In 1969, the Canadian Government increased its annual contribution to UNHCR to $400,000 from the previous figure of $350,000.[23]

The "global policy," despite the 1967 restriction, continues to provide resettlement opportunities for refugees from all over the world. The new policies, in fact, while tending to discourage immigration from countries which formerly gave asylum to many refugees, encourage it rather from those nations in which the UNHCR now finds it greatest problems. Thus in 1967, immigration figures, which include refugees, list 5,767 immigrants from Hong Kong, 679 from Malta, 399 from Cyprus, and 7,962 are listed from the West Indies, 2,054 from Africa and over 6,000 from the Middle East. Many still come from European countries, the greatest number from Italy.[24] Canada also continues to keep in close contact with UNHCR in order to be able to respond to refugee needs throughout the world. Thus in 1968, when the Czech crisis threatened Europe with new refugee groups, Canada sent special teams of immigration officers to European countries to facilitate the movement of the more than 12,000 Czech refugees who wished to resettle in Canada. And in 1969 Canada admitted 274 Tibetan refugees from India. As further indication of its continuing concern for refugees, Canada, in 1969, ratified both the 1951 Convention and the 1967 Protocol. Not only do refugees who resettle in Canada find chances for integration into that country's economic and social life, but Canada stands as the potential home for future victims of political turmoil.

Notes

1. The movements for which statistics are available are those under the IRO, from 1946 to 1951, 123,479 refugees and DPs. Those under UNHCR from 1951 to 1960, 115,055. Many of both groups were handicapped persons or required medical and welfare

assistance. GA, Ex. Com. (VI), A/AC.96/Inf. 4, 16 October 1961. Canada admitted in WRY, 325 tubercular refugees and their dependents. Canadian participation in WRY resulted in the admission to Canada of over 5,000 refugees, including 1,097 from camps in Italy and West Germany. As of 7 July 1969, Canada had also admitted 11,165 refugees from Czechoslovakia who had left that country at the time of the Soviet intervention in August 1968.

2.   Statistical Supp. to ICMC News, Mar.-Apr. 1970, No. 73.

3.   Freda Hawkins, Canada and Immigration, Public Policy and Public Concern, Montreal, 1972; Joseph Kage, "The Canadian Immigration Policy: A Historical Appreciation," JIAS, No. 5, May 1963: 9.

4.   Canada, Dept. of Citizenship and Immigration, Annual Rep. for the Fiscal Year ended 31 Mar. 1951: 19.

5.   Canada, HC Debates, 1 May 1947: 2763-5.

6.   Ellen L. Fairclough, "The Social Implications of the New Immigration Regulations" Social Planning Council of Metropolitan Toronto, Immigration Conf., Mar. 9, 1962: 39.

7.   Vernant, The Refugees in the Post-War World: 557.

8.   Ibid.: 570.

9.   The Immigration Act of 1910, rendered awkward by many revisions and new regulations added over the years by Orders in Council, was superseded in 1952 by the present Immigration Act [R.S.C. 1952, c. 325] to which additional amendments and regulations have, from time to time, been added.

10.   CYB, 1964-65, Dominion Bureau of Statistics, Year Book Division.

11.   George F. Davidson, to the annual meeting of the AICC, NY, 24 Mar. 1961 in UNHCR, Ref. Serv., No. 23, Sept. 1961.

12.   Dept. of Citizenship and Immigration, "Canada's

Refugee Programs--1945-1961, " JIAS, Statements and Documents on Immigration and Integration in Canada, No. 1, May 1962, Montreal: 3.

13. W. B. Nesbitt, "WRY--The Government Program, " to the Canadian Com. for WRY, 29 June 1960.   Statements and Speeches, Inf. Div. of Dept. of External Affairs, No. 60/28.

14. J. Kage, "Canadian Immigration Policy Today, " UNHCR, Ref. Serv. No. 5, May 1963:   12.

15. CYB, 1964-65.

16. Ellen L. Fairclough, Minister of Citizenship and Immigration, May 9, 1963, JIAS, No. 3: 42.

17. S. F. Rae, Statement to Ex. Com. (X), Oct. 1963.

18. Jean Marchand, Min. of Manpower and Immigration, White Paper on Immigration, Oct. 1966.

19. Passed by Order-in-Council, 16 Aug. 1967, and made effective on 1 Oct. 1967 as PC 1967/1616.

20. Marchand, op. cit.:   8.

21. Davidson, "Humanitarian Immigration and Problems of Integration, " Rep. on Conf. convened by CWC, 26 Oct. 1961, JIAS, No. 8, June 1964: 18.

22. Marchand, op. cit.:   16.

23. CYB, 1969.

24. For discussion of the new policy see Freda Hawkins, "Canadian Immigration Policy, " "Canada's Immigration Policy Re-examined" and Martin Joney, "Canada's Immigration Policy" in Race 1971, also Freda Hawkins, "The Canadian Experience" in Venture, Vol. 23 (1) Jan. 1971: 32-35.

ANNEX 24.1

CANADIAN IMMIGRATION:
MAJOR SOURCE COUNTRIES, 1966/1969

1966 Total Admissions	194,743	1969 Total Admissions	161,531
1. Britain	63,291	1. Britain	31,977
2. Italy	31,625	2. US	22,785
3. US	17,514	3. West Indies- Antilles	13,093
4. Germany, Fed. Rep. of	9,263	4. Italy	10,383
5. Portugal	7,930	5. China	8,272
6. France	7,872	6. Portugal	7,182
7. Greece	7,174	7. Greece	6,937
8. China	4,094	8. Germany, Fed. Rep. of	5,880
9. West Indies- Antilles	3,935	9. France	5,549
10. Australia	3,329	10. India	5,395

SOURCE: Freda Hawkins, "Canadian Immigration," Race
Today, Mar. 1971: 89.

Chapter 25

REFUGEES IN AUSTRALIA AND NEW ZEALAND

I: Resettlement in Australia

Since the end of WWII, Australia has provided a
unique opportunity for over 350,000 refugees to start their
lives anew by becoming a vital element in this developing
nation. Australia has, since the establishment of the first
penal colony in 1788, been populated mainly by immigrants
and their descendants, but by the end of WWII the "empty
continent" still had a population of only 7.5 million, including some 300,000 aborigines remaining from a once vast
population.   For a land the size of the US (excluding Alaska)
such a population was extremely sparse.   Although the government had specifically encouraged immigration since shortly after WWI, by a joint Commonwealth State scheme for selecting migrants and contributing to their transport costs,
and by an agreement in 1925 with the UK (from which a majority of immigrants continued to come), nevertheless, Australia's growth through immigration continued to be subject
to sharp fluctuations.   Immigration was brought to a virtual
standstill first by the world depression in the 1930s, and
then by the outbreak of WWII.

By the end of the war, shortages of a wide range of
goods and supplies and a backlog of housing, power, and
other needs which these shortages in turn gave rise to,
pointed up the nation's isolation and the urgent need not only
for extensive and rapid development of the economy, but especially for a sizeable increase in the labor force, and in
the population in general.   In 1945, with all major parties
for the first time unanimous in their support of immigration,
the Commonwealth Government decided upon a vigorous immigration program that would be planned on a continuous
basis, and would be supported by industry--both management
and trade unions--and by all sections of the Australia community.[1]   The resulting planned effort, led by the Commonwealth Government, has made the Australian immigration

program unique. By 1970, more than one-fifth of Australia's total population of 12. 3 million people was made up of post-war migrants.

Immigration Policy and its Implementation

The fundamental principles underlying immigration policies have concerned "homogeneity of its population, readiness of absorption, familiarity of religion, the same fundamental attitude of living. "[2] Three basic policies are corollaries to these principles. First, that it is the right of every nation to determine its own racial and cultural composition, which in Australia is predominantly of persons of British stock and a smaller number of Europeans, with aboriginals and members of other racial stocks forming a small percentage.

Second, immigration has been regarded as part of a program of national development of which population increase is an important element. Thus, the government has aimed for a high rate of economic and population growth, with full employment, increasing productivity, external viability, and stability of costs and prices. In view of the urgent need for population growth it set a target for an annual intake of one percent by immigration: an increase of 75, 000 per year on the basis of its population of about 7. 5 million in 1945.

Third, in view of the first two premises, immigration must be deliberately and carefully planned so as to further the development of both a homogeneous society and a stable economy. Immigrants must be those who can contribute to this economic development and who can be easily integrated into Australian social and cultural life, and who will not disrupt the welfare of "old" Australians by generating economic or social friction. Furthermore, special care must be taken in planning for their integration into the economy and into the society. Immigration policies based on these objectives have been drawn up by the Commonwealth Government, and particularly by the Department of Immigration within the framework of the Migration Act of 1958, which repealed and consolidated previous legislation.

Immigration legislation in Australia, as in Canada, has provided a flexible framework within which the Minister of Immigration sets policy and determines from year to year the actual flow of migrants to Australia. Before 1958 the

major legal provision (in the Immigration Act of 1901 and
the Alien Deportation Act of 1948) stated that, to gain admission, an immigrant must pass a "dictation" or written
English language test.   This requirement was effective in
maintaining a considerable homogeneity of population.   In
1958 the new Migration Act eliminated all language requirements, but required instead that all persons (with certain
exceptions, such as diplomats and the crews of ships in
Australian harbors) must obtain an entry permit from immigration authorities at the port of entry.   Although there is
no mention of race, nationality, or numbers in the law itself, the mechanism of the entry permit provides control:
anyone can be admitted who has an entry permit; but whether
the permit is granted or refused is at the discretion of the
Minister of Immigration and his officials.   Nothing is explicitly stated as to the grounds on which permits will be granted
or refused, although certain categories (such as convicted
criminals) are still "prohibited immigrants, " and can be refused entry. [3]

To implement these objectives within this legal framework, a Department of Immigration was established in 1947.
The Minister of Immigration is responsible: (1) for determining the absorptive capacity of the economy at any given
period; (2) for encouraging programs to assist in the economic and social integration of new Australians; and (3) for
planning recruitment techniques according to availability of
potential immigrants, and facilitating the transportation of
migrants.

To achieve the first objective, analysis of absorptive
capacity, the Minister established an advisory body of top
level industrialists, trade unionists, and leading figures from
the universities and from primary industry.   This Immigration Planning Council serves the dual purpose of advising the
Minister on matters relating to the economic and industrial
absorption of migrants and of providing private enterprise
with reliable data on which it can base its own planning for
development.   It advises the Minister on the types of immigrants most urgently needed to break industrial bottlenecks,
on priorities in allocating immigrant labor, and on the desirable location for immigrant hostels in relation to key industries, etc.

Working with the information given by this Council,
the Minister of Immigration can adjust annual objectives to
existing conditions.   In the immediate post-war years, for

instance, when returning veterans accentuated the already
serious housing shortage, immigrants were recruited who
were skilled in the building trades, and so could not only
help achieve the desired increase in population but at the
same time assist in solving a serious Australian problem.
Likewise, when employment opportunities were limited by a
recession in the early 1960s and the effects of the post-war
"baby-boom," so that admission of new members of the
working force would have had an adverse effect on old Australians and previous immigrants, the Department of Immigration could stress family reunion and still maintain the
annual population increase. Because there has long been an
imbalance in the sex ratio, the Department also seeks propitious occasions for encouraging migration of single women
to offset earlier recruitment of single men for the labor
force. Thus, the mechanism of the Immigration Planning
Council provides the opportunity for refined adjustment both
of recruitment to absorptive capacity and of available man
power to economic development, while still allowing a continuous annual population increase through migration.

     The Immigration Department, with the assistance of
the Commonwealth Immigration Advisory Council, has also
led the nation in planning for the social integration of immigrants. It has recognized that integration itself is a two-
sided process. Not only must the immigrant be assisted in
adjusting to the new society but the society itself often needs
help in adjusting to newcomers. Combined government and
citizen efforts in both aspects of the problem of integration
have resulted in a high degree of harmony between new Australians and their old Australian hosts in communities
throughout Australia.

     Before the war, migration to Australia from countries
other than the UK was very small. Even in the years of
highest migration in the 1920s only about one-tenth, or 3,000
to 4,000 of the immigrants, were from other European countries. No special attempt was made to assist adjustment,
but it was assumed that any adjustment would be on the part
of the newcomers. They were to abandon their language and
customs and become assimilated by becoming as much like
their hosts as possible. After WWII the situation changed
radically, especially when Australia received nearly 200,000
refugees from Europe within a period of only two years.
From that time onward, a very large number of European
immigrants have come each year, some to join relatives, but
others, sponsored by the government, alone. The concept of

"assimilation" has had to be replaced by one of "integration, " implying mutual, rather than one-sided adjustment. Recognizing that the situation called for deliberate action, the government has taken special measures to assist in immigrant integration.

Many government agencies and private organizations play a role in this integration effort.   The State Department of Labour, as well as the National Employment Service assist in placement of immigrants.   State Housing Commissions assist in finding accommodation.   Private banks, also, often provide Migrant Information Services which include translation of trade certificates and documents.   National clubs, churches and voluntary organizations aid in personal adjustment and education, and the Good Neighbour Movement (see below) plays an outstanding role in this field.   In addition, because of the importance of the social aspects of immigration, the government, in 1957, set up the Commonwealth Immigration Advisory Council to conduct investigations and report to the Minister on all aspects of the social integration of migrants into the Australian community.   The Council includes representatives of such bodies as the National Council of Women, the Australia Council of Social Service, the Australian Council of Employers Federations, the Australian Council of Trade Unions, the Council of Local Governments Association, and the Country Women's Association.

Specific responsibility for carrying out measures for social integration, however, rests with the Citizenship Division of the Department of Immigration.   It investigates complaints about discrimination due either to misapplication of regulations or to unfair results of such regulations.   It provides welfare counselling to assist immigrants in taking advantage of the provisions to which they are entitled.   Nationality and residence requirements still operate to limit the welfare benefits available to immigrants, but they nevertheless do enjoy many benefits such as maternity and child endowment, unemployment and sickness benefits, and certain medical and rehabilitation services.   Old age and widows' pensions are limited to British subjects, although the government assists private organizations in the construction and purchase of homes for the aged. [4]   The Citizenship Division also provides translation and foreign-language press services. More recently it has developed a Field Officer Service for interviewing a cross section of immigrants on a continuing basis in order to provide the information necessary for assessing immigration policies and regulations insofar as integration is concerned.

An important task of the Citizenship Division is the Adult Migrant Education program, which is mainly concerned with helping immigrants to learn English. Australia has recognized the fact that a good knowledge of English, though no longer required for admission, is a basic requirement for true integration. In addition, it is a legal requirement for citizenship, for which immigrants can apply after five years' residence. The Division provides teachers on immigrant ships coming to Australia and conducts classes at its Bonegilla Migrant Center, where most immigrants spend some time upon arrival. It also helps to arrange night classes all over Australia, often carried out by voluntary organizations as part of the Good Neighbour Program.

The Division's most vital function is its role as coordinator and leader of the national voluntary effort in behalf of immigrants. Through its sponsorship of the annual Citizenship Convention, and its support and encouragement of the Good Neighbour Movement, the Citizenship Division Department has been a central force in promoting the necessary adjustment on the part of both immigrants and the receiving communities. It is this mutual adjustment that has served to keep the "returnee" rate of migrants extremely low, especially among non-British migrants, and has contributed to Australia's continuing ability to attract a sufficient number of immigrants to more than fill its annual targets.

The Citizenship Convention

In 1949, recognizing the need for a deliberate effort on the part of all segments of the Australian community to promote the successful integration of new Australians into the community, the government approached the voluntary organizations and called the first annual Citizenship Convention. This Convention, which has met annually since 1950, is attended by members of Parliament, of Commonwealth and State Governments, and of the Immigration Planning and Advisory Councils, as well as by representatives from churches, community organizations, commerce and industry, the press, radio and television, and by a substantial number of persons from the Good Neighbour Movement itself. Representatives from this cross section of the nation gather to discuss their separate integration problems, and to hear lectures by top

national and international figures on whichever special topic
has been made the central concern of the year's convention.
Guest speakers have included such persons as Mr. Pierre
Jacobsen, Deputy Director of ICEM, and both UN High Commissioners, Dr. Auguste Lindt and Dr. Felix Schnyder, as
well as many other prominent international figures. [5]   A report of each Convention, printed in the Australian Citizenship
Convention Digest, is available to communities throughout the
nation.   The widespread publicity given to the annual Convention helps to provide the public with factual information on
developments in the field of immigration and to stimulate interest in immigrants, and gives migrants an indication of the
interest taken in their welfare. [6]

The Good Neighbour Movement

Recognizing that "the introduction of nationals from
many lands would call for special measures to bring about,
in the short term, the satisfactory settlement of newcomers
and, in the long term, their economic social and cultural integration into the community without loss of desirable ethnic
characteristics, the Commonwealth Government "sponsored a
nation-wide movement to insure the speedy and smooth integration of all newcomers. "[7]   In 1950 the Good Neighbour
Movement was officially created, with branches known as
Councils set up in each of the six states and in the Capital
Territory.   This organization coordinates and promotes the
existing organizations interested in immigrant welfare.   The
councils draw together the work of all voluntary organizations
and individuals working in behalf of immigrants who wish to
become members of the Council.   In each community, church
organizations, the Boy Scouts, YMCA, Rotary, Chamber of
Commerce, ethnic groups formed by immigrants themselves,
societies formed by commerce, industry and trade unions,
returned soldiers' clubs, etc. may become members of the
movement through local Good Neighbourhood Councils.   Cooperation between State Councils and their branches in local
communities is achieved by means of continuous correspondence, conferences, and the annual national Citizenship Convention sponsored by the Department of Immigration.   The
government also appoints a Coordinator to provide personal
liaison between the parts of the movement and between them
and the Department, and underwrites all administrative expenses.

The task of the Good Neighbour Movement is two-fold:

on the one hand, recognizing that any efforts on the part of persons interested in helping immigrants would bear little fruit unless the community itself were receptive to immigrants and aware of their problems, the movement endeavors to educate members of the public. Through its monthly periodical, The Good Neighbour, the Department of Immigration has been able to allay many fears of receiving communities concerning immigrants--fear of economic competition, of foreign influence undermining Australian customs, etc. It has fostered an appreciation of the contribution which immigrants can make to the society and, consequently has stimulated efforts on the part of citizens to assist in the task of alleviating the inevitable adjustment problems of immigrants.

On the other side its work concerns the immigrants themselves.   "In general the members of the Good Neighbour Movement endeavor to insure that newcomers receive neither better nor worse treatment than Australians in normal community affairs. "

The work of the Good Neighbour Movement starts with the arrival of the immigrant in Australia, when a contact worker greets and visits him and offers preliminary help in the practical business of getting settled. Other services involve giving advice on legal matters, social service, housing, naturalization, etc. In addition, members of the movement organize social functions, assist in language training, plan activities for youth, and set up informational programs with speakers, exhibits and films to acquaint the immigrant with his new home. In all these activities, the actual work is carried out by members of the separate groups which form the Council, but, more recently, the Councils themselves have, upon occasion, actually organized programs for which members were not able to assume responsibility. All in all, despite certain weaknesses, such as a concentration on new arrivals and a tendency to neglect immigrants who have already become "settled, "[8] the Good Neighbour Movement has made immigrant integration the business of the entire Australian community.

Planning Recruitment and Facilitating Transportation

Ability to attract and absorb continuing large numbers of immigrants results not only from these vigorous and well-planned efforts to gear immigration objectives to economic and social conditions, and to mobilize the nation for promoting the integration of immigrants, but also from a complementary program of recruitment and transportation assistance. The framework within which this program operates is set, not by legislation or by decree, but by policy decisions taken from time to time by the Cabinet--usually at the time of the Budget debates. The Minister of Immigration is given broad discretionary powers in applying these policies. Flexibility, therefore, is an outstanding characteristic of the operation of Australia's immigration program. 9

While Australia has been able to control both the economic and the social aspects of immigration from within the nation, it can exercise only limited control over the availability of desired immigrants. Vigorous publicity and recruitment campaigns guided by the Immigration Publicity Council, and generous assisted passage schemes arranged with other governments and with ICEM have been used to attract desired immigrants. But flexible application of policies is probably mainly responsible for Australia's ability to find suitable immigrants, even in the face of growing manpower shortages in the countries which have traditionally been the sources of its migrants.

As in Canada, immigrants come to Australia in several categories: Some--private nominees--are nominated by relatives, friends, employers or groups in Australia. Others--Commonwealth nominees--are nominated by the Commonwealth for specific purposes such as labor requirements, balance of sex-ratio, family reunion, or for compassionate purposes. Of these migrants a very large proportion (over half in some years) receive assistance in meeting the high cost of their passage to this land whose distance from most source countries would make migration impossible for most potential migrants. Some persons come to Australia unassisted and on their own, however, and may be permitted to enter if they meet health and character requirements and can show that they will not become a financial charge on the nation within a predictable period. Over these immigrants the government exercises control through the entry permit requirement. Over other categories of potential immigrants the government can exercise control through setting eligibility requirements for assisted passage, and defining the closeness of relationship required for private sponsorship. Thus, persons from the UK, highly desired by Australia, are eligible for private sponsorship and for assisted passage with virtually no restrictions. The same has been the case with citizens

from many of the countries of northern Europe with whom
Australia has drawn up assisted passage agreements.   In
other areas, Italy and Greece, for instance, where the population pressure makes available a constant supply of more
potential migrants than Australia feels could be socially and
economically absorbed, only close relatives or persons with
particular skills can be privately nominated, and assisted
passage is granted only to the kind and number of persons
desired by Australia. [10]   In areas where the national culture
is most different from the traditional British-oriented way of
life, or in communist areas, no assisted passage schemes
are drawn up, and no specific, clearly defined regulations
are stated as to who will be accepted for private sponsorship.   Decisions in individual cases are at the discretion of
the Minister, and can be exercised quite arbitrarily.   The
same applies to non-European nations, from which immigration is deliberately kept at a minimum. [11]

The need to maintain a steady annual intake has forced
Australia to put this potential flexibility to the test over the
years as changing conditions in Europe have affected the
sources from which Australia can attract immigrants.   The
assisted passage agreements indicate the direction in which
Australian policies have shifted since its immigration program recommenced in 1947.   Although exceptions were always made in the case of refugees by particular arrangements, these shifts in general recruitment policies have increased the opportunities for refugees to migrate to Australia as regular immigrants.

Negotiations with the UK during the war resulted in
both the free passage scheme for ex-servicemen and their
wives and children, and the renewal of pre-war assisted
passage schemes for other selected migrants resident in the
UK, in which a distribution of costs was established between
the two governments, in the first case, and between them
and the immigrant in the latter.   In the assisted passage
schemes, immigrants nineteen years old or over were to pay
a fixed portion of their passage while the two governments
shared the major part of the cost.   If the migrant chose to
leave Australia before the end of two years, he agreed to
repay the entire government share of his passage costs.
Persons under nineteen paid nothing.   Both private and Commonwealth nominees were eligible for assisted passage.

Shipping immediately after the war was extremely
limited, but arrangements were made with commercial

British lines which customarily travelled to the Orient, and even with BOAC and Qantas Airlines, for allocating a fixed number of berths per year to assisted or free passage migrants. After the advent of ICEM, most travel arrangements were made in conjunction with that organization. The free passage scheme came to an end in 1954, but the assisted passage scheme has been renewed repeatedly, and serves as the model for bilateral agreements made with several other governments in subsequent years, the first of which was with Malta, in 1949, for the benefit of British subjects residing there.

Because of the shipping shortages after the war, movement of migrants from Britain was far below the potential level, and there remained for many years a backlog of potential migrants who could not be brought to Australia. When the IRO appealed to Australia in 1947 to take migrants from among the refugees in Europe, Australia used the opportunity for the double purpose of fulfilling her annual population growth targets and providing relief for refugees. Under the agreement, Australia agreed to take 5,000 refugees annually, to be transported by the IRO. Selection missions in Europe were set up to screen immigrants for health and character, and to eliminate former members of the Nazi party, and also, to pick from among refugees those, especially male workers, who could contribute to the labor needs of the Australian economy. This arrangement continued until the closing of the IRO in 1951.

As the number of refugees decreased, however, and in spite of the increasing availability of shipping the number of migrants from Britain was insufficient to meet Australian targets, and Australia had to look elsewhere for immigrants. In 1951 the first assisted passage schemes for non-British migrants were negotiated--with the Netherlands in April 1951 (under which the Netherlands was responsible for finding shipping from among its own commercial lines), with Italy in August of that year, and with Germany in August 1952. Assisted passage arrangements, in conjunction with ICEM, were developed with Austria and Greece from August 1952 onward, with Spain in August 1959, and with Belgium in February 1961. The great majority of Australia's non-British European assisted immigrant intake is achieved under these agreements and arrangements. Furthermore, in 1954 Australia decided upon a system whereby selected persons from countries which could not or would not enter into formal arrangements might also receive assistance for their passage

to Australia. Under this General Assisted Passage Scheme
Australia agreed to subsidize the passage costs up to $160
per person and smaller amounts per child. With the con-
currence of their governments, the General Assisted Passage
Scheme was made available for migrants from the US, Denmark, Norway, Sweden, Finland, Switzerland, France and
Ireland, and countries in the British Commonwealth not already eligible under the agreement with UK.

Through these arrangements and with an average annual expenditure of $13.3 million, and offices set up in thir-
teen countries to administer them (Germany, the Netherlands,
France, Austria, Italy, Malta, Belgium, Spain, Greece,
Scandinavia and Finland, Switzerland, Egypt, and Hong Kong)
Australian immigration authorities can select the kinds of
persons they wish, and control the numbers from each country. There has been little consistency in the policies by
which immigrants have been either accepted or refused admission to the assisted passage schemes; a person who is
rejected one year may be needed another and may be accepted if he tries again. Thus, with the flexibility of the
arrangements for Commonwealth nominees, and restrictions
which can be placed on, or removed from private or family
nomination possibilities, Australia has been able to control
any excess of persons from any given area or of any given
type in order to maintain population and economic equilibri-
um. And, with vigorous publicity campaigns (which have
been likened to Madison Avenue techniques) it has, in most
years, been able to adjust its immigrant intake to its set
goals.

In the twenty-five years between 1945 and 1970, Australia received 2.6 million immigrants, of whom approximately half were British, and of whom approximately half came
on assisted passages. Of the non-British arrivals, nearly
500,000 had been naturalized by 1965. The composition of
the annual intake of immigrants has varied over the years,
with Northern European countries at first providing the largest numbers of non-British migrants (12,000 from Germany
in peak years, 17,000 from Holland, and 38,000 from Poland
in the peak years around 1951). Italy, Greece, and Yugoslavia succeeded these northern countries, and have also remained prime sources of non-British migrants for Australia.[12]
As through the entire period, refugees have swelled the ranks
of immigrants, not only as immigrants under regular schemes,
but also by special arrangements made with the UNHCR for
relief of the special refugee problems with which it has had
to deal over the years.

By 1969, during which year alone 184,000 new settlers arrived, Australia once again felt the need for a reappraisal of immigration needs and of the policies which had
governed the program over the preceding twenty-five years.
"Increasingly--the implications of immigration must be related more closely to total progress rather than to economic
progress in isolation."[13] To the continuing factors determining immigration programs must now be added the problems of urbanization, population distribution and "the great
discovery of the sixties," man's effect on his environment.[14]
This broader based approach called for a far-reaching round
of investigations and studies, which were announced by the
Minister on 26 July 1969, and for the addition of authorities
on urbanization and environment as consultants to the Immigration Planning Council. The studies, to be carried out by
the research staff of the department over a period of several
years, include investigation into desirable future population
levels and the role of immigration in achieving them, a cost-
benefit analysis of immigration, and time-span surveys of
some 10,000 immigrants during their first three years in
Australia.   These surveys were to employ techniques pioneered by Canadian authorities.   In this connection, closer
liaison with Canada's migration authorities was also proposed, including exchange of survey results and other information.

Australia's new requirements, as well as changed
conditions in source countries, called for changed recruitment efforts.   As in Canada, the need was felt for addition
to Australia's labor force of persons with technical and professional skills--also in demand elsewhere.   Recognizing the
need to revise its attitude to European professional and trade
qualifications, the Minister for Immigration, in 1969, established a Committee on Overseas Professional Qualifications,
as well as a committee to study the training of skilled workers in Europe.   In June 1970, the Minister himself visited
a number of countries with a view to drawing up further migration agreements.   With immigration offices operating in
twenty-eight countries, Mr. Lynch emphasized the "need to
take office operations to the doorsteps of potential migrants"
and to extend both counselling services and advisory services
for professionals.[15] Thus again, "at the beginning of a
period as significant, in its own way, as that in which the
present immigration programme was planned,"[16] Australia
strives to adjust its immigration program to current needs
at home, and present conditions abroad.

Australia's Contribution to the Resettlement of Refugees

From the point of view of the UNHCR the Australian immigration program has provided a constant outlet for overseas resettlement of European refugees from many areas of the world. Not only have flexible policies permitted relief at times and in places where the severest pressures for resettlement have arisen, but the nation-wide integration program for all migrants has made Australia a most satisfactory resettlement country. Australia has responded generously to appeals from the UNHCR for assistance in solving particular refugee problems, notably those of the refugees of European origin in China, of handicapped refugees after WRY, of Hungarian refugees in 1956, and of Czech refugees in 1968. More recently Australia has helped an increasing number of cases of refugees from the Middle East and Africa.

Special Considerations for Refugees under General Immigration Programs

In proportion to its population Australia has led the world in accepting refugees for resettlement.[17] Between October 1945 and December 1963, of the 2,044,014 permanent arrivals, 278,905 (13.6 percent) were refugees. More than two-thirds of these came to Australia on assisted passage schemes (see Annex 25.1). Between 1952 and 1963 nearly one-fourth of the total number of persons coming to Australia under ICEM were refugees (see Annex 25.2).

Although many of these were selected like regular immigrants, according to occupational skills, many were accepted without regard to these considerations. In 1953, Australia agreed to select refugees from Eastern Europe who were living in refugee camps in Trieste. Approximately 5,000 such refugees were selected, including a large number of unaccompanied youths sponsored by NCWC. Under similar arrangements Australia agreed to accept 5,000 German East Zone refugees as assisted immigrants within the framework of the Australian-German bilateral agreement. Many such refugees were non-German. In 1956, 500 visas were set aside for refugees from Italy under Australia's bilateral agreement with that country. In May 1956 Australia requested permission from the Governments of the USSR, Hungary, Poland, Rumania and Czechoslovakia for persons residing in these countries to rejoin relatives in Australia, and streamlined its immigration procedures to facilitate the movement of those relatives for whom exit permits might be granted.   By December 1963, 41,359 nominations had been made, and 22,779 exit permits granted.

During WRY, the UNHCR acknowledged that Australia's acceptance of refugees in connection with camp clearance programs in Austria and Italy was a significant factor in reducing camp population despite the continuing influx. [18]

Special Refugee Groups

Australia was among the leading countries of resettlement for Hungarian refugees.   Of the 27,937 who had come to Australia by 1963, 14,060 were admitted after the 1956 October uprising.   In March 1957, considering the difficulties faced by European residents from Egypt, the Australian Government permitted their nomination by residents of Australia, even though they did not fall within the normally accepted classes from that area.

The special needs of European refugees in China have been met with outstanding generosity by Australia.   Not only were 15 percent (2,907) of those settled whom the IRO moved to Australia between 1947 and 1951, but under the joint UNHCR/ICEM Far Eastern Operation of 1952-1963, Australia accepted 44.7 percent of those moved (8,746 persons).   This movement was made possible by special arrangements following UNHCR's appeal whereby individuals and religious bodies in Australia might nominate refugees from mainland China without regard to numbers or qualifications.   Furthermore, Australia provided 50 floating visas, enabling refugees to secure exit permits from China in order to encourage the nomination of refugees from that country.   In 1953 the UNHCR allocated the sum of $11,000 to the WCC with which resettlement opportunities for 602 refugees were provided. The UNHCR also contributed $12,667 to the LWF for promoting nomination of these refugees by Australians.   When the new Three Rivers crisis arose in 1964, Australia stated that it would consider sympathetically any of the 1,400 refugees from Sinkiang province who might be able to reach Hong Kong.

Handicapped refugees have also benefited from sympathetic interpretation of immigration policies, especially since WRY.   Following representations by Dr. Lindt during

his visit to Australia in 1958, Australia agreed to accept 50
cases from among refugee families in Europe who had previously been rejected for health reasons. The scheme was
eventually extended, and 300 families had been sponsored by
relatives, friends, or voluntary organizations in 1963. In
addition, Australia agreed to accept 10 families with no relatives in Australia, one of whose members suffered a disability which disqualified the entire family. Over 200 families eventually benefited from this scheme. Australia, during WRY, abolished visa fees for refugees and extended the
age limits under which refugees could be considered for assisted passage schemes. And in 1961 Australia made available to the UNHCR the services of Dr. Jensen for the purpose of examining in detail those cases of "old refugees"
still under the HC's mandate; of those presented for resettlement, Australia accepted a significant proportion.

In recognition of the great contribution made by Australia to the solution of refugee problems, the Nansen Committee awarded to Sir Tasman Heyes, Secretary of the Australian Department of Immigration from its formation in 1946
until his retirement from office in November 1961, the Nansen Medal for 1962.

Since that time Australia has continued to assist the
UNHCR in the solution of refugee problems. By 1969 it had
accepted over 350,000 refugees as such, and thousands more
had come under family reunion and other regular immigration schemes. Special measures were taken in 1968 to permit entry of refugees from Czechoslovakia after the 1968 uprising, bringing the total accepted from that country to over
3,000. In addition, the government has, on the basis of
representations by the UNHCR, approved special schemes for
admission of small groups of refugees such as Albanians
from Yugoslavia and Assyrians from Lebanon, who are being
sponsored by the Australian Council of Churches. [19] Permission was also granted for Cuban refugees in Spain to apply
for migration to Australia.

The UNHCR has continued to allocate funds to Australia for promotion of resettlement opportunities, in varying
amounts according to needs; in 1966, $94,840 was allocated[20]
and in 1967, $22,211 was granted for sponsorship promotion
and $1,000 for supplementary assistance. The UNHCR has
also assisted in financing the building of old-age homes for
refugees. [21] But in general Australia has been able, with
assistance from agreements with ICEM and the bilateral

assisted passage schemes, to carry most of the burden of
resettling refugees.   The UNHCR report for 1969 states:
"Australia continued to serve as one of the leading countries
for refugee migration.   The extensive facilities in the field
of reception and assimilation which are provided by the Australian Government, with the support of many community
groups such as the Good Neighbour Council, have made it
possible for the government to maintain without interruption
its policy of large-scale population building in which refugees
form an important component. "22

II: Resettlement in New Zealand

New Zealand, too, has been a steady supporter of
UNHCR endeavors to find permanent solutions for the problem of refugees.   Since WWII, 7,000 refugees have found
new homes in that country.   New Zealand was a leader in
the HC's drive to ease immigration restrictions for handicapped refugees.   In addition to its steady support of the
UNHCR, the government has contributed generously to projects to aid refugees throughout the world.   Voluntary organizations united under the Council of Organizations for Relief
Service Overseas (CORSO) have not only raised vast sums
of money for refugees abroad, but have established invaluable services for those in New Zealand, including the Nansen
Home for older refugees in Wellington.

The growth of New Zealand's population from 664,419
in 1886 to 2,857,862 in 1970 has depended more upon natural
increase than immigration.   Nevertheless, of the number of
immigrants entering between 1945 and 1966, a total of 6,934
were refugees, moved to New Zealand with international assistance under IGRC, UNRRA, IRO, and ICEM.   Although
New Zealand immigration laws favor immigration of persons
from the UK, many have also come from other European
countries, notably from Holland, among whom were many
refugees.23   In 1966 alone, 1,000 Hungarian refugees were
admitted.   And in 1967 the government agreed to examine
dossiers of refugees from Yugoslavia.   Those of four large
family groups (74 persons) were submitted in that year.

"As far as European refugees are concerned, New
Zealand's main significance is as a migration haven for the
handicapped. "24   High Commissioner Lindt visited New Zealand in January 1958, appealing for resettlement opportunities
for refugees from the Camp Clearance Program in Europe.

In March 1959, New Zealand became the first overseas country to accept handicapped refugees and their dependents without requiring individual sponsors to guarantee that the refugees would not become liabilities to the state. Twenty families, each with one handicapped member, were admitted under government responsibility. "This was a breakthrough of
paramount importance, for it opened the doors to refugees
who had been rejected time and again under normal immigration criteria."[25] This example set off a chain reaction,
with a succession of other countries following suit with similar concessions, especially during WRY. In New Zealand,
itself the success of the first venture prompted the government within a few months to take a further contingent of
families with handicapped members. Four successive
schemes followed, in each of which 100 families were brought,
with assistance from ICEM, for resettlement in New Zealand.
Voluntary agencies have contributed greatly to the success of
this program. The St. Vincent DePaul Society, for instance,
has sponsored the admission of many handicapped refugees
and, in addition, operates a hostel for them until they are
placed in other accommodation and employment. At the
present time, as for many years past, there is no quota for
handicapped refugees--Jensen cases; dossiers are submitted
by WCC or UNHCR to the New Zealand authorities who judge
each case according to its merits. By May of 1967 seven
cases, comprising twenty persons, had been accepted.

In 1964, New Zealand also assisted the UNHCR in
finding permanent solutions for European refugees in the Far
East. Not only did the government accept eleven families of
"Old Believers" comprising 91 persons, some of whom were
handicapped, but in addition it accepted many handicapped
refugees from among those under UNHCR care in Hong Kong
and in mainland China. UNHCR assisted in the resettlement
of these refugees by a grant of $40,000 to the NCC, which
was officially handling the "Old Believer" cases. The government further aided the HC in his search for a solution
for the very serious problem of Chinese refugees in Hong
Kong. In August 1962 it permitted the NCC to sponsor admission of 50 Chinese orphans. Sponsorship for 10 of these
orphans was assumed by the St. Vincent DePaul Society,
which placed them in foster homes in New Zealand. The
UNHCR granted $2,200 toward the transportation of these
children from a contribution by the Catholic Churches in the
Netherlands. In 1969 the government permitted the Council
to sponsor the admission of 20 Chinese families from South
East Asia, for whose movement UNHCR paid the cost. In

the same year, a special scheme was completed for admission of 100 Czechoslovak refugees. [26]   Thus, in relation to its size and population, New Zealand has played an important role in the reception of refugees.

The Nansen Home

The "handicap" of many refugees from the Far East was age.   Since WRY, the Rev. Dr. Ian Fraser, Chairman of the Refugee Homes Board, had worked toward establishing a home for aged refugees.   In December 1962, he succeeded in obtaining government approval and the promise of private financial support for such a home.   The UNHCR contributed $37,500 toward the cost of construction.   In May 1963, High Commissioner Schnyder officially opened the Nansen Home near Wellington.   Odd Nansen, son of Dr. Fridtjof Nansen, was also present at the ceremony.   The home, with an original capacity of 16, later enlarged to 25, is run by the Refugee Homes Board, which provides lifelong care and maintenance for residents.   Originally designed for aged European refugees from the Far East, the Nansen Home now cares for refugees from other countries as well.

The Work of CORSO

As leader and coordinator of voluntary action for refugees, both in New Zealand and overseas, CORSO, uniting thirty-six religious and social welfare agencies, has made an outstanding contribution to refugee welfare.   CORSO conducts a yearly fund-raising campaign for refugees, both in New Zealand and throughout the world.   For many years a large proportion of the funds gathered has gone directly to the UNHCR.   In 1956, £15,000 was made available to UNREF, and equivalent contributions have followed. [27]   Financial support for the UNHCR has come in nearly equal strength over the years from the government and from CORSO.   The government's annual contributions have averaged $65,000 (not including the special contribution of $14,002 made in 1956 for Hungarian refugees, or the many contributions which the government itself has made to CORSO, and which have benefited refugees through that organization).   CORSO's contribution to the UNHCR has averaged $71,000 annually.   This sum represents a part of the funds gathered by CORSO which have benefited refugees through FAO, UNICEF, or through projects sponsored directly by CORSO or the other voluntary agencies throughout the world.

CORSO's most outstanding achievement, however, was the raising of $1.3 million for refugees during WRY. On the basis of per capita contributions, New Zealand ranked second only to Norway. The sum included a donation of $10,000 from the Government, which cooperated with CORSO in the drive through the actions of the Prime Minister, the Rt. Hon. Walter Nash, who served as patron of the campaign, and the Rt. Hon. K. J. Holyoake, then leader of the Opposition, who was vice patron. In his report to CORSO on the projects to which these funds had been applied, Dr. Schnyder declared that CORSO "stands in the very first rank, on a world-wide basis, in terms of what it has accomplished in favor of refugees." Of this money, the $448,000 entrusted to the UNHCR benefited 11,700 refugees in various countries ranging from Austria to Hong Kong. CORSO sponsored the clearance of two camps in Austria and one in Germany with a total of 268 persons. The money designated for the UNHCR's Far Eastern Operation was used mainly for care and maintenance of refugees in transit in Hong Kong, and to assist destitute refugees in mainland China. In addition, CORSO's contribution went, through the UNHCR, to assist the work of other voluntary agencies operating programs in favor of refugees: to the AFSC and WCC for their work in Austria, to the Chinese Methodist Church for Chinese refugees in Hong Kong, and to the Hong Kong government for improvement of a refugee village in Hong Kong.

In 1963, in the framework of the Freedom from Hunger campaign, and on the occasion of the opening of the Nansen Home, CORSO announced an additional contribution of $160,000 to the UNHCR, of which $100,000 was to aid in the resettlement of refugees of European origin on farms in Brazil, and the remainder for assistance to refugees from Rwanda in the Congo. Voluntary efforts in New Zealand also associated themselves with the 1966 European Refugee Campaign. The UN Association of New Zealand led an information drive to stimulate interest in refugees, and CORSO included an insert in a special refugee edition of its publication CORSO News inviting contributions to the UNHCR for projects to be financed by CORSO. This publicity, supplemented by radio, television and other public relations drives, resulted in the collection of $86,004.

In the words of Dr. Schnyder, "The people of New Zealand have consistently shown an outstanding awareness of the need for concerted international action to deal with refugee problems. "[28]

Notes

1. Dept. of Immigration, "A Post-War Immigration Pro-
    gram: A Survey of Policy, Effects, and Future
    Planning," Apr. 1964: 2-3.

2. A. R. Downer, Minister of Immigration, 28 July 1960,
    reprinted in Kenneth Rivett, ed., Control or Colour
    Bar. Melbourne UP, 1962: 159.

3. The Immigration Reform Group, in Rivett: 28.

4. W. Wryell, "Social Services and the Migrant." ICEM,
    Course on Migration for Officials from Argentina
    and Chile, Dept. of Immigration, Oct. -Dec. 1963,
    Lecture No. 19.

5. The annual topics have concerned "Prejudice and the
    Migration Program" (1961), "Migrant Youth in the
    Australian Environment" (1963), "Every Settler a
    Citizen" (1965), and in 1966 the theme was "Aus-
    tralia, New Dimensions" which dealt with the na-
    tion's ability to attract and hold new immigrants.

6. P. C. Purcell, in ICEM, Course on Migration, Lecture
    No. 16.

7. G. G. Sutcliffe, in ibid., No. 17: 1.

8. Price, ibid., No. 17A: 5.

9. Ibid., Lecture No. 6: 10.

10. Australia has thus avoided the problem of "mushroom-
    ing" to which Canada's 1963 non-restrictive policies
    gave rise.

11. Immigration Reform Group, in Rivett: 30-31.

12. Australia in January 1970 signed a bilateral agreement
    with Yugoslavia to provide a framework for the or-
    ganized migration of Yugoslavs to Australia (UNHCR
    Report for Australia and New Zealand, June 1970).

13. Phillip Lynch, M. P., Minister for Immigration, Immi-
    gration in the Seventies, an address to the Metal
    Trades Industry Association, Melbourne, 30 July
    1970. Canberra, GP: 16.

14.   Ibid. : 7.

15.   News Release, Dept. of Immigration, Canberra, 13
      June 1970.

16.   Lynch: 19.

17.   Dept. of Immigration, Australia's Contribution to the
      Relief of the Problem of Refugees, 1964: 2.

18.   HC's Annual Rep. for 1959, GA, Off. Rec. (XIV) Supp.
      11, A/4104/Rev. 1 1959.

19.   Ex. Com. (XX), A/AC.96/417, 1969: 13.

20.   HC's An. Rep. for 1967, GA, Off. Rec. (XXII), Supp.
      11, A/67aa, 1967: p. 63.

21.   During Dr. Lindt's visit to Australia in 1958, he laid
      the cornerstone for a home for aged Rumanian ref-
      ugees from the mainland of China.   For detail see,
      UNHCR, Ref. Serv. , No. 6.

22.   HC's An. Rep. for 1969: 13.

23.   "New Zealand, Its Place in a Changing World, " The
      British Survey, Main Series No. 232, British Soci-
      ety for International Understanding, London, July
      1968: 17.

24.   Felix Schnyder, Report to New Zealand on Projects Fi-
      nanced from National Appeals for WRY Organized by
      CORSO, May 1963: 2.

25.   Ibid.

26.   Rep. of Ex. Com. (XX), A/AC.96/1961: 15.

27.   Dr. Lindt's visit to Australia and New Zealand, Jan.
      1958, UNHCR Ref. Serv. No. 5: 13-14.

28.   Ibid. : 6.

ANNEX 25.1

REFUGEES ENTERING AUSTRALIA ON ASSISTED PASSAGE SCHEMES
FROM 1945 TO 1963

	Assisted	Unassisted	Total
Albanian	279	114	393
Bulgarian	742	224	966
Czechoslovak	9,232	2,813	12,045
Estonian	5,330	932	6,262
Hungarian	23,277	4,660	27,937
Latvian	19,422	613	20,035
Lithuanian	9,898	253	10,151
Polish	64,950	15,582	80,532
Rumanian	1,976	615	2,591
Russian	7,063	9,306	16,369
Ukrainian	10,569	276	10,845
Yugoslavian	28,131	16,457	44,588
Stateless	26,798	19,393	46,191
Total	207,667	71,238	278,905

SOURCE: Australia, Dept. of Immigration, 1964.

ANNEX 25.2

IMMIGRANTS TO AUSTRALIA UNDER ICEM, 1952-63

Year	Non-Refugees	Refugees	Total	Refugees As % of Total
1952	12,584	2,963	15,547	19.1
1953	10,781	2,546	13,327	19.1
1954	28,512	9,261	37,773	24.5
1955	50,854	2,923	53,777	5.4
1956	34,744	6,317	41,061	15.4
1957	21,420	22,234	43,654	50.9
1958	18,458	9,546	28,004	34.1
1959	26,087	13,422	39,509	34.0
1960	28,674	12,047	40,721	29.6
1961	19,204	8,347	27,551	30.3
1962	17,159	6,777	23,936	28.3
1963	16,427	7,275	23,702	30.7
Total	284,904	103,658	388,562	26.7

SOURCE: Australia, Dept. of Immigration, 1964.

Chapter 26

REFUGEES IN LATIN AMERICA AND THE CARIBBEAN

Since WWII, Latin American states have been among the important reception countries for refugees from Europe and other areas. Continuing the immigration policies by which their national economies had been built up over past decades, many Latin American countries welcomed European refugees as agricultural settlers, industrial workers, or technicians. As a result of IRO's mass movement and subsequent ICEM resettlement of post-war refugees to overseas countries, 133,000 had found resettlement opportunities in Latin American countries by 1963. When the UNHCR took over from IRO in 1951 there were some 100,000 mandate refugees under the HC's protection in various Latin American countries: Argentina, 33,000; Brazil, 40,000; Chile, 5,000; Paraguay, 6,000; Peru, 2,530; Uruguay, 1,500; Venezuela, 18,000.[1] In recent years a growing proportion of refugees have been those fleeing from one Latin American country to another; these Latin American refugees totalled some 7,000 by 1971.

The UNHCR operates in these areas through BOs set up in Bogota, Colombia, in March 1952; in Rio de Janeiro, Brazil, in 1953; and in Buenos Aires, Argentina, in June 1970.[2]

Conditions in South American Countries since 1951

Immigration policies and economic conditions differ from one receiving country to another. In general, however, the opportunities for resettlement had been considerably reduced since the late 1940s and early 1950s, a period when the economic outlook for the area as a whole had seemed promising. Changed economic conditions in some countries, often reflected in a sharp rise in the cost of living, have adversely affected refugee migrants since that time. Refugees, once firmly settled, now need once again to turn to

SOUTH AMERICA
AMÉRIQUE DU SUD

MILLER CYLINDRICAL PROJECTION
PROJECTION CYLINDRIQUE DE MILLER

the UNHCR for assistance when old age pensions are insufficient, or when illness prevents them from working.[3] Furthermore, the rate of population growth in Latin America is now one of the highest in the world.   UN projections indicate that by 1975 Latin America will have a population of 303 million people, compared to 240 million for the US and Canada combined.[4]

Although these factors have reduced the possibility for mass immigration, uneven distribution of population in many countries leaves areas of potentially valuable land sparsely populated, whose settlement would be advantageous to the economic development of the country.   In Latin American countries, especially Argentina, Brazil, and Venezuela, it has been possible for the UNHCR to find many opportunities for placement of refugees under his mandate.

Argentina.   With a population almost wholly of European origin (and by 1970, totalling over 24 million), Argentina has some of the world's best agricultural and grazing land, as well as rich mining and crude oil resources which settlers have been encouraged to tap.   Vast stretches remain unsettled and undeveloped.   Its economy, while based largely on the export of agricultural products (Argentina has been called the granary of Europe), is also strengthened by a large set of industries (cement, pig-iron, crude steel, textiles, chemicals, etc.).

Argentina admitted 33,000 refugees under the IRO and 15,000 ex-servicemen of Polish origin under an agreement with the UK, a large majority of whom were satisfactorily settled in 1951.   Bilateral agreements have been made with Spain, Italy, and Germany, which provide for the annual admission of a given number of immigrants, including refugees, from these countries.   In 1952, for instance, an agreement with Italy provided for the admission of 500,000 Italians over a five-year period.   However, since admission is now restricted to technicians, agricultural workers, and stock farmers, and now depends upon private sponsorship rather than government colonization schemes, the actual number of immigrants is much smaller than permissible quotas.   Responsibility for refugee migrants is shared by the various government departments which carry out regular social welfare tasks.[5]

Brazil.   Brazil is the largest country in South America in area as well as in population.   It is a land of rich,

largely untapped natural resources, stretching over an area
larger than that of the continental United States, and including a range of land types and climate from equatorial rain
forest to prairie with rich crop land in the temperate zone.
Its population (over 92 million in 1970), is one of the world's
fastest growing, and consists of the merging of three racial
stocks: Mongoloid (American Indians and recent Japanese
settlers), Negroid (Africans brought originally by Portuguese
colonists), and Caucasian (predominantly Portuguese). In
addition there is a continuing influx of immigrants from
Italy, Germany, and Spain, and to a lesser extent Austria,
the USSR and other European nations, as well as from several Middle Eastern countries, and from Japan.

More than 42 percent of the 1967 population of almost
85 million were under seventeen years of age and therefore
not yet self-supporting. Of those over seventeen, only half
are literate. The population is unevenly distributed, with
some 34 percent living in the agricultural lands along the
southern coast while the rich interior lands are sparsely
populated. As in Argentina, settlement and development of
this potentially valuable agricultural land has been encouraged
with a view to improving the national economy as a whole.
While Brazil's economy is based mainly on the export of
agricultural products--sugar, coffee, and tea--as in Argentina, mining and such industries as textiles, metallurgy and
the petroleum industry have also become important. [6]

Brazil has been the foremost recipient of UNHCR refugees in Latin America. In 1954 there were over 40,000
refugees, most of them settled under the IRO. Until 1954
Brazil had an open-door policy on immigration, without discrimination. It still has great potential for absorbing refugees. In January 1954 the Congress created the National
Association of Immigration and Colonization, centralizing
responsibility for all immigration, naturalization, land settlement, and placement of immigrants, including refugees,
in one federal agency. Furthermore, the Brazilian Red
Cross initiated the formation of a Committee for Aid to Refugees which has direct access to the federal authorities on
matters affecting refugee welfare. In that year the UNHCR
also set up a second Latin American BO in Rio de Janeiro
with the approval of the Brazilian Government. Between
1952 and 1954 active work on the part of voluntary agencies,
assisted by funds from the Ford Foundation grant, effected
the admission of 5,449 refugees, including 2,193 refugees of
European origin from China under the Joint Far Eastern

Program. After this period, however, opportunities for settlement in Brazil were shut off altogether for a while, and
later limited to those who qualified under government immigration programs, to refugees wishing to come for family
reunion, and to those with sponsors in Brazil, provided they
obtained the approval of the National Association of Immigration and Colonization. [7]

During WRY a total amount of $185,000 was collected
from a variety of international sources for the settlement of
Chinese farmers in a colony in Brazil. (The UNHCR received $62,000 toward this project from the National World
Refugee Committees in Australia, West Germany, New Zealand and the UK. The WCC, which played a major role in
carrying out the project received a contribution of $115,300
from Brot für die Welt, a West German voluntary organization, and a further contribution of $9,700 from the Anglican
Church in Canada.) Qualified refugee farmers were pre-
selected by WCC in Hong Kong with the assistance of the
Department of Agriculture of the Hong Kong Government.
The Evangelical Confederation of Brazil has the responsibility of administering the colony. The WCC also made arrangements for a small colony near Santa Cruz in Bolivia,
where 7 families (30 persons) were settled in July 1963.

Chile. A 2,635-mile long strip of land between the
Andes mountains and the Pacific Ocean (at no point wider
than 225 miles) Chile has become one of Latin America's
leading industrial nations. Three-quarters of the population,
a homogeneous blend of Spanish Basques and Indians, with
the addition of certain English, Scottish, and other European
elements, inhabits the arable areas of Middle Chile. Small
but influential German colonies have partially opened up the
inhospitable southern section to agriculture and industry, and
the northern section is increasingly exploited for its rich
mineral resources. However, the latter two areas are still
frontier regions whose settlements and development the government is encouraging not only for their economic potential,
but to relieve population pressures in Middle Chile. Chile
has a very high birth rate; its population more than doubled
between 1920 and 1960, and by 1970 had reached 9,780,000.

Refugees in Chile have benefited from advanced and
comprehensive social legislation designed (and codified in
1945) to combat severe economic and social problems. Welfare legislation covers almost any contingency of life for
wage workers and salaried employees and their families

(housing for labor is an accepted part of industrial planning).
Despite vigorous measures, however, economic and social
problems--illiteracy, generally poor health, illegitimacy and
alcoholism--and a low standard of living still persist, especially in rural areas. Refugees especially suffer from such
economic maladjustments.

At the time when the UNHCR took up its role the
5,000 IRO refugees in Chile were, for the most part, satisfactorily settled. In addition to Government welfare agencies, they received assistance from several private organizations, including the YMCA and the ICMC. The Standing
Immigration Board, set up in 1948, advises the Government
on the number and kind of immigrants which should be admitted. Small numbers of carefully selected, Government-
sponsored refugees, of German and Latin stock, have been
admitted for settlement in agricultural colonies in the undeveloped areas. Between 1952 and 1954, through bilateral
agreements with Germany and Italy, Chile admitted 406 settlers. During 1954 the government initiated the establishment of 130 families in a farming colony. The Director of
Immigration of the Ministry of Foreign Affairs is responsible
for their reception and admission, and in addition, a joint
ICEM/ICMC project has set up a hostel to aid in their reception. [8]

Colombia. Colombia's advantageous trade position,
with sea ports on both the Atlantic and the Pacific coasts,
is offset by the difficulty of developing the rugged Andean
terrain and equatorial rain forests which cover a large proportion of the country. Nevertheless, government efforts
since WWII have assisted agricultural production, which en-
gages half of the population--over 20 million in 1970, of
which 70 percent are of mixed Spanish and Indian descent,
20 percent white, 5 percent Negro and 5 percent Indian. The
government has also contributed to the extremely rapid development of industry. Although agricultural products, especially coffee, are still the country's leading export, Colombia ranks second only to Venezuela in oil production; in 1955
heavy industry was introduced by the government's construction of a steel mill. Through the growth of industries (now
employing 15 percent of the labor force) Colombia is now
almost self-sufficient in textiles, food products, and other
consumer products.

Colombia's standard of living is still among the lowest
in Latin America. Social welfare legislation enacted since

WWII provides comprehensive benefits for workers but these
are unevenly distributed among the population. Education is
free, but not compulsory, and is still inadequate, especially
in the rural areas. Vigorous government efforts are gradually improving these conditions.

Government development schemes included the creation, in 1953, of the Institute of Land Settlement and Immigration, with a rotating capital of $40 million to open coloni-
zation centers, grant loans to settlers, engage technical
personnel, create selection missions, and dispose of state
land. The Institute compiles data on the need for skilled
workers and technicians and has given ICEM responsibility
for preliminary selection of immigrants (including refugees)
to fill openings for which sponsors are available. The Colombia consul in Rome makes the final selection. Voluntary
organizations such as Caritas Colombiana, the Colombia
Catholic Immigration Committee (which no longer operates
as an autonomous institution) and the ICMC are assisted by
the Institute in seeking sponsorships of migrants, especially
for refugee families, by rural and semi-rural parishes, and
have set up, with Institute support, a reception center near
Bogota. In 1955 the government approved a standing quota
of one hundred visas monthly for refugees whose placement
could be guaranteed by the Colombia Catholic Immigration
Committee. Active publicity is required to fill this quota.
By 1954, 200 Hungarian refugee families from West Germany
and Austria were admitted, and visas were granted for 300
refugees from Trieste.

Other Latin American Countries. Ecuador government officials have informed the UNHCR that a small number
of well-selected refugees for settlement in industry, agriculture, and fishing can be accepted.

Paraguay, one of the least densely populated and
least developed countries in Latin America, presents many
opportunities for settlers. Political instability, war, and
disease have kept the population low (2,386,000 in 1970) with
an average density of only eleven persons per square mile.
Of the present population, mainly of mixed Indian and Spanish
descent, with a smaller number of Argentinians, Italians,
and Germans, 80 percent are engaged in agriculture and
animal husbandry, often using primitive methods and living
in primitive conditions.

Since 1940, heavy government investment in the

economy has speeded up Paraguay's development. Encouragement of industry and urban-improvement programs have
attracted many from rural areas into occupations in industry
and transport. (Paraguay has access to the Atlantic Ocean
through the Paraguay/Panama River system, flowing southward through Argentina.) Furthermore, the Institute for
Agrarian Reform, the government agency responsible for immigration and colonization, including the distribution of state
lands, granting of visas, and so on, operates some 126 agricultural colonies. Under the IRO more than 6,000 refugees
were absorbed in these colonies. In 1954 the Institute set
up a scheme for the settlement of 500 Europeans from China, and assisted the WCC in establishing an old-age home
for some of these refugees. With the prospect of technical
assistance and capital from such foreign sources as the US
Point IV Program, the Institute has planned for the settlement of 10,000 Italian and 15,000 German farm families and
has officially accepted the family reunion plan. However,
as in other Latin American countries, refugees have been
the hardest hit by the rise in the cost of living, and immigration schemes have been slowed down.

In Peru, 2,350 IRO refugees are satisfactorily settled, and further immigration is limited to a few specialists
under contract to local employers. Although the Sierra area
east of the Andes has great potential for agriculture, inadequate transportation facilities prevent its development for the
present.

Uruguay, a prosperous and politically stable country,
has provided excellent conditions for settlement of some
1,500 IRO refugees. Its population (nearly 3 million in 1970)
is mostly of European origin, mainly from Spain and Italy.
Unlike that of other Latin American countries, a large proportion of this population is considered to be middle class;
only 37 percent of the people are involved in agriculture.
Inflation and a severe slowdown in economic development,
however, have affected salaried workers, including refugees,
as elsewhere in Latin America. A $140 million development
plan drawn up in 1960 and backed by US technical assistance
programs has been partially successful in overcoming a tendency to economic stagnation.

In the early years of UNHCR operation Uruguay admitted some 6,000 immigrants from Italy and Spain. Since
1954 many refugees have been admitted under the government's family reunion plan, operated with the advice of

ICEM. But dense population and limited area of undeveloped land have made further immigration on a large scale both unnecessary, and undesirable.

Immigration to Venezuela for settlement in agriculture has, since the war, been encouraged and subsidized by the government. Much rich land is available; not only has the development of the oil industry drawn many workers away from prime agricultural land, thus reducing food production, but the 1958 land reforms have broken up vast estates to provide opportunities for many small holders in agriculture and stock farming. In addition, much undeveloped grassland still exists. While the flow of immigrants into Venezuela has at times been high, more than half of those arriving since WWII have moved to other countries for final settlement. In an attempt to counter severe economic and social maladjustments, government funds have, since 1958, been increasingly diverted into social welfare and educational programs. The Ministry of Health and Social Welfare has waged a successful war against malaria and tuberculosis, and has set up over 400 health centers and a network of local health facilities. In addition, the Bureau of Social Security has its own health services for welfare cases. Over 55 percent of the adult population (the majority of which is of Spanish-Indian descent) is still illiterate, although the school construction program begun in 1951 is beginning to have an effect.

When UNHCR operations began in Venezuela, most of the 18,000 IRO refugees had been satisfactorily settled in Venezuela or elsewhere. Of the 21,000 received by 1954, 2,500 became citizens. The UNHCR, by means of discussions with government representatives, the Venezuelan Red Cross, and the Archdiocese Bureau for Refugees, assured more effective assistance to individual refugees still in UNHCR care. Some further immigration is possible through procurement of work contracts and private sponsorships, as well as through government colonization schemes operated by the National Agrarian Institute. The Institute is responsible for all government immigration and colonization, and for selection, transportation and reception of refugees in centers it operates, and for their placement. Voluntary agencies are active in seeking private sponsorships.

Participation of the UNHCR in South America

     The UNHCR's role in South America has been three-
fold: to promote resettlement opportunities for European
refugees who remained unsettled in Europe and in China after
the close of the IRO; to render assistance in local integration, both to new settlers and to those previously settled for
whom economic reverses in Latin American countries have
caused severe hardship; and to assure them international
protection under the terms of the 1951 Convention and the
1967 Protocol. UNHCR has also assisted in the voluntary
repatriation of a number of refugees. Such assistance was
given when the costs of the journey could not be covered either by the refugee himself or by the country to which he
returned.

     Promotion of Resettlement. Mindful of the enormous
untapped potential of many Latin American countries for absorbing refugees, the HC turned to them after the close of
the IRO to seek opportunities for resettlement of refugees
under his mandate. By 1951, the post-war mass movement
of refugees had come to an end, and thereafter the major
part of overseas resettlement was carried out by voluntary
agencies on the basis of individual migration. Because few
refugees in Europe had friends or relatives in Latin American countries who could give the sponsorships which most
governments now required as a condition for admission, voluntary agencies were obliged to make great efforts to promote resettlement opportunities. This placed a heavy burden
on them in Latin American countries where local agencies
lacked resources, and internationally organized voluntary
agencies did not have branches.

     Assistance to voluntary agencies, therefore, was one
of the first efforts of the UNHCR in Latin America. Funds
made available under the Ford Foundation grant were given
to WCC, LWF, and NCWC to establish small offices and
pay trained personnel for encouraging sponsorship of refugees and for providing for their reception and establishment
locally. Through their efforts during 1953-55, voluntary
agencies managed to secure government approval for the admission of several thousand refugees who could not otherwise
have been admitted. [9] Between 1955 and 1961 a further 608
were settled in Latin American countries.

     UNHCR representatives in Colombia and in Brazil
maintained a continuous dialogue with officials in the

governments of Latin American countries in an effort to obtain openings for refugees and to liberalize immigration restrictions and promote the welfare of those who were admitted.   In 1955, the HC himself visited nine Latin American countries (Argentina, Brazil, Chile, Colombia, the Dominican Republic, Ecuador, Peru, Venezuela, and Uruguay) not only to encourage further accessions to the 1951 General Convention on the status of Refugees and to stimulate contributions to UNREF but also to urge governments to grant more opportunities for resettlement, especially for the handicapped.   These consultations also fostered the especially valuable willingness of Brazil, Chile, Paraguay, and Venezuela to receive European refugees from China under the joint UNHCR/ICEM Far Eastern Program. [10]   In 1962 the Argentine Government agreed to admit 700 refugees of European origin from the Far East.   A small farming colony has been established at La China in the south of Argentina for Old Believers.   Brazil has continued to admit refugees of European origin from the Far East on an individual basis. In 1962, 1,600 Old Believers were successfully established in two land colonies in the State of Paraguay, in addition to 100 Chinese refugee families from Hong Kong.

To facilitate visa availability the UNHCR also circulated copies of the special travel document which had been accepted by many European countries, among Latin American governments, and at meetings of the OAS.   Its use was accepted first by Ecuador, and later by Colombia and Peru.

In general, Latin American governments, in accordance with GA Res. 832 (IX), agreed to give priority to refugees seeking admission for family reunion, but were unwilling to commit themselves to acceptance of a specified number of refugees. [11]

By 1961, as a result of continuous efforts and of the stimulus of WRY for liberalizing immigration restrictions, resettlement was possible for virtually any refugee for whom a sponsor could be found, rather than for only the few with particular skills or capabilities.   The number of refugees resettled as a result of WRY stimulus rose in Latin America, as elsewhere.   During 1961 alone, over 900, including 240 Europeans from China, were settled in Latin American countries.   After that time, until political events in the Caribbean created new refugees in the area, the number of "old refugees" seeking resettlement was progressively smaller, and because many of them were handicapped they were more difficult to place. [12]

Local integration. Up until 1961 the UNHCR's role
in promoting local integration consisted mainly in stimulating
government and voluntary-agency services to assure the inclusion of refugees in public welfare programs. Consultations with governments were designed to encourage government participation in such services as well as to promote
legislation favorable to refugees. In some countries, naturalization laws were liberalized so that refugees could more
easily become citizens. Under Argentina's October 1954
naturalization laws for instance, immigrants could, by applying, become citizens after only two years of residence, and
after five years, they became citizens automatically in some
cases. In Venezuela the government established and supported a panel of young lawyers to serve in counselling and
legal-aid programs run by voluntary agencies. Voluntary
agencies themselves were setting up or strengthening programs for assisting refugees in local integration. The
UNHCR initially allocated $100,000 from Ford Foundation
funds to assist their efforts. Programs of counselling and
legal aid were especially important for bringing refugees
more quickly within the scope of public welfare programs.

In general, however, a serious gap existed between
the emigration services refugees received in European countries and services in the receiving countries in Latin America, designed to expedite satisfactory final settlement. International funds, public and private, were available in Europe for such programs as vocational, rehabilitation and
language training, placement assistance, establishment loans,
legal aid, etc. In Latin American countries, where such
programs would have been most useful, except for some
ICEM funds for transportation and for covering the administrative costs of reception, no international funds were available to cover establishment costs except for refugees under
USEP.[13] Furthermore, although many Latin American countries had comprehensive social legislation, unequal distribution of population and uneven economic development within
each country often prevent effective administration of this
legislation. When Ford funds were exhausted, voluntary
agencies faced staggering and rapidly increasing demands for
social welfare assistance with very limited local resources
to meet them.

By 1961 the sharp rise in the cost of living had created serious hardship for many settled refugees. Some,
who had been self-sufficient since their arrival (in some
cases twenty years before), were forced to apply to the

UNHCR for material assistance, whether because their incomes could not keep up with rising prices or because, having reached retirement age, or having become chronically ill, they nevertheless did not qualify for regular public old age or illness benefits and had exhausted their savings. An increasing number of ill refugees needed treatment and care. In 1962, although the total number of refugees settled under UNHCR programs was only 1,946, assistance was being given to 4,099 refugees. [14]

Neither the governments nor the voluntary agencies had complete statistics on refugees in Latin American countries. The statistics published by ICEM on refugees transported under their auspices did not include the number of refugees who immigrated to Latin America independently. However, on the basis of all available data the number of refugees from Europe was estimated to be 133,000 during the period from 1947 to 1963, of which 26,500 emigrated between 1952 and 1963. [15]

In April 1964, Deputy High Commissioner Prince Sadruddin Aga Khan undertook an extensive fact-finding mission to five Latin American countries: Venezuela, Peru, Argentina, Chile, and Colombia. He was accompanied by the HC's Regional Representative for the Americas, Francisco Urrutia Holguin (Colombia). He reported to the Eleventh Session of the Ex. Com. in April 1964 (A/AC.96/229) that although refugee conditions varied from country to country, they had one point in common: "had [the refugees] remained in Europe they would have benefited from international aid on a much more extensive basis, whereas once they had migrated they were considered as having been settled, and, therefore no longer of international concern." He emphasized the importance of legal assistance to refugees in helping them to become naturalized without excessive cost, and in bringing them within the scope of public welfare benefits. But he noted that these benefits alone often did not enable the refugees to achieve stability.

On the basis of these findings, High Commissioner Schnyder recommended an amount of $410,000 for material assistance for needy persons for the year 1965:

Assistance toward local settlement	$370,000
Counseling	10,000
Legal Assistance	20,000
Supplementary aid	10,000

The Ex. Com. adopted a number of principles which were to
govern the action of the HC as far as material assistance
was concerned, stressing the need of operational partners,
concentration of efforts on the aged and mentally ill, the
constructive character of solutions to be proposed, and the
encouragement of a collective undertaking.

The UNHCR programs for both individual and group
solutions include counseling, legal assistance, support for
construction or administration of homes for the aged and
hospitals for the care of chronically ill, handicapped, or
mentally ill refugees, as well as support of voluntary agency
self-help schemes in agriculture and education, etc.   In
some cases direct financial assistance was given for individual settlement, or for emergency relief.   These projects
were administered either through voluntary agencies, or directly by the UNHCR BOs in Bogota or Rio de Janeiro.

Mental Health Services.   Parallel to the material difficulties faced by refugees was the growing difficulty of obtaining treatment and care for mental illness.   Prompted by
reports of serious mental-health problems among refugees
in Latin American countries, the UNHCR in 1965 asked Dr.
Peter Berner, UNHCR Mental Health Consultant, to undertake a survey of the mental health problems of certain refugees in Chile, Argentina and Brazil, where large concentrations of refugees made the situation most acute.   Dr. Berner reported that because of the steady and heavy increase in
population, mental health institutions were seriously overcrowded and were reserved for most urgent cases among the
total population.   Private treatment, when available, was
very expensive.   There was virtually no public health system for social-psychiatric aftercare or for care of patients
outside hospitals.   For numerous reasons the situation was
particularly difficult for refugees.   They were less familiar
than the indigenous population with means of availing themselves of existing facilities.   Since many lived alone, those
released from hospitals were unlikely to find the sheltered
home conditions necessary for preventing relapse.   Many
who were mentally ill had been partially handicapped at the
time of their arrival.   Since many had been unable to obtain
regular work, they could not now benefit from insurance.
There were an estimated 200 cases in Argentina, 100 known
cases in Chile, and 375 cases in Brazil, for whom Dr.
Berner recommended the establishment of services under the
1966 program, according to given priorities.   Immediately
imperative were expansion of existing facilities, the

appointment in Brazil and Argentina of consultant psychiatrists, and the admission of certain emergency cases to private hospitals where public facilities were overcrowded. Long-range programs involving community organization for follow-up services, sheltered workshops, etc. were also recommended. [16] Immediate efforts were made to begin an attack on these problems.

Refugees in Caribbean America

Initially the UNHCR was little involved in the Caribbean, where only two countries had accepted refugees. Costa Rica accepted a very limited number of refugees, who were generally able, with the help of a program run with the cooperation of churches and civil authorities, to settle satisfactorily. The Dominican Republic accepted many refugees under the IRO, but most of them subsequently resettled in other Latin American countries. Those remaining were well settled in trade and industry at the time when the UNHCR began operation in the area; only a few individual refugees have been settled there since that time.

Refugees from Cuba

From mid-1962 on, the problems of local integration in the Latin American countries were again added to by those of resettlement as political events in Cuba and in the Caribbean area caused new groups of refugees to flee their homes. Many Cubans fled to the US and to Spain, but some 20,000 to 30,000 sought asylum in Latin American countries. The HC was called upon to lend his good offices to assist the governments concerned in dealing with the problem with a view to preventing it from growing into unmanageable proportions. [17]

Of those who sought first asylum in Latin American countries, 1,931 refugees were resettled with UNHCR assistance during the latter part of 1963 and the beginning of 1964, the majority in the US. [18] In addition, assistance was given to 28 refugees in Venezuela and 2 in Ecuador. In the US, where most of the Cubans found asylum, the Office matched assistance in the resettlement of a number of refugees working to join relatives or friends in Latin America.

Cuban refugees continue to flee to various countries

in the Caribbean area. The only permanent solution for
most of these people is immediate resettlement in other
countries, mainly the US. They continue to receive UNHCR
and ICEM assistance for transportation and maintenance while
in transit. The UNHCR, accordingly, has been devoting increasing sums annually to refugees in Mexico, Jamaica,
Curaçao, and the Bahamas who are awaiting resettlement.
During 1965 the UNHCR assisted 876 refugees in Mexico and
in Jamaica awaiting settlement in the US, at a cost of
$21,000. In 1966, 900 persons in a similar situation were
assisted by an allocation of $22,000, while the sum of
$10,000 was allocated to 95 refugees in transit from US to
Latin American countries. In 1968 the number awaiting resettlement in the US increased to 2,000. The UNHCR continues to seek resettlement opportunities for such refugees
and to assist them in the meantime.

Similarly, at the request of the Bahamian authorities
the UNHCR developed, in cooperation with the governments
concerned, a plan for resettlement of 107 Haitians. The US
(46), Belgium (8), Canada (28), and France (25) responded
to the HC's appeal for migration opportunities. ICEM and
a number of voluntary agencies took care of transportation
and reception services. The operation was implemented under the direction of UNHCR's correspondent in Nassau.

UNHCR Assistance since 1969

The UNHCR program for permanent settlement in
Latin American countries accelerated during 1969, and that
momentum continued in 1970. A plan of action was evolved
aimed "at an increased use of local resources as well as
the intensification of cooperation with UN agencies active in
that region and a progressive approach to the remaining
problems by establishing priorities. "[19]

The HC established a Regional Office in Buenos Aires
in 1970 and strengthened the existing staff. The Regional
Program Officer and the Consulate on Social Services have
concentrated on program planning and implementation with
two specific goals: to provide solutions for the remaining
needy persons and to establish a mechanism which would insure that assistance could be provided to refugees who may
require settlement aid in the future.

With regard to the remaining needy refugees, with the

cooperation of voluntary agencies and assistance by governments, great progress has been made in developing a network of places in new or existing old people's homes and
institutions for the mentally handicapped. Some 824 places
are occupied by refugees in various Latin American countries. The average turnover in the population of the homes
is estimated at 10 percent annually. Thus the possibility
has been provided for the yearly placement of sixty to eighty
refugees in vacancies occurring in such homes, at no further cost to the UNHCR. These facilities are located in six
countries, mainly in Brazil (40 percent), Argentina (35 percent) and Chile (16 percent), the three countries in which
about three-fourths of the refugee population in Latin America resides.

Refugees also continue to benefit from the revolving
funds which were launched in 1969 in Argentina, Brazil,
Chile, and Venezuela to assist professional establishment,
housing, rehabilitation, and other amenities, with a view to
local integration. The revolving funds are administered in
each country by an inter-agency committee.

Counselling assistance continued in Argentina, Brazil,
Chile, and Venezuela, which implemented counselling projects in former years. In addition, funds were provided by
the HC to strengthen the services of agencies operating in
Colombia and Peru. Counselling assistance covers a wide
range of services such as advice on economic and social integration, and on family, health, and housing problems.
The legal and administrative problems of refugees continued
to require attention. The provision of documents or certification of papers, and advice on naturalization and social-
security entitlements were the main areas in which refugees
required assistance.

Through an allocation of $3,500 from the UNHCR
Education Account a project was initiated in 1969 for educational assistance in Latin America. Fifty-one students benefited from this assistance, most of them in vocational and
technical training, and some were helped to continue or complete studies at secondary or university level. Assistance
financed from the Refugee Education Account enabled 33 persons to continue their secondary education, 24 university
students to pay fees and purchase books, and 11 persons to
follow vocational training courses. The assistance was provided at the cost of slightly over $9,000, of which 70 per-
cent was in the form of loans.

Every effort has been made to reduce supplementary aid in favor of more permanent solutions, in order to avoid the development of a case load dependent on relief. [20]

In formulating the 1971 UNHCR Program for Latin America the following factors were taken into consideration: (1) Priority was to be given to assistance and care for socially handicapped and mentally-ill refugees. With over 600 places in old-age institutions available in 1970, additional places were to be created only on the basis of specific needs. (2) Housing projects were being considered for those living in sub-standard conditions with no prospect of improvement, and for those who had adequate housing but were unable to make ends meet. (3) Further establishment assistance was to be made available for employable refugees by way of tools and equipment, loans, retraining of handicapped persons, and funds for equipping a workshop or setting up a small business. [21] A total allocation of $325,000 was provided for these constructive measures.

From 1969 to 1971, in general, progress has been made in Latin America. While the HC is still concerned with 110,000 refugees--mainly a defined case load of aged and handicapped refugees--his annual allocations could be reduced. Under the Latin American and Caribbean programs around $3 million was spent from 1963 to 1971. It is hoped that solutions will be found for the remaining problems of European refugees by 1974. [22]

Notes

1. HC's Annual Rep. for 1953, GA (IX) Off. Rec., Supp. No. 11.

2. The BO in Bogota operated from Mar. 1952 to May 1970. Since that time a consultant has been stationed there. BO's have also operated in Santiago, Chile (Apr. 1959 to June 1961), and in Quito, Ecuador (Oct. 1962 to Dec. 1965).

3. UN Inf. Serv., P. Rel. No. REF/839, May 1964.

4. Population Ref. Bureau, Population Profile, "Latin America: World's Fastest Growing Region," 18 Feb. 1960.

5. "Argentina, " The British Survey No. 219, British Soc.
    for International Understanding, London, June 1967.

6. Population Ref. Bureau, "Brazil--Latin America's
    Growing Giant, " 2 Apr. 1962.

7. HC's Annual Rep. for 1953 GA (VII) Off. Rec., Supp.
    No. 11; A/2394; and for 1954; Supp. No. 13, A/
    2648.

8. Ibid.

9. HC's Annual Rep. for 1954, GA (VIII), Off. Rec.,
    Supp. No. 13; A/2648/Add. 2.

10. HC's Annual Rep. for 1956; GA (XI), Off. Rec. Supp.
    11 A/3123/Rev. 1.

11. Ibid.

12. HC's Annual Rep. for 1962, GA (XVII), Off. Rec.
    Supp. 11; A/5211/Rev. 1.

13. HC's Annual Rep. for 1956, GA (XI); Off. Rec. Supp.
    11; A/3123/Rev. 1.

14. HC's Annual Rep. for 1963, GA (XVIII), Off. Rec.
    Supp. No. 11; A/5511/Rev. 1.

15. Ex. Com. (XII), A/AC.96/263, 21 Aug. 1964: 16.

16. "Report on the Mental Health of Refugees in Certain
    Latin American Countries, " to Ex. Com. (XVI);
    A/AC.96 INF. 63, 6 Oct. 1966.

17. HC's Annual Rep. for 1964; GA (XIX), Off. Rec. Supp.
    No. 11, A/5811/Rev. 1: 11.

18. A/AC.96/229.

19. A/AC.96/396.

20. A/AC.96/428, Rep. of UNHCR Current Operations in
    1969; GA (XXIV), Ex. Com. (XX), UNHCR Assist-
    ance Program for 1971, A/AC.96/429: 37 ff.

21. For more detail, see UNHCR Assistance Programs for

1971, Ex. Com. (XX), 12 Aug. 1970, A/AC. 96/
429: 37.

22. Ex. Com. (XXII) A/AC. 96/455; 30; and Ex. Com.
(XXIII), A/AC. 96/467: 32.

ANNEX 26. 1

LATIN AMERICA AND THE CARIBBEAN AREA:
VALUE OF UNHCR CURRENT PROJECTS 1963-71
(IN US DOLLARS)

UNHCR Current Programs	1, 678, 457
Emergency Fund	35, 000
Supporting contributions from other sources	183, 275
UNHCR Special Trust Funds (for operations outside the programs)	21, 985
Total (rounded)	2, 919, 000

SOURCE: Ex. Com. (XXII), A/AC. 96/449: 26; and Ex. Com. (XIII) A/AC. 96/467, 6 Aug. 1972.

PART VI

REFUGEES IN ASIA AND THE NEAR
AND MIDDLE EAST

Words that are not translated into effective action are so many insults to the human beings who look to the United Nations with fresh hope and faith which so many seem to lack.

Prince Sadruddin Aga Khan

INTRODUCTION

In seeking solutions to refugee problems in Asia and the Middle East the HC was compelled to create responses different from those developed in his work in Europe. The overwhelming need in the case of refugee movements in Asia was for immediate material assistance. Relief measures at the basic level were necessary simply to assure the survival of millions of people. Foodstuffs, provisions for shelter, and medical attention had to be secured internationally and distributed without delay.

In these circumstances a significant concept emerged for the activities of the UNHCR: that of securing material assistance and of coordinating the aid extended through the UN system and by governments and concerned international and non-governmental agencies through use of the HC's good offices (see Chapter 18).

With the exception of European refugees from the People's Republic of China in transit through Hong Kong, most refugee groups in Asia did not fall within the HC's mandate under the Statute. The UN was urged to act, however, in order to mitigate their urgent need for material assistance. By lending his good offices, the HC was able to seek immediate aid for specified groups of refugees regardless of their legal status. Thus the Statute was not altered, but the HC was given a new authority that was to expand the effectiveness of his office in helping to cope with the wave of emergencies created by unforeseen circumstances. The concept of good offices was applied first in relation to the needs of Chinese refugees in 1957 and reached its fullest development in the massive Focal Point program undertaken in India in 1971-72 on behalf of refugees from East Bengal.

Because of the tremendous size of refugee influxes into Asian host countries and the fact that the underdeveloped economies of those countries were already overburdened by population pressures, local resettlement was not envisaged as

657

a feasible solution to most refugee problems.   Nor were
less populated states prepared to welcome large numbers of
Asian immigrants.   Local integration of a specific nature
has occurred in the case of protracted non-resolution of
political questions, as in the case of the Chinese in Hong
Kong and Macao and of the Tibetans in India and Nepal; in
general, however, eventual voluntary repatriation of refugee
groups has been the primary objective of the governments
concerned, of the UNHCR, and of the refugees themselves.

Another factor characterizing the work of the HC in
the Far East, and later in Africa as well, was the frequent inaccessibility of the refugees and the almost overwhelming technical and logistic problems involved in providing them with material aid.   European refugees in China,
for political reasons, and Tibetan refugees in India and especially Nepal, for reasons of terrain, were often impossible
to reach with assistance; even information about them was
difficult to obtain.   In the Focal Point program of assistance
to some ten million East Bengalis in India, the HC was
compelled to find means to transport vast quantities of
material although an effective transportation network was in
some areas virtually non-existent.

By utilizing his good offices, the HC was thus able
to aid millions of refugees who strictly speaking did not fall
within his mandate.   The growing acceptance by the international community of the concept of good offices has provided
the HC with an increasing flexibility of action with regard
to the vast numbers of refugees in Asia and in Africa whose
eligibility for the status of refugee could not be specifically
determined.   New applications for the HC's good offices, endorsed by the competent organs of the UN, have enabled the
HC to place the expertise of his Office at the disposal of the
UN system and to offer a wider type of assistance and more
efficient coordination than would have been possible under the
limited provisions of his mandate.   The high point in such
service came when the HC was requested to act as Focal
Point for the coordination of assistance to the East Bengali
refugees in India and to assist in their repatriation.

Other emergencies have led to special requests for
the HC's assistance.   In Southeast Asia, military operations
over the last decades between North Vietnam and South Vietnam and spreading over into Laos and Cambodia have forced
thousands of people to leave their homes.   Many were DP's,
who were cared for by their own countries, but others were

refugees. The UNHCR has been called upon by the Governments of Laos, of the Republic of Khmer, and of the Republic of Vietnam to lend his good offices at different times, in
particular to stimulate and coordinate the extension of material assistance.

      Somewhat different demands have arisen in the Mid-
dle East. This area of long-standing political tensions,
military disturbances and economic difficulties has had many
different refugee movements. The major refugee group consists of the Palestinian Arab refugees. Under Art. 7(c) of
the Statute, these refugees do not fall within the HC's mandate. However, the UNHCR inherited a number of IRO refugees in this area from WWI and WWII. This number has
increased during periods of consecutive political unrest and
military upheavals. Due to the intensified Arab nationalism
and the restrictive policies of some Arab states, many foreigners, including settled refugees, became destitute and
were persecuted. Although these refugees were not numerous, they have involved the UNHCR in issues of international
protection and in securing material assistance and in seeking
resettlement opportunities for them in Europe and overseas.
The resulting intricate diplomatic negotiations and complicated operations have demanded much time and effort.

      The UNHCR's activities in Asia and the Middle East
have thus been extensive and diverse. A unifying thread related to all Asian refugee movements has been the use of the
concept of good offices, which has provided the HC with a
new flexibility in responding to emergencies. The growing
confidence of the international community and of individual
governments in the usefulness of the good offices concept, in
light of the manner in which the HC has used it, has also
greatly expanded the range of his international responsibilities.

Chapter 27

REFUGEES IN HONG KONG

The British Crown Colony of Hong Kong has been the site of two refugee problems of quite different nature. Since WWII it has been the primary point of exit from mainland China, the "bridge of hope" for some 30,000 refugees of European origin in transit elsewhere and the destination of over three million Chinese seeking refuge from economic and political conditions on the mainland.[1] Taking into account its physical limitations and political problems, the Colony has endeavored to live up to the traditions of the right of asylum. But the stress of this population movement on the Colony's resources and limited space has affected every aspect of its economic, social, and political life.

The Host Country

The British Crown Colony of Hong Kong, founded in 1841, lies to the southeast of China's Kwangtung Province, and 40 miles northeast of the Portuguese Island of Macao. Of its total area of about 400 square miles, Hong Kong Island (on which is located the capital City of Victoria) and a number of small adjacent islands constitute 33.3 square miles. One-quarter mile across the harbor, the City of Kowloon on the mainland (which contains the Colony's only flat land) and adjacent Stonecutter's Island make up another three and three-quarter square miles. The remaining 370.4 square miles constitute the New Territories, a barren, hilly terrain on the peninsula between Kowloon and the Chinese border, and some 230 small islands leased from China in 1898 for a period of 99 years. The lease expires in 1997. While the British view Hong Kong as a Crown Colony, the People's Republic of China considers Hong Kong to be an integral part of China, administered by the British.

Eighty percent of the total area of the colony is

660

wasteland, steep, rocky hillsides or swamps, unsuitable for agriculture, and developable for other purposes only by means of heavy expenditures for site construction and land reclamation. Of the remainder, 55 square miles comprise agricultural land, and 25 square miles are urbanized, particularly in the areas of Victoria and Kowloon. On these 25 square miles, and on thousands of boats in bays and harbors surrounding Hong Kong Island, 4.1 million people live today, in conditions of unparalleled congestion. Irregular rainfall and limited water resources are a constant deterrent to the Colony's development. The fishing grounds in adjacent waters are virtually its only natural resource. [2]

Population. Hong Kong has traditionally served for the Chinese as a place of free movement to which they have come in search of work, sometimes temporarily, returning home for harvests or for other reasons, and sometimes permanently. This traditional movement, usually strongest in times of economic and political crisis, has resulted in a fluctuating population. From the 1930s onward, political events on the mainland caused hundreds of thousands of mainland Chinese to seek asylum. The major influx of population into Hong Kong began after WWII when the population of the city had dropped to 600,000 from the pre-war figure of 1,000,000. Some were old residents returning home after the Japanese occupation. [3] A significant number were immigrants, part of the historic rural-urban population movements which had been interrupted by WWII. The largest portion, however, was refugees in the political sense, individuals and families responding to increasingly unsettled conditions in China as the intensity of the Civil War mounted. An unprecedented and sudden influx of refugees followed the Communist takeover in 1949. During the succeeding ten years the flow continued at the rate of 90,000 annually despite the government's Immigration Control Ordinance which attempted to restrict entry into the colony.

Although border control procedures were further tightened in the 1960s, a large migration from the mainland into Hong Kong occurred in 1962. Revolutionary social and economic policies and land reform programs in mainland China in the late 1950s contributed to this increase in the number of persons seeking refuge or new livelihoods in Hong Kong, and economic recession and agricultural crises in China in the early 1960s precipitated the huge and critical influx of refugees in early 1962, when 500,000 attempted to enter the colony. By 1970 the population had climbed, a

result of immigration and natural increase, to over four
million people, nearly tripling the 1941 high point. [4]

The non-Chinese persons living in the Colony never
exceeded 2.5 percent of the population. In the first post-
war census in 1961, out of a total of 3,128,004, the non-
Chinese population numbered 25,500, including 16,000 British, 2,436 Americans, and 1,750 Portuguese. Unlike the
Chinese who, once they reach the Colony, are permitted to
stay, and whose Hong Kong born children are automatically
British subjects, the non-Chinese are subject to strict immigration control, and must obtain a visa from the Colonial
Government before entering. Whereas Chinese immigrants
have never officially been regarded as refugees, those persons of European origin fleeing China have been so regarded
and, for the most part, have been permitted to enter the
Colony only as transients.

The Economy. Culturally, economically, and politically Hong Kong has long been the "crossroads of the Far
East." Until 1951 it was a booming free-trade center between East and West through which China's goods passed for
export to the rest of the world, and through which came
most of its imports. Ship building was its only notable industry. The ability of the Colony to absorb nearly three
million new inhabitants since 1945 is attributable mainly to
a virtual transformation of this traditional economic structure. The Korean War and the UN embargo on shipments
to mainland China choked off Hong Kong's trade after 1951.
Unemployment, resulting from decreased trade and increasing population, became a cause for serious alarm, one which
has contributed to Hong Kong's development since then as a
manufacturing center. The population movement from the
mainland brought additional manpower and in many cases
technical skill and capital, and made development of alternate
means of subsistence both necessary and possible. [5] Since
1959, although entrepôt trade still provides almost one-third
of the Colony's revenue, Hong Kong has gradually developed
a wide variety of local industries, especially textiles and
consumer goods, which are exported throughout the world. [6]
Industry has been Hong Kong's economic salvation. It has
also meant salvation for the Chinese refugees, since it was
able to provide them with at least a bare subsistence as long
as markets were available for Hong Kong's products.

But the subsistence which the economy provides for
the masses of Hong Kong's poor is meager indeed. The

prosperity enjoyed by a small minority of the Colony's residents is far beyond the reach of refugees. Despite the visi-
ble prosperity, and the "modern miracle" which has produced a shoppers' paradise for visitors, "the majority of
the population is still ill-housed, undernourished, and under-
paid. " The spectre of unemployment is always present. In
the first place, the labor force itself is constantly growing.
New immigrants of working age continue to enter the Colony,
and the children of earlier immigrants and former residents
are reaching maturity in increasing numbers. Secondly, the
economy itself is constantly threatened by the demands of
Western countries that Hong Kong reduce the volume of its
exports--demands against which Hong Kong must continually
defend itself if it is to maintain the possibility of even minimal subsistence for its inhabitants.

The Government. Through its effort to meet the basic
needs of a vastly swollen population the Government of Hong
Kong has been a key factor in this industralization and has
itself undergone considerable professionalization. The government derives its authority from Letters Patent passed
under the Great Seal of the UK. These provide for a Governor, an Executive Council, and a Legislative Council.
Royal Instructions from the Sovereign to the Governor prescribe the membership of these councils. The main function
of the Executive Council is to advise the Governor, who
must consult its members on all important matters. The
laws of the Colony and financial policies are enacted by the
Governor with the advice and consent of the Legislative
Council. The principles of English Common Law and Equity,
and the Statutes of England are the foundation of Hong Kong's
legal system. Under the general direction of the Colonial
Secretary, the administrative functions of government are
discharged by some thirty departments. Thus, although
overall policy for the Colony is controlled by the UK through
the Secretary for Colonial Affairs, considerable authority
rests with the local authorities. The Colony is financially
autonomous, except for external defense. It has its own
courts, schools, medical and social services, housing authority, and public works department.

After 1949 it became increasingly evident that government services were totally inadequate for the requirements
of the enlarged population--that unless the government took
positive action the new residents could not be absorbed, as
they had been in the past, into the society and into the
economy as it existed. The government, therefore, set

about planning for modification of the economy and for the administration of programs which would permit this absorption. During the last twenty years it has undertaken land reclamation and site formation projects, and has built dams and reservoirs in an attempt to alleviate Hong Kong's two most severe shortages--land and water. [7] It has supplemented private construction of housing by a program of multiple-storied low-rent housing estates. It has engaged in a campaign of school building and has considerably enlarged the Colony's medical facilities. In cooperation with the voluntary agencies it has developed its social welfare services to the community. These undertakings have been financed mainly out of revenue from the Colony's exports. But the task has not been easy, nor has it been possible to keep abreast of the constantly increasing needs of the rapidly growing population.

Refugees of European Origin in China

Over 20,000 refugees of European origin from mainland China passed through Hong Kong under the auspices of the IRO between 1945 and 1952 on their way to resettlement countries. The problem remained unsolved, however, and became one of the most critical confronting the UNHCR when it became his concern in 1952. At that time their total number was uncertain, but was estimated to be 15,000, of whom 3,000 were registered with the IRO. Others, although they had for various reasons never registered were, nevertheless, prima facie within its competence. Some did not register because they considered that the new regime in China would not last; others did not require assistance in the early days, and some were prevented from registering because of the great distance that separated them from any existing IRO offices within China, especially those large numbers of refugees who lived at the time in northern China.

A great majority of the refugees were stateless persons of Russian origin who, in the early 1920s, had fled from Soviet Russia into China. In addition, there was a smaller number of nationals and ex-nationals from countries in eastern and southeastern Europe, including Austria, Greece, and Spain. Most had settled in Manchuria and in northeast China, where many thousands were employed by the Manchurian Railway and resided principally in the vicinity of Harbin and the three eastern Provinces of Girin, Zizikar, and Chabar. After the occupation of Manchuria by the USSR

in 1945, the situation for many of them began to deteriorate,
and before long, several thousand were dismissed from their
positions by the influx of newly arrived officials, engineers,
advisers, and workers who came to Manchuria from the
USSR to take over control of the Chinese Eastern Railway.
From 1949 onward, when the Government of the People's
Republic assumed full control in mainland China, economic
and political conditions made the position of all foreigners
extremely difficult.

Those refugees who had been retained in employment
by the railway were dismissed in large numbers.   Foreign
business houses were gradually closed down resulting in additional unemployment with little or no chance for these refugees to find work elsewhere.   Many of those who had been
dismissed earlier had already experienced great economic
stress and were now in critical need.   Those who were able
and had the means began to leave for the larger cities of
the south, particularly Shanghai, hoping to secure some assistance from the IRO.   Many of this earlier group were
fortunate in securing assistance and were subsequently resettled from China to the US, Canada, Brazil, and Paraguay. [8]

In Manchuria alone, there were an estimated six to
seven thousand refugees who were formerly railway employees and were now deprived of any means of earning their
livelihood.   Reports from this area mentioned that many had
resorted to begging in the streets, and that others had sought
employment as servants in Chinese households and were
forced to accept degrading and humiliating jobs.   A number
of those who were reduced to complete destitution had died
as a result of the bitter cold, hunger, and sickness and
others had committed suicide.   Expressions of dissatisfaction
with conditions was a crime against the government which
might lead to punishment or imprisonment or even to forced
labor.

Many of these refugees managed to leave China and
obtain a resettlement visa; others, among them many able-
bodied technicians, professional, and clerical workers, were
a potential asset to the economy of any receiving country,
and had not given up hope that help might yet reach them before it was too late.   The situation existing in China was
well substantiated by the desperate appeals which reached
the Offices of the HC in Shanghai and Hong Kong.

International Assistance Through UNRRA and IRO

      The predecessors of UNHCR had evolved programs of emergency assistance and resettlement. In 1945 UNRRA instituted a program of emergency assistance and by 1947 had given financial assistance to approximately 11,500 refugees in China. In July of 1947, when the IRO assumed responsibility for this problem, it undertook a financial assistance program to 9,300 registered European refugees, of which 3,000 were settled by the end of the year.

      From the beginning of the IRO operation in July 1947 requests for registration were received by the thousands, great numbers of which were from the northern area around Harbin. However, the distances prevented many from ever reaching the IRO offices established for the south and becoming registered. By the end of 1948 there were still 8,400 persons receiving financial assistance out of a total of 13,000 registered.

      Following the takeover of Manchuria and of the cities of Peking, Nanking and Shanghai in 1949, the political situation in China was for a while stabilized. Although other offices in China were closed down the IRO was able to continue its cash assistance program in Shanghai with a small staff. By the end of December 1949, 11,000 persons had been either resettled or repatriated.

      As of 1 January 1950 there remained approximately 6,000 registered refugees, of whom 3,400 were receiving assistance. This number slowly decreased through 1950 and 1951. At the end of its operation in China on 21 January 1952, the IRO had registered or assisted 29,000 refugees of European origin. Of this number 19,000 were resettled (including 5,500 evacuated to Samar in the Philippines), 1,800 were repatriated, 2,900 were reported dead or missing, and 3,800 were left in China.

      With the fall of Manchuria and its capital in 1949, the IRO had considered it necessary to initiate emergency action by evacuating as many refugees as possible (particularly those of Russian origin against whom there had been mounting animosity) from Shanghai. In the beginning of 1949 the IRO had concluded an agreement with the Philippine Government to give temporary (no longer than four months) asylum in Samar to 6,000 refugees from China until their permanent resettlement could be arranged in other countries.

Accordingly, in the early months of 1949 the evacuation of
5, 500 of these took place, but the last evacuation ship was
refused port clearance by the Shanghai administration, and
a group of 500 was obliged to remain behind.   They remained as part of the IRO caseload to be assumed by the
UNHCR.

When the IRO ceased operation in Samar, on 31 December 1951 (after repeated difficulties and delays), all but
130 of the original 5, 500 refugees had been resettled.   Responsibility for these was given to the WCC to whom a fund
of $400, 000 was entrusted to provide for their final settle-
ment.   By April 1953, the last of these refugees had been
resettled.

UNHCR/ICEM Joint Office

The Shanghai Operation 1952-55.   At its last session
the General Council of IRO allocated a sum of $235, 000 to
UNHCR to provide a limited program of emergency assistance
for European refugees in China.   It also established a Trust
Fund of $500, 000 to be administered by ICEM for resettle-
ment of IRO refugees from China.   To continue IRO operations in behalf of these refugees UNHCR and ICEM established a joint office in Hong Kong as of 1 February 1952,
with a special representative in Shanghai.   UNHCR was to
be responsible for care and maintenance of refugees in China
and in transit through Hong Kong to resettlement countries.
ICEM was to be responsible for their transportation.

The original case-load for the new office was based
on the 3, 800 refugees registered with the IRO and still in
China at its closure.   In addition, an unknown number (estimated at seven or eight thousand but, as subsequent years
revealed, the number was actually much greater) of unregistered refugees of European origin were known to be in China
who were potentially prima facie eligible within the mandate
of the IRO, or the eligibility criteria established for the Joint
Program.   It was not immediately possible to register the
prima facie case-load, but those refugees who applied for assistance to the Shanghai office were documented and assisted
on an ad hoc basis.

Active cooperation on an operational level was established during 1952 between the Joint Office and the voluntary
agencies, especially through the LWF/WCC Joint Service to

Refugees. [9] The complicated operation of arranging for resettlement of refugees has been shared primarily by these
two agencies--the Joint UNHCR/ICEM Office, and WCC, although other agencies, such as NCWC and the YMCA have
assisted in the task.   WCC initially contacted the refugee in
China and kept in touch with him from that time until final
settlement was completed.   It compiled the necessary visa
data both for entry into Hong Kong and for onward movement.   When the refugee arrived at the China-Hong Kong
border the Communist-owned China Travel Service telephoned
WCC whose Russian-speaking representative immediately
visited him in the lodgings to which the Travel Service had
escorted him, and began the necessary counseling and assistance with problems of health, material needs, and resettlement procedures.   WCC took full responsibility for
visa production through its field offices, consulates, sponsors or organizations abroad.   The Joint Office, for its part,
contacted the British Chargé d'Affaires in Peking and arranged for transit visas for Hong Kong.   It arranged and
paid for board and lodging in Hong Kong, finalized visa documentation and took care of all movement arrangements including the payment of passage.   It was also responsible for
medical expenses incurred by refugees in Hong Kong. [10]

     With information gained mainly through the "grape-
vine, " applications for visa production and assistance began
to flow in from China to the Joint Office in Hong Kong.
Agency case-loads were established and active visa production resulted in the movement during 1953 of 3,264 persons.
As a consequence, increasing numbers of applications for
registration were subsequently received by the Joint Office.

     The early years of the Joint Operation were a period
of financial crisis and of technical problems retarding visa
production, during which requests for registration poured
into the Shanghai office from all over China.   The Chinese
Government required that the emigrant possess a visa for the
resettlement country before he could apply for an exit permit, but even those with visas were never certain whether
their permits would be granted before the expiration of the
visa, if at all.   For entry into the Colony, Hong Kong authorities required refugees of European origin to obtain a
transit visa for Hong Kong, but they granted such visas only
to those who already possessed proof of the transitory nature
of their stay in Hong Kong, namely, a visa for some other
country.   Furthermore, the Hong Kong visa expired six
months after issuance.   It was difficult at best to process

refugees for such visas in Shanghai, but, in addition, some
countries which did not maintain consulates in China, notably
the US and Canada, still insisted on a consular interview in
Hong Kong.   Thus, until some place could be found where
refugees could be interviewed by competent consuls, the
situation was at an impasse.

A partial solution was found through the action of
Belgium, Norway, Denmark, Sweden, and Switzerland, which
agreed to issue alternate visas to refugees to enable them
to come to Hong Kong in small numbers for processing.
When a refugee holding an alternate visa found placement,
the alternate visa was freed for use by another refugee who
could then apply for an exit permit from China.

There were long delays in obtaining exit permits from
China, even for refugees holding visas.   During such delays
waiting refugees relied almost entirely on UNHCR emergency
aid for their survival.   Every delay in moving these refugees to their destination increased the cost to UNHCR for
their care and maintenance, and raised the long-term cost
of the operation.

The most constant and serious threat to the success
of the Shanghai Operation was lack of funds.   The limited
funds transmitted from IRO to UNHCR were exhausted by
November 1952.   By the beginning of 1953 the UNHCR estimated that, at the rate at which refugees were being resettled, and given the growing need for financial assistance to
those awaiting exit permits, the operation might last over
five years and cost between $1 million and $1.5 million.
The HC appealed to governments to relax immigration restrictions and to make openings available to the difficult
cases.   He also stated that unless funds were forthcoming
the operation would have to cease before the end of the year.

Receipts from the HC's many appeals totaled
$1,487,112 (including the IRO allocation, private sources,
and government contributions to the UN Emergency Fund).
Expenditures amounted to $1,248,581 (including maintenance
of European refugees in China, payment to ICEM for Shanghai refugees in transit, cash payments to voluntary agencies
working in China, and administrative expenses for the Hong
Kong and Shanghai offices).   The operation continued precari-
ously, often on a month-to-month basis.   When, on 21 October 1954, the GA established UNREF (GA Res. 832[IX]) and
merged the special Emergency Fund for most needy cases

(GA Res. 538[IV]) with the new fund, it was hoped that sufficient funds might be made available to speed up the operation. By 1955 the Joint Operation, with the assistance of the voluntary agencies, had resettled 5,915 persons, mostly in Australia, Brazil, Canada, Greece, Israel, Paraguay, Turkey, and the US.

There remained, however, a huge unsolved problem. It was now estimated that there were 14,000 refugees in China, of whom more than 6,000 had already obtained visas or promise of visas and were in various stages of processing for resettlement. Many were blocked only by lack of exit permits from China. Seven hundred of these were maintained in Shanghai by UNHCR funds. In addition, 50 of the 500 stranded Samar-bound refugees still waited in the Shanghai staging center for resettlement opportunities; 40 refugees were hospitalized in Shanghai for whose expenses the UNHCR reimbursed the Shanghai authorities regularly. The voluntary agencies had turned over to UNHCR the care of 400 refugees whom they no longer had funds to support. And, finally, a continuous average of 200 refugees was maintained in Hong Kong while in transit to countries of final asylum.

The Far Eastern Operation, 1956-59. The year 1956 brought a major change in the policy of the People's Republic of China which altered the nature of the Shanghai Operation (known henceforth as the Far Eastern Operation). The policy of the mainland government toward European refugees and its expectation concerning their final destination had never been clearly definable. Until 1956, although there had always been a small flow of refugees from China, it was difficult for Europeans to qualify for exit permits. The former IRO Shanghai Office was permitted to operate on a semi-official basis after 1952, and much of the information required for visa production and for exit permits was gathered through the voluntary agencies in China.

In May 1956, however, not only did the China People's Relief Association take over the Joint Office in Shanghai, thus forcing all resettlement procedures to be operated by UNHCR through the Hong Kong office, but the government suddenly increased the number of exit permits for Europeans in China. In 1955 only 594 entered Hong Kong and were resettled; in 1956 the number jumped to 1,191; and during 1957 a total of 4,120 entered Hong Kong to await onward movement. 11

The result of these changes was twofold. First, the unexpected flood of refugees could not immediately be moved by ICEM, whose funds from IRO were nearly exhausted by 1957. In spite of funds received from a joint UNHCR/ICEM appeal in the summer of 1957 the number of refugees entering Hong Kong continued to exceed by hundreds the numbers which could be moved by ICEM. The flood of Europeans coincided with a still greater influx of Chinese refugees at the same time, and thus contributed to a crisis situation for the tiny colony. Hong Kong authorities threatened to turn away refugees who did not have Hong Kong transit visas, and to reduce the number of those to be issued. Thus, as Dr. Edgar Chandler of the ICVA pointed out, "failure to provide funds would result in untold misery for thousands of human beings who now, for the first time, have regained hope for a new life in the free world."[12] The burden of maintaining this flood of European refugees from China fell on the UNHCR. The allocation from UNREF for care and maintenance of refugees in Hong Kong during 1957 had to be increased by $81,000. The cost of maintaining a refugee for six months in Hong Kong was estimated to exceed the cost of transporting him to his final destination.

A second long-range result of the closing of the Shanghai Office was the increased difficulty of obtaining information on unregistered refugees in China, which was required both for visa production and for exit permits from China. After its closing, all processing had to be undertaken through direct correspondence with refugees in China. In the case of many refugees the only information available was the name and composition of the family. Medical reports and other required data could not be obtained until refugees reached Hong Kong. The system of alternate visas covered only some 50 refugees at any one time.

Special Problems. Two special problems were accentuated by the surge of refugees arriving in Hong Kong after 1956. The problem of difficult cases had been with the UNHCR since the beginning of the Joint Operation. The problem of "Old Believers" did not become acute until 1956. Difficult cases included individuals who, because of old age, chronic illness, or physical or mental handicaps, were not an economic asset to receiving countries and would in fact need institutional care or some degree of financial assistance throughout the remainder of their lives. The number of such cases had increased constantly over the years since 1952. By 1956 it had reached major proportions and placed

severe demands on UNHCR funds.   In addition to individual
difficult cases were their dependents who had to relinquish
possible resettlement offers rather than abandon a family
member who was not accepted for resettlement.

Since European refugees in Hong Kong were considered transient, integration was not a feasible solution, and
it was necessary for the UNHCR to seek placement for these
individuals in institutions in European countries.   The HC
made personal approaches to governments in his search for
placement opportunities.   He often granted up to $500 per
capita to assist in the initial placement of these cases.
Some places were made available in old-age homes, but it
was extremely difficult to find places in institutions equipped
to care for the chronically ill, and openings in mental institutions were found only in two countries--Denmark and the
Netherlands.

As openings in existing installations (government institutions or those administered by private agencies) were filled,
it became necessary to set up new homes, thus adding to the
per capita cost of placement.   The HC deplored the impression, implicit in the offer of financial assistance to any country which would assume the care of difficult cases, that human beings were being treated as merchandise.   Yet it
seemed the only method which enabled countries to take these
cases.   He was, therefore, all the more grateful to a country like Denmark, which offered to take ill refugees, but refused the UNHCR grant.

As modern treatment methods were discovered which
would enable many of the chronically ill or handicapped to
regain their health and independence, it seemed all the more
tragic that lack of funds for moving them to places for treatment and for meeting the costs of the treatment should be
the major reason for their being left behind in China or in
Hong Kong.   By 1959, some 900 had been placed in homes,
mostly in European countries and in Australia.   But in the
years immediately following the influx of refugees into Hong
Kong, the numbers of difficult cases in UNHCR care in Hong
Kong and in Shanghai became a severe burden.

The second problem, that of the Old Believers, became acute after 1956, and was not entirely resolved until
after 1965.   Old Believers belonged to a sect which had, in
the early seventeenth century, refused to accept innovations
in Russian Orthodox liturgy and had broken away from the

Church. They guarded their religious identity through political changes, first in Russia and then in China, to which they
migrated after WWI. They settled in Sinkiang and Manchuria
in self-contained communities as horse breeders, trappers,
and subsistence farmers, retaining their special customs and
rarely marrying outside their own sect.

Before 1956 few had obtained exit permits from China. But during 1957-58 some 1,500 left northeastern China
and trekked 3,500 miles southward to Hong Kong where they
had to be maintained by the UNHCR until resettlement opportunities could be found for them. For the most part they
sought resettlement in large groups so as to be established
in colonies. They resisted the UNHCR policy of seeking the
integration of refugees into the community in which they were
resettled. Special efforts were made in their behalf. The
WCC, with the support of UNHCR and ICEM, approached
several governments before a sympathetic response was received from Brazil. The WCC bought 5,000 acres of virgin
land in the Parania Plateau in central Brazil. By May 1958
the ground had been prepared and formalities attended to;
as a result of special appeals, funds were available for the
first 500 to set out for Brazil. The refugees were given
tools and surplus food by WCC, and seeds, tools, and some
livestock by the Brazilian Government. Within two years
they had become self-supporting and were considered an asset to the country. Eventually more than 1,000 Old Believers (a name which they had chosen for themselves) went to
Brazil, several hundred to Australia, and smaller contin-
gents to Argentina, Bolivia, Canada and the US. [13] But in
the meantime those not yet resettled were maintained in
Hong Kong at UNHCR expense, thus adding to its difficulties
at a time of grave crisis in the Far Eastern Operation.

In May and June 1964, after a lapse of several years
during which no Old Believers came to Hong Kong, the main
body of the remainder of the sect, numbering around 360
persons, was granted permission to leave Sinkiang. On arrival in Hong Kong they stated their determination to settle
as a single colony in Canada or in Argentina. It was impossible for the UNHCR to make such arrangements, and the
group refused offers made for settlement in other countries.

In February 1965 a special commission of representatives of UNHCR and WCC was sent to Hong Kong to attempt
to break the deadlock. After considerable effort the HC
drew up lists for Argentina, Australia, Brazil, and New

Zealand, where openings had been made available for members of the sect. All but 57 of the refugees accepted the plans. The remaining 57, for whose maintenance in Hong Kong considerable money had already been spent, continued to refuse available resettlement opportunities. However, since they were self-sustaining, the UNHCR was able to discontinue material assistance.

Aid to the Joint Operation. In November 1957 all these problems faced the Joint Office at once. Recognizing the seriousness of the situation the GA authorized the HC to use his good offices to encourage arrangements for contributions. It authorized UNHCR to use funds received for European refugees in China in any way the HC saw helpful for long-term solutions, rather than just for care and maintenance, including allocating sums to ICEM for the transportation of refugees. It urged concentration on the movement of refugees and a speed-up of the operation, as conditions appeared to be growing worse with time. Estimates were made of the cost of moving all remaining registered refugees of European origin out of China by the end of 1960: If ICEM could move 2,550 during the last half of 1958 and 4,000 during each of the years 1959 and 1960, transportation costs were estimated at $1,325,000 for 1958 and $2,087,500 for each of the two following years. If the average caseload of refugees in transit in Hong Kong could be maintained at 250 persons and the average transit time held to three weeks, the cost of care and maintenance to the UNHCR would reach $525,000.

In response to the appeal many countries offered financial assistance. The US gave ICEM a grant of $450,000. Switzerland offered to accept some difficult cases, and Swissair gave their free passage (transport by air was often the only way of moving the ill or aged). CWC loaned ICEM $180,000 to carry out its operation. These efforts considerably relieved the emergency.

The result of this upsurge of attention to the Far Eastern Operation was to cut the problem almost in half by the time WRY focused the world's attention on refugees everywhere. On 1 June 1959, on the eve of WRY, 8,400 European refugees, including some 900 aged and infirm, still awaited emigration from mainland China. Funds were available for moving over 3,000 of these, and visas had been obtained for 3,700. An additional $4 million was necessary to move all these people to new homes, including $3 million

for ICEM to provide overseas transport, and \$1 million for
UNHCR for care and maintenance in Hong Kong.   An additional 4,700 immigration visas were still needed, including
visas for some 900 aged and infirm.   It was hoped that these
requirements would be met during WRY.[14]   The contributions
received during WRY were almost double the amount which
had previously been obtained and, as a consequence, in 1960
the problem of European refugees known to be in China was
all but overcome.

The Three Rivers Crisis.   Before the end of 1962 a
new crisis arose with regard to European refugees.   Another
apparent change in policy of the People's Republic of China
Government sent a new wave of refugees from the distant
Three Rivers area in Sinkiang on their way to Hong Kong.
Many of them were Old Believers.   On arriving in Hong
Kong, many reported having been called suddenly to the government office where they were handed an exit permit and
given 48 hours notice to leave.   Before their arrival little
was known about these people.   There were no medical records, no documents.   They had apparently lived in isolated
communities to such an extent that their lack of immunity to
common diseases became a serious problem.

The first wave of some 300 arrived in September
1962; a further 1,500 arrived several months later.   The
Hong Kong authorities were very lenient in their policy
toward them and permitted their lack of documents to be
covered by affidavits.   But without immediate relief a repetition of the 1956 crisis threatened to occur, since it was not
known how many more might arrive, or when.   The UNHCR
at once sought admission for them into Australia.   Not only
did the Australian Government grant permission for the admission of 1,000 refugees but, when it became known that
the Orthodox Church in Australia could not finance their
passage, the Australian Government offered to treat them
as government-sponsored immigrants and pay for their transportation.   The UNHCR set up a joint fund of \$20,000 with
the Australian Council of Churches to help finance their establishment in Australia.   By March 1963, 1,300 Three
Rivers refugees had reached Australia, where they found
jobs as semi-skilled laborers.   At the beginning of 1963 an
estimated 2,500 refugees of European origin remained in
China, some 100 of them in the Three Rivers area.

After that time the case-load of the Far Eastern Operation dwindled.   In 1964, 2,000 remained, and by 1967

only 1,032 were still in China.   But even though visa production continued and many of those remaining held visas,
the number who managed to obtain exit permits from China
also dwindled.   In 1966 only 48 reached Hong Kong.   In
1969, of the 852 who held visas, very few were allowed to
leave China. With a few new registrations continuing to be
made annually, and a few managing to leave China, the case-
load has for several years remained at about 1,000 persons.
The UNHCR allocated $43,602 in 1969 for maintaining refu-
gees in transit in Hong Kong, for assistance to refugees in
Harbin, and for the operation of the Joint Office.   In 1970
$45,000 were allocated for these purposes.

        The Joint Far Eastern Operation had, by 1969, set-
tled over 20,000 refugees at a cost of $7 million.   Over
half of these were taken by Australia, and one-quarter of
them by Brazil.   The remainder were settled in various
European countries (especially the chronically ill), in other
Latin American countries, and in the US, Canada, and Israel.   In the words of the HC, the Joint Office "will be required as long as there is hope that further European refugees will be granted exit facilities from China."[15]

The Chinese Refugees in Hong Kong

        A problem of far greater complexity and volume is
that of the Chinese refugees in Hong Kong.   The general
background differs from refugee problems in some other
parts of the world.   These refugees are not, generally
speaking, distinguishable from the majority of Hong Kong
residents, in language, customs, or mode of life.   Furthermore, Hong Kong has traditionally been a place of free immigration for Chinese.   In keeping with this tradition the
Hong Kong authorities have admitted almost any refugee who
succeeded in reaching the Colony.   Recognizing no legal refugee status, the policy has been to integrate new arrivals
as fully as possible into the life of the Hong Kong community.
Even should the Hong Kong Government desire to distinguish
refugees from ordinary members of the community, such a
differentiation would be impracticable.   The UK Government
has not extended to Hong Kong its ratification of the 1951
Convention and, consequently, Chinese cannot claim any
rights accruing to refugees under this international instrument.

        On the other hand, the refugees do not develop a real

sense of belonging to or of having a stake in Hong Kong.
Like de facto refugees elsewhere, they have for two decades
sought in Hong Kong merely a safe haven and protection
from what they consider to be a hostile force constituting a
constant threat to their life and liberty.   Whether considered to be refugees or not from the humanitarian point of
view, the almost insurmountable problem which their sheer
numbers pose in an area ill suited physically and ill prepared economically to accommodate them, has almost inevitably become a matter of international concern.

The problem is further complicated by the fact that
two governments claim to be the legal government of China;
one seated in Taipei, Taiwan, and one in Peking, China.
This and other complicated factors are responsible for the
fact that the Chinese refugees in Hong Kong are not under
the mandate of the UNHCR.   Nobody is in a legal position
to give the Chinese refugees diplomatic protection in case
political difficulties should arise in Hong Kong.

The Chinese refugees have come from every province
of China (although the majority are from neighboring Kwangtung Province) and from all walks of life--from farms, river
boats, city shops, and universities, from every trade and
profession.   Some who had been landlords fled China when
land reforms threatened their lives.   Some were peasants
who could no longer make a living under the new agricultural
system.   Others were industrialists from cities like Shanghai, former army personnel, or professors and their students who had been members of the resistance.   Some managed to bring with them a few possessions and even, in
some cases, capital.   But the great majority arrived destitute. [16]

Arriving in post-war Hong Kong simultaneously with
returning residents, refugees accentuated existing shortages
and competed with local residents for severely limited food
and water supplies, medical and social services, employment opportunities, and especially for housing.   A considerable number of refugees who had some capital bought accommodations from Hong Kong tenement residents who, in their
turn, became homeless and joined refugees in seeking shelter
in "squatter" communities.   Most of the refugees were
forced to improvise shelters out of scrap material.   Huts of
mud, tar paper, wood scrap or tin sprang up in all available
spots, on the steep hillsides, under the cliffs, and on the
rooftops of existing buildings.   Many refugees slept on the

streets, on stairways or in doorways. The squatter communities had no sanitary facilities and no water, and were vulnerable in the extreme to fires. Tuberculosis and other
sickness affected up to 50 percent of the population. Although medical facilities and services compared favorably
with those of other Asian nations, even at times of greatest
population pressure, they were grossly inadequate for Hong
Kong's needs (although there has never been an epidemic of
the types which frequently accompany such population crises).
Education was in great demand, but it was expensive, and
facilities even in the late 1950s could accommodate less than
one-half of the Colony's primary school children. Opportunities for steady work were limited. Eight percent of the
indigenous population was unemployed and a further twenty-
two percent were underemployed. For refugees the percentage was twenty-three and thirty-six percent, and for these,
wages were so low as to provide a bare subsistence. 17

Emigration from this vastly overpopulated area was a
solution urged both by the UK Government and by the Government of the Republic of China in Taiwan. Hong Kong
places no legal restriction on emigration. But emigration
depends upon the willingness of governments to admit refugees, as well as on the willingness of refugees to be resettled. Opportunities for resettlement were extremely limited.

It may be thought that the very difficult conditions
refugees met in Hong Kong would have led many to repatriate to mainland China, but so far only a handful have chosen
to do so. A much greater number have expressed a desire
to emigrate to other countries. But most have preferred to
remain in Hong Kong where they are among their own people and, in the case of the majority who came from nearby
provinces, among people who, like themselves, speak Can-
tonese. (The official language of Taiwan is Mandarin; while
educated people throughout China are likely to know Mandarin, it is not the mother tongue of most refugees.) Furthermore, refugees have hesitated to relinquish their last remaining contact with the mainland, which would be the result of a move even to Taiwan.

Between 1949 and 1954 about 150,000 refugees were
admitted to Taiwan. Since that time the movement has
dropped considerably. Taiwan itself is, moreover, one of
the most densely populated areas in the Far East, and one
with a high rate of natural increase. Although the government has assisted voluntary agencies, especially through the

Free China Relief Association, in resettling many of those admitted, it has always considered the admission of Chinese refugees from Hong Kong as a problem of military and political security. Most of those admitted had been members of the Nationalist army.

Although Australia, Canada, the US, and some countries of South America were willing to receive Europeans, Asians were not welcomed as regular immigrants. Certain South American countries have been willing to accept Chinese for reunion with their immediate families, or if they have acceptable skills, or can prove that they will be self-supporting. In 1963 and 1965, LWF/WCC helped to resettle 77 persons in Bolivia, and over a period of fifteen years they helped in the resettlement of 1,026 Chinese refugees in other South American countries, mostly in Brazil. Canada accepts Chinese for reunion with immediate family, and those whom the government selects for pre-arranged employment. Australia began to accept a few Chinese with the required educational background. In Britain a limited number of work permits (necessary for immigration) are issued for Chinese. New Zealand also has a small quota which the Labour Department can fill with selected Chinese refugees.

The most concrete prospects of emigration for Chinese refugees have been offered by the US Government. Some 5,000 were admitted under the 1953 RRA, and Public Law 85-316 in 1959 allowed the entry of some 3,000. This was followed in 1962 by the Parolee Program which allowed the entry of over 10,000 from Hong Kong. In addition to these three refugee programs, the US accepted 105 persons annually on the regular immigrant quota. In 1968 this quota was changed so that oversubscribed countries now share the benefit of unused quotas from undersubscribed countries.

Prospective emigrants have not lacked assistance in Hong Kong. In 1954 the WCC opened an office in Hong Kong in order to assist in processing applications under the first US RRA. This office has been responsible for both Chinese and European refugees since that time. Between 1954 and 1969 more than 14,500 Chinese applied to it for emigration, of whom 7,497 were successfully placed, 6,206 in the US. The office assists in all aspects of the process of resettlement--selection of suitable applicants from among those registered with it, finding sponsorship in the country of reception, full documentation, travel arrangements, often with ICEM, and in some cases providing financial assistance with fares.[18]

However, the small proportion of refugees who find
opportunities for resettlement are usually not the most destitute.   Nor is their number sufficient to relieve significantly
the pressure of population on the Colony.   Thus, while immigrants continue to enter the Colony in large numbers, only a few are able to find resettlement opportunities which
will permit them to emigrate.   For the vast majority of
Chinese refugees the only course open to them is integration
locally.

Government Policy in Local Integration

In view of these circumstances the government has
been obliged to make some attempt to limit the volume of
immigration.   The Immigration Control Ordinance, established in a treaty with the Government of the People's Republic of China in 1949, permits the entry into the Colony
of a maximum of 50 immigrants daily (thus approximately
18, 250 annually).   Temporary visas may also be issued for
visitors and businessmen, as they are for refugees of European origin.   Immigrants entering within the quota are registered and given an entry permit.   Thereafter, they enjoy
the same legal rights and the same economic and social opportunities as residents.

But the borders of Hong Kong are difficult to patrol,
and controls are almost ineffectual against the illegal entrants, that is, persons without an entry permit within the
daily quota who arrive in junks and sampans, or frequently
by swimming from island to island from mainland China or
from the peninsula of Macao, forty miles to the west.   Of
these illegal immigrants the Hong Kong authorities estimate
that for every one who is arrested three manage to slip by
border patrols and marine police.[19]   In 1962, 500,000 persons attempted to enter the Colony, of whom 250,000 were
turned back at the border.   The rest "merged with the general population and became, for all intents and purposes indistinguishable from older residents."[20]   In general, immigration policy permits "illegal immigrants"--any who have
entered without registering since the 1949 Ordinance became
effective--to legalize their position by applying for entry
permits and registering.

Thus, refugees are not placed in any special legal
category.   Like other immigrants they are distinguished from
British subjects--persons born in Hong Kong or in other

British territories (or those descended from or married to such persons), who now form more than one-half of the population of Hong Kong--only by the fact that they may be deported if they become a charge on or a danger to the Colony, and that for travel outside of Hong Kong, instead of a British passport, they must use special travel documents. Children born to immigrants in Hong Kong are British subjects.

Given this legal position, government efforts to facilitate local integration have inevitably, and intentionally been bound up with measures to improve economic and social conditions for all Hong Kong residents. In 1962, Mr. Claude Burgess, British Colonial Secretary, stated:

> The fundamental point in our policy hitherto is that the government has never distinguished in any way between the immigrant population and the population which has its roots there. All have the same rights, and the same opportunities. Once an immigrant has been admitted he will take his turn for our resettlement housing if he needs it. Our schools, our clinics, our hospitals are available to him on precisely the same terms as apply to people who were here before he came. [21]

The government's role in assisting in the local integration of refugees, thus, has consisted mainly in instituting a vigorous program for improvement and development of these facilities, and in supporting the development of voluntary agency programs in the fields of health and education, and a comprehensive range of social services.

When the refugees began to arrive by the hundreds in 1949 the help they received came from many private relief organizations. Early in 1950, however, these organizations appealed to the government, which agreed to undertake a feeding program for some 7,000 refugees living in the Rennie's Mill Camp (mostly escaped army personnel, former government officials, and intellectuals) for whom the voluntary agencies had been caring as best they could. [22] Government relief and rehousing measures began in earnest, after the "Christmas fire" which in one hour on 25 December 1953 swept through a squatter settlement, leaving 50,000 persons homeless once again. Having once recognized the appalling plight of the refugees, and the dislocation and privations their arrival caused among Hong Kong's poor, the Government

undertook a vigorous program of redevelopment for Hong
Kong, attacking first the most serious problem--housing.

Housing. Taking advantage of the land that had been
cleared by the Christmas fire, the government set about
building the first of a series of multi-storied dwellings which
would house more than the 50,000 who had been made homeless by the fire. It undertook to provide food for the homeless until they could be resettled. These dwellings--only
slightly modified in subsequent projects--provide a cubicle of
between 120 and 150 square feet for a family of five or
more, with communal cooking, bathing and washing facilities
for residents of each story. Water and electricity are provided in the communal areas and residents may install their
own electricity in their rented quarters. These blocks are
capable of housing from 2,000 to more than 6,000 people.
This housing, while only substandard, is a considerable improvement over "squatter" housing, but it is relatively expensive. [23]

In 1954 the government established the Hong Kong
Housing Authority to arrange for sites and construction of
similar blocks, and for allocation of space to applicants. In
the seven years that followed, the Housing Authority constructed 200 additional blocks. The program continued at
the rate whereby one block was opened every nine days, and
by 1969, one-quarter of Hong Kong's population (or 1,092,000
persons) were similarly housed. Space was allocated on the
roofs and sometimes on the ground floor for government and
voluntary agency social welfare programs--nurseries, clinics,
community centers, food distribution points, counselling,
etc.--and in some cases also for workshops and retail out-
lets.

In addition to these measures undertaken by the government through the Hong Kong Housing Authority, two other
non-profit organizations also contributed to the solution of
the serious housing shortage resulting from the influx of immigrants. The Hong Kong Housing Society, with funds from
the UK Colonial Development Fund, and the Hong Kong Settlers' Corporation, constructed apartment housing for more
than 65,000 persons. Furthermore, following a report in
1958 on the serious deterioration of pre-war tenement housing in which a large proportion of Hong Kong's poorest residents lived, the government undertook a program for the
gradual replacement of these dwellings so that persons in the
lowest income groups could be resettled in low-cost housing.

This government program was administered by the Housing Authority.

Education. The expansion of educational facilities was "no less dramatic." In 1954 the government initiated a seven-year school construction program, especially of primary schools, which resulted in the opening of 180 full-sized, government-built or subsidized schools with total capacity for 215,000 pupils. During 1961, schools were completed at the rate of one a week, and enrollment reached 484,000 in primary schools and 90,200 in secondary schools. By 1968 the combined enrollment had reached 1,133,000.

Post-secondary education also received assistance from the government. In 1957 a joint effort of the University of Hong Kong and the government initiated a seven-year program for the University of Hong Kong designed to nearly double its capacity--bringing it to 1,800. The government agreed to underwrite deficits from recurrent costs while the University, with the help of the UK Colonial Development Fund, agreed to improve and expand its installations. The government also decided to assist certain Chinese colleges and technical schools in raising their educational standards with a view to their eventual union in a second Chinese-medium university. Both projects were designed to assist in meeting the needs of the rapidly growing post-secondary school population. By the end of 1962, 6,000 students were enrolled in the University of Hong Kong and in the various colleges.

Nevertheless, there is still a shortage of educational opportunities, especially at the secondary and post-secondary level. Because of the shortage, and because education is expensive and not compulsory, and low economic standards force many children to work at an early age, many children and young people are still without schooling.

Medical Services. To improve medical services, the government in 1955 made plans to supplement existing facilities--11 government hospitals and a number of private and subsidized ones whose combined capacity was 3,900 beds. By 1961 it had constructed three additional hospitals, bringing the total to 9,940 beds; and in 1963 it opened a 1,320-bed hospital which also has comprehensive clinic and out-patient facilities. Creation of new facilities since that time has increased the capacity of hospitals so that in 1968 the ratio was about three beds per thousand of population. This

considerable increase in facilities still leaves medical services seriously inadequate for Hong Kong's needs.   To match
Western standards four times the present number of beds
would be required.

Partnership of Government and Voluntary Agencies
in Developing Social Services

Long-range economic development and individual self-
sufficiency, rather than relief, have been the goal of both
government and private social welfare programs.   Yet after
1949 the needs of the population were so overwhelming that
emergency relief was essential.   Such government programs
as existed were carried out through the Social Welfare Office
of the Secretariat for Chinese Affairs.   Emphasis was on
direct relief for the most urgent cases.   The government
relied almost entirely on the many voluntary agencies for
on-going services such as orphanages and old-age homes,
as well as for supplementing its emergency relief.

The voluntary agencies were, in fact, the only source
of aid to which many refugees could turn before the government turned its serious attention to their needs.   More than
one hundred agencies had programs in Hong Kong.   The
Catholic Welfare Commission of China, for instance, operating through nearly 100 centers in various parts of the Colony,
the LWF/WS through its twenty-two centers, the CWS, and
the British Red Cross had distributed food, clothing, and
medical supplies to those who were either unemployed or
could not earn sufficient incomes to afford these.   They had
run nurseries and day-care centers, and in some cases primary schools, and had had operated clinics. [24]   The government had subsidized such agencies as the Family Welfare
Society in its program of granting loans to individuals for
establishing them in business.   Chinese neighborhood organizations (Kaifongs) had also been active both in emergency
assistance and in community development.   Voluntary agencies had approached the housing situation with innovative development schemes, but the magnitude of the problem far
exceeded their capacities.

Among the responsibilities assumed by voluntary agencies was the distribution of assistance from abroad.   Since
1953, for instance, when the US Department of Agriculture
released surplus food for distribution abroad, voluntary agencies have paid for its shipment to Hong Kong, and attended

to its distribution. CWC and LWF took on the task of interviewing and registering applicants for emigration to the US
under the RRA. The US Far Eastern Refugee Program, begun in 1954, is administered through the voluntary agencies.
Likewise, contributions from OXFAM have been handled by
Hong Kong agencies.

In the decade after 1949 an emergency approach characterized the social welfare programs of both government
and voluntary agencies. As the economy improved, however, providing more employment for immigrants, this approach gradually gave way to one of coordination and planning for more comprehensive services. A first step in this
direction was the creation in 1958 of a new Department of
Social Welfare to replace the Social Welfare Office of the
Secretariat for Chinese Affairs. Since that time the government has become increasingly involved, not only in direct
services but also in financial support for voluntary agency
programs. The private agencies also coordinated their efforts through the Hong Kong Council of Social Service, to
which 84 of the more than 100 agencies belonged.

The partnership between public and private welfare
agencies matured steadily in the following years, and in
1966 the government, recognizing that effective social welfare services could only be achieved through the joint planning and combined efforts of the government and the voluntary agencies, established the Joint Planning Committee with
members from both the Department of Social Welfare and
the Hong Kong Council of Social Service. The Committee,
after careful assessment of welfare resources in the context
of the social needs of the Colony, drew up a five-year plan
for development of social welfare services, through which it
hoped not only to attack the backlog of needs, but to be able
to keep up with new problems. Under the plan the Social
Welfare Department broadly speaking,

> assumes responsibility for those functions which
> are required by statute and for public assistance,
> registration of the disabled, and a variety of case
> work, group and community services ... while the
> voluntary agencies assume responsibility over a
> range of services as wide in scope--financial and
> supplementary relief assistance, vocational train-
> ing, rehabilitation, day care, institutional services
> for young and old, aftercare of prisoners and drug
> addicts, social research and a host of essential

services which supplement and complement the official services.[25]

Projects were agreed upon for services to youth, community organization, probation and juvenile correction, family and child welfare, moral welfare, welfare for the disabled and counselling services. These projects were to be implemented either directly by the Department of Social Welfare or by one or more of the members of the Hong Kong Council of Social Service with generous government subvention. During 1965-66, out of a budget of HK $15 million, HK $6 million was disbursed to voluntary agencies for projects undertaken within the framework of the five-year plan. HK $2 million went to projects carried out by the Social Welfare Department. In 1966-67 the amount of subventions reached nearly HK $7 million. The Department of Social Welfare reports annual progress in all areas of social welfare resulting from this planning and cooperation.

Yet, as with government efforts in housing, education, and medical services, social services in Hong Kong still cannot meet the still growing needs of the Colony. Furthermore, Hong Kong still lacks certain basic social services which have for decades been taken for granted in most Western nations. There is no free, compulsory education, no employment exchange or minimum wage law, no comprehensive public social service even for special groups--the aged or chronically ill.

The Eligibility Question Before the UN

In the years between 1949 and 1959 the needs of the Hong Kong poor, swelling annually in numbers as a result both of continuing immigration and natural increase, grew at a faster pace than resources for meeting these needs. The financial burden on the government increased annually and its services continued to be inadequate for the emergency. To voluntary agencies and to the government itself, it was clear that from a practical standpoint, the situation merited the sympathy and assistance of the international community.

Discussion of the Chinese refugees in Hong Kong had taken place intermittently in the GA, in ECOSOC (8 July 1952), and in the UNHCR Adv. Com. meetings over several years.[26] Official recognition of the problem was not given, however, until 1954 when the HC was authorized to send a

team to investigate the situation and to report on it to the
Adv. Com.   The undertaking was financed by private funds
($50,000 from the Ford Foundation).

Debate in the Adv. Com. revealed a broad division
of opinion between those (such as France and Belgium) who
felt that the issue of legal status of the refugees in relation
to the UNHCR mandate must be determined before the HC
could take any action in their behalf, and those, on the other
hand (such as Turkey and the observer from the Republic of
China), who felt that humanitarian considerations were paramount. 27   They wished to avoid the appearance that the HC
was geographically or racially discriminatory.   The HC himself considered that his Statute should be interpreted to include these refugees, whose plight no one doubted.   But it
was pointed out that, regardless of the ultimate resolution
of this question there were in fact insufficient funds at the
disposal of the HC to carry out even his present undertakings.   At the same meeting the delegate of the UK underlined
the fact that local integration was impossible for scores of
thousands of refugees to whom asylum had been granted, and
that the UK and the Hong Kong authorities would welcome
practical schemes for the removal and resettlement of these
refugees.

The delegate from the Republic of China declared that
his government had already given shelter to thousands of
refugees under IRO but that there was a limit to the numbers Formosa could absorb and that international assistance
must be forthcoming if the UNHCR was not to be considered
discriminatory.

The HC emphasized the complexity of the situation,
stating that the work of his Office was based on the assumption that a refugee was a person who had left his country,
and hence could not claim the protection of its government.
But as everyone knew, there were two Chinese governments
in existence, and therein lay the source of the difficulty.
He also pointed out that voluntary organizations had frequently stressed the extreme difficulty and impracticality of arriving at a proper breakdown of the refugee population in the
Hong Kong context.   He suggested that since insufficient information was at hand, a team of experts in social, legal
and economic matters be sent to Hong Kong to make a comprehensive study and to report back to him.   After some
discussion the Committee adopted the suggestion that the HC
"endeavor within his budgetary possibilities, and to the extent

to which other resources might make it possible for him to
do so, to prepare a report on the refugee problem in Hong
Kong in cooperation with local authorities and to present it
to the Committee as soon as possible. "28

　　　　The Hambro Report.　The HC appointed Dr. Edvard
Hambro, former Registrar of the International Court of Justice, to lead a mission which included a representative of
the UNHCR, Dr. Gilbert Jaeger.　Its purpose was:　to ascertain as far as possible the number and composition of the
refugee group among the Chinese population of Hong Kong,
Kowloon and the New Territories; to investigate all possible
solutions to the problems of these refugees; to ascertain all
the necessary facts which would permit a decision to be taken
whether all or any part of these refugees come within the
mandate of the UNHCR; and to submit a report to the
UNHCR. 29

　　　　Dr. Hambro submitted the report on 15 November
1954 to the HC who transmitted it to the Adv. Com. for
consideration at its Fifth Session (6-10 December 1954).
Discussion was deferred to the First Session of UNREF Ex.
Com. , May 1955.

　　　　The UNREF Ex. Com. (I) concluded, in its turn, that
it was not yet in a position to decide on the eligibility of the
Chinese refugees.　But noting its appreciation of the thor-
oughness of the report, it adopted a resolution requesting the
HC to give sympathetic encouragement to governments and
organizations with a view to their assisting in alleviating the
problems of the Chinese refugees in Hong Kong, and to report to the Committee any progress made in implementing
the resolution. 30

　　　　The issue did not rest there, however, for the UN
Association in Hong Kong and the China Refugee International
Council cabled requesting the UNREF Ex. Com. at its Third
Session to devise measures to provide international assistance
to Chinese refugees in Hong Kong in accordance with the
recommendations submitted in the Hambro Report.　Although
the matter was not on the agenda, the Chairman brought it
up at the Third Session in May 1956.

　　　　It was suggested in the course of the ensuing discussion that a distinction might be made between eligibility under
the Statute of the HC and eligibility under the UNREF Program, as had been done already in the case of other groups

of refugees.   The HC quoted one section of the Hambro Report concerning their legal position:

> From a strictly legal point of view the Chinese refugees may fall outside the HC's mandate, but from a broader and humanitarian point of view it may be added that a factual situation cannot be without influence on the legal position.   If it is a fact that the Government of Taipei is incapable of protecting these persons, they are de facto refugees.   They would thus seem to be in a worse situation now than they would be even if they had no government at all to protect them.   If this result is good law, it is still somewhat startling to the common sense of people who do not benefit from a profound knowledge of international law.[31]

Still unable to reach agreement on the status of the refugees, committee members suggested that the question be referred to the International Court of Justice for an advisory opinion, or even to the GA itself.   Most members of the Committee agreed, however, that such a course would involve too long delays, whereas the question of assistance to these refugees should be decided as soon as possible.   It was decided that the matter should be taken up at the Fourth Session of the UNREF Ex. Com. and that a short summary of the Hambro Report should be prepared on the question of eligibility of the refugees.   In the meantime, the HC was to inquire from the UK Government whether the situation of these refugees was such as to warrant taking special measures.   The HC was also to report to the next session if any funds were available to help these refugees.   The Committee hoped by these steps to be able to reach a decision at its next session as to whether it should, and could, assist the Chinese refugees in Hong Kong.

The Fourth Session of the UNREF Executive Committee.   Between the Third and Fourth Sessions of the UNREF Ex. Com. "two new notes were sounded in this long drawn-out discussion."[32]   The 1956 Annual Report of the Governor of Hong Kong, Sir Alexander Grantham, contained an implicit plea for assistance.   In it he stated, referring to the refugee problem,

> It is remarkable how much we have done.   I venture to add that it is also remarkable how little help we have received from outside.   I am aware

of, and most grateful for, the large and generous
assistance that has been given by the voluntary
agencies, but the problem is too vast for them and
ourselves alone to solve.

In February 1957, one month prior to the Fourth
Session of the UNREF Ex. Com., a detailed report on the
needs of the Hong Kong refugee was drawn up by Pastor K.
L. Stumpf, leader of the LWF in Hong Kong. [33] He worked
for both European and Chinese refugees in Hong Kong. On
behalf of WCC he had travelled to Japan, Australia, Thailand, Malaya, the US, Brazil, and through Europe to investigate and help with the resettlement of refugees. Endorsed
by the China Refugee International Council, his report was
presented to the Hong Kong Government which sanctioned its
use as the official document for circulation and for presentation to the UNREF Ex. Com. [34] These statements were reinforced by appeals at the opening of the Fourth Session in
February 1957 from the Hong Kong UN Association and the
WFUNA. [35]

　　Position of Concerned States. The legal status of the
Chinese refugees in Hong Kong still proved too intricate for
the Ex. Com. to settle at its Fourth Session. The summary
of the Hambro Report revealed, first, that criteria for determining the eligibility of a refugee under UNHCR mandate
turned mainly on the question of whether the refugee's motive
for leaving his country was a "well-founded fear of being
persecuted for reasons of race, religion, nationality or political opinion." (Some refugees had asserted that their departure was motivated by a desire for economic betterment--
a fear of poor economic conditions in China--rather than by
political persecution.) It would be impossible without individual screening of the 385,000 persons in Hong Kong estimated to be refugees in 1954, to decide on the motives for
their departure from China. Second, even if such screening
were possible, the duality of Chinese Governments posed
another problem. For those governments which recognized
the Government of the People's Republic of China, the refugees could legally be considered within the UNHCR mandate
since it was reasonable to assume that most had fled for
fear of persecution by that government. Governments which
recognized the Government of the Republic of China in Taiwan, however, could not consider these refugees to be within
the mandate since in theory they could avail themselves of
the protection of their government (Taiwan) without fear of
persecution. Furthermore, because the Government of the

Republic of China was the one which, up to 1972, had the seat in the UN, it would hardly be logical for the UN to act as though a government which had its seat in that organization were not the legal government of its country. But neither could the mere fact that the Government of the Republic of China had recommended UNHCR assistance to these refugees lead to the conclusion that the refugees did come within the mandate.

The position of the British Government itself was ambiguous. On the one hand, because of the British policy toward immigrants in Hong Kong, the exclusion clauses of the UNHCR Statute could not be invoked to exclude these refugees from HC competence. [36] Although the Hong Kong authorities had generously given all immigrants the same opportunities as British subjects, they did not grant them British citizenship. On the other hand, neither could the refugees be included in the HC's competence, since the British Government did not categorize them as refugees, and moreover had not included Hong Kong in its ratification of the 1951 Convention relating to the Status of Refugees.

The views of Dr. Hambro himself were given in the concluding chapter of the report: "These refugees are of international concern, and it is inconsistent with the large measure of international interest in other groups of political refugees that this important group should fail to receive international assistance on account of a legal technicality. "[37]

The observer from the Government of the Republic of China exhorted the Committee to face the problem and to reach a decision on the issue which had been repeatedly shelved. Pointing to the Hambro conclusions, he urged that an immediate start should be made to bring relief to most needy cases among the refugees.

In response to the second question--whether the British Government felt that conditions in Hong Kong called for special UN consideration, the UK representative summarized the serious situation in Hong Kong. Refugees at that time numbered nearly one-quarter of the Hong Kong population. In spite of all government and voluntary efforts, provisions for assisting these people, and for meeting their housing requirements were inadequate. The representative stated that what might be done internationally still depended on whether the refugees were considered eligible for assistance under UNHCR. But, if that assistance should be made available, the most suitable type would be a contribution toward the cost of one of the Hong Kong Government's housing schemes. Such a grant should be administered in close cooperation between the Hong Kong Government and the UNHCR.

The third question, concerning the availability of funds, was answered in the negative. The economies which had been expected in the Far Eastern Operation had been consumed in care and maintenance of the refugees whom ICEM had been unable, for lack of funds, to resettle.

After considering the legal and practical situation of the Chinese refugees in Hong Kong, the UNREF Ex. Com. drafted a resolution to be presented to the Twelfth Session of the GA, agreeing that while it had not been able to reach a clear decision in the matter of the eligibility of these refugees, and although it recognized that no funds were available at the time to assist them, it nevertheless considered "that the plight of these refugees is such as to be of concern to the international community" and suggested that the GA should examine the question.

Two GA Resolutions. The GA resolution resulting from this examination (Res. 1167 [XII], 1957) avoided the legal aspect of the question, but agreed that the problem was such as to be of concern to the international community. It authorized the HC to use his "good offices" to make arrangements for contributions. But "the response of the international community to this resolution was negligible until 1960 when the impetus of WRY began to be felt."[38]

This resolution was followed two years later by the WRY Res. 1388 (XIV) of 20 November 1959 which expanded the concept of good offices to all non-mandate refugees. These resolutions opened the way for the first time for the UNHCR's active involvement in the problems of the Chinese refugees in Hong Kong.

World Refugee Year Aid to Hong Kong

During WRY the HC asked the Government of Hong Kong to draw up a list of priority projects to which the international community could contribute which would be of benefit to refugees. The Hong Kong Government listed projects totaling about $7,280,000 for which no money was available at the time from either government or voluntary sources, and which could therefore not be undertaken without outside assistance. The HC publicized this list and invited contributions, either through his Office, or directly to the Hong Kong Government. These projects were not aimed specifically at refugees, but were designed to benefit all of Hong Kong's poor. Since housing was, in fact, the major requirement, a majority of the projects were in this field.

Conditions in Hong Kong were widely publicized in the world press and television. [39] As a result a total of $4 million was contributed by governments, voluntary agencies, and private sources for Chinese refugees. Most of the funds went directly to projects already being operated by voluntary organizations, rather than to the new undertakings suggested by the Hong Kong Government. However, $943,000 were channelled through the HC for distribution to the competent authorities and the voluntary agencies.

After WRY, with worldwide emphasis placed on camp clearance and on the solution of "old" refugee problems, interest in Hong Kong slackened. In spite of the HC's plea for continued aid, "the voluntary agencies which had previously instituted programs of assistance continued them, but the international community left the Hong Kong Government to face its problems alone."[40] However, a pattern of giving had been established during WRY, which foreshadowed the future role of the HC in Hong Kong.

The Establishment of a Revolving Fund

At the Third and Fourth Sessions of the Ex. Com. -- April and October 1960--a suggestion was made by the representative from the Republic of China that the HC set up a revolving fund for grants and loans to individuals for assistance in establishing themselves in trades. No action was taken on this suggestion. The Committee requested more information on the situation. The delegate from the UK expressed the fear that the Chinese request might entail undesirable interference with the Hong Kong Government's arrangements for material assistance. The Committee merely agreed on a statement to the effect that it hoped the Chinese refugees would continue to receive full attention.

Recognizing this slackening of interest in non-mandate refugees the GA in December 1960 passed a further resolution (GA Res. 1499[XV[), in which it reminded member governments of the UNHCR's role in the question of non-mandate refugees, and invited them to "continue to devote attention to refugee problems still awaiting solution." This resolution was in effect an appeal to member governments to follow up the considerable success achieved during WRY in solving refugee problems. At its Fifth Session, the Ex. Com. established the requested revolving fund.

Reaction to the Influx of May 1962

Though WRY and the GA resolutions helped to focus attention on the problem of the Hong Kong refugees, their effect was "less dramatic than the sudden influx of would-be refugees in May 1962."[41]

In May 1962, an unprecedented number of persons suddenly sought entry into Hong Kong. Authorities were faced with the decision as to whether to continue their customary policy of granting asylum, at the risk of reversing hard-earned economic and social gains, or to refuse entry to all but the agreed 50 per day, at the risk of breaking the traditional policy of non-refoulement, and "delivering up these people to their executioners" (in the words of the Chinese representative in the Fourth Session of the Ex. Com.). They officially took the latter course, turning back refugees at the border but, as before, not those who had once managed to enter the Colony unnoticed. In fact, during 1962, instead of the 18,000 who would have been admitted legally, a total of 300,000 managed to enter the Colony--over the border by boat or sampan, and from Macao.

The international community, while sympathizing with the predicament of the Hong Kong Government, criticized its choice of policy, feeling that the right of asylum should have been given precedence over the domestic needs of Hong Kong itself. However, it was pointed out by Duncan Wood (Director of the Friends International Centre in Geneva) at the 1963 ICVA General Conference that the Hong Kong Government had, during the past decade, made capital expenditures equivalent to 20 percent of its annual revenue for provision of housing and expansion of social services, while operating costs had absorbed a further 10 percent. "It seems doubtful" he said concerning the criticism of the international community, "whether this view can be upheld, unless the international community shows itself much more ready than in the past to promote the development of Hong Kong so as to increase its absorptive capacity."[42]

Voluntary agencies, even during WRY, had continued to urge the UN to determine the mandate status of the Chinese refugees, not only so that the HC should be able to assist them, but especially so that he could help to promote measures for their resettlement. Now, with the broadened competence of the UNHCR through resolutions concerning use of his good offices, the successful use of WRY contributions for economic and social projects, and recognition of the fact that Hong Kong Chinese refugees were virtually indistinguishable from the rest of the population, ICVA emphasis changed. "What is important is that they should be assisted irrespective of their legal status. "[43]

At the Seventh Session of the Ex. Com. (14-22 May 1962) the UK delegate presented to the Committee the policy of the Hong Kong Government concerning refugees and measures which it had taken to meet the problem. The report reviewed the background of the influx up to the end of 1961 and reiterated its policy of integrating new arrivals as fully as possible into the life of the Hong Kong community. It reviewed the measures which had been taken to implement this policy: vast expenditures had been made since 1949 to relieve shortages of housing, medical and educational facilities, and water supply. Land reclamation schemes were in progress. The report also described Hong Kong's economic progress and the consequent increase in employment possibilities for immigrants. But, it added, "How long this relative freedom from unemployment can hold out in the face of restrictions on Hong Kong manufactured goods which other countries are seeking to impose, and against the increasing numbers of young persons of employable age in the next few years, is a matter for some uneasy speculation. "[44]

In the face of world criticism the Hong Kong Governor stated in his Annual Report for 1962,

> Nothing could wreck our plans and our achievements more rapidly or more certainly than a further flood of immigrants. ... We have accepted our heavy burden and we are willing to bear it, but we cannot allow that burden to be intolerably increased, and we must be allowed to pursue our policy of containment in the immigration sphere. If the conscience of the world is stirred by the needs of the people affected by that policy, then it would seem that the needs of those people can only be met elsewhere than in Hong Kong. [45]

This statement again suggested emigration as a solution for Hong Kong's refugee problem.

The new influx reawakened international concern. On 24 May 1962, President Kennedy decided to parole Chinese refugees into the US, Canada and Australia, and some Latin American countries also made special provisions for some Chinese refugees. The representative from the Republic of China to the UN announced that his government was prepared to receive new refugees; that it would send one thousand tons of rice to the Hong Kong Government for distribution; that it was anxious to cooperate with other governments and with relief organizations and that it had established a special committee to administer funds appropriated for the relief and resettlement of Chinese refugees in Hong Kong.

On the same occasion Felix Schnyder announced, in response to publicity in the world press, that he had received many requests for information on ways of alleviating the new emergency situation. He stood ready, in accordance with GA Res. 1167 (XII), to undertake anything, however modest, to assist in agreement with the wishes of the authorities directly concerned. 46

Accordingly, the HC discussed the matter with the Minister of State for Foreign Affairs of the UK, who agreed to ask his government what international assistance it might suggest. The UK Government transmitted to the HC a statement containing a full exposition of the policy of the Hong Kong Government on its immigration problem, and an invitation to any government wishing to assist the Hong Kong Government with this problem, to contact that government directly. The Hong Kong Government was prepared to furnish interested governments with full details of the range of projects for which international financial assistance would be welcomed.

The UNHCR Since 1962

In December of the same year the GA passed its second resolution specifically pertaining to Chinese Refugees in Hong Kong (GA Res. 1784 [XVII]). It reaffirmed its concern over the situation of Chinese refugees, appealed to member governments of the UN, to the Specialized Agencies, and to non-governmental organizations, to increase their contributions, and requested the HC to continue his good offices,

in agreement with the governments of the countries concerned, to provide assistance to the Chinese refugees in
Hong Kong.

The implementation of this resolution, based mainly
on consultation between the UNHCR and interested governments, followed the pattern begun during WRY. In his report covering the year 1962, the HC reported that a total of
$129,386 was channelled through his Office for Hong Kong
refugees. During 1963 he listed specific projects which had
been supported by international contributions amounting to
$475,000. In 1964 contributions were made to the revolving
fund which had been set up by the Ex. Com. at its Fifth
Session totalling $77,000, but other assistance went directly
to the Hong Kong Government. Reports since 1965 have
merely stated that the HC continues to follow with interest
the situation of Hong Kong refugees who continue to benefit
from measures enacted by the Hong Kong Government for the
benefit of all residents. The HC reported in 1971 that the
number of refugees of European origin on the mainland of
China remained at about 1,000 during recent years. Owing to the continued suspension of exit permits only a few
have left the mainland for Hong Kong. Where their resettlement to other countries was being arranged, the UNHCR
committed small sums for the maintenance and medical expenses for refugees in Hong Kong. [47]

Towards the end of 1971, a marked increase in the
number of European refugees with exit permits, issued by
the Government of the People's Republic, arrived in Hong
Kong for completion of migration formalities for permanent
settlement in other countries. The UNHCR provided therefore a total of $147,000. [48]

Notes

1.   See Edgar H. S. Chandler, The High Tower of Refuge,
        London: Oldhams P., 1959, Ch. 15.

2.   Hong Kong An. Rep., 1967. Also, "A Problem of
        People," revised from final chapter of Hong Kong,
        An. Rep., 1956.

3.   Wells C. Klein, "The Hong Kong Refugee Problems,"
        in Background Paper, National Conference on World
        Refugee Problems, 1969: 29, and K. L. Stumpf,

"Report on Hong Kong's Refugee Assistance Programme," ibid., 1969: 2.

4. Wm. E. Collard, Director of Immigration, in an interview with Frank Ching, The Times, London, 11 Oct. 1970.

5. "Chinese Refugees in Hong Kong, a Summary of Recent Developments," Ex. Com. (VII), 1962 A/AC.96/Inf. 8: 13 (in French).

6. In 1948, 1,160 factories employed 60,000 persons, whereas by 1966, there were 11,232 factories which employed 576,440 persons. Additional employment opportunities were created by the construction of housing, schools, factories, etc. Hong Kong An. Rep., 1967: 21-22.

7. Between 1951 and 1967 three reservoirs were constructed. For further water resources the government will be obliged to invest in dams and conversion plants for sea water.

8. Holborn, IRO History: 186-87.

9. This Service was initiated in the spring of 1952 and operated until, in the spring of 1954 sole responsibility for its functions was transferred to WCC. LWF, since that time, has concerned itself with rehabilitation and local integration of Chinese refugees in Hong Kong.

10. K. L. Stumpf, "Resettlement of Stateless European Refugees of Russian Origin from the Mainland of China." WCC Service to Refugees, Hong Kong, June 1969.

11. HC's Annual Rep. for 1958, GA (XIII) Off. Rec., Supp. No. 11, A/3828/Rev. 1.

12. ICEM News #225, 9 Oct. 1957.

13. UNHCR Monthly Newsletter No. 45, Apr. 1967, and UNHCR, Meeting the Challenge, Geneva, 1961; and Chandler, op. cit., Ch. 17. Unable to make a living in South America some of the group left to start again in Oregon. In 1967, to protect their children

from what they felt were corrupting influences, Old
Believers purchased land in the Alaskan wilderness
for a new village (see Jim Reardon, "A Bit of Old
Russia Takes Root in Alaska," National Geographic,
Sept. 1972: 401-24.

14. WRY/INF/22 "To End an Odyssey."

15. An. Rep. for 1969, GA (XXIV) Off. Rec., Supp. No.
    12, A/7612: 35.

16. R. Donders, "The Forced Migration and the Refugee
    Problem of Hong Kong, 1949-54." Catholic Confer-
    ence, Dec. 1954: 261-70. See also, "Report by
    the HC Concerning the Question of Chinese Refugees
    in Hong Kong," UNHCR Adv. Com. (III), A/AC.36/
    25, Mar. 1953.

17. USEP News No. 16, Oct. 1957.

18. Stumpf, "Short Description of the Problem of Chinese
    Refugees in Hong Kong," June 1969: 5.

19. Collard, op. cit.

20. Klein, op. cit.: 29.

21. Ex. Com. (VIII), 1962. A/AC.96/INF. 11, Annex: 3.

22. In Oct. 1952 Mr. James Read, the Deputy HC visited
    the Camp when he was informed that the feeding
    program was to cease. See, "Report by HC Con-
    cerning the Problem of Refugees in HK. For detail
    on the voluntary organizations associated with the
    Hong Kong Council of Social Services, see Ex. Com.
    (XII) A/AC.96/INF. 8, Annex A: 1-2.

23. K. L. Stumpf, Rep. on Hong Kong's Refugee Assistance
    Program: 3.

24. The Free China Relief Association, set up in 1950 with
    headquarters in Taipan, carried out various projects
    of assistance and relief for Chinese refugees in
    Hong Kong, allocating money for such purposes as
    child welfare, education, medical expenses and pur-
    chase of clothing. This association depends for its
    resources primarily on contributions by Chinese

people throughout the world. In addition, "Aid Refugee Chinese Intellectuals, " an organization set up in March 1952 by US Congressman, Walter Judd, concerned itself specifically with registration, rehabilitation and resettlement of professionals, intellectuals and specialists. Its rolls had over 15,000 persons. "Report by the HC Concerning the Question of Chinese Refugees in Hong Kong, " op. cit. : 5.

25. Hong Kong Social Welfare, op. cit. : 5.

26. GA (VI), Third Com. Off. Rec., 7 Jan. 1952.

27. 29 Apr. 1954, Third Session A/AC.37/SR. 23.

28. Ibid. : 11.

29. A/AC.36/25.

30. A/AC.79/7, 12 May 1955.

31. E. Hambro, The Problem of the Chinese Refugees in Hong Kong, Rep. submitted to the UNHCR, 1955.

32. Elfan Rees, We Strangers and Afraid: 65.

33. Pastor Stumpf, born in Mannheim, worked there for a pharmaceutical concern which, in 1937, appointed him scientific representative in Shanghai. Ordained in 1951 in Shanghai, he was one of those to assist Jewish families through church funds. In 1951 the German Church in Shanghai was confiscated, and he was ordered to leave China. He arrived in Hong Kong on 13 Jan. 1952 and was jointly appointed by LWF and WCC as Director of their Joint Services to Refugees in Hong Kong.

34. Letter from Colonial Secretary to LWF as quoted in Elfan Rees, op. cit. : 66.

35. A/AC.79/55.

36. Clause 7b states that HC competence shall not extend to any person "who is recognized by the competent authorities of the country in which he has taken residence as having the rights and obligations which

are attached to the possession of the nationality of that country...."

37. Hambro, op. cit., 127, par. 488.

38. D. Wood, "The Problem of Chinese Refugees in Hong Kong and Macao," ICVA Gen. Conf., Doc. 10 R, 1963: 2.

39. For example, a model street from a Hong Kong squatter settlement was set up in central London as a means of encouraging donations.

40. HC's Annual Rep. for 1962, GA (XVII), Off. Rec., Supp. No. 11, A/5211/Rev. 7.

41. Wood, op. cit.

42. Ibid.: 3.

43. Ibid.: 4.

44. Ex. Com. (VII), 1962 A/AC.96/INF. 8: 12.

45. Quoted in Wood.

46. HC's Annual Rep. for 1962, GA (XVII), Off. Rec., Supp. No. 11, A/5211/Rev. 1, An. III: 34.

47. HC's Annual Rep. for 1971, GA (XXVI), Off. Rec., Supp. No. 12, A/8412.

48. Ex. Com. (XXIII), A/AC.96/471, 24 Aug. 1972.

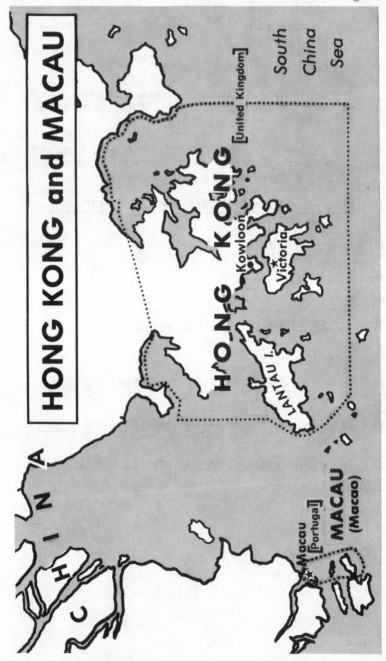

Chapter 28

REFUGEES IN MACAO

During and after WWII a disproportionate number of
Chinese refugees moved into the Portuguese Province of
Macao. In 1961 at the Fifth Session of the Ex. Com., the
observer of Portugal requested the HC to lend his good offices in securing international support for a long-range plan
for assistance of refugees in Macao. In fact, the refugee
problem in Macao was even more serious in certain respects
than the problem in Hong Kong but, being overshadowed by
the latter, it had been neglected.

Host Country

The tiny Portuguese Province of Macao lies on the
south coast of China in the estuary of the Pearl River, sixty miles downstream from the City of Canton, and thirty-
five miles to the southwest of Hong Kong. The province
comprises the City of Macao on a peninsula three miles long
by a mile wide, and the nearby Islands of Taipa and Coloane
--a total land area of 5.5 square miles. Since the relatively
barren land supports little agriculture a large part of Macao's food, except fish, is imported, mostly from mainland
China. Its water also comes from the mainland through
pipes running along the narrow causeway connecting the two.

The oldest, and for many years the richest outpost of
European trade in the Far East, the territory was granted in
1557 to Portuguese traders who acted at the time as middle-
men in trade between China and Japan. Macao's geographic
location and its excellent harbor were major assets. Chinese businessmen traveled freely between the mainland and
Macao, and many established businesses there, including
match, firecracker, and footwear factories. Much of the
world's gold trade was centered in Macao. These activities,
and especially trade, were the main sources of its rich
revenues until the mid-nineteenth century, after which Hong

Kong's development gradually outstripped Macao.   After that
time its entrepôt trade dwindled, but revenue from other
sources--gambling and tourism, as well as exports and the
gold trade--partially made up for the decrease.

Since the early 1950s the economic structure of Macao has gradually undergone a further change as a result of
new trends in trade movements and the growth of local manufacturing industries--especially furniture and plastic pro-
ducts--financed by Chinese capital.   By 1960, as a result of
the increase in the number of industries, including development of the fishing industry, revenue from exports covered
about one-third of the value of merchandise imports; by
1965, it had risen to one-half their value. [1]   The export of
some two-thirds of the annual catch of fish brings in almost
13 percent of this revenue. [2]

The gold trade, which continues to play an important
role in the economy, in 1960 brought 20 percent more income than did exports, whereas by 1965 the situation was
almost reversed.   Concomitantly, by 1964 income from
salaries and wages, and from small businesses were the
leading sectors in terms of gross national product. [3]   As in
Hong Kong, this gradual shift to local industries has provided employment for an increasing number of people, including refugees.   Yet, even with this growth in employment
possibilities, a large proportion of the population, swollen
by the influx of refugees from mainland China, was unable
to find work.   In 1964 over 10,000 families were living entirely on relief. [4]

The Province has a Portuguese administration with a
Governor and a Government Council.   A Legislative Council
was established for the first time in 1963, consisting of
twelve members, of whom three are ex-officio, eight are
elected either by direct suffrage, or by special interest
groups, and one is nominated by the Governor to represent
Chinese interests.   Except for the latter, members must be
"original" Portuguese citizens.   In the two municipal councils of the Province, members are elected according to law
"with due representation of Chinese interests. "[5]

Until recently the role of the Portuguese administration has been mainly one of maintaining law and order.   But
in the last two decades the Government of Portugal has taken
positive steps to further the economic development of Macao,
and the local government has allocated increasing funds to

the creation or improvement of social services. In a series of Development Plans (1953-58, 1959-63, and 1965-67) the Government of Portugal invested considerable sums for such programs as improvement of harbor facilities (including dredging and the construction of port facilities), extension of roads and electric power, urbanization, improvement of fishing, horticulture, and agriculture, and for reclamation of land intended for intensive agriculture. Furthermore, the ordinary budgetary expenditures of the Government of Macao itself, drawn from the province's own resources, have risen by an average of 20 percent annually (1955-64). [6]

Government welfare and relief services are carried out through the Social Welfare Department, Assistencia Publica, whose annual budget in recent years has been approximately 20 percent of the total provincial budget. [7] Assistencia Publica undertakes direct health and welfare services and relief programs for refugees and residents alike. In addition, it supports the programs of numerous voluntary agencies, especially CRS. The Diocese itself also provides direct and indirect services from its own resources which cannot be measured in cash. For many years CRS has implemented projects for all types of refugee assistance, in many cases with matching contributions from the government, from the Diocese, and from overseas agencies and governments. (The largest contributions to CRS have come from the US Government.) This combined effort to provide welfare services has, however, been severely challenged by the influx of refugees, many of whom are handicapped by special problems of health or age.

Although only about 3 percent of Macao's annual budget is allocated directly to education, schooling has not been seriously deficient in the province. [8] In addition to the official system, which consists of both a few government-run schools and many government-subsidized parochial schools as well as some provision for higher and technical education, there is also the Chinese school system in which almost one-half of the Province's children are enrolled. Even before Portugal's 1964 educational reform--making primary education compulsory--was introduced to Macao, 90 percent of school-aged children were enrolled in various schools. [9] Nevertheless, the arrival in the Province of thousands of refugee children has necessitated the creation of many additional places, and has pointed up the need for greatly increased opportunities for vocational and technical training.

Portugal has always recognized the Chinese character of Macao. Chinese have always outnumbered the Portuguese. At the time of the 1960 census the resident population (excluding refugees) was 169,299, of whom about 8,000 were Portuguese or Makanese (of mixed Portuguese and Chinese stock). The Chinese own and operate most of the businesses, schools, and hospitals in the province. Macao's trade with Portugal is almost negligible (although its exports to Angola and Mozambique have increased considerably since about 1961), so that although all persons born in Macao are considered Portuguese subjects and could, in theory, enter Portugal, few in fact have occasion to do so. Portugal claims legal "sovereignty" over the province, but it is clearly recognized that "if we leave the sphere of legality and take into account other factors, it is true that whatever resistance we might make, Macao would finally be absorbed by China, on which it depends in its daily life. "[10]

Severe disturbances which took place in December 1966-January 1967 point up the tenuous nature of this sovereignty. At that time, Portuguese police shot into a crowd of demonstrators who were protesting earlier official actions (in November the police had disbanded a group of Chinese who were said to be building a school on Taipa without authorization). Eight persons were killed in this incident, and over one hundred wounded. It was followed by the imposition of a curfew and some 3,000 troops armed with automatic weapons were called in to join Portuguese police in patrolling the streets. Chinese leaders, following these measures, presented to the authorities a series of demands: that the government apologize and compensate the families of victims; that it punish the officials responsible for the deaths (including four high-ranking persons); and that it suppress the activities of groups supporting the Republic of China and hand over seven persons accused of being political agents. When the government did not immediately accede to these demands (there was difficulty over the wording of the statement the Governor was to sign) further demonstrations, including the massing of 15,000 people on the mainland side of the border and the appearance of Chinese gunboats in near-by waters, occurred. Towards the end of January some residents began to take economic measures against Portuguese: refusing to sell them food, boycotting Portuguese-owned busses and refusing to pay taxes to the local government. It was also announced that electricity and water supplies to Portuguese residents would be cut off. However, before this happened the Governor signed an agreement meeting most of the

demands.   In addition to compensating victims' families with
a total of $360,000 and announcing that the responsible offi-
cials had been returned to Portugal for trial, the government agreed to put a stop to activities of groups in sympathy
with the Republic of China, to hand over the seven persons
in question and, furthermore, to turn back persons attempting to enter the Province without exit permits from the Chinese People's Republic.   After that time, various Chinese
schools, trade unions, and refugee centers were given notice
to close down, and a certain number of refugees were turned
over to authorities of the Chinese People's Republic at the
border.

In defending itself against the accusations by UN members, particularly the Republic of China, that Portugal violated the principle of non-refoulement of the 1951 Convention
to which it is a party, the Government of Portugal maintained
that the action was taken to prevent illicit activities by persons who style themselves as refugees but whose true purpose is to endanger the security of lives and property.   In
Macao at the opening of the Legislative Council in April
1967, the Governor noted that while the good understanding
of the local population, both Chinese and Portuguese had
made it possible to settle the crisis, the government would
continue to base its policy on good neighborliness, and would
not permit acts against the People's Republic of China.[11]

Refugee Influx

Through the centuries Macao has been a haven for
the unfortunate and the oppressed, including persecuted
Christian converts and, during WWII, refugees from Japan-
ese-occupied Hong Kong.   Until recently the Province set
no restrictions on the inward or outward movement of people.   As in Hong Kong, this freedom of movement was not
a significant problem until after 1949, when many thousands
of persons began to flood into Macao, coming either with
legal exit permits from China, or arriving clandestinely by
boat or by swimming from the mainland.   Between 1949 and
1959 an estimated 75,000-80,000 persons entered Macao,
many on their way to Hong Kong.   As in Hong Kong, the influx reached a peak in 1962, when in one month alone 1,200
persons entered Macao.   In the period between 1961 and
1965, police registers indicate that 120,000 persons entered
the Province.

Until 1962 a large proportion of the newcomers continued onward, especially to Hong Kong where conditions were somewhat more favorable. But after 1962 Macao, acceding to Hong Kong's request, established some control over permanent departures for Hong Kong, drastically reducing the numbers who left Macao--to between 1,000 and 2,000 annually. At the same time the influx from China continued to be very heavy, until by 1964 refugees were estimated to number 75,000 and to compose 35 percent of the population. There was no serious effort to restrict the number of new arrivals until 1966, when the Government of the People's Republic of China requested Macao to return to Chinese authorities all persons attempting to enter Macao without exit permits from China. In the intervening years, however, the population of the Province, especially the City of Macao into which most of the newcomers crowded, had reached alarming size and produced serious social and economic conditions.

The great majority of persons entering Macao were single, able-bodied young men, most of whom, before 1962, moved on to other areas. However, there was in addition a high proportion of handicapped persons, "useless mouths," to whom it has been the policy of the Government of the People's Republic of China to grant exit permits more readily than to others. These persons, including not only the aged, blind, or chronically ill, but also drug addicts and mental cases were, for the most part, unable to move on to other places and now, forming a very large percentage of the new population, pose serious problems for the government and the voluntary agencies. There are also many school-aged children, split families, and widows among the arrivals. Furthermore, some 3,000 Indonesians of Chinese origin had fled to China after the Dutch withdrew from Indonesia; eighteen months later 1,300 of them began to trickle into Macao. They were at a particular disadvantage since they knew no Chinese and had to compete with other refugees through the medium of Dutch or Malay, the languages of Indonesia. Under Indonesia's new nationality law they are no longer considered Indonesians, even though they were born there, and so cannot return to their homeland.

For able-bodied persons who remained in Macao there were very few employment possibilities, even in a growing economy. Most of them were farmers for whom no land was available in Macao, and who did not possess the qualifications required for the few jobs which did exist in the tourist trade and in factories. Those who might have supported themselves by fishing usually did not have the means to purchase the necessary boats or equipment. These unemployed persons and the large number who could never hope to become self-supporting, placed a severe burden on public and private welfare resources.

The Government of Macao and the voluntary agencies were very sympathetic toward the newcomers and, although outside assistance was limited in comparison with Hong Kong, made great efforts to assist them. The government set up two refugee camps, one accommodating some 200 ex-army officers and their dependents, and the other housing some 900 persons. It made available dormitory-type buildings for a reception center where refugees were housed and fed for a two-week period after their arrival. Assistencia Publica administered the center, which was partly equipped by a $15,000 grant from the US Government through the NCWC. On the Island of Taipa the government established a center for the treatment and rehabilitation of narcotic addicts which could handle 600 patients at a time. Although the government did its own fund raising for this project, CARE financed its kitchen and bakery and OXFAM financed a building to house the refectory and recreation rooms. The US has provided surplus food in support of this and other projects.[12] Voluntary agencies expanded their programs for the education of refugee children and for the medical care of refugees.

But these efforts did not go far toward alleviating the situation. After their two-week stay in the government center, refugees had to move on to make way for new arrivals, and to seek housing and employment on their own. As in Hong Kong, housing had to be improvised out of scrap materials, and shelters were constructed on stilts out over the tidal flats surrounding the crowded peninsula. With employment opportunities almost nil, a very large number of refugees had to rely entirely on relief. The need for emergency relief made it impossible for the government or the private agencies to undertake any projects for the rehabilitation or permanent local settlement of refugees.

UNHCR Assistance to Chinese Refugees in Macao

Under the circumstances, Portugal turned for assistance to the international community. At the Fifth Session of the Ex. Com. (7 June 1961) the observer from Portugal,

drawing attention to the fact that since 1937 Macao had admitted over 80,000 refugees from China, announced that his
government had drawn up a long-range plan for assisting
30,000 of these and of setting up certain light industries
through which the refugees could become self-sufficient. Under this $11 million plan the Portuguese Government agreed,
inter alia, to donate land worth a total of $8 million for
housing, schools, and industrial premises. When the new
influx in 1962 threatened to make even this ambitious plan
seem inconsequential Portugal requested the HC to lend his
good offices in order to secure international financial support for the plan, details of which were given to members of
the Seventh Session of the Ex. Com. The HC responded
that, as was the case with other refugee problems, the contribution the HC could make would depend upon the interest
shown by the international community. [13]

In response, Belgium offered to contribute $14,000
and the Holy See $410,000. The Ex. Com. decided to con-
tribute $20,000 from the receipts of the Stamp Plan and,
in addition, allocated $14,000 for assistance to Macao refu-
gees under the good-offices resolution. Private sources
also initiated projects, such as that of the Norwegian Refugee Council which undertook to supply surgical instruments
for a clinic for eye diseases, one of the most prevalent
problems among refugees in Macao.

As refugees continued to enter Macao in large numbers during succeeding months the Portuguese Government
again expressed to the Ex. Com. its hope that the UNHCR's
initiative would stimulate further action. The representative
from the Republic of China emphasized that his government
had been cooperating for years both with local authorities
and with the voluntary agencies in Macao, but that concerted
efforts were now essential. After further discussions between the HC and the Portuguese Government, a UNHCR
representative was sent to Macao in February 1964; with the
assistance of the joint ICEM/UNHCR representative in Hong
Kong, he investigated conditions in Macao and made recommendations on possible UNHCR assistance to refugees there.

In his report, presented to the Eleventh Session (17
April 1964), the representative applied the term refugee not
in the sense of its definition in the UNHCR mandate, but
rather in consideration of the refugees' social conditions, as
had the GA in relation to refugees in Hong Kong concerning
the refugees benefiting from the UNHCR's good offices. He

found that refugees, considered from this standpoint, had indeed aggravated social and economic conditions in Macao and created serious problems for the authorities, whose considerable efforts still left refugees little hope of permanent settlement.   The report also stated that although housing was the most pressing need, provision of housing alone would not solve the problem unless refugees could be made self-supporting through suitable employment opportunities.

On the basis of this study the HC submitted to the Eleventh Session of the Ex. Com. a proposal for, inter alia, the building of fishing boats, the provision of housing and of heavy equipment to implement the land reclamation, water storage, and other projects, and the extension of a social rehabilitation center on the Island of Taipa.   He requested an allocation of $259,000.

The projects were approved by the Ex. Com. for implementation under the 1964 Program, but because of a delay in Portugal's signing of the agreement, the UNHCR BO in Macao was not officially opened until March 1965, and none of the projects were begun until then.   It was estimated that through these projects 350 persons were firmly settled, and 500 additional cases were treated in the rehabilitation center.   The equipment was used for construction of a causeway linking Taipa and Coloane--a project which provided employment for many refugees--and after the project was eventually completed in 1968, with additional funds from the 1965 program, the equipment was used for still other projects. The housing project, eventually completed in August 1968, benefited 852 persons.   During 1965 a further $105,000 from the HC supported these and similar projects.

Because of the high proportion of "uneconomic units" among the refugees, relief operations continued to be of great importance.   Nevertheless, HC assistance was based as much as possible on principles whereby, first, the government of the asylum country assumed the major responsibility for refugees and UNHCR help constituted only a fraction of the expenditures in their behalf; and second, UNHCR-supported projects were designed to further long-range local integration and in themselves provide employment for refugees.   Thus the projects approved under the 1966 Program included

1.   The establishment of a vocational training center for some 850 girls on the Island of Taipa
2.   A similar, smaller project on the Island of

Coloane
3.   The establishment of a rehabilitation workshop
where inmates of the government's center could learn
such crafts as tailoring, shoemaking, and basketmak-
ing so that they might become self-sufficient on leaving the center
4.   Establishment of a revolving fund for assisting
refugees to establish themselves in small enterprises
5.   Construction of a hostel-vocational school for refugee girls and women.

The UNHCR's contribution for these projects totaled
$130,000, which in almost all cases was generously matched
by funds from the Government of Macao, from voluntary
agencies in Macao and overseas, and from other governments.   These projects were implemented either through the
Social Welfare Department, Assistencia Publica, or through
local or overseas church groups such as the Camera Ecleci-
astica of Macao or NCWC/CRS.

The disorders in Macao during 1966-67 caused a
serious setback to the development projects being undertaken
for refugees and most of those being financed by UNHCR
were deferred until stability returned.   The 1966 program
was resumed during 1967 with $145,000 additional funding.
In announcing the 1967 allocation, however, the HC noted that
while he was aware that the Portuguese authorities were under considerable pressure to send back all new illegal entrants, he was "extremely concerned and had repeatedly
drawn attention of the Portuguese Government to the necessity of maintaining the generally accepted principle of 'non-
refoulement'."[15]   In view of the general uncertainty in the
area, although projects from previous years were carried
forward, no new projects were presented for 1968, and the
program for 1969 was in the amount of $43,000 only, pend-
ing a return to more settled conditions.

For 1970, however, with a return to stability and ac-
celeration in the economic growth of Macao, the general
emphasis shifted away from housing, and UNHCR assistance
had as its main objectives in 1970 the promotion of social
improvement through support for various welfare projects,
and the preparation of young refugees to compete for the
growing number of jobs through the creation of better educational and vocational training facilities.   Thus, while $15,000
of the total allocation of $115,000 related to the establish-
ment of a second revolving fund, the balance was devoted to
social welfare projects:

1. The establishment of a home for unmarried refugee mothers to be run by the Institute de Assistencia
Social de Macao (a branch of the administration)
2. The establishment of a home for aged and invalid
men
3. A home to care for some of Macao's 800 blind
persons.

For these projects the Macao Government provided land and
also substantial support for the voluntary agency, the Santa
Casa da Misericordia, which was to operate the homes.

Finally, a day nursery was to be established which
would permit refugee mothers to take advantage of the increased employment opportunities in Macao.

Continuing to collaborate closely with the Department
of Social Welfare in drawing up the 1971 program, UNHCR
allocated a total of $238,000 for similar projects, including
a home for the mentally handicapped, and also, at the advice
of the Department and of voluntary agencies, for a further
housing project for needy refugee families, many of whom
were still living in temporary, improvised shelters.

In preparing the 1970 program it was noted that the
majority of the projects undertaken since 1965 had been successfully implemented indicating that it was possible with
modest funds, and using to the full other sources of assistance, to improve in a significant manner the economic situation of a considerable number of refugees and to help them
to become self-supporting. Most of these projects have been
of long-term value, and continue to serve succeeding groups
of beneficiaries, thus contributing largely to the permanent
social resources of the Province.[16]

Notes

1. Territories Under Portuguese Administration, "Macao
and Dependencies," Special Com. on the Situation
with Regard to the Implementation of the Declaration
on the Granting of Independence to Colonial Countries
and Peoples, A/AC.; 09/L.388/Add., 4 May 1967:
5.

2. Hong Kong takes a large proportion--one-third in 1965--
of Macao's exports, many for transshipment to other
destinations, and is also the present source of some

two-thirds of Macao's merchandise imports.   A
regular hydrofoil service operates between the two,
underlining the closeness of their tie.

3. Ibid.

4. 1964 Program, "New Projects for Chinese Refugees in
    Macao, Ex. Com. (XI), 17 Apr. 1964, A/AC.96/
    237: 3.

5. Territories under Portuguese Administration, op. cit.

6. Although these expenditures include Macao's contribu-
    tion to Portugal's military expenditures, neverthe-
    less, increasing sums have been allocated for hous-
    ing, public health, schools, and welfare services
    in Macao.

7. In 1965 the Department's budget was $1 million.

8. This allocation does not include the value of land which
    the government provides for school construction.

9. Territories under Portuguese Administration, op. cit. :
    8.

10. Oliveira Salazar, "The Portuguese Overseas Terri-
    tories and the United Nations Organization," speech
    delivered on 3 June 1961, Lisbon, quoted in Terri-
    tories under Portuguese Administration, op. cit. :
    2.

11. Ibid. : 2-4.

12. The Free China Relief Association gave a small cash
    grant (20 patacas, or about $3.40) to each refugee
    who registered with them.

13. Ex. Com. (VII) 19-22 May 1962, App. : 27.

14. UNHCR, Program for 1964: 2.

15. HC's Annual Rep. to ECOSOC (XLIII), June 1967.

16. UNHCR Program for 1970, GA (XX), 15 Sept. 1969,
    A/AC.96/412: 43, and Rep. on UNHCR Current
    Operations in 1969, GA Ex. Com. (XXI) 1970, A/
    AC.96/428: 47.

Chapter 29

REFUGEES IN THE ASIAN SUBCONTINENT

I. Tibetan Refugees in India

Little known to the world until they were caught up in
international tensions between the Government of the Chinese
People's Republic and that of India, Tibetans had long lived
in relative isolation on the high plateaus and valleys of the
Himalayas ("the abode of snow") under the spiritual leadership of the Dalai Lama.[1] Supporting themselves and a large
number of religious men, the lamas, by farming, herding of
yak, and trading, these descendants of a once powerful empire had been able, in spite of repeated invasions, to retain
a culture quite distinct from that in other parts of China,
and considerable political autonomy.

When the Chinese People's Republic was established
in Peking on 10 October 1949, one of its first public an-
nouncements was its intention to reestablish control over
Tibet by sending in its army, a statement against which India
reacted sharply.[2] Early in 1950 the Tibetan theocratic Government appealed to the UN against Chinese pressure which
it charged had created an emergency.[3] Although El Salvador
also brought the question to the UN in the same year, no
action was forthcoming. In May 1951, the Tibetans were
forced to sign a 17-Point Agreement whereby the Peking Government took control of Tibet's external affairs while pledging itself to respect the region's autonomy, religious beliefs,
and customs.

The situation was particularly complicated as far as
the international community was concerned by two facts:
that mainland China was not a member of the UN until 1972
and that there had always been great ambiguity regarding the
relations of China and Tibet. The Chinese People's Republic
claims that Tibet has always been an integral part of China
and that therefore the international community has no right
to interfere.[4] It seems likely, however, that its 1950 action

715

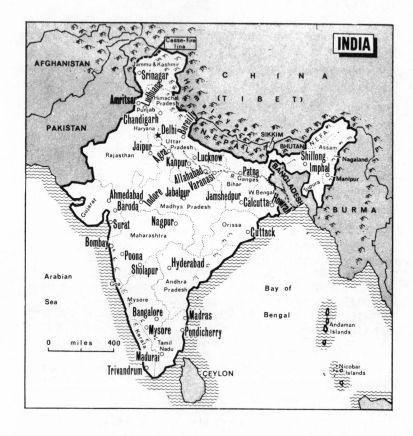

regarding Tibet was enduced not only by its desire to reassert its sovereignty but also to transform Tibet's parochial economy and institutions, that is, in Mao's words, to "liberate it."[5]

The Chinese thus proceeded, despite increasing resistance, to reorder the internal life of Tibet.   In March 1959, following increasing pressure on the Dalai Lama to move to Peking, a violent uprising led by Khamba tribesmen, and severe reprisals by the Chinese, the Dalai Lama fled with some one hundred members of his government and household to India.   He has been followed by more than 85,000 Tibetans fleeing from the southern borders of Tibet into India and Nepal, and later also into the semi-autonomous regions of Sikkim and Bhutan.[6]

Deliberations in the UN

The situation was brought before the UN three times between 1959 and 1965.   In 1959, Ireland and Malaysia, stressing that the GA had "a duty to call for the restoration of the religious and civil liberties of the people of Tibet,"[7] proposed a resolution (1353 XIV) which, after long and often heated debate, was adopted by 45 to 9, with 26 abstentions. It called for "respect for the fundamental human rights of Tibetan people and for their distinctive cultural and religious belief."[8]

Further outbursts of fighting, leading to an additional 1,000 refugees fleeing to India and some 5,000 to Nepal, motivated Thailand and the Federation of Malaysia, in June 1960, to ask the UN for "renewed consideration of the question" with a view to paving the way "for the restoration of the religious and civil liberties of the Tibetan people."[9]   At its Sixteenth Session the GA adopted a further resolution recalling Res. 1353 and again calling for respect of the fundamental human rights of the Tibetan people.[10]   Discussion in the Twentieth Session of the GA in 1965 brought about the adoption of a third resolution drafted by El Salvador, Ireland, Malaysia, Malta, Nicaragua, the Philippines, and Thailand. In addition to its previously expressed concern for the rights of the Tibetan people this resolution also declared its conviction that violation of rights and suppression of the traditional freedom of the Tibetan people "increase international tension and embitter relations between peoples."

Each of these resolutions avoided reference to the political questions involved, not only because of the ambiguous juridical status of Tibet, but also in the interest of international harmony. Each stressed instead those aspects of the problem which related to the rights of Tibetans to pursue their own way of life and their traditional religion. These resolutions were a strong factor in the generous response of the world community to the plight of Tibetan refugees in the countries to which they had fled.

The Policy of the Government of India

When the Tibetan refugees began to arrive in India in 1959 the immediate problem was to keep them alive and India provided relief to the thousands of Tibetans crossing the border. Many, especially women and children, died on the way, or soon after arrival. Those who survived the gruelling trek over the rugged 16,000-foot Himalayan passes were starving and utterly exhausted. None could speak any of the major Indian languages, nor could their hosts understand Tibetan. The few who had managed to bring with them saleable items soon exhausted the money these brought in local markets. Unaccustomed to the hot climate and low altitude, the majority developed skin diseases and gastric disorders. All needed food and shelter, and most needed medical care. With as many as 1,500 arriving every week, it was necessary for the government to take immediate steps for handling the emergency.

Responsibility for the refugees was, at first, placed in the Ministry of External Affairs. Forewarned of the imminent arrival of large numbers of refugees, the Ministry had set up transit camps, one at Misamari in Assam, and one at Buxa in West Bengal, each with an Indian Government official in charge. Three hundred bamboo huts were hastily constructed, and food, clothing, and medical supplies were rushed in, often from great distances. When the refugees arrived at the camps they were provided with rations, clothing, and cooking utensils, as well as some medical care. Serious cases were sent to hospitals in nearby towns. Within a few weeks 6,000 persons had arrived at Misamari and 1,000 at Buxa, most of them via Bhutan and Sikkim. Although the government, in an attempt to avoid an accumulation of large numbers of refugees in the camps, made frequent dispersals of refugees to other areas, the population of Misamari was, at one point, over 7,000. Between May and June 1959 the camp handled a total of 15,000 Tibetans.[11]

The government was assisted in this effort by voluntary agencies in India, and especially by the Central Relief
Committee of India (CRC[I]).   The CRC(I) worked in close
cooperation with the Ministry of External Affairs, and
through it, the sympathy of the world community was expressed in the form of aid from the major voluntary organizations.   During its eight months of operation CARE provided 90 percent of the rations for all refugees at Misamari.
The American Emergency Committee for Tibetan Refugees
(AECTR), hastily formed in the US in 1959 under the direction of Lowell Thomas, provided medical supplies, including
4,000 pounds of antibiotics, and raised $15,000 in cash
within a month of the Dalai Lama's flight.   CWS and LWR
assisted by providing the total supply of powdered milk.
CRS and YMCA also played their roles.

Misamari wound up its operation in July 1960 and
refugees were dispersed to the Himalayan colder regions (including some 4,000 to Sikkim) where most were absorbed,
temporarily, on road work.   The elderly lamas, numbering
about 700, were settled in Dalhousie, and a residential
academy was set up at Buxa in West Bengal where over
1,200 junior lamas were able to pursue their theological
studies.   CRC(I) and several voluntary agencies set up a
handicraft training and production center which trained some
500 Tibetan youths in various trades.   A small transit camp
at the border was retained to accommodate the steady trickle
of refugees still making their way out of their homeland despite the fact that the border was sealed from the other
side.[12]

On 30 March 1959, the Government of India granted
asylum to the Dalai Lama, who was officially welcomed at
Tezpur in Assam.[13]   On 4 April the Prime Minister, Mr.
Nehru, stated at a Press Conference in New Delhi that India's policy was governed by three factors: the preservation
of the security and integrity of India; India's desire to maintain friendly relations with the People's Republic of China;
and India's deep sympathy for the people of Tibet.   The Indian Government and the Tibetan refugees hoped, in fact,
that the political problem would be resolved so that the refugees might return to their homeland.

The formulation of policy for the care of Tibetan refugees in India involved a delicate weighing of factors.   For

many years, in the interest of both harmonious foreign relations and smooth internal development, the government handled the emergency cautiously. While attempting to maintain
the cultural autonomy of the Tibetan people, it nonetheless
sought to avoid large concentrations of unsettled refugees
which might attract attention. It refrained from officially
seeking help from the international community, and sought
to retain control over the use made of the very considerable
assistance proffered by local and overseas voluntary agencies
and their personnel. It did not seek UNHCR assistance, and
in the GA, it abstained from voting on both the 1959 and the
1961 resolutions concerning the treatment of the Tibetan people by the Chinese People's Republic. During this period,
policy was based on the hope that matters could still be arranged diplomatically so that the Tibetan refugees in India
might return to their homeland.

        In 1962 there was an exchange of hostilities between
India and the Chinese over the border, and Indian policies
in the UN were changed thereafter. [14] At the Twentieth Session of the GA in 1965 India joined the forty-three nations
which supported the GA resolution concerning Tibetans. Mr.
Zakana, the Indian Delegate to the UN, in his address maintained that:

        Although the relationship between Tibet and India
        ... has flourished all through the ages ... we
        have always taken care not to make that relation-
        ship a political problem ... we have exercised the
        greatest caution, for we believe that what should
        concern all of us is the much larger human prob-
        lem, namely, the plight of these good and innocent
        people who are being victimized merely because
        they are different, ethnically and culturally from
        the Chinese. [15]

It was the position reiterated by the Indian Government in
1972 in response to the Chinese charges that Tibetans had
gone to India "under the coercion of the Indian Government. "[16]

The Search for Permanent Solutions, 1960-63

        The search for permanent solutions in India, and in
Sikkim and Bhutan, was made difficult not so much by the
size of the Tibetan refugee problem, as by its nature. In
October 1964 the estimated number of Tibetan refugees in

India was 40,000.[17] In addition to the political implications of this problem, in terms of both domestic and foreign policy, the refugees themselves had special needs.

An ideal solution in India for the great majority, who had been farmers or herders in Tibet, would have been in agriculture; but available arable land was not easy to obtain. For the large number of refugees who had been traders, employment opportunities were rarely available since this field was highly competitive among Indians themselves; only a very few of the Tibetan refugees were equipped for the technical jobs which were available in small industries. A further problem was the large number of lamas, between 7,000 and 8,000, a number out of proportion to the normal ratio of lamas to non-lamas in Tibet. Their role at home had been to study and pass on the religious knowledge of their ancestors and to carry out the stringent demands of their religion. They were not accustomed to any manual work. The Dalai Lama was very concerned over the fact that many of them at the outset were employed in road construction work. In addition to these difficulties, almost all the Tibetans, accustomed to the cold, high-altitude conditions of the Himalayas, suffered severe physical effects from the Indian climate, and became extremely susceptible to tuberculosis. There were also special problems such as those of the 2,000 children who were either orphans or unable to accompany their parents to the rugged road construction camps, and of the more than 3,000 aged and infirm persons who could never be expected to become fully self-sufficient.

Since the Tibetan refugees themselves were not at first resigned to the fact that they would have to remain in India, they resisted efforts to settle them permanently in the country of asylum. The motive for the flight of the Tibetans and the continued concern of the Dalai Lama was to preserve the identity of the two-thousand-year-old culture of the Tibetan people. Like the Old Believers who fled from mainland China to Hong Kong, the Tibetans were only prepared to accept permanent solutions in India which would permit them to settle in large, relatively isolated communities, and like the Indian Government they continued to look forward to ultimate repatriation.

From the outset it was evident, however, that whatever plans were adopted to insure the wellbeing of Tibetan refugees and to relieve the Indian Government of the burden of their care, some means had to be found which would

enable them to be more or less self-sufficient during their
period of exile, whatever might be its duration. The Government of India sponsored three approaches to this objective.
The most effective was resettlement in agriculture, horticulture, or animal husbandry, which is discussed in detail below. Two alternate solutions--establishment of centers for
training refugees in the production and sale of Tibetan handicrafts, and the creation of small industries to be run and
operated by Tibetans--were also proposed. Although handicraft workshops sprang up spontaneously in many settlements,
and the Government of India itself opened a small center in
1959, these alternative approaches were not tried extensively
until after 1965.

Agricultural Settlements. During 1960-63 the groundwork was laid for the development of five major agricultural
settlements in India and several smaller ones in Sikkim and
Bhutan. The Government of the State of Mysore was the
first to reply affirmatively to the Central Government's request for land on which to settle Tibetan refugees in India.
An agreement was reached between the State and Central
Governments (in consultation with representatives of the Dalai
Lama) to settle 3,000 refugees on a 3,000-acre tract of land,
2,500 feet above sea level at Bylakuppe in Mysore. Rs
37,84,000 was allocated to this project.

Later in 1961 land was located and settlement begun
at two other sites in the heavily forested areas of the North-
East Frontier Agency--Changlang and Tezu. These settlements were originally planned for the resettlement of 1,200
refugees each. Both are in what are classified as "protected
areas"--areas close to the border into which the free movement of foreigners is not permitted. This fact has had a
marked effect on the amount of assistance forthcoming from
private agencies, as well as on the establishment of government services. Settlers had to be moved out of these areas
during the 1962 hostilities. The difficulty of clearing the
heavily forested land and serious erosion also contributed to
the slow progress of these communities, although a good
local market for eggs, milk, and goats somewhat offset the
difficulties at Tezu.

The Government of India has also been the major
source of relief to refugees in Sikkim and Bhutan. Sikkim,
in terms of similarity of climate and local culture, is an
ideal area for settlement of Tibetan refugees. Some 3,400
refugees went there directly from bordering regions in Tibet,

and the Government of India sent an additional 3,300 from
India, especially from Camp Misamari; but sufficient land
has not been available to provide for permanent settlement
of more than a small proportion of these refugees.

Many of those who came to Sikkim directly from Tibet
were able to bring their animals with them, and with the
proceeds from the sale of these animals to set themselves
up in small trades, or restaurants.   A special relief committee under Mrs. Phunkhang Lacham (sister of the Mahara-
ja of Sikkim) at first provided free food for some 3,000 old
and infirm persons, and schooling for 150 children.   Those
sent to Sikkim by the Government of India, mostly on road
work, were provided with rations by the CRC(I), which also
set up two dispensaries for them.   A certain number have
since that time left the country of their own accord.   Many,
however, remained unsettled.

At the request of the Dalai Lama, the Government of
India made plans to bring the remaining unsettled refugees
to India for resettlement in agriculture.   In 1962, the first
group of 800 was brought by Bylakuppe.   Since the completion of road construction in 1965 the condition of the remaining 3,600 unsettled refugees in Sikkim has been difficult.
Efforts have been made to resettle them; in 1970, 500 were
resettled in Mysore.

Settlement of Tibetan refugees in Bhutan has met with
greater success.   The main route by which Tibetan refugees
first came to India was through Bhutan.   In 1961, however,
the Government of India closed its borders to refugees coming via Bhutan.   At the same time, fearing too great an influx into the small country, Bhutan also refused entry to
Tibetans seeking to cross the Bhutan-Tibetan border.   Refugees would not return, and could not go forward.   Under
these circumstances the Dalai Lama asked the Government of
India for assistance, either in permitting the refugees to enter India, or in helping them to settle in Bhutan.

At a meeting at Calcutta in June 1962, attended by the
Prime Minister of Bhutan, the Political Officers of Sikkim
and Bhutan, and representatives of the Government of India
and of the Dalai Lama, it was agreed that these refugees
(numbering about 3,000) should be settled on land given by
the Government of Bhutan and with funds made available by
the Indian Government.   Accordingly, two settlements were
established in 1963 for the settlement of 1,060 refugees.

Both were put under Tibetan management. They were able
to become at least minimally self-supporting within two years
and have received no outside assistance since 1965. They
have not, however, been provided with educational and medical facilities. In 1967 two additional settlements were established for a further 1,000 refugees, and in 1969 these were
well on the way to being self-supporting. The remaining
940 unsettled refugees were expected to be settled within
another two years. It is possible, however, that a further
1,000 refugees near the border may also need to be resettled in the interior.

At another settlement begun in 1961 in the Bomdila
area of Northern Assam, also a "protected area" close to
the Indo-Tibetan border, clearing of the jungle and construction of houses had already begun when renewed fighting in
1962 forced refugees once again to flee. After this, all
plans for resettlement in this area were abandoned.

In 1963 land was made available at Mainpat in Madhya
Pradesh, at Changragiri, and at nearby Mahendragarh in
Orissa, each a settlement of 2,500 refugees. Later, a further 1,400 were settled at Mahendragarh. Many refugees
from the Bomdila settlement were placed in these new projects, which were organized along the lines of the Bylakuppe
settlement. At Mainpat, however, refugees arrived before
preparations had been made for them and, in March 1963,
700 were sent back to the road camps of Kulu and Kangra,
and 548 to the State of Orissa. The refugees who remained
were paid a daily wage by the Government of India for their
work in setting up the colony, constructing houses and roads,
digging wells, and clearing land. To supplement these
wages, and for those for whom there were no jobs, the government provided food rations, as in the other settlements;
relief assistance from voluntary organizations such as the
CRS was provided through the CRC(I).

Following the open border hostilities between India and
the Chinese People's Republic in 1962, the Government of
India gradually opened up possibilities whereby the international community could assist in finding a satisfactory solution. From the domestic point of view, the presence of unsettled and dependent Tibetan refugees could only add to India's already complex developmental problems. Furthermore,
this problem now seemed unlikely to disappear quickly, or
to be easily resolved, even with the efforts so far devoted to
that end. Experience in the agricultural settlements indicated

that refugees, even when land and certain minimal services were made available to them, could not become independent on their own. Technical assistance and considerable outlays of funds appeared necessary, at least during the initial stages of any rehabilitation project. This was equally true for handicraft training centers, and for the establishment of small industries. Furthermore, by this time the refugees themselves had begun to realize that their exile was likely to be much longer than they had hoped, and that even to maintain their cultural and religious traditions during this exile they must find a more satisfactory and secure way of life in India.

India's change in policy led to the representation of twelve major overseas voluntary agencies on the Advisory Committee of the CRC(I), which had been set up in 1959 to coordinate the limited assistance from abroad and to act as the agent for distributing government and voluntary agency contributions. With representatives from donor agencies assisting in drawing up plans, one major drawback to the former system was overcome. While the Government of India retained control of the general handling of activities within its territory, the voluntary agencies could now determine the uses to which their contributions were put. They could now also draw up individual projects and submit them to the Master Plan Sub-committee for its approval, thereby encouraging projects which fitted into the coordinated rehabilitation scheme.

Aid from the Voluntary Agencies

During the years after the flight of Tibetans from their homeland, many voluntary agencies had become concerned with relief efforts and new agencies had sprung up in India and abroad for aiding Tibetan refugees.[18] These agencies, working through CRC(I), rendered valuable services through their support of government programs financially and in kind. In addition, some had developed programs for training Tibetans overseas for occupations which they could pursue upon their return to refugee communities in the host countries.

Several voluntary agencies, in India and from overseas, assisted the government by providing farm equipment and animals, vocational training, schools and clinics, and help in financing self-help projects and in providing child

care. The RCS(I) handled the government's medical programs and distributed most of the medical supplies received
from overseas. AECTR, in addition to providing drugs during the emergency period, continued its assistance by financing the establishment of full-fledged hospitals in the various land settlements, and generously supported the Vocational Training Institute in Dalhousie and the Self-Help (Handicraft) center at Darjeeling, both of which were started in
1960. It continued its program until 1968. The CRS/USCC,
the only major overseas agency to continue its services after
the emergency period, took part in specific rehabilitation
projects and, working through the CRC(I), distributed a large
proportion of the relief supplies from overseas. CWS and
LWF shared on a fifty-fifty basis with the Government of
India the cost of hospitalized TB patients. Most of the aid
took the form of food distributed by the various agencies
which were members of the CRC(I). This included considerable surplus food from the US.

        After the first emergency, however, assistance from
the major voluntary agencies, which was channeled through
CRC(I), fell off sharply. The flow of refugees continued to
be heavy in these years, with some still managing to come
directly over the Indo-Tibetan border and many others coming from Nepal, Bhutan, and Sikkim. This fact among others made it difficult for the CRC(I) to develop an overall
plan for permanent solutions. Lack of such a plan inevitably
resulted in certain inequities in the distribution of assistance.
Nevertheless, it was during this period that many lines of
action were formulated which served as the basis for subsequent programs.

        In 1963 the voluntary organizations, recognizing the
fact that their efforts to date had been less effective than
they might have been with greater unity of approach, asked
ICVA to assume the role of an interim coordinating body in
an effort to work out permanent solutions. ICVA accordingly
set up, under its Committee on Refugees, a sub-committee
on Tibetan Refugees which, after studying the situation, presented its findings to a special seminar convened by ICVA
in April 1963 in Geneva. The seminar was attended not only
by the forty voluntary agencies involved, but also by representatives of the UNHCR, the Government of India, the Dalai
Lama, and ICEM. The conference, considering various solutions for the pressing needs of Tibetan refugees--vocational
training overseas, resettlement overseas for some, and resettlement projects in India and Nepal--concluded that one of

the principal aims of the international community should be
to assist the Indian Government in its plans for the creation
of additional settlements to absorb upwards of 15,000 more
Tibetans. While this seminar did not in itself lead to noticeable practical results, it served the important function of
once again focusing world attention on the Tibetan refugees,
thereby undoubtedly contributing to the increase in assistance
after 1963.[19]

The CRC(I)'s Master Plan
and International Assistance

With this increased assistance from overseas agencies and governments the CRC(I)'s Master Plan carried forward further plans for permanent solutions.   In 1964 the
CRC(I) drew up a detailed plan for rehabilitation of the
Tibetan refugees in India.

It proposed that a total of 12,000 refugees should be
settled in the five existing agricultural settlements at Bylakuppe, Tezu, Chandragiri, Mainpat and Changlang.   With
6,600 already in these settlements, provision had to be made
for an additional 5,400.   There was, therefore, immediate
need for land-clearing equipment, and for financial assistance
to refugees until such time as the land became productive.
Additional bullock, poultry, and other livestock were also required to assist in agricultural operations and to provide additional sources of food and income for the settlers.   Fertilizers and high-yielding seeds were needed, as were additional food supplies.   To further supplement income from
agriculture, assistance in initiating cottage industries was
essential.   Weaving, cane work and wood work, and Tibetan
art crafts were considered.

Because the amount of land available for agriculture
was limited, and because many refugees had more aptitude
for non-agricultural occupations, India proposed to establish
industrial centers where refugees could engage, with minimal training, in industries especially those requiring foreign
machinery, materials, or technical assistance.   The Government of India agreed to participate in the very heavy expenditures which would be required to set up such industrial
communities.   It was hoped that a large percentage of the
refugees who were at the time in road construction work
could be re-established in these centers.   If employment for
1,000 could be created, it was estimated that 1,000 families,

or 5,000 refugees would be supported. Successful enterprises could later be expanded, and ultimately all would be
turned over to Tibetan management.

The Tibetan Schools Society drew up a three-year
vocational training scheme for 475 Tibetans. If the scheme
could be put into operation it could, in the future, absorb
Tibetans as they finished school and prepare them for a variety of occupations. Funds from voluntary agencies for such
an undertaking were needed to hasten its implementation.
Funds were also needed at existing centers for training Tibetans as mechanics, electricians, etc. whose services were
immediately needed in these communities.

Other needs in the field of education were outlined--
assistance for higher technical studies, and for the nurseries
then being run by the Dalai Lama with the cooperation of
voluntary agencies such as Save the Children, Civil Service
International, the CRS and the NCWC. It was expected that
Tibetan children, if they remained in India, would eventually
study in Indian schools.

Basic medical necessities would be provided by the
Government of India. Although the AECTR had taken on a
great part of the responsibility for medical services, it was
felt that alternate resources should also be available to assure ongoing financial support. Finally the Outline Plan
mentioned the possibility of settling some of the refugees
outside India in projects such as that undertaken by the
Swiss Foundation.

The formulation of this Master Plan, coupled with the
government's shift in attitude toward assistance from the international community, permitted renewed efforts on the part
of overseas voluntary agencies for projects both in India and
in their own countries.

For a number of reasons most of the agricultural settlements at first made little progress. The task of clearing
the land by hand, or even by bullock, was slow. Water
shortage was a major problem in several of the settlements,
and the refugees were unaccustomed to the new methods of
farming which their new land needed. As a result, agricultural yields were generally low, and the time envisaged for
settlers to become self-sufficient had to be extended indefinitely.

Bylakuppe, however, is considered a kind of model agricultural settlement. The Master Plan called for similar development at the other settlements. And, indeed, although the program of land clearing progressed gradually, several thousand more refugees were more or less firmly settled in agriculture each year, and every year new groups of settlers met the government's criteria of self-sufficiency and their rations were discontinued.

Bylakuppe Settlement. At Bylakuppe, in Mysore, some 3,000 refugees were settled in 1961 in what was to become a model agricultural settlement. Six colonies of one hundred households each were set up. Every family received a small house and five to seven acres of land. Refugees were to receive food rations until they became firmly settled in agriculture, that is, after two consecutive successful harvests. The settlement was administered by a special officer of the Government of India. Representatives of the Dalai Lama acted as liaison between the refugees and the administration. Provision of relief supplies and services was administered through the CRC(I), and the RCS(I) ran the medical program for the government.

After 1963 the agricultural settlement at Bylakuppe made great progress toward self-sufficiency. In order to increase agricultural production, steps were taken to introduce scientific farm methods. Supplementary income-producing projects were started and community services were improved. Projects drawn up in the Master Plan were assisted by the US and by the UNHCR.

By agreement with the government, an adviser from the Swiss Technical Cooperation Association (STCA) made a soil survey to determine the suitability of the land for various kinds of cultivation. Following STCA's recommendations, voluntary agencies provided eleven tractors for more efficient ploughing, and the settlers supplemented their regular crops with the cultivation of maize. By 1966, agricultural activities yielded a surplus over consumption which was sold either directly by the settlers, or through their cooperative-- started in 1961 with the help of a loan from the settlement's Special Officer, and funds from the Dalai Lama.

Other sources of income are a poultry farm started in 1964 with YMCA funds, a carpet weaving factory set up in the same year by Swiss Service for Technical Cooperation (SSTC) (with the expectation that it would eventually convert to

Tibetan management), and horticultural operations begun in
1967 with the donation by CRS of 65,000 fruit tree saplings
(distributed on a 50-50 basis between individual settlers and
the Cooperative Society). Two other sources of potential income are the community center at which sewing classes
train Tibetans to become tailors (both the building and the
sewing machines were provided in 1965 by the YMCA) and
the work center for the aged by means of which they can become at least partially self-sufficient, opened in 1967 by
AECTR and maintained after 1968 by CRC(I). A flour mill
intended for the settlers' use, but also potentially income-
producing, was established in November 1966 with funds
from both CRC(I) and the settlement itself.

Services to refugees also improved after 1963. Swiss
Aid Abroad provided trucks to facilitate transport within the
settlement. The schools, under the direction of the Tibetan
Schools Society of the Ministry of Education, were enlarged
and provided with more teachers. Medical services were
transferred from a tent to a permanent building in 1964, and
in 1965 a small hospital was opened. AECTR provided for
construction and operation of all medical services until the
end of its program in India in March 1968, at which time
services were carried on with the help of a number of voluntary agencies--Individuell Manniskohjalp of Sweden, SSTC,
SATA SHARAN (a subsidiary of the National Christian Council of India (NCC), which in turn was supported by funds from
WCC, LWF, and CWS), and CRS, among others. The NCC
in Delhi covered costs for refugees who had to be hospitalized in Government hospitals.

By the end of 1965 rations were discontinued in certain sections of the Bylakuppe settlement, and by March 1967
the government stopped rations to all but a few old or infirm. The refugees were considered now to be independent,
although it was in fact necessary for voluntary agencies to
continue providing gift rations for many. In June 1968 the
Special Officer of the Government of India was withdrawn
from the settlement which thereafter came under the authority of the State Government of Mysore.

Mundgod Settlement. In 1965 efforts of the Indian
Government and of the Dalai Lama had produced an agreement with the State of Mysore proposing the settlement of
4,000 refugees on a 4,000-acre tract of land at Mundgod,
267 miles north of Bylakuppe. The STCA began clearing the
land in late 1966 and settlers began to arrive shortly

thereafter from road camps in Himachal Pradesh, and from
among groups who had been isolated in Ladakh; in 1967 1,000
were brought from Sikkim where the completion of road work
had left them unemployed.

Many voluntary agencies shared the cost of early developments. SHARAN provided water (which had to be
trucked in), as well as sixteen tractors. STCA looked after
cultivation when sufficient land had been cleared for this
purpose. OXFAM and the UNHCR provided farm machinery.
In addition the Public Works Department drilled wells, but
these were found to be dry. Provision of permanent housing
was not possible until after 1967.

It was soon evident that the very first necessity for
the settlement was an overall irrigation scheme, without
which intensive agricultural production would be impossible.
In 1968 the ERC, together with the Central Government, the
State of Mysore Government, and the Dalai Lama's Tibetan
Rehabilitation Office, formed an agency--the Mysore Resettlement and Development Agency (MYRADA)--to supervise
the overall development of the settlement. MYRADA is, in
a sense, a counterpart of the Board of Trustees of the Common Project of the ERC. One of its primary tasks at Mundgod has been supervision of the construction of a dam which
irrigates 3,700 acres of the total 4,000. Construction of
this dam was undertaken with the help of funds from ERC
and many voluntary agencies, and the labor of 683 Tibetans.
There are at present 5,000 settlers at Mundgod.

The first crops have been harvested, and a school
for 600 children is operating, although it has not yet been
taken over by the Tibetan Schools Society. A forty-bed
hospital, set up and run by CRC(I), provides for the needs
of the local Indian villages as well as of the refugees.

Spurred by the success of the Mundgod settlement,
and an urgent awareness of the need to settle the thousands
who were still subsisting on relief or in the road work
camps, the Government of India continued its search for land
on which to set up similar projects. In 1969 the State of
Mysore provided another vast area of land on the Cauvery
River, only a short distance from the Bylakuppe settlement,
for the eventual settlement of 10,000 refugees. A fourth
Mysore settlement was also proposed.

In the case of the Cauvery River project, MYRADA,

rather than purchasing the land from the State Government, has used available funds to help settle tribal groups and landless people of Mysore. Furthermore, as with the hospital at Mundgod, facilities constructed under MYRADA such as wells, and tractor stations were intended also for Indian villages in the area. Thus the resettlement of Tibetan refugees is being integrated into the general development plans for the area. The cost to the government of resettling Tibetan refugees in these projects has been kept well within the Indian Government's guidelines--$400 per person--for settling its other refugees, such as those from Ceylon and Burma.

Settlement Projects in Handicraft Centers and Small Industry. With a view to providing alternate means for refugees to achieve self-sufficiency, the Government of India, in 1959, opened the Tibetan Handicraft Training Center in Dalhousie. Five hundred refugees from the Misamari transit camp were placed in this center where they received training in the production of traditional handicrafts whose sale was to provide them some income. The government provided housing and daily rations for the workers. By 1962 the Center had made little progress and was turned over to the Dalai Lama, under whose auspices it still operates to train workers.

Alternate schemes for rehabilitation--settlement of refugees in communities centering about a small industry, or in handicraft centers--also made less than the desired progress in the beginning. It was not until 1965 that an administrative mechanism, Tibetan Industrial Rehabilitation Society (TIRS), was created to serve as a framework for initiating and operating such communities, and as a channel for both government and voluntary agency funds destined for them. TIRS, like the CRC(I), is essentially a voluntary agency with very close ties to the central government. One member of its Ex. Com. is also the Secretary of the CRC(I), and can be said to represent the opinions of the government.

TIRS planned a number of projects intended to settle some 4,500 people. A woollen mill in Kangra Valley was the first to be completed. Others were the Bir Tea Estate, a fiberglass industry at Paonta, a hydrated lime plant at Sataun, and a lime quarry at Kumrao. In 1966 all these projects were either still incomplete, or not even begun. Without considerable capital expenditures refugees in these projects could not for many years have earned sufficient

incomes to support themselves. The same is true of the
handicraft centers set up by the government or by voluntary
agencies. In addition to production problems these also had
the problem of having their products accumulate for lack of
buyers, and thus delaying the time when these centers could
become economically independent of financial assistance from
government or voluntary organizations.

For the settlement of refugees in industry the ERC
contribution to TIRS by November 1968 totalled Rs
32,80.288.18. This was 40 percent of the total contributed
to TIRS up to that time. By 1969, with the help of these
funds, the seven projects begun or operated by TIRS since
1964 were consolidated, and three others begun. Schools
and medical facilities were improved or created, coopera-
tives and marketing agencies were developed, and most of
the settlements, while they were still not ready to be turned
over to Tibetan management, were no longer on government
rations. In all, some 5,000 refugees are being accommodated in these settlements.

A related area which has assumed increasing importance has been that of vocational training. As the refugees
came closer to being self supporting in the agricultural, industrial, and handicraft settlements, it was essential that
properly trained Tibetan leaders and auxiliaries be prepared,
on termination of outside assistance, "to direct and sustain
the economic and social programmes elaborated on their behalf by governmental, inter-governmental and non-governmental bodies."[20]

Overseas Settlement Projects. In the early period of
settlement efforts a number of small-scale programs were
set up abroad for the benefit of Tibetan refugee children or
young people who were expected to return to India after a
given period of training. In Denmark, for example, the
Training Center in Aalsgaarde was started in 1960 with
twenty-two children (the UNHCR contributed $6,000), and by
1964 one hundred Tibetan children were being trained in
centers in other Scandinavian countries as well. Ia Coume,
a home for twenty Tibetan children was established at the
end of 1962 in the Pyrenees-Orientale in France. The Ockenden Venture in UK, jointly with the Tibet Society of the
UK and Swiss Aid to Tibetans, pursued a policy of bringing
to England for further training, students who had already received some training in English. The Tolstoy Foundation in
the US established a Lamaist Buddhist Monastery in New

Jersey for four lamas. In addition, a limited number of
young Tibetans went, mainly for study purposes, to Australia,
Ceylon, the Federal German Republic, Japan, and the US,
etc. [21] A small number settled in lumber camps in Maine
in the US. The most ambitious schemes, however, were
carried out in Switzerland where some 800 Tibetans were
permanently resettled in several communities.

In 1961 several Swiss industrialists, alpinists and
civic leaders formed the Association for Tibetan Home-
steads. [22] Their purpose was to resettle Tibetan refugees
in colonies of some fifty persons in Switzerland under the
administrative care of a local "home leader" chosen by the
Swiss Red Cross, and one lama, selected (as were the immigrants themselves) by the SRC and the Dalai Lama's Office of Home Affairs (an organization established in India to
aid Tibetans in exile). Owners of small factories and other
industrialists provided refugees with jobs, and in some cases
with housing.

It was at first thought that the Tibetans would prefer
to establish themselves in agricultural and herding communities in the Swiss Alps, resembling as much as possible the
situation in their homeland. But they resisted such settlement, preferring to find jobs in small industry where the
pay was better. Thus they assisted Switzerland in overcoming a manpower shortage among its thriving small industries.

The Swiss Government agreed, in March 1963, to allow 1,000 Tibetans to be received, provided that the com-
munes and cantons in whose territory they were to be settled
gave their consent. The SRC, which assumed responsibility
for their financial support until they could become self-sufficient, and the Swiss Government agreed to participate in
the financing of their transportation from India. [23] Under
Swiss law refugees can apply for citizenship after twelve
years' residence.

By 1968 there were ten communities in eastern Switzerland in the area of Zürich, in which some 430 Tibetans
were settled, and applications from 300 more, many of them
relatives of Tibetans already in Switzerland, had been received by the SRC. In accordance with the hopes of the Dalai
Lama and of refugees themselves, the Red Cross stated that
"while we want them to be a part of the Swiss scene, we are
anxious that they not lose their very special cultural identity
and heritage. "[24] As one measure for assuring against this

loss, the refugees themselves, in September 1968, opened
the Tibetan Monastic Institute in Rikon to preserve and further Tibetan culture.   It is run by five lamas selected personally by the Dalai Lama.   Although plans for the resettlement of 3,000 Tibetans under this project did not material-
ize, there are today some 800 Tibetan settlers in Switzerland.

   In a separate program initiated by another industrial-
ist, Charles Atschimann, 200 Tibetan children were brought
to Switzerland to be placed in Swiss foster homes.   Twenty
were placed in the Pestalozzi Children's Village in Trogen
in houses run by two lamas.   The program was discontinued,
however, because Tibetan leaders and the Dalai Lama himself feared that the children were in danger of losing their
spiritual and cultural heritage.   Although these programs
helped to draw attention outside India and Nepal to the plight
of Tibetan refugees, they solved the problem of only a small
fraction of the total number.   The question also has arisen
as to whether, in the long run, it is a wise solution to either
train or settle the Tibetans in an entirely strange civiliza-
tion.

   Education and Child Welfare Programs.   After 1961,
although overall responsibility for Tibetan refugees remained
in the hands of the Ministry of External Affairs, responsibility for their education was placed in the Ministry of Education and a special sub-division of the Ministry was created--
the Tibetan Schools Society--which is funded by the Indian
Government.   The Society has developed and administered an
outstanding program for Tibetan refugee education.

   The Society at once took over three residential schools
which the Dalai Lama had started in Mussourie, Simla, and
Darjeeling, and it later opened or took over four others in
addition.   By 1969 a total of 4,170 children attended these
residential schools, and the sum of Rs 60. million was allocated annually for their operation.

   In many of the government land settlements the refugees themselves established makeshift schools.   After 1961
the Society also took over these schools, and established
others where none existed.   For these day schools the government allocated Rs 50 per month per child.   A noon meal
was served to the children, the food in most cases provided
by voluntary agencies through the CRC(I).   Dispensaries were
also established to handle minor illnesses.   Serious cases
were sent to the nearest government hospital.

The curriculum in all schools run by the Society was similar to that of Indian Government schools and, with the exception of Tibetan teachers for the Tibetan language courses, the teaching staff was Indian.[25] While the preservation of the unique Tibetan culture is a goal of the education program, gradual assimilation of Tibetan children into Indian society through the schools is anticipated in the second and third generations.

Other educational facilities run by the Dalai Lama are also assisted by the government with rations, and by the voluntary agencies with clothing, and medical and relief supplies. The largest of these is the Transit School in Dharamsala, originally a center for care of children whose parents were unable to care for them. Although the children are placed in regular schools as soon as there are places for them, the number at the transit schools has continued to grow. In 1969 there were 350 children. In addition, in May 1960, the Dalai Lama opened a nursery, especially for the children of refugees in the Chamba road camps. Since that time, 3,200 children have passed through the nursery and on into regular schools.

In November 1962 three homes for orphaned children, or children unable to remain with their parents, were also opened by the Dalai Lama, and in April 1963 the Tibetan Homes Society, inaugurated by him to carry out the work, was officially registered with the Government of India. The many homes which have since been set up by the Society are given substantial assistance from voluntary agencies, and the Government of India has provided a regular grant of Rs 50 per month per child. These homes have cared for thousands of Tibetan children over the years, and in 1968, when overcrowding forced the government to limit their enrollment, the number of applicants was still increasing.

The Tibetan School Society is also taking important steps not only to relieve the shortage of teachers but also to foster Tibetan culture by offering scholarships for university training to Tibetan refugees.[26]

The Role of the UNHCR

The first tentative acceptance of the idea that the UNHCR could aid in the settlement of Tibetan refugees in India, Bhutan and Sikkim was expressed during the visit of

High Commissioner Schnyder to India in July 1963.   The
government expressed interest in any assistance which might
be made available from the sale in India of the "All Star
Festival" record.   It was agreed that sale of the record in
India would begin on UN Day, 24 October 1964. [27]

   In order to assess the situation, and to plan for the
allocation of funds coming from the sale of "All Star Festival, " the HC, on the invitation of the Indian Government,
sent his Director of Operations to India in November 1963,
and again in September 1964.   After his second visit Mr.
Jamieson reported on the advances made in planning for the
rehabilitation of the refugees, particularly through the reor-
ganization of the CRC(I).   Because of continued tension over
the Chinese-Indian border, the Indian Government preferred,
however, not to have an official representative of the UNHCR
based in its country at this time.

   At the end of 1967 the HC, on request, again sent a
representative to India and to Nepal to re-evaluate the position of Tibetans in the light of new developments resulting
from the Common Project of ERC.

   The refugee situation itself had not remained static.
In 1967 alone the government gave asylum to a further 1, 500
Tibetans.   It was also apparent that others might come any
time, and in unpredictable numbers, for whom immediate
assistance and resettlement must be planned.   By now many
of the refugees had been in India for a decade and their
hopes of returning to Tibet had become all but extinct.   They
now accepted the need for well established settlements, but
experience had shown that this development required not only
viable schemes but also considerable resources.   An important corollary was that the Indian Government's earlier
guarded acceptance of assistance from international sources
had now changed to one of positive welcome, provided still
that this assistance did not provoke undue diplomatic comment.

   Another aspect of the problem, which was likely to
increase in importance as more refugees became self-sufficient was that of their legal status in relation to the local
economic structure.   Refugees held land on the ad hoc basis
of a fifteen-year lease, seven of which had already elapsed.
Fundamental to any worthwhile agricultural venture is the
need to obtain both short- and long-term credit for improvement of the land.   The Bylakuppe Cooperative, for instance,

had received a generous loan ($530,000) from CRS for agri-
cultural purposes, but this loan had to be repaid within a
year.   Further development of the land for irrigation, for
instance, would require similar loans.   Short-term loans
might be arranged by tying the Cooperative in with the existing banking structures in the area.   For long-term loans,
however, a change in the land-holding arrangements would
be necessary if refugees were to benefit from the State Land
Mortgage Bank.   This matter, part of the wider issue of
legal protection, increasingly required study.

Discussions with the HC of all these circumstances
led the Government of India to suggest that more material
assistance from the HC would also be welcomed.   Since a
prerequisite of such assistance was proper supervision of
UNHCR funds and careful coordination of international efforts,
the government agreed that the presence of an on-the-spot
UNHCR representative was desirable.   On 1 February 1969,
therefore, a BO was officially opened in Delhi, and Mr.
Frederik L. Pijnacker-Hordijk (Netherlands) was appointed
UNHCR representative.   It was thought that the UNHCR Program in India would be required for at least two or three
years before the problem of the Tibetan refugees could be
permanently resolved. [28]

In 1970 the role of the UNHCR assumed new importance as attempts were made to consolidate and speed up the
permanent settlement of Tibetan refugees.   Projects from
previous years were carried forward in the fields of agricultural settlement, housing for the aged, and for the Buxa
lamas, and for the improvement of medical facilities.   From
the $300,000 allocated in 1970 the UNHCR provided a total
of $20,000 for vocational training for young Tibetans, par-
ticularly in the fields of agriculture, cooperative management, and simple bookkeeping and accounting.

After his third mission to India, made in 1970, Mr.
Jamieson could report that the needs for which UNHCR assistance was required had been identified and a substantial
program of assistance drawn up.   Although the work toward
Tibetan rehabilitation was by no means complete, and the
task of affording legal protection to the refugees in such matters as naturalization, ownership of property, and the rights
and obligations of citizenship still needed to be thought out,
the work of the UNHCR in India was developing in an encouraging way. [29]   Above all, a close working relationship
between the UNHCR and the government had been established.

Funding International Assistance
in Resettlement Programs

In spite of the surge of interest in Tibetan refugees after 1966, the resources available were far from adequate for resettlement of them all.   Of the 55,000 Tibetan refugees now in India, Sikkim, and Bhutan, some 25,000-30,000 were more or less firmly settled.   That left as many again in need of resettlement.

Common Project of ERC Contribution.   The most important development in terms of foreign aid to Tibetan refugees was the Common Project for Tibetan Refugees of ERC. On 4 January 1966 a Board of Trustees of the Common Project of ERC was established to administer the International Tibetan Fund.   It was composed of one representative each from the Netherlands Committee for Aid to Refugees and an equivalent committee of a second country, one representative from the ICVA, and one from UNHCR.   Prince Bernhard of the Netherlands was the Honorary President; the Coordinating Secretary was Mr. C. Brouwer, a Dutchman.   The Board acted as an intermediary for all committees and national organizations which wished to contribute to permanent solutions for Tibetan refugees; it not only ensured the most productive use of funds collected for this purpose, irrespective of the account to which such committees transferred their funds, but it established financial rules for the administration of the Fund, and saw that donating committees were consulted before their funds were actually spent. [30]

For resettling the remaining 25,000 refugees, the Common Project had drawn up twelve priority schemes whose total cost was estimated to be around $6 million.   The 1966 ERC drive had yielded $3.5 million which was sufficient to carry out projects for the resettlement of only 17,000.   Mr. Brouwer, Coordinating Officer of the Common Project, was attempting to secure the additional funds from non-campaign sources, of which some $1.5 million was expected, but not assured, in matching funds from the US.   There was, therefore, a prospect of considerable short fall of funds for completing the twelve projects for long-range rehabilitation.

These projects were not intended to cover recurring expenses.   In spite of the evident wisdom of assisting refugees to become independent, there were, nevertheless, many who were in serious need of immediate assistance for which voluntary agency funds were also uncertain or inadequate.

These included the 950 lamas at Buxa for whom resettlement
was essential, and the many aged and infirm persons who
could never become totally self-sufficient.   Furthermore, it
was now necessary to cover the cost of medical programs
which AECTR had supported from 1959 until the end of 1967.
While the government was gradually assuming responsibility
for this medical program, $50,000 was required in 1968 for
its continuance.   The HC had already allocated $7,000 dur-
ing 1967 for continuing the hospital at Mundgod, and there
were other such urgent needs.

        UNHCR Financial Aid.   In 1964 as a result of the
visits and talks mentioned above, the HC had agreed with the
CRC(I) and the RCS(I) on the allocation of the $100,000 pro-
ceeds from sale of the "All Star Festival" record as follows:

    1.   In agreement with the RCS(I) and through the
          LRCS, UNHCR provided $50,000 toward a medi-
          cal relief operation in the Simla area where some
          3,200 refugees were living.

    2.   In agreement with the CRC(I), the Government of
          India and the Swiss Aid Program, UNHCR pro-
          vided $30,000 for the purchase of a special
          tractor for land clearing which would supplement
          one provided by the Swiss, and would be looked
          after by them.

    3.   Ten thousand dollars were used for purchase of
          seeds, fertilizer, poultry, and livestock for 500
          refugees at Bylakuppe who were then to stop re-
          ceiving rations, and for other settlers in Mainpat
          and Chandragiri.

    4.   The remaining $10,000 provided pumping equip-
          ment and piping for irrigation at Chandragiri, as
          well as two tractors for use by CRC(I) at either
          Chandragiri or Mainpat. [31]

        In subsequent years, the HC continued to stimulate in-
terest in projects suggested by the CRC(I) under the Master
Plan, to support agencies which undertook to carry out these
projects, and to channel funds to these projects from private
sources.   Thus in 1965, $57,000 from the proceeds of "All
Star Festival" and $5,000 from the Holy See assisted RCS(I)
medical programs in one agricultural settlement, the installation of a flour mill in another, and the procuring of tents

for road camps. In 1966 the UNHCR provided two bulldozers for land clearing at Mundgod, and $9,000 from the HC's Program for 1967 were allocated for supporting IRC programs throughout India. Furthermore, the ERC Common Project not only acted as a powerful spur to rehabilitation efforts, but also provided opportunities for the UNHCR to assist in the final settlement of Tibetan refugees.

During the first nine months of 1969 the newly appointed HC representative was able, in collaboration with the Government of India, to develop projects for which the Ex. Com. had allocated $300,000 from the 1969 HC's Program. These plans were coordinated with the Board of Trustees of the Common Project, and consultations were held with the voluntary agencies still working for Tibetan refugees in India. Funds were allocated as follows:

1. In 1968 $7,000 had been allocated for medical assistance so that the CRC(I) could continue to operate the hospital at Mundgod no longer operated by AECTR. This hospital treated an average of 150 patients per day. An additional $20,000 was allocated for this purpose in the 1969 Program, and for other hospitals and clinics in Bylakuppe and Darjeeling, and for the tuberculosis hospital in the Lama Camp at Buxa until it closed at the end of the year, the lamas having been moved. The hospital at Bylakuppe was handed over to the State Government of Mysore at the end of 1969.

2. During 1969 construction of housing for 1,100 aged and infirm persons was begun at Mundgod. The total cost of this housing, estimated at $183,576, was shared by the Common Project and the UNHCR. The Mundgod project for 600 was completed in time for Mr. Jamieson to officiate at the opening ceremonies during his visit in April 1970.

3. For permanent settlement of refugees in industry, $28,266 was appropriated in 1969. Part of these funds were allocated through TIRS for repair of houses at the Bir and Chautra industrial communities which had suffered severe storm damage. The remainder, $26,666, was given as a grant to provide working capital in the form of

revolving loans to five industrial rehabilitation
units in the north of India.

4.   For assistance to land settlements the UNHCR
      allocated $25,000 to three main projects.   A
      heavy truck was purchased to enable the inhabi-
      tants of Tezu to market their produce, and two
      other similar projects were financed for im-
      provement of the overall food and health condi-
      tions in Chandragiri, where successive bad har-
      vests had caused undernourishment and bad
      health.

5.   One hundred thousand dollars was allocated for
      the rehabilitation in agriculture of 900 of the
      lamas at Buxa in the Ashram of west Bengal in
      which health and climatic conditions, never very
      satisfactory, had deteriorated seriously.   During
      1969 600 lamas were moved to Mundgod, and 300
      to Bylakuppe, and 400 to a settlement in South
      India.   (Mysore State made available 400 acres
      of land in Mundgod and 200 acres in Bylakuppe
      for this purpose.)   UNHCR funds provided hous-
      ing, seeds and fertilizers, livestock and agricul-
      tural equipment.   The Government of India pro-
      vided rations and transportation, and the State
      governments provided the land.   In 1970 an addi-
      tional $100,000 was appropriated by the UNHCR
      for completion of these schemes.

6.   A sum of $200,000 was also allocated for imple-
      mentation in 1970 of projects at Mainpat land set-
      tlements (which had experienced difficulties for
      several years, mainly due to climatic factors),
      designed to strengthen the economic infrastruc-
      ture.

      In 1970 the UNHCR allocated again a total of $200,000.
The major contribution to settlement in agriculture in 1970
was through projects carried out jointly with STCA in the
settlements at Chandragiri and Mahendragarh in Orissa.
Considering the inability of these two settlements, especially
the latter, to support themselves by agriculture, the Government of India decided to develop the agricultural potential of
the area through irrigation.   During 1970, $50,000 from
UNHCR funds assisted this project by providing for the purchase of tractors, seeds, fertilizers, livestock and other

agricultural requirements, as well as supplementary food and medical supplies.   Furthermore, through these funds a cooperative store was established for the 3,000 refugees living in these settlements.

Since that time the UNHCR program has focused mainly on the non-recurring needs of refugees who are not being assisted, either independently or through the Common Project, by other international sources.

II.   Tibetan Refugees in Nepal

The situation in Nepal differed in several respects from that in India.   The topography of Nepal, with its massive hills and gigantic mountains, generally made internal communications possible only by foot or by air.   (Mt. Everest, the highest of the lofty Himalayan range in which much of Nepal is situated, is only a few miles from the capital city of Kathmandu.) Consequently it has never been possible to determine accurately the number of refugees who sought asylum in Nepal at any one time, or their condition and needs.   It has been equally difficult until recently to be of help to those who did not come down from the heights to seek assistance.   Unlike India, where all but a small proportion of the Tibetan refugees passed through official reception centers where they could be registered, and their needs at least assessed, there were no such centers in Nepal.   Less than half of the estimated 12,000 refugees came to areas where they could receive assistance from such voluntary programs as were set up for them.   The majority remain in inaccessible mountain areas, living as best they can, some as nomads, and others subsisting on what the local population is able to spare them.   Since the agricultural potential of these regions is severely limited by topography, poor soil, and inadequate rainfall, the local population, with the best of intentions, has little surplus to offer the newcomers. [32]

Emergency Relief, 1960-63

More often than in India, refugees coming to Nepal were able to bring with them some animals and supplies. With these they managed to survive the first year or so of exile.   The only assistance they received from outside the area came from the Indian Red Cross Society, which

air-dropped some food and supplies. By 1961, however, not
only were the refugees' supplies exhausted, but the Chinese
soldiers had left little for the Nepalese, and less for the
refugees. Many of the refugees came down from the mountains to seek assistance. A considerable number subsequently returned to Tibet. (The Chinese treated Tibetans in border regions less rigorously than they did those in the interior.) More than one hundred were estimated to have died
of starvation.

        Under these circumstances the Government of Nepal,
in May 1960, asked the ICRC to undertake an emergency relief program for as many of the refugees as could be reached.
There was no official feeding program as in India, but ICRC
set up feeding stations at the major refugee gathering spots
and on their known routes through Nepal. The mainstay of
this program was provided through the US AID Food Program in Nepal, which also made a grant of $50,000 annually
for transportation and distribution of the food within Nepal.
Through the Swiss Red Cross (SRC) ICRC parachuted supplies, from special planes designed for mountain flying to
refugees in the remote areas. For those in more accessible
areas it set up a medical program as well and distributed
clothing and other necessities. In several of these relief
stations, the rudiments of settlements initiated at the time
have formed the basis of those existing today. The UNHCR,
at the request of ICRC, assisted in this relief operation
through its good offices. From 1960 to 1963, when the
ICRC concluded its refugee operation in Nepal, UNHCR was
able to make available to ICRC an amount of $129,295 con-
tributed from various sources (including funds from WRY)
for refugees in Nepal.

Assistance from Voluntary Agencies

        In May 1963, a bilateral agreement was concluded
between the Governments of Nepal and Switzerland whereby
SATA and the SRC undertook direct responsibility for assistance to Tibetan refugees. Both these organizations were
operating programs for refugees supplemental to that of
ICRC, whose program they now jointly assumed.

        SATA, whose refugee activities were financed by the
Swiss Government, operated the largest program at the
time, at an annual cost to the Swiss Government of
$230,000. Beginning in 1960, SATA had established

rehabilitation centers at Chialsa in Solu Khumbu, Dhorpatan in northwest Nepal, Kathmandu, and Pokhara. By 1963 the SRC was providing some degree of maintenance and medical assistance to some 3,300 refugees in these four centers and those at Janakpur and in Trisuli, at an annual cost of $7,500. By 1964, 1,000 refugees were receiving rehabilitation and technical training assistance in spinning, carpentry, carpet making, boot making, tailoring, and in agriculture. In the latter projects SATA maintained close contact with the FAO and WHO representatives in Nepal.

Two other voluntary organizations were also operating programs to assist refugees. The United (Protestant) Mission provided medical care for refugees along with Nepalese in its hospitals at Kathmandu, Okhaldungs, Pokhara, and Tensen. The Nepal International Tibetan Refugee Relief Committee (NITRRC), under the chairmanship of Father M. D. Moran, S. J. concentrated its efforts on providing teachers and other facilities for the elementary education of some 715 refugee children.

In September 1963, the Nepalese Red Cross Society (NRCS) was constituted under the chairmanship of Princess Prinsep Shaha, with Dr. N. P. Singh, Minister of Health, as Vice-Chairman, and Dr. Jaya Giri as Secretary. The NRCS undertook relief programs for refugees who were not yet receiving relief from other sources. Although at its inception the society needed considerable technical and financial assistance from outside sources, it was accepted into the LRCS by the end of 1964. As the operational partner of UNHCR after 1965 and with the help of funds from UNHCR and other sources, especially the SRC, NRCS was able to expand its program very rapidly. In 1969 Princess Prinsep Shaha was awarded the Nansen Medal in recognition of the exceptional services rendered to refugees by herself and her country.[33]

Permanent Solutions

In Nepal, with its very limited resources, opportunities for refugees to engage in their traditional occupations were even more limited than in India. Agricultural land for settlements like those in India was almost totally unavailable. If creation of privileged refugee communities was to be avoided, any measures taken to assist refugees necessitated over-all schemes for raising the general standard of living

of the Nepalese population, as well as access for Nepalese
to facilities created for refugees.   Furthermore, whereas in
India a variety of self-help projects could be developed, with
programs of emergency relief receding gradually, in Nepal
the main activity from which Tibetans could derive a livelihood was the production of handicraft items and their subsequent sale overseas.   Termination of relief measures, thus,
depended not only on the development of these industries,
but on the development of overseas markets as well.   Nevertheless, handicraft centers, begun either by the refugees
themselves, or by the various organizations assisting them,
have been the foundation of subsequent efforts for permanent
solutions.

UNHCR Programs in Nepal

Another major difference between Indian and Nepalese
efforts for permanent solution of the refugee problem was
that in Nepal the UNHCR played a role almost from the beginning.   Help at first was given indirectly through ICRC but
in February 1964 the Government of Nepal requested the HC
to send a representative to Nepal to study the situation.   Accordingly, from 11 March to 6 April 1964, Mr. J. D. R.
Kelly visited all the centers in Nepal where assistance was
given to refugees.   His visit resulted in proposals to the
Ex. Com. whereby UNHCR, operating through the newly
formed NRCS, would undertake a gradually expanding program for refugees who were not receiving assistance from
other sources. [34]   With government approval, a permanent
UNHCR representative opened a BO in Kathmandu in August
1964 to provide liaison between the UNHCR and the various
parties involved in aid to refugees--its operational partner
the NRCS, the SRC, SATA, US AID, UN agencies (such as
FAO and WHO) and the Government of Nepal.

The UNHCR immediately set aside $50,000 from its
Emergency Fund for aid to Tibetan refugees in Nepal.   Some
of this money was spent through the SRC, for improving
health conditions among refugees in the Trisuli area.   This
center, located some forty-six miles north of Kathmandu,
was operated by SATA and the SRC.   Refugees there depended mainly on employment in the construction of a hydro-
electric plant under the Indian Aid Program to Nepal which
was completed in 1965.   Of the estimated 11,000-12,000 refugees in Nepal, some 4,300 in or near established settlements were found to be receiving varying degrss of

assistance from SATA, the SRC or other programs. Some 4,000 were known to be living on the northern border of Nepal in the far west of the country. Little was known about their condition, since it was extremely difficult to reach them. Finally there were about 3,700, mainly on the Nepal borders to the north and north-east of Kathmandu, who were in immediate need and for whom it was proposed that the UNHCR undertake an assistance program.

It was also agreed that the UNHCR would assist the NRCS to develop two small multi-purpose centers for these refugees at Kathmandu. The money required was allocated from the balance of some $20,000 still available from the $50,000 referred to above. Each center comprised a small school, a clinic, a milk station and a food distribution point and these were made available also to Nepalese.[35] They were developed in cooperation with the other interested parties; including the US AID Food Program and UNICEF.

During 1965 three important changes took place which led to greatly increased UNHCR participation in projects for permanent solutions, and which aroused the hope that the Tibetan refugees might soon be set on their way to self-sufficiency. In April, 4,000 refugees moved from Nepal to India, thus reducing the previous total to between 7,000 and 8,000. Secondly, the Government of Nepal agreed to provide land for settling those of the remaining refugees who chose to stay. Although land was not immediately available, this move by the Nepal Government made it possible for SATA and the NRCS to draw up, with the government, a comprehensive plan whereby refugees might become self-supporting and relief measures be tapered off. Third, under these circumstances the HC, always anxious to convert relief measures into long-range projects leading to permanent solutions, allocated funds for the first time from his Program for 1965 for projects designed to help 1,000 Tibetan refugees in Nepal to achieve permanent settlements. He concluded an agreement with NRCS (May 20) under which the latter undertook to implement UNHCR-financed projects. This first allocation, of $143,750, was used to build some one hundred dwellings for refugees, who were still living in tents, in three areas close to centers at Jawalakhel, at Pokhara-Pardi and at Chialsa, where they could find employment, and where hospitals and schools for Tibetans and Nepalese had previously been set up. From 1965 onward the HC has included allocations to Tibetan refugees in Nepal in his regular annual Program. Whereas the UNHCR's total contributions for relief efforts through 1964 had been $163,522, its participation increased as the emphasis swung to permanent solutions so that the 1965 contribution almost matched the total of all previous contributions. [36] Total contributions through UNHCR in the period 1963-71 were $526,500 (see Annex 29.2).

Internationally Assisted Settlement Programs

UNHCR projects have been planned, not as a global solution, but rather as a series of measures carried out within a network of other assistance which would, as quickly as possible, lead refugees to economic independence. Although one or another of the many partners may have been primarily responsible for the establishment or development of a particular settlement each has played some part in most of them. They work in close collaboration with one another so as to take maximum advantage of the other's efforts.

Jawalakhel. At Jawalakhel (Kathmandu) the close working relationship between the Government of Nepal, the NRCS, SATA, and the UNHCR undoubtedly contributed to its success. There were 600 refugees living in this settlement. The work for which the UNHCR contributed $45,000, for construction of housing, a school, and a hospital, was completed in 1967. The school has over eighty pupils, including some Nepalese, and has been supported by the Norwegian Refugee Council's "Action 7,600." The hospital, run by NRCS, added an extra room as a TB ward. Refugees working in the handicraft center earn a wage comparable to that of Nepalese in the area, and SATA guided not only the production but also the sale of products from the center, which benefits from its location near an area frequented by tourists. Because the refugees work full-time and can buy their food in the market, land which had originally been set aside for their use for cultivation remained unused, and has been returned to the government.

Pokhara. At Pokhara there are two settlements: Tarshi Palkhiel (Pokhara Hyangja) with 506 refugees, completed by SATA in 1964, and Tashi Ling (Pokhara Pardi), which was established in 1966 and financed almost entirely by UNHCR. Both these settlements benefit from their location in a growing tourist area which is only five hours by bus from India, and is also accessible today by road from Kathmandu.

Tarshi Palkhiel.   At Tarshi Palkhiel UNHCR assistance has been marginal only.   Thus $7, 500 was made avail-
able to provide permanent roofing to replace the thatch which
had caused a number of fires and destruction of several
dwellings.   Otherwise, the consistent support of SATA permitted this community to become ultimately self-sufficient.
A cooperative store sells a considerable variety of goods.
The carpet-making industry is well established.   A restau-
rant/hotel is making good profits.   In 1969 the community
also acquired some land for agricultural purposes.   The
NRCS runs a first-class clinic with the help of a nurse from
the SRC.   A workshop also gives work to a number of Tibetan carpenters and artisans.   It has been suggested that
should the community require further UNHCR assistance it
could be granted on the understanding that the community itself would make a matching contribution.

Tashi Ling.   The Tashi Ling settlement was originally
a temporary camp set up by the UNHCR in which at one time
1, 000 refugees were gathered, but many of them left after
1965 for India or other places in Nepal.   The development,
begun in 1966, was carried out by NRCS with UNHCR funds.
A school is operating for both Tibetans and Nepalese, with
a Nepalese teacher assisted by a Tibetan lama.   A dispensary, a nursery, and a handicraft center have all been completed.   There is also a poultry farm, a noodle factory, a
small animal husbandry scheme, a tea room, and a restau-
rant.   Being in a tourist area, the handicraft center is making a good profit; the other projects are barely holding their
own and need continued assistance to develop into profit-mak-
ing projects.   A carpentry workshop, built by the Danish
Refugee Council, still lies unused as there is little work of
this nature in the area.   It is proposed that the building
should be used to expand the handicraft center.   For the
present, most of the refugees have been in road construction.   But plans were drawn up to diversify the economic
activities of the community, especially since the road work
will soon be finished.

Dhorpatan.   Dhorpatan, in northwest Nepal, lying at
9, 500 feet just below the snow-capped peaks of 26, 800-foot
Dhaulaoiri, is the oldest Tibetan settlement in Nepal, established in 1961 when groups of refugees first began to cross
over into Nepal.   It reflects more closely than other settlements the traditional Tibetan way of life.   There are 400
Tibetans living at Dhorpatan.   Begun by the ICRC, the settlement was continued by SATA.   In 1967 the administration

was taken over by the Government of Nepal and is the responsibility of the Ministry for Home and Pahchayat Affairs.

The Swiss program settled the original 275 refugees
in adequate housing and established a cooperative store and
a handicraft center which have done well. In view of the
proposed development of the northern areas of Nepal, this
center may well become an important trading center from
which the commercial activities of the Tibetans may prosper.
Agricultural schemes, an animal husbandry scheme and a
dairy farm have helped to diversify the settlement's economy,
although they have been in need of assistance. SATA also
runs a dispensary for the settlement with the support of the
SRC. A new school, built by the government with funds
from the UNHCR for both Tibetan and Nepalese students, is
to be included within the regular program of the Ministry of
Education.

When an additional 125 Tibetans joined the community
they met with considerable difficulty in finding housing and
employment. To alleviate this situation the UNHCR contributed $6,000 in 1968 for housing and to assist the settle-
ment's cooperative in broadening its activities so that these
new settlers could find employment.

Chialsa. The settlement at Chialsa had its origin in
a handicraft center established in 1961 by the refugees themselves. It was first developed by the ICRC along with its
program for the 6,000 refugees then in the Solu Khumbu area. It was turned over, in 1963, to SATA, which developed
it in cooperation with the SRC after that time. Since many
refugees migrated to India in 1965, the number in the area
dropped to only 650. The handicraft center itself employs
270 workers. UNHCR funds in 1965 provided for the construction of dwellings for a total of 99 families. A dispensary was constructed in 1963 by the NRCS with funds from
the SRC. NITRRC constructed and supported a school until
1967 when it was taken over by Swiss Aid to Tibetans. A
cooperative society, originally started by Tibetans to support
the aged and infirm of the community, profitably operates a
retail shop and three restaurants. Cultivation of some
eighty-five acres of land (half of it provided by the government) began in 1967, and has yielded relatively good results.

These five settlements were sufficiently established
by the end of 1967 so that rationing could be discontinued in
all of them. Since 1969 the ministries concerned with

housing, health, education, and agriculture have also cooperated in UNHCR projects.

Economic Diversification in Settlements

In spite of the success of the established settlements,
there remains a continuing need for some assistance in such
projects as housing, schools, and especially in the area of
medical services. Moreover, a serious problem has arisen
as a result of the unreliable market for the products of these
centers. As many of the centers are almost totally dependent upon income from sale of these products, any fluctua-
tion in the market has serious consequences in the settlements.

At Jawalakhel, the carpet center which usually provides work for between 300 and 500 workers was operating
only five days a week in January 1968 and there was a large
stock of unsold carpets in the warehouse. At Tarshi Palkhiel, the center which had provided work for 140 workers
had stopped functioning and over $12,000 had to be borrowed
from the cooperative to pay workers their wages. Over one
hundred settlers had moved away to a nearby area to work
on road construction. In Chialsa, too, the center was closed
and workers were being employed in wool transportation
work.

The Tibetan Carpet Trading Corporation (TCTC) was
formed in 1966 to supervise the quality of production in all
centers, and to arrange for marketing their products overseas. The Board of Directors includes Tibetans, Nepalese,
and a Swiss adviser. Only if this corporation is able to
maintain a steady and increasing market for the products of
these centers, will they continue to be viable economic units.

Attempts are being made, therefore, to diversify the
economic life of all settlements to make them less dependent
upon the overseas market for their products. The UNHCR,
in 1967, allocated $40,000 for a fund for permanent solu-
tions. Half was used during 1967-68 mainly for training
refugees in trades whereby they could earn their living locally. The remaining $20,000 was used for this purpose dur-
ing 1969, and for establishing other self-help projects. In
addition, the UNHCR established a revolving fund to enable
individual refugees to set up independent enterprises. In the
HC's Program for 1970, $10,000 was set aside for each of

these funds, while $6,500 was allocated for medical care, and $3,500 for management and counselling to enable Tibetans to take over management of their own projects. Similar amounts were allocated for the 1971 program.

Efforts for Refugees in the Northern Area

With solutions for the nearly 3,000 settled refugees making good progress in 1967, the HC turned his attention to the needs of the estimated 4,000 scattered in the mountains as well as some new arrivals from Tibet. The refugees in the northern mountain tracts have affinity with the local inhabitants, and hundreds of them descend from the mountains every winter some of them to remain permanently in the lower valleys. In the winter of 1966 some 60 to 80 of the nomadic refugees decided to stay on in Tashi Ling, and it was possible to absorb this group into the settlement. But the UNHCR had to set up a new project for the 500 who stayed behind in the Kathmandu area after the winter of 1967. Considering this project part of the Urban Development Program of Kathmandu Valley, the Government of Nepal provided land in two areas in the valley, Balaju and Swayambunath, which, with UNHCR funds and operational assistance from the Ministry of Housing and Physical Planning, are now being developed to settle over 500 refugees. Benefiting from training provided under the Fund for Permanent Solutions, they were already operating a well-run handicraft center by 1969. It is expected that periodic arrivals such as these will continue until the needs of the scattered refugees can be met.

Of the various groups of Tibetan refugees scattered in the remote northern areas, some 550 are gathered at Rasua in the Province of Trisuli. Other small groups are scattered in the areas of Dolpo, Mustang, Walung, Chum, Solu Khumbu and Western Nepal. In Rasua, through the collaboration of the Government's Northern Zonal Development Board, the UNHCR has provided $40,000 for the initiation of a settlement project whereby refugees will be integrated into the zonal development of the region. Refugees and the local inhabitants also benefit from the programs of other UN agencies such as WHO's campaign against goiter which is prevalent in the area. The Trisuli Watershed Project, undertaken by FAO/UNDP, has covered half the costs of a health center for the area, and for the Thangmujet Health Center (opened in 1969), and UNICEF has agreed to

supply medical equipment and medicines through the Ministry
of Health.   A school, for Tibetan and Nepalese children,
constructed on land given free by the local panchayat, is being aided by the Remote Areas Development Board and
UNICEF working through the Ministry of Education.   The
FAO is undertaking a feasibility survey for sheep or yak
breeding.   The UNHCR has made allocations of $45,000 in
1969, $20,000 in 1970, and $35,000 in 1971.[37]

Although the refugee population remained at a level of
about 8,000 for many years, some still manage to come in
from Tibet every year.   In the closing months of 1967 about
300 braved the Tinker Pass to cross into northwestern Nepal.
Their need for emergency aid led the UNHCR to allocate
$5,000 from the Emergency Fund.   Similarly, a new group
of 500 arrived in the Trisuli area, requiring not only emergency assistance, but ultimate arrangements for permanent
settlement.

Planning for the 1971 program was influenced by two
factors.   Efforts must continue to assist the scattered
groups of Tibetan refugees in northern Nepal, where the
UNHCR Director of Operations made another extensive survey during 1970.[38]   Marginal assistance to established settlements has also been necessary, particularly in such fields
as medical care, management and counselling services, and
promotion of the handicraft industry.   Projects totalling
$65,000 were planned for these needs.   In 1971, $55,000
was allocated, and in 1972, $46,000.

Increasing progress has been made by the established
settlements.   The Government of Nepal has made major efforts to solve the refugee problem with the assistance of
interagency cooperation.   The lasting solution is seen to be
through local integration.   In the light of these advances the
HC was able to announce at the Twenty-third Ex. Com. that
UNHCR assistance could be discontinued in 1973.

The generous hospitality of the Governments of India
and Nepal, and their resettlement policies, have thus provided not only for the survival of thousands of Tibetan refugees but have also, with the aid of the international community, given them the possibility of becoming contributing
members of the societies of their host countries, while at
the same time preserving their own identity.

III.   The Focal Point Program in India, 1971-72

In April 1972 the UN family was called upon by the
Indian Government to assist in bringing relief to the massive
refugee movement from East Pakistan into its Eastern territory, thus involving the HC in one of the largest and most
difficult humanitarian emergency actions in the history of his
office. [39]

Political events, internal conflict, and a long period
of increasing unrest in East Pakistan (East Bengal) had culminated in a systematic campaign, launched by the Pakistan
Government on 25 March 1971, to suppress political opposition in East Bengal.   On 26 March, in response to West
Pakistan military action, the Bengali nationalists declared
East Pakistan to be the independent state of Bangladesh, with
Mujibar Rahman as its leader.   East Bengalis in increasing
numbers sought refuge from the struggle in the neighboring
states of India. [40]   The movement soon assumed major proportions, and when it reached its peak in December 1971,
the refugee population numbered near ten million.   In this
period, military buildups by both Pakistan and India along
the East Pakistan border led to a series of infiltrations and
reprisals and ultimately, on 6 December, to a full-scale
war.

The uprooting of millions of persons was the third
disaster to befall East Bengal in little more than a year.
In the summer of 1970 floods had destroyed crops and thousands succumbed.   In November a cyclone had hit the coastal
region killing an estimated 400,000 persons and rendering an
additional two million homeless.   Rehabilitation projects following the 1970 flood and cyclone were still underway at the
beginning of the massive refugee movement of 1971.

The 1971 eruption of deeply seated social tensions had
political as well as humanitarian aspects which were of concern to India, Pakistan, the UN, and ultimately the UNHCR.
Throughout the crisis these aspects were intimately intertwined.   While the immediate involvement of the international
community centered around the relief action for the refugees
in India and for the civilian population in East Pakistan, a
simultaneous concern was promotion of political solutions
which would establish peace between India and Pakistan on the
one hand and, on the other hand, reestablish stable conditions in East Pakistan.

The Secretary-General of the UN became the center
for international action in the confused and fluid situation
which existed in the Asian subcontinent from March to December of 1971. While awaiting SC and GA action with respect to political and military aspects of the situation--ac-
tion which was not taken until December 1971--the Secretary-
General himself initiated direct contact with India and with
Pakistan, offering his good offices in seeking political solutions between India and Pakistan and between West Pakistan
and East Pakistan. Above all, however, the Secretary-
General was the initiator of humanitarian actions taken by
the international community through the UN and its related
agencies.

Among these initiatives was the establishment of the
Focal Point operation for humanitarian assistance to the refugees from East Pakistan then in India. The UNHCR was
called upon in April 1971 by the Secretary-General to lead
this massive relief program in India, which was conducted
during the months from May 1971 to February 1972. In
June a parallel unit, the UN East Pakistan Relief Operation
(UNEPRO), was established by the Secretary-General to relieve the plight of civilian populations in East Pakistan.

Indian Response in the Early Days of the Emergency

In the immediate period following the events of 25
March, the movement of East Bengalis seeking refuge in India did not seem alarming. Only a few thousands were reported. However, by the end of April, more than 1,200,000
refugees had entered India, and by May the movement had
become a massive exodus, with an average influx of 83,000
persons daily. The refugee tide was swelled as a result of
Pakistani military action and terrorism against civilian populations. Hindus were predominant among the refugees, as
the Hindu community had been singled out for decimation by
the Pakistan army, together with intellectuals, students, and
members of the politically active Awami League (the principal
East Pakistani party). Although the majority of the refugees
proceeded to West Bengal, nearly a million and a half moved
into the State of Tripura.

From the beginning India's Prime Minister, Indira
Ghandi, insisted that the refugees could not remain as permanent residents in India. [41] However, the Indian Government and the Indian people did their utmost to bring relief

to the refugees. Measures of assistance were taken immediately by the Indian authorities at local and state levels, and
also at the Central Government level under the Department
of Rehabilitation, supported by other operational ministries
and by the Indian Red Cross Societies (IRS).

The first efforts were made in haste, and were improvised. At checkposts established at the main points of
entry arrangements were made to register the refugees and
some food and medical attention were given that they might
continue their journey inland. Refugees were temporarily
housed in schools, colleges, government buildings and other
vacant compounds. Food was issued from reserves--"buffer
stocks" intended to meet famine and scarcity conditions which
often occurred in certain pockets of the country--but this
supply served to meet only the immediate demands.

The problem soon reached such dimensions that a
Central Coordination Committee for Refugee Relief (CCC)
was set up within the Rehabilitation Department of the Central Ministry of Labour and charged with the task of establishing camps and of coordinating the relief programs. This
organization worked in conjunction with seven state governments, twenty-four Indian voluntary organizations and twelve
international agencies. In less than nine months 896 refugee
camps were set up (some later consolidated, reducing the
number to 825). By the end of the emergency, accommodations in camps had been provided for 6.8 million refugees.
The remaining refugees (approximately 3 million) were registered by the organization and provided with rations and
medical assistance from the camps, but found shelter with
friends or relatives. The majority of camps were located
in West Bengal and Tripura; to relieve crowded conditions
in those states camps were also established in Assam,
Meghalaya, Bihar, Uttar Pradesh and Madhya Pradesh (annex 29.3).

A great number of Indian voluntary agencies played a
valuable role in helping the refugees. Thousands of volunteers helped in setting up the voluntary services. They
served with great efficiency, ingenuity, and devotion. At the
beginning they began to organize community kitchens and
medical assistance at border checkposts. When the influx
continued and more camps were opened away from the border,
they widened the scope of their operations. They undertook
feeding, medical assistance, and social education. They also
administered a number of camps with their volunteers and

helped in this way the government's overburdened administrative machinery in a critical time.   They attended to social problems and educational needs of the refugees: homes
and vocational training centers were established for unattached
women and social education centers were opened in various
camps, where refugees were taught health measures to prevent spreading diseases and children were given elementary
education.

Because of the strong public desire to bring assistance
as rapidly as possible, some private foreign voluntary agencies initiated relief action independently and some sent out
teams of volunteers without the knowledge and approval of the
Indian Government which was in charge of the operation.
The authorities informed the foreign agencies that while they
welcomed their support, those who previously had not been
working in India should channel their aid through the IRS or
through such voluntary agencies as were authorized to continue their operations predominantly with Indian personnel,
such as OXFAM, CARE, CRS, LWF, and others.

The Indian Government allocated 600 million rupees
(US $80 million) for aid to the refugees within the budget
presented on 28 May.   Three hundred million was earmarked
for grants-in-aid to the states affected by the influx and the
other half for the administration of federal camps.   The
Government of India insisted, however, that the problem was
not of its making but the result of developments which had
taken place in another country.   While India, due to its geographical situation and to human solidarity, was assisting
refugees, it was also a responsibility of the international
community to provide the urgently needed resources.

West Bengal is a poverty-stricken, politically unstable,
and extremely heavily populated area which was unable to
support the increasing refugee population.   In addition to the
shortage of food, friction developed between the refugees and
the people of West Bengal when refugees began to filter into
local labor markets, further depressing wages in areas already burdened by severe indigenous unemployment and underemployment.   The resources of the Indian Government, like
those of the voluntary agencies working in India, were soon
strained to the utmost, and the extraordinarily heavy burden
imposed by the flow of refugees came to threaten India's own
prospects for economic, political, and social development. [42]

Throughout the early days of the crisis the Permanent

Representatives to the UN of both India and Pakistan had
been in frequent communication with the Secretary-General,
and on 22 April the Indian Government, through its Permanent Representative to the UN, formally requested aid from
the UN and its Specialized Agencies. The Representative
suggested also that preliminary discussions should take place
in New Delhi between the Indian authorities and the Representative of the UNHCR. On 27 April the Indian Government
approached formally the UNHCR and LRCS for assistance to
East Pakistan refugees in India.

Three UN agencies in a position to help took immediate action at the request of the Government in early May
1971. WFP released several thousand tons of butter oil and
milk powder for a value of over $1 million from its re-
serves. UNICEF made an immediate appropriation of
$300,000 for the supply of relief goods, including medicines
and jeeps, and paying for an airlift of badly needed relief
goods, and UNHCR allocated $500,000 from its emergency
fund.

Establishment of the Focal Point Program

Immediately after the outbreak of the civil strife in
East Pakistan in March 1971, the Secretary-General expressed his concern over the situation to President Yahya
Khan and thereafter remained in continuous contact with the
Governments of Pakistan and India, both through their Permanent Representatives to the UN and through other contacts,
as it became increasingly clear that international assistance
on a large scale was needed.

Following the request of 23 April 1971 by the Indian
Government, the Secretary-General initiated the UN humanitarian effort. He stated publicly that "the civil strife which
erupted in East Pakistan in March 1971, and its aftermath,
are of deep concern to me as Secretary-General of the UN.
While the civil strife in itself is an internal affair of Pakistan, some of the problems generated by it are necessarily
of concern to the international community." In consultation
with members of the ACC, the Secretary-General decided
that the HC should act as the principal office for the coordination of assistance from and through the UN, and on 29
April he appointed the UNHCR as Focal Point for Assistance
to Refugees from East Bengal in India.

As in other refugee emergencies the HC was confronted with two facets of his task: a better coordination of the UN system in the realm of relief operation and the promotion of voluntary repatriation, at the earliest possible time--the only long-term solution envisaged by the UN and by the governments both of India and Pakistan. The HC stated at his press conference, held in Geneva on 5 May 1971, that "We cannot afford to just set up huge feeding programmes and temporary housing which tends to be permanent.... We have to find out quickly what the ultimate solutions will be, and no one has to be a prophet to see that the best solution would be to help the people to return to their homes, if and when the situation allows [this] to take place.... My office can play a role here as we have in so many other situations." However, his immediate concern was the emergency operations for the refugees in India.

On 19 May the Secretary-General appealed to the international community. He called "on behalf of the entire UN family ... to governments, intergovernmental, and nongovernmental organizations, as well as private sources, to help meet the urgent needs for humanitarian assistance in this tragic situation." He expressed the hope that voluntary repatriation would be possible at the earliest possible time, but "pending such repatriation, massive external assistance would be required on an emergency basis." The HC, reiterating the Secretary-General's appeal, proceeded to mobilize and secure international support and contributions, and to set up the intricate machinery of the Focal Point operation.

Under the Focal Point arrangement, a program entirely distinct from the normal duties of the HC was created. The agencies directly involved--UNICEF, WHO, FAO/WFP-- agreed to coordinate fund-raising and assistance activities related to the relief action with the HC at the international level and entrust the HC with liaison both with the Government of India and with the governments which contributed to the relief effort in cash and kind. At the request of the Indian Government the operations in India were carried out and coordinated by the Indian authorities.

At the time of the crisis the HC and the Specialized Agencies were represented in India, the latter by the UNDP resident representative. WFP and UNICEF had also some field staff in India; the HC was closely in contact with his own representatives in New Delhi and in Islamabad.

To mobilize from the world at large the massive help needed, it was necessary to establish first of all a detailed list of requirements and to organize the coordination of the international action on a firm basis. In the face of the multitude of relief goods required, governments in particular needed guidance as to priorities, in addition to a global assessment.

Thus after conferences with the Secretary-General, the HC sent a fact-finding mission composed of the Deputy HC, Mr. Charles Mace; Mr. Thomas Jamieson, Director of Operations; and Dr. Paul Weis, Legal Consultant. The three-man team visited India from 7 to 19 May to assess the nature and magnitude of the needs of refugees and to discuss with officials of the Indian Government the ways in which the assistance could be effected.

An analysis of the situation and the views of the Indian and Pakistan Governments made it clear that the UN action was to concentrate on two matters, previously defined: urgent relief measures for refugees in India and promotion of voluntary repatriation. The report on the findings of the UNHCR mission was shared with the governments through their Permanent Representatives to the UN and through representatives of UNHCR or the Residential Representatives of the UNDP in the various capitals.

The overall coordination of the relief program was to operate at UNHCR Headquarters and at the field level. A Focal Point unit was set up in UNHCR Headquarters in Geneva as a small separate group of five officers, headed by the Director of the Afro-Asian Division, Mr. Gilbert Jaeger; this unit was to carry out the administrative functions of recording and transmitting contributions and collating information. It met almost daily. Coordination with the other UN agencies was insured through a Standing Interagency Consultation Unit (SICU) which met once a week in Geneva--for the first time on 8 May 1971. In addition to UNHCR, representatives of the UN Secretariat, UNICEF, FAO/WFP, and WHO, as well as LRCS and occasionally ICVA, discussed practical matters relating to the relief action. Each agency had its own specific responsibilities. WFP advised on the availability of various food commodities and arranged for purchase and shipping; UNICEF, in addition to its functional duties of caring for children and women, acted as the purchasing agent for commodities such as shelter material, vehicles, and baby food, and arranged shipment; WHO, in addition to advising on health matters, purchased and shipped vaccine and medical equipment, often in cooperation with UNICEF and LRCS. LRCS undertook supplementary programs in terms of food, milk, medicaments, clothing, and shelter. The UNHCR maintained liaison with the governments in obtaining contributions in cash and kind. It apportioned contributions received on the basis of a statement of needs and related information provided by the Indian Government to UNHCR officials in New Delhi.

The HC mobilized the governments and the public. He traveled widely to contact the governments in the UK, US, and France. The Office kept diplomatic representatives of donor countries constantly informed of developments. The world-wide network of Resident Representatives of the UNDP and of the UNHCR, as well as those of the Specialized Agencies played a valuable role in passing information to member governments advising them of needs, and assisting them with the dispatch of relief goods. By holding press conferences in Geneva, New York, London, and Paris, the HC enlisted the essential support of the mass media on the refugee question. [43]

At the field level, a Focal Point mission was set up in New Delhi. Mr. Thomas Jamieson, who went to India on 5 June, headed this mission with a small team and kept liaison with the Indian Government, mainly through the CCC and its four subcomittees: health, housing, transportation, and food. The UNHCR and the Specialized Agencies were represented on this committee. The UNHCR unit kept daily contact with the Indian authorities, the IRS and the voluntary agencies.

Thus within a brief time the mechanism of the assistance channel was laid, with CCC in New Delhi as the coordinating source of information and action in India, directly linking the Ministry of Rehabilitation to the relief operation's headquarters in Calcutta; with SICU in Geneva as the platform where information from India, from donors, and of the activities by UN agencies was exchanged; and with the UNHCR as the fund-raising and decision-taking body.

The HC described the threefold functioning of the coordinating mechanism that had been set up at the Focal Point as being to mobilize and secure international support and contributions; to arrange for the procurement of supplies in a coordinated manner and to deliver the supply to India; to maintain close liaison with the Indian Government.

In the beginning of June (6-17 June) Prince Sadruddin himself visited Pakistan and India for consultation with the governments on relief measures required, and, seeking the return of the refugees, the HC, in agreement with the Secretary-General, tried to initiate a dialogue between the two countries concerned as "an intermediary of good will. " The HC was well aware that voluntary repatriation could only be the result of reaching a consensus between the host country and the country of origin, and that both sides would have to agree not only on the solution, but also on the means for achieving this solution. In past experiences a system of mutual cooperation and help had been established with the active participation of UNHCR which facilitated repatriation. In visiting India and Pakistan the HC was able to make a personal assessment of the emergencies on the spot and consult with both governments. In both capitals he held discussions at the highest level; he also saw the border areas on both sides and visited some refugee camps in India and some reception centers in Pakistan.

In the interval between the onset of the crisis and the activation of the machinery through which government contributions would be channeled, voluntary agencies in India, as elsewhere, filled the time gap inevitable in the emergency operations.

At the beginning of the refugee influx some international organizations which were running normal programs with India provided emergency relief to refugees. In most cases they received their guidelines from their headquarters in Europe and the US. The local coordination of their work was secured through regular meetings, especially in Calcutta. The respective Indian Government officials, as did the representatives of the UN organizations, participated in these meetings. In the case of the contributions of the various national and Red Cross Societies, LRCS carried out the coordination and assisted in this way the IRS. The largest organizations in India included Caritas India, which in cooperation with CRS was the organ of the Catholic Church; the Christian Agency for Social Action (CASA), the executive organ for most non-Catholic churches; CARE; Cooch Behar Refugee Service (CBRS), the organ of LWP; OXFAM; Rette das Kind (Feed the Children); War on Want; Rädda Barnen; and others in Europe and overseas countries. Not all voluntary organizations were operational, some helped the relief programs through contributions in cash and kind, either to Indian or to international organizations already working in

India. Many of these organizations launched appeals through radio, press, and television. They organized several power- ful fund-raising appeals in many countries. (By June 1972 the total of contributions by non-governmental organizations amounted to $5.7 million, in cash and kind.)

Parallel with the establishment of the Focal Point operation, a UN relief program was initiated on behalf of the civilian population in East Pakistan. On 22 April the Secretary-General had addressed a letter to Yahya Khan, the President of Pakistan, in which he expressed his concern at the situation in East Pakistan and offered on humanitarian grounds on behalf of the UN family of organizations assist- ance to the government in bringing urgently needed relief to the population of East Pakistan. Yahya Khan, in a letter of 3 May, replied that adequate supplies of medicines, food- stuffs and other daily necessities were available, but assess- ment of future possible assistance which might eventually be needed was under consideration.

The Secretary-General received through the Perman- ent Representative of Pakistan on 22 May a communication detailing the extent of relief requirements needed from the international community. The Secretary-General asked the Assistant Secretary-General for Inter-Agency Affairs to travel to Pakistan and to discuss with the government au- thorities matters for relief assistance to East Pakistan from and through the UN. He was received by the President and had discussions with senior government officials, both in Islamabad and in Dacca. The Pakistan Government endorsed the resumption of the UN relief operation for the civilian population of East Bengal. This humanitarian action, cre- ated to meet the emergency following the November 1971 cy- clone, had been interrupted by the March events. Full agreement was reached on the manner in which the operation should be organized and the President promised full coopera- tion of his government at all levels to the UN personnel. [44]

On 16 June the Secretary-General appealed to govern- ments, intergovernmental and non-governmental organizations and private sources to contribute in cash and kind to the UN humanitarian effort in East Pakistan. The UN East Pakistan Operation was set up in Dacca as a program separate from that of the Focal Point in India. The Secretary-General made clear that the two operations were distinct, but were related to the extent that "as conditions improve, a better possibility of arresting and reversing the flow of refugees

would occur. " On 15 July the Secretary-General issued a
comprehensive UN review of the relief needs of East Pakistan, indicating that $28.2 million would be required to meet
the initial needs.

At the time of the HC's June visit the Pakistan Government agreed that the HC would provide assistance to
Pakistan in arranging the return and rehabilitation of the
refugees and that a representative of the HC could be stationed at Dacca with a small team to maintain contact with
the local authorities of East Pakistan.   The HC appointed a
senior officer, Mr. John Kelly, as his representative in
Dacca.   He arrived in Dacca in early August and worked in
coordination with UNEPRO through the Secretary-General's
Representative, Paul-Marc Henry.

On 21 and 24 May and again on 18 June the President
of Pakistan had appealed to the refugees to return home.
The Governor of East Pakistan made similar appeals on 10
June and on 5 September.   A general amnesty was declared
for civilian, military, and police personnel, with certain
exceptions.   In a further appeal on 14 September the Governor of Pakistan announced measures for facilitating the
voluntary repatriation of refugees, particularly in regard to
restitution of property, and reception centers were established.   In the early October meeting of the Ex. Com. the
observer from Pakistan stated that his Government most
anxiously desired the return of the refugees and had taken
a number of "positive and constructive steps" to this end.
The actual number repatriated before the December settlement, however, was virtually nil.

Humanitarian Basis for UNHCR Operations

The hope and the attempts of some governments to
influence the Governments of India and Pakistan through
"quiet diplomacy" to reach a political settlement had been
without success.

The position of the UN and the HC was in the early
day of the crisis--and was to remain--a delicate one.   There
were inherent in the situation intricate political controversies.   Passions ran high not only in the Asian subcontinent
but also throughout the international community.   The refugee problem was inextricably linked to the political and
military situation, and in executing the massive humanitarian

relief program and seeking a permanent solution through voluntary repatriation the HC had to steer a narrow course in the international arena.

The HC in particular came under criticism by segments of the world press. His Office, as the spearhead of the international community, was accused alternately of not acting quickly enough to bring relief to millions of destitute and homeless persons and of acting precipitously and thus interfering in the internal affairs of sovereign states.

In his efforts to maintain what became the largest and most difficult relief operation in the twenty-year history of his Office, the HC followed from the beginning the initiative of the Secretary-General, who acted without any supporting resolution by the deliberative organs of the UN to establish the Focal Point operation for assistance to Bengali refugees. The Secretary-General justified his independent actions on the manifestly humanitarian principles of the UN system. He stated, ''I have felt that an initiative on my part was essential to fill the gap until more regular arrangements can be made, and that the Secretary-General's obligation under the Charter must include any humanitarian action that he can take to save the lives of large numbers of human beings. '' His initiative had been supported by ACC, including the Executive Heads of the UN agencies and programs, at its meeting in Bern on 26 April 1971.

The HC forcefully reiterated the Secretary-General's concern that a strict neutrality was implicit in the humanitarian relief action to be implemented under the Focal Point operation. He stated in his press conference of 5 May that ''as in all previous action this office will be stressing very much once more the humanitarian, non-political role of the UNHCR. This may be a political problem, but the role of my Office here, and ... also [that of] other humanitarian agencies ... will be dealing with the problem in a humanitarian and non-political spirit. ''

From the beginning the Secretary-General and the HC, together with the UN and the governments concerned, considered the relief program to be a palliative. Ultimately repatriation of the refugees was seen to be the only possible solution, a solution wholly contingent on the achievement of a political settlement. To this extent the activities of the HC and the means by which implementation of his programs occurred threaded constantly through and around the political framework of the problem.

The humanitarian concern was first voiced in the Social Committee of the ECOSOC by Ambassador S. Sen, Permanent Representative of India to the UN, on 12 May 1971.
He drew attention to "a current example of violation of human rights of many million people on an unprecedented scale
in our age," and went on to say that "the foremost consideration which my country has in mind is the need for urgent
humanitarian relief measures." "The problem," he said,
"has assumed such proportions and the suffering of these
people has been so enormous that it cannot but be a matter
of international concern." Five days later he reiterated before the ECOSOC the urgent need for international action and
placed in complete form suggestions as to how the international community might deal with the matter. The overtones
of the debate, however, were more political and no action
was taken.

However, the actions of the Secretary-General and the
problems in the Asian subcontinent were considered by
ECOSOC at its meeting on 16 July 1971. The HC gave the
Council a factual account of his Focal Point activities and
the Assistant Secretary-General reported on the action of
UNEPRO. Ambassador N. Krishan, the Observer for India,
stressed at that meeting that plans for accelerated economic
and social development had been severely jeopardized by the
massive influx of refugees. (Thirty percent of the taxes
paid in his country were already channelled to meet needs
arising from the refugee influx.) He mentioned that by the
end of June the figure had risen to 6.3 million people and
that relief efforts, even on an expanded scale, could at best
be only a temporary matter. "The real and timely and humanitarian solution lies in stopping the flow of refugees and
in expediting their return to their homeland, a condition
which would assure them full freedom and security and create in them confidence and faith for the future."

The chairman of ECOSOC expressed the unanimous
feeling of the delegates of "profound concern" and sincere
support for the Focal Point. "I cannot overemphasize the
duty of the international community when faced with this
problem of unprecedented magnitude," he said.

Planning and Implementation of the Relief Program

The relief program under Focal Point developed to
meet a human problem of a magnitude greater than any yet

faced by the UNHCR. Although the Office had dealt with refugee problems in Europe, Africa, Asia, and Latin America--
many of a very large scale--at no time had it had to cope
with such a massive number of uprooted people in such a
short time span. The refugees streaming across the borders
numbered several millions. The majority were utterly destitute; they travelled by foot, and without sustenance. Arriving in an area already burdened by overpopulation, the refugees were spent by fatigue and disease, emaciated, and clad
in rags. If the desperate need of millions hovering on the
brink of starvation presented a seemingly insuperable task to
the UNHCR, the magnitude of the problems were increased
manyfold by the imponderables of the political situation, the
constant threat of epidemic disease, and the impending onset
of tropical rains which would reach monsoon proportions.
Relief efforts were even further complicated by the enormous
distances over which supplies had to be procured and distributed, often virtually without an existent infrastructure of
rail, road, water, or air transport.

    Although the need for food and shelter remained con-
stant and urgent throughout the operation, unanticipated conditions and new emergencies forced continually shifting priorities to the forefront. In late May, for instance, cholera
broke out among the refugee population, and a massive airlift of vaccine had to be immediately mobilized and administered. Then the monsoon rains struck with an unexpected
ferocity, necessitating the relocation of thousands of temporary shelters and requiring the construction of more camps
and new groups of basha huts and tents. ("The need of the
hour here now," said the director of health services in West
Bengal, "is not for inoculations but for tarpaulins.") In the
North-East the cold season descended, and more and more
blankets had to be procured. Throughout these crises, the
need for special care for hundreds of thousands of undernourished children deepened.

    Costs and Finance. In order to assess the continually
shifting requirements of the refugees, both qualitatively and
quantitatively, three factors were surveyed by the Indian
Government: the size of the refugee caseload, the expected
duration of their stay in India, and the norms to be applied
in providing relief. The caseload, throughout the period,
was determined by regular and detailed reports by the Government of India. However, up to December 1971, future
influxes could not be predicted with accuracy. Because the
Indian Government from the beginning of the influx stressed

that the refugees would have to return to their homeland
within a period of six months (that is, by September 1971),
contingency plans for a longer period were not made.

The Indian Government was determined to ensure that
the refugees were, to the extent feasible, protected from
hunger, malnutrition, major epidemics, heat, rain and cold;
and, on the basis of approved norms, successive lists of
requirements for food rations, shelter, medical assistance,
transportation, etc. , were prepared by the Indian Government.
These lists were used as a basis for the appeals for international contributions launched by the Secretary-General and
followed up by the HC in his capacity as UN Focal Point.
The lists reflected the estimated composition and size of requirements for a six-month period.   The first list, totalling
$175 million, was presented in May 1971, based on a case-
load of three million refugees; the second, submitted on 26
June, totalled $400 million for six million refugees; and the
third, 1 October, totalled $558 million for eight million ref-
ugees.

In this fluid situation the purchasing process was a
most complicated one.   Ideal specifications, approximations,
and alternatives had to be balanced against availability and
urgency.   Financial considerations too played their part.
Liquid funds were constantly overcommitted and the search
for free airspace--in regard to charter costs involved--com-
plicated the procedure.   Focal Point's main worry became
the allocation of funds to individual items.   This "balancing"
of requirements against liquid funds was to mark the whole
history of UN assistance.

The costs of the assistance program fell into two
categories: recurrent costs (food and medical assistance)
and non-recurrent costs (shelter, transportation, sanitation
facilities, and others).   Eventually the total direct cost of
the relief program amounted to about $440 million, of which
international contributions transferred to the Indian Government covered slightly more than one half.   The deficit was
borne by India.   Contributions (in cash and kind) from abroad
were made principally by governments, but also by UN organizations and agencies (from their own emergency resources), by international and national non-governmental organizations, and by private bodies and individuals.   Sixty-
four countries donated $183. 2 million in cash and kind
through the UN system.   Of these, the US gave over $82
million, UK nearly $26 million, and the Federal Republic of

Germany $17.6 million. In all, each of eleven countries
gave over $1 million (see Annex 29.4). Bilateral arrange-
ments were also made by a number of countries and inter-
governmental organizations. For example, the USSR provided 50,000 tons of rice and 1,000,000 units of smallpox
vaccine; and Japan, the Federal Republic of Germany, the
German Democratic Republic, Canada, Sweden, Norway, the
UK, and US directly or through support given to voluntary
agencies rushed cash, food, shelter, and medicaments to the
subcontinent. By December 1971 some $60 million in as-
sistance had been given bilaterally, and an additional $46
million had been contributed by voluntary agencies, including
LRCS, bringing the total international effort in the relief
program to a value of more than $280 million.

There were several crises in the provision of aid.
In August the Office had to inform the press that it had
practically exhausted all the resources, then valued at $100
million, placed at its disposal. On 13 August the Secretary-
General called a special meeting of potential donors, presenting them with a memorandum outlining both the requirements of Focal Point and those of UNEPRO. At the Twenty-
sixth Session of the Ex. Com. (4 to 12 October) the HC
gave an overall report on the activities up to that date.
The Committee expressed "deep concern at the magnitude of
the tragic problem of refugees in India" and appreciated
greatly the HC's activities under the Focal Point. With the
backing of the Ex. Com. the HC sent a new list of priorities to the governments and appealed over radio and television for contributions in order to continue the program.

Food. WFP acted as a food adviser to Focal Point
and handled almost all food secured through the UN system.
It also provided a "pipeline" through which the commodities
were channeled. WFP's staff worked closely with the Indian
Government from the middle of April 1971 with the CCC and
its Food Sub-Committee. They were frequently consulted on
all matters concerning food supplies, logistics, the phasing
of food shipments, the composition of the daily per capita
ration, etc.

The daily per capita ration was established by the
Government which designated the IRS as its executive agency
for supplementary feeding. Each head of family received a
ration card. On distribution day refugees lined up at distribution points to collect their rations, often waiting for hours.
Milk was distributed at milk-feeding centers specially set up

and run by IRC or by voluntary agencies working under the
direction of IRC under a special nutrition program. Even
in the best weather, the logistics of moving large quantities
of food to remote areas was a tremendous problem (see
transportation).

Shelter. The Government's position that the refugees
would have to return to their country within six months had
implications for the measures taken with regard to shelter
as well as for other aspects of the relief program. (The
temporary character of the camps was implied by designating
them "Transit Relief Camps.") The Indian Government instructed that all accommodation for the refugees was to be
of a short-term nature and that costs of construction should
be kept to a minimum by the use of inexpensive, locally
available materials. The Government encouraged the refugees to provide voluntary labor with a view to reducing the
cost and to generate a spirit of self-help and also shorten
the delays resulting from the fact that private builders could
not meet the heavy demand.

UNICEF, entrusted with selection and procurement of
material, placed orders for suitable plastic sheeting. This
material, light in weight and reasonably durable, could be
used to cover a bamboo or wooden frame and provide immediate shelter. The first air shipment through the UN system
of this material took off in two chartered cargo jets from
New York to Calcutta on 22 June. This was the beginning
of a massive airlift of polythene from Europe, Japan, the
US, Canada, and Australia.

The shelter problem was aggravated by the exception-
ally heavy monsoon rains in West Bengal and in other states
in the northeastern region, which started earlier than usual
and were heavier than usual. The low-lying camps in West
Bengal were completely flooded by the rains, and makeshift
arrangements had to be made on the main roads for the refugees, thus endangering the traffic of supplies. Although the
main emergency was met, the need for shelter continued to
be a priority problem because of the continuous flow of refugees.

Transportation. The logistic problems involved in
moving supplies and equipment to millions of refugees in India, from places as remote as the US and Japan, were enormous. Goods--which included shelter materials, food grains,
medicine, trucks and jeeps, and blankets, clothing and

utensils--were equally diverse.   Airlifts, because of cost,
were kept to the minimum.   However, when a cholera epidemic occurred anti-cholera drugs and saline fluids were
flown in, either by chartering commercial planes or by using
space made available by air companies on their scheduled
flights.   Shelter materials were flown in when the monsoon
broke out.   Large numbers of refugees were still living in
the open, and a third airlift in November and December delivered blankets for the refugees in the colder regions.   One
of the significant contributions made was free shipment to
India.   Contributions in the form of free cargo space were
estimated at $235,117.   The Indian Government carried sup-
plies like anti-cholera drugs and milk powder from Europe
by Indian Airlines from Bombay and Delhi to Calcutta.

Within India rail transportation posed great problems.
The principal lines run on broad-gauged track, while many
of the other lines, particularly in the North-East region,
are run on meter-gauged track.   Railway transports from
Bombay to the North-East, therefore, involved shifting the
cargo to meter-gauged trains.   Furthermore, the main railway line from Calcutta to North Bengal and Assam crosses
the Ganges River at Faraka where, until the completion of a
bridge in December 1971, a ferry had to carry passengers
and goods over the river, thus incurring long delays.   Furthermore, the operation of the ferry had to be suspended for
three months because torrential rains had flooded the Ganges
Plains.   In addition, railway cars were not always available
on short notice.   These factors made overland transportation
slow at best, and often entirely unreliable.   The logistic
problems involved were not only the transportation of essential equipment and supplies to more than 800 camps in the
four different states neighboring East Bengal, but the re-
grouping of the refugees from the border areas to larger
camps further inland.   In all, over 259,000 refugees were
moved by rail from West Bengal and from Gauhati to central
camps in Assam.

Because of the poor overland communications between
the State of Tripura and the rest of the country, the only
rapid means of moving refugees out of Tripura was by air.
By arrangement with the Indian Government, the US Government provided four planes which flew in urgent relief supplies to Agartala, the capital city of Tripura, and brought
back refugees to Gauhati in Assam where they were taken by
train to nearby camps.   The USSR flew two planes from
West Bengal to Mana Camp in Madhya Pradesh.   Since the

supply situation had become critical, the Indian Air Force, which had carried out airlift operations in the eastern states, continued to airlift refugees and relief supplies between Assam and Tripura after the US aircrafts had terminated. Additional airlifts transported urgently needed medicines, milk powder, and sometimes food grains from Calcutta to North Bengal, Meghalaya, Assam, and Tripura. These airlifts were often complicated because the airports in these areas were not equipped to receive heavy aircraft: thus small planes had to be used, further increasing the cost. The North-East of India is an area of heavy rainfall, and during the monsoon vital supply lines, linking Calcutta with the camps along the 1,700 mile border were broken as road conditions became almost impossible.

Because of the difficulties involved in air and rail transportation, often the most dependable transport was by road. In Tripura trucks were regularly used over the 150 miles of road between the railhead at Dharamagan and Agartate. The requirement for vehicles, estimated by the Indian Government, was 630 jeeps, 244 trailers, 935 trucks, and 121 ambulances. On the basis of this need, the UN Focal Point made funds available to UNICEF which ordered the vehicles through its world-wide procurement channels.

The total cost for vehicles and transportation provided to the Indian Government through the UN system was valued at $10,105,272 for which 1,885 vehicles were provided. The ownership was transferred to the Indian Government which also assumed responsibility for the operation and maintenance of the fleet. In addition, the Government made 145 vehicles available to the relief operation.

Health. Health problems were severe and worsened as time went on and the influx of new refugees continued. Chronic under-nourishment gave rise in the course of time to protein-deficiency diseases, particularly among children. Overcrowding, the lack of safe drinking water, and unsanitary conditions resulted not only in infectious diseases (cholera, diptheria, smallpox and others) but also produced gastro-enteritis and skin diseases.

The first cases of cholera were reported toward the end of April. A large-scale immunization program was made possible by the constant flow of cholera vaccine from abroad. With immediate help of WHO, sending urgently needed drugs, medical supplies, and equipment by airlift, the

cholera epidemic was somewhat contained by August, but
6,144 out of 49,840 patients died. Throughout the duration
teams of Indian doctors and nurses worked around the clock
carrying out this vaccination program. In all, nearly 21
million doses of anti-cholera vaccine were provided through
the UN system.

Two outbreaks of smallpox were reported among the
refugees, the first at the end of April 1971 in West Bengal
(out of 764 cases reported, 392 died). Some 200 cases were
reported in other states. A mass vaccination program
brought the epidemic to a halt. The second outbreak occurred in the Salt Lake Camp near Calcutta. Mass vaccination was undertaken and the epidemic quickly subsided.

The high incidence of severe protein-calorie malnutrition was observed among children by UNICEF staff in June
1971. According to a report made in July by a team from
the All India Institute of Medical Sciences, New Delhi, nearly fifty percent of the infants and pre-school children examined suffered in some degree from protein malnutrition.
Nutritional therapy centers were established for children under five years who had signs of moderate and severe malnutrition. And large-scale milk feeding centers were set up
to protect those children who were suffering from early
stages of malnutrition.

The existing medical facilities of the states where
refugees had sought asylum were soon strained to the maximum. The Central Ministry of Health, therefore, created
new health facilities in the camps themselves. For a camp
of 50,000 refugees--a central camp--a 25-bed hospital was
set up as well as two health centers or dispensaries. In
all, 1,700 new hospital beds were provided in existing and
new hospitals and nearly 700 dispensaries were erected.
The medical equipment contributed by the UN system included a field hospital, 1,384 hospital tents, 80 barracks,
and an equipped mobile unit.

In the early days of the crisis, the Central and State
Governments provided, as a matter of Indian Government
policy, medical personnel from their existing medical es-
tablishments or from medical colleges and other medical institutions. As time went on, the Government welcomed the
cooperation of voluntary agencies and designated camps where
they carried out their programs. In addition, the Government recruited special medical teams for short periods of
time.

Deliberations in the Security Council
and the General Assembly

On 20 July when he saw the situation had taken on threatening proportions, the Secretary-General sent a confidential memorandum to the President of the SC, expressing his fear that the situation constituted a threat to international peace and security and his feeling that it had bearing on the future of the UN as an effective instrument for international cooperation and action. He believed that the UN, with its experience in peace-keeping and with its various resources for conciliation and persuasion, should play a more forthright role to avert further deterioration of the situation. The nature of the crisis, however, was reflected in divisions within the SC and the SC did not, in fact, meet on the question of UN action until 4 December, two days before war broke out between India and Pakistan.

On 2 October, with the situation continuing to worsen, the Secretary-General sent identical messages to the heads of the Governments of India and Pakistan in which he expressed increasing anxiety that the situation might give rise to open hostilities, posing a threat to the wider peace. He offered his good offices to both in the hope of averting any development that might lead to disaster. He suggested the placement of civilian UN observers along both sides of the India-Pakistan border. On 22 October the President of Pakistan welcomed the offer of good offices and assured full cooperation. However, the Prime Minister of India replied on 16 November that Pakistan had sought to divert attention from the situation in East Bengal by projecting it as an India-Pakistan dispute and stated that India could accept the Secretary-General's offer of good offices only in regard to a political solution.

The HC made a second journey to India and Pakistan in the beginning of November. The mission was so timed as to permit an up-to-date presentation to the GA, meeting in November and December. The two humanitarian programs on the Asian subcontinent were considered on 18-22 November by the Third Committee of the GA, in connection with the reports of the HC and of the Assistant Secretary-General in charge of UNEPRO. Mr. Henry in his report on UNEPRO humanitarian activities referred to the military developments that had affected the work of that operation, causing the situation to reach a critical stage. The HC gave an account of his activities as Focal Point, including his efforts to arrange for the voluntary repatriation of refugees. In his oral presentation before the Third Committee, Prince Sadruddin reported the findings of his second journey to India and Pakistan, saying that "neither needs nor numbers have stood still since [the beginning of the emergency], and our efforts have had to race against them and time." The problem, he said, "has grown in dimension and anguish almost beyond comprehension and endurance."

After two further days of debate, the Third Committee presented a Draft Resolution strongly supporting the efforts of the HC.

On 29 November the Permanent Representative of Pakistan conveyed a message from his President stating that Indian armed forces were carrying out large-scale attacks on the borders of East Pakistan. The Secretary-General who had been continuously in communication with the President of the SC, informed the President about his offer of good offices and the reactions to it, and transmitted to him the Pakistan message on the same day with the comment that the stationing of observers would require authorization by the SC and that in the light of its primary responsibilities under the Charter for the maintenance of peace and security, the SC should give serious consideration to the situation in the Asian subcontinent.

On 3 December, three days before the outbreak of war between India and Pakistan, the Secretary-General reported to the SC that the situation constituted a threat to international peace and security and stated that the President of the SC had been kept informed of his efforts under the terms of Art. 99 of the Charter. Later in November the problem of peace and security in the subcontinent had become a matter of deep concern at the UN Headquarters. The worsening atmosphere and the increasing number of armed clashes between India and Pakistan prompted representatives of nine countries, including the UK and US, to request, in a letter of 4 December to the SC, a meeting of the SC.

The SC met on the same day and invited the representatives of India and Pakistan to participate in the debate without a vote. Several draft resolutions were introduced and lengthily debated, among them one introduced by USSR and one by China which, because of a negative vote of a permanent member of the Council, were not adopted. A

Six-Power draft resolution was introduced by the representative of Somalia (sponsored by Argentina, Burundi, Japan, Nicaragua, Sierra Leone) which was adopted by a vote of 11 to none, with 4 abstentions. Under this resolution the SC transferred the question to the GA as provided for in GA Res. 377A (V) of 3 November 1950.

On the 6th of December the GA reviewed the Res. drafted by the Third Com. and passed it unanimously as 2790 (XXVI). This Res., concerned with UN assistance to East Pakistan refugees through Focal Point and UN humanitarian assistance to East Pakistan, recognized that voluntary repatriation would be the only satisfactory solution to the refugee problem, and endorsed the designation of the HC to be the Focal Point for coordination of assistance to East Pakistan refugees in India. It further endorsed the Secretary-General's initiative in establishing the UNEPRO. It requested the Secretary-General and the HC to continue their efforts and appealed to the international community to intensify its assistance efforts. Finally, it urged all Member States "to intensify their efforts to bring about conditions necessary for the speedy and voluntary repatriation of the refugees to their homes. "

Throughout the relief operation, a political solution that would permit repatriation of the refugees had been seen as the ultimate goal, and implementation of the humanitarian relief programs had from the beginning been inextricably intertwined with the complex political and military situation. In late November and early December--simultaneous with the long-awaited GA endorsement of Focal Point and UNEPRO-- military actions forced temporary suspension of aspects of the relief operation but led finally to acceptance of the independent state of Bangladesh, enabling the HC to assist the repatriation of millions of refugees.

In late November as hostilities escalated, UNEPRO had to withdraw all its non-essential personnel in Dacca, and the UNHCR team, with the exception of Mr. Kelly, flew out with them to Bangkok to await further developments. UNEPRO supply ships were redirected from Chittagong to Singapore. On 3 December Calcutta and New Delhi airports were closed, and blankets urgently needed in the North-East had to be unloaded at Bombay. The Indian Government advised UNHCR to hold up further shipments for 72 hours.

War between India and Pakistan broke out on 6

December.   After consultation with the Secretary-General it
was announced in New York on 7 December that "in view of
the prevailing situation shipments of relief commodities and
equipment" were being interrupted "until the situation permits resumption of deliveries. " The conditions of the war
had seriously interrupted the airlift and shipment of supplies
and equipment.

On 7 December the Secretary-General reported to the
GA and SC about the evacuation of 46 UNEPRO and other international personnel who had stayed in Dacca after open
warfare had begun (37 UN officials had remained as volunteers).   After consultation with the Indian and Pakistan Governments four neutral zones were established in Dacca, under the protection of the UN and the Red Cross, as temporary safe havens for evacuee groups and for humanitarian
purposes.

The GA considered the outbreak of open hostilities at
two meetings held on 7 December.   Most representatives
spoke in favor of an immediate cease-fire and withdrawal of
the troops of both India and Pakistan to their own territories.
The majority agreed in principle that a political settlement
was needed that would allow voluntary repatriation, but dis-
agreed on how that settlement should be achieved.   At the
end of the debate the GA adopted the revised 34-Power Draft
Resolution introduced by Argentina by a vote of 104 to 11,
with 10 abstentions, as Res. 2793 (XXVI).   Res. 2793 recognized the need to take measures to bring about an immediate cessation of hostilities between India and Pakistan and
effect a withdrawal of their armed forces to their own sides
of the borders.   It urged intensification of efforts to bring
about conditions necessary for the voluntary return of the
East Pakistan refugees to their homes and called for the full
cooperation of all States in rendering assistance to and relieving the distress of the refugees.

On 9 December in a letter the Pakistan Government
informed the Secretary-General that it accepted the call for
immediate cease-fire and withdrawal of troops.   However,
the Prime Minister of India informed the SC on 16 December
(during a second series of meetings) that the Pakistan armed
forces had surrendered in East Pakistan and India had recognized the independent State of Bangladesh.   The fighting
stopped on 17 December.

The SC met again on 21 December and passed a

Six-Power Draft Resolution by 13 votes to none as Res. 307
(1971). In this Res. the SC called for "international assistance in the relief of suffering and the rehabilitation of refugees and their return in safety and dignity to their homes, "
and for full cooperation with the Secretary-General to that
effect. On 25 December the Secretary-General reported that
in accordance with the SC Resolution and in the light of developments in the subcontinent he had appointed a special
representative for humanitarian good offices for Bangladesh
and to set up the UN Relief Operation in Dacca (UNROD).

Repatriation

Mr. John Kelly with a number of other UN officers,
including Paul-Marc Henry, the head of UNEPRO, had remained in Dacca after the fighting broke out. Mr. Kelly
served as intermediary between the Indian and Pakistan
military forces in seeking a cease-fire. With the end of the
hostilities the UN officers returned to their headquarters in
New York and Geneva. But soon they were back in Dacca
to resume the UN humanitarian relief operation under a new
name, UNROD, and to coordinate UNHCR aid in the massive
movement of refugees back to their homeland.

Repatriation had begun spontaneously even while the
fighting was going on. Refugees whose homes were in the
border areas traveled by foot; some had bicycles; others
pulled rickshaws carrying aged parents and young children.
However, for the mass of the refugees provisions had to be
made for an organized return.

The Indian Government in cooperation with the authorities in Dacca organized the return movement and made great
efforts to facilitate its speedy implementation. The officially
assisted movement began on 1 January when some train services were opened and plans were made for the creation of
staging centers where groups on their way home could find
food, medical services, and other assistance. Those of the
refugees who were not transported by the Government were
given journey allowances. For the majority, however, transportation had to be provided. Special trains for those living
in outlying "central camps" in the North-East were run;
3,500 trucks and 30 launches, steamers, and barges were
used in January for the evacuation of refugees from South
Bengal and Assam.

The refugees received two weeks' basic rations for
the journey, and some provisions to get them through for a
short time on their return to Bangladesh. They turned in
their ration and registration cards and border slips and
received in exchange a "refugee return card, " with which they
were admitted into Bangladesh and entitled to further help
there.   Once in Bangladesh, refugees on the trek home could
transit through "staging camps" where they could stay for
one or two days and where they found cooking facilities,
clean water, and medical facilities.   Some 271 such camps
operated in Bangladesh in January and February.   Arriving
home with only a little food and no immediate means of supporting themselves, the returnees often found their homes
destroyed.   The Bangladesh authorities gave the returnees
food, and with financial assistance from the Indian Government, cash grants and allowances were made toward the reconstruction of houses.   Relief committees were set up at
all levels of the local administration in order to ensure
proper supervision and distribution of aid.

Once the massive return movement had begun, in addition to his functions as Focal Point for assistance to the
refugees in India awaiting return, the further responsibility
fell to the HC of mobilizing international resources needed to
facilitate repatriation.   On 20 January 1972 the Indian Government, in an aide-memoire to the UNHCR, stressed that
although international assistance had so far "contributed in
no small measure, " it did not reach one half of the total
estimated expenditure for relief in India alone and stated that
a further expenditure estimated at $80 to $100 million was
required for the repatriation phase.   The HC, after consultation with the Secretary-General, sent a letter on 22 January
to the member governments of the UN enclosing the Indian
aide-memoire and broadcasted an appeal to the public on 26
January.   By the end of May 1972 contributions pledged to
the Focal Point toward repatriation amounted to $14 million,
$6. 3 million of which was transferred to the Government of
Bangladesh for aid in financing relief and rehabilitation of the
returnees.

Immediately after the cease-fire the Focal Point informed the Indian Government that the returnees could carry
back with them clothing, blankets, and utensils distributed to
them in India from contributions provided through the UN.
Similarly, the Focal Point endorsed an agreement between
IRS and the Bangladesh Red Cross under which the equipment
and supplies operated in India could be transferred to the

Bangladesh Red Cross. Also, 800 trucks, 300 jeeps, and
136 ambulances received from Focal Point were transferred
as a grant to the Government of Bangladesh.

On 15 February 1972 the Secretary-General gave an
account of action taken under GA Res. 2790 (XXVI) and the
humanitarian provisions of SC 307 (1971). Under the activities of Focal Point, out of nearly ten million refugees, more
than seven million had by that time returned to Bangladesh.
On 29 March, one day before the HC left for a visit to Dacca and other areas in Bangladesh, he received a significant
message from Mr. T. E. Roman, Deputy Secretary of the
Rehabilitation Department of the Indian Government. In this
message the HC was informed that "the last refugees from
the central camp at Panchanpur ... in Bihar left for Bangladesh on 25 March 1972. With this, all the refugees accommodated in both central and state camps have been repatriated." Thus, on 25 March the organized return movement
of the East Bengal refugees was completed. An additional
60,000 refugees who were staying with relatives were expected to return on their own.

Focal Point's task had thus come to an end, except for
the administrative winding up of the operation. Some monies
and relief goods were still in the pipe-line and the final report had to be written (dated 23 June 1972) which the Secretary-General submitted to the GA and SC in August 1972.
The HC marked the end of his responsibilities as Focal Point
by making a personal visit to the returnees, to the authorities in Dacca, and to UNROD and the Indian Government and
the UN representatives in New Delhi, and finally to the new
leaders of Pakistan. 45

Notes

1.   Lowell Thomas, High Mountains, N.Y., Simon &
        Schuster, 1964, Ch. 15: 223. Lowell Thomas is a
        renowned global traveler, newscaster and commenta-
        tor whose journey to Tibet, "The Roof of the World,"
        is recorded in this work.

2.   Neville Maxwell, India and the China War, N.Y., Dou-
        bleday, 1972: 63.

3.   Office of the Dalai Lama, Tibetans in Exile, Bureau of
        the Dalai Lama, 1969: i.

4. Statement made by the Delegate of the Permanent Mission of the Chinese People's Republic at the Fifty-third Sess. of the ECOSOC, 27 July 1972; see also Maxwell: op. cit. : 63.

5. Michael Peissel, Cavaliers of Kham, London, Heinemann, 1972: 10 and 14; Maxwell, op. cit. : 62.

6. GA (XIV), Doc. A/4234, 29 Sept. 1959.

7. GA Res. 1353 (XIV), 21 Oct. 1959.

8. UN Doc. A/4444, 19 Aug. 1960: 13.

9. GA Res. 1723 (XIV), 12 Dec. 1961.

10. GA Res. 2079 (XX), 1965.

11. Bureau of the Dalai Lama, op. cit. : 2.

12. CRC(I) Vol. 2(4), Mar. , 1968: 2.

13. In anticipation of the day when repatriation would be possible the Dalai Lama maintains a government in Dharamsala. This administration "exists only as a non-political and private organization devoted mainly to the cultural development, rehabilitation and general welfare of Tibetan refugees, " and serves also as a consultant to the Government of India in the execution of its Tibetan refugee policy. Tibetans in Exile, op. cit. , iii-xii.

14. Maxwell, op. cit. , Chs. 3 and 5: 269-478.

15. Quoted in Tibetans in Exile: 301-66.

16. Communication by the Permanent Mission of India to the UNHCR, 12 Oct. 1972, Geneva.

17. Dispersed as follows: 6, 600 in agricultural settlements; 4, 000 in schools, not including those in agricultural settlements; 3, 000 aged and infirm; 3, 000 lamas not in full self-supporting occupations; 3, 000 in miscellaneous self-help centers and similar projects or in employment in the Indian economy; 20, 000 on road work in India and Sikkim. "Outline Plan for Rehabilitation of Tibetan Refugees Now in

India," as quoted in A/AC.96/INF. 31, 23 Oct.
1964.

18.   e.g. Schweizer Tibethilfe, the Tibet Society of Great
        Britain, the Tibetan Aid Society of Canada, and
        similar organizations in Australia, New Zealand,
        and in Scandinavian countries. CRC(I) mentions the
        following voluntary agencies actively associated with
        the relief and rehabilitation of the Tibetan refugees
        in India: CRS; Christian Agency for Social Action/
        CWS (US); CORSO (New Zealand); ERC; Help the
        Aged (UK); Individual Mannisköhjälp (Sweden); Junior
        Chamber International; Norwegian Refugee Council;
        Save the Children Fund (UK); Sharan (India); Swiss
        Aid to Tibetans; Swiss Technical Aid Mission;
        Spangenberg Sozialwerk (West Germany); Tibetan
        Children Relief Fund (New Zealand); Tibetan Refugee
        Aid Society (Canada); Tibet Society of UK. ICVA
        News No. 43, Sept.-Oct. 1969: 25-26.

19.   An example of foreign aid after this time was reported
        by the Canadian Tibetan Aid Society which spent over
        $90,000 from 1963-1969 in India and Nepal. ICVA
        News, Mar.-Apr. 1969, No. 40: 15. OXFAM con-
        tributed £105,000 from 1960/61 to 1966/67. ICVA
        News, Mar.-Apr. 1969, No. 40: 5.

20.   Ibid.: 6.

21.   A/AC.96/412: 38.

22.   Laura and Fred Mayer Pilarski, "Little Tibet in Swit-
        zerland," Nat. Geog., 134 (5), Nov. 1968: 711.

23.   UNHCR Reports, Monthly Newsletter No. 27, Nov. 1963.

24.   Ibid.: 722.

25.   Difficulty in finding Indian teachers, especially in the
        remote settlements, has proved a persistent prob-
        lem. In addition to learning Tibetan and one major
        Indian language, Tibetan pupils also learn English,
        and thereby become tri-lingual.

26.   In 1970, 15 Tibetans benefitted from such scholarships
        under the condition that after the completion of their
        training, they serve for two years as teachers in a
        Tibetan school.

27. Ex. Com. (XII) A/AC. 96/INF. 31, 23 Oct. 1964.

28. In Oct. 1969, India for the first time designated an Observer to attend sessions of the Ex. Com.

29. Jamieson, "Mission to India and Nepal," April 1970.

30. ICVA Communiqué, par. 22 of the minutes of the meeting of 4 Apr. 1967: 21.

31. Ex. Com. (XII) Account of the Mission of the Director of Operations to India and Nepal. A/AC. 96/INF. 31, 23 Oct. 1964.

32. Ex. Com. (XI).

33. UNHCR Bulletin, Supp., Oct. 1969.

34. The UNHCR Director of Operations paid a visit to Nepal at the end of Sept. 1964 at the invitation of the Government of Nepal, for further discussions with the HC's representative and the government and for visiting the settlements. Ex. Com. (XII) A/AC. 96/INF. 31, 23 Oct. 1964.

35. Ex. Com. (XI) A/AC. 96/247, 4 May 1964.

36. UNHCR Newsletter No. 42, Mar. 1966.

37. Ex. Com. (XXI) 1970, Rep. on UNHCR Current Operations in 1969, A/AC. 96/428, June 1970: 51ff and Ibid., 12 Aug. 1970, UNHCR Assistance Program for 1971, A/AC. 96/429: 45ff.

38. See Thomas Jamieson's "A visit to Nepal," in HC Bulletin, No. 10, Apr.-June 1970.

39. For official documentation of the Focal Point operation in India see UN, GA (XXVII) SC, A. 8662/Add. 3, 11 Aug. 1972; UN, GA (XXVII) SC, Off. Rec.; UN, GA (XXVII), ECOSOC (LI), Oct. 1971; UN, GA (XXVII) Off. Rec. Supp. 1, A. 8701, Report of the Secretary-General on the Work of the Organization, 16 June 1971-15 June 1972: 69-75; UN, GA (XXVI), Off. Rec. Supp., 12A, A/8412/Add. 1, Addendum to the Report of UNHCR: 4 and 31-4; UN, Monthly Chronicle, Dec. 1971, VIII (12) and Jan. 1972, IX

(1): 3-45, 89 and 170; UNHCR, HCR Bulletin, Third
Quarter 1971, No. 15, Nov. 1971; UNHCR, HCR
Bulletin, Fourth Quarter 1971, No. 16, Feb. 1972;
UNHCR Report, A Story of Anguish and Action, The
UN Focal Point of Assistance to Refugees from East
Bengal in India, UN, NY, Nov. 1972; UNHCR, Pr.
Rel.; US, 92nd Cong. 1st Sess. HR Hearings, Sub.
Com. on Asian and Pacific Aff., Crisis in Pakistan,
11 and 25 May 1971; US, 92nd Cong. 1st Sess. S.
Hearings, Sub. Com. to Investigate Problems Con-
nected with Refugees and Escapees, Relief Problems
in East Pakistan and India, Parts I-III, 28 June, 30
Sept., 4 Oct., 1971, and Report to the Sub. Com.
by Senator Edward Kennedy, Crisis in South Asia,
Nov., 1971; US, Interagency Committee on Pakistan
Refugee Relief Situation Reports; International Commission of Jurists, The Events in East Pakistan,
1971, Geneva, 1972; India, Ministry of External Affairs, Bangladesh, Documents, New Delhi, n. d.;
Yvonne von Stedingk, "Situation der Flüchtlinge aus
Ostpakistan in Indien," AWR Bulletin, Dec. 1971:
169-83. For detailed reports of the US Government
on the emergency assistance and aid in repatriation
and on activities of US voluntary agencies, see
ACVIA, Report on Assistance to East Pakistan and
to Pakistani Refugees in India, NY, Oct. 1971;
ACVIA, Report on Assistance to East Bengal and to
Bengali Refugees in India, NY, Dec. 1971; ACVIA,
Report on Assistance to Bangladesh and to Bengali
Refugees in India, NY, Apr. 1972.

40. The Indian population at the time of the refugee influx
numbered 559 million; East Pakistan's population was
75 million, and that of West Pakistan was 62 million. The Indian population is predominantly Hindu
(84 percent); Islam is the state religion of Pakistan,
and is practiced by 96 percent of the population.
Hindus, however, comprised 13 percent of the population of East Pakistan, and religious divisions were
reflected in the tensions within that state.

41. The Indian Government referred to those persons as
evacuees, in order to stress that they had sought
temporary refuge in India and would be returned as
soon as the conditions in their homeland would permit.

42. In June IBRD held a meeting in Paris at which Mr. Mace, the Deputy HC, and the Resident Representative of UNDP, brought to the notice of economic experts the potentially dangerous side effect on India's future economic development if that country were not to receive sufficient international assistance toward the relief operation for the East Bengali refugees. On 26 Oct. in Paris at another meeting of IBRD, the Indian Secretary of the Department of Economic Affairs stated that all non-plan expenditure (that not directly concerned with development) had been cut 5 percent, civil servants' salaries reduced by 20 percent, and tax collection increased. IBRD estimated that the volume of relief required from the Indian Government equalled 12 percent of the economic plan and observed that the whole development plan was severely disrupted.

43. After his return from India and Pakistan on 19 June, the HC held press conferences in New York on 23 June, in Geneva on 25 June, in London on 30 June, and in Paris on 2 July.

44. For the text of the Agreement between the Secretary-General and the Government of Pakistan on Conditions for Discharge of Functions of UNEPRO, see UN, Monthly Chronicle, VIII (1) Dec. 1971: 116-18.

45. After the resignation of General Yahya Khan on 20 Dec. 1971, Zulfikar Ali Bhutto as Prime Minister formed a new government.

ANNEX 29.1

INDIA, 1963-71

Value of UNHCR Current Projects (US Dollars)

UNHCR Current Programs	951,627
Supporting contributions from other sources	226,000
UNHCR Special Trust Funds (for operations outside the programs)	280,995
Total (rounded)	1,468,700

SOURCE: Ex. Com. (XXII), A/AC.96/449, 28 June 1971 and Ex. Com. (XXIII), A/AC.96/467, 8 Aug. 1972.

ANNEX 29.2

NEPAL, 1963-71

Value of UNHCR Current Projects (US Dollars)

UNHCR Current Programs	427,549
Emergency Fund	24,858
Supporting contributions from other sources	50,500
UNHCR Special Trust Funds (for operations outside the program)	23,594
Total (rounded)	526,500

SOURCE: Ex. Com. (XXII), A/AC.96/449, 28 June 1971 and Ex. Com. (XXIII), A/AC.96/467, 8 Aug. 1972.

ANNEX 29.3

Refugee population by State
Subdivided between refugees in camp and out of camp
on 1 December 1971

(Source: Government of India)

State	Number of camps	Living in camps	Number of Refugees	
			Living with friends and relatives	Total
West Bengal	492	4,849,786	2,386,130	7,235,916
Tripura	276	834,098	547,551	1,381,649
Meghalaya	17	591,520	76,466	667,986
Assam	28	255,642	91,913	347,555
Bihar	8	36,732	-	36,732
Madhya Pradesh	3	219,298	-	219,298
Uttar Pradesh	1	10,169	-	10,169
TOTAL	825	6,797,245	3,102,060	9,899,305

SOURCE: Report of the Secretary-General, 11 August 1972,
Table 1: 118.

ANNEX 29.4

STATUS OF CONTRIBUTIONS THROUGH THE UN SYSTEM

Situation as of 21 June 1972
in US Dollars

DONOR GOVERNMENTS	PLEDGED CASH	KIND	TOTAL	CASH RECEIVED
Argentina(1)		00.00	00.00	
Australia	595,521.68	1,760,145.18	2,355,666.86	501,293.48
Austria	164,789.58	-	164,789.58	99,789.58
Barbados	2,500.00		2,500.00	2,500.00
Belgium	1,082,110.00	62,553.19	1,144,663.19	1,082,110.00
Botswana	8,333.33		8,333.33	8,333.33
Brazil	-	17,204.23	17,204.23	
Canada & Provinces	4,806,930.69	4,096,930.69	8,903,861.38	4,806,930.69
Ceylon		336,134.45	336,134.45	
Chile	3,000.00		3,000.00	3,000.00
Colombia	-	3,000.00	3,000.00	
Cyprus	11,999.04		11,999.04	11,999.04
Denmark	4,680,893.62	-	4,680,893.62	4,680,893.62
Dahomey	3,968.25	-	3,968.25	3,968.25
Fiji	5,000.00	-	5,000.00	5,000.00
Finland	577,783.09	-	577,783.09	577,783.09
France	2,908,114.91	-	2,908,114.91	2,908,114.91

Gambia	235.00	235.00	-	235.00
Germany (Fed. Rep.)(2)	17,471,226.25	17,671,226.25	200,000.00	17,471,226.25
Ghana	25,009.80	20,000.00	20,000.00	25,009.80
Guinea		7,680.00	5,180.00	
Guyana	2,500.00		-	2,500.00
Holy See	5,000.00	5,000.00	-	5,000.00
Iceland	8,594.79	8,594.79	-	8,594.79
Iran		183,606.56	183,606.56	
Ireland	134,852.42	254,842.82	119,990.40	134,852.42
Italy	23,828.97	23,828.97	-	23,828.97
Jamaica	12,745.10	12,745.10	-	12,745.10
Japan		4,891,700.00	4,891,700.00	
Kenya	27,678.22	27,678.22	-	27,678.22
Khmer Republic	-	1,000.00	-	-
Kuwait	60,000.00	60,000.00	-	60,000.00
Liberia	30,000.00	30,000.00	-	30,000.00
Libya	200,204.15	200,204.15	-	200,204.15
Liechtenstein	10,037.77	10,037.77	-	10,037.77
Luxembourg	15,957.45	15,957.45	-	15,957.45
Malaysia	27,099.60	27,099.60	-	27,099.60
Mauritius	1,869.16	51,869.16	50,000.00	1,869.16
Monaco	5,434.78	5,434.78	-	5,434.78
Nepal	2,450.98	2,450.98	-	2,450.98
Netherlands	4,423,318.12	5,755,630.71	1,332,312.59	4,423,318.12
New Zealand	115,170.79	115,170.79	-	115,170.79
Nigeria	70,000.00	70,000.00	-	70,000.00
Norway	3,781,804.96	3,781,804.96	-	3,781,804.96
Oman (Sultanate of)	25,000.00	25,000.00	-	25,000.00
Peru		184,898.15	184,898.15	
San Marino	1,602.56	1,602.56	-	1,602.56
Senegal	7,194.24	7,194.24	-	7,194.24
Singapore	13,147.08	13,147.08	-	13,147.08

| DONOR GOVERNMENTS | PLEDGED | | | CASH RECEIVED |
	CASH	KIND (cont.)	TOTAL	
Spain	-	42,857.00	42,857.00	
Swaziland	1,199.90	-	1,199.90	1,199.90
Sweden	9,559,836.05	-	9,559,836.05	9,559,836.05
Switzerland	2,258,665.29	-	2,258,665.29	2,258,665.29
Tanzania (United Rep. of)	8,403.36	-	8,403.36	8,403.36
Thailand	-	24,800.00	24,000.00	
Togo	1,167.31	-	1,167.31	1,167.31
Tonga	282.61	-	282.61	282.61
Trinidad & Tobago	10,058.44	-	10,058.44	10,058.44
Uganda	14,005.60	-	14,005.60	14,005.60
United Kingdom	25,863,411.98	-	25,863,411.98	25,863,411.98
United States(3)	35,750,000.00	46,425,000.00	82,175,000.00	35,444,887.30
Uruguay	2,000.00	-	2,000.00	
Vietnam (Rep. of)	15,000.00	-	15,000.00	15,000.00
Yugoslavia	-	20,000.00	20,000.00	
Zambia	28,003.36	-	28,003.36	
Sov. Order of Malta	10,801.28	-	10,801.28	10,801.28
SUB TOTAL	114,876,741.56	59,776,312.44	174,653,054.00	114,381,397.30
NON GOVERNMENTAL ORGANIZATIONS:				
Australia	458,764.75	76,822.30	535,587.05	458,764.75
Belgium	105,803.19	13,285.53	119,088.72	105,803.19
Canada	97,212.01	-	97,212.01	97,212.01
Cyprus	783.30	-	783.30	783.30

France	1,130,006.66	1,130,006.66	–	1,130,006.66
German (Fed. Rep.)	1,535,607.66	1,535,607.66	–	1,535,607.66
Guyana	.	2,500.00	2,500.00	–
Ireland	1,199.60	1,199.60	–	1,199.60
Israel	1,226.19	1,226.19	–	1,226.19
Italy	849.61	849.61	61,609.03	849.61
Japan	55,454.54	117,063.57	–	55,454.54
Luxembourg	1,004.98	1,004.98	–	1,004.98
Netherlands	1,592,722.27	1,592,722.27	–	1,592,722.27
New Zealand	143,082.29	173,456.29	30,374.00	143,082.29
Norway	153,996.92	153,996.92	–	153,996.92
Sweden	124,740.12	124,740.12	–	124,740.12
United Kingdom	13,120.84	62,625.79	49,504.95	13,120.84
United States	304,522.26	304,522.26	–	304,522.26
SUB TOTAL	5,720,097.19	5,954,193.00	234,095.81	5,720,097.19
OTHER DONORS:				
- Air Companies				
- Gift Coupon Progr.		235,116.90	235,116.90	–
- UNESCO	9,730.00	9,730.00	–	9,730.00
- I.C.F.T.U.	1,463.02	1,463.02	–	1,463.02
- UN Staff Ass.	29,740.69	29,740.69	–	29,740.69
SUB TOTAL	40,933.71	276,050.61	235,116.90	40,933.71
PRIVATE DONORS:				
Canada	1,885.23	1,885.23	–	1,885.23
Malaysia	1,308.26	1,308.26	–	1,308.26
Switzerland	2,518.59	2,518.59	–	2,518.59

PRIVATE DONORS	PLEDGED (cont.)		TOTAL	CASH RECEIVED
	CASH	KIND		
United States	20,986.34	–	20,986.34	20,986.34
United States	13,539.72	–	13,539.72	13,539.72
Zaïre	3,707.98	–	3,707.98	3,707.98
Other countries				
SUB TOTAL	43,946.12	–	43,946.12	43,946.12
UN AGENCIES:				
– UNHCR	500,000.00	–	500,000.00	500,000.00
– UNICEF	–	600,000.00	600,000.00	. .
– WHO	–	166,540.00	166,540.00	. .
– WFP	–	2,782,111.00	2,782,111.00	. .
SUB TOTAL	500,000.00	3,548,651.00	4,048,651.00	500,000.00
GRAND TOTAL(4)	119,476,338.59	63,794,176.15	183,270,514.74	118,580,994.33

(1) The original pledge from Argentina (4,000 metric tons of wheat) has been transferred to UNROD, Dacca.
(2) Not including DM 7,200,000 (US $2,168,674.70) utilized by German voluntary agencies in Bangladesh.
(3) Not including US $10,232,000 i.e., the value of metric tons 40,000 sweetened CSM/WSB sent directly to Bangladesh.
(4) After substraction of US $1,705,379.99, as certain contributions transited through more than one donor.

SOURCE: Report of the UN Secretary-General, 11 August 1972: 120-22.

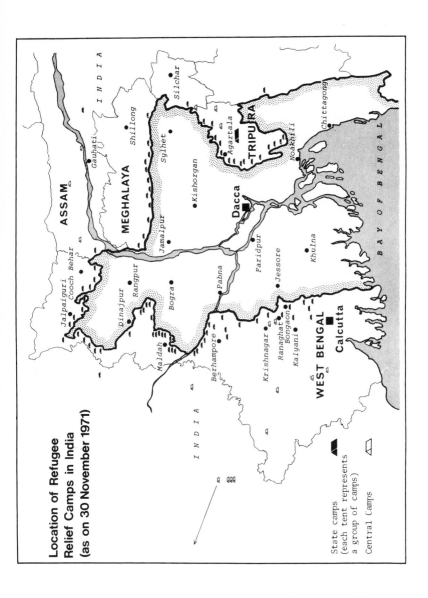

Location of Refugee
Relief Camps in India
(as on 30 November 1971)

State camps
(each tent represents
a group of camps)

Central Camps

Source: UNHCR Report, A Story of Anguish and Action, Geneva,
Nov. 1972: 43.